STUDIES IN THE HISTORY
OF CHRISTIAN MISSIONS

R. E. Frykenberg
Brian Stanley
General Editors

STUDIES IN THE HISTORY OF CHRISTIAN MISSIONS

Alvyn Austin
China's Millions: The China Inland Mission and Late Qing Society, 1832-1905

Chad M. Bauman
Christian Identity and Dalit Religion in Hindu India, 1868-1947

Michael Bergunder
The South Indian Pentecostal Movement in the Twentieth Century

Judith M. Brown and Robert Eric Frykenberg, *Editors*
Christians, Cultural Interactions, and India's Religious Traditions

Robert Eric Frykenberg
*Christians and Missionaries in India:
Cross-Cultural Communication Since 1500*

Susan Billington Harper
*In the Shadow of the Mahatma: Bishop V. S. Azariah
and the Travails of Christianity in British India*

D. Dennis Hudson
Protestant Origins in India: Tamil Evangelical Christians, 1706-1835

Patrick Harries and David Maxwell, *Editors*
The Spiritual in the Secular: Missionaries and Knowledge about Africa

Ogbu U. Kalu, *Editor,* and Alaine M. Low, *Associate Editor*
*Interpreting Contemporary Christianity:
Global Processes and Local Identities*

Donald M. Lewis, *Editor*
*Christianity Reborn: The Global Expansion of Evangelicalism
in the Twentieth Century*

Jessie G. Lutz
Opening China: Karl F. A. Gützlaff and Sino-Western Relations, 1827-1852

Steven S. Maughan
*Mighty England Do Good: Culture, Faith, Empire, and World in the Foreign
Missions of the Church of England, 1850-1915*

Jon Miller
Missionary Zeal and Institutional Control: Organizational Contradictions in the Basel Mission on the Gold Coast, 1828-1917

Andrew Porter, *Editor*
The Imperial Horizons of British Protestant Missions, 1880-1914

Dana L. Robert, *Editor*
Converting Colonialism: Visions and Realities in Mission History, 1709-1914

Wilbert R. Shenk, *Editor*
North American Foreign Missions, 1810-1914: Theology, Theory, and Policy

Brian Stanley
The World Missionary Conference: Edinburgh 1910

Brian Stanley, *Editor*
Christian Missions and the Enlightenment

Brian Stanley, *Editor*
Missions, Nationalism, and the End of Empire

John Stuart
British Missionaries and the End of Empire: East, Central, and Southern Africa, 1939-64

T. Jack Thompson
Light on Darkness? Missionary Photography of Africa in the Nineteenth and Early Twentieth Centuries

Kevin Ward and Brian Stanley, *Editors*
The Church Mission Society and World Christianity, 1799-1999

Timothy Yates
The Conversion of the Māori: Years of Religious and Social Change, 1814-1842

Richard Fox Young, *Editor*
India and the Indianness of Christianity: Essays on Understanding—Historical, Theological, and Bibliographical—in Honor of Robert Eric Frykenberg

Mighty England Do Good

Culture, Faith, Empire, and World
in the Foreign Missions of the
Church of England, 1850-1915

Steven S. Maughan

WILLIAM B. EERDMANS PUBLISHING COMPANY
GRAND RAPIDS, MICHIGAN / CAMBRIDGE, U.K.

Published 2014 by

Wm. B. Eerdmans Publishing Co.

2140 Oak Industrial Drive N.E., Grand Rapids, Michigan 49505 /
P.O. Box 163, Cambridge CB3 9PU U.K.

Printed in the United States of America

20 19 18 17 16 15 14   7 6 5 4 3 2 1

Library of Congress Cataloging-in-Publication Data

Maughan, Steven S., 1962-

Mighty England do good: culture, faith, empire, and world in the foreign missions
of the Church of England, 1850-1915 / Steven S. Maughan.

pages   cm.   — (Studies in the history of Christian missions)

Includes bibliographical references and index.

ISBN 978-0-8028-6946-3 (pbk.: alk. paper)

1. Church of England — Missions — History — 19th century.

2. Church of England — Missions — History — 20th century.

I. Title.

BV2500.M38   2014

266'.309034 — dc23

2013049155

www.eerdmans.com

Contents

vii

Contents

List of Illustrations

Preface and Acknowledgments

Contrasting agendas have complicated the story of Christian expansion in the modern age of empires: Those interested in understanding imperial processes, those determined to denounce empire, those preoccupied with religion as a social phenomenon, and those focused on and often involved in the growth of Christianity as a world faith have historically talked past each other in the study of foreign missions. Recently, rising interest in the British Empire as providing a historical pattern for understanding contemporary international relations and development has encouraged the study of imperialism from diverse disciplinary perspectives. Uncritical "revisionism" advanced by popularizers of the imperial past demands challenge, as does the tendency to vilify as neo-imperialist any who would argue for complexity and ambiguity in the experience of empire. This study aims to examine the power of religion and religious organization, as well as languages of faith, to convey meaning and spur action, particularly focusing on English society and culture in the "high imperial" era. Through an examination of both local and national religious and ecclesiastical politics, a picture emerges of cultures of faith and empire shot through with fissures of conflict and uncertainty regarding definitions of family, community, class, gender, race, nation, and humanity. The multifacetedness of religion is what made and makes it such a powerful and flexible formulator of identity, particularly in the rapidly shifting circumstances of opportunity and resistance that characterized the late Victorian British Empire.

Historical writing aims for analytical rigor and attention to evidence. It brings what a detailed study of the past can offer to understanding the messy intersection of forces and identities that human experience always entails. Here, that messiness is increased by the enormous disparities of power and the inherent transcultural encounter that was central to missionary and imperial experience. While missionary and imperial activity never shared a single identity, their often close overlap — particularly in the Victorian high imperial period — was so persistent and pervasive that, despite the equalitarian ideology embedded deeply in Christian belief, the languages of difference constructed through understandings of gender, nation, class, and race were so powerful that even the best intentions of the age were corroded and redirected in ways that were fascinating, unexpected, sometimes empowering, and often deplorable. At the heart of imperialism, as I hope this study ultimately demonstrates, is both the crass exercise of power and the unexpected opening of opportunity to challenge power throughout colonial fields — and in this case, in the metropolitan center — that is contingent upon precisely that unsettling of accepted structures of authority that religious iconoclasm, imperial adventurism, and innovation in the production of knowledge so typically produced.

This book has been long in the making; my debts are correspondingly deep. Many sources of funding over many years have made possible its research and writing, most notably the Fulbright and Woodrow Wilson Foundations, Pew Charitable Trusts, and Idaho Humanities Council, as well as faculty research funds provided by The College of Idaho. The help of many archivists and librarians has also been critical, but I owe particular debts to the staff of the Heslop Room at the University of Birmingham, the Bodleian Library of Commonwealth and African Studies at Rhodes House, Lambeth Palace Library, the Archives and Special Collections at the School of Oriental and African Studies, the Day Missions Library at Yale University, Terteling Library at The College of Idaho, the now relocated Partnership House Library in London, and to Rosemary Keen and Jean Woods, CMS archivist and librarian, who early in the project provided particular direction and access to the collections they know so well. I also want to gratefully acknowledge the United Society for the Propagation of the Gospel, the Dean and Chapter of Windsor, the Trustees of Lambeth Palace Library, Interserve, and the United Reformed Church for access to the collections and permissions granted to cite from archives and to reproduce photographs. In the case of photographs it has not always been possible to trace original copyright holders. Portions of chapters four and eight were previously published respectively in Frank Trentmann, ed., *Paradoxes of Civil Society: New Perspectives on Modern German and British History* (New York: Berghahn Books, 2000) and in Daniel O'Connor and others, *Three Centuries of Mission: The United Society for the Propagation of the Gospel, 1701-2000* (London: Continuum, 2000).

From my undergraduate years onward I have been fortunate in my mentors. Both Howard Berger, with his conviction that ideas matter, and Franklin Specht, with his insistence upon the force of lived experience, encouraged my interest in history, religious and otherwise. In graduate school, under the guidance John Clive, Simon Schama, and Susan Pedersen I learned from the example of graceful, astute historical thinking and writing. The conception, research, and writing of the book were supported by many scholars: Advice from Jeff Cox as well as Peter Marshall and the members of the Imperial History seminar at the Institute of Historical Research has been formative, as were the comments over the years on various conference presentations, particularly by Antoinette Burton, David Savage, Rhonda Semple, Rowan Strong, and Brian Stanley. Many colleagues, friends, and students have read and commented on parts of the manuscript, among them Kelly Boyd, Arthur Burns, Jeff Cox, Sean Eudaily, Benjamin Fischer, JuNelle Harris, Rowan McWilliam, Daniel O'Connor, John Rember, Rosemary Seton, Mark Smith, Jeff Snyder-Reinke, Taylor St. John, and Frank Trentmann. To the anonymous readers for Eerdmans publishing I am grateful for thoughtful comments and suggestions for improving the manuscript. Research assistance has come from many students over the years, most notably Alexandra Grande and Nicole Watson. Linn Wallace and Savannah Ottmar provided copyediting on the manuscript, as did Cassandra Painter, who also supplied valuable assistance on statistical charts and appendices. Anne Goldgar has provided advice, shelter, and moral support throughout the years, particularly during many a research stint in London. The College of Idaho has provided a stimulating, supportive, and companionable community in which to work through the completion of this book. To Andrew Porter I owe a debt that is difficult to overstate. From the earliest to the latest stages he has given advice and criticism that have sustained and improved the book. Use of the academic research software suite NotaBene enormously assisted its production. Despite long and generous support from many quarters, I of course remain responsible for any errors that follow.

Finally to Debi, Theo, and Zoë I owe more than gratitude for their patience, love, and inspiration throughout a long, long process that too often took me away from family, with its many joys and consolations.

Abbreviations

BCCU	British College Christian Union
BMS	Baptist Missionary Society
CEZMS	Church of England Zenana Missionary Society
CICCU	Cambridge Inter-Collegiate Christian Union
CIM	China Inland Mission
CMS	Church Missionary Society
CSU	Christian Social Union
CWW	Committee for Women's Work (of the SPG) (from 1866 to 1895, known as the Ladies' Association of the SPG; from 1895 to 1903 known as the Women's Mission Association)
ECU	English Church Union
FES	Society for Promoting Female Education in the East (Female Education Society)
GFS	Girls' Friendly Society
IFNS	Indian Female Normal School and Instruction Society (renamed Zenana Bible and Medical Mission in 1881)
JCMA	Junior Clergy Missionary Association (of the SPG)
LMS	London Missionary Society
MSUW	Missionary Settlement for University Women
MU	Mothers' Union
OICCU	Oxford Inter-Collegiate Christian Union
RBMU	Regions Beyond Missionary Union
RTS	Religious Tract Society
SCM	Student Christian Movement
SPCK	Society for Promoting Christian Knowledge

SPG   Society for the Propagation of the Gospel in Foreign Parts
SVM   Student Volunteer Movement
SVMU   Student Volunteer Missionary Union
UMCA   Universities' Mission to Central Africa
WMA   Women's Mission Association (of the SPG) (from 1866 to 1895, known as the Ladies' Association of the SPG; renamed the Committee for Women's Work in 1903)
WMMS   Wesleyan Methodist Missionary Society
YMCA   Young Men's Christian Association
YWCA   Young Women's Christian Association
ZBMM   Zenana Bible and Medical Mission (from 1861 to 1881, known as the Indian Female Normal School Society)

Note on Capitalization: Throughout this text the term "evangelical" has been capitalized when it refers to the evangelical party within the Church of England, and "church" has been capitalized when it refers to the Church of England itself. Both words have been left uncapitalized when they refer to the broader spiritual movement or to the English churches more extensively. Following the practice of contemporary sources, descriptors such as "High Church" and "Ritualist" have also been capitalized when they refer to (in the minds of contemporaries) individuals or groups associated with clearly understood religious parties. Similarly, "Nonconformist" and "Dissenter," capitalized, refer to the Protestant English churches and sects that existed outside the fold of the Church of England.

CHAPTER 1

The Foreign Missions of the Church of England: Reconceptualizing Anglicanism in Imperial Culture, 1850-1915

The English nation cannot but be a nation of Missionaries; the only question is, What is the nature of the message it shall carry to every part of the world?

B. F. Westcott, 1885[1]

Unprecedented growth in foreign missions, colonial churches, and popular imperial culture profoundly influenced the late Victorian and Edwardian Church of England. Contests over religious identity and the relationship of church and state, challenges to orthodoxy from revivalism, biblical criticism, and theological liberalism, and attempts to adjust religious institutions to urban and industrial society operated in the context of conspicuous British imperial and ecclesiastical expansion. The major Anglican parties — from Evangelicals to Anglo-Catholics; from High Church traditionalists to Broad Church modernists — were all deeply affected by this expansion. When at the turn of the century Handley Moule, the influential Evangelical scholar and future bishop of Durham, published a short history of the "evangelical school" in the Church of England, central to his story was the shift that had occurred when the majority of Evangelicals turned their energies in the final three decades of the nineteenth century to foreign missions as the pivot of their identity and politics.[2] Similarly,

---

1. Brooke Foss Westcott, *Speech of the Rev. Professor Westcott at the Anniversary Meeting of the Cambridge Church Missionary Association, on May 11th 1885* (n.p., n.d.).
2. H. C. G. Moule, *The Evangelical School in the Church of England: Its Men and Its Work in the Nineteenth Century* (London: Nisbet, 1901), 5-12, 33-38.

when the High Church bishop of Tasmania, Henry Hutchinson Montgomery, arrived in London to assume leadership of Anglican missions directed by the Society for the Propagation of the Gospel, he carried with him an ambitious plan to "make the ancient Church of England more completely an Imperial Church" by coordinating international Anglican missionary effort.[3] Even Anglican modernists, like the Anglo-Catholic Charles Gore, the Christian Socialist B. F. Westcott, and the Broad Church liberal Hensley Henson, emphasized the importance of the Church as a force for improving imperial morality and unity through spiritual and ecclesiastical expansion the world over.[4] Prominent English Churchmen, otherwise notoriously divided over standards of belief, styles of worship, and the role of the Church in national life, could nevertheless agree that, like the Victorian city, the Victorian empire and the world beyond it required vigorous engagement if the future health and prospects of the Church of England, and England itself, were to be safeguarded.[5]

At the same time that Church leaders were pondering and contesting the relationship of Anglicanism to nation, empire, and world, women in the Church of England were consolidating an unprecedented expansion of women's missions and female missionary institutions while attempting to carve out an acceptable place in missions and the Church itself.[6] The subordinate place of women within Church institutions and their hierarchies had been, since the early nineteenth century, justified in new ways that emphasized the contained power of an elevated feminine spirituality directed within the Christian family and, outside the family, toward "domestic" concerns structured around it.[7] Be-

3. Montgomery to SPG Standing Committee, 17 Aug. 1901, Randall Thomas Davidson Papers, vol. 151, fols. 322-23, Lambeth Palace Library, London (hereafter cited as Davidson Papers).

4. "Charles Gore: Bishop of Mr. Chamberlain's Kingdom," *The Review of Reviews* 24 (14 Dec. 1901): 593; Brooke Foss Westcott, et al., *The Church and New Century Problems* (London: Wells, Gardner, Darton, n.d., ca. 1900), 27-30; H. Hensley Henson, "The Church of England," in *Church Problems: A View of Modern Anglicanism*, ed. H. Hensley Henson (London: Murray, 1900), 25-27.

5. For convenience and clarity, throughout this study I will use the term "Anglican" to refer to those in communion with the Church of England. In the nineteenth century this was a contested term: early in the century to many Evangelicals it suggested High Church sacerdotalism while to Tractarians it had overtones of "high and dry" complacency. Most Anglicans referred to themselves as "Churchmen," but by the end of the century all parties increasingly used the term. Peter Benedict Nockles, *The Oxford Movement in Context: Anglican High Churchmanship, 1760-1857* (Cambridge: Cambridge University Press, 1994), 39-43.

6. See, for example, the extended discussion on the "Vocation and Training of Women for Foreign Missions" and "The Need and Scope of Women's Missions," in George A. Spottiswoode, ed., *The Official Report of the Missionary Conference of the Anglican Communion* (London: SPCK, 1894), 570-631.

7. Sean Gill, *Women and the Church of England: From the Eighteenth Century to the Present* (London: SPCK, 1994), 28-31, 77-84; Leonore Davidoff and Catherine Hall, *Family Fortunes: Men*

tween 1870 and 1900, however, the ideal of the deferential missionary wife and daughter was eroded as British foreign missions experienced an explosion in funds and missionary recruits, the closest parallel to which had been the heady days of the 1830s when evangelical triumphs culminated in the final success of the anti-slavery movement, African and West Indian settlement schemes, and the victory of evangelically inspired reforms of religious practice in India.[8]

Women had always been important to the movement, both as organizers and contributors in England and as missionary wives abroad. They played critical roles in missions from the start, primarily as teachers of girls but also as one of the figurative anchors of the domestic establishment's missionary societies judged as crucial to successful mission stations in the field. Nevertheless, their role was systematically downplayed in the missionary publicity controlled by male clerics. Late Victorian missionary expansion continued to rest disproportionately on women's interest and activism, but it was also characterized by a new factor: accelerated recruiting of unmarried female missionaries. The sheer volume of missionary women overseas and their increasing independence began by the final decades of the century decisively to shift missionary theory and practice — always practically oriented toward education from its origins — toward schools and social service as growing, powerful missionary institutions carried women's concerns and approaches into action.[9] Insiders knew what society propagandists never publicized: that, in the words of international student leader John Mott, "the missionary movement is largely a women's undertaking."[10] Women provided the foundation for what came to be called the "new age" of missions in late Victorian England.

---

and Women of the English Middle Class, 1780-1850 (London: Hutchinson, 1987), 114-18, 450-51; Alison Twells, *The Civilising Mission and the English Middle Class, 1792-1850: The "Heathen" at Home and Overseas* (Basingstoke, UK: Palgrave Macmillan, 2009), 7-9, 103-14.

8. On the first great age of British Protestant missionary expansion, see Andrew Porter, *Religion Versus Empire? British Protestant Missionaries and Overseas Expansion, 1700-1914* (Manchester: Manchester University Press, 2004), 136-62.

9. North American missionary women have attracted substantial scholarly notice; only more recently has comparable attention been directed to their British counterparts, most notably Fiona Bowie, Deborah Kirkwood, and Shirley Ardener, eds., *Women and Mission: Past and Present; Anthropological and Historical Perceptions* (Providence, RI: Berg, 1993); Myra Rutherdale, *Women and the White Man's God: Gender and Race in the Canadian Mission Field* (Vancouver: University of British Columbia Press, 2002); Rhonda Anne Semple, *Missionary Women: Gender, Professionalism and the Victorian Idea of Christian Mission* (Woodbridge, UK: Boydell, 2003); Eliza F. Kent, *Converting Women: Gender and Protestant Christianity in Colonial South India* (Oxford: Oxford University Press, 2004); and Elizabeth E. Prevost, *The Communion of Women: Missions and Gender in Colonial Africa and the British Metropole* (Oxford: Oxford University Press, 2010).

10. J. R. Mott, *The Home Ministry and Modern Missions: A Plea for Leadership in World Evangelization* (London: Hodder and Stoughton, 1905), 73.

Foreign missions were one of the largest charitable undertakings in the Victorian era, but histories of English religion and women have largely ignored both the impact of foreign missionary practice and ideology on the churches and the impact of women's interest and agency on missions.[11] The English churches, however, and most extensively the Church of England, were transformed in the nineteenth century by women's charitable activity, including support for foreign missions both inside and outside the British Empire.[12] Throughout the nineteenth century, and especially after the 1870s, Christian expansion generated imperial and international concerns among both Anglicans and Nonconformists as the overseas commitments of British religion multiplied.[13] Yet the imperial and international context of the Church of England, or the British churches more generally — including the independent Protestant Nonconformist churches of "Old Dissent" (Baptists, Congregationalists, and Presbyterians, most prominently) and new dissenting groups associated with the Methodist connection — has seldom been adequately acknowledged in histories of British religion.[14] Similarly, scholarship on nineteenth- and twentieth-century national and imperial culture has also largely ignored the impact and complexity of religious attitudes, identity, and deeply

11. In national charitable giving, foreign missions were third at 12.4 percent (behind elementary education [26.2 percent] and church building [43.1 percent]) of an aggregate of £81,573,237 donated between 1860 and 1884. *Official Year-Book of the Church of England* (London: SPCK, 1886), table, p. xv.

12. The terms "English" and "British" are not, of course, identical in meaning or interchangeable. Within Anglicanism they remained in tension as English Churchmen operated within a larger British Protestant tradition, the British Empire, and a larger international, though predominantly Anglo-American, Protestant connection. Most members of the Church of England identified themselves as English, but readily adopted the term British when it served their purposes. I attempt to use the terms with precision, but ambiguity in the self-identification and uses at the time can make this an inexact practice. For a discussion of religion and British nationalisms, see Keith Robbins, *History, Religion, and Identity in Modern Britain* (London: Hambledon, 1993), 85-103, and John Wolffe, *God and Greater Britain: Religion and National Life in Britain and Ireland, 1843-1945* (London: Routledge, 1994), 204-12.

13. Stephen E. Koss, "Wesleyanism and Empire," *The Historical Journal* 18, no. 1 (1975): 105-18; David W. Bebbington, *The Nonconformist Conscience: Chapel and Politics, 1870-1914* (London: Allen & Unwin, 1982), 106-26.

14. Little has changed over the four decades since Owen Chadwick opened his monumental history of the Victorian church by commenting on the "extraordinary and romantic endeavour to care for new people overseas" that gripped the Victorians only to mention the two major Anglican missionary societies — the CMS and the SPG — a scant three times and the Nonconformist societies not at all. *The Victorian Church: Part One, 1829-1859*, 3rd ed. (London: SCM Press, 1971); *Part Two, 1860-1901*, 2nd ed. (London: SCM Press, 1972), 1:5, 68-69; 2:89. More recently see Callum Brown, *The Death of Christian Britain: Understanding Secularisation, 1800-2000* (London: Routledge, 2001) where foreign missions receive but minimal passing attention.

gendered missionary action as expressions in Britain of nation and empire.[15] John Wolffe's *God and Greater Britain* represents an important contribution to the study of religion, empire, and national identity. Characteristically, however, the extraordinarily large foreign missionary effort considered as a constituent force in the development of national and religious identity in "Greater Britain" is examined only cursorily in this broad and synthetic study.[16] And while the missions of Nonconformists, as an expression of an emerging middle-class culture of liberalism and respectability, have attracted increased attention, the missions of the Church of England have not.[17]

The process of constructing an integrated narrative about the missionary movement as a British cultural force, and particularly the Anglican role within it late in the century, has hardly begun. There is a long tradition of investigating the Church of England, often with an eye to class, often in the early to mid-nineteenth century, but little on late Victorian Evangelicalism or the Church.[18] The undisputed growth of imperial culture in this era reinforced a more aggressive late Victorian imperial expansion, which paralleled the spread of missions and domestic missionary culture. In this atmosphere, as English missions inevitably became increasingly engaged with the British Empire, they also grappled with the reality that the mission field extended well beyond the empire where other European and American missions considered this world an

15. Repeated calls for a reassessment and investigation of metropolitan missionary Christianity may be found in Torben Christensen and William R. Hutchison, "Introduction," in *Missionary Ideologies in the Imperialist Era, 1880-1920,* ed. Torben Christensen and William R. Hutchison ([Aarhus, Denmark]: Aros, 1982), 5-10; Andrew Porter, "Religion and Empire: British Expansion in the Long Nineteenth Century, 1780-1914," *Journal of Imperial and Commonwealth History* 20, no. 3 (1992): 374; Norman Etherington, "Introduction," in *Missions and Empire,* ed. Norman Etherington, The Oxford History of the British Empire Companion Series (Oxford: Oxford University Press, 2005), 13-18.

16. Wolffe, *God and Greater Britain,* particularly chap. 8. Wolffe's edited volume in the *Religion in Victorian Britain* series provides case studies and a general overview of missionary and imperial influence on British religious experience. *Culture and Empire,* ed. John Wolffe, vol. 5 of Religion in Victorian Britain (Manchester: Manchester University Press, 1997).

17. See Susan Thorne, *Congregational Missions and the Making of an Imperial Culture in Nineteenth-Century England* (Stanford: Stanford University Press, 1999) for an ambitious argument for imperial mindedness among Congregationalists, and Catherine Hall, *Civilising Subjects: Metropole and Colony in the English Imagination, 1830-1867* (Chicago: University of Chicago Press, 2002) for an examination of evolution in the conception of civilization through the missionary relationship of Midlands Baptists and West Indians.

18. John Wolffe, "Anglicanism," in *Nineteenth-Century English Religious Traditions: Retrospect and Prospect,* ed. D. G. Paz (Westport, CT: Greenwood, 1995), 23-28. One notable recent exception is Martin Wellings, *Evangelicals Embattled: Responses of Evangelicals in the Church of England to Ritualism, Darwinism, and Theological Liberalism, 1890-1930* (Carlisle, UK: Paternoster, 2003).

intensely competitive open field, creating a persistent, intrinsic tension between the imperial and the international in English missionary vision. Over the course of the nineteenth century, foreign missionary societies came to command a complex, integrated, and nationally extensive organizational structure designed to deliver clearly formulated messages to socially targeted audiences with the goal of supporting massive overseas operations; however, the priority of focus and ambition — empire or world — was never clearly resolved. English missionary societies were at the cutting edge of Victorian charitable development, and none were more successful or had more resources than the Church Missionary Society (CMS) and the Society for the Propagation of the Gospel (SPG); however, the conflict over whether these societies should operate primarily as an imperial enterprise, or work to transcend the empire, remained a centrally contested issue.

This book examines the ideological, institutional, and cultural realities of the foreign missions of the Church of England primarily as they developed in England in the late Victorian and Edwardian era of "high empire." Central to my text is an evaluation of the religious party context — in its theological, social, and political dimensions — in relation to the development of Anglican missions, emphasizing internal dynamics within the Church among its characteristic parties, constituencies, and factions as they operated in dynamic tension with failures, successes, and transformative experiences of multiple missionary encounter in worldwide fields of proselytizing. I argue that the development of Anglican "missionary religion" grew from a complex interaction of religious, social, and ideological factors that require detailed examination if the movement is to be fully understood. In the remainder of this chapter, then, I aim to provide first an overview of the historiography of British foreign missions and second an introduction to the relationship of missions to religious sectarianism, nationality, gender, and empire in order to set the frame for the following analysis. In Chapters 2 and 3, I follow by unraveling the relationship between evangelicalism and emerging varieties of "High Churchism" in the context of debates and controversies emerging out of religious competition at home and abroad. Chapter 4 features the foundational importance of women and gender constructs to the strategies and structure of Anglican missions, with the impact of professionalization and engagement with the universities the focus of Chapters 5 and 6. Chapter 7 details the impact of women's mission and gendered strategies on the movement and the intensifying conservative religious backlash against "modern" missionary methods. The final chapter examines the emergence of an aggressive but contested project to transform the Church of England into an "imperial church."

The detailed subjects of the chapters are bound together by the overarching perspective of the book: that the cultural contest to structure Anglican missionary effort operated in a multivalent encounter of ideologies and forces that required responsiveness to a complex series of interests. These ranged from varied theological and ecclesiastical commitments to shifting patterns of imperial opportunity as well as from particular cultures of faith and historical identity to constructs of national identity and social ideology fed by strongly gendered visions of Christian service. These interests appealed to overlapping but clearly differentiated communities. Thus, while a generic embrace of the idea of "England's mission" could and did have broad, cross-class appeal by the 1880s, the specific application of the idea of mission to strategies for religious expansion, as well as the ideals and ends to which it was applied, varied considerably.[19] Emphasis on missions as a critical component of religious life could be applied to very different purposes. Focus on the Church of England as an English church in relation to the operation of its foreign missions, the British Empire, and its associated episcopal churches throughout the world leads to key questions: Why did the Anglican missionary movement take on the shapes and styles it did? Why did it grow so successfully in England after 1870? What were the extent and nature of its influence on British religious and imperial culture? What was its impact on the development of a clearly English nationalism within the British isles and empire? What were the limits of Anglican and imperial identity in pushing forward and sustaining the movement?

Recently a new critical scholarship of missions has begun to emerge, emphasizing the importance of the "missionary encounter" to both "metropole" and "periphery" in Britain's empire and its wider set of international relations.[20] Much of this work has drawn on the perspectives of Africanists such as Jean and John Comaroff and their introduction of a new, fluid conception of culture as an interactive, transformative process, shifting the focus of studies of colonialism to the "colonial encounter." Additionally, Edward Said's insistence on the centrality of the production of colonial knowledge to imperial processes of control has transformed the study of empires, both in the centers of imperial power and within and between indigenous groups which assimilated and used that knowledge for local purposes.[21] Study of missionary encounters in

19. On newly aggressive, self-justifying ideas of divine mission to rule, though in tension with continuing "federal" thinking in imperial organization, see C. C. Eldridge, *England's Mission: The Imperial Idea in the Age of Gladstone and Disraeli, 1868-1880* (Chapel Hill: University of North Carolina Press, 1974), 242-46.

20. Notably, see Elizabeth Elbourne, *Blood Ground: Colonialism, Missions, and the Contest for Christianity in the Cape Colony and Britain, 1799-1853* (Montreal: McGill-Queen's University Press, 2002) for her skillful drawing of metropole and colony into a single analytical frame.

21. Edward Said, *Orientalism* (New York: Pantheon, 1978); Jean Comaroff and John L. Coma-

a variety of colonial locales, from Africa and India to the Pacific, has clearly demonstrated the complexity of the subject across both time and space, forcing an elaboration of Said's monolithic and historically static conception of power and discourse. For example, as the progressively greater power of converts to construct an indigenized Christianity molded for local purposes emerged, the complex ways rhetorical and institutional power was deployed by Europeans, and the equally complex ways it was utilized or subverted in part or whole by indigenous populations, has also become more apparent.[22] This new set of approaches has reinforced the importance of understanding that "metropolitan" and "imperial" contexts were not separate but intimately interactive and often transcended by transnational discourses and dynamics.[23] At the same time, however, understanding that missions were more than a "mere reflection of monolithic cultural structures or social forces" has become clearer not only with regard to indigenous or imperial society but also with regard to British society itself.[24] The missionary movement had the range and scope it did because millions of Britons supported it with their sustained interest and substantial

roff, *Of Revelation and Revolution: Christianity, Colonialism, and Consciousness in South Africa*, vol. 1 (Chicago: University of Chicago Press, 1991); Edward Said, *Culture and Imperialism* (New York: Knopf, 1993); Jean Comaroff and John L. Comaroff, *Of Revelation and Revolution: The Dialectics of Modernity on a South African Frontier*, vol. 2 (Chicago: University of Chicago Press, 1997). These represent a postcolonial strand and a historical anthropology strand, but both are primarily concerned with the cultural play of ritual and language. On the postcolonial strand and imperial studies, see Dane Kennedy, "Imperial History and Post-Colonial Theory," *Journal of Imperial and Commonwealth History* 24, no. 3 (1996): 345-63. On the strengths and limitations of the anthropological work of the Comaroffs for historians, see Elizabeth Elbourne, "Word Made Flesh: Christianity, Modernity, and Cultural Colonialism in the Work of Jean and John Comaroff," *American Historical Review* 108, no. 2 (2003): 435-59.

22. For examples from a large field of work, see Geoffrey A. Oddie, *Hindu and Christian in South-East India* (London: Curzon, 1991); Paul Stuart Landau, *The Realm of the Word: Language, Gender, and Christianity in a Southern African Kingdom* (Portsmouth, NH: Heinemann, 1995); Richard Elphick and Rodney Davenport, eds., *Christianity in South Africa: A Political, Social, and Cultural History* (Berkeley: University of California Press, 1997); J. D. Y. Peel, *Religious Encounter and the Making of the Yoruba* (Bloomington: Indiana University Press, 2000). For an assessment of this literature emphasizing the ambiguous relationship of missionary Christianity to empire, see Porter, *Religion Versus Empire*, chap. 12. On the ways indigenous Christians negotiated their place and agency in traditional and emerging national societies, see the many individual chapters in Norman Etherington, ed., *Missions and Empire*, The Oxford History of the British Empire Companion Series (Oxford: Oxford University Press, 2005).

23. Mrinalini Sinha emphasizes, for example, the operation of "imperial social formations" where categories of identity interact in uneven, often contradictory ways. *Colonial Masculinity: The 'Manly Englishman' and the 'Effeminate Bengali' in the Late Nineteenth Century* (Manchester: Manchester University Press, 1995), 2.

24. Jean and John Comaroff, *Of Revelation*, vol. 1, 10.

financial contributions. What follows is an investigation of the conditions under which this set of projects was carried out within the Anglican Church and, while conceived as an excavation of a broader consciousness of "missionary religion" and its consequences across many fields, it focuses primarily on the sites of institutional, ideological, and social power in England that were necessary to sustain the effort. In doing so, I hope to contribute to an expansion of the understanding of religion and its impact in England, Britain, the empire, and beyond.

Comprehending missionary influence across colonial fields requires, then, a deeper analysis of what was brought to the encounter, including those under-evaluated aspects of the metropolitan foundations of the missionary project. Within the Church of England this means, among other things, deconstructing the many evolving meanings of "Anglicanism," including the party distinctions between the interdenominationalism of "holiness"-based Evangelicals and "neo-Evangelical" establishmentarianism as well as the divide between the independent internationalism of Anglo-Catholicism and the continuing old High Church commitment to nation and empire. With such an orientation, this study necessarily tells us more about the culture of religion, nationalism, and empire in England than it does about missions and missionaries in the overseas fields where they worked. It suggests that, not for the first or last time, when intensely scrutinizing foreign peoples the British were deeply engaged in a self-reflective process of comparative self-construction. The exchange of ideas between metropole and colony and the power of that exchange in the context of broader imperial and internationalist Christian cultures is also an important dynamic. Yet while acknowledging the critical importance of indigenous and international voices to the shaping of the missionary encounter, this book primarily attempts to excavate the mentalities, strategic challenges, institutions, and conditions that formed an Anglican consciousness of church, nation, empire, and world. My analysis concentrates primarily upon the center of Anglican membership and power in England, and it focuses on bringing religious identity and languages of belief, as well as Church institutions, back into the story of English religion and the British Empire.[25]

Taking this approach has advantages. In particular it gives an important perspective on a critical question in imperial history: What was the impact of empire and imperial culture upon Britain in the nineteenth and twentieth

25. As Hall and Rose note, despite dangers of scope and omission inherent in focusing on the metropole, there is considerable value in reexamining British history in the light of the transnational perspective that imperial and cross-cultural dynamics brings. Catherine Hall and Sonya O. Rose, "Being at Home with the Empire," in *At Home with the Empire: Metropolitan Culture and the Imperial World,* ed. Catherine Hall and Sonya O. Rose (Cambridge: Cambridge University Press, 2006), 2-5.

centuries? This question remains vigorously contested between "maximalist" and "minimalist" lines of interpretation.[26] Minimalists emphasize the sectional, diffusive, and limited impact of empire on Victorian domestic culture, making Britain less of an imperial society than many might assume because, as Bernard Porter argues, the working classes were not significantly affected by imperial knowledge, and those in the middle and upper classes who were imperially minded were far more ambivalent about imperialism than has generally been recognized. Thus Britain, while "obviously an imperial power, *never* became a genuine imperial society."[27] Maximalists, on the other hand, insist that imperial knowledge and attitudes had culture-wide incidence, that empire was, in Antoinette Burton's phrase, "a fundamental and constitutive part of English culture and national identity," and that empire enjoyed conscious, pervasive, and functionally critical support throughout the Victorian era and into the decades that followed.[28] Partisans on either side of this debate will find little of comfort here. What a close study of the Anglican experience shows is that imperial attitudes and knowledge were both far more widely dispersed, at least in the quite impressive channels of influence that "missionary religion" affected, than the minimalists suggest. However, within this shared communion there were much more variety, ambiguity, and contradiction than the maximalists might comfortably accept. By a broad definition, all Victorians were imperialists; by a narrow, few. But labeling the Victorians as deeply cognizant of empire or largely ignorant of it tells us very little about precisely how the indubitable lines of imperial force that radiated through England's culture, society, and economy actually influenced the surprisingly complex array of cultures, communities, and coteries that made up the multilayered, variable reality of lived empire residing in the Victorian experience.[29]

26. The contours of this debate have been usefully outlined in John M. MacKenzie, "Empire and Metropolitan Cultures," in *The Nineteenth Century*, ed. Andrew Porter, vol. 3 of The Oxford History of the British Empire (Oxford: Oxford University Press, 1999), 270-93. See also Andrew Thompson, *The Empire Strikes Back? The Impact of Imperialism on Britain from the Mid-Nineteenth Century* (Harlow, UK: Pearson/Longman, 2005), 3-4.

27. Bernard Porter, "'Empire, What Empire?'; or, Why 80% of Early- and Mid-Victorians Were Deliberately Kept in Ignorance of It," *Victorian Studies* 46, no. 2 (2004): 262; Bernard Porter, *The Absent-Minded Imperialists: Empire, Society, and Culture in Britain* (Oxford: Oxford University Press, 2004), vii-xvi, 310-12.

28. "On the Inadequacy and the Indispensability of the Nation," in *After the Imperial Turn: Thinking with and through the Nation*, ed. Antoinette Burton (Durham, NC: Duke University Press, 2003), 3.

29. For recent emphasis on pluralism in the Empire and Britain, as well as the complex and even contradictory effect of empire on British society, institutions and identity (including a brief investigation of missionary influence), see Thompson, *Empire Strikes Back*, 4-8, 105-11. This work

In order to begin a project that aims to tell us something both concrete and nuanced about English culture in an undeniably imperial age, a closer consideration of several key issues is therefore necessary. In this chapter I will begin by examining the surprising absence of analyses of the missionary enterprise in studies of English religion, in examinations of national and imperial culture, and in the history of women and gender in the Victorian and Edwardian eras. From there I will suggest a beginning point for understanding the missionary movement in the context of English religious culture and national identity as a gendered project developing out of a professionalizing society with wide-ranging imperial ambitions and opportunities.

Invisible Influence? Anglican Foreign Missions in the Victorian Era

The history of British Protestant missionary outreach parallels in timeframe and cultural influences the emergence of modern Britain, and its empire, with the longest continuous tradition associated with the Church of England.[30] By the closing decades of the eighteenth century, in the midst of the late evangelical revival and the age of democratic revolutions, the various English Protestant denominations had all initiated foreign missionary work, but the initiative clearly lay with the dynamically expanding Nonconformist denominations.[31] Despite the intense competitive pressure it experienced from Nonconformity throughout the nineteenth century, however, the Church of England remained unmatched in institutional and cultural presence in the English religious world. And within the Church, foreign missionary societies grew over the nineteenth

---

is one of several that have called for greater precision in the writing on empire's impact on and entanglement with British life, for example, Linda Colley, "The Difficulties of Empire: Present, Past and Future," *Historical Research* 79 (2006): 367-82.

30. British Protestant foreign missions began with the founding by English Anglicans of the Society for the Promotion of Christian Knowledge and the Society for the Propagation of the Gospel in 1699 and 1701. Craig Rose, "The Origins and Ideals of the SPCK, 1699-1716," in *The Church of England c. 1689–c. 1833: From Toleration to Tractarianism,* ed. John Walsh, Colin Haydon, and Stephen Taylor (Cambridge: Cambridge University Press, 1993), 172-90.

31. The Baptist Missionary Society (BMS) was founded in 1792, the (largely) Congregationalist London Missionary Society (LMS) in 1795, and the Wesleyan Methodist Missionary Society (WMMS) in 1816 (although Methodist missions had been active for three decades). Anglican evangelicals, unwilling to join either High Churchmen or the London Missionary Society, formed the CMS in 1799. Scottish and American Protestant societies also started early, and Canadian, Australian and other colonial societies later in the century. Kenneth Scott Latourette, *The Great Century, A.D. 1800–A.D. 1914: Europe and the United States of America,* vol. 4 of *A History of the Expansion of Christianity* (New York: Harper, 1941), 65-93.

century to be one of its chief institutional forces, accounting for nearly 5 percent of Anglican clergy.[32]

Yet when missionary enterprise has been noted at all in general studies of imperialism the tendency has been to focus on Nonconformity, leaving the mistaken impression that foreign missions were mainly a dissenting cause.[33] Additionally, in general studies of the missionary movement the pattern has been to concentrate on evangelicalism, leaving out of consideration both the second largest missionary agency of the age, the SPG — which functioned as the institutional home of the majority of moderate High Church missionary activity — and also dynamic and influential Anglo-Catholic missions, such as the Universities' Mission to Central Africa (UMCA). These non-evangelical societies directed by bishops, particularly the SPG with its relatively stronger focus in "white-settlement" colonies (in contrast to the evangelical partiality to Indian and "tropical" missions), represent a significant but largely neglected section of the missionary movement.[34] By the end of the century, however, Anglicans sent the majority of English missionaries abroad, contributed the bulk of funds supporting missions, and by 1899 accounted for over half of the expanding army of nearly 1,500 unmarried English female missionaries who profoundly transformed the movement in the late Victorian age.[35] Originally a movement largely of evangelical Nonconformity (with support from a minority of influential Anglican evangelicals), missions had transformed into a majority Anglican project by the turn of the twentieth century, garnering deep sympathy from a broad range of establishment-minded supporters.[36] And until the inter-

32. The figure is close to 4.5 percent, calculated from clergy numbers in Alan Haig, *The Victorian Clergy* (London: Croom Helm, 1984), 3, and numbers of Anglican ordained missionaries (1,100), James S. Dennis, *Centennial Survey of Foreign Missions* (Edinburgh: Oliphant, Anderson and Ferrier, 1902), 22-25. If 551 "ordained natives" are added, the figure rises to almost 7 percent.

33. On the misperception of missions as mainly Nonconformist and marginalization of the reach of missionaries as a factor in imperial culture, see Porter, *Absent-Minded Imperialists,* 85, 89. The tendency of imperial historians generally to ignore missionary influence is widespread and of long standing. Norman Etherington, "Missions and Empire," in *Historiography,* ed. Robin W. Winks, vol. 5 of *The Oxford History of the British Empire* (Oxford: Oxford University Press, 1999), 303-8.

34. High Church missions have tended to be easily dismissed as accounting for only about ten percent of Victorian missionary giving, although David Bebbington concedes that, within the Church of England, such dismissal distorts the dynamics of influence in a rapidly changing intellectual landscape. "Atonement, Sin, and Empire, 1880-1914," in *The Imperial Horizons of British Protestant Missions, 1880-1914,* ed. Andrew Porter (Grand Rapids: Eerdmans, 2003), 16.

35. Calculated from Dennis, *Centennial Survey,* 22-25, 257-60. See also Appendix I, Figures 5 and 6.

36. By century's end Anglicans certainly made up well over half of missionary support based on CMS, SPG, allied Anglican mission and missionary diocese incomes, and Anglican support to

war period when superseded by the Americans, Britain supplied the largest and leading force in global Protestant missions (see Appendix I, Figure 1).

British and imperial studies have recently begun to emphasize the connection of religion, nation, and empire as well as the interconnectedness of the histories of metropole and colony, shifting attention back to the missionary enterprise.[37] Growing interest has been fueled by cultural approaches to the study of empire and imperial culture,[38] increasing attention to the role of women in national and imperial life,[39] and a deepening appreciation of the power of religious belief and institutions to influence and structure culture, society, and politics.[40] Despite these shifting patterns of study, particularly within studies of religion in the British Isles, the general neglect of imperial culture and international Christian cooperation as forces in metropolitan Christianity has continued to obscure the importance of foreign missions to the construction of religious identity. The rapidly growing and changing missionary movement, one of the most generously and fervently supported of the Victorian philanthropies, was characterized by a complex set of internal divisions along denominational,

interdenominational missions. On the early-nineteenth-century atmosphere of anti-authoritarian Nonconformist evangelicalism in missions, see Elbourne, *Blood Ground*, 28-43.

37. Notably beginning with Thorne, *Congregational Missions* (1999); Brian Stanley, ed., *Christian Missions and the Enlightenment* (Grand Rapids: Eerdmans, 2001); Hall, *Civilising Subjects* (2002); Andrew Porter, ed., *The Imperial Horizons of British Protestant Missions, 1880-1914* (Grand Rapids: Eerdmans, 2003); Brian Stanley, ed., *Missions, Nationalism, and the End of Empire* (Grand Rapids: Eerdmans, 2003), and following with others.

38. Most notably, John M. MacKenzie, *Propaganda and Empire: The Manipulation of British Public Opinion, 1880-1960* (Manchester: Manchester University Press, 1984), MacKenzie, ed., *Imperialism and Popular Culture* (Manchester: Manchester University Press, 1986) and the more than twenty volumes that followed in the Manchester Studies in Imperialism and Popular Culture series.

39. The literature on gender and empire is substantial. Significant general studies include Margaret Strobel, *European Women and the Second British Empire* (Bloomington: Indiana University Press, 1991); Clare Midgley, ed., *Gender and Imperialism* (Manchester: Manchester University Press, 1998); Philippa Levine, ed., *Gender and Empire,* The Oxford History of the British Empire Companion Series (Oxford: Oxford University Press, 2004); Clare Midgley, *Feminism and Empire: Women Activists in Imperial Britain, 1790-1865* (London: Routledge, 2007).

40. Emphasis on the importance of religious views to the formation of political identity and government policy has pushed the study of British religiosity beyond the social history of religion that dominated the field until the 1990s. For only a few of the works that began the trend, see J. C. D. Clark, *English Society, 1688-1832: Ideology, Social Structure, and Political Practice During the Ancien Regime* (Cambridge: Cambridge University Press, 1985); Jim Obelkevich, Lyndal Roper, and Raphael Samuel, eds., *Disciplines of Faith: Studies in Religion, Politics, and Patriarchy* (London: Routledge & K. Paul, 1987); Boyd Hilton, *The Age of Atonement: The Influence of Evangelicalism on Social and Economic Thought, 1795-1865* (Oxford: Oxford University Press, 1988).

theological, regional, social, and gender lines, making it a dynamic site for the fashioning of religious, national, and imperial life.

Missionary support, while concentrated in the Victorian middle classes, significantly transcended class boundaries and included nearly every religious denomination, attracting enormous resources and attention.[41] Though primarily founded in the late eighteenth century, British Protestant missions grew most vigorously after 1870, and by the turn of the century they were truly imposing, involving sixty missionary societies, over 6,000 missionaries, and over £1.6 million annually.[42] By the late Victorian era a multiform missionary movement with multivalent social and institutional associations had emerged, yet the core of the missionary effort in England developed in its five largest denominational societies: Baptist, Congregationalist, Wesleyan Methodist, High Church Anglican, and Low Church Anglican, with overlapping organization on similar lines in Northern Ireland, Scotland, and Wales. Thus denominational societies, attracting 71 percent of domestic giving to missions in England at century's end, remained the heavyweights of the movement, and the Anglicans were the heaviest of the heavyweights.[43] In sheer volume of contributions they far exceeded any other single benevolent or reform-oriented philanthropy — one informed observer estimated around one-fourth of the total of charitable giving — and they sent, along with the Colonial Office, the most highly educated agents into the British Empire and the "regions beyond" it.[44] Missionaries of all

41. Brian Stanley has demonstrated for earlier in the century that missionary support crossed class as broadly as religious observance. "Home Support for Overseas Missions in Early Victorian England, c. 1838-1873" (Ph.D. diss., University of Cambridge, 1979), 196-99. Frank Prochaska suggests that the missionary and Bible societies were the most effective Victorian philanthropies in gaining support from the poor. F. K. Prochaska, "Philanthropy," in *The Cambridge Social History of Britain, 1750-1950: Social Agencies and Institutions,* vol. 3, ed. F. M. L. Thompson (Cambridge: Cambridge University Press, 1990), 367.

42. Dennis, *Centennial Survey,* 22-25, 257-60. Dennis reports over 9,000 missionaries, but unorthodox returns for the Salvation Army inflate his totals by about 2,700. Total British missionary giving had increased from £543,628 in 1861. W[illiam]. B[innington]. B[oyce]., *Statistics of Protestant Missionary Societies, 1861* (London: Nichols, 1863), 79-81. For caveats on the use of missionary statistics, see Appendix II.

43. Computed from Dennis, *Centennial Survey,* 22-25. The domestic income of the Evangelical CMS alone was more than the combined incomes of the Nonconformist BMS, LMS and WMMS; the income of the High Church SPG was more than any single one of them. The other 29 percent of income was accounted for by 41 additional independent societies, several of which — the CEZMS, ZBMM, Colonial and Continental Missionary Society, and South American Missionary Society, for example — very closely allied to the Anglican societies.

44. In the year 1880 when the Anglican evangelical Church Missionary Society registered an income of £221,723, Dr. Barnardo's Homes received £36,000, the London City Mission £46,990, the Mildmay Institutions £19,378, and the London Bible and Domestic Female Mission about

denominations outnumbered employees of the various colonial services four to one, and the movement commanded funds equivalent to almost 2 percent of central government gross expenditures, or the same as annual outlays for all civil service salaries.[45] And in the foreign missionary movement, by the year 1899 the two flagship Anglican missionary societies accounted for over 60 percent of the British funds contributed to the five major denominational missionary societies (see Appendix I, Figure 5).

Beyond simple statistics, and perhaps most importantly, the foreign missions of the British churches were a significant element in the networks of religious associational life and the broader imagination of millions of Britons. The massive publishing and educational arms of the missionary societies created an astonishing volume of words through which supporters at home viewed the empire and the world, structuring the ways foreign cultures were pictured and judged.[46] The cause of missions supplied "zeal and purpose" that was cultivated in Sunday schools and reinforced by sermon, religious publication, and social life surrounding Anglican church and Dissenting chapel. Most British Christians came to see empire as endowing a unique set of opportunities and special responsibilities upon the denominations, which rapidly adopted imperial roles.[47] The overseas commitments of the churches, quite simply, were of considerable significance not only to religious institutions and identity but also to national and imperial life more broadly conceived.

Marginalized Missionaries

Until recently scholarly study of foreign missions has fallen through several gaps in the historiography of modern Britain and its empire. Lately it has be-

---

£10,000. W. F. Howe, *The Classified Directory to the Metropolitan Charities for 1880* (London: Longmans, Green, 1880), 6-8, 13. For the one-fourth estimate, see Meredith Townsend, "Cheap Missionaries," *Contemporary Review* 56 (Jan. 1889): 3.

45. Porter, "Religion and Empire," 372.

46. By 1881 the CMS alone, with over 1,000 local associations, organized annually for over 7,500 sermons and 4,000 public meetings. In 1898 the CMS had a monthly magazine circulation — targeted differentially to the educated, popular, laboring, and youthful reader — of 216,000 per month, and distributed in total over 7.5 million magazines, tracts and papers. E[ugene]. S[tock]., "The Church Missionary Society at Home," *Church Missionary Intelligencer,* n.s., 7 (Apr. 1882): 194 and "Report of the Centenary Review Committee. Section XI," in *Centenary Review Reports* (n.p.: private printing, 1899), 78, Church Missionary Society Archives, G/CC b 15, University of Birmingham, Birmingham, Eng. (hereafter cited as CMS Archives).

47. P. J. Marshall, "Imperial Britain," *Journal of Imperial and Commonwealth History* 23, no. 3 (1995): 381-82.

come commonplace to emphasize that the empire was not something fundamentally outside of and separate from the metropole, but that its enterprises,
institutions, and ideologies were of significant, if uneven, importance to domestic British culture and society.[48] However, while studies of imperial culture
have increasingly challenged the insularity of traditional approaches to British
social and political history, the history of British religion has remained largely
isolated from the history of its overseas influence through foreign missions and
"daughter" colonial churches. Foreign missions were one of the most conspicuous aspects of British overseas commitment, yet the historiography of missions
in the field, while voluminous, has remained marginal and largely ignored by
scholars of the religious or imperial dimensions of the recent history of the
British Isles.

There appear to be several factors which, when taken together, account for
this. The first is simple distaste at the extraordinarily uniform defamatory presentation of non-Christian religions, and often non-Western cultures, made
by so many missionaries.[49] Along with the self-righteous, dogmatically propa-
gandistic Christian paternalism and triumphalism that characterize Victorian
missionary literature, missions as a subject have sat extremely poorly with liberal, pluralistic post-war academic cultures.[50] Combined with a set of Marxist
analyses dating from the era of decolonization that construct missions as simple
auxiliaries to capitalist imperialism, the willingness to think of missionary religion as an understood quantity, and thus dismissible, has been almost palpable.[51]
As Jeffrey Cox has noted, writing about missions and empire has tended to fall
into one of two historiographical camps. The first is a "providentialist" apolo-

48. Ann Laura Stoler and Frederick Cooper, "Between Metropole and Colony: Rethinking a
Research Agenda," in *Tensions of Empire: Colonial Cultures in a Bourgeois World* (Berkeley: University of California Press, 1997), 1-56.

49. Jeffrey Cox, *The British Missionary Enterprise Since 1700* (New York: Routledge, 2008),
chap. 6. This persistent defamation was in part a legacy of early-nineteenth-century evangelical
discourses, particularly about slavery, which focused on transformation from the degradation of
slave society to the liberty of emancipation. The development of these narratives entailed imagining a variety of foreign societies as having embraced enslaving tyrannies.

50. Andrew Porter, "Church History, History of Christianity, Religious History: Some Reflections on British Missionary Enterprise Since the Late Eighteenth Century," *Church History* 71, no.
3 (Sept. 2002): 556-57. For discussions of "missionary literature" as a literary genre, see Anna Johnston, *Missionary Writing and Empire, 1800-1860* (Cambridge: Cambridge University Press, 2003),
and Benjamin Fischer, "A Novel Resistance: Mission Narrative as the Anti-Novel in the Evangelical
Assault on British Culture," in *The Church and Literature*, ed. Peter Clarke and Charlotte Methuen,
vol. 48 of Studies in Church History (Abingdon, UK: Boydell, 2012)

51. Brian Stanley, *The Bible and the Flag: Protestant Missions and British Imperialism in the
Nineteenth and Twentieth Centuries* (Leicester, UK: Apollos, 1990), chap. 1.

getic narrative, characteristic of religiously committed observers. It emphasizes the "otherworldliness" of the missionary task and thus glosses over the intertwining of foreign missions in processes of imperial domination and colonial resistance. By emphasizing that missions, much in keeping with the worldview of the evangelicals who drove the movement, should be understood primarily in terms of faith and altruistic personal commitment, "providentialists" obscure the worldly agendas, commitments, and entanglements of both missionaries and indigenous Christians.[52] The second camp employs a "Saidian" unmasking narrative, common to many recent histories of empire or imperial culture, that often dismisses missionaries as marginal to imperial processes directed by imperial elites or assumes that the primary task in assessing missions is to uncover their roles as imperial functionaries tied to a simple and generic cultural imperative of ordering and dominating foreign peoples.[53]

Put bluntly, missionaries and their supporters have tended to be historically constructed either as the otherworldly Christian conscience of Western expansion or as the accessories to a sophisticated ideological and institutional project of hegemonic imperial domination. As Cox further notes, however, just as the act of missionary persuasion, pursued under extremely varied conditions throughout the world, has a complex relationship to imperial coercion, so too do forms of missionary religion, constructed within the contested, free-associational life characterizing Victorian England, have a complex relationship to denominational identity and imperial culture. The nature of those relationships has only recently begun to be plumbed with any depth and, because so often concerned with Nonconformity, has tended to focus on the industrial middle classes. In the main, both religiously "committed" histories and recent imperial studies provide incomplete analyses of the British missionary project both abroad and at home. The former neglects to engage with issues of nation, empire, race, class, ethnicity, or gender in revealing or satisfying ways.[54] The

52. Jeffrey Cox, *Imperial Fault Lines: Christianity and Colonial Power in India, 1818-1940* (Stanford: Stanford University Press, 2002), 11-13.

53. The "Saidian" approach, of course, is traceable to Edward Said's deeply influential *Orientalism* and *Culture and Imperialism*. Cox suggests these contemporary scholarly "master narratives" are overlaid and intersect with other perspectives on missions and religion in empire: those of a pro-imperialist past that emphasized a set of modernizing processes as being at the heart of ultimately beneficial imperial encounters and those of anti-imperialists who, whether nationalist or post-colonialist, identify missionaries as imperial functionaries. "Were Victorian Nonconformists the Worst Imperialists of All?" *Victorian Studies* 46, no. 2 (2004): 247-48, 251-53.

54. Protestant missionary historiography dates back to the first nineteenth-century society-commissioned studies, which focused largely on the exploits of white clerical missionaries, with scant attention to women, non-Western workers, and domestic culture and organization. The major works on Anglicans for the period 1870 to 1914 are C. F. Pascoe, *Two Hundred Years of the*

latter, despite frequent attention to contested discourses and shifting language, often ignores the internal complexities and dynamics of formal religious communities and the power of religious belief, language, and culture to structure meaning and behavior.[55]

As Gauri Viswanathan has pointed out, however, the analytical marginalization of religious languages and identities reduces our ability to understand historical processes of change, particularly because "religion shares features with the analytical categories of race and class in that each assumes certain established criteria for determining rank, position, and membership in a national community." Yet shifting religious identities, she cautions, are resistant to easy classification, and the discussion of belief in current secular cultural studies suffers from a lack of adequate vocabulary.[56] The relative paucity of fully developed studies of missionary culture and encounters has meant that as an older, dimensionally flat vision of missions (as uncomplicated followers of spiritual imperatives and pure motives) receded, it was largely replaced by a similarly reductive set of assumptions that constructed missions as fully complicitous agents of imperial and colonial domination.[57] It is easy to discover in case after case missionary complicity with the Western imperial establishment, but identifying these alone does little to advance the project of working through this phenomenon with historical precision and analytical rigor.[58] Nor does it advance our understanding of how missionary Christianity could also — if only occasionally — contribute to developments that ultimately criticized, weakened, and overturned colonialism.[59]

S.P.G. (London: SPG, 1901) and Eugene Stock, *The History of the Church Missionary Society,* 4 vols. (London: CMS, 1899-1916). Of all missionary histories in the nineteenth century, only Stock features the domestic context of missionary organization.

55. This argument derives much from Jeffrey Cox, "The Missionary Movement," in *Nineteenth-Century English Religious Traditions: Retrospect and Prospect,* ed. D. G. Paz (Westport, CT: Greenwood, 1995), 198-202.

56. Gauri Viswanathan, *Outside the Fold: Conversion, Modernity, and Belief* (Princeton: Princeton University Press, 1998), xii-xiv.

57. Characteristic among those seeing missionaries as simple, unambiguous cultural imperialists have been (from an anthropological and a nationalist perspective, respectively) T. O. Beidelman, *Colonial Evangelism: A Socio-Historical Study of an East African Mission at the Grassroots* (Bloomington: Indiana University Press, 1982) and Arun Shourie, *Missionaries in India: Continuities, Changes, Dilemmas* (New Delhi: ASA Publications, 1994). For a problematization of this formulation, see Andrew Porter, " 'Cultural Imperialism' and Protestant Missionary Enterprise, 1780-1914," *Journal of Imperial and Commonwealth History* 25, no. 3 (Sept. 1997): 367-91.

58. The general point about analytical rigor is Edward Said's, which he articulates in *Orientalism* and then ignores with regard to missions by reducing them to a minor part in a larger British mechanism of state-sponsored domination (pp. 100, 123).

59. E.g., the examples of Harriette Colenso's involvement with the founders of the African

Bringing Missionaries Back In

Missionary organizations, supporters, theoreticians, and enthusiasts were a constant and surprisingly heterogeneous presence in the British churches. Ferocious self-critical debates that yielded no single common missionary method characterized missionary activity.[60] The ambiguity of the role of the missionary is implicit in the differences of approach over the course of the nineteenth century to a variety of issues, including, for example, West Indian slavery, African colonialism, and China's Boxer Rebellion, to name but a few contested subjects.[61] Furthermore, while the European missionary, deeply enmeshed in Western cultural prejudices, could often act as an ideological and functional supporter of westernization and empire, missions had far less control over missionary institutions and converts than they pretended. The significant spread of Christianity in the non-Western world was primarily dependent upon converted indigenous agents, the "new Christians" responsible for the striking success of church growth particularly in Africa and the Pacific; and the complex ways that converts used Christianity, often at odds with the intentions of the missionaries who preached it, further complicate a story now understood to be of multiple encounters and peculiarly contingent outcomes.[62]

Because there was no uniform, simple metropolitan missionary culture or approach, because the variability of local conditions from mission to mission meant a range of relations to colonial governments from collaboration to conflict on a wide array of policy issues, because significant divergences existed over definitions of Christian "civilization" and culture, of Church authority, of

---

National Congress and the influence of Christian friendship in the midst of crude racism on the developing thought and practice of M. K. Gandhi. John Wolffe, "Victorian Religion in Context," in *Culture and Empire,* ed. John Wolffe, vol. 5 of *Religion in Victorian Britain* (Manchester: Manchester University Press, 1997), 16. See also R. S. Sugirtharajah, *The Bible and Empire: Postcolonial Explorations* (Cambridge: Cambridge University Press, 2005), chap. 3 on the cases of Anglican missionaries John Henry Colenso and James Long.

60. On the debate over promoting commerce to aid the spread of Christianity, for example, see Brian Stanley, " 'Commerce and Christianity': Providence Theory, the Missionary Movement, and the Imperialism of Free Trade, 1842-1860," *Historical Journal* 26, no. 1 (1983): 71-94 and Andrew Porter, " 'Commerce and Christianity': The Rise and Fall of a Nineteenth-Century Missionary Slogan," *Historical Journal* 28, no. 3 (1985): 597-621.

61. On varieties of approach in these three cases, see Stanley, *Bible and Flag,* 85-98, 116-32, 136-42.

62. Peggy Brock, "New Christians as Evangelists," and Robert Edgar, "New Religious Movements," in *Missions and Empire,* ed. Norman Etherington, The Oxford History of the British Empire Companion Series (Oxford: Oxford University Press, 2005), 132-52 and 216-37.

theology and orthodoxy, it becomes very problematic to reduce the missions of a communion as diverse as Anglicanism to a simple extension of some generic metropolitan imperial culture of control.[63] Catherine Hall's study of Midlands Baptists and West Indian missions demonstrates that interest in the complex ideological and social encounters catalyzed by missions is beginning to influence the study of religion and imperial culture in Britain in relation to its colonies and other international commitments.[64] For some time, awareness has been growing that reified bipolarities of colonizer and colonized alone cannot comprehend the complexities of interaction in colonial realms and imperial cultures. Yet the contemporary urge to denounce the forms of cultural and racial arrogance exhibited by many missionaries may yet be the most significant factor in sidetracking broader historical inquiry that seeks to determine how missionary systems came into operation, how they were sustained, and how they changed over time.

Studies of the religious fields in which missions operated have clearly demonstrated that colonized populations were deeply divided by class, age, gender, ethnic, regional, and other differentiators, creating a multisided dynamic of engagement both within and outside of their communities.[65] This reality is no less true in and of Britain among the communities and coteries of influence that sent missionaries abroad and that fought vigorously over money, inspiration, and competing visions of the future. These divisions were primarily expressed through languages of faith (theology and popular religious loyalties and attitudes) and their power to construct common cultures based on shared religious identity and values. Central to missionary support, these communities reflected the enormous cultural variety of not only metropolitan but also colonial Christianity.[66] With such rapid mutability in religious identities and

---

63. On the "ambiguity, contradiction, and paradox" that characterized missionary attitudes toward imperial governments and international politics, see James G. Greenlee and Charles Murray Johnston, *Good Citizens: British Missionaries and Imperial States, 1870-1918* (Montreal: McGill-Queen's University Press, 1999), xii and passim.

64. *Civilising Subjects.* See also her earlier *White, Male and Middle-Class: Explorations in Feminism and History* (New York: Routledge, 1992), 207 and passim, which emphasizes the importance of religious language, if not theology itself, to the construction of middle-class Nonconformist evangelical confidence, activism, and audacity in their campaign to influence English national life and the British Empire.

65. Nancy Rose Hunt, "Introduction," in *Gendered Colonialisms in African History,* ed. Nancy Rose Hunt, Tessie P. Liu, and Jean H. Quataert (Oxford: Blackwell, 1997), 4-5.

66. Gareth Stedman Jones delineates a parallel reality in his analysis of the thought and language of participants in popular radical activity. *Languages of Class: Studies in English Working Class History, 1832-1982* (Cambridge: Cambridge University Press, 1983). On the importance of the "language of belief" to understanding religiosity, see Sarah C. Williams, "The Language of Belief:

the cultures that surrounded them, it becomes essential to understand English missionary culture in terms of its own languages of identity and difference. At the center of these languages were debates regarding the place and values of fundamental Christian identities, ranging from Catholicism to Protestant Non-conformity, with Anglicanism placed centrally, proclaimed by many a national *via media*. Because of this position, Anglicans formed the religious grouping with the most varied and significant differences of identity.

Despite the complexity and variety of missionary vision and practice, as well as indigenous response and appropriation, the movement did share a set of ideological commitments with continuity over time. It was, despite High Church efforts, a majority evangelical movement, and overall, even with very significant differences, missionaries almost without exception shared a central set of ideas tied deeply into progressivist Enlightenment assumptions of a uni-formly rational human nature whereby all peoples, although arranged hierar-chically into categories of cultural development, were capable of improvement under universal laws of social and economic change.[67] Universalizing princi-ples, including a core presumption of spiritual equality, were focused into an astonishingly ambitious program — nothing less than the conversion of the entire world to Christianity — but ironically this universalizing set of ideas also rested on deeply partisan interpretations regarding their practical application.

Missions formed a set of crucial overseas causes and an armory of social examples against which discussions of religion, respectability, civilization, race, and gender could be framed. As the missionary project of the Church of En-gland grew in importance, it became a critical platform supporting discussion of contested ideals for church, society, nation, empire, and international order. Analysis of the foreign missionary movement and the essentially spiritual im-pulses that originated and sustained missionary ambitions needs to be balanced against an understanding of the power of religious belief and practice, linked to the social position and influence of its leading groups, to direct and shape thought, institutional agendas, and individual and group action.[68] Sophisticated and extensive domestic bureaucracies took on their own logic and institutional

An Alternative Agenda for the Study of Victorian Working-Class Religion," *Journal of Victorian Culture* 1, no. 2 (1996): 303-17.

67. Brian Stanley, "Christianity and Civilization in English Evangelical Mission Thought, 1792-1857," in *Christian Missions and the Enlightenment*, ed. Brian Stanley (Grand Rapids: Eerdmans, 2001), 169-97.

68. This approach emphasizes the Weberian insight into the "purposive rationality" of religious belief and its power to switch particular behaviors into particular channels of development in the context of other ideological, associational and cultural forces. *Max Weber, Selections in Translation,* ed. W. G. Runciman, trans. E. Matthews (Cambridge: Cambridge University Press, 1978), 66, 86, 136.

force. At the core of the influence of domestic missionary societies was the apparatus they generated to raise interest and cash, calling forth emotional commitment and a habitual sense of duty through the management of popular imagery and religious identity, particularly directed at women, supported by deeply gendered theology.

Central to the powerful presence of missions within the Church was one crucial idea that missionary advocates had effectively entrenched in religious thinking over the course of the century: that missionary expansion was a demonstration of religious success.[69] A constant tension, however, existed in this movement and within the Anglican Church between the evangelicalism that in principle united the vast majority of supporters of foreign missions and the denominational identities and competition that separated and differentiated them. As the established "official" church of the nation, the Church of England claimed a corporate identity that, embodying "the Englishness of English religion," cut across evangelical identity within the larger movement.[70] Its comprehensive nature meant that the Anglican Communion represented a broad variety of religious styles contributing to foreign missions. And its identity as the national church made it a natural home for those in the late Victorian period who saw the Church as central to reforming nation and empire. But generating a program that could satisfy a Church that was composed of energetically antagonistic parties, ambitious women, and eager professionals remained a significant difficulty, as the following chapters in this book will demonstrate.

The Tensions of Late Victorian Missionary Religion

Although many Anglicans claimed that the Church of England had been a "national church" well before the Reformation, it was the Reformation process that created close bonds of formal Church power and association with the state. By the eighteenth century, as much recent work has emphasized, the core national identity of Britain as a Protestant nation had solidified, even if there was disagreement over what precisely Protestantism entailed.[71] The problem

69. This idea was deeply tied into Victorian ideologies of progress and postmillenial optimism expectant of peace and prosperity prior to the Second Coming. David W. Bebbington, *Holiness in Nineteenth-Century England* (Carlisle, UK: Paternoster, 2000), 44-45.

70. Robbins, *History, Religion, and Identity,* 87.

71. Linda Colley, *Britons: Forging the Nation, 1707-1837* (New Haven: Yale University Press, 1992); Kathleen Wilson, *The Island Race: Englishness, Empire, and Gender in the Eighteenth Century* (London: Routledge, 2003). For cautions on the unanimity of any "Protestant Englishness,"

of the relationship of religion to national identity is a complex one because, as David Hempton notes, religion has had a crucial but variable impact on evolving conceptions of national, regional, and local identity, providing broad planks of support upon which many separate cultures that share a core of "religio-moral homogeneity" could rest.[72] Rather than simply providing a common culture within which a homogeneous national identity developed, religion and especially religious conversion generated clear, critical dissents from dominant cultures, as Nonconformity and anti-materialist critiques of culture inherent in both evangelical and Anglo-Catholic piety movements demonstrated.[73] In the "mission field," both Low and High Church "holiness" could translate into suspicion of westernization in mission practice on the part of missionaries and nationalist appropriations of a biblically sanctioned egalitarianism that justified reform and autonomy on the part of indigenous churches.[74] Church leaders rapidly discovered that national identity alone was insufficient to bind the communion together as the Church transcended the boundaries of the British Isles. The common perception of a national role, however, was one of the central ideas tying all the Church parties together.[75]

In an age of nationalism and empire the strongly English character of the Church generated unsettled energy and dynamism within missionary religion, as both High and Low Church parties sought to define a set of parameters for international religious action and identity. As Geoffrey Rowell notes, the deep concern that characterized Anglican attitudes toward authority and order within the Church was tied to a broader concern to construct a new Anglican identity appropriate to a modern environment.[76] Difficulties arose, however, due to the very breadth and comprehensiveness of the Church, making the problems of forging an Anglican identity comparable to those of forging a national identity. That is,

---

however, see Tony Claydon and Ian McBride, eds., *Protestantism and National Identity: Britain and Ireland, c. 1650–c. 1850* (Cambridge: Cambridge University Press, 1998).

72. David Hempton, *Religion and Political Culture in Britain and Ireland* (Cambridge: Cambridge University Press, 1996), 136.

73. Bebbington, *Holiness*, 13, 22, 81-82. More generally on the subversive power of conversion, see Peter van der Veer, "Introduction," in *Conversion to Modernities: The Globalization of Christianity*, ed. Peter van der Veer (New York: Routledge, 1996), 1-21.

74. Andrew Porter, "Cambridge, Keswick, and Late-Nineteenth-Century Attitudes to Africa," *Journal of Imperial and Commonwealth History* 5, no. 1 (Oct. 1976): 5-34 and "The Universities' Mission to Central Africa: Anglo-Catholicism and the Twentieth-Century Colonial Encounter," in *Missions, Nationalism, and the End of Empire*, ed. Brian Stanley (Grand Rapids: Eerdmans, 2003), 79-107. On indigenous churches, see Edgar, "New Religious Movements," 216-37.

75. Wolffe, "Anglicanism," 29-31.

76. Geoffrey Rowell, *The Vision Glorious: Themes and Personalities of the Catholic Revival in Anglicanism* (Oxford: Oxford University Press, 1983), 8.

parallel to broader English political culture, this dynamic within Anglicanism became fundamental to the culture of a communion that, more than any other in Britain, had a deep and abiding sense of national role and at the same time held profound transnational ambitions for planting churches both inside and outside the British Empire. Missions carried out in the empire and beyond had a double effect on nationalist culture: partisan struggle sharpened and strengthened debates over the type of national identity that should be projected through the church overseas while at the same time divisions at home were often softened overseas in pursuit of common objects, reinforcing broad consensus over the beneficence of the English nation and its imperial and international roles.[77]

Church, Nation, and World

The deep sense of historical English Anglicanism created a strong, pervasive vision of the positive cultural potential of the Church at home and abroad. But as I will argue in Chapter 2, the program of internationalizing the Church was contested, drawing as it did upon contrasting core ideals: pan-denominational evangelical unity, Broad Church comprehensiveness, High Church exclusivity, anti-Erastian church independence, and church/state partnership. Even the presumption of a common sacramental practice was challenged in the 1860s by the emergence of controversy over Ritualism, leaving as the only common glue a generalized sense of shared English culture and supposed racial affinities with colonial societies, although even these were undermined by urges to Christian universalism.[78] These contrasting ideals were assembled at different times and places as different mixes with different emphases. After Catholic Emancipation in 1829, the Church, previously an unambiguous focus for anti-authoritarian Nonconformist agitation, became for growing numbers of English Protestants a key bulwark against "popish tyranny" and thus an essential element in defining and defending a Protestant nation. Emerging populist anti-Catholic Anglicanism could in this manner unite Evangelical with High Churchmen.[79]

77. C. A. Bayly, *Imperial Meridian: The British Empire and the World, 1780-1830* (London: Longman, 1989), 137. However, settlement colonies tended to replicate and even amplify sectarian differences, as the examples of Canada and Australia demonstrate.

78. On the persistence of universalist developmental thought in British debate over civilization, see Peter Mandler, " 'Race' and 'Nation' in Mid-Victorian Thought," in *History, Religion, and Culture: British Intellectual History, 1750-1950*, ed. Stefan Collini, Richard Whatmore, and Brian Young (Cambridge: Cambridge University Press, 2000), 227.

79. Walter L. Arnstein, *Protestant Versus Catholic in Mid-Victorian England: Mr. Newdegate and the Nuns* (Columbia: University of Missouri Press, 1982), 1-8, 74-87.

In the early Victorian era the Church increasingly grew as a symbol and structure supporting Protestant truth and independency while its missions were increasingly constructed as a means of taking the battle against idolatrous error — both Catholic and "pagan" — on the offensive. But the concurrent emergence of the Oxford Movement, with its focus on reviving Anglican piety by reclaiming the pre-Reformation Catholicism of the Church of England also generated fears for the Protestant character of the Church itself, forcing the divisive energy of anti-Catholicism into the internal dynamics of the Church as an emerging Anglican Anglo-Catholicism became the focus of popular "Protestant" agitation.[80] The Church of England became a crucially contested ground for defining the Protestant nation, and while Anglican missions became increasingly important in giving ideological legitimacy to the British Empire, there was no simple formula surrounding missions or any other religious cause for creating a unifying Victorian Protestant nationalism or a clear vision for the development of empire. Particularly after 1860, as the evangelical domination of missions was challenged by the entrance of High Church missions and the resurgence and growing legal (if not popular) acceptance of Catholicism at home and abroad, the party passions and divisions of missionary Christianity increased, throwing into greater doubt any assumed natural affinities between religion and empire.

At the extremes of the party spectrum, both High and Low Churchmen posited an independent internationalism for the Church. Moderates, on the other hand, tended to extend national identity and duty (and thus the national character and duty of the Church) into the empire, maintaining the bonds of Church and nation by elaborating the imperial component of English, and by extension British, national identity. Because of its historic role as a *via media* in English religious culture, the Church provided a strong center with Nonconformity to one side and Roman Catholicism to the other. As such it tended to push out radicalism in either direction, and, as the century wore on, it became progressively more attractive to young educated Nonconformists.[81] With its generally broad support, and the strengths and actions of its own Evangelical wing operating in conjunction with the broader evangelicalism favored by most Nonconformists, the Church was able to weather ongoing Nonconformist criticism calling for disestablishment by strengthening itself as a national institution at the center of the increasingly elaborate national and imperial ritual

---

80. John Wolffe, "A Transatlantic Perspective: Protestantism and National Identities in Mid-Nineteenth-Century Britain and the United States," in *Protestantism and National Identity,* ed. Claydon and McBride, 291-95.

81. Eugene Stock, *My Recollections* (London: Nisbet, 1909), 281.

of the high Victorian era.[82] Yet ecumenical affiliations and a broad, inclusive nationalism were also suspect within churches where the intensifying heat of controversy and insistence on credal distinctiveness continued to characterize Victorian Christianity. Furthermore, Anglicanism remained an international movement with international ambitions and thus essential colonial ties. International controversies, such as that over the "heresies" of Bishop Colenso of Natal, drew the communion closer together institutionally through the international Lambeth conferences (established in 1867) and the ongoing correspondence of a worldwide web of bishops connected through the archbishop of Canterbury at Lambeth Palace. Underlying much of the tension within the Church was the question, as much an emotional as an intellectual one, of whether Anglicanism was essentially national, imperial, or global.

Thus, in important although poorly understood ways, the development of church congregations in the colonies, the empire, and the world had a powerful impact upon the metropolitan church and the communion as a whole. From the challenges to Christian unity presented by prejudicial racial attitudes, to the cultural and ideological impact of returning Anglo-Indian and other colonial families, to late-century schemes for Anglican imperial federation, the worldwide sweep of the Church created powerful and transforming effects on the Church in Britain as a national church. The growth of the Church of England into a global communion, William Sachs suggests, was accomplished largely as the institutions of the Church provided expression for the emergence by the late twentieth century of a generally nonpartisan and pluralistic global Anglicanism, mainly uniform in its ecclesiastical identity.[83] However, despite Sachs's emphasis on the common elements tying Anglicanism together, this transformation was anything but smooth and inevitable because the dynamics of party division and the ambiguities produced out of a contested Anglican identity created intense conflict. In the late Victorian era dissension swirled particularly around the ongoing project of assigning a role for evangelicalism within the Church because at this time Anglican evangelicals faced both continued internal divisions over the appropriate response to Ritualism and anxiety over what many perceived as

82. On the critical role of the Church in the development of ritual around the institution of the monarchy, see David Cannadine, "The Context, Performance and Meaning of Ritual: The British Monarchy and the 'Invention of Tradition,' c. 1820-1977," in *The Invention of Tradition*, ed. Eric Hobsbawm and Terence Ranger (Cambridge: Cambridge University Press, 1983), 131-32.

83. Sachs's argument depends on assuming the inevitable dominance of one section of the Anglican spectrum, Anglo-Catholic internationalists, wherein he sees an inherent "whiggishly" liberal commitment to indigenize the Church culture by culture, breaking Anglicanism from the snares of empire. William L. Sachs, *The Transformation of Anglicanism: From State Church to Global Communion* (Cambridge: Cambridge University Press, 1993), 166, 182, 190, 247-54.

their declining influence within the Church.[84] Thus the deployment of nationalist, imperialist, and internationalist rhetoric became critical in the contest to define the Victorian and Edwardian Church. For in their radical and energetic forms, both Anglo-Catholicism and holiness-based Evangelicalism resisted the notion of a simple English cultural identity; instead, they defined what they saw as a universal Church that would transcend national and imperial bonds. This placed missionary radicals at odds with domestic Broad Church leaders who grew in influence as the definers of the domestic establishment order. Party identity and its distinctive theological emphases — Evangelical, High Church, and Anglo-Catholic — influenced how missionary organizers incorporated imperial attitudes, how they related to class and social character among their supporters, how they structured the role of women in religion, and how they attempted to structure the institutions, hierarchies, and work of their mission stations.[85]

Anglican resurgence was a notable feature of religion in Britain after midcentury, but so was a sharpening of distinct, aggressive party identity and organization dedicated to advancing specific standpoints within the Church. The divisions that were to define the terrain of late Victorian Anglican missions had developed by the 1870s into low and high traditions with several shades of variation. Of these, the most dynamic were the revivalistic variants of evangelicalism that came to be institutionalized in the holiness-oriented Keswick Convention; the Anglo-Catholicism shading into new styles of High Church activism, which from the late 1850s generated new urban missions and missionary societies; and the Anglicanism of the public schools, which, inspired by Thomas Arnold and Rugby School, carried into the late nineteenth century a strong English nationalism, establishmentarianism, and vision of a comprehensive national church.[86] All of these variants presented challenges to older styles of Evangelicalism and High Churchmanship, particularly in

84. Evangelicalism as a coherent, powerful culture within the church is significantly downgraded by Sachs who, for example, fails to mention traditional party oppositions in his description of a culminating Evangelical and Anglo-Catholic conflict, the Kikuyu Controversy of 1913-15. Sachs, *Transformation of Anglicanism,* 187-90.

85. Francis Knight's useful corrective regarding Anglican religious experience at the parish level which de-emphasizes the importance of party notwithstanding, among missionary organizers Church party formed a critical marker of identity and ideology around which to structure the work. Cf. Frances Knight, *The Nineteenth Century Church and English Society* (Cambridge: Cambridge University Press, 1995), 19-20, 209-10.

86. On Thomas Arnold, the public schools, and the vision of the Church of England as a national institution for refining national goodness (as developed in the liberal Broad Church strains of Matthew Arnold and A. P. Stanley, Dean of Westminster, 1864-1881), see Ruth apRoberts, *Arnold and God* (Berkeley: University of California Press, 1983), 56-62, 157-58, 257-59.

the form of new missionary societies. Most notable of these were the fervently interdenominational (but significantly Anglican-supported) evangelical "faith" missions, such as the China Inland Mission (1865) and Regions Beyond Missionary Union (1872), and the Oxbridge-associated "gentlemanly missions" supported by Anglo-Catholics, such as the Universities' Mission to Central Africa (1859) and the Oxford Mission to Calcutta (1880). These differences in emphasis, I will argue in Chapter 3, led to significant differences in approach in missions, forceful debates over how missionary Anglicanism should operate, and intense competition that spurred late-century missionary expansion. Between the extreme parties resided moderates of high, low, and broad persuasions, as well as most of the English bishops, who were influenced by the need to maintain the cohesion of the Church while being also newly aware of missionary theory through the development of orientalist scholarship and interest in the ancient Church in its early centuries.

Anglican Women, English Society, and the Professionalization of Mission

The backdrop against which Anglican missions operated, however, included more than internal Anglican party divisions. Other factors were also critical as the missionary societies, following the institutional logic that large charities often adopt, sought to maximize their appeal to an increasingly affluent national public. As the Victorian Church confronted the problems of the industrial system and the city, a broader shift in social attitudes had clear relevance to a Church that also faced questions of imperial involvement and religious competition outside the nation, most notably from Roman Catholicism and Islam.[87] The response was to send larger numbers of women and young clerics, each armed with widening and professionalizing social roles, to meet the Church's organizational challenges.

Theologies suggesting that Christians follow the incarnate Christ of service, Boyd Hilton shows, were on the rise following a sterner early Victorian "age of atonement," and they provided a model for social action well suited to missionary religion, which was being reinforced by accumulated experience in a mission field that suggested the implausibility of rapid, complete, and unprob-

87. On perceptions of religious crisis and insecurity at home and abroad, see Andrew Porter, "Late Nineteenth Century Anglican Missionary Expansion: A Consideration of Some Non-Anglican Sources of Inspiration," in *Religious Motivation: Biographical and Sociological Problems for the Church Historian*, ed. Derek Baker, vol. 15 of Studies in Church History (London: Blackwell, 1978), 349-65.

lematic conversion of entire societies to Western moral and social standards.[88] As doubts grew in educated circles about the literal truth of the Bible and the simple transformative power of preaching, emulation of the incarnate human life of an ethical Christ in pursuit of a romantically intuitive personal spirituality also grew, both among Anglo-Catholics and "higher-life" evangelicals where, significantly, there was a particularly strong appeal to women.[89] It was especially, although not exclusively, attractive to High Church thinkers emphasizing Anglican communalism as a path to shared religious identity and social harmony (thus, the conversion of society) over evangelical individualism (thus, the conversion of the individual). In the context of the social interventionism of the later Victorian state, this appeal tended to supersede an earlier, simpler moralistic exhortation to piety and frugality.[90] But emotional, incarnational theologies also had a growing impact on Evangelical leadership and key congregations, which were increasingly enthusiastic, suburban, and southern.

As the missionary movement faced both the social and colonial problems of the later Victorian era, many within it became more acutely aware of and troubled by issues of class, cultural, and racial difference. Social class within Britain and cultural difference overseas, often understood in overlapping ways tied to ethnicity or race, were key concerns of missionary leaders but, characteristically, were understood in religious terms. Anxieties over class and culture were sharp for all Anglicans as they faced persistent Nonconformist challenges to the establishment, which were coming largely from outsider groups and the lower classes. Such anxieties were particularly acute for evangelicals at the CMS, who feared both the competition from and the methods of nondenominational lower-middle- and working-class movements such as the Salvation Army, which launched massive evangelistic initiatives in the 1880s and extended to Asia and South Asia in the 1890s, and the China Inland Mission, which drew heavily on enthusiastic evangelical Anglicans for both support and missionaries, while advocating that missionaries adopt iconoclastic postures such as non-Western indigenous dress. Evangelicalism and Anglo-Catholicism, both influenced by their own varieties of holiness radicalism, were energized in this era. But as Chapters 4 and 5 will explore, they also presented challenges to the Church and its missionary societies because holiness pietism dangerously transgressed class and gender norms, providing extraordinary new levels of authority to women and new patterns of conduct

88. Hilton, *Age of Atonement*, 332-39.

89. Bebbington, *Holiness*, chaps. 1 and 4. Nonconformity was also affected (pp. 65-69).

90. G. Kitson Clark, *Churchmen and the Condition of England, 1832-1885* (London: Methuen, 1973), chap. 12.

for men while at the same time generating a robust backlash from social con-servatives. The new roles authorized by holiness pietism raised the question of what kind of society and what variety of civilization English Church mis-sions sought to create overseas, particularly in colonial societies. At the heart of what it meant to be a nation in late Victorian Britain lay the question of how — for men and, especially within the Church, for women — the nation was expressed through, supported by, and informed in the construction of the British Empire.

The worldwide growth of Anglican institutions, inherent in Anglican eccle-siastical and missionary expansion, was given impetus in the late Victorian era by the feminization of missionary religion.[91] Historians now widely recognize that British imperial expansion was reinforced by justifications and institutions fundamentally gendered and conditioned by British understandings of class, respectability, civilization, and race.[92] But missions were both deeply embedded in English understandings of empire and constructed by mission advocates as transcending imperial concerns and structures. From their origins missions, like Christianity itself, were profoundly gendered, from the division of official and ministerial work to strategies for proselytizing that demanded separate targeted methods for men and women, and the building of the domestic life of Christian converts along lines theoretically solidified under a Victorian ideal of separate gender spheres: male, largely public, and female, largely domestic.[93] However, while prescriptive literature may have encouraged the withdrawal of women from public life, the extraordinary growth of women's missions, women's par-ticipation in missionary endeavor, the deeply gendered divisions of missionary institutions, and the fundamental gender assumptions of an essentially mater-nalist movement as a whole were critical to the shape and influence assumed

91. On gendered patterns of church attendance and work, see Hugh McLeod, *Religion and Society in England, 1850-1914* (New York: St. Martin's, 1996), 66-70. On the feminization of British Congregationalist missionary religion and American missions, respectively, see Thorne, *Congre-gational Missions,* 92-101; Jane Hunter, *The Gospel of Gentility: American Women Missionaries in Turn-of-the-Century China* (New Haven: Yale University Press, 1984), 11-14.

92. Philippa Levine, "Why Gender and Empire?" in *Gender and Empire,* ed. Philippa Levine, The Oxford History of the British Empire Companion Series (Oxford: Oxford University Press, 2004), 1-13.

93. For a foundational interpretation of the operation and function of this ideology of "sep-arate spheres" see Davidoff and Hall, *Family Fortunes,* 187-92, 429-36. But cf. work that has chal-lenged the degree to which binary oppositions were operative in the lived experience of Victorian women wherein gendered practices consistently cut across any simple public/private distinction. Amanda Vickery, "Golden Age to Separate Spheres? A Review of the Categories and Chronology of English Women's History," *Historical Journal* 36, no. 2 (1993): 383-414 and the essays in Sue Mor-gan, ed., *Women, Religion and Feminism in Britain, 1750-1900* (Basingstoke, UK: Palgrave, 2002).

by missions and the expanding roles that women forged for themselves within them.[94]

As I will argue in Chapter 4, perhaps the single most important factor in the growth of the late Victorian missionary movement is the degree to which changing gender roles and strategies designed to unlock imagined possibilities for conversion within the "native" home came to drive the movement. Late Victorian missions were differentiated by an overlapping and reinforcing set of developments: the emergence of women — especially unmarried women — as visible and publicly acknowledged members of the movement, the rapid infiltration of the university world as a recruiting ground for both women and men, and the increase in enthusiasm for engaging the British Empire as a source of inspiration, support, and direction. While the vast majority of missionary women were involved primarily in girls' education, the most resonant particular call was to the Indian *zenana*, or isolated upper-caste Hindu and Muslim female domicile, where they encountered a social institution resistant to change and open only to women. As time went on and zenana women remained resistant, female missionaries pursued enhanced qualifications in education and professional training (notably in medicine) as the simple demonstration of a presumed superiority of English manners failed to transform Indian homes, families, and society.[95]

Such missionary activity was part and parcel of the larger set of processes by which women in Victorian England built upon and extended their perceived domestic and moral power into public pursuits. By emphasizing that foreign women were the essential "leaven" in societies resistant to the Christian message, missions came to engage British women even more fully by highlighting women's conversion as the critical element in missionary strategy. While Anglican women from the evangelical and High Church traditions developed different approaches to mission — the former favoring strategies of cultural change through education and evangelization that would transform "heathen" society, the latter protectionist strategies centering on boarding school and family ed-

94. On the expansive, energetic, often public nature of "missionary domesticity," see Twells, *Civilising Mission,* chap. 3. Missionary ideology and its relationship to gender norms has received some attention, but until recently British women's missions have not been examined with the thoroughness of other women's history topics. See, however, Mary Taylor Huber and Nancy C. Lutkehaus, eds., *Gendered Missions: Women and Men in Missionary Discourse and Practice* (Ann Arbor: University of Michigan Press, 1999).

95. Despite the fact that *zenanas* were not representative of Indian women's social reality, they became central to the ideology and justifications for women's missions. Ruth Compton Brouwer, *New Women for God: Canadian Presbyterian Women and India Missions, 1876-1914* (Toronto: University of Toronto Press, 1990), 100-101, 188.

ucation that would reform colonial society, creating safe spaces from which to develop Christian community — growing women's missions reinforced a broader emerging theology of service, based on the maternal powers of caring and morality that underpinned women's reformist activism at home.[96] This set of approaches advanced the further creation in both High Church and evangelical fields of influence institutions dedicated to a social mission — schools, orphanages, hospitals, dispensaries.[97] This set of developments paralleled the emergence of a secular British internationalist feminism, which constructed its legitimacy upon English women's claims to rehabilitate indigenous women in the empire and beyond.[98] Arguably, however, it had a direct impact upon vastly more women by providing a substantial new weight of support to an emerging imperial "trusteeship" vision within English missions.

Women's influence, though systematically erased and downplayed in the missionary records before 1900, was transformative, as the available figures (themselves probably underestimated) clearly indicate. In the British missionary movement as a whole, women made up at least 55 percent of the missionary force in 1899, and by 1907 single women missionaries outnumbered ordained ministers in the field 2,332 to 1,980. At the CMS, where by the turn of the century women made up nearly 65 percent of mission agents from Europe, possibly over 70 percent when systematic undercounting is taken into account, the figures are even more striking and significant.[99] The rapidly expanding missionary movement of the late century — what some enthusiasts called the "new era" of missions — must be understood as driven by women's concerns, reinforced by the deeply gendered religious languages of women's domestic reform agendas, from opposition to the Contagious Diseases Act to the urban culture wars fought by the Salvation Army. As Anglican women expanded their roles in public life they developed overseas interests, and missionary reformism became their primary route into a burgeoning realm of foreign work that was also of considerable

96. On High Church protective strategies in Madagascar versus Evangelical transformative strategies in Uganda, see Prevost, *Communion of Women*, 11-12, 35-44, 85-97.

97. For this process in the High Church Cambridge Mission to Delhi, see Jeffrey Cox, "Independent English Women in Delhi and Lahore, 1860-1947," in *Religion and Irreligion in Victorian Society: Essays in Honor of R. K. Webb*, ed. R. W. Davis and R. J. Helmstadter (London: Routledge, 1992), 172-76. On maternalist politics underpinning European social reform, see Seth Koven and Sonya Michel, eds., *Mothers of a New World: Maternalist Politics and the Origins of Welfare States* (New York: Routledge, 1993).

98. Vron Ware, *Beyond the Pale: White Women, Racism, and History* (London: Verso, 1992), 119-64.

99. For the 1907 figures, see *Encyclopedia Britannica*, 11th ed. (1911), s.v. "Missions." CMS percentages include returns from its de facto auxiliaries the CEZMS and ZBMM. For all data on women, see Appendix I, Figure 6.

significance to the construction of Christian, English, and imperial identities. The impact of what Barbara Bush calls "missionary feminism," which over time helped to soften the edge of cultural arrogance and colonial coercion, spread in the late Victorian era as a missionary women's movement with millions of adherents and followers grew in its potential to encourage the construction of a modern, progressive missionary movement, and by extension, a progressive empire and world.[100]

Analysis of how religious identity intersected with gendered ideals of empire is complicated by the fact that evangelicalism and the ideologies that surrounded it were not unitary, were often not unifying, and were deeply affected by the sectarian tendencies of Victorian religion. It is, of course, easy to overstate the depth of impact of religious controversy upon average believers; however, it is clearly the case that controversy itself opened possibilities for women within a missionary movement susceptible to "the almost limitless potential [of] domestic ideology . . . to authorize aggressive projects."[101] Women, more adept than men at transcending and traveling the boundaries of public and private divisions in Victorian society, exploited and filled the fissures created by clerical infighting, thereby serving as an integrating influence within the Church. Constructing religious identity in distinctive ways, they provided much of the activist enthusiasm and support for the radical subcultures of holiness evangelicalism and ritualistic Anglo-Catholicism, taking advantage of the broader trend of increasing lay activism and influence within the Church. As the professionalization of clerical power progressed, lay expansion into the voluntary, social roles of the Church also advanced. Nowhere did Anglican women experience more opportunity than in the mission field.

The power that women attained as the most rapidly growing force in the missionary movement was reliant upon and conditioned by several social, cultural, and religious forces, the most influential being the development of professional standards tied to educational credentials in religion, medicine, and the actual management of missions. For some, the enthusiasm generated by imperial vision — often supported by ideologies of race — was important. However, to what was arguably the largest constituency of support — women — missions needed to be explicable in the context of prevailing expectations about family and gender roles. Theological party, imperial program, and policy toward the use of women all became important areas contested largely by clerics within the

100. Barbara Bush, "Gender and Empire: The Twentieth Century," in *Gender and Empire*, ed. Philippa Levine, The Oxford History of the British Empire Companion Series (Oxford: Oxford University Press, 2004), 82-83.

101. Mary Poovey, *Uneven Developments: The Ideological Work of Gender in Mid-Victorian England* (Chicago: University of Chicago Press, 1988), 189.

Anglican missionary effort, but these contests were generally secondary to the women who made the movement work. As Chapter 4 will show in greater detail, women's missionary activity came to have a critical impact on the Christian and imperial imagination of the late nineteenth century, as female missionaries and their supporters assumed roles as legitimate participants in debates over the nature of indigenous societies and the "civilizing" processes operating through the family that were taken up by feminists, colonial reformers, and indigenous nationalists in the decades that followed.

As missionary recruitment of university graduates, including women, grew in the 1870s and 80s, university engagement came to define the Anglican missionary movement. As detailed in Chapters 5 and 6, professionalism advanced alongside an increasingly university- and student-based missionary culture, and earlier emphasis on the transforming power of faith alone, although still critical to English local support and enthusiasm, waned among missionary leaders. Institutional progressivism, imperial reformism, and clerical professionalism influenced an evolution away from simple evangelical proclamation of the word. These forces were central, for example, to solidifying missionary understandings of race, which were more complex than has previously been acknowledged. With respect to other cultures, missionaries commonly used "civilization" as a standard of judgment and hierarchy, thereby developing a paternalist attitude to race and national culture that differed from scientific racism, both in its emphasis on civilizational development and its refusal to accept the notion of inherent racial inferiority.[102] By the late nineteenth century a vocabulary of paternalistic ethnocentrism, often shading from relatively soft to harder and outright racism, pervaded optimistic missionary oratory and almost universally promised development and "civilization" to benighted races.[103] Thus, for some missionaries, theories of race did become vehicles for explaining cultural difference, but missionaries, more than other imperial groups, consistently resisted deterministic racial theory.[104]

In the complex missionary response to questions of race, nation, and empire, as well as the rise of technocratic mission strategies encouraged by an

102. While Stuart Hall has argued persuasively that differences registered on cultural and religious grounds and on scientific racist grounds are two interconnected logics, this was not a distinction without a difference when it came to formulating strategies of engagement with overseas peoples or representing those strategies in England. "The Multi-Cultural Question," in *Un/Settled Multiculturalisms: Diasporas, Entanglements, Transruptions,* ed. Barnor Hesse (London: Zed Books, 2000), 209-41.

103. C. Peter Williams, *The Ideal of the Self-Governing Church: A Study in Victorian Missionary Strategy* (Leiden: Brill, 1990), 181-82, 188-89.

104. Cox, "Missionary Movement," 216-17.

emerging "mission science," growing numbers of young clerical professionals embraced liberal theologies (often tending toward a new "fulfillment" theology) and emphasized ecumenical cooperation.[105] In doing so, however, they also sowed the seeds for schism and controversy in the missionary movement, paralleling conflicts that had been brought on by modernist controversies in broader religious culture between traditionalists and innovators, often split between older and younger generations. Clerical forces clashed in the Edwardian era over modernist challenges to the "Bible religion" of a growing extreme Protestantism in evangelical circles, and once again religious party and contest over deeply gendered missionary ideals had a profound influence. When Evangelicals split between more traditional and more liberal interpretations of their creed — between an emphasis on the immediate, miraculous transformative process of atonement-based salvation and the work-in-this-world approach of incarnation-based engagement — missionary professionalism played a powerful role in the general process whereby High Church and Anglo-Catholic impulses increasingly defined the central culture of Anglicanism. As Chapters 5, 6, and 7 make clear, professionalization drove the leadership of the Anglican missionary movement away from a focus on private faith to an emphasis on the building of institutions, the amelioration of social ills, and the inculcation of public civilized virtues in the mission field, but only at the cost of schism in the evangelical core of the movement.

The Problems of Empire

The change toward a more public, institutional vision of missions can, in part, be seen in its most developed form in the imperial vision that grew fulsomely among many High and Broad Church Anglicans in the final decade of the nineteenth century. By this time foreign missions had come to be strongly influenced by the desires and aspirations of clerical professionals and activist women. With the rising financial requirements that rapid extension in the mission field in the final two decades of the century brought, many influential Anglicans, both high and low, began advocating a vision

---

105. Eric R. Sharpe, *Not to Destroy but to Fulfil: The Contribution of J. N. Farquhar to Protestant Missionary Thought in India Before 1914* (Uppsala: Swedish Institute of Missionary Research, 1965). A few missionaries developed into open anti-imperialists, for example, C. F. Andrews and Roland Allen. Daniel O'Connor, *Gospel, Raj and Swaraj: The Missionary Years of C. F. Andrews, 1904-14* (Frankfurt am Main: Lang, 1990) and Hubert J. B. Allen, *Roland Allen: Pioneer, Priest and Prophet* (Grand Rapids: Eerdmans, 1995).

of a national church operating in "Greater Britain."[106] This ideal was constructed partially on the assumptions of High Churchmen, who emphasized the ability of the corporate church to bring religious, national, and imperial unity, and partially on the spiritual ambitions of moderate Evangelicals, who envisioned the creation of an orderly church and empire bound together by common evangelical commitments. By such means, a growing but far from overwhelming cadre of Anglican imperial enthusiasts hoped to regain a level of unity and commitment that could support the continuing growth of the overseas missionary project and, more important to some, revive a church seen as embattled at home by theological division and declining religious observance.[107]

The potential for a developed Anglican missionary-imperial project had been evident from the early decades of the century, when the vigor and social ordering of imperial rule was reinforced by a shared Anglicanism operating as "a national and imperial faith" directed particularly to British nationals and their descendants.[108] By late in the century, when imperial language and imagery suffused the missionary world, the vast majority of both missionaries and Britons approved of empire in a general way. Many also approved of it in far more specific and concrete ways, but as there was no single missionary movement (given the wide variety of churches and religious societies supporting disparate projects), there was also no single missionary-imperial project, but rather a variety of them. Some missionaries, as the premillennial conviction spread, wanted to get beyond empire to preach the pure gospel in expectation of the impending millennium.[109] Others fell into groupings perhaps usefully divided into the broad categories identified by Peter Marshall as authoritarian — emphasizing "hierarchy, obedience and order" tied to military and nationalistic aggrandizement — and libertarian — emphasizing liberal market values and individual opportunity offered as freedom "under British tutelage."[110] Missionary societies generally, if cautiously, embraced imperial libertarian values and supported empire conducted on such lines, which were understood to allow a benevolent, peaceful provision of freedoms that flowed from Western Christian

---

106. The cautious attitudes to imperial cooperation that characterized Anglican evangelicalism prior to 1870 shifted perceptibly to a recognition, even at the CMS, of the inevitability of imperial entanglements and the need for explicit imperial strategies. Greenlee and Johnston, *Good Citizens,* 4-5, 39-40, 53-56.

107. G. K. A. Bell, *Randall Davidson, Archbishop of Canterbury,* 2 vols. (London: Oxford University Press, 1935), 1:136.

108. Bayly, *Imperial Meridian,* 143.

109. For a definition and the development of premillennialism, see Chapter 3.

110. Marshall, "Imperial Britain," 389-90.

society and civilization as an exemplar to all humanity.[111] Within the Church of England, however, the proportion of missionary support for the authoritarian division, including a radical protectionist variety, rose significantly higher than among Nonconformists.

Missionary imperial initiatives tied to authoritarian styles were launched within the Church of England in the 1890s, but as I argue in Chapter 8, they proved less successful than enthusiasts and society bureaucrats, many of decidedly High Church sentiments, had hoped. Relying on an easy translation of diffuse imperial sentiments into concrete action, they discovered there was no natural or simple connection between missions and aggressive support for authoritarian empire, and after the turn of the century, definite lines of doubt grew regarding association with any clearly imperial project. When, for example, the Prime Minister Lord Salisbury, at no less an event than the 1900 SPG Bicentenary celebration, saw fit to criticize missionaries for their disruptions in China and elsewhere, some missionary leaders believed the apparent distancing between imperial officials and missions to be ominous.[112] New problems also arose out of financial crises as, after the turn of the century, earlier Anglican evangelical growth registered itself as insistent, apparently unsustainable demands on fundraising. Discomfort in missionary circles, more acute among Nonconformists than Anglicans, arose out of the sense that governmental involvements in conflicts like the Second South African (Boer) War and Boxer Rebellion in China made uncritical association with empire more and more problematic. Shifting circumstances led many, ranging from an internationalist like J. H. Oldham to an imperialist like Henry H. Montgomery, to develop a vision of incipient colonial nationalisms as carriers of distinct cultural forms of church and Christian faith.[113] The imperial context of Tariff Reform and imperial preference united the interests of social reform and imperial strength and suggested a model of transnational Church federation that could strengthen both home and missionary churches.[114] But

111. Max Warren, "The Church Militant Abroad: Victorian Missionaries," in *The Victorian Crisis of Faith,* ed. Anthony Symondson (London: SPCK, 1970), 65, who points to John Henry Newman's "The Idea of a University" as perhaps the most resonant, characteristic, and influential expression of this "astonishing presumption."

112. Greenlee and Johnston, *Good Citizens,* 113-14.

113. Timothy E. Yates, *Christian Mission in the Twentieth Century* (Cambridge: Cambridge University Press, 1994), 30, 247; Henry H. Montgomery, "Introduction," in *Mankind and the Church: Being an Attempt to Estimate the Contribution of Great Races to the Fulness of the Church of God,* ed. H. H. Montgomery (London: Longmans, Green, 1907), xii.

114. Stock, *Recollections,* 394-95. For general background, see Bernard Semmel's classic *Imperialism and Social Reform: English Social-Imperial Thought 1895-1914* (Cambridge, MA: Harvard University Press, 1960), though it largely lacks consideration of religion.

as with Tariff Reform, the key difficulty lay in converting those still ideologically committed to free trade — among many Evangelicals, both spiritual and
material — as well as the additional reality that the Church had transnational
ambitions and reach that ultimately transcended imperial boundaries.[115]

The failure of High Church enthusiasts to create effective missionary-
imperial programming within the Church is suggestive of the problematic
relationship that Anglican missions and the Church had to imperial culture.
While most Anglicans undoubtedly believed that England was one of the few
nations capable of Protestant international morality (an attitude that supported
an aggressive national pride), missionaries reflexively kept a distance from secular institutions and secular ideologies.[116] If the empire provided providential
openings to the gospel, imperialists themselves, so bound up in worldly and
secular concerns, often seemed problematic allies. In Chapter 8, the story of the
forced re-molding and dilution of grandiose plans for an "imperial Christianity"
shows how competing domestic religious priorities, renewed religious party
friction, and contrasting visions of empire created an environment in which
the "culture of empire" became a particularly contested terrain, even in this
age of "high imperialism."[117] This is not to deny John MacKenzie's observation
that, in the wake of the growing militarist language of evangelical revivalism
and the growth of pseudo-military organizations like the Salvation Army and
Church Army, many of the churches were swept up into "the tidal wave of race
patriotism" of the late 1890s and Edwardian years. It is to suggest, however,
that what patriotism meant varied from denomination to denomination and
from church party to church party, and that what could be concretely accomplished in the name of church, nation, empire, or Christianity was contingent
on domestic factors such as religious politics, home imperatives, and divided
ideals concerning imperial engagement.[118] The enthusiasm for imperial strate-

115. On the developing Edwardian debate over free trade ideology, see Frank Trentmann, "The
Strange Death of Free Trade: The Erosion of 'Liberal Consensus' in Great Britain, c. 1903-1932," in
Citizenship and Community: Liberals, Radicals and Collective Identities in the British Isles, 1865-1931,
ed. E. F. Biagini (Cambridge: Cambridge University Press, 1996), 221-33.

116. John Wolffe, "Evangelicalism in Mid-Nineteenth-Century England," in *Patriotism: The
Making and Unmaking of British National Identity*, ed. Raphael Samuel (London: Routledge, 1989),
196-97.

117. It has long been recognized, of course, that the idea and nature of empire was deeply
contested even at its height of popularity. A. P. Thornton, *The Imperial Idea and Its Enemies: A
Study in British Power*, 2nd ed. (New York: Anchor, 1968), 57-122, while commenting insightfully
upon the importance of the sense of mission to empire (p. 79), pays little attention to religion,
and no attention to missions or the Church. This holds generally true for the standard works on
imperial ideology.

118. MacKenzie, *Propaganda and Empire*, 5. On the contrast between missionary emphases

gies evident among at least an influential section of missionary support shows that English Churchmen were hardly aloof and disinterested in their imperial attachments. But complications and failures in imperial projects also suggest the English Church was not so permeated by imperial imperatives, enthusiasm, and duty as to be carried away by any uncomplicated, unified imperial program or culture.[119] The empire itself was so significantly diverse as to be difficult to encompass in any single program or inspiration, as demonstrated by the basic (although not exclusive) division of overseas religious work among Anglicans into provision for colonial settlers and provision for "the heathen," taken up as a special responsibility by the SPG and the CMS, respectively.

There is no doubt that Victorian missionaries and missionary societies were conscious of the empire as a field of considerable opportunity, but they also often saw it as a potential minefield. Should missions act as a vanguard of empire or as the conscience of civilization? As supporters of tightened imperial control or liberalization guiding toward independence? These questions unleashed a complex imperial Anglican dynamic that was entangled in conflict between Church parties, colonial nationalisms, and the obvious need to engage with the challenges of race implicit in dealing both with settlement colonies and their frontiers and with extending churches in the "tropical" fields of Africa and South Asia. Thus in the Church of England, which had deeper and more loyal ties to the idea of an establishment and an established empire than any other denomination, these were profoundly influential issues.

Conclusion

The foreign missions of the Church of England represented a set of channels through which intense English religious preoccupations were transmitted beyond English shores and religious encounters overseas transmitted back to England. The Church itself provided an incubator and forum for metropolitan and colonial discussions surrounding religious, cultural, social, and economic development. In the context of growing nineteenth-century denominational rivalry — including contests between Church and Nonconformity, between Protestantism and Catholicism, and within Anglicanism between Evangelicals and High Churchmen — opportunities for growth and the demonstration of

on "spiritual free trade" and "Imperial Christianity," see Greenlee and Johnston, *Good Citizens*, chaps. 1 and 2.

119. Cf. John MacKenzie's treatment of missionaries primarily as advocates for pro-imperial agendas, *Propaganda and Empire*, 32-33.

vitality provided by the mission field sharpened the public contest of religion and support for missions. While a precise definition of what a "missionary church" was to do or to be remained elusive, the importance of distinctive denominational or theological identity was critical to effective propagandizing and organization. Of all the churches by the end of the nineteenth century, the Church of England was the most successful at supporting missions.

By focusing on the shifting concerns and conflicts within the Church of England, I aim to reveal a religious culture that, even within its evangelical wing, was far from monolithic and fixed. It was in fact precisely the competitive diversity of views and approaches, operating within a larger set of assumptions about English religion, civilization, and empire, that drove the success and thus the influence of a multivalent and constantly changing movement in the metropole. This was an encounter of English religion, imperial culture, and global ambition constituted at the intersection of religious preoccupations with Anglicanism as an ideal national, imperial, and international community.[120] The discourses of missionary professionals of all sorts were, of course, conditioned by and responsive to dynamic colonial and transnational exchanges that were multiplying in a heady age of empire, from the impact of a rising Indian nationalism that contested missionary discourses on Indian civilization to the power of arguments and ideals brought back to Britain by colonial bishops and returned missionaries. Thus metropolitan culture, with a series of traditional dynamics, remained powerfully influenced by colonial experience, just as transatlantic colonial dynamics and correspondence had influenced religious culture in the era of the first British Empire.[121] The vision of non-English, non-Christian cultures that English Anglicans sought to define was central to the English religious and social imagination. This was true not only in building the ideologies of difference that underpinned religious, national, and imperial identities but also in creating realms of debate about operative similarities between a historically imagined, evolutionary English identity and other world cultures.[122] In the tensions of

120. In this emphasis, I echo the later-nineteenth-century work suggesting that the ambiguities in eighteenth-century Protestantism disrupted confidence in the existence of a unitary "British" or "English" identity, but also provided the languages for a unifying debate over appropriate prescriptive aspirations for the nation. Tony Claydon and Ian McBride, "The Trials of the Chosen Peoples: Recent Interpretations of Protestantism and National Identity in Britain and Ireland," in *Protestantism and National Identity*, ed. Claydon and McBride, 26-27.

121. W. R. Ward, *The Protestant Evangelical Awakening* (Cambridge: Cambridge University Press, 1992), 3-10, 275-76.

122. On the importance of the projection of British domestic understandings through the lens of a romanticized past upon the Empire, particularly in the settlement colonies, see David Cannadine, *Ornamentalism: How the British Saw Their Empire* (Oxford: Oxford University Press, 2001), 6-10. Although some historians have found the argument unpersuasive as a unifying theme

such debates, instabilities in imperial confidence and disposition were often highlighted.

While the underlying logic of the conversion of the individual had a natural parallel to imperial projects emphasizing the transformation of societies, the missionary project also unleashed a deep, interconnected internationalism based on common religious concerns that formed a continuing basis for the extensive networks of a new humanitarianism that grew in the late Victorian and Edwardian eras.[123] Shifting attitudes toward proper gender roles were crucial to the imperial dimension of Anglicanism and the general shift to social service over itinerant proselytizing within Anglican missions. However, the ways in which women's missionary work was structured and justified, as well as the way "daughter churches" were envisioned as fitting into an Anglican future of a multiplicity of national churches adapted to national needs, were tied intimately to core visions of religious identity and Church politics. Although Anglicanism was the English religious tradition most closely associated with empire *qua* empire and English governing traditions, even within the Church of England "missionary Christianity" was an ambiguous instrument used by different groups and individuals for often conflicting purposes. The fact that the High Church wing of Anglicanism alone could generate two figures as widely diverging in view as Henry H. Montgomery and C. F. Andrews — the first an ardent imperialist and advocate of the creation of "racial churches," the second a supporter of the Indian National Congress and advocate for intercultural religious exchange — demonstrates the breadth and diversity of view within the Church.[124] The contest over what it meant for the Church of England to be a "national Church" was deeply influenced by the visions of its future as an "imperial Church" and, potentially, as a transnational federation of churches in worldwide Anglican Communion. Thus questions of historical identity, issues of freedom versus authority, and the contest between Christian witness and imperial power all became crucial fields of discourse by which Anglican missions and Anglican identity were formed.

Anglicanism proved in the Edwardian period to be less functionally malleable as a reinforcing imperial ideology than imperial enthusiasts had hoped. It also provided unexpected resources to those interested in challenging received conventional notions of religion, society, and empire. This was not least because

throughout Victorian imperial culture, such forms of historical understanding were critical to Anglican imperial thought, particularly among High Churchmen.

123. Kevin Grant, *A Civilised Savagery: Britain and the New Slaveries in Africa, 1884-1926* (New York: Routledge, 2005), 29-37.

124. Montgomery, "Introduction," in *Mankind and the Church*, xxi; O'Connor, *Gospel, Raj and Swaraj*, chaps. 6 and 7.

central among other tensions at the heart of Anglican missionary thinking was friction between the implicit spiritual equality and human similitude contained in the Christian conversionary message and what Partha Chatterjee calls the "rule of colonial difference," the ongoing imperial and colonial project of inscribing difference between Britons and colonial subjects in order to create a logic of rule, whether of race or "civilization."[125] As Elizabeth Elbourne has reminded us, religious languages could be and were constructed into bifurcating systems of cultural difference, but the discussions surrounding these were mediated by a "politics of interpretation" in the mission field, the metropole, and the transnational networks that tied them together.[126] As I argue in this book, what the missionary societies did and desired to do was in large part a product of fundamentally metropolitan concerns about the state of the churches, the nature of English society, and the future of religious influence at home and in an expanding world church that was envisioned to outlive nations and empires.

Anglican foreign missions were rooted in domestic English ecclesiastical institutions, and a taxonomy of missions reflects the variety of opinions within these establishments. By the final decades of the century missionary strategists clearly understood the importance of this variety to the shape missions took, as echoed in the report on home support commissioned by the 1910 Edinburgh World Missionary Conference: "[T]he missionary enterprise is the projection abroad of the Church at home. It shares in a much larger measure than is usually recognised the ideals and spirit of the Home Church, and carries their influence into the life of the Church which it creates in the non-Christian world."[127] Anglican missionaries and their supporters believed their message to be of universal import. In this they shared a broad and homogeneous message with the rest of Protestant missions that was perhaps no better expressed than in the message delivered by an African servant of the quintessential Victorian missionary hero, David Livingstone.[128] Jacob Wainwright was one of the "faithful

125. Partha Chatterjee, *The Nation and Its Fragments: Colonial and Postcolonial Histories* (Princeton: Princeton University Press, 1993), 10. Gauri Viswanathan notes that the "civic equality" constructed in the Victorian liberal position had the force of "forever complicating national loyalties" by giving religious minorities commonalities with those outside the nation (or a comprehensive church). Viswanathan, *Outside the Fold*, 7-9.

126. Elbourne, *Blood Ground*, 18-19.

127. "The State of the Home Church in Its Bearing upon the Work of Carrying the Gospel to all the non-Christian World," in *Report of Commission I: Carrying the Gospel to All the Non-Christian World*, vol. 1 of *[Report of the] World Missionary Conference, 1910* (Edinburgh: Oliphant, Anderson and Ferrier, n.d.), 344.

128. David Livingstone (1813-1873), although a Scot employed originally by the Congregationalist LMS, became a largely freelance explorer and proselytizer from 1857, and was, incongruously, particularly adopted as missionary inspiration for the foundation by High Churchmen of the

Negro servants" who in 1873 had carried the salt-preserved corpse of Britain's greatest missionary paragon out of the depths of Africa for its symbolic interment in "the national cathedral," Westminster Abbey. On the missionary circuit following his delivery of Livingstone's body, Wainwright described the strange last journey of Livingstone's remains. He brought his tale to culmination, as a CMS missionary recounted, with a characteristic missionary message: " 'The countries of this world are like the coaches in a Railway Train — Of this Train England is the Engine, the station to which England is drawing them is Heaven, and the Bible is the Time Table.' He concluded by crying out 'Mighty England do good.' He was rapturously applauded."[129] This general message — that through its fundamental Christian character England could be the "Engine" for good in the world — provided the foundation for the construction of a system of cooperation between missions and missionaries and for a steady flow of donations from an increasingly affluent Christian nation. Yet despite widely shared general sentiments that might suggest homogeneity in English missions, considerable variations in missionary style were critical to stimulating support, and new developments from the 1870s onward, particularly in changing patterns of gendered understanding of mission labor, led to new currents in English Protestant expansion. The analysis of generalized forms of propaganda and ideology can be useful, but it is inadequate to explain fully the nature of foreign missions, the nature of English religious culture, and the changes they underwent during the high imperial era.

Until World War I all the denominations largely agreed on the broad contours of a progressive Christian program for the world, yet significant differences regarding the uses to which missions could be put were clear and powerful. As Susan Thorne has demonstrated, it was natural for the evangelical, nonconformist Congregationalist middle classes to see in Christian missions a reflection of a liberal, expansive, respectable, industrial society advanced by a kind of progressive imperialism, and some evangelical Anglicans also supported this species of political liberalism.[130] Most bodies of Anglican opinion, however, were much more closely associated with the Conservative party and the traditional establishment, although there were groups that seriously ques-

---

Universities' Mission to Central Africa. He, in fact, stood as a national and missionary icon largely above denominational identity. Andrew C. Ross, *David Livingstone: Mission and Empire* (London: Hambledon, 2002), chap. 15.

129. Deputation Diary of A. H. Lash (hereafter cited as Lash diary), 15 Sept. 1874, Walsall, Augustus Henry Lash Papers, CMS Archives, Acc 348 F 1/5A, fol. 29.

130. Thorne, *Congregational Missions*, 19-22; David W. Bebbington, *Evangelicalism in Modern Britain: A History from the 1730s to the 1980s* (London: Unwin Hyman, 1989), 137.

Jacob Wainwright, one of explorer David Livingstone's African servants,
with Livingstone's coffin on the homebound steamer, 1874.
Council of World Mission (LMS) Archives, Home, Livingstone
Pictures, Box 1, School of Oriental and African Studies, London.

tioned the wisdom of any imperial entanglements at all.[131] The broad range
of Anglican attitudes shows a variety of national, imperial, and transnational
commitments not easily bound up in a single English "culture of empire," as
"missionary religion" drew much of its power from its very flexibility and
ambiguity. Thus, while the support of Church and empire established by Disraeli as one of the new foundations of Conservatism from the 1870s remained
a strong set of commitments among Tories, support for "Church Defense"
dropped off amidst the embarrassments of continuing Ritualist controversies,
and the question of precisely what kind of empire to create was never effec-

131. The Church of England, in T. B. Macaulay's trenchant phrase, was long understood as
"the Tory Party at prayer"; the Anglican clergy were overwhelmingly Conservative voters. Hugh
McLeod, *Religion and the Working Class in Nineteenth-Century Britain* (London: Macmillan, 1984),
44. The general association of Anglicanism with the Conservative Party is well established. Robert
Currie, Alan D. Gilbert, and Lee Horsley, *Churches and Churchgoers: Patterns of Church Growth
in the British Isles since 1700* (Oxford: Clarendon Press, 1977), 57-58.

tively pinned down, as the diversity of missionary attitudes to empire late in the century suggests.[132]

Changes in the style and emphasis of religious party and cultures of piety, in attitudes toward women's work and professionalization, and in the possibility of an "imperial church" all had profound effects on styles of foreign mission both within and without the Anglican Church. By integrating mission work into a more comprehensive Anglican framework it is possible to comprehend more fully these dynamics and, in this broader context, integrate previous work on missions, which has tended to more partial views focusing on particular missions and societies, aspects of the Church of England, or single themes such as imperialism or women. Foreign missionary institutions, with their variety of approaches to these and other issues, had a complex dialectical effect on domestic mission institutions, Anglicanism, British society, and the British Empire. Even as the foreign missions of the Church suffered division and distraction in the years prior to World War I and as liberal and conservative evangelical factions fought over "modernist" issues, missions remained one of the primary fields for arguing and articulating Anglican, and thus English, identity in an era of growing imperial anxiety. While not all Anglicans were enthusiastic missionary supporters, the ecclesiastical and missionary institutions that the Church produced shaped the response of the British to the social and imperial challenges the nation faced in the twentieth century. No Anglican who worked to imagine and secure a future for the Church and nation could avoid engaging with the programs and questions that foreign missions generated regarding contested aspirations for the Church in the world. And as modernist controversies, combined with the growth of a commercialized, politicized, and secularized culture, led churches to fight ever harder for relevance in English life, missionary matters retained their relevance, if only because they seemed to demonstrate through example just how churches and religious life could be maintained and extended in hostile environments. Foreign missions drew on a reservoir of loyalty and support that sustained them in their Victorian form well into the 1930s. This resilience is testimony to the central place that foreign missions assumed in Victorian religion and culture and the impact that they were to have on English national, imperial, and religious identity and life at the height of the imperial age.

132. Freda Harcourt, "Disraeli's Imperialism, 1866-1868: A Question of Timing," *The Historical Journal* 23, no. 1 (Mar. 1980): 87-109; E. H. H. Green, *The Crisis of Conservatism: The Politics, Economics and Ideology of the British Conservative Party, 1880-1914* (London: Routledge, 1995), 13-15. Anglo-Catholics formed the one Anglican party that generally supported Gladstonian liberalism because of Gladstone's Parliamentary support in the 1870s for the freedom of Ritualist priests to worship as they chose. C. Brad Faught, *The Oxford Movement: A Thematic History of the Tractarians and Their Times* (University Park: Pennsylvania State University Press, 2003), 123-25.

CHAPTER 2

Faith, Authority, and the Sectarian Spirit
of Anglican Foreign Missions

The spirit which, in politics, we call "party" has a great deal to do with the
interest and vehemence and energetic success of the [missionary] Societies.

E. W. Benson, 1894[1]

On the morning of 29 May 1894 Edward White Benson, the archbishop of Canterbury, addressed an impressive gathering of Church notables at the inaugural meeting of the Missionary Conference of the Anglican Communion. This was a groundbreaking occasion. Never before had a general assembly of all the divergent shades of Anglican opinion been gathered for common consultation on the foreign missions of the Church. Benson was expected to exhort the conference with a conventional missionary homily that urged the Church to greater missionary effort.[2] The crying spiritual and moral needs of the "heathen" were common themes known well by respectable Victorians who attended missionary meetings and read the letters of returned missionaries to the *Times* or the *Guardian*. Optimism, cooperation, and duty were the common fodder of pious missionary advocates on the public platform. Benson, however, was addressing Anglican missionaries, missionary administrators, and missionary supporters who were intimately involved in a movement that had increasingly come to prominence within the Church in the previous three decades. With every

1. E. W. Benson, "President's Address," in *The Official Report of the Missionary Conference of the Anglican Communion*, ed. George A. Spottiswoode (London: SPCK, 1894), 13.
2. Eugene Stock, "The Anglican Missionary Conference," *Church Missionary Intelligencer*, n.s., 19 (July 1894): 485.

Church party extending foreign missionary work, Benson focused on what he saw as the key ingredient driving and defining Church missions: the consuming passions of religious parties for combative Church politics.[3] Church parties in their late Victorian manifestations were largely shaped by the reverberations of Church reform in the 1830s, but they also had much deeper roots leading back to the English Reformation which, with its imagined lessons regarding tyranny, individual conscience, and Godly governance, was a taproot of thinking about ecclesiastical, national, and even imperial governance.

The archbishop's speech excited considerable comment both at the conference and in the religious press. This was because Benson, in assessing the prospects for united effort in the missions of the Church, openly acknowledged that the bishops must see such unity as a utopian project achievable only in an unspecified future. He thus frankly admitted the degree to which party divisions between Evangelicals, High Churchmen, and Anglo-Catholics permeated mission work. While he lamented the sectarian temper bred by the parties, the jealous control of "native churches" they encouraged, and the rigid, inefficient bureaucracies they proliferated, he more importantly emphasized that the fierce rage of religious party they engendered solidified loyalty and spurred action in support of Protestant missions. The archbishop's position as chief referee in Church party disputes led him wryly to compare the CMS to the fanatical Jesuits and the SPG to the rigid *de Propaganda Fide* in Rome. More revealingly, however, he stressed that the impressive success of independent missionary societies in generating support for foreign missions was tied precisely to their reputations as agents of party identity. The bishops recognized the power of party in Church philanthropy as a reality, leading Benson to comment: "The Societies are banded together upon principles. They engage enthusiasm; they even enlist fanaticism; and they have a very considerable power of bringing to bear the riches of rich men." Party division led to competition between the societies and this competition led to growth. The societies became "the Mission-conscience of the Church" and did the work that most Anglicans agreed was an obligation, but an obligation that the Church, as a corporate body, was too preoccupied and divided to accomplish.[4] The bishops held up the ideal of a peaceful and unified Anglican Communion, but they found themselves ceaselessly striving against party divisions that, in an irony not lost on Benson, animated interest, loyalty, and activism.

3. Benson obviously believed the subject to be of continuing importance. The 1894 conference address was in substance a reiteration of points he had made nine years earlier in a speech in Cambridge. Stock, *History of the CMS*, 3:651.

4. "President's Address," in Spottiswoode, ed., *Anglican Missionary Conference, 1894*, 10-17.

Party controversy affected virtually every Anglican voluntary activity in the nineteenth century, but none more so than the work of foreign missions. Issues of right doctrine and Church order were at the very core of the tasks of proselytizing and institution building overseas. The growth of the Church in the developing "second British Empire" of the nineteenth century was substantial, as an accelerating process of creating new bishoprics — most notably Calcutta (1814), Jamaica and Barbados (1824), Madras (1835), Australia (1836), Bombay (1837), and New Zealand and Jerusalem (1841) — made evident. The existence of fifty-one overseas bishops by the time of the first Lambeth Conference, in 1867, was cause for intensifying debate regarding the shape of the Anglican Church overseas and its relationship to the Church and English society at home.[5] The urgency of this debate was reinforced by the unparalleled success of evangelical Anglicans, largely through the agency of the CMS, in spreading Christian missions, but operating under the Evangelical assumption that Christian conversion and the spread of the faith by evangelical witness operated prior to (and by implication was superior to) the founding of fully episcopal churches considered by High Church Anglicans as essential to orthodoxy. Difficulties between the CMS and colonial bishops thus set the terms for later party controversies to come swirling out of the mission field, radicalized by the passionate, litigious response of evangelicals to the introduction of "popish" ritual by Anglo-Catholics in English parishes from the 1860s onward.[6] Maintaining a workable balance between the liberty under law that protected evangelism, due respect for episcopal authority inherent in Anglicanism, and achievement of the ultimate goal of creating independent indigenous churches consumed the career of the CMS's influential honorary clerical secretary, Henry Venn (1841-72).[7] Thus, Evangelical missionary vision operated beyond the structures of the established national church. High Church vision, however, rested squarely within the logic of historic institutional authority and power, meaning that contests over the relationship of ecclesiastical, priestly, and voluntary associational power were built into Anglican missionary expansion. So too, by natural extension, were

---

5. Subsequently the bishoprics of Australia and New Zealand were specified as Sydney and Auckland, respectively, as other sees were added. For a full list of eighty-seven new dioceses created up to 1894, see C. F. Pascoe, *Classified Digest of the Records of the Society for the Propagation of the Gospel in Foreign Parts, 1701-1892*, 5th ed. (London: SPG, 1895), 758.

6. James Bentley, *Ritualism and Politics in Victorian Britain: The Attempt to Legislate for Belief* (Oxford: Oxford University Press, 1978).

7. Timothy E. Yates, *Venn and Victorian Bishops Abroad: The Missionary Policies of Henry Venn and Their Repercussions Upon the Anglican Episcopate of the Colonial Period, 1841-72* (Uppsala: Swedish Institute of Missionary Research, 1978), 47 and passim. Venn saw evangelism and indigenous growth as the foundation of overseas churches; bishops as a final "crown" achievement (p. 18).

the relationship of these debates to questions of national identity and imperial goals and practice.

Division over doctrine, belief, and practice within the home churches profoundly affected their strategies toward foreign missions, both the divisions between the Church and Nonconformity and the general Protestant "crusade" against Catholicism that also fuelled much conflict within a Church of England troubled by its own increasingly strident Anglo-Catholics. The cleavage between church and chapel was the most profound expression of religious social division in Victorian England, while attitudes toward Catholicism and its presumed threat of heresy, moral corruption, and tyranny were the most profound imaginative division.[8] Each deeply affected the state of the late Victorian Anglican church. Fundamental orientations on these cleavages in religious and national categories defined how Anglicans imagined, supported, and attempted to carry out mission work. The perceived vitality of competing religious traditions and the imagined future of the English nation appeared to be at stake. These debates incorporated other deeply emotive issues involving the appropriate use of women in mission work and the best methods of transmitting Christian models of domestic and community order, morality, and "civilization." Party identities within the Church also engaged critical organizational strategies, most notably whether missions would operate through diocesan structures at home and abroad or through voluntary association. In essence, the question was whether they would embrace a traditional authoritarian, community-oriented model of church extension — that tended to be associated with High Church attitudes — or a modern libertarian vision of free associational and individual action — that tended to be connected with Evangelical attitudes. For Evangelicals in particular the unmatched success of the CMS in the English missionary world indicated the continued vitality of an Evangelical party under a deepening siege within the Church, as well as offering a continued proof of the Protestant vigor of Church, nation and empire.[9] The foundations of this success, however, lay deep within a pan-denominational evangelical tradition long suspected of disloyalty to the corporate Church.

The English church was both the model and context for Anglican missions, from its various imagined histories and internal divisions to its significant dependence on voluntary societies to organize resources and activism. Propagandists for foreign missions produced heroic stories of missionary effort bringing

8. Edward R. Norman, *Anti-Catholicism in Victorian England* (New York: Barnes & Noble, 1968); John Wolffe, *The Protestant Crusade in Great Britain, 1829-1860* (Oxford: Clarendon Press, 1991); D. G. Paz, *Popular Anti-Catholicism in Mid-Victorian England* (Stanford: Stanford University Press, 1992).

9. On the decline of Evangelical influence, see Bebbington, *Evangelicalism*, 141-43.

light and civilization to the heathen world; leaders of missionary effort crafted a religious and cultural orientation that channeled competitive religious identity into concrete support at the local level.[10] The pious men and women who worked to maintain and extend enthusiasm for foreign missions and gather the prayers, pounds, shillings, and pence that supported the effort were at the center of a movement based fundamentally on shared religious experience. The dynamic of religious parties was crucial to the renewed Anglican commitment to foreign missions that grew from the 1870s onward. This was, of course, also an age that witnessed the emergence of an undeniably popular and extensive enthusiasm for empire as evidenced by growing fascination with imperial subjects, from the career of African explorer and missionary David Livingstone to the question of control of the Suez Canal, and from the question of the identity of an imperial nation (raised by Prime Minister Benjamin Disraeli in 1874) to the spate of high-profile colonial wars against the Ashanti, Afghani, and Zulu.[11] As Eric Hobsbawm and Terence Ranger have shown, the process of constructing a community of shared values rooted in an imagined past and reinforced by common rituals and practices was at the very center of national and individual life in Victorian England.[12] This was no less true for missionary enthusiasts and supporters, but the cloth from which a missionary vision of the world was cut was woven primarily of threads of religious conviction, party loyalty, and an intensely Christianized vision of the world that was shot through with lines of regional, national, imperial, racial, gender, and class identifications. Responsiveness to the popularity of faith-based movements, as well as the demands of authority in the Church, was essential to those who sought to devise a strategy to amplify Anglican interest and commitment at home to world proselytizing and the building of "daughter" Churches abroad.[13] This was the reality that

10. For details on the elaborate and extensive nature of local organization, see Steven S. Maughan, "Regions Beyond and the National Church: Domestic Support for the Foreign Missions of the Church of England in the High Imperial Age, 1870-1914" (Ph.D. diss., Harvard University, 1995), 189-213.

11. John M. MacKenzie, "Introduction," in *Imperialism and Popular Culture,* ed. John M. MacKenzie (Manchester: Manchester University Press, 1986), 2-6.

12. Eric Hobsbawm and Terence Ranger, *The Invention of Tradition* (Cambridge: Cambridge University Press, 1983), 7-12. See also Clifford Geertz on theologies, parties, and institutions that create human "webs of significance" in *Interpretation of Cultures: Selected Essays* (New York: Basic Books, 1973), 14 and passim.

13. This approach parallels work on earlier, more thoroughly studied eras of Anglicanism, emphasizing the centrality of religious concerns to educational, social, and political debate. Piero Corsi, *Science and Religion: Baden Powell and the Anglican Debate, 1800-1860* (Cambridge: Cambridge University Press, 1988); Richard Brent, *Liberal Anglican Politics: Whiggery, Religion and Reform, 1830-1841* (Oxford: Oxford University Press, 1987).

Archbishop Benson understood when he addressed the 1894 Anglican missionary conference — that sectarian religious identity, even within the church itself, was of utmost importance to support for missions, and it required careful manipulation in an age when many religiously committed enthusiasts were pressing aggressively for the extension of Christianity.

Voluntarism and the Origins of English Protestant Missions

The sectarianism that characterized Anglicanism late in the nineteenth century was a reflection of much deeper historical roots in the transformations of modern British religion, from which the missionary movement developed. The massive growth of Victorian foreign missions was linked to the eighteenth-century emergence of evangelicalism, but it was also driven and shaped by a growing industrial and imperial society that extended its influence and formal power far beyond the bounds of that so-called second British Empire, which had been produced by a "swing to the East" following the loss of the American colonies.[14] Evangelicalism, strongly transatlantic and increasingly transnational, produced a cooperative, ambitious program that extended evangelism and the development of churches beyond nation and empire in a broadly unified cultural vision that was quite often at odds with the deference to authority implicit in traditional Anglican social vision and thus corrosive of the established church.[15] High Church Anglicans thus largely rejected the evangelical vision, focusing instead on the stability of institutions, the apostolic authority of the Church, pastoral care resulting from a view of an organic relationship between religion, society, and the state, while also exhibiting a deep suspicion of "enthusiasm," understood as an uncouth expression of spiritual emotionalism that too often suggested ungovernability.[16] Before the 1790s, English missions were sporadic and limited, focusing primarily, although not exclusively, in North America.[17] Later Evangelical analyses of the eighteenth

14. P. J. Marshall, "Britain Without America — A Second Empire?" in *The Eighteenth Century*, ed. P. J. Marshall, vol. 2 of *The Oxford History of the British Empire* (Oxford: Oxford University Press, 1998), 576-77, 583-84.

15. David Hempton, "Evangelicalism in English and Irish Society, 1780-1840," in *Evangelicalism: Comparative Studies of Popular Protestantism in North America, the British Isles, and Beyond, 1700-1990*, ed. Mark A. Noll, David W. Bebbington, and George A. Rawlyk (New York: Oxford University Press, 1994), 160.

16. Nockles, *Oxford Movement*, 25-26, 30-32.

17. Over the course of the eighteenth century, the SPG sent out over 400 ordained clergymen primarily to serve settler populations; the Society for the Promotion of Christian Knowledge

century tended to overemphasize the dearth of Protestant missionary influences prior to the 1790s. The Protestant missionary impulse, however, if not the popularity and successful staffing characteristic of the nineteenth century, was alive and well developed by the mid-eighteenth century among Anglicans.[18] Nevertheless, until the later decades of the century (with the growth of an evangelical theology emphasizing engagement with the world, the foundation of voluntary religious associations supporting reform and charity, and the extension of the second British Empire) the theological, organizational, and political foundations were lacking for vigorous, extensive missionary activity.

Colonial expansion movements under Crown patronage aimed to revive Anglican piety and had inspired the earliest organized attempts to advance Christianity overseas. This took place with the founding in 1699 and 1701, respectively, of the Society for Promoting Christian Knowledge (SPCK) and the SPG, both of which, despite the attention to formal association with royal sovereignty, functioned primarily as voluntary societies.[19] While committed to propagating Christianity to colonist and heathen alike, the SPCK and the SPG found little success in extending mission beyond the provision of Anglican colonial clergy for English settlements in North America and garrisons throughout the empire.[20] They operated in what Jeffrey Cox has labeled the "confessional worldview" in which churches, supported by states and socially dominant elites, built places of worship for subordinate populations, providing religious services and instruction in a competitive effort to undermine the spread of dissenting forms of Protestantism. From the beginnings of late-seventeenth-century voluntary efforts to reform the manners, morals, and religious beliefs of social subordinates, Anglicans had imagined a broad missionary mandate as a core responsibility operating at the heart of church life, and they created an innovative mix of voluntary and mandatory religious agencies for its support.[21] And while early efforts may have been, by nineteenth-century standards, limited by the loss of the American colonies, more Anglicans had begun to imagine the

---

(SPCK) sent over fifty Lutheran missionaries to Tamil speakers in the Indian subcontinent. Cox, *British Missionary Enterprise*, 46.

18. See, for example, the impact of the work of the Moravians and High Church SPG in the eighteenth century, in Porter, *Religion Versus Empire*, 16-32, and Rowan Strong, *Anglicanism and the British Empire, c. 1700-1850* (Oxford: Oxford University Press, 2007), chap. 2.

19. On Thomas Bray, founding member of the SPCK and SPG, and his non-partisan, voluntaristic Anglicanism, see Rose, "Origins of the SPCK," 172-90.

20. Boyd Stanley Schlenther, "Religious Faith and Commercial Empire," in *The Eighteenth Century*, ed. P. J. Marshall, vol. 2 of *The Oxford History of the British Empire* (Oxford: Oxford University Press, 1998), 131-33.

21. Cox, *British Missionary Enterprise*, 23-30.

Church of England as a potential buttress for British colonial rule outside the bounds of European colonial society.[22]

Early Missions and the Evangelical Revival

The missionary explosion of the nineteenth century had its origin and impetus in eighteenth-century evangelical revivals operating in the context of revolutionary turmoil and rapidly extending market societies. While Anglicans may have originated and given institutional form to a growing missionary impulse in the early eighteenth century, one of the chief impediments to rapid growth was the difficulty of recruiting the ordained male missionaries that clerical prejudice insisted were necessary for the effective spread of Christianity. The evangelical revival provided the impetus to precisely that recruitment. Drawing on German pietism, such as that cultivated among the Lutherans at Halle in Saxony or in the community of the Moravian Brethren, evangelicalism rose in social and cultural influence by emphasizing personal religion and responsibility. Revivalism, influenced deeply by John and Charles Wesley, popularized a "methodistical" formula for assured salvation based on an atonement-oriented Arminian theology that focused on the free choice, extended by God to sinners, of choosing the community of the saved or the damned. By the early nineteenth century evangelicalism drew many Anglicans away from sacramentalism and many Nonconformists away from rationalistic Calvinism to a vision of social transformation achieved through individual activism, preaching, and conversion.[23] Militant emphasis on combating slothful corruptions and religious formalism meant the growth of a universalistic social agenda at home aimed at reforming human "depravity," comprising both aristocratic and lower-class immoralities ranging from licentiousness and gaming to drink and impiety, in which the touchstone was always the assumption of a moral or spiritual cause underlying worldly difficulties or distress. This also tended toward the development of a pan-evangelical political program, with significant leadership by Evangelical Anglicans of the influential Clapham Sect — prominently Henry Venn, William Wilberforce, Zachary Macaulay, Charles Grant, Granville Sharp, and Hannah More — to abolish slavery and extend enthusiastic Christian evangelism, particularly in India.[24]

22. Strong, *Anglicanism and the British Empire*, chap. 3.

23. Bebbington, *Evangelicalism*, 27-34, 63-65; and Deryck W. Lovegrove, *Established Church, Sectarian People: Itinerancy and the Transformation of English Dissent, 1780-1830* (Cambridge: Cambridge University Press, 1988), 17-22 on the varieties of early evangelicalism.

24. John Clive, *Macaulay: The Shaping of the Historian* (New York: Knopf, 1973), 16 and passim

The unity of core evangelical ideas, reformist impulses, and global ambitions did not, as might be expected, create an organizationally unified movement. In England in particular, the strength of the religious establishment and the emergence of politically independent radical dissenting movements meant that while evangelicalism grew rapidly, it did not achieve the same level of religious hegemony as it did in other North Atlantic regions, and it was particularly contested within the Church of England.[25] Thus, in Britain, religion was reinforced as a fundamentally disputed area of public life. British civil society legitimized the formation of voluntary associations, the most widespread and influential being those associated with churches and religious groups. While the religious discourse of the era was dynamically contested between several Nonconformist communities and the national church, which retained considerable power and influence in public institutions but not a monopolistic relationship to the state, these conflicts only amplified the relevance of religious institutions and their missionary contributions to national life. The most important organizations through which the adherents of sectarian British religion advanced their public rivalries were the freely supported voluntary societies. And the foreign missionary society was arguably, over the full course of the century, the most successful class of voluntary society in manipulating and extending the religious associational network upon which so much of Victorian public life depended.

In an emerging environment of voluntary religious associational life, British missions balanced between an ecumenism encouraged by common domestic and foreign reformist agendas and a competitive sectarianism fundamental to the growth of Anglo-American styles of Protestantism. The generally accepted understanding that missionary vision and missionary success were important indicators of denominational strength and cultural legitimacy, perhaps more than any other factor, ensured the centrality of missions to the British churches. Robust free associational social behavior and religious voluntarism defined Victorian public life.[26] Foreign missions were associated consistently

---

for a particularly insightful account of Evangelical psychology and circumstance in the Clapham Sect of the 1790s and 1800s.

25. Mark A. Noll, "Revolution and the Rise of Evangelical Social Influence in North Atlantic Societies," in *Evangelicalism: Comparative Studies of Popular Protestantism in North America, the British Isles, and Beyond, 1700-1900*, ed. Mark A. Noll, David W. Bebbington, and George A. Rawlyk (New York: Oxford University Press, 1994), 122.

26. Voluntarism, the fundamental commitment to voluntary, as opposed to compulsory, association and action, operated at the core of emerging British and European civil society. From the eighteenth century, and most completely in the nineteenth, it fundamentally transformed religion and the philanthropy associated with it. See Frank Trentmann, "Introduction: Paradoxes

with humanitarian projects for social reform, most notably abolition, and in the early decades of the century their assumptions, methods, reformist goals, and expectations bound together a largely middle-class movement that also promoted temperance, monitorial schools, and visitation of the poor in parishes and slums. As such, foreign missions and humanitarianism operated as an important expression of the commercial and expanding industrial societies of northern Europe and the Atlantic world, where strengthening national identities, centered on the legal rights of free citizens and free labor, reinforced the Protestant cultures of independency and social reform that spiritual regeneration was imagined to produce.[27] Furthermore, evangelical reformist culture emphasized the role of women as defenders of domestic purity and religious integrity in establishing the conditions for Christian civilization. When these conditions were not met, evangelically inspired reformism could mobilize women to energetic reform activity.[28] In connection with this broader culture of religious reformism, missions were responsible for the forceful direction of the English charitable impulse overseas. And in the minds of the first generations of evangelical reformers, home and overseas activities were constructed as a universalistic assault on sinful behavior, operating as a single project with intertwined local and global reformist agendas.[29]

Developed evangelical thought and organization supporting foreign missions, while heavily dependent on earlier example, such as that offered by the Moravians, began to emerge with a new clarity in the 1780s as part of a growing abolitionism and emphasis on the responsibility of the saved — particularly the laity — to actively engage the world. Traditional "orthodox" High Church Anglicans, focused on the sacramental necessity of clerical leadership and tied to the patronage of established social elites, were thus fundamentally out of sympathy with early evangelical missionary emphases.[30] New evangelical theological formulations were ultimately distilled into their most famous exposition

---

of Civil Society," in *Paradoxes of Civil Society: New Perspectives on Modern German and British History*, ed. Frank Trentmann (New York: Berghahn Books, 2000), 34-39; and F. K. Prochaska, *The Voluntary Impulse: Philanthropy in Modern Britain* (London: Faber and Faber, 1988), 21-31.

27. On the dynamism, restlessness and quest for respectability of early "middling class" missionaries, see Stuart Piggin, *Making Evangelical Missionaries, 1789-1858: The Social Background, Motives and Training of British Protestant Missionaries to India* ([Abingdon, UK]: Sutton Courtenay, 1984), 40-54.

28. Women played a substantial role in the abolition movement by advancing middle-class domestic ideals and free wage labor as the basis of reconstituted slave societies. Midgley, *Women Against Slavery*, chap. 5.

29. Twells, *Civilising Mission*, 4-7, 25-43.

30. Cf. the Moravians, in J. C. S. Mason, *The Moravian Church and the Missionary Awakening in England, 1760-1800* (Woodbridge, UK: Boydell, 2001).

in William Carey's *An Enquiry into the Obligations of Christians to Use Means for the Conversion of the Heathens* (1792), which advanced the moderate Calvinist argument that human responsibility provided a channel through which God's sovereignty could spread Christianity. This was the most widely influential early theory of Protestant missions. Carey's emphasis on voluntarism to secure mass lay and clerical support — drawing on the model of the chartered trading company — and his insistence that missions would advance civilization along with "the spread of civil and religious liberty," set a tone that, despite missionary advocacy from the more respectable Anglicans who were associated with the East India Company, such as Charles Grant, raised alarm bells among establishment conservatives who were mobilizing to oppose French Revolutionary and Painite radicalism.[31] Fear of religious radicalism formed a key context in the 1790s when missionary appeals led to the creation of the new evangelical missionary societies; in particular, fears of Methodism animated many Anglicans who saw popular religion and political radicalism as pressed from the same potentially disloyal mold. But the idea that missions would be the most effective means of spreading civilization among savages continued to provide an argument for commercial and imperial utility beyond that of simple religious duty, the claim made since the 1720s by Anglicans associated with the SPG.[32] Evangelical Anglicans also advanced this core argument, expressed in the words of the Reverend Melville Horne in 1811 as "PROTESTANT RELIGION is the bulwark, shield, sword, and glory of Britain."[33] In this, evangelicalism represented an expression of the restless "aspirations of the mobile classes of a new society" coalescing into new formations of denominational organization.[34]

Whether or not the foreign missionary societies attempted to channel radical reforming vision to safer, more respectable fields overseas, the creation in 1799 of a rival Anglican missionary society to the "venerable" SPG was certainly a result of the desire to represent Anglican evangelicals as loyal to Church authority, which the extremely careful and conservative operation of the CMS through the era of the Napoleonic wars further demonstrates.[35]

31. William Carey, *An Enquiry into the Obligations of Christians to Use Means for the Conversion of the Heathens,* reprint, 1792 (London: Carey Kingsgate, 1961), 70, 79-83. Carey was a Baptist missionary to India.

32. David Hempton, *The Religion of the People: Methodism and Popular Religion, c. 1750-1900* (London: Routledge, 1996), 8 and passim; Strong, *Anglicanism and the British Empire,* 65-71.

33. Quoted in Bernard Semmel, *The Methodist Revolution* (New York: Basic Books, 1973), 154.

34. Clyde Binfield, *So Down to Prayers: Studies in English Nonconformity, 1780-1920* (London: Dent, 1977), 12.

35. Bernard Semmel argues that for the Methodists from 1813 to 1818 foreign missions represented "a way to reconcile the Enthusiasm inherent in Methodist evangelism, with its revolution-

Spearheaded by Charles Simeon, the elder John Venn, and other leaders of the influential Clapham Sect, the formation of the CMS in 1799 represented a withdrawal from a purely evangelical alliance on the part of Anglicans eager both to maintain credal loyalty and to extend evangelical influence within the Church.[36] By the 1820s a wave of missionary enthusiasm had led to the widespread creation of voluntary missionary societies throughout Northern Europe and North America in a broad pan-evangelical movement of nevertheless separate, denominationally distinct missionary efforts. By the mid-Victorian era, virtually every British denomination had created independent missionary societies that, while generally willing to accept state aid throughout the mission field, resisted state control. The relationship of missions to imperial power thus would remain ambiguous and situational, as missionaries advocated for the moral exercise of imperial power designed to benefit indigenous populations. This generally libertarian approach to empire derived from the era of Parliamentary debates over the right conduct of the British Empire in the 1770s and 1780s, influenced by the rebellion in the American colonies, and early in the nineteenth century contrasted with higher church tendencies to see the church overseas as a limited extension of confessional responsibilities and formal British power rather than an ambitious force for Christian growth and reform.[37] Despite a decided suspicion among traditionalist Anglicans toward mission, both a general English Christian belief that rising "atheistical" French influence in the age of Napoleon must be countered and a growing millenarianism fostered by an age of continuous warfare fuelled the evangelical missionary impulse. By the early nineteenth century, missionary initiatives, and evangelical support for them, had become one of several forces to engage and condition imperial power and expansion.

---

ary, Antinomian tendencies, with an obsession with order in both Church and state." In contrast, he seems to suggest that Anglican Evangelical enthusiasm for missions from 1813 onward was tied to a kind of millenarian triumphalism boiling up in the wake of the downfall of Napoleon, perceived widely as Antichrist. *Methodist Revolution*, 144-45, 154-55, 167-69. On eschatological responses to the French Revolution and Napoleon, see Stuart Semmel, *Napoleon and the British* (New Haven: Yale University Press, 2004), chap. 3.

36. Originally named the "Society for Missions to Africa and the East," the CMS was officially renamed in 1812 to emphasize its Anglican identity. Elizabeth Elbourne, "The Foundation of the Church Missionary Society: The Anglican Missionary Impulse," in *The Church of England, c. 1689-c. 1833: From Toleration to Tractarianism*, ed. John Walsh, Colin Haydon, and Stephen Taylor (Cambridge: Cambridge University Press, 1993), 248, 261-62. The Religious Tract Society (1799) and Society for Promoting Christianity Among the Jews (1809) were similarly constituted as formally Anglican.

37. Marshall, "Britain Without America," 583-84, 590-92.

Early Evangelical Missions and the Anglican Establishment

Because of the ongoing suspicion of missionary activity among establishment-oriented Anglicans prior to the 1830s and the undeveloped nature of missionary support mechanisms, the activities of the CMS received only the most grudging backing from those outside the Evangelical fold who instead advocated, as did the High Churchmen of the Hackney Phalanx, staunch support of the SPG.[38] The SPG had developed an influential set of ideas about the role of the Church of England in imperial expansion over the eighteenth century, insisting that church and state alike had a responsibility for the spiritual welfare of colonists and "colonial heathens," that the riches of empire entailed duty to God to extend the Church as the one best form of religion, and that the maintenance of empire depended on creating bonds of common religious culture and morality that would be pleasing to God.[39]

Nevertheless, Anglican and Nonconformist alike faced the scorn of Church critics such as Sydney Smith, whose 1808 *Edinburgh Review* articles, which argued that missions advocated by evangelicals under the inspiration of "visionary enthusiasm" created danger of rebellion in the precarious Indian empire, reflected higher and drier church conservative fears that support for mission was tainted by association with political radicalism and its threats to traditional authority. To social and political conservatives the logic of mission itself — by which enthusiast forms of persuasion led individuals to a fundamental transformation of belief and lifestyle — represented a danger to political and social order both at home and abroad.[40] Early evangelical successes, such as the foundation of the Crown Colony of Sierra Leone in 1806 for settlement of ex-British slaves, the 1807 abolition of the slave trade, and the insertion of pro-missionary clauses in the renewed East India Company charter in 1813, were achieved only with spirited agitation against resistance in government circles where officials, while supporting Anglican ecclesiastical expansion when it seemed to support colonial authority, shrank from

38. Other societies included in the web of associations that held the early-nineteenth-century High Church connection together included the SPCK, the National Society (1811) dedicated to Church education, and the Church Building Society (1818). Nockles, *Oxford Movement*, 19.

39. Strong, *Anglicanism and the British Empire*, 211.

40. Sydney Smith, "Publications Respecting Indian Missions," *Edinburgh Review* 12 (Apr. 1808): 170-80. Smith, co-founder and editor of the *Edinburgh Review*, was no Tory; nevertheless, his views echoed those of establishment-minded Anglicans. On the Whig politics of the *Edinburgh Review*, including consistent opposition to the slave trade, if not support for foreign missions, see John Clive, *Scotch Reviewers: The Edinburgh Review, 1802-1815* (Cambridge, MA: Harvard University Press, 1957), chap. 4.

the "enthusiasm" of the evangelical connection.[41] Evangelicals, for their part, deplored the "rationalism" of the higher church, a form of Christian expression that suggested no true direct experience of God and no conversion to true religion.

Despite this fundamental experiential divide and the resulting mutual denigration, general observation of religious neutrality by government officials at home and abroad allowed freedom of development to missions and emerging Christian communities of all denominations. As missionary activity grew, it became more difficult to ignore the implications for Church strength and structure that were coming from the missionary activity of these "canting hypocrites and raving enthusiasts."[42] Alliances on common objectives soon developed between evangelical and High Church Anglicans, as shown by their combined efforts in successfully agitating for the admission of missionaries to India and establishment of an Indian bishop and three archdeacons in the reauthorization of the East India Company charter in 1813.[43]

The difficulty of attracting respectable traditionalist support for the mission cause was in part a reflection of the difficulty of recruiting missionaries. The CMS, for example, resorted to German missionary recruits and, like Nonconformist societies, the CMS relied heavily on artisanal and lower-middle-class missionary candidates because the more "gentlemanly" regular clergy avoided the stigma of missionary service.[44] Furthermore, early problems in establishing control over missionaries abroad led to controversies over apparently self-serving missionary commercial trading and missionary liaisons with "native" women. But as all the societies developed more effective bureaucratic control over missions from the 1820s forward, missions were placed on a surer footing, relying on a stricter vetting and training standards for recruits (mirroring training for home ordination) and on a general acceptance of the principle that missions needed to be supported primarily through voluntary contributions, not direct involvement in local or colonial commerce.[45] By the 1830s then, the

41. Andrew Porter, "Religion, Missionary Enthusiasm, and Empire," in *The Nineteenth Century*, ed. Andrew Porter, vol. 3 of *The Oxford History of the British Empire* (Oxford: Oxford University Press, 1999), 223-29.

42. Sydney Smith, "Strictures on . . . Methodism and Missions," *Edinburgh Review* 14 (Apr. 1809): 43.

43. Kenneth Hylson-Smith, *High Churchmanship in the Church of England: From the Sixteenth Century to the Late Twentieth Century* (Edinburgh: Clark, 1993), 119-20.

44. Paul Jenkins, "The Church Missionary Society and the Basel Mission: An Early Experiment in Inter-European Cooperation," in *The Church Mission Society and World Christianity, 1799-1999*, ed. Kevin Ward and Brian Stanley (Grand Rapids: Eerdmans, 1999), 43-51.

45. For a more detailed history of the development of the early missionary movement in Britain, see Porter, *Religion Versus Empire*, chaps. 2-4.

basic outlines of missionary culture and missionary organization had been established: clerical standards of operation, responsiveness to the voluntary associational life central to English denominational communities, and racial and cultural separation from indigenous populations and converts.

If some society secretaries favored a cooperative pooling of resources, most supporters showed greatest comfort by giving to societies that mirrored their sectarian identities. This principle held true within the Church of England as well, where the concerns of High and Low Church parties became the most important determinant in defining the nature of Anglican missionary activity and motivating missionary support. The general atmosphere of sectarianism in British religion set the context and provided much of the energy behind the emergence of the Protestant missionary movement in England. Spirited competition between the Church of England and the Nonconformists, contained for two decades by the fears of social revolution and political repression seemingly required by the Napoleonic Wars, burst forth in the late Georgian era. This created a dynamic of social and political change and reform that destroyed any realistic expectation that the "confessional state" dear to High Church Anglicans, wedded to an ideal of divine and traditional — rather than popular political and religious — legitimacy, could be revived.[46]

The transformations of this turbulent social and political era shook the Church of England to its foundations as its special status and prerogatives were challenged, a circumstance that High and Low Churchmen responded to very differently. Scholarship in the past few decades, however, rather than emphasizing the failings of the Church in responding to social, political, and organizational challenges, has noted the effectiveness of the Church, particularly after mid-century, in adjusting to these changes.[47] Evangelical reformism, however, was a deeply ambiguous phenomenon for the Church. Although the growing influential "school" of evangelical Churchmen professed continued loyalty to the *Ecclesia Anglicana* and Evangelical enthusiasts brought dynamism to its culture through their home and foreign missionary activity, their association with evangelical Dissent reinforced fears of sectarian decay within the Church itself.

46. Clark, *English Society*, 408-20.

47. K. D. M. Snell, *Church and Chapel in the North Midlands: Religious Observance in the Nineteenth Century* (Leicester, UK: Leicester University Press, 1991); Mark Smith, *Religion in Industrial Society: Oldham and Saddleworth, 1740-1865* (Oxford: Clarendon Press, 1994); Arthur Burns, *The Diocesan Revival in the Church of England, c. 1800-1870* (Oxford: Oxford University Press, 1999). But cf. David Clark, *Between Pulpit and Pew: Folk Religion in a North Yorkshire Fishing Village* (Cambridge: Cambridge University Press, 1982); and Albion M. Urdank, *Religion and Society in a Cotswold Vale: Nailsworth, Gloucestershire, 1780-1865* (Berkeley: University of California Press, 1990).

The emergence of the Oxford Movement in the 1830s as a High Church revival aiming at a purified Anglicanism both reinforced and significantly complicated stiffening resolve to support Church defense among High Church Anglicans. The Oxford Movement and its heirs fundamentally realigned the Anglican party terrain, redefining the meaning of High and Low Church Anglicanism and the relationship of the Church establishment to popular religion. The subsequent evolution of deeply emotional responses to Anglican Church reform revitalized the missionary societies and ultimately set the context for Anglicanism, and Anglican missions, in late Victorian Britain.

Reform, Missions, and the Shape of Victorian Church Party

Looking back from the 1890s, R. W. Church, the early Tractarian turned progressive Anglo-Catholic sympathizer and Dean of St. Paul's Cathedral, saw the origin of the Oxford Movement in John Keble's Assize Sermon of 1833. With its critique of the "national apostasy" committed by the English state in usurping Church authority through the Irish Temporalities Bill, the Oxford Movement resonated with older forms of High Churchmanship in its emphasis on the unique apostolic authority of the Church of England and its priestly orders in the face of Church reform.[48] The supporters of the Oxford Movement are the most thoroughly studied party within the modern Church of England, not least because they helped reinforce a spreading wave of reforming Anglican thought with profound effects, not only among avowed Tractarians and their later Ritualistic and Anglo-Catholic heirs, but also among High Churchmen of continuing establishmentarian loyalties. Evangelicals were also deeply affected, both in responding to renewed High Church attacks on their supposed deficiency of loyalty to the Church and in acting on their fears that the Oxford Movement had revived a creeping "Romanizing" influence within Anglicanism that threatened Reformation principles within the Church.[49]

48. The followers of the Oxford Movement were also known as Tractarians (after the ninety *Tracts for the Times* published from 1833 to 1841) and Puseyites (after notable Tractarian leader Edward Bouverie Pusey). R. W. Church, *The Oxford Movement: Twelve Years, 1833-1845* (London: Macmillan, 1891), 1-2, 28-29, 82-83. Church, a stalwart supporter of toleration for evolving High Church practices, was also the co-founder of the *Guardian* newspaper, the mouthpiece of High Church politics. The Irish Temporalities Bill abolished and amalgamated several Irish bishoprics and made other reforms to decayed, mismatched Church offices. Cheered by the Irish and Radicals, ultra-Tory Anglicans deplored it as a tyrannous robbery of the Church and precedent for further assaults. Chadwick, *Victorian Church: Part One: 1829-1859*, 56-60.
49. Conflict was sharpened by early Oxford Movement leader John Henry Newman's attack

The divisions that the Oxford Movement enlivened had such force, however, because of the long and well-articulated historical character of pre-existing divisions that continued as a legacy of the English Reformation. A church pre-dominantly Protestant in theology, Catholic in administrative logic, and pro-foundly mixed in liturgical practice had rapidly developed "low" and "high" pressure groups from the sixteenth century onward, dedicated to pressing the Church in either Protestant or Catholic directions. The seventeenth-century High Church triumph during the Restoration of Charles II drove substantial numbers of the Low Church party out into the swelling dissenting sects; how-ever, the Revolution of 1688 crippled High Church power when a substantial number of nonjurors (Churchmen who refused to take the oath of allegiance to William III) were deprived of office. In the aftermath, Low Church influences revived within the Church in the eighteenth century under the force of Meth-odist evangelical revival.[50] By the late eighteenth century, when the Protestant evangelical missionary movement began in earnest, British religious society had settled into patterns of coexistence that reinforced an expanding civil society founded in the legacies of the late seventeenth century: religious toleration and general social consensus about the desirability of free associational life.

Church Parties and Foreign Missions in the Age of Reform

By the 1830s denominational identity, deeply linked to an emerging class-based cultural politics of reform, had become central to the intellectual milieu in which missionary administrators devised strategies for mission work, revenue collection, and administration.[51] Critical to the nineteenth-century transfor-mation of Anglicanism was the constitutional revolution caused by Church reform. The repeal of the Test and Corporation Acts in 1828 and the Catholic Relief Bill of 1829, which formally admitted non-Anglicans into national life, was followed by the Parliamentary Reform Act in 1832, which drew Anglicans of all party persuasions into denominational competition. Reform, however, bred fear that the entire Anglican edifice was soon to be dismantled, from the rationalization of Church offices engineered by the Ecclesiastical Commission

---

on the creation of the Jerusalem bishopric as bringing the Church into cooperation with heresy through the unification of Anglicans with Lutherans (with whom the CMS had closely associated for decades). W. M. Jacob, *The Making of the Anglican Church Worldwide* (London: SPCK, 1997), 112.

50. Nigel Yates, *The Oxford Movement and Anglican Ritualism* (London: Historical Association, 1983), 5-8.

51. Lovegrove, *Established Church, Sectarian People*, 154-61.

to local parochial reorganization, church building, and educational initiatives. It was from this atmosphere that the Oxford Movement arose, but its formulation of a newly authoritative Church of England drawing its strength from its pre-Reformation continuity with the apostolic church of early Christianity drew the fearful, organized opposition of evangelical "Puritans" within the Church of England.

In the wake of Parliamentary reform in the 1830s, vigorous Nonconformist pursuit of disestablishment of the Church further stoked the Victorian politics of religion; this issue continued to fire denominational friction through to the end of the century.[52] Anglican Church defense crossed Church party lines, complicating bonds of alliance and perceived allegiance both within the Church and evangelicalism more broadly. Thus, by mid-century, Tractarians could find common cause with Evangelicals in defending the legitimacy of the Church and biblical authority, opposing modernist doubt, and extending the Anglican Church overseas, even while they were bitterly opposed on the extent of the authority of bishops and the state as well as on the loyalty of "Romanist" doctrinal and liturgical innovations.[53] At the same time there emerged a Broad Church movement, drawing on the ideas of Anglican philosopher Samuel Taylor Coleridge regarding the need for a "clerisy" of sophisticated religious, educational, and professional leaders to develop the civilizational genius of England through a comprehensively imagined, universal, tolerant national church. Finding substance in Thomas Arnold's reforms at Rugby School and hopes for a public school movement that would moralize public life through Church reform, the inspiration of ecclesiastical statesmanship, and the ultimate vision of a Christian commonwealth, Anglicanism rapidly became an imaginative space within which the rebuilding of national unity could be both pursued and contested.[54]

For most Anglican thinkers by mid-century, confronting the question of the proper nature of the Church of England and its role in the nation became an underlying focus. The dynamism of missionary Churchmanship, however, tended

---

52. The significant issues of religious political agitation by the late Victorian era were disestablishment, education and Ritualism. G. I. T. Machin, *Politics and the Churches in Great Britain, 1869 to 1921* (Oxford: Oxford University Press, 1987), 7 and passim.

53. The unification of the parties in opposition to the publication of *Essays and Reviews* in 1860, with its theological modernism, and also against John Colenso, bishop of Natal, for his liberal biblical criticism, drew the mission field into controversy over modernism. Bernard M. G. Reardon, *Religious Thought in the Victorian Age: A Survey from Coleridge to Gore,* 2nd ed. (London: Longman, 1995), 237-37, 251-55.

54. Claude Welch, *Protestant Thought in the Nineteenth Century: Volume 1, 1799-1870* (New Haven: Yale University Press, 1972), 121-23, 186-89.

to be tied not into intellectualized systems of thought associated with the well-known figures of Anglican intellectual history — Newman, Coleridge, Pusey, Arnold, Maurice — but into the emotionally insistent systems of righteousness associated with charismatic evangelicalism and emergent advanced Ritualism. The English Anglican missionary societies, at mid-century exclusively the CMS and SPG, confronted this confused atmosphere and found themselves vessels for competing visions of right religion, national mission, imperial duty, and international responsibility.

Anglican party politics thus became both more potent and more diverse, drawing the missionary societies into contests over theological, ecclesiological, eschatological, political, social, and reformist concerns. Perhaps the clearest representation of what the divisions of the Church had come to by the 1850s is to be found in Anglican essayist and wit W. J. Conybeare's famous 1853 article "Church Parties," which attempted to outline the new channels along which Anglican politics flowed.[55] Because of his comprehensive approach and tax-onomical precision, it is worth looking at Conybeare in more detail to get at least a broad outline of the state of Church parties at mid-century. Conybeare divided these parties into three major categories, each subdivided into enthu-siastic extremists, sensible, principled moderates, and lethargic, uninspired for-malists: High Church (subdivided into "Tractarian," "Anglican," and "High and Dry"); Low Church (subdivided into "Recordite," "Evangelical," and "Low and Slow"); and Broad Church (subdivided into "concealed infidels," "theoretical and antitheoretical," and "Stagnant type").[56]

Extremists set the tone of a party and reinforced loyalty through aggres-sive tactics. Second-generation Tractarians, pushing beyond the leaders of the Oxford Movement into innovative Anglo-Catholic theories and Ritualistic practice, were inspired by study of the ancient church and Roman Catholi-cism; Recordites, following the evangelical newspaper the *Record* into violent "no-popery" agitations, were inspired by the Protestant martyrdoms of the Reformation; and theoretical Broad Churchmen, following Thomas Arnold and the public school vision of an organic, reforming moralism, were inspired by a rationalistic approach to reviving national church institutions aiming at social unification. Tractarianism and an emerging Ritualist style of worship shaded, however, into a more "orthodox" but also innovative and activist High Churchmanship. They faced often aggressive evangelicals devoted both to op-

55. Conybeare's article first appeared in 1853, but was subsequently reprinted and revised. W. J. Conybeare, "Church Parties," *Edinburgh Review* 98 (Oct. 1853): 273-342.

56. These are the subdivisions of Conybeare's later 1857 revision of the article. Arthur Burns, ed., "W. J. Conybeare: 'Church Parties,'" in *From Cranmer to Davidson: A Church of England Mis-cellany*, ed. Stephen Taylor (Woodbridge, UK: Boydell, 1999), 357.

posing "Romanist" innovation within the Church and to promoting evangelical doctrines. Between them, and growing in dynamism, Conybeare argued, was an emerging Broad Church movement dedicated to institutional reform and common social action to tackle the problems of industrial society, particularly the "regeneration of the humbler classes." Conybeare's assessments of the strength of these parties within the 18,000 clergy of the Church of England were debated and denounced, but they probably provide as broadly indicative a picture as any other source.[57] Roughly, Conybeare estimated that High Churchmen made up about 40 percent of the clergy, Low Churchmen around 35 percent, and Broad Churchmen 20 percent (see Appendix I, Figure 3).[58] By mid-century, then, the Church found itself clearly divided between significant, strongly self-identifying parties with often antagonistic agendas. These were tied directly to missionary societies and their strategies as fundamental markers of identity and programs of action.

Tellingly, Conybeare argued that the parties showed their power for good most significantly in their missionary and social outreach. Conybeare suggested that Evangelicalism, in its most valuable formulation, was associated with philanthropic success at home and abroad, as in India where "Hindoo widows are no longer burnt alive," and in the remainder of the empire where "natives of the most distant and barbarous colonies know that they will not appeal in vain to English sympathy against English oppression."[59] Central to Evangelical consciousness was awareness of a national responsibility to create "centres of religious truth and of civilisation" among "heathen populations" brought into contact with the Church by imperial commercial involvement.[60] Evangelical stimulus to Church reform in England and expansion overseas through the creation of Anglican voluntary societies arose from the logic of mission: the CMS, the first Diocesan Church Building Society in Chester, the Church Pasto-

---

57. Attempts to determine the strength of Church parties by a strict counting approach suffer from the ambiguity of religious identities and the reality that moderates of all parties supported many causes that crossed party lines. Detailed annotations on the original 1853 and subsequent 1855 and 1857 versions of Conybeare's article, as well as a valuable interpretive essay including an assessment of Conybeare's accuracy and the pitfalls in assigning individuals to parties, are to be found in Burns, ed., "Conybeare," 213-385. On the redefinition of Church parties and confusion of terminology caused by the Oxford Movement, see Nockles, *Oxford Movement*, 33-43.

58. Conybeare also noted that of twenty-eight bishops, thirteen were High Church, ten Broad Church, and five Evangelical, although, again, questions of definition exist here as well. Conybeare, "Church Parties," 338.

59. Conybeare, "Church Parties," 227.

60. Conybeare, "Church Parties," 278. For Conybeare the greatest challenges of the colonies, however, were not those of "heathenism," but "the Mammon-seeking and Jacobinical population" of Europeans (p. 282).

ral Aid Society (formed in the committee rooms of the CMS), and the order of Scripture Readers who win back "baptized heathen to the pale of Christendom" were all defining organizations.[61] In pious Evangelicals' minds the regeneration of the heathen, at home and abroad, always began with the gospel.

High Churchmen, on the other hand, emphasized the power of apostolic bishops to develop and regenerate the Church and its institutions. Thus they focused their energies on establishing colonial bishoprics, transferring the Church to "nascent empires," and encouraging the "good government" and moral energy of the episcopal office overseas. This approach, Conybeare argued, brought enormous revitalization to the SPG, in part linked to the founding of St. Augustine's College at Canterbury (1848) for the training of missionaries. Both Low and High Churchmen could boast self-denying and successful overseas bishops: Evangelicals had the selfless Charles Perry of Melbourne and High Churchmen had the committed George Augustus Selwyn of New Zealand. In contrast, Conybeare's Broad Church sympathies led him to suggest that Robert Gray of Cape Town, aggressively Tractarian abroad and at home, made the colonial episcopate ridiculous.[62] For Conybeare, as for so many other moderate Churchmen, piety and parochial duty were becoming the measure by which to judge religious vigor both at home and overseas.

Clearly the crisis brought by Church reform was a galvanizing force among Anglicans of all persuasions. However, this was particularly true for High Churchmen. Early in the century support of the SPG and SPCK as established, dignified organs of Church extension was a marker of High Church orientation. And through the 1830s supporters of the SPG were able to remain largely disdainful of voluntarism, viewing it as an enthusiastic cultural expression of a rising tide of evangelicalism. But as Nonconformist foreign missions drew intensifying support, boosted by antislavery agitation and particularly by controversies surrounding Nonconformist missions to West Indian slaves, the shifting sands of popular politics and the assaults on establishments of all kinds stirred dangerous waters for the "high" view of the church. Anglican attitudes toward emancipation, for example, were deeply divided, with Evangelicals mostly supporting abolition, and many High Churchmen, particularly West Indian colonial clergy, supporting white planters.

The SPG's ownership of Codrington Plantation and College in Barbados, a slave-plantation bequest supporting colonial education, made profoundly ambiguous its relationship to the wave of evangelical reformism cresting in

61. Conybeare, "Church Parties," 279. Burns notes that the Chester society was not actually the first diocesan church-building society. Burns, ed., "Conybeare," 265nn25-26.
62. Conybeare, "Church Parties," 282, 311, 323.

the 1830s, as did the often enthusiastic support of slavery by many of the main-line Anglican clergy in the West Indies. Throughout the eighteenth century, the SPG and the Anglican bishops proved willing to operate the plantation routinely and thus gave their implicit support to the slave system and white, landowning privilege.[63] Parliament's 1834 abolition of slavery, the culmination of four decades of agitation catalyzed by the Evangelicals of the Clapham Sect, was tied to currents of middle-class liberal political reform that had brought democratic extension of the franchise in the Reform Bill of 1832. Fear for the Anglican establishment among Tory Churchmen was one key result of liberal reform in the 1830s, and it generated contrasting responses within the Church. Progressive humanitarian optimism and focus on evangelical spirituality ani-mated evangelical Anglicans — embodied in the career of William Wilberforce's collaborator and influential successor, Thomas Fowell Buxton — who saw the CMS, but also leading Nonconformist missionary societies like the LMS, as crucial supports for ongoing colonial reforms.[64] Church reform and defense of Church prerogatives, on the other hand, a program which increasingly saw the SPG as an essential foundation, obsessed High Churchmen, especially leading reformers as diverse as Edward Bouverie Pusey, Samuel Wilberforce, Charles Blomfield and Henry Phillpotts.

In the divide that grew within Anglican missions, origins mattered. The CMS grew out of the evangelical revival's late-eighteenth-century activism, bib-licism, and conversionism. The SPG, however, was founded much earlier and catered to a significantly different clerical culture of deference to established authority more temperamentally suited to an *ancien regime* environment than to a modern, mass voluntarist one. Of all the English missionary societies, the SPG was the oldest, receiving its Royal Charter in 1701. Known to supporters as "the venerable society," through the eighteenth century the SPG, as the of-ficial Church agency for supporting Anglican clergy overseas, had relied on Parliamentary Grants and Church-wide collections under Royal Letters of ap-peal.[65] With Church reform, however, in 1832 the Whig government made clear that colonial church establishments would soon be deprived of parliamentary

---

63. Daniel O'Connor and others, *Three Centuries of Mission: The United Society for the Prop-agation of the Gospel, 1701-2000* (London: Continuum, 2000), 36-37; and Mary Turner, *Slaves and Missionaries: The Disintegration of Jamaican Slave Society, 1787-1834* (Urbana: University of Illinois Press, 1982), 10, 13-16.

64. On Buxton, see Porter, *Religion Versus Empire*, 82, 124, 137-41, 149-52. Buxton, though deeply influenced by the Quakerism of his mother and wife, remained a Churchman influential among evangelical Anglicans.

65. Thompson, *History of the SPG*, 104-5. The SPG received its last Parliamentary Grant in 1845 and its last collection under Royal Letter in 1853. *Report of the SPG, 1880*, 120.

grants. After 1846 the state withdrew all support from the SPG, forcing the Society to engage in the popular fundraising methods pioneered by evangelical voluntary societies.[66] In an atmosphere rife with paranoia fuelled by the larger political reform agendas of the day — from Whig liberal governmental reforms to popular radical Chartist demands for sweeping democratic change — the SPG and the CMS came to be associated within a Church itself deeply connected to Tory conservatism and paternalism with contrasting approaches: the SPG with traditional deference to authority in the name of stability and the CMS with innovative appeal to spiritual power working broad cultural change beyond the reach of institutions. Extremists on either side of the divide imagined catastrophic conspiratorial plans on the part of their opponents: Evangelicals feared that High Churchmen, infected with Tractarian papism, would reintroduce the tyranny of Rome to the heart of English culture; High Churchmen feared that Evangelicals, in league with disloyal Dissenters, would launch a "Puritan" overthrow of established Church authority, bringing chaos in its wake. Moderates of the parties, even if they dismissed the more paranoid vision of extremists, saw the fundamental direction of the Church and the nation at stake in these disputes.

The renewed sense that Church institutions and Church principles required strengthening, which in the 1830s and 1840s produced significant church building campaigns and expansion of the clergy, increased support for the SPG as the "legitimate" organ for overseas Church extension. Thus, from the highest realms of High Churchmanship, the SPG was reauthorized as the chosen agency for Church missions, with E. B. Pusey, leader of the Oxford Movement in the aftermath of John Henry Newman's shocking conversion to Rome, anointing the SPG as "the accredited organ of the whole Episcopacy of our branch of the Church Catholic."[67] Controversies involving Church defense had the effects of mobilizing High Church support as never before as well as organizing the party sense of High Churchmen around the SPG and allied bodies, such as the Colonial and Continental Church Society, founded in 1823. Whereas the era of the 1830s and 1840s was clearly good for evangelicals and the CMS, which doubled its income over the twenty-year period, income growth in excess of 400 percent for the SPG was a mark of how seriously High Churchmen began to take the need to operate competitively in an undeniably

---

66. Stanley, "Home Support," 77-81.

67. Pusey voiced these sentiments in 1838 in a pair of sermons detailing proper Anglican expansion abroad. E. B. Pusey, "The Church the Converter of the Heathen," in *Parochial Sermons Preached and Printed on Various Occasions*, vols. 11 and 12 (Oxford: Parker, 1865), quoted in Faught, *Oxford Movement*, 134.

changed atmosphere requiring mobilization of voluntary support.[68] From a society that prior to the 1830s supported virtually no local association network, no public meetings, and no popular periodicals, by 1850 the SPG had revolutionized its operations.

Within a High Church connection influenced by the stridency of the Oxford Movement, the centrality of the Church and the primacy of its principles, in the words of Samuel Wilberforce, "to send out the Church, and not merely instructions about religion," was a means of reclaiming an apostolic missionary heritage, as was his controversial campaign to send out "missionary bishops, i.e. bishops and a missionary clergy as a visible Church" as the vanguard, rather than the completion, of church extension.[69] The culmination of this vision was the 1841 creation of the Colonial Bishoprics Fund, at the public behest of several High Church bishops, and, subsequently, the passage of the Colonial Bishoprics Act, which enabled the Church to create bishops who would provide for colonial church extension.[70] Accepting the voluntary principle to be necessary in the face of growing government reluctance to act, the supporters of the Fund — including SPG Standing Committee member (and future prime minister) William Ewart Gladstone, its treasurer until his death in 1898, and Ernest Hawkins, its first secretary (an office he held concurrently with the secretaryship of the SPG) — acted to bring their vision of the Church's future before a public deeply concerned with advancing Christianity overseas. From this point onward, the creation and consecration of bishops became a high-profile public celebration of Church extension held in Westminster Abbey, St. Paul's Cathedral, or Canterbury Cathedral. Despite the divisions within the Church, organizational advancement grew out of a new voluntaristic effort tied directly to a missionary vision for the future of Anglicanism that saw the creation of a wave of new overseas bishoprics.[71]

It was in the context of this program that Samuel Wilberforce, later the influential bishop of Oxford (1845-69) and Winchester (1869-73), so often

68. Between 1830-31 and 1850-51, the SPG increased its income from £17,370 to £89,245. The CMS in the same period increased from £47,959 to £103,914. See Appendix I, Figure 4 for CMS and SPG incomes.

69. Arthur R. Ashwell and Reginald G. Wilberforce, *Life of the Right Reverend Samuel Wilberforce, D.D., Lord Bishop of Oxford and Afterwards of Winchester,* 3 vols. (London: Murray, 1880-82), 1:129. The American Church sent out the first missionary bishop in 1835. Rowell, *Vision Glorious,* 161-62.

70. Strong, *Anglicanism and the British Empire,* 210-11.

71. In twenty years, the Fund endowed thirty-three bishoprics, fifty-four by 1900, each with a substantial missionary component, particularly as "tropical" imperial and extra-imperial dioceses were formed. W. F. France, *The Oversea Episcopate: Centenary History of the Colonial Bishoprics Fund, 1841-1941* (Westminster, UK: Colonial Bishoprics Fund, 1941), 9-23.

at the center of High Church reforming efforts, launched in 1838 and 1839 energetic deputation tours for the SPG, in the process also consolidating his rising reputation as a speaker and young Churchman of consequence.[72] As part of a larger campaign to support an expansion of colonial bishoprics and the resources of Anglican bishops generally, the SPG proved a rallying point for reforming bishops, despite differences they may have had on other matters of Church and social reform. It thus provided common ground for episcopal leaders like Charles Blomfield of London (1828-56) and Henry Phillpotts of Exeter (1830-69) — intensely divided, for example, over poverty relief and the workhouse under the Poor Law Amendment Act — to push jointly for Church growth both at home and abroad.[73] Though an early supporter of the CMS, Wilberforce grew into a combative backer of the SPG and became its most consistent and influential champion through the 1860s, seeing it as an embodiment of church order through the authority of apostolic succession. Despite an Evangelical campaign led by the *Record* to encourage withdrawal of support for the SPG after the appointment of reportedly Tractarian secretary Ernest Hawkins, the SPG, moving into mid-century, enjoyed a rich and successful environment produced by the invigorated party atmosphere.[74] Success of the SPG was based upon its clear association with spirited High Church ecclesiastical reformers such as Wilberforce — in his outspokenness as a liberal Tory defender of the organic community of the Church — and Henry Phillpotts — in his paternalistic defense of the parish system in the face of the harsh economic effects of political economy. Thus the SPG, claiming exclusively to spread the distinctive truths of the Church, created a clear identity based on Wilberforce's counsel to Hawkins that it "act as little as possible as a <u>society</u>: to remember & carry out the principle that you are <u>the</u> missionary of the Church."[75]

By representing "high" Anglican reserve, the SPG relied on the unique authority of the Anglican episcopacy and sacraments, disconnecting the Society doctrinally and temperamentally from the evangelical mainstream of foreign

72. Wilberforce, along with Bishop John Inglis of Nova Scotia, promoted popular tours to cultivate voluntary lay support. Standish Meacham, *Lord Bishop: The Life of Samuel Wilberforce, 1805-1873* (Cambridge, MA: Harvard University Press, 1970), 36-37.

73. On the drive for more English bishops and dioceses, see Burns, *Diocesan Revival*, 196-98. On differences over the New Poor Law, see R. A. Soloway, *Prelates and People: Ecclesiastical Social Thought in England, 1783-1852* (London: Routledge & K. Paul, 1969), 172-76.

74. Meacham, *Wilberforce*, 83; Stanley, "Home Support," 80-91.

75. Sam[ue]l Wilberforce to Ernest Hawkins, 12 Nov. 1839, United Society for the Propagation of the Gospel Archives, H 94, Bodleian Library of Commonwealth and African History, Rhodes House, Oxford (hereafter cited as USPG Archives).

missions. Exclusive reliance on conversion and the Bible united the Nonconformist societies and the Evangelicals within the Church of England; as one
contemporary noted, the British & Foreign Bible Society (BFBS) conference
rooms — dedicated to the worldwide distribution of the Bible — were "sacred
territory within which denominational distinctions disappear."[76] Such biblicism
and ecumenism, however, repelled both the Tractarians and the more "orthodox" High Church supporters of the SPG. Early Oxford Movement leader John
Henry Newman, for example, resigned from the BFBS in 1830, reasoning that
missionary effort outside the Church was damaging to its strength. He later
encouraged Wilberforce, saying that "the only right way of missionary-izing
is by bishops" and that he should like to "try the powers of at least *colonial*
bishops to do without the State."[77] In Bible distribution the SPG worked exclusively with the Anglican SPCK, refusing cooperation with the BFBS. In theology,
temperament, style, and constituency the CMS — with its commitment to the
Reformation principles of preaching the cross, fearing Rome, emphasizing the
depravity of humans, distributing Bibles and tracts, insisting on justification
by faith alone, and pressing for the conversion of the world — was closer to
the LMS than to the SPG. Anglican evangelicals thus stood united culturally
with the mainstream dissenting sects. Their continued loyalty to the Church remained a lasting concern, not least within the episcopal leadership of a Church
that feared losing members not only to Rome but also to Dissent. That the CMS
had come under the leadership of the irenic secretary Henry Venn, who was a
clerical leader rather than a layman, in 1841 was of considerable and continuing significance to maintaining a viable and loyal evangelical party within the
Church.[78]

As High Churchmen became engaged with the overseas Church as part
of a common heritage and a commonly imagined future, the controversies
that arose within the Church of England were also exported overseas. From
the 1830s the animating waves of Anglican innovation and reaction generated by the Oxford Movement rippled out into the colonial and missionary
churches, not least because the emphasis on reviving catholic principles within

76. *Report of the Centenary Conference on the Protestant Missions of the World*, 2 vols.,
ed. James Johnson (London: Nisbet, 1888), 1:x. On the BFBS, see Leslie Howsam, *Cheap Bibles:
Nineteenth-Century Publishing and the British and Foreign Bible Society* (Cambridge: Cambridge
University Press, 1991).

77. David Newsome, *The Parting of Friends: A Study of the Wilberforces and Henry Manning*
(London: Murray, 1966), 217.

78. Venn and Bishop Blomfield of London arranged that disagreements between colonial
bishops and the CMS would be settled by binding adjudication by the archbishops of the Church
of England and Ireland. Yates, *Venn and Victorian Bishops*, 77-78.

the Church was itself inherently missionary. The problem of Church identity was most clearly revealed in the missionary project. The origins of the Oxford Movement were themselves tied into missionary matters that suggested the need to formulate clearer visions of essential Churchmanship in which the advancement of Anglican doctrine rather than evangelical enthusiasm was paramount.[79] Almost inevitably, certain exclusivist Tractarian colonial bishops, most notably Robert Gray of Cape Town, engineered diocesan policies focused on driving out Evangelicals in acts of purification inspired by the Oxford Movement.

The lines, however, between Tractarian extremists and High Church reformers could be very fine: establishment-oriented reformers could find inspiration in the enthusiasm of young, Ritualist Anglo-Catholics who built an energetic countercultural clerical movement, even if excesses of ritual practice also caused troublesome public controversy with evangelicals.[80] At the same time, colonial bishoprics, along with American sees, were often poorly endowed. The growing visibility of returned colonial bishops and the more frequent visits of American bishops became a focus for Church reformers to advocate for more generous Church provision and for more Church independence through the development of synodical governance, a cause that both moderate and Tractarian High Churchmen, urged on by charismatic colonial bishops like Selwyn of New Zealand and Gray of Cape Town, could support.[81] The SPG's Third Jubilee observances, begun in the Great Exhibition year 1851 and concluding with celebrations in the summer of 1852, symbolized the new program by bringing to England American, Scottish, and colonial Episcopalians united in the moderate High Church project of developing the unity of the Anglican Communion, not least as a defense against Roman Catholic criticisms of the disunity of the English Church.[82] The SPG, as symbolic mother of the American Episcopal Church, became one key institution around which an Anglican self-consciousness grew in the wake of Church reform. The validation of the claims of the parties to contribute to that identity lay substantially in the decade that followed in overseas and missionary effectiveness.

79. Faught, *Oxford Movement*, 131.

80. On emerging Anglo-Catholicism as a countercultural youth movement self-consciously opposed to Evangelicalism, see John Shelton Reed, *Glorious Battle: The Cultural Politics of Victorian Anglo-Catholicism* (Nashville, TN: Vanderbilt University Press, 1996), 76-84.

81. Burns, *Diocesan Revival*, 198, 234, 244; Rowell, *Vision Glorious*, 166-70.

82. Alan M. G. Stephenson, *Anglicanism and the Lambeth Conferences* (London: SPCK, 1978), 18-25. As Stephenson notes, the Jubilee marked the beginning of the systematic use of the term "Anglican Communion" by Churchmen (p. 16).

Anglican Identity, History, and Imperial Boundaries

Voluntarism and denominationalism thus became crucial to defining the nineteenth-century Anglican missionary movement. Despite examples of practical cooperation between societies, particularly evangelical ones, and even a desire among some society secretaries to build ecumenical accords, there were clear limits to collaboration between organizations that operated under the core assumption of English philanthropy: that a charity was to be organized by voluntary societies, funded by voluntary contributions, and dependent on the good will of supporters.[83] The cultivation of sectarian identity secured the good will of supporters on its most basic level. And within the Church of England the process by which the Church parties emerged — Tractarian, High, Broad, or Low Church — was of particular importance because the definition of Anglicanism, above the broad minimal requirements of the communion, was ever more fiercely contested, a reality that must be taken into account if the late Victorian Anglican missionary movement is to be at all understood.

One of the most significant outcomes was the way in which the Anglican societies imaginatively divided the mission field to build support. The SPG, emphasizing its commitment to English settlers and immigrants — an emphasis that operated in accord with its goal to present the visible Church as a bulwark of stability and morality — carved out a particular appeal to English support based on shared cultural and racial affinities, as well as support for colonization and the formal empire. The SPG's strong "establishment" links and the historical consciousness as an organization deeply involved in the eighteenth-century colonial empire in North America are evident in Samuel Wilberforce's assertion that no one "can doubt that if England will not maintain a colonial Church for the benefit of her own sons settled abroad, & for the gathering in of the Heathen, she will be deprived of all her colonies."[84] This sense of the particular duty of the SPG to Britain's colonies in providing spiritual care for the accelerating flood of British immigrants to North American and other "white settlement" colonies was designed to ensure the expansion of the English Church with the English people. In this the SPG consistently associated itself with the particular responsibility of securing divine sanction for empire, and the missionaries of

83. The working secretaries of the major evangelical foreign missionary societies had met for private conferences every winter since 1819 to negotiate cooperative policies. John H. Ritson, "The Things They Talked About," in *Records of Missionary Secretaries: An Account of the Celebration of the Centenary of the London Secretaries' Association* (London: United Council for Missionary Education, 1920), 29, 46, 51, 58.

84. S[amuel] Wilberforce, draft letter from the SPG to the Parochial Clergy, 5 Sept. 1839, USPG Archives, H 94.

the SPG showed a far greater willingness than missionaries of other societies to associate themselves directly with colonial authorities and the imperial idea. And as ecclesiastical growth continued, the obvious parallels to military conquest under empire grew in importance, particularly to those tied loyally to the SPG and its close association with the Colonial Bishoprics Fund and its purposes, despite the fact that many Evangelicals, with their expanding roster of overseas bishops, also often supported the Fund. In this association with empire, however, it is worth noting that High Churchmen saw their role as purifying an empire in which "England's too irreligious colonization" had corroded the positive, godly influence of higher forms of imperialism.[85] This core identity persisted into the late Victorian era as local organizers stressed the SPG's distinct identity as a buttress of Christianity in the colonies. Thus in Birmingham, a CMS stronghold, Bishop Mitchinson (late of Barbados) emphasized at the SPG anniversary that "the work of the two societies was now distinct enough, the one cared for our Colonists and the fringe of heathen; the other carried the means of grace to the great mass of the heathen."[86]

In contrast, the CMS had from its origins highlighted its commitment to the "perishing heathens," often emphasized as existing beyond the bounds of empire. In the spirit of evangelical universalism, the CMS developed an identity in accord with its stress on the invisible spirit, the unseen realm of spiritual power, and an insistence on the impermanence of human institutions that underlay much of the millenarian thinking of evangelicals throughout the century.[87] Thus the CMS was often at pains to emphasize its primary function of bringing the gospel to utterly isolated peoples who had little or no exposure to Christianity.[88] The CMS's particular appeal to English support was based on an intense spiritual vision tied, as often as not, to an at least theoretical rejection of the material world and to an understanding of England as God's chosen spiritual instrument. Nevertheless, the agency of the CMS could not avoid entanglements with British imperial power. As well, the CMS experienced particularly acute dilemmas of identity and action, given the contrast between its deeply held voluntarist principles and its association with an Anglican Church established under law in England, India, and other colonies

85. Samuel Wilberforce preaching the SPG's 151st Anniversary Sermon, quoted in O'Connor, *Three Centuries*, 52.

86. *Birmingham Daily Gazette*, 2 Nov. 1886, press clipping, Birmingham SPG Association Minute Book, USPG Archives, X 184.

87. Diary of A. W. Bauman (hereafter cited as Bauman diary), 30 Nov. 1886 (on deputation in England), Augustus William Bauman Papers, CMS Archives, Acc 323 F/1.

88. Deputation Diary of William Crompton (hereafter cited as Crompton diary), 1 Mar. 1890, USPG Archives, X 562/1, fol. 30.

without self-governing legislatures. In addition, the CMS also struggled with the contradiction between its commitment to spiritual equality and its participation in a Church structure that generated deeply elitist views of religious influence and social hierarchy.[89]

Given conflicts over theology, style of worship, and Church authority, it was only natural that the two societies developed distinctive visions of their work abroad. The SPG was tied to "white-settlement colonies," the CMS to "tropical" colonies and the "regions beyond." For each society, contrasting core identities not only expressed different priorities but also served the pragmatic purpose of providing justification for making appeals for support even in hostile parishes.[90] The division between the societies was not simply one made on theological grounds, and there is clear evidence that clergy often would collect for and support both societies based on their distinct tasks, as the evidence of High Churchmen supporting the CMS in a number of parishes in Oldham and Saddleworth suggests.[91] But in addition, the contrasting visions of the English nation abroad developed by High Churchmen and Evangelicals — establishing a church structure and pastoral responsibilities on English lines as opposed to proclaiming a gospel truth in providentially opened territory as a universal message — meant that Anglican missions and the communities that supported them developed distinct cultures of Christian action. This was true even if both, in their relationship to a privileged established Church, came almost reflexively to resort to elite support, official influence, and hierarchical theories of control put into action in the creation and extension of local institutions like churches, schools, hospitals, and printing presses.

The relationships at the core of Anglican missionary evolution and growth through the mid-Victorian period, then, were bound up directly with the emerging party politics that characterized this unsettled period. Suspicions of SPG supporters about the loyalty of the CMS to the Church were clearly articulated by the forthright Samuel Wilberforce when he urged support for the SPG because "the poor and the middle classes are led to give their pence or sixpence or shillings to Societies of a temper hostile to the Church or doubtfully attached to it: & through these societies they grow allied to the parties they represent & which seem to them living & spreading communions whilst the Church appears but a dead name." Nonconformist successes were had "under the guise of zeal for Missionary enterprise abroad," thus implicating the CMS in the process that

89. Cox, *Imperial Fault Lines*, 31-32.

90. Reports for Chester, Ely & Oxford Dioceses, 5 July 1871, in Minutes of the Home Organisation Committee, USPG Archives, X 63. All these reports refer to competition with CMS for churches as a major challenge.

91. Smith, *Religion in Industrial Society*, 276-78.

had undermined the power of the Church in the late eighteenth and early nineteenth centuries.[92] The fact that by the late 1830s there were many who "*hate* the *C.M.S.* with a godly hatred" had allowed the SPG to build support on the basis of party feeling, Church expansion, and "Church defense" particularly focused on the extension of a colonial episcopate imagined as halting the advance of colonial Nonconformity and Roman Catholicism.[93]

It has been observed that English evangelicals, with their preoccupations with the millennium, had a particularly historicized view of their place in the world as they contemplated their future within God's plan.[94] Their vision of the future, however, was contingent upon an extremely refined view of the past that developed and sharpened in competition with High Churchmen and Anglo-Catholics. The several Anglican parties appealed to specific historical constructions of Christian and English identity that rested on contrasting ideals of national life. The Anglo-Catholic vision stood upon a presumption of organic unity in the original apostolic church, encoded in the ancient patristic writings of the church fathers, and imagined as laying the foundation for a lost, harmonious society that had grown to maturity in the antiquity that preceded the Reformation.[95] Evangelicals, for their part, emphasized the biblical purity and importance of individual conscience in the post-Reformation settlement, certain that "whatever England is among the nations of the earth as a Christian country, — whatever political liberty we have, — whatever light and freedom in religion, — whatever purity and happiness there is in our homes, — whatever protection and care for the poor, — we owe it to the Protestant Reformation."[96] Moderate High Churchmen attempted to steer a middle course by emphasizing the historic nature of an ancient national church purified but not fundamentally altered by its break from Rome, a church in which, increasingly, resort to the example of the earliest church fathers became a reflexive impulse, although not

92. Draft letter, Wilberforce to the Parochial Clergy, 5 Sept. 1839, USPG Archives, H 94.

93. A. M. Campbell to Ernest Hawkins, 31 Aug. 1839, USPG Archives, H 94.

94. Kent, *Converting Women*, 97.

95. Anglo-Catholic attitudes to history can be difficult to characterize because of their variety and rapid evolution. Anglo-Catholics looked both to the ancient church and to Rome, with varying emphasis, in varying eras. Peter Hinchliff, *God and History: Aspects of British Theology, 1875-1914* (Oxford: Clarendon Press, 1992), 104-11. Early Tractarian leaders such as Hurrell Froude abhorred the Reformation as disaster for an organic English society, and among many Anglo-Catholics this attitude long persisted. Desmond Bowen, *The Idea of the Victorian Church: A Study of the Church of England, 1833-1889* (Montreal: McGill University Press, 1968), 48-49.

96. J. C. Ryle, *What Do We Owe to the Reformation?* (London: Shaw, 1877), 15. For the development of the "Reformation Tale" as a subgenre of Victorian women's popular writing, see Miriam Elizabeth Burstein, "Reviving the Reformation: Victorian Women Writers and the Protestant Historical Novel," *Women's Writing* 12, no. 1 (2005): 73-84.

an exclusive foundation for reform.[97] For Broad Church liberals the progressive idea of history, bound up in a national church of romantically English, sensibly tolerant improvement, formed the foundation of a rationalized English sense of destiny and duty that moved past the old forms of authority.[98]

In particular, Evangelicals and many reforming High Churchmen were concerned to use missions and colonial churches to demonstrate the vigor of their principles in areas of vital contest: world civilizations (Eastern religious systems, Islam, and pan-theistic "heathenism"), European religious traditions (Protestantism and Catholicism), and English sectarian divisions (Nonconformity and the Church). They also included their parties within the Church as vital to these contests. In the late Victorian era, many Anglicans, drawing on the parallels they saw in these other contests and their histories, sought to buttress their claims to preeminence within the Church by reference to imperial and international circumstance as being a demonstration of God's providential movement in history.[99] Thus evangelicals saw in mission the opportunity to demonstrate religious charisma as a mainstay of faith operating prior to church order, unbounded by political subdivision, and generating the liberty of individual salvation. Anglo-Catholics, on the other hand, saw mission as an opportunity to seize ecclesiastical independence from the state, allowing the application of an innovative "apostolic" Church organization beyond the reach of the too often Erastian English episcopal bench, thus creating autonomous societies of organic stability. "National" Anglicans, in contrast, saw the mission field as an opportunity to extend and proliferate an essentially English religious culture of duty and service into a colonial environment disordered by religious heterodoxy and secularism.[100]

Religious aims also were often tied tightly to social ideas and cultural practices, operating none-the-less with their own dynamic power. Many Conser-

---

97. Bowen, *Victorian Church*, 50-51. On the persistence of historical argumentation in the contest over diocesan reform (including the breadth of historical sympathy of Orthodox High Churchmen), see Burns, *Diocesan Revival*, 265-66, 272-73. Note also High Churchmen, such as Hugh James Rose, who argued, in the face of Tractarian contempt for the Reformation, that it had purified and liberated the apostolic church. On the growing resort to the ancient church among a new, pious, educated High Churchmanship led by E. W. Benson, B. F. Westcott, and J. B. Lightfoot, see Hinchliff, *God and History*, chap. 4.

98. Duncan Forbes, *The Liberal Anglican Idea of History* (Cambridge: Cambridge University Press, 1952), 103-5.

99. Hinchliff, *God and History*, 19-20.

100. The Long Judgment of the Privy Council in 1865 definitively removed Anglican colonial churches from control of the Church of England, defining them as equivalent to other voluntary religious bodies, unless established by law by colonial legislatures. Stephenson, *Lambeth Conferences*, 14-15.

vative rural and paternalist professional communities tended toward higher church clerical pastoral ideals that developed out of a high Tory reaction to the "christian" political economy of liberal Tories such as Bishops Blomfield and Sumner in the 1830s and 1840s.[101] High Church missionary policies that were centered around settled church structures and order appealed particularly to these supporters. Yet while Anglicanism was most often associated with the Conservative Party and its base of support within the Church of England, urban middle-class lay evangelical activism could also be associated, through its connection to Nonconformity, with political liberalism. More than merely political positions, these cultural styles allowed, for example, Evangelicals to tie emphasis upon personal freedom and responsibility to free trade arguments in both spiritual and economic realms. Such positions were often opposed by High Church and Anglo-Catholic emphases on hierarchy, order, and communalism, which frequently extended to support for the revived male and female monastic religious communities that grew in numbers from the 1840s onwards.[102] As such each resonated with distinctive responses to the Victorian urban and industrial crises: Evangelicals emphasized evangelistic missions to identifiable groups in need — seamen, street traders, prostitutes — while Anglo-Catholics focused on settled residential mission experiments in depressed communities.[103] And each style resonated with a particular missionary vision that engaged empire in distinctive ways.

As the distinctions between High Church and Evangelical missions sharpened through the 1850s, one of the emerging critical lines of debate came to revolve around gender, home, and male authority, as women inspired by the Oxford Movement (with the support of Tractarian leaders) pursued the reestablishment of Anglican sisterhoods. Despite the denunciations of "Romanism" that sisterhoods inspired in evangelicals, as well as continuing lurid fascination with imagined sexual depravities behind the cloister, by the 1860s High Church reformers strengthened support for revived Anglican orders, arguing they were clearly allowed for under Church formularies. Although sisterhoods (communities of women united in common labor) potentially provided a model for female missionary work in High Church missions, they proved to be particularly contentious. Their association with Catholicism ensured that Protestant con-

101. Kitson Clark, *Churchmen*, 296-99; Peter Mandler, "Tories and Paupers: Christian Political Economy and the Making of the New Poor Law," *The Historical Journal* 33, no. 1 (Mar. 1990): 98-103.

102. On Anglican religious orders, see Michael Hill, *The Religious Order: A Study of Virtuoso Religion and Its Legitimation in the Nineteenth-Century Church of England* (London: Heinemann, 1973), chaps. 2 and 3.

103. David Newsome, *The Victorian World Picture: Perceptions and Introspections in an Age of Change* (London: Fontana, 1997), 219.

troversialists would see in them a dangerous "papist" priestcraft that threatened legitimate paternal authority. Thus debates over missionary methods continued to be suffused with deeply gendered languages of home and femininity. The politics of Church party, with all their imaginative power, particularly structured religious action within missions and influenced the paths of development available to men and women alike.[104]

For all Churchmen, the prosecution of missions was part and parcel of a larger set of arguments about authority, episcopal and paternal, its relation to orthodoxy and church order, and the way that directing church growth could define the nature of Anglicanism both as a system of belief and of social ordering.[105] Tied directly into debates over the significance of the English Reformation, Anglican interest groups that clustered around missionary societies developed variously expansive senses of Englishness that, in connection with developments in settlement colonies and "tropical" spheres of influence, could serve as transimperial and transnational visions of Christian community.[106] There was, however, considerable variety within the movement because of the different ways Englishness was constructed, advanced, and contested. The comprehensive nature of the Church meant that Anglicanism served a variety of religious identities that developed a strong missionary impulse. Late in the century, the more extreme wings of Evangelical and Anglo-Catholic communities became very concerned with finding indigenous cultural forms through which Christian theology could be effectively transmitted, while more centrist High Churchmen and even many moderate Evangelicals were less interested in conversion and cultural adaptation than in transplanting the Church and its forms — often constructed as "English" or "Anglo-Saxon" — in foreign lands.[107] Controversy and contrasting Churchmanship thus underpinned new developments in mission practice and new ways of conceptualizing English influence overseas.

In all of these debates Englishness remained a critical touchstone, and High

---

104. For a more detailed discussion of these dynamics, see Chapter 4.

105. This was particularly evident to the Broad Church bishop of London A. C. Tait when in 1861 he warned of the dangers to breadth and toleration in the Church if colonial churches were allowed to follow independent bishops. Rowell, *Vision Glorious*, 164.

106. See Benedict Anderson, *Imagined Communities: Reflections on the Origin and Spread of Nationalism* (London: Verso, 1983) for a foundational argument about the dimensions of imagination that produce communities.

107. On the Oxford historical school of Stubbs, Freeman, and Green and the rise of racial theory and Anglo-Saxonism, see Anthony Brundage and Richard A. Cosgrove, *The Great Tradition: Constitutional History and National Identity in Britain and the United States, 1870-1960* (Stanford: Stanford University Press, 2007), 41-55.

and Low Church Anglican politics at the local, national, and imperial levels was often closely related to debates over the Church's relationship to Dissent and to Roman Catholicism. Too close an association to either was constructed as un-English: association with Dissent was imagined to be supportive of socially destabilizing radicalism, which was linked backwards to the seventeenth- and eighteenth-century English and French revolutions; association with Catholicism was seen as endorsing aristocratic continental tyranny and corruption, with the papacy imagined at its heart. Religious, political, and social order in nation, empire, and world was assumed to be at stake in the battles between High Churchmen and Evangelicals to define the basic dogma and style of the Church, while bishops and moderates worked to prevent schism by deploying overarching conceptions of Church unity resting in common cultures of church, race, society, and home. This portentous sense of importance contributed to the emergence of an extraordinarily diverse and powerful missionary upsurge late in the century.

Within this context, the CMS emerged as the most successful of the Protestant missionary societies worldwide, collecting by 1860 nearly £150,000 a year (about a quarter of the British total) and sending out 423 missionaries over sixty years. Spurred on by crisis and competition inside and outside the Church, the SPG also began a rapid transformation, despite its reputation for dry, formulaic, dutiful support of Church extension, and by 1860 it was swiftly approaching an income equal to its chief rival, the CMS. Humanitarian activism, political reform, interdenominational rivalry, internal party strife, and contested visions of Christian community acted as sharp spurs to growth.

Rome, Revival, and Later Victorian Missionary Identity

The basic opposition of High Church and Evangelical missions set by the developments of the 1840s persisted into the 1870s, but at a new level of animosity created by evangelical attempts to challenge the "strange and extravagant forms" of extreme High Church worship — conducted by advanced Ritualist priests, encouraged by Tractarian innovations — by intimidation and legal proceedings.[108] Two significant broader developments lay behind these changes: the

---

108. Bentley, *Ritualism*, 20, 37-40, and passim. Theologically based Tractarianism began to shade into a connected, parallel movement known as Ritualism, focused on enhanced ceremonialism, with the founding at Cambridge in 1838 by John Mason Neale of the Camden Society (known from 1845 as the Ecclesiological Society), with its influence on reviving medieval religious ceremonial and Gothic architecture. The controversy over Ritualistic worship at St. Saviour's, Leeds in 1846, which implicated E. B. Pusey, but failed to draw him into vigorous support, publicly

emergence by the 1860s of an Anglo-Catholic movement that was increasingly Ritualist in commitment; and the spread of a highly emotional American-style evangelical revivalism. Both of these developments existed in a complex relationship of antagonism and competition. In 1859 advanced Ritualists founded the English Church Union (ECU) "to defend and maintain unimpaired the doctrine, discipline, and ritual of the Church of England against Erastianism, Rationalism, and Puritanism."[109] In doing so they anchored a core Anglo-Catholic identity that crystalized by the 1870s into defense of six points of contested ritual practice, but also included distinctive attitudes inherited from Tractarianism: open antagonism to the Protestant Reformation and a sympathetic orientation to Roman Catholicism as a larger fellow catholic faith.[110] Opposing these developments, in 1865 activist Evangelicals founded the Church Association, dedicated to obstructing "Romish" ritual innovations by publicity and by legal prosecutions.[111] Missionary administrators quickly perceived the extremism of both, and the culture wars that they animated, as a threat to their societies.

In the missionary world in the 1860s the centripetal, sectarian tendencies among the extremists at either end of the Anglican spectrum expanded alongside growing support for two newly created societies: the Anglo-Catholic-leaning UMCA and the China Inland Mission (CIM), which was an avowedly revivalistic "faith" society. While the influence of "high" and "low" pietism on missionary strategies and growth will form the focus of the following chapter, it is important to understand the context of party among Anglicans in the 1870s, which swirled around legal and legislative action against ritual innovation. Anglo-Catholics and Evangelicals both sought to remake the Anglican Communion by insisting on contrasting formulations of piety, while energized young High Churchmen supported many (but not all) Anglo-Catholic innovations towards enhanced sacramentalism, sacerdotalism, and historically validated au-

---

launched Ritualism and began the division of the movement into loose groupings of old Tractarians and Anglo-Catholic ritual innovators. By the 1860s well-known Ritualist priests, notably A. H. Maconochie of St. Alban's, Holborn, had crystallized a new generation of support for the Anglo-Catholic movement, as enthusiasts vigorously defended him against prosecution by evangelicals, and on principle even older Tractarians like Pusey stood to his defense. Faught, *Oxford Movement*, 44-46, 70-71, 117-19.

109. Stock, *History of the CMS*, 2:348. Originally the Church of England Protection Society, the ECU adopted the new name in 1860.

110. The six points were: (1) the eastward position of worship; (2) the priestly use of vestments; (3) the use of lights (candles); (4) the mixture of wine and water in the communion chalice; (5) the use of unleavened bread for the communion wafer; (6) the use of incense. G. Bayfield Roberts, *The History of the English Church Union, 1859-1894* (London: Church Printing, 1895), 173.

111. By 1876 the ECU had nearly 14,000 members; the Church Association 7,000 by 1869. Machin, *Politics and Churches, 1869-1921*, 4-5.

thority. Thus sectarian passions grew further in the 1870s as conflicts over ritual exploded, causing many members of the Evangelical party to believe dangerous "Romanist" tendencies were pushing them to the margins of the Church. At the same time, many High Churchmen struggled to synthesize moderate ritual innovation with a continuing hostility to Catholicism and an appreciation for Reformation principles. In this environment, demanding constituencies shaped the CMS and the SPG: the societies operated to create a party identity that would motivate support, but at the same time the majority of patrons demanded loyalty to the Church of England, which was at the same time being challenged as illegitimate by Nonconformists and Roman Catholics alike. These competing forces required the missionary societies to cultivate identities that were sectarian but not schismatic. This resulted in moderate party programs designed to balance delicately party identity against denominational loyalty. To a very substantial degree, developments in the universities in the 1870s dovetailed with the emergence of workable missionary programs. Of considerable importance was, for example, the growth of new, "gentlemanly" missionary programs organized around celibate missionary brotherhoods, drawing on the diffuse public school and university Anglican culture associated with B. F. Westcott, Thomas Valpy French, and the younger Edward Bickersteth at Cambridge University, as well as on the developing strains of Anglo-Catholicism associated with Cuddesdon College and Oxford University.[112]

The Problems of Anglican Breadth

The claim of the Church of England to be a comprehensive national church required toleration of the broad range of theological positions that a minimum requirement of adherence to the Thirty-nine Articles and the Prayer Book allowed. This was the ambiguous position reinforced by law with the contentious Gorham Decision in 1850 when High Church Bishop Henry Phillpotts of Exeter refused to confirm Evangelical George Gorham's appointment as a priest in his diocese (over Gorham's refusal on evangelical principles to admit the unconditional regenerative power of sacramental baptism). The bishop's refusal, however, was overturned by the Judicial Committee of the Privy Council on the grounds that Gorham's interpretation could be consistent with accepted doctrine.[113] The decision, opposed by many High Churchmen as both intolerably

---

112. Developments surrounding High Church brotherhoods will be explored in greater detail in Chapters 3 and 8.

113. Chadwick, *Victorian Church: Part One: 1829-1859*, 250-71.

Erastian and anti-sacramental, confirmed Evangelical insistence that Anglicanism be as wide as the nation. Moderates perceived the trickle of High Church conversions to Rome that followed the decision as more than compensated for by the maintenance of Evangelical loyalty. Given the challenge of new "papal aggression" that was represented by the reestablishment of a Catholic hierarchy in England in October of 1850, moderate High Churchmen and bishops, tarred with the "popery" of Tractarianism by their "Puritan" antagonists, found reason to grudgingly accept that continued establishmentarian cooperation between Church and state was at least valuable in preventing the secession of a "free" evangelical Church of England. Meanwhile Evangelicals cried that a dangerous trend to "Romanism," evidenced in elaborate church services and growing emphasis on the sacraments, was undermining essential Reformation principles. The anti-Catholic scares of the 1850s hardened these positions and left the Church of England divided between the simple enthusiasm for the gospel of the Evangelicals and the sacramental Ritualism of the emerging new generation of Anglo-Catholics, with a large body of less committed traditionalist clergy, stretching either low or high, content to occupy a middle ground.

The mid-Victorian years saw a dynamic process by which the Oxford Movement (Tractarianism) evolved into the moderate Ritualism of the older E. B. Pusey but also was more aggressively developed into increasingly elaborate Anglo-Catholic worship by younger enthusiasts, with support from a fringe of more adventurous members of the "Tractarian generation." The Tractarians and later Anglo-Catholics overlapped and shared much doctrinally, but the innovative edge of the movement encompassed the intransigent, law-defying Ritualist priests, who raised the ire of evangelicals through the 1860s and 1870s, adopting various forms of "advanced Anglicanism."[114] As Tractarianism evolved, much old-fashioned High Church commitment to authority and tradition shifted with it to support diocesan reform and the enhanced ceremonialism of moderate Ritualism. And as High Churchism was divided between aggressive Anglo-Catholic and moderate Church principles (that nevertheless shared much common ground), Evangelicalism was similarly divided between a growing revivalistic emotionalism, often associated with dramatic premillenarian belief, and a doctrinal school of support for traditional evangelical beliefs and the moral reform implicit in the work of the early Clapham Sect, continued in the mid-century career of leading public Evangelical, Anthony Ashley Cooper, Seventh Earl of Shaftesbury. The constituencies of missionary organizations reflected these divisions, forcing the societies to attempt to comprehend the

114. On the personnel and geography of Victorian Ritualism, see Nigel Yates, *Anglican Ritualism in Victorian Britain, 1830-1910* (Oxford: Oxford University Press, 1999), chap. 3.

influence of extreme elements in their parties. Whereas the CMS stood openly upon Evangelical principles and opposition to ritual innovation in the Church, the SPG sought to balance the support of the less enthusiastic "high and dry" middle ground and an emerging Anglo-Catholic party devoted to reclaiming the order and ritual of the pre-Reformation Church.

Missions, Parties, Identities

The contest of church party thus remained important in the late Victorian era, but it also grew in complexity. Religious competition and the problems of adaptation to it became particularly acute during the 1870s. In this decade the continuation of aggressive Evangelical legal assaults on Ritualism combined with the new challenges presented by the "modernism" of an emerging Broad Church party to produce serious disturbances in Anglicanism. At the first Lambeth Conference, in 1867, the range of issues proposed for discussion and the opposition to the conference from different quarters indicated these divisions. The bishops of various persuasions attempted to get hearing for their particular fears and complaints: from demands for a discussion of Ritualism in the colonies as an insidious force (supported by Evangelicals) to the desire that Bishop Colenso of Natal be condemned for the heresies of his modernist biblical criticism (supported by moderate High Churchmen and Evangelicals alike). The Declaration issued by the bishops on the goal of intercommunion between the various worldwide Anglican Churches and the debates it generated suggest the core historical lines that many imagined to be critical to the communion. E. B. Pusey, aging Tractarian leader and inspiration to many Anglo-Catholics, deplored the Declaration for its positive mention of the English Reformation, and moderate High Churchmen insisted upon reference to the ancient church's first four general councils, while Evangelical bishops (many of whom declined even to attend what they saw as a possibly illegal assembly that presaged similarly illegal synods advanced by High Churchmen) expressed alarm at its inadequate attention to Scripture and to the Thirty-nine Articles.[115]

These divisions had been brewing through the 1850s, as High Churchmen like Bishop Wilberforce of Oxford sought to pass Parliamentary bills authorizing colonial synods and missionary bishoprics; they were successfully opposed, however, by evangelicals, led by Lords Shaftesbury and Kinnaird, who feared Tractarian excesses would come to dominate the overseas

---

115. Stephenson, *Lambeth Conferences*, 33-34, 37-38. In the end the conference did support synodical government as the favored approach to developing the colonial churches.

Bishops at the first international Lambeth Conference, 1867, assembled to consider grounds for intercommunion between the emerging worldwide Anglican churches.
From USPG Archives, Photograph 5363, Bodleian Library of Commonwealth
and African History, Rhodes House, Oxford. Courtesy of the
United Society for the Propagation of the Gospel.

churches.[116] Still, while evangelicalism had been the rising cultural force of the early nineteenth century, by the 1860s it was often assailed from within the Church — by Anglo-Catholic and Broad Church antagonists — and from without — by liberal culture and modernist ideals, particularly within Britain's universities. The transformation of Anglicanism into a distinct English denomination and the evolution of Evangelicalism into a distinct minority subculture within Anglicanism became increasingly evident. In the 1860s Lord Palmerston — on the advice of Lord Shaftesbury, England's most significant Evangelical humanitarian — had elevated Evangelicals to the episcopal bench in unprecedented numbers. But this favor subsided by the 1870s, and the Evangelical party in the Church of England passed out of the phase of its greatest public power.[117]

116. Jacob, *Anglican Church Worldwide*, 132-35.
117. Moderate High Church bishops made up the great bulk of episcopal appointments from 1865 to 1900, when only six thorough Evangelicals became bishops; instead, moderate High Churchmen, the heirs of moderate Tractarians, filled the episcopal bench. Bebbington, *Evangelicalism*, 146.

Central to the broadest circles of late Victorian Evangelical identity were cooperative institutions such as the Church Pastoral Aid Society and the CMS, which unlike the Church Association — formed to prosecute advanced Ritualists — engaged in constructive projects that could form the basis of loyal Churchmanship. The CMS itself grew more completely identified with the fortunes of the Evangelical subculture to the degree that financial shortfalls at the Society meant, in the words of the Evangelical bishop of Rochester, Anthony Wilson Thorold, that "Evangelical Religion is on its trial." Money troubles, Thorold argued, gave their enemies the opportunity to claim publicly that Evangelical spiritual principles were losing their power.[118] Maintaining finances meant cultivating the support of the most eager patrons, who needed reassurance from CMS secretaries "that the principles of this Society are thoroughly Protestant & Evangelical."[119] "The whole constitution of our Society," asserted CMS Secretary Christopher Fenn, "is to give power to those who subscribe to its funds. The voluntary support of those who help us . . . is what we must humanly speaking depend upon. The money test is a rough one, & is often delusive as regards individuals; but in the long run when spread over numbers it is fairly correct."[120] In adherence to the voluntary principle, the CMS constructed a position from which to defend its Evangelical identity and the validity of an independent but loyal evangelical Anglicanism.

In contrast to the CMS, the SPG laid emphasis on ecclesiastical authority and the unified corporate action of the Anglican Church. The secretary and committee of the SPG claimed a broad mandate to represent the entire Church of England, and more extreme High Churchmen maintained that the SPG was its only legitimate foreign missionary society. Rather than taking direction from largely lay voluntary boards, SPG identity rested in maintaining the continuity of the historic episcopal leadership of the Church. Whereas the CMS proclaimed the unity of the Protestant faithful in spreading the Word, SPG organizers instead emphasized the unique authority of the Church and its "definitely Anglican stance."[121] Nonconformists were particularly sensitive to the aggressive pursuit of these claims, so that when Archbishop Tait of Canterbury attempted to work out jurisdictional problems between SPG and LMS missionaries, the LMS secretary sarcastically informed him that meetings would be useless because of the SPG's uncompromising commitment to "go &

118. *Church Missionary Intelligencer,* n.s., 5 (Jan. 1880): 1.
119. Henry Wright to T. B. L. Browne, 27 Nov. 1872, CMS Archives, G/AC 1/18. Wright succeeded the long-serving Henry Venn as Honorary Clerical Secretary in 1872.
120. Fenn to Mr. Stead, 2 Apr. 1875, CMS Archives, G/AC 1/19.
121. Ely Diocesan Report, 5 July 1871, in Minutes of the Home Organisation Committee, USPG Archives, X 63.

establish missions where they will, because 'their Church is the divine body on which the Holy Ghost descended and to whom the ends of the Earth shall be given.'"[122] This approach, while confirming the SPG in its Church principles to High Churchmen, raised indignation in evangelical circles both inside and outside the Church.

Exclusivity and the dignity of position — the decorum and distinction that traditional authority implied — produced a temperament at the SPG in which rejection of the cultural style of "ranting dissenters" became a mark of identity. The SPG central office projected a serene assurance of position, but at the cost of coldness and formality, its local committees too often becoming "mere business machinery and very inefficient [ones] even for mere money getting purposes."[123] With a careful, respectable "high and dry" stance, the SPG often found itself taking "seconds" in the parish church, with the result that SPG advances vis-à-vis the CMS in the 1840s began to reverse in the 1870s, as the Society stood off from enthusiasm, evangelical and Anglo-Catholic alike.[124] On the other hand, the CMS tapped a warmth and enthusiasm that was characteristic of evangelicals — and as the century wore on, characteristic of energetic suburban congregations. Even enemies had to concede that Evangelical diligence, devotion, and labor often redeemed their unseemly emotional conduct. But the difference in outlook and principles between the two Anglican societies meant that each suffered persistent sniping criticism within the Church.

Sectarian differences in English Anglican missions rested on the contested issue of how one established loyalty as a Churchman, which had important ramifications for how the societies organized support. Charges of schism made against the CMS during the difficult era of Church reform in the 1830s had led the Society to acknowledge the authority of English bishops in the mission field, preventing serious quarrels through the mid-1870s.[125] Earlier compromise, however, began to break down in the heat of Ritualist controversies, fuelling

122. SPG Secretary W. T. Bullock, Tait was informed, officially embraced this position. Joseph Mullens to A. C. Tait, 25 Feb. 1873. LMS Secretaries were fearful that the same friction that Anglo-Catholic bishop T. N. Staley had produced between the Hawaiian missions would be replicated in Madagascar. Mullens to Bullock, 8 Feb. 1870, Council for World Mission Archives (London Missionary Society), Home: Outgoing Letters (Home Office), Box 1, School of Oriental and African Studies, London (hereafter cited as CWM Archives [LMS]).

123. Walter Blunt, to A. C. Tait, 14 Feb. 1879, Archibald Campbell Tait Papers, vol. 245, fols. 141-42, Lambeth Palace Library, London (hereafter cited as Tait Papers).

124. Statement by J. C. Betham, Ely Diocesan Report, 5 July 1871, in Minutes of the Home Organisation Committee, USPG Archives, X 63. While in 1851 SPG home income had been £89,245, or 14 percent behind CMS home income of £103,697, by 1871 SPG income of £97,604 had dropped to 37 percent behind the CMS's £156,065.

125. Edgar Jacob to [Christopher W.] Wordsworth, 30 Aug. 1876, USPG Archives, H 96.

anew the differences between the parties, as when in 1876 the aggressive, inexperienced Anglo-Catholic "Boy Bishop" R. S. Copleston of Colombo withdrew preaching licenses from CMS missionaries in Ceylon. The missionaries opposed the bishop's Ritualistic practices and the bishop insisted upon the cessation of cooperation with Nonconformists as well as the complete control of bishop over clergy within his diocese, making for an unambiguous struggle over Anglo-Catholic and Evangelical understandings of episcopal power.[126] The evangelical *Record* expressed alarm that Copleston, along with Bishop L. G. Mylne of Bombay, both appointed by High Church Lords Carnarvon and Salisbury, were part of a plot to advance Anglo-Catholicism in the colonies just as it was being thwarted in England.[127] This, they felt, must be opposed because Evangelicals saw Ritualism as a far more insidious form of disloyalty to the Church of England than their own sympathy with Nonconformists. Ritualism, after all, was thought fundamentally un-English because it brought Anglicanism within the sway of tyrannous Romanism.[128] Edgar Jacob, commissary to the bishop of Calcutta, fearing a general evangelical backlash against advanced Anglo-Catholicism in the mission field, commented to Christopher Wordsworth, the orthodox High Church bishop of Lincoln, that the whole Colombo affair, which had led to "sermons advertised for CMS in schismatic chapels, will do the Society [SPG] a world of harm."[129] In the battle to seize the high ground of "loyalty," Roman Catholicism typically became the anti-English doppelganger, as so many Protestants imagined it devoted to immorality and tyranny.[130] Party controversialists commonly denounced their opponents as being in thrall to "popery." Both societies weathered such charges, the SPG for association with Ritualists, the CMS because its efficient central control of speakers and local agents allowed critics to compare the authority of the Pope to that of the CMS's London secretaries, and in this detect "the very essence of 'popery.'"[131]

The refusal at the CMS to support an SPG plan — strongly promoted by Bishop Wilberforce, the highest profile supporter of episcopally led High

126. Charles Perry, *A Review of the Controversy Between the Bishop of Colombo and the Missionaries of the Church Missionary Society* (London: Hatchards, 1877); M. E. Gibbs, *The Anglican Church in India, 1600-1970* (New Delhi: ISPCK, 1972), 262-75. Coplestone (1845-1925) was consecrated bishop at the earliest possible age in 1875. The controversy was only resolved with the intervention of a panel of English bishops under Archbishop Tait.

127. Williams, *Self-Governing Church*, 71.

128. On the extent and depth of anti-Catholic feeling in mid-Victorian England, see Norman, *Anti-Catholicism*, 54-62 and passim.

129. Jacob to Wordsworth, 30 Aug. 1876, USPG Archives, H 96.

130. Wellings, *Evangelicals Embattled*, 48-54.

131. Walter Blunt to A. C. Tait, 8 Feb. 1879, Tait Papers, vol. 245, fols. 135-38.

Church missions — for the creation of an Anglican bishopric in Madagascar accentuated the party divide at the beginning of the 1870s.[132] For the CMS, the Madagascar bishopric question boiled down to a choice: it could sanction the plan, place its few missionaries in Madagascar under a High Church bishop, and break an agreement made in the 1830s that gave the Congregationalist LMS exclusive occupation of the capital city; or it could oppose the plan, reassure its supporters of its defense of Evangelical principles, and maintain good relations with evangelical Nonconformity. In a situation where either its Anglican or its Evangelical identity would be compromised, the CMS chose to withdraw its missionaries entirely from Madagascar and, despite its sympathy with the LMS position, refuse to participate publicly in the debate.[133] Despite such strategic moves, the CMS's cozy relations with Nonconformists infuriated High Church supporters of the SPG. On the other hand, the aggressiveness of High Church Anglicans, and their willingness to break agreements that regulated cooperation in the mission field, appalled CMS supporters. Such controversies, which extended to the wrangling over the authority of bishops in China, widened even further the rift that had grown between the two missionary societies in the 1840s.[134] Secretaries in the central offices worked to present at least a veneer of cooperation between the CMS and SPG, but extreme Evangelical and Anglo-Catholic supporters engaged in vituperative combat on the local level and used the societies as platforms from which to launch attacks — a practice that, though publicly deplored, suited the interests of the London secretaries.[135]

Loyalty to the Church implied larger loyalties to be defined through the Church's mission. For High Churchmen loyalty to Church often implied loyalty to England and English people. As William Crompton emphasized in his deputation tours for the SPG, the key focus was urging Christian duty to "our Settlers . . . from England" through the SPG as "the only society which made its chief aim to be the taking care that . . . our own countrymen, our own relatives had the means of Grace." This was pressed directly against the CMS and

132. On Wilberforce as the arch-opponent of CMS Secretary Henry Venn, theorist of voluntary lay-directed missions, see Wilbert Shenk, *Henry Venn — Missionary Statesman* (Maryknoll, NY: Orbis, 1983), 36.

133. For further details on the Madagascar controversy, see Randall Thomas Davidson and William Benham, *Life of Archibald Campbell Tait, Archbishop of Canterbury,* 2nd ed., 2 vols. (London: Macmillan, 1891), 2:341-46. On CMS sympathy with the LMS see Henry Wright to Dr. Sale, 14 Oct. 1872, CMS Archives, G/AC 1/18. Ultimately the Scottish bishops created the bishopric, despite opposition from Lord Shaftesbury and refusal of government endorsement. Jacob, *Anglican Church Worldwide,* 183.

134. Stock, *History of the CMS,* 3:35-36.

135. See, for example, Henry Wright to Sydney Gedge, 30 Apr. 1873, CMS Archives, G/AC 1/18.

its "claptrap about the Heathen" in preference to "our own flesh and blood . . . in one of our colonies."[136] For Evangelicals loyalty to the Church often implied loyalty to the destiny of the English as one of God's chosen peoples, to carry forward a vision of the Church that transcended the nation as a spiritual, moral force, rather than a visible set of institutions. That the CMS proselytized to the "heathen," which evangelicals stressed was the last command of Christ to his followers, meant that advocates such as the celebrated Evangelical preacher H. W. Webb-Peploe could emphasize that the CMS, in contrast to the SPG, was a " 'Missionary' & not a 'Pastoral Aid' Society."[137] This was not an entirely fair comparison, since the SPG also conducted the majority of its missions to the "heathen," but distinctions between the SPG and the CMS on matters of theology, ecclesiology, and range of work tended to divide the societies, as they envisioned differently the national role bound up in the missionary project.[138] The substantial overlap between the two societies meant an ongoing ideological interaction that generated competing visions of missionary work designed to appeal to constituencies that valued different things and imagined Christian community in different ways.

Managing Sectarianism

Owen Chadwick has identified "a strong desire to find and obey lawful authority" as a pervasive and deeply held attitude in the Anglican clergy as a whole.[139] The difficulty, of course, was building consensus over precisely what the basis of this lawful authority was to be: Scripture interpreted by the laity as advocated by Evangelicals, or enacted by the clergy and episcopacy as pressed by High Churchmen of all shades. Because the leaders of the CMS and the SPG retained a basic loyalty to the idea of the Church, both resisted schism (toward Nonconformity or Rome) and rejected the programs of the most extreme elements of their own parties. Although each society relied on sectarian impulses to mobilize support, carrying sectarianism too far risked destroying the overarching Anglican identity and establishment that each party sought to define and control. Society leaders, much like the bishops, found themselves engaged in a delicate balancing act between encouraging the enthusiasm and support

136. Crompton diary, 1 Mar. and 23 Apr. 1890, USPG Archives, X 562/1, fols. 29, 47-50.

137. H. W. Webb-Peploe to "Dear friends," 30 May 1887, CMS Archives, G/AC 4/5/884. Emphasis in original.

138. By the turn of the century the SPG spent approximately two-thirds of its income on foreign missions to unevangelized groups. Dennis, *Centennial Survey*, 22n2.

139. Chadwick, *Victorian Church: Part Two: 1860-1901*, 315.

that sectarianism bred, and retaining the respectability and stability conferred by the Anglican establishment.

The CMS consistently proclaimed its loyalty and Churchmanship and worked to maintain a position of distinct but moderate Evangelical Anglicanism with deep connections to the respect for Church order exhibited by the revered founding fathers of the Clapham Sect. In the four-year controversy that raged in the late 1870s around the withdrawal of the licenses of CMS missionaries to preach in Ceylon by the young, brash, acknowledged Ritualist bishop of Colombo, R. S. Copleston, leading CMS officials — including William Barlow, principal of the CMS College at Islington, Secretary Henry Wright and prominent committee member Canon Edward Hoare of Canterbury — had the unenviable task of maintaining CMS principles at sufficient levels of "purity" to satisfy the majority of supporters while resisting "friends who desired to carry on a more aggressive war against the bishop than was thought, by the more moderate section, to be consistent with loyal churchmanship."[140]

The SPG experienced similar stresses. For example, in the midst of the ongoing emotional battles being fought over Archbishop Tait's ultimately failed attempts to curb Ritualistic liturgical practice by the legal prosecutions that were authorized under the Public Worship Regulation Act of 1874, radicals from the ECU packed the SPG General Committee in 1878 to try to force the Society to accept missionary candidates with extreme Ritualist views. In the process, they used SPG meetings as a public platform to denounce the treatment of Ritualists by the archbishop of York and the bishop of London.[141] The bishops, however, were quick to respond to ensure that the SPG remained a distinctively High Church society, but a moderate rather than an extreme one. George Moberly, bishop of Salisbury, recognized High Church leader and intimate of Keble, commented that the actions of the advanced Anglo-Catholics represented a "carefully organized & determined move on the part of extreme Ritualists to obtain command of the S.P.G."[142] Bishop Magee of Peterborough urged decisive

---

140. Margaret Barlow, ed., *The Life of William Hagger Barlow, D.D., Late Dean of Peterborough* (London: Allen, 1910), 100.

141. The SPG vetted candidates through a Board of Examiners appointed by the archbishops of Canterbury and York and the bishop of London. Outram Marshall, organizing secretary of the ECU, denounced "the unfair conduct of the Bishop of London to the Ritualists" and pushed through a vote (35 to 29) to annul the power of the SPG Committee of Examiners over the selection of missionary candidates, a maneuver possible under the SPG Charter of 1701 that allowed the packing of an often poorly attended London Standing Committee meeting. "The Holy Cross Society and Foreign Missions," *The Standard*, 15 Nov. 1878, press clipping, Tait Papers, vol. 239, fol. 391.

142. Moberly to A. C. Tait, 1 Nov. 1878, Tait Papers, vol. 239, fols. 387-90.

action, arguing that success by extremists at the SPG would be a serious blow for the Church because the episcopate "should have been publicly censured & corrected by the S.P.G. at the bidding of the extreme Ritualists!"[143] True extremism harmed overall support, as the SPG discovered when the news of its alleged takeover by the ECU led to its being refused pulpits, damaging its standing among loyal moderate Churchmen. With pressure from the bishops and assistance from moderate Anglo-Catholics who perceived the dangers of pushing the bishops too far, the SPG expelled extreme Ritualists from the General Committee and aligned itself with the progressive program to regenerate church life, exemplified by R. W. Church, who in 1871 had launched far-reaching reforms as Dean of St. Paul's Cathedral.[144]

Time and again the societies found themselves caught between vocal groups of sectarian supporters and the establishment, represented by the bishops. Just as sectarian battles defined the national life of the Church at large, so battles between moderates and extremists within Church parties multiplied, with the result that both extreme Evangelicals and extreme Anglo-Catholics hoped to capture the missionary movement. This had to be defended against, for while the CMS and the SPG were necessarily organs of party identity and protectors of party principles, they could not become locations for defiance of the episcopacy without risking the destruction of the Church. Thus, while defined by party, the societies became locations for the growth of gradualist moderate evangelicalism and moderate Anglo-Catholicism.

The Impact of Party Extremism

The rise of extreme party strife ultimately proved more damaging to the SPG than to the CMS. This was linked to the rising conflict over state influence and control over the Church. Broad Churchmen and Evangelicals as a body supported church and state connection as a legal protection for breadth of belief and against an imagined Romanist takeover of the Church. High Churchmen, however, were divided, because advanced Anglo-Catholics saw dises-

143. Bishops E. H. Browne of Winchester, C. J. Ellicott of Gloucester, R. Bickersteth of Ripon, and J. Jackson of London, all moderate High or Low Churchmen, concurred. William Magee to A. C. Tait, 25 Nov. 1878, Tait Papers, vol. 239, fols. 400-404.

144. A. C. Tait to Henry Tucker, 23 Nov. 1878, Tait Papers, vol. 239, fols. 394-97. A peaceful recapture of the SPG Committee was engineered by influential committee member Robert Gregory, Canon of St. Paul's from 1868 and close associate of moderate Anglo-Catholic–leaders H. P. Liddon and R. W. Church. On Gregory, Church, and Liddon's Anglo-Catholic–inspired High Church reforms at St. Paul's, see Trevor Beeson, The Deans (London: SCM Press, 2004), 63-72.

tablished churches as being freed to recover the lost catholic heritage of the pre-Reformation Church. Focusing criticisms on the missionary societies gave extreme High Church activists the opportunity to advance the independent authority of English and colonial bishops and their visible churches against state interference, to undermine what they saw as the "congregationalist" voluntarism of the society system, and to strike a blow at evangelical "puritan" excesses. In the struggle that developed around these issues, the SPG was caught in the middle: it was obligated to maintain higher church missions and overseas dioceses from moderate to extreme, while also being attacked by advanced Anglo-Catholics for its very existence as a voluntary society. Ideologically committed to operation through the established diocesan structures of the Church, which were controlled by independent local clergy, the SPG was limited in its ability to emulate successful CMS strategies, which were directed by London-based bureaucracies and required building local voluntary lay organization and increasing local interest by working it up through paid and honorary field agents.[145] Despite relative caution, the SPG still generated outrage among socially conservative Anglicans and extreme Anglo-Catholics due to the extent that it did adopt popular and voluntary methods. With its legitimacy as a Church organ questioned by extremists of the very party that had built up its importance over the 1840s, the SPG turned to the bishops to make an authoritative call to the Church for support and prayer for the efforts of the missionary society system. In 1872 SPG Secretary W. T. Bullock forwarded a plan for a "Day of Intercession for Foreign Missions" in honor of the "martyr bishop of Melanesia," J. C. Patteson, whose murder in the South Seas had created a sensation of feeling among High Churchmen, who knew of his sympathies not only with Keble and Pusey but also with his former metropolitan bishop, Selwyn of New Zealand (bishop of Lichfield from 1868).[146] To be observed throughout the Church of England, the day was designed to emphasize episcopal authority — both through martyrology and the leadership of the bishops — while also advancing the Society. On one designated Sunday (20 December 1872) nationwide Church prayer, led by the bishops, aimed to reverse the "insufficiency of present missionary agency."[147]

However, while extreme Anglo-Catholic aggression against voluntarism hampered the SPG, it aided Evangelicals who used its perceived threat to mobilize grassroots support. Anglo-Catholics and reforming High Churchmen aimed to subordinate voluntary Church societies under the Church order of

145. Reports for Chester, Ely & Oxford Dioceses, 5 July 1871, in Minutes of the Home Organisation Committee, USPG Archives, X 63.

146. William Ewart Gladstone, "Art. VI," review of *Life of John Coleridge Patteson, Missionary Bishop of the Melanesian Islands,* by Charlotte Mary Yonge, *Quarterly Review* 137 (1874): 458-92.

147. W. T. Bullock to A. C. Tait, 6 May 1872, Tait Papers, vol. 182, fols. 138-40.

the diocese and its bishop, claiming that growing indifference to missionary endeavors in the 1860s issued from a "notoriously deep rooted distrust of the manner in which they are worked." Cyrus Packman asserted, "[n]o one likes contributing to institutions which, by their wasteful system of 'travellers' and 'office salaries' first of all take three, four, or even five shillings out of each pound subscribed for 'cost of collection'; and whose affairs are practically managed by a small and, perhaps, narrow-minded clique."[148] At the CMS, suggestions like Packman's appeared as an insidious attack on liberty of conscience and the evangelical independence guaranteed under the historically loose formularies of the Church. Assaults on the CMS as the premier organ of Evangelical identity generated an animated defense and redoubled CMS development of its voluntary networks. William Barlow, a rising leader in the Evangelical connection, defended the society system by emphasizing the long-standing historic divisions of the Church of England, the past success of the societies, and the danger of lukewarm diocesan Boards of Missions to missionary zeal and evangelical principles. "The Society [CMS]," Barlow stated, "has never been anxious to win public favour, otherwise than as it may have deserved it by its steady upholding of Evangelical truth. . . . All we ask for is, to be allowed to go on as we are."[149] On this ground the Evangelicals fought to protect their most successful public institution.

In this atmosphere, the CMS treated the Day of Intercession as a dangerous innovation and, while conceding to observe it, declined to employ any of its associations or personnel to support the initiative.[150] On the principle that they represented independent voluntary societies, the CMS refused to share the public platform with Nonconformist and High Churchman alike, and thus, as in the controversy surrounding the Madagascar bishopric, sought neutral ground to protect itself from accusations by its own extremists of cooperation with papist sympathizers, as well as from High Church criticisms of disloyalty in cooperating with Nonconformists. Even after the success of the 1872 observance, the CMS continued to object, largely because of fears that Church-wide mission programs such as the Day of Intercession deadened missionary enthusiasm with routine and encouraged the growth of dreaded diocesan organization in

148. Cyrus H. L. Packman, *The Establishment of a General Board of Missions: Being a Paper Read Before the Chapter of the Deanery of Liverpool North, September 26, 1871* (Liverpool, 1871).

149. W. H. Barlow, *Diocesan Mission Boards: A Paper Read at the 14th Annual Conference, Cheltenham, June 6, 1871* (n.p., 1871), 8-12. "Church Missionary Society. Proposed Convocation Board of Missions. Memorandum of Committee of C.M.S.," Tait Papers, vol. 272, fols. 222-23.

150. Henry Venn to W. T. Bullock, 14 June 1872, printed in "Proposal for Observing Friday, 20th December 1872, as a Day of Intercession for an Adequate Supply of Missionaries," Tait Papers, vol. 182, fols. 146-47.

the form of Boards of Mission.[151] Success of the Boards, Evangelicals worried, would allow High Church bishops too much influence in the one area of Church life where Evangelicals showed growth and strength. When, with the support of the archbishop of Canterbury, the Day of Intercession continued to be observed, the CMS shifted tack and worked to broaden the observance of the Day by securing the participation of Nonconformists.[152] CMS secretaries aimed to dilute the attempts of High Churchmen to commandeer the missionary movement as well as to legitimate CMS participation in the Day in the broader evangelical world. The CMS, in the face of extremism issuing from the outer reaches of both High and Low Church parties, attempted to pour oil on troubled religious waters while simultaneously maintaining an acceptably evangelical identity.

The threat to voluntarism presented by High Church exclusivism continued through the 1870s and strongly influenced foreign missions. The CMS resisted persistent attempts to draw it into unified Anglican missionary organizations that replaced control by the societies with direction by bishops or diocesan organizations. When Bishop Moberly of Salisbury, a moderate High Churchman and intimate of Keble, invited participation in a proposed united Church Diocesan Missionary Festival, CMS Secretary Henry Wright refused to cooperate with a movement that "foresees the ultimate extinction of Societies."[153] At stake, he believed, was the independence of "voluntary individual action, for which united Church action, however attractive in appearance, would in the long run be a poor exchange . . . [and] would be simply a step toward the extinction of the C.M.S. . . . with a loss to the Church of her choicest members."[154] In the end, however, CMS secretaries found it hard to resist what rapidly became a widespread Anglican observance. For Evangelicals, despite the dangers, there were also clear advantages and compelling theological reasons for closer associations within the Church. This left the CMS balanced delicately between the evangelicalism that fired Protestant missions and loyalty to the Anglican Church that most CMS followers both felt and feared in varying degrees.

While Evangelicals faced challenges from High Church diocesan reformers and champions of a "high" doctrine of ecclesiastical authority, these develop-

151. Minutes of the General Committee, special committee meeting, 18 Feb. 1873, CMS Archives, G/C 1, vol. 40; Henry Wright to W. T. Bullock, 19 Feb 1873, CMS Archives, G/AC 1/18.

152. Henry Wright to Lord Chichester [Henry Pelham], 21 July 1873, and Wright to A. C. Tait, 3 July 1873, CMS Archives, G/AC 1/18.

153. Wright to N. Catheast, 5 June 1874; Wright to [Anthony Ashley Cooper], Earl of Shaftesbury, 8 Apr. 1874; Wright to George Moberly, bishop of Salisbury, 9 July 1874, CMS Archives, G/AC 1/19.

154. Henry Wright to W. Doyle, 22 Oct. 1873, CMS Archives, G/AC 1/18.

ments also had importance for the SPG. Leaders at the SPG found themselves assailed not only by Evangelicals for perceived snobbish exclusivity but also by Anglo-Catholics for their imperfect acquiescence to episcopal authority, especially when the SPG London office found itself in conflict with overseas bishops holding advanced Anglo-Catholic views. Unable to appeal to the emotional pietism within the High Church connection — Anglo-Catholicism — the SPG aimed to appeal to regional and imperial interests through the cultivation of "special mission funds" earmarked for specific missions overseas. Over the course of the 1870s this strategy raised the income of the SPG's Special Funds over 300 percent (from £12,954 to £42,569). However, this was cash that the Society did not control; rather, the SPG acted as financial agent to independent missions or dioceses — Central Africa, Cape Town, Melanesia — that were sometimes controlled by aggressive Anglo-Catholic bishops who, battling to expand their authority and control, tended to argue that the SPG should merely distribute funds and leave all strategy and decision making to the bishop on the spot.[155]

Enthusiasm for High Church missions rose by taking advantage of growing interest over the 1870s in Africa, but by the early 1880s a serious problem developed when SPG secretaries clashed with Anglo-Catholic bishops, particularly Bishop Steere presiding over the UMCA, over control of Special Fund money. When the SPG, under the direction of a new secretary, Henry W. Tucker, moved in 1881 to receive a new supplementary Charter from the Queen, it was a change primarily designed to prevent further embarrassments like the 1878 seizure of the Society by extremist Ritualists, as well as raise the centralized efficiency of society operations, seen by many as too beholden to often indifferent parish clergy and sadly inadequate in comparison to the impressive organizational sophistication of the CMS.[156] But the resulting controversies that arose over tighter central control by the SPG, between independent-minded overseas bishops and a society pursuing bureaucratic reorganization inspired by the diocesan reform movement, caused an ongoing set of troubles, specific to the SPG, that halted High Church missionary expansion in its tracks.

While partisanship seemed to pull Evangelicals closer together, High Church divisions seemed instead to push the SPG into damaging conflict, as those "orthodox" Churchmen who supported a continued state establishment,

155. Report of the SPG, 1880, 120.

156. Election of the executive Standing Committee was to be by ballot of all members rather than by voice vote at the Annual Meeting, and the archbishop of Canterbury was made the president of the Society, the bishops vice-presidents, ex officio. "Petition of SPG to Queen in Council" and Henry Tucker to E. Harrison, Privy Council Office, 22 July 1881, Tait Papers, vol. 276, fols. 223-28, 236.

with the special national and imperial rights and responsibilities it entailed, squared off against Anglo-Catholics who pressed toward episcopal and clerical independence. This reality militated against the creation of a unified High Church missionary project. For most Anglicans operated on the assumption that continued support in the broader religious culture depended on defending the established legitimacy of the Church of England in the face of both Nonconformist calls for disestablishment and Catholic calls for reunion.[157] Such pressures tended the Church of England toward internal reforms encouraging more efficient self-government and lay control, more effective Church organization, and better educational provision. But extreme Anglo-Catholics who endorsed both disestablishment and Catholic reunion remained an indigestible element on the High Church side. While moderates might endorse some enhancements of ritual and a stronger organizational hierarchy in diocese and church, their vision fell far short of the full program endorsed by advanced Ritualists.[158]

Just as moderates began to assert themselves at the SPG in the 1870s, so a new group began to define itself at the CMS. Rather than insisting on principled separation from the "pre-Reformation" practices of High Churchmen, the so-called "neo-Evangelicals" stressed participation in Church Congresses and Convocation in order to make claim upon influencing the formal structures of the corporate Church.[159] This strategy aimed to counter both High Church claims that Evangelicalism was rapidly dying and the tendency of older "Puritan" Evangelicals to separatism. The neo-Evangelical position was strongly supported by CMS Secretary Henry Venn and influential members such as Bishop J. C. Ryle of Liverpool and Canon Edward Hoare of the Claphamite Evangelical banking family.[160] The earlier decision of the CMS under Henry Venn in the 1840s to cultivate episcopal cooperation continued in the 1870s, if such cooperation would not, as CMS secretaries carefully judged the matter, place it in a false position with its Evangelical supporters.[161] Thus by 1880 the CMS led a retreat of "neo-Evangelicals" from the aggressions pressed by the

157. By the 1870s Anglicans, with the exception of advanced Anglo-Catholics, uniformly argued that great damage to national morality and religiosity would be caused by disestablishment. Machin, *Politics and Churches, 1869-1921*, 2-4.

158. On Anglo-Catholic disestablishmentarianism versus mainstream Anglican support of establishment (as a proof against schism in the Church), see Bowen, *Victorian Church*, 125-36.

159. The term "neo-Evangelical" was coined in the 1870s by the extreme Protestant publication *The Rock* to denounce "traitors to the Evangelical cause" who were too willing to cooperate with High Churchmen and countenance ritual innovations. Stock, *History of the CMS*, 3:8-10.

160. Moule, *Evangelical School*, 68-71. The Church of England restored Convocation in 1854 and held its first Congress in 1861. Henry Venn was appointed as the only Evangelical to the Ritual Commission in 1867.

161. See, for example, Henry Wright to A. C. Tait, 4 Jan. 1873, CMS Archives, G/AC 1/18.

Church Association, refusing to support openly prosecution of Ritualists who defied the law through innovative use of Catholic elements in Anglican worship. This strategy drew savage criticism from the most extreme evangelicals, who attacked the CMS position of neutrality on continuing Ritualist prosecutions, its cooperation with the High Church bishops of Japan and Ceylon, and its toleration of the revived Jerusalem bishopric under High Churchman G. F. P. Blyth.[162]

The controversial appointment of moderate Broad Churchman A. C. Tait, Arnoldian public school, university, and Church reformer, as archbishop of Canterbury (1868-82), reinforced the Evangelical reassertion of familiar methods: voluntarism and public activism. With Tait's penchant for open-air preaching experiments and his support for novel methods for inner-city missions, developed during his term as bishop of London (from 1856), Evangelicals seemed to have felt that Tait, even if very far from a keen evangelist himself, implicitly supported Evangelical methods.[163] In addition, moderate Evangelicals felt increasing uneasiness that the rising heat of Church controversy, including aggressive legal proceedings against Ritualists, was pushing the party into extremism, bitterness, and sheer spite, thus harming the Evangelical position within the Church, not least because it alienated many young university-educated Anglicans.[164] Redoubling efforts to prove their continued strength and vitality, Evangelicals combined home challenges with exciting new foreign projects in Japan, East Africa, Persia, and Palestine to reinvigorate enthusiasm and activity in the 1870s.[165]

Under the impact of renewed party conflict, the missionary effort rapidly became the chief location of Evangelical influence and activity within the Church, as the CMS provided the most important leadership and the primary graphic example of vitality in the party. While High Church Anglicans consciously separated themselves from evangelical missionary efforts, and while this stance helps to explain the much greater influence of the CMS in the broader world of foreign missions, High Church missions, linked in dynamic contest with evangelicalism, also brought a fuller range of the established Church's resources to bear on Anglican Church extension overseas into the colonies, empire, and beyond. SPG missions accounted for about 10 percent of missionary revenues compared to 25 percent for the CMS, yet High Church missions altogether carried greater weight than income figures for the two societies can convey, partly because the SPG was in contention with several smaller Anglo-Catholic

162. Stock, *History of the CMS*, 3:279-80, 336-45, 489-90.
163. Davidson and Benham, *Tait*, 1:253-64, 502-4.
164. Barlow, *Barlow*, 115.
165. Davidson and Benham, *Tait*, 2:337; Stock, *History of the CMS*, 3:36-37.

societies and bishops' funds, while CMS efforts were much more consolidated. Moreover, High Church invigoration itself catalyzed energetic reactions from evangelicals of all persuasions.[166] Nevertheless, because it was the largest and wealthiest missionary society and was also linked into the missionary efforts of evangelical Nonconformity, many saw the CMS as the flagship of the entire missionary movement. By drawing on the structure of strong organization in the Church of England and channeling "respectable" female charitable activism into Church missions, the CMS, in dynamic competition with High Church missions, led an organizational revolution that fuelled unparalleled missionary expansion in the 1880s and 1890s, known among contemporaries as the "new age" of transformative growth.

Conclusion

In 1873 the Anglican antiquarian and Honorary Canon of Canterbury W. A. Scott Robertson published figures designed to demonstrate the magnitude and religious distribution of British support for foreign missions. Robertson indicated that the movement — in the form of sixty-five separate societies — had received £1,032,176 from the British public in 1872. Of this, nineteen Anglican societies received the lion's share when compared to fourteen Nonconformist societies. The CMS, with an annual income of over £200,000, was the largest, fastest growing, and most impressive of these societies. Denominational pride led Robertson to emphasize that when CMS income was added to that of the SPG, the two major missionary societies of the Church of England accounted for £350,117, compared to the £237,627 raised by the three major societies representing Nonconformity — the Wesleyan Methodist Missionary Society (WMMS), the London Missionary Society (LMS), and the Baptist Missionary Society (BMS).[167]

The separation of the missionary effort into competitive organizations whose distinguishing features and claims to support were primarily denominational or party-oriented is the most obvious fact that emerges from Robertson's tabulations. His primary intention was to contrast the missionary zeal of Protestants to that of Catholics, with a clear secondary purpose of demon-

166. W. A. Scott Robertson, *British Contributions to Foreign Missions. Analysis and Summary of the Receipts of Sixty-Five Societies for the Year 1872* (London: Church Printing, n.d., ca. 1873), 1.

167. Robertson, *British Contributions to Foreign Missions,* 1-2. For partisan reasons Robertson focused on domestic contributions; Nonconformist societies typically received 20 to 30 percent of their income from overseas. The Anglican societies did not, because overseas Anglican funds were funneled into overseas diocesan funds or colonial missionary societies. See Appendix I, Figure 2.

strating that the importance of Anglicans to the cause was greater than that of their Nonconformist counterparts. In arranging income figures in this way, however, Robertson, exhibiting his higher church sympathies, purposely over-looked the most important affinity in the English missionary movement in the 1870s: evangelicalism. While the evangelical missionary societies did compete for support, their competition was generous in tone and mutually supportive, based on shared commitment to broad evangelical principles. The SPG, how-ever, vigorously rejected evangelicalism. Some extreme evangelicals considered this divide within the Church of England over foreign missions — between the Evangelical CMS and the High Church SPG — to be nearly as great as that between Protestantism and Rome. If the established Church represented the greatest repository of support for foreign missions in the Victorian age, it was in many respects a house divided against itself. The breach corresponded to divisions within the home Church with respect to doctrine, history, religious style, and attitude to episcopacy. Anglican missionary societies reflected the sectarian problems of the Church of England, but these divisions were in fact also the great motivator for support and the guide to policy within the Church's formidable mission force.

The missionary movement directly reflected divisions within the Church and debates over national identity tied to Victorian religious styles. Tensions were persistent and acute within the Anglican Communion, where they were constantly recharged by the ecclesiastical exclusivity and universalist claims of High Church Anglicans. Evangelicals challenged this exclusivity and engaged in pan-evangelical alliances to support specific charitable objects. Because of their Anglican affiliation, however, they also experienced qualms about their participation in broad alliances constructed on the basis of evangelical "princi-ple," such as the Evangelical Alliance, and with many this reticence grew stron-ger over the course of the century.[168] The tension was constant, but through missionary and other charitable societies, characteristic in their insistence on voluntarism as the basis of the public realm, Evangelicals could maintain their independence within the communion, sustain pan-evangelical links, and dis-play their strength. Reliance on voluntary charitable contributions reinforced evangelical populism and independence in a liberal society of "free" property and labor where churches continued to form the central social institutions. Brit-ish Protestant missionary societies arose in an era when European religion was shifting to a modern pattern that dissolved assumptions about the necessity for

168. John Wolffe, "The Evangelical Alliance in the 1840s: An Attempt to Institutionalise Chris-tian Unity," in *Voluntary Religion*, ed. W. J. Sheils and Diana Wood, vol. 23 of Studies in Church History (Oxford: Blackwell, 1986).

state church sponsorship in favor of a new environment of public contestation of dominant religious ideologies — a free market of religious ideas.[169]

In this environment even previously state-sponsored Anglican societies such as the SPG were forced onto a purely voluntary footing. Vigorous competition, productive of voluble and ongoing conflict, came to characterize even more fully much of British religious life. For as religious tolerance grew as a core practice that drew religious minorities into civil participation in the nation, sectarian conflict operated as a language of political contest as well as an expression of social class. What the history of Anglicanism suggests is that broad religious dynamics of interaction between Evangelicalism and other faith styles in late Victorian England — that is, between disestablishment-oriented Nonconformists, "national" Churchmen, interdenominational evangelicals, High Church traditionalists, and Anglo-Catholic internationalists — catalyzed public controversy that carried not only subcultural religious significance but also regional, national, and imperial overtones. The missionary movement in Britain was divided along several axes of identity: evangelical charisma and individualism conflicted with ecclesiastical formalism and sacerdotalism; nonconformist evangelical independence conflicted with Anglican establishmentarianism; Anglo-Catholic independence conflicted with traditionalist English devotion to cooperation between church and state; and Protestant interdenominationalism and internationalism conflicted with loyalty to church, nation, and empire. In such an environment the construction of mission ideology and policy became a complex process of matching overseas tasks with a domestic ideology able to resonate compellingly with existing constituencies of support.

While the 1860s formed a decade of general stagnation in missionary society incomes, public attitudes toward foreign missions began to shift perceptibly soon after that decade. A growing general acceptance in English public life of the legitimacy of Christian missions led Archbishop Tait, speaking in Exeter Hall at the 1877 CMS Annual Meeting, to comment, "I am old enough to remember the time when it was a fashionable thing rather to sneer at missionary success and at missionary work. Thank God, I believe that time has greatly gone by." By the 1890s such reminiscences by old mission hands had become stock-in-trade at missionary meetings, indicating an overarching qualitative improvement in the public perception of foreign missions.[170] In part this shift was the result of the increasing importance of missionary work to the refinement of party identity. The activities of Church parties and the adjustments of

169. Cox, "Missionary Movement," 200-204.

170. The change in attitude was just beginning in the early 1870s. Davidson and Benham, *Tait*, 2:359.

missionary societies to reflect their concerns strongly mediated the growth of Anglican foreign missions in the late Victorian period. In the 1870s both the CMS and the SPG responded to the shifting ground of Church partisanship, as deeply emotional battles over Ritualism combined with growing anxieties over the emergence of modern doubt, as well as urban mass society, with all its obvious social challenges. The societies grew in the later Victorian period along the lines that their identities as Church societies allowed and encouraged. The CMS emphasized voluntarism, through which it could maintain a separate evangelical identity within the Church of England and encourage a broader national and imperial identity along the lines of a Protestant liberty that its supporters imagined as its primary inheritance and legacy. The SPG emphasized its loyalty to the visible Church and leadership by the episcopacy, but it suffered in comparison to the CMS as much higher church activism focused on diocesan reform efforts and parochial duties rather than evangelistic work of all types. For the enthusiasts among High Churchmen, the SPG was not a particularly inspiring model, and more vigorous partisans turned their support to new missions like the UMCA, with its avowed Anglo-Catholic principles, splitting High Church missions over the key issue of the relationship between religious and state authority.[171] Conflicts over ritual, the authority of bishops, the orthodoxy of evangelical belief, and establishmentarianism all contributed to the dynamics driving Church missions. The partisans who collected to contest these issues provided leadership within the constituencies that the societies organized. Rivalry of an acute and particular type drove the missionary organizations of late Victorian England.

This pattern of activity inside the Church of England is also relevant to the missionary movement more generally, for just as Evangelicals within the Church defined themselves against Anglo-Catholics, so evangelical Dissenters, who saw their chapels and missions as "bastions of freedom, democracy and equality," defined themselves against the established Church, with its pretensions to a superior patriotism, culture, and learning.[172] The Evangelicals in the Church of England had the advantage of drawing on both the lively spirit and countercultural brio of evangelicalism and the respectability and organization of the Church. But they also had a complex series of negotiations to perform in order to maintain a position of loyalty to the Establishment, and they had to carry them out in the context of intra-Church conflict and crisis. This situation

---

171. See Chapter 3 for more on the 1859 founding and subsequent growth of the UMCA.

172. McLeod, *Religion and the Working Class*, 42. In most districts elections represented a contest of strength between church and chapel corresponding to the vote for the Conservative and Liberal parties, respectively. David W. Bebbington, "Nonconformity and Electoral Sociology, 1867-1918," *Historical Journal* 27, no. 3 (Sept. 1984): 633-34, 655.

was not, however, a detriment to the growth of foreign missions supported by large, organized, bureaucratic missionary societies. The societies prospered as national symbols of party identity and, as Brian Stanley has noted, their growth was often much more closely linked to crisis in the home denomination than to external influences. Under the threat of Church reform in the 1830s, for example, both the CMS and the SPG grew as Church missionary societies; in the face of denominational schism in the 1850s, Methodist per capita giving to the WMMS rose significantly.[173] Similar correlations can be made in the later Church of England. With the growth of Ritualist controversies in the early 1870s, the late 1880s, and the late 1890s, both the CMS and the SPG, although at different phases, made major funding and recruitment advances as the Church parties faced off against one another and used the CMS and the SPG as platforms in cultural and theological battle.

Extension provided energy and vision, but it also challenged Anglican cohesion. The tensions within Anglicanism, tied as they were to pragmatic needs surrounding Anglican church operation in Britain and overseas, led to the rise of moderate, pragmatic parties within the Church. Among Evangelicals closely associated with the CMS, a "neo-Evangelical" party that sought to balance evangelical principles with participation in the corporate Church emerged. Similarly, a centrist position, associated with the SPG and the majority of the English bishops, also developed within the High Church tradition. It focused on avoiding the public excesses of what many evangelicals characterized as "popish" Ritualism while also emphasizing the unique apostolic authority of a worldwide Anglican Church. The traditional missionary societies became the bases of these moderate parties, where missionary policy centered on attempts to increase quietly the efficiency of society organization while retaining distinctive but non-schismatic party identities. The more extreme fringes, however, also generated missionary programs, from a committed new Anglo-Catholic missionary enthusiasm — associated with the Universities' Mission to Central Africa (1859) and several overseas Anglo-Catholic dioceses and their emphasis on the "bishop in mission" — to the new charismatic "faith" ideals of interdenominational evangelical activism — associated with the China Inland Mission (1865) and supported keenly by the zealous premillennialist vision of many extreme evangelical Anglicans. The tensions between these forms of missionary religion set the context of Anglican missionary development in the final decades of the century.

Party identity influenced how missionary supporters incorporated imperial attitudes, how they responded to social hierarchies, how they structured the

---

173. Stanley, "Home Support," 36-39.

role of women in religion, and how they developed the goals and institutions of their mission stations. Evangelicalism, "orthodox" High Church attitudes, and Anglo-Catholicism were fundamental to the identity of Church organizations, if not always individuals and congregations, and competition between these parties was essential to building enthusiastic support. By the 1870s the divisions that were to define the terrain of late Victorian Anglican missions had coalesced. The most dynamic visions were tied either to the revivalistic variants of evangelicalism that came to be institutionalized in new "faith" missions and the Keswick holiness conventions or to the Anglo-Catholic styles of High Churchism that generated new home and foreign missions alike. Both presented persistent challenges to the respectable Evangelicalism of the later Clapham connection that had been institutionalized at the CMS, as well as the "higher and drier" institutional Anglicanism characteristic of the SPG. Whether enthusiastically innovative or traditionally reserved, Anglican clergy ultimately determined on what terms missionary propaganda was delivered to parishioners, and thus, crucially, how religion and empire were merged into a cultural message in Victorian England.

Anglican foreign missions grew rapidly from the 1830s, peaking in domestic social power by the end of the century and in worldwide reach in the 1920s. The size of Anglican missionary work and the sophistication of society administration — particularly at the CMS — were impressive. By the late 1880s missionary advance at the CMS led some to declare the arrival of a qualitatively different "new era" in foreign mission, promising that the twentieth century would be a golden age of opportunity.[174] After the turn of the century the SPG also saw substantial growth; however, late Victorian and Edwardian success in the foreign missions of the Church of England arose out of the context of heated controversies over Church order, authority, and ritual that made the 1860s and 1870s decades of intense Church conflict. The response to that conflict, an intensification of the deep pietism that characterized both the Evangelicalism and Tractarianism of earlier in the century, was one of the realities of the second half of the nineteenth century, as both Low and High Church revivalism developed after the 1860s with major implications for the late Victorian missionary movement.

---

174. E[dward] Lombe, *How Is the Present Need of Missionaries to Be Met? A Paper Read Before the Cambridge Church Missionary Union, Oct 23, 1888* (London: CMS, 1889), 9.

CHAPTER 3

Revivalism and Church Order:
Late Victorian Anglican Missionary Expansion

If any despondent minds had been tempted to think that the "Word of the Cross" had somehow had its day and lost its power, and that the modern soul must be reached and transfigured by some means more consonant with "the wisdom of men," they had good cause to be reassured.

H. C. G. Moule, 1901

[T]he sign of Empire for nations, as for men, is not self-assertion but self-sacrifice.

B. F. Westcott, 1900[1]

Late Victorian evangelical Anglicans fundamentally reoriented their identity and the focus of their enthusiasm and resources. Commenting in 1899, the moderate High Church Bishop Henry H. Montgomery was struck by the intensity of Evangelical interest in foreign missions, virtually to the exclusion of constructive domestic social action.[2] This transformation was also celebrated within the "evangelical school." Handley Moule, Norrisian Professor of Divinity at Cambridge University, wrote of late-century Evangelicalism as an evolutionary transformation out of earlier phases of development.[3] Over the course of

1. Moule, *Evangelical School*, 62; Westcott, *The Obligations of Empire* (London: Macmillan, 1900), 7.
2. Montgomery to Randall Davidson, 12 July 1899, Davidson Papers, vol. 519, fols. 244-47.
3. Moule preceded his appointment in 1899 to the Norrisian professorship with nearly two decades as principal of the preeminent Evangelical training college, Ridley Hall, Cambridge, and

the century, three periods had characterized the party. In the age of William Wilberforce, Charles Simeon, and the Clapham Sect slavery was eradicated and the insistence on moral rectitude (demanded both by evangelical Anglicans and Dissenters) combined with the rise of the middle classes to purify the culture of the country. In the following age of Lord Shaftesbury, enthusiastic urban revivalism and organized Christian philanthropy were brought to bear on the problems of the modern city and modern doubt. And in the final decades of the nineteenth century Anglican evangelicalism had transcended charismatic leaders, parochial concerns, and petty infighting to rally its energies around the CMS, "our great Evangelical Institution." Central to this transformation, Moule argued, was the impact of new charismatic forms of revivalism that called growing numbers of volunteers, most notably women and university graduates, into missionary service, allowing the CMS to develop "its resources, its energy, and its influence, as to form a phenomenon of commanding import in our Evangelical history." By directing energy overseas, in combination with new efforts on the part of High Churchmen to call the church and nation to its missionary duties, Evangelicals were galvanized by a new spirit that made the final decades of the nineteenth century truly the "age of the Church Missionary Society."[4]

In the late Victorian era Anglican missionary interest grew not only among Evangelicals but also among higher varieties of High Churchmen, who became missionary-minded to an unprecedented degree. Just as a new revivalism that proceeded from reinvigorated emphasis on personal piety had transformed British evangelicalism, so too had new forms of pietism in High Church circles, from the urban missionary enthusiasms of Ritualist slum priests to the historicist mystical piety of the circle surrounding B. F. Westcott, acknowledged missionary visionary, biblical scholar, Christian Socialist, and ultimately the bishop of Durham (1890-1901).[5] Realignment in Anglican missions was influenced by imperial and international realities, but it was also driven by the intertwined, competitive revivalisms of Evangelicalism and Anglo-Catholicism. The conflict between these "schools" fired growth that from the 1870s launched a "new era" of expansion, peaking in the 1890s with the new imperialism of the late century.

---

succeeded it as bishop of Durham from 1901 to 1920. As bishop of Durham he was the clear successor to J. C. Ryle, bishop of Liverpool, as the episcopal leader of the Evangelical party. F. W. B. Bullock, *The History of Ridley Hall Cambridge,* 2 vols. (Cambridge: Cambridge University Press, 1941), 1:326-29.

4. Moule, *Evangelical School,* 5-6, 33-38, 64-65, 86, 104-8.

5. Westcott was supported by four devoted sons who became missionaries to India, two subsequently bishops: George Herbert Westcott of Lucknow and Foss Westcott of Calcutta. Westcott was appointed bishop of Durham, following his former student, friend, and partner in critical biblical studies, J. B. Lightfoot (bishop, 1879-89).

From a modest ten denominational societies in 1840, new missionary societies proliferated, numbering by 1910 nearly sixty in England alone and over 160 within the empire.[6]

The British missionary movement, bred of official religious toleration and voluntarism, developed support from a bewilderingly diverse set of religious and social milieux. Anglo-Catholic, Evangelical, and High Church Anglicans all contributed, as did a legion of Baptist, Methodist, Congregationalist, Presbyterian, Quaker, and other Nonconformist denominations and sectarian splinter groups. This diversity was reinforced from the 1860s onward by the missionary operations of notable interdenominational missions (although heavily Anglican-subscribed), such as Hudson Taylor's China Inland Mission (CIM) and Henry Grattan Guinness's Regions Beyond Missionary Union (RBMU), as well as by independent, often Anglo-Catholic, overseas Anglican dioceses.[7] In contrast with American and continental European societies, which tended largely toward denominational organization, the late-century expansion of independent agency within the movement added to the discordant competition that characterized British missions. Increasingly divided between higher church Anglican Protestants and evangelicals of all denominations, while also influenced by the sectional successes of smaller societies and missions that proliferated in large numbers after about 1870, novel approaches and methods had growing influence to change the style, emphases, and even direction of an entire movement, which had evolved into an alphabet soup of societies. Thus emerged a dizzying array of different, smaller societies run on "distinctive lines," such as the Anglo-Catholic UMCA and the holiness-oriented evangelical Livingstone Inland Mission. Both were formed in response to the appeals of Livingstone in the late 1850s and after, but they were dedicated to deeply contrasting styles: settled, Anglican, indigenized community building versus itinerant, interdenominational, proclamatory gospel preaching. Such developments substantially complicated the world of missionary endeavor.[8]

---

6. In 1910, 58 primary missionary societies and 118 auxiliary societies and committees operated in England, 82 and 156 respectively in Britain, 164 and 280 within the British Empire, and 377 and 618 across the world (including American and Continental societies). James S. Dennis, Harlan P. Beach, and Charles H. Fahs, eds., *World Atlas of Christian Missions* (New York: SVM, 1911), 78.

7. The CIM was routinely described by contemporaries as "non-denominational," although, as F. Howard Taylor remarked, it was more accurate to understand it as an "inter-denominational" body. *These Forty Years: A Short History of the China Inland Mission* (Philadelphia: Pepper, 1903), 24-25.

8. Briefly on the UMCA and Livingstone Inland Mission respectively, see H. Alan C. Cairns, *Prelude to Imperialism: British Reactions to Central African Society, 1840-1890* (London: Routledge & K. Paul, 1965), 218-22; and Andrew Porter, "Evangelical Enthusiasm, Missionary Motivation and

The histories of missions and missionary societies deliver the impression of a unified movement advancing a common project of spreading Christianity and modernizing Western culture beyond English shores, but in fact smaller and often highly individualistic societies tended to erode uniformity and act as catalysts for change. While relatively small in their overall numbers of missionaries, these societies were large in influence and generated challenges to prevailing mainline institutional theory and practice. Most notably, "outsider" movements tended toward the questioning of standard models of evangelical missionary modernization from earlier decades, although conventional attitudes that assumed the superiority of Western society remained widespread throughout the missionary movement. Influenced by the greater weight of women and university students among their supporters, newer forms of missionary experimentation often expressed deep suspicion of the ungodly corruptions developing in Western society, drawing into question prevailing wisdom regarding collaboration with empire and widespread assumptions of European cultural and racial superiority.

By the 1860s the CMS and SPG had come to represent among Anglican evangelicals and High Churchmen, respectively, distinct, respectable, "establishment" styles. They were challenged by more radical developments within their own connections: on the evangelical side, by new activist holiness pietism arising from waves of American-style revivalism; on the High Church side, by holiness emphases inspired by the several streams of influence issuing from the Oxford Movement, most notoriously the "advanced" Ritualism that increasingly advocated for Anglican independence from the state.[9] In addition, less extreme impulses toward enhanced ceremonialism and romantic appreciation of the Church's ancient past and communal potential were also growing, particularly among Anglicans connected to the universities. While the High Church SPG embraced this new reverence for the Church's antiquity and apostolic dignity, as well as a strong connection to the "old Tractarian" clergy whose influence stretched into the 1880s, it vigorously resisted the influence of advanced Anglo-Catholicism (severing in 1882 its connection with several troublesome "special missions" — including the Central Africa and Melanesia funds). The CMS, in contrast, was able to embrace and manage the enthusiasms of evangelical spiritual radicalism, and in that achievement it invigorated and enlarged its missions to an unprecedented degree.

The dominant Anglican missionary ideologies were tied to several varie-

---

West Africa in the Late Nineteenth Century: The Career of G. W. Brooke," *Journal of Imperial and Commonwealth History* 6, no. 1 (1977): 28.

9. Bebbington, *Holiness*, chaps. 1 and 4.

ties of Church reformism, from those focusing on institutional reconstruction to those drawing energy from the reforms and revivals associated with the new pietism of late Victorian Britain. These new ideologies served to reinforce pre-existing party oppositions. The growing division between the holiness revivalism of evangelicals and the growing Ritualism within the Anglo-Catholic connection led extremists in both parties to define their opposites as disloyal to the Anglican Communion. While problematic for moderates, such approaches drew forth new enthusiasm, especially from the young, which could not be ignored. In the 1860s and early 1870s, as stagnation in both interest in and support for missions became obvious, two crucial questions arose for evangelical Anglicans: How far should suspect evangelical enthusiasm, often revivalistic and undenominational in thrust, be encouraged in the movement? And what limits should the Anglican establishment be allowed to put on enthusiastic proselytizing?[10] Among High Churchmen two related questions arose: To what degree should experimental Anglo-Catholic and evangelical methods be endorsed and emulated? And how could High Church principles of episcopal control be reconciled to Anglo-Catholic enthusiasms and thus be focused into a successful missionary program? New circumstances, then, led to reorientation and significant expansion after the 1870s, as the convergence of enthusiast holiness movements, transforming gender ideologies and norms, growing pressures of professionalization, and new insistent forms of imperial enthusiasm led to a late Victorian phase of rapid growth.

The New Pietism: Revivals, Settlements, and New Missionary Departures

The 1850s and 1860s formed a period of relative stagnation in missionary interest due to a combination of causes, notably the high-profile missionary and commercial disaster represented by the Niger Expedition of 1841, the rising Chartist agitation in the midst of economic depression through the following decade, and an intensifying perception of missionary culpability in imperial failures, particularly the Indian insurrection of 1857 and Jamaican Morant Bay uprising of 1865.[11] In this context radical experiments in mission — most nota-

10. Missionary recruiting was also stagnant in this period; 1872 was the low point for the CMS in an era of generally receding mission support. C. Peter Williams, "The Recruitment and Training of Overseas Missionaries in England Between 1850 and 1900, with Special Reference to the Records of the CMS, WMMS, LMS and the China Inland Mission" (Master's thesis, University of Bristol, 1976), 1-17.
11. Howard Temperley, *White Dreams, Black Africa: The Antislavery Expedition to the River*

bly the Anglo-Catholic UMCA and the faith-based, interdenominational CIM — were able, by developing and channeling emerging spiritual movements, to engineer what were over time often startlingly successful new missionary enterprises. Despite their relatively small size, these missions, inspired by new cadres of supporters who were driven by reanimated religious and imperial enthusiasms, had a decisive impact on the broader world of foreign missions.

The most influential activists in this era came from a growing evangelical subculture galvanized by fervent, apocalyptic premillennial expectations focused through organized religious revivals as the way forward to the Second Coming of Christ and the end of history.[12] From the 1850s the overlapping revivalist and holiness movements, drawing energy from feared Catholic threats and emerging challenges made by Anglo-Catholics to "Puritan" ideas and practice, increasingly rooted themselves in English evangelicalism and became institutionalized through holiness conferences, most famously the annual Keswick Convention held from 1875 in the Lake District.[13] Significantly for the evangelical societies, the impatient temperament of revivalism for large-scale and instantaneous Christian conversion also came by the 1880s to be expressed as a vocal yearning for a "Pentecostal season" in overseas missions. In self-conscious contrast to these fevered developments, the growing social conscience of Broad and High Church men and women, who were deeply influenced by Anglo-Catholic pietism, provided an alternative vision for the development of institutionalized overseas Anglicanism. This vision was nourished not by the revival tour but the revitalization of parochial care and the attempted cultural adaptation to urban working-class populations embodied in inner-city settlement movements.[14]

Critical interaction between highly contrasting styles of missionary approach gave new life to retooled religious styles and identities, reinforced by historical models that informed alternative visions of the missionary enter-

---

Niger, 1841-1842 (New Haven: Yale University Press, 1991); Hall, *Civilising Subjects*, 243-64, 370-79.

12. In contrast to postmillennialists, who believed Christ's Second Coming would be preceded by a 1000-year period of increasing righteousness, premillennialists believed a rapid, cataclysmic struggle would bring the Parousia — Second Coming or Advent — preceded by signs of the times (foretold in coded scripture) and worldwide proclamation of the gospel. This set of beliefs was new, but growing, at mid-century, and owed much to the millennial ministry of Edward Irving and his following. Bebbington, *Evangelicalism*, 78-92.

13. John Kent, *Holding the Fort: Studies in Victorian Revivalism* (London: Epworth, 1978), 125-28.

14. On the incipient social reformism displayed in Tractarianism, accelerated by mid-century in the development of Ritualism, see Paz, *Popular Anti-Catholicism*, 141-47. As Paz notes, Anglo-Catholicism challenged both the conversionary theology and *laissez-faire* economics favored by many Evangelicals.

prise. Low Church evangelical Anglicans tended to focus on the first century of Christian history, when itinerancy and spiritual charisma were imagined to have reigned. The result was a reinforced confidence in proclamatory preaching of a gospel message believed to possess universal power to transform individuals and societies. Anglo-Catholics emphasized the importance of the church fathers and their patristic writings, also pointing to the role of the missionary bishop who carried Christian missions to the British Isles and Northern Europe. Within this vision, emphasis rested on settled missionary strategies centering on the parochial model of community life and service. While many orthodox High Churchmen shared this preference with Anglo-Catholics, others with a more Erastian bent emphasized the importance of the ecumenical church councils, which started in the fourth century when doctrinal discipline and creeds were established and then extended into a bureaucratic, imperially favored church. Such models favored collaboration with empire and elites to advance Christian civilization.[15] These constructed lineages had profound implications for the way mission strategies developed.

By the 1870s evangelicalism, previously more powerful in national politics, was regrouping to conserve its past influence. Increasingly it did so by emphasizing its special relationship to foreign missionary endeavor. Anglo-Catholicism, more in tune with traditional orthodox High Churchism, was in comparison rising in influence as it challenged for a place in the communion, emphasizing a contrasting, church-based missionary strategy. The societies achieved modest growth in mission incomes by the mid-1870s — spurred by the public attention surrounding, first, the martyrdom of High Church Bishop J. C. Patteson in Melanesia in 1871 and, second, the death of evangelical and national hero David Livingstone in 1873. But general stagnation in revenue followed. Both the SPG and CMS struggled to pay for new overseas programs that had been launched in the disappointed hope that the enthusiasms surrounding imperial heroism and martyrdom might alone support them.

The potent new influences that transformed this situation were tied, then, not primarily to imperial heroics but, more crucially, to an identifiably new set of revivalistic patterns within the Church of England. The foundations were laid in the 1860s, as Evangelical responsiveness to new American styles of holiness revivalism fuelled dynamic new missionary initiatives and as High Church missionary enthusiasm was channeled into settlement strategies in both English inner-cities and overseas dioceses.[16] Both Evangelical and High Church

---

15. The other historical lineage dividing Anglicans, of course, was that of the Protestant Reformation. Hinchliff, *God and History,* 11-30 and passim.

16. John Venn, *The Revival in Wales* (London, 1860), 13-24; James Edward Vaux, "Missions and

patterns of pietism faced off, often defaming their opposite as superstitious or simplistic, while energizing party feeling and contrasting styles of Anglican devotion. Both animated new missionary visions, sharpened aspirations for Church growth, and imagined a Christian future in which Englishness and the bounds of empire would be transcended in new waves of enthusiastic Christian universalism. Implementing such pietistic visions of mission was nearly always deeply problematic, however, because of the difficulty of transporting culturally inscribed, prescriptively Western religious languages to foreign cultures as well as problems arising from the often enormous social and cultural distances, which the vast disparities of wealth and power characteristic of imperial environments produced between missionaries and indigenous populations. Nevertheless, such new movements profoundly altered the force and focus of late Victorian and Edwardian Anglican missions.[17]

The creation in particular of two new missionary societies, the China Inland Mission (CIM) and the Universities' Mission to Central Africa (UMCA), each drawing on ideals conceived as an explicit rejection of established missionary organization and strategy, catalyzed new thinking about missions that challenged accepted wisdom on the need to civilize and develop commerce with indigenous peoples. Among evangelicals, the faith-based CIM, founded in 1865 by the enthusiastic interdenominationalist James Hudson Taylor (1832-1905), called into question the highly structured bureaucracy and organizational formalism of denominational societies such as the CMS. Similarly the founding of the Oxford and Cambridge Mission to Central Africa in 1859 (soon renamed the Universities' Mission to Central Africa) brought new focus and new energies to High Church missionary effort. While the culture of the CIM ultimately was successfully co-opted in the 1880s by Evangelicals at the CMS, High Churchmen found it more difficult to harness and extend Anglo-Catholic ideals to general mission practice. Only when a strategy for incorporating these energies under the SPG system was eventually developed in the final decade of the century did a parallel process of growth and reorganization result. Essential to the transformation and notable in each case was an effective response to the public enthusiasm of middle- and upper-class women for women's missions, supported as a critical component of Church extension and social outreach.[18]

Preaching Orders," in *The Church and the World: Essays on Questions of the Day in 1868,* ed. Orby Shipley (London: Longmans, Green, Reader, and Dyer, 1868), 152-88.

17. On intractable problems created in the field by missionary privilege, see Cox, *Imperial Fault Lines,* 88-105.

18. For more detail on this phenomenon, see Chapter 4.

Anglo-Catholicism and High Church Overseas Ambition

In the 1860s innovating High Church bishops — most notably Wilberforce of Oxford in England, Gray of Cape Town, and Selwyn of New Zealand in the colonies — launched a bid to seize Anglican missionary initiative. Initially they received enthusiastic support from the founders of the Oxford Movement, John Keble and E. B. Pusey. But even at this stage the early leaders of Tractarianism were no longer the avant-garde of High Church practice, and a contest developed to define this High Church missionary initiative. The Tractarianism of the 1840s had at its core the reassertion of apostolic authority in the Church and necessarily elevated the role of the episcopacy and the priesthood. Rapidly, as it found episcopal sympathizers, an advanced "orthodox" High Churchism emerged, with several "old Tractarians" in its ranks. However, a still more radical set of Ritualist variations developed as priests at the parish level, advancing the more general authority of priestly orders, carried the movement forward to new levels of provocative public display that even the founders, Pusey and Keble, found difficult to support. One particular practice emerging by the 1860s, defiant administration and public defense of habitual confession, came to mark the growth of an advanced Anglo-Catholic identity. This practice challenged the authority of the bishops, who proscribed it, and it became the target of "anti-popery" campaigners in the evangelical ranks.[19] The firestorms of controversy unleashed by the second generation of Tractarians, the ritually innovating Anglo-Catholics of the 1860s, provided the context for late mid-century High Church missionary initiatives.

While advanced Anglo-Catholics saw missionary and overseas dioceses as laboratories in which to work out radical reformulation of the Church — from severing colonial Churches from England, allowing them free pursuit of a more complete Ritualistic revival of the ancient church to advancing the most energetic competitive emulation of Roman Catholicism within the overseas dioceses[20] — more orthodox High Churchmen balked at such radicalism. While they could also see the utility of overseas dioceses in elevating the dignity of the

19. While Pusey acted as confessor to many, and while even moderate High Church bishops like Wilberforce allowed that occasional confession in extreme cases of need was allowable practice, Pusey's lack of enthusiasm for ritual (until his final years), and his frustration at what he saw as actions likely to draw further state intrusions into Church affairs, marked the older Tractarians off from the new generation of strident "Ritualists." Meacham, *Wilberforce*, 175-76; Faught, *Oxford Movement*, 30-31.

20. Edmund Huff, "Public Laws and the Colonial Church," in *The Church and the World: Essays on Questions of the Day in 1867,* 3rd ed., ed. Orby Shipley (London: Longmans, Green, Reader, and Dyer, 1867), 113-44.

Church — in enhanced ceremonialism of services, increased exclusivism of the Church's claims to authority, and the advancement of an educated, upper-class vision of symbiosis between Church and colonial culture — they recoiled from too close an approach to Roman Catholicism.[21] Thus was born a divided bid to advance the High Church missionary profile, a bid that was nevertheless formulated in direct and explicit contrast to evangelical methods and assumptions.

The Anglo-Catholics specifically staked their claim to legitimacy upon a reconceptualized ideal of mission, both at home and abroad. All those within High Church realms understood this and were to some degree affected by it, not least because it was rooted in older High Church and Tractarian insistence that the distribution of Scripture to the unlearned without adequate guidance produced little but misunderstanding and heresy.[22] Proclaiming Evangelicalism to be the culturally deficient religion of the lower middle classes, and insisting that "High and Dry" Anglicanism was maintained in the countryside only by the "feodal [feudal] pressure exerted by the squirearchy," Anglo-Catholics argued that only their vision of the Church was truly universal — transcending class in England and national culture in the world. Further, the essentials of Christianity could only be communicated in symbolic language adapted to changing times and cultures, both at home and abroad, so that the Church "not merely be fully capable of adaptation to the habits of all climates and nations, but that in each nation it should meet the wants of all classes of society and all types of mind."[23] Suggesting that the fate of the empire lay in missionary choices, advanced Anglo-Catholics such as R. F. Littledale pointed to the stability of episcopacy as reinforcing both authority and the civilizing process. He proclaimed evangelicalism to be "a purely subjective religion, fatally weighted with the most anti-missionary and anti-Christian of dogmas — the Lutheran doctrine of Justification — [which] has been offered to men who needed to be taught by externals to rise gradually into the conception of spiritual life."[24] Preaching the cross alone, then, was inadequate when listeners did not have

21. Samuel Wilberforce, *A Sermon Preached at Westminster Abbey, on the Feast of the Purification, Feb. 2, 1863, At the Consecration of the Bishop of the Mission to Central Africa and the Bishop of the Orange River Free State* (Oxford: Henry and Parker, 1863), 15-17; Charlotte M. Yonge, *Life of John Coleridge Patteson, Missionary Bishop of the Melanesian Islands*, 2 vols. (London: Macmillan, 1874), 1:404-5; 2:49-50.

22. W. S. F. Pickering, *Anglo-Catholicism: A Study in Religious Ambiguity* (London: Routledge, 1989), 68-71; Nockles, *Oxford Movement*, 198-200.

23. Richard Frederick Littledale, "The Missionary Aspect of Ritualism," in *The Church and the World: Essays on Questions of the Day*, ed. Orby Shipley (London: Longmans, Green, Reader, and Dyer, 1866), 32-33.

24. Littledale, "The Missionary Aspect of Ritualism," 49.

the cultural vocabulary to understand the message or its implications. This interpretation represented the evangelical conversion experience, both within the working classes and the heathen masses, as little but empty theater.

While there was considerable variation within the emerging Anglo-Catholic missionary movement regarding the relationship that missionary settlements and dioceses should have to empire (diversity that developed with growing and varied experience overseas — from south and central Africa to India and Melanesia), the fundamental rejection of what was styled the excessive individualism and anti-intellectualism of evangelical missionary theology and practice was ubiquitous.[25] One prominent feature of the movement was advocacy for female communal life through the emergence of Anglo-Catholic sisterhoods, which empowered women and provided a mechanism for the employment of single women in missions. But preserving orthodox Church order was also key, and Anglo-Catholics insisted the missionary bishop was necessary to ensure sophisticated, educated, apostolic leadership. This fundamentally paternalistic vision was also, somewhat ironically, productive in the longer run of growing cultural sensitivity and sophistication within the missionary movement. Its legacy proved to be a complex and mixed one.

The idea of the missionary bishop had appeal in both Low and High Church Anglican circles, but for significantly different reasons. At the CMS, Henry Venn evolved a position supporting missionary bishops in order to allow independence for indigenous churches under separate, even overlapping episcopal districts. For High Churchmen, however, missionary bishoprics were a strategy to ensure what they saw as the integrity of the Church and its order as it expanded overseas. Thus the Evangelical emphasis at the CMS came to embrace the ideal of separate racial churches, with independent bishops specifically intended to counter inevitable Western missionary paternalism and condescension. Among High Churchmen, however, such paternalism under bishops appointed from England, embodying the orthodox learning that underlay the High Church position, was precisely the point.[26] Advocacy for missionary bishops in England developed as a Tractarian ideal designed to advance the High Church position that incorporation into the Christian church and Christian society preceded the growth of Christian faith. This idea had received forceful advocacy through the preaching tours and writings of Samuel Wilberforce in the 1840s, but it only began to bear fruit with the elevation of High Churchmen to colonial dioceses

---

25. See, for example, Yonge, *Patteson*, 1:404-5, 2:92; Brooke Foss Westcott, *On Some Points in the Religious Office of the Universities* (London: Macmillan, 1873), 35, 38-39.

26. On the CMS's policy under Venn as it evolved from 1840s through 1860s, see Williams, *Self-Governing Church*, chap. 1.

— notably Selwyn to New Zealand in 1841 and Gray to Cape Town in 1847 — and their initiation of synodical government within the colonial churches as a means of advancing High Church reform. In forcing the clarification of the legal relationship of church to state in the colonies, they opened the way to the consecration of missionary bishops under colonial episcopal authority.[27]

It was precisely within this context of rapid evolution in the colonial church that the UMCA was conceived and founded. Its inauguration, celebrated with extensive fanfare, was tied to the highly publicized return to England of intrepid African missionary and explorer David Livingstone. Arriving in 1856, Livingstone inspired audiences with his famously electrifying challenge in 1857 to university Christians to save a newly opened Africa from slavery "for commerce and Christianity."[28] To Bishop Robert Gray, ambitious to advance High Church missions, the incongruity of collaboration with a Scots Presbyterian previously employed by the LMS was clearly overweighed by the opportunity to seize the moment and generate support within the universities.[29] In 1859 he urged the creation of a committee in Cambridge to establish a mission along the Zambezi river, and the committee was rapidly joined by supporters at other universities.[30] Gray had recently been raised to the position of a controlling metropolitan over two new dioceses, Grahamstown and Natal, giving him a geographical interest in the area of Livingstone's ambitions for a new commercial and missionary project to open East Africa. The opportunity to launch a high-profile, High Church missionary experiment had appeared suddenly, and Gray seized it.

Despite later criticisms from his High Church partners, Livingstone, after the CMS declined to sponsor a proposed new highland mission, initially had few qualms about collaborating with High Churchmen. From 1859 the UMCA project received vigorous support from Samuel Wilberforce, now widely acknowledged as a key episcopal leader of the High Church connection in England. Wilberforce travelled the country touting the project — sometimes in the

27. Emulating the Protestant Episcopal Church of the United States and the Protestant Episcopal Church of Scotland, Selwyn called a synod of his New Zealand clergy in 1844. In following years he and several other colonial bishops — in Australia, Canada and South Africa — led the further development of colonial church governance under provincial synods. Alan M. G. Stephenson, *The First Lambeth Conference, 1867* (London: SPCK, 1967), 66-79.

28. David Livingstone, *Dr. Livingstone's Cambridge Lectures*, 2nd ed., ed. William Monk (Cambridge: Deighton, Bell, 1860), 12.

29. Livingstone, under Royal Geographical Society patronage, was made a British consul in central Africa in 1857 and resigned from the LMS, formally removing the objection to interdenominational cooperation that High Churchmen generally adopted. Tim Jeal, *Livingstone* (London: Heinemann, 1973), 189-90, 223-24.

30. [Henrietta Louisa Lear], *Life of Robert Gray, Bishop of Cape Town and Metropolitan of Africa*, 2 vols., ed. Charles Gray (London: Rivingtons, 1876), 1:438.

face of angry evangelical public protest — as a means of bringing civilization, commercial development, and true religion to Africa.[31] From its inception, the UMCA operated on the premise that a mission field should be under the direct supervision of an Anglican bishop and that missionary societies should advocate for, but not control, missions. Its creation was a logical outgrowth of the Tractarian ideal of elevating sacramental and priestly power as the locus of reform. Samuel Wilberforce, the most influential of the energetic "orthodox" High Church bishops, supported the SPG as a corporate expression of the Church. He also advocated for the UMCA as an alternative to the emphasis on proclamatory evangelism and individual conversion prior to the establishment of the episcopacy that reigned at the CMS. Wilberforce insisted that missions, if they were to be scriptural and apostolic, must be conducted under a bishop and advanced by communities of dedicated Churchmen. Supporters of the UMCA also included many Anglo-Catholics who avowed episcopal independence from the State, which Evangelicals feared would leave "papists" on the bench free to inaugurate ritual innovations without checks provided by law.[32] This program established the UMCA as an ultra-high Anglican pietist missionary foil to the CMS but also to the SPG. The more centrist SPG rapidly found itself criticized by UMCA loyalists for what were seen as its ongoing Erastian loyalties and staid, respectable profile.

With Wilberforce and Gray collaborating in England to press the mission forward, and with Livingstone dreaming of and developing an ambitious endeavor under sponsorship of government and the Royal Geographical Society for commercial development of the hinterlands of the Zambezi river, the Anglo-Catholic mission was organized to piggyback on the official Zambezi Expedition and designed both to "civilise as well as Christianize."[33] Gray consulted with the continuing spiritual leaders of the Oxford Movement, Pusey and Keble, securing their support. He was careful also to get government assurances of his liberty to consecrate missionary bishops, advancing Pusey's long-held views on right principles of Church extension under episcopal authority.[34] In 1861 the agreement of the archdeacon of Natal, Charles Mackenzie (1825-62), to become the Church of England's first missionary bishop must have seemed to High

31. Ashwell, *Wilberforce*, 2:419-22, 443-45, 449-50, 460, 3:51-54.

32. Stock, *History of the CMS*, 2:17-21.

33. Henry Rowley, *The Story of the Universities' Mission to Central Africa: From Its Commencement, Under Bishop Mackenzie, to Its Withdrawal from the Zambesi* (London: Saunders, Otley, 1866), 2-4.

34. C. Brad Faught, "Tractarianism on the Zambezi: Bishop Mackenzie and the Beginnings of the Universities Mission to Central Africa," *Anglican and Episcopal History* 66, no. 3 (Sept. 1997): 307-9.

Churchmen the final piece necessary to begin the construction of a glorious new phase in the history of Church missions.[35] Combined with the consecration of J. C. Patteson by Bishop Selwyn as missionary bishop to Melanesia just seven weeks later in February of 1861 (without Letters-Patent from the Crown) and with the launch of a new mission to Hawai'i in cooperation with the American bishops (undertaken at the express invitation of King Kamehameha IV and Queen Emma), the building blocks were in place for a new High Church and Tractarian initiative to challenge Evangelical dominance in Church missions.[36] Rapidly, however, the hopes of the mixed High Church party were dashed in the most disastrous of ways.

The failure of the Zambezi Expedition and the fate of the Church of England's first missionary bishop — profoundly ignorant of local African politics, compromised by violent entanglement in complex slaving conflicts, repeatedly led astray by Livingstone's questionable judgment, and dead of malarial fever within a year of the inauguration of the mission — have been often recounted, most elegantly in Owen Chadwick's classic *Mackenzie's Grave*.[37] Beyond the immediate disaster of the bishop's death, which required that the mission withdraw and regroup in Zanzibar under Mackenzie's more prudent successor, Bishop William Tozer (1863-74), the fallout from this failure had profound consequences for emerging Anglo-Catholic missionary support in England.[38] Horrified by the failure of the mission and scandalized by the missionaries' local alliances, which employed violence and armed, retaliatory raids against presumed slaving villages (resulting in military forays, deaths, and burnt settlements), leaders of the emerging Anglo-Catholic connection expressed grief and mortification. Pusey, in a public meeting in Oxford in 1862, declared that blood shedding through the agency of the mission was a "frightful thing" that militated against the power of the true blood of martyrs. This opened the floodgates of criticism.[39] The irony that the bishop as agent of order had proven so

35. Mackenzie had sealed his "high" credentials by preaching in Durban in "popish" surplice, eliciting fevered evangelical opposition. Harvey Goodwin, *Memoir of Bishop Mackenzie* (Cambridge: Deighton, Bell, 1864), 123-25.

36. Samuel Wilberforce, with the support of Manley Hopkins, the Hawaiian consul in London, pressed forward the Hawaiian mission through SPG channels from the summer of 1860. Robert Louis Semes, "Hawai'i's Holy War: English Bishop Staley, American Congregationalists, and the Hawaiian Monarchies, 1860-1870," *Hawaiian Journal of History* 34 (2000): 115-16.

37. Owen Chadwick, *Mackenzie's Grave* (London: Hodder & Stoughton, 1959).

38. On the bitter controversy between Tozer and Livingstone over responsibility and the conduct of the mission, see Dorothy O. Helly, *Livingstone's Legacy: Horace Waller and Victorian Mythmaking* (Athens: Ohio University Press, 1987), 35-39.

39. Faught, "Tractarianism," 316, 319, 324-25.

Final image from *Memoir of Bishop Mackenzie* captioned "Dr Livingstone
planting the Cross on Bishop Mackenzie's Grave. (From a sketch made on the spot.)"
Harvey Goodwin, Memoir of Bishop Mackenzie (Cambridge: Deighton, Bell, 1864), 439.

fallibly human was glaringly obvious to the UMCA's supporters, but even more significantly to its evangelical detractors.

Similarly the Hawaiian experiment, so appealing in theory, rapidly unraveled in a blizzard of negative press. Thomas Nettleship Staley sailed from England in August 1862 already dreaded by American Congregationalist missionaries of the ABCFM as a high-handed bishop. Upon his arrival in Honolulu he almost immediately alienated the missionaries by publicly prohibiting his clergy from cooperating with those who denied the divine ordinance of episcopacy and the unique authority of Anglican sacraments. Displaying high and uncompromising behavior characteristic of advanced Anglo-Catholicism, Staley was perceived and publicized by the American Congregationalist missionaries, already forty years in residence, as the embodiment of all that was bad and dangerous among Ritualists: an insistence on the exclusive apostolic authority of the Church, a refusal to recognize the missionary "comity" that unofficially divided the mission field between Protestant societies, and a snobbish superciliousness in ecclesiastical matters that was read as the essence of tyrannical, popish, overbearing arrogance. Americans in Hawai'i with their own imperialistic republican designs on the islands saw in Staley, despite the mission's cooperative foundation by American and English bishops, the face of British imperial scheming, and they deeply resented the Hawaiian royal family's open preference for Anglicanism as more compatible with monarchy. In particular, Staley's toleration and encouragement of "heathen" customs such as the hula dance disgusted evangelical advocates of stamping out "savagery," who also disparaged the ceremonialism of Anglo-Catholicism.[40] Staley protested to the bishop of London about the highly prejudicial treatment he had received from "Puritans" upon arrival in the islands, and he recounted the many overtures he had made for cooperation. But his manner and behavior, seen as characteristic of the most extreme Anglo-Catholicism in England, led Mark Twain to criticize a lack of judgment "which might be forgiven a restless, visionary nobody, but not a bishop."[41] Similarly, Rufus Anderson, the secretary of the ABCFM and Staley's most persistent critic, vigorously denounced him, having been informed even before his arrival by former LMS Pacific island missionary William Ellis that the bishop "associated with that section of the Church of England from which the greatest number of perverts to Popery has proceeded, and between whom and the Roman Catholics the difference is reported to be slight."[42]

With the memory still strong among Nonconformists of French Catholic aggression in the South Pacific — particularly at the LMS, which had been driven from one of its most successful missionary stations on Tahiti by the French in 1839 at the urging of expelled Roman Catholic missionaries — feelings ran high among Pacific evangelicals against what they saw as popish imperialism and its presumed English analogue within Anglican High Churchism.[43] Furthermore, the Hawaiian mission, specially supported by Pusey and Keble, showed extremely disappointing growth due to intense competition from already established Congregationalist, Roman Catholic, and Mormon congregations and unremitting criticism and hostility from the American missionaries and community.[44] Staley had heartily joined battle with evangelicalism, stating

40. Semes, "Hawai'i's Holy War," 118-25.

41. T. N. Staley to A. C. Tait, 29 Sept. 1866, Tait Papers, vol. 170, fols. 144-49; Letter to the *Sacramento Union*, 30 July 1866, in A. Grove Day, ed., *Mark Twain's Letters from Hawaii* (New York: Appleton-Century, 1966), 171. Twain's opinions represented an endorsement of American republican imperialism, a general stance he was later to repudiate. Clifford Putney, "Man in Both Corners: Mark Twain the Shadow-Boxing Imperialist," *Hawaiian Journal of History* 40 (2006): 55-73.

42. Ellis quoted in Semes, "Hawai'i's Holy War," 119.

43. Jane Samson, *Imperial Benevolence: Making British Authority in the Pacific Islands* (Honolulu: University of Hawai'i Press, 1998), 46; Niel Gunson, *Messengers of Grace: Evangelical Missionaries in the South Seas, 1797-1860* (New York: Oxford University Press, 1978), 144, 174-80. In 1886 official French obstructionism further drove the LMS to withdraw much of its missionary force from Tahiti.

44. Henry Boyd Restarick, *Hawaii, 1778-1920, from the Viewpoint of a Bishop* (Honolulu: Paradise of the Pacific Press, 1924), 68, 91-92.

shortly after his arrival in Hawai'i that "in this remote spot of the globe" the mission was ready to fight "the battle between modern Puritanism and primitive Catholicism," but the death of the mission's chief patron, King Kamehameha IV, in November of 1863 (prior to an expected land endowment to support the Church) proved a serious blow to Staley's ambitions.[45] While the mission retained the support of Queen Emma and Anglican stations were established on all of the main Hawaiian islands, redoubled American Congregationalist attacks meant years of ongoing roadblocks, hardships, and a deteriorating relationship between the queen and the bishop. Emma, who cultivated a devotion to English culture as one bulwark against American cultural and political aggression, remained deeply committed to Hawaiian independence, and she ultimately denounced Staley for incompetence in raising the funds and support necessary for Anglican success. Following Staley's failed cathedral fundraising trip to England, she accused him of a willingness to deliver Hawaiian Anglicans into the hands of the American Episcopal Church in order to salvage his own reputation.[46] When a worn-down T. N. Staley — family finances ruined, diocese disruptively divided over Churchmanship, and personal reputation destroyed — withdrew from the bishopric in 1870, the church was in tatters, and the appointment of Alfred Willis to the bishopric of Honolulu in 1872 could do little to reverse the collapse.[47]

With the exception of the quiet work of the deeply unworldly J. C. Patteson in Melanesia, High Church experiments overseas seemed to deliver little but failure, especially when compared to more successful Anglo-Catholic English slum settlement work. And while advanced Anglo-Catholics relished confrontation, more moderate High Churchmen, the bishops, and the SPG did not. These episodes undoubtedly contributed to the cooling of enthusiasm and a critical reassessment of missions being developed along lines influenced by Anglo-Catholicism. The lessons of the Central African mission in particular were important, leading to a distancing of missionary practice from "worldly" collaborations with commerce, "civilization," and Western culture. As Andrew Porter has pointed out, the Anglo-Catholic mission pattern was distinctive. Rejecting the voluntary society, the bishop in the field (although frequently

45. Thomas Nettleship Staley, *A Pastoral Address, by the Right Reverend the Bishop of Honolulu* (Honolulu: Hawaiian Gazette Office, 1865), 31, 61; *Occasional Paper of the Hawaiian Church Mission (Sandwich Islands)* (London: Rivingtons, 1865), 29-32, 56.

46. George S. Kanahele, *Emma: Hawai'i's Remarkable Queen: A Biography* (Honolulu, HI: Queen Emma Foundation, 1999), 240-41.

47. George Mason, letter to the editor, 24 Nov. 1870, *The Net Cast in Many Waters* 6, no. 1 (Jan. 1870): 15-16; Mildred E. Staley, *A Tapestry of Memories: An Autobiography* (Hilo, HI: Hilo Tribune Herald, 1944), 18-19; Kanahele, *Emma*, 241, 369.

present in the metropole to rally support and recruits) became the focus, aiming to build the church beyond the corrupting influence of irreligious white settlers in self-contained godly communities reliant on an organic community sustained by the Christian ethic.[48] While the disaster of Mackenzie's mission may have stopped dead the enthusiastic expansion of Anglo-Catholic missions, it arguably formed a critical moment of reinforcement for a counter ethic of Anglo-Catholic independency and an increasing suspicion of SPG comprehensiveness. In some ways this was a development appropriate to Livingstone's own positive vision for an independent, developed African civilization, which rested heavily upon his deep, appreciative assessment of African potential.[49] But in the shorter term, Anglo-Catholics primarily directed their attention to parochial missions in English inner-city slums, checking the expansion of High Church foreign missions that had been so evident at the SPG through the 1840s and 1850s. In comparison to setbacks overseas, the Twelve Days' Mission to London (1869), which utilized the pre-existing parish structure, Anglo-Catholic priests, and populations already acculturated to Church-oriented forms of religious practice, was comparatively an enormous success for the Anglo-Catholic pattern of mission.[50]

The UMCA remained the highest profile Anglo-Catholic mission, and as it developed under Bishop Tozer it distanced itself rapidly both from the westernizing model and from mainstream High Church missionary attitudes. Tozer rejected the notion that Christianity relied on Western culture or required any comprehensive assault on indigenous customs, and he criticized the overwhelming domination of the overseas church and episcopate by those "English either by birth or extraction." Writing in 1869 to the Brotherhood of the Holy Trinity, Oxford, he pled for missionary recruits. Arguing that "civilization" was defined by humanistic communal morality, not technology, Tozer stated that "[n]othing can be so false as to suppose that the outward circumstance of a people is the measure either of its barbarism, or its civilization. The chief ornaments of the Apostolic Church would certainly be considered uncivilized at the present. . . . [The Church] has no commission to bring all nations to any other uniformity than that of the faith."[51] Combined with his Ritualism, however, such beliefs and behaviors drew scorn akin to that showered upon Bishop Staley. Explorer Henry Morton Stanley, for example, declared that "[t]he Bishop in his crimson robe, and with his sacerdotal title 'Missionary Bishop of

---

48. Porter, *Religion Versus Empire*, 227.

49. Ross, *Livingstone*, 241-44.

50. Kent, *Holding the Fort*, 258-71.

51. Gertrude Ward, ed., *Letters of Bishop Tozer and His Sister Together with Some Other Records of the Universities' Mission from 1863-1873* (London: UMCA, 1902), 187, 191.

Central Africa' . . . in the queerest of all head-dresses . . . is the most ridiculous sight I have seen anywhere outside of a clown show. I as a white man protest against the absurdity."[52]

Despite such criticism, the trends established at the UMCA were reinforced under Bishop Edward Steere (1874-82), who, in pressing aggressively for the ordination of indigenous Christians, envisioned the Church as independent of state (and empire), as developing in the purity of early apostolic forms and pre-Reformation organization (such as the use of celibate orders for men and women), as separate from modern civilization and all its corruptions, and as an appropriate substitute to modernizing missionary models.[53] By the mid-1870s the UMCA had reinforced its identity as an Anglo-Catholic stronghold, emphasizing cultural assimilation, an indigenized missionary economy, and the creation of an organically spiritual Church community. Known for the simplicity and self-sacrifice of its missionary brethren, it resisted the original intention of its organizers and refused to transfer its work to the SPG.[54] It was upon an alternative model — not that of "Christianity and civilization," which had characterized the rhetoric of early supporters like Samuel Wilberforce — that the UMCA subsequently developed itself, recruited, and raised money. Steere, for example, emphasized that missionaries have "no right to go with arms in . . . hand," should hold no land, and should form "a Church," not "a statelet," while observing and honoring African law and governments, which were in essential principles, he argued, identical to those of Europeans.[55] Developing a strategy that sought to retain only the essentials of the Christian faith while building indigenized mission communities around Christian families and the Church, the Anglo-Catholic ideal drew on a romantic medievalism prevalent among admirers of the Oxford Movement, and this in turn made Anglo-Catholics more sympathetic to "primitive" forms of culture. Anglo-Catholic historicism was important to this orientation, focusing as it did on the processes by which a purer apostolic church was imagined to have spread in its first several centuries through missions to "primitives" past, namely the Germanic Anglo-Saxon "barbarians" of ancient Europe.

52. Henry Morton Stanley, *How I Found Livingstone: Travels, Adventures, and Discoveries in Central Africa* (London: Sampson Low, Marston, Low, and Searle, 1872), 19-20.

53. Steere as an undergraduate was deeply attracted to the romance of the ancient church, and he founded a short-lived Anglican brotherhood in a ruined chapel near Tamworth. Reed, *Glorious Battle*, 55.

54. Richard Symonds, *Oxford and Empire — the Last Lost Cause?* (Oxford: Clarendon Press, 1986), 209-10. The amalgamation of the SPG and UMCA only occurred in 1965.

55. R. M. Heanley, *A Memoir of Edward Steere, D.D., LL.D.: Third Missionary Bishop in Central Africa* (London: Bell, 1888), 326-29.

Theory and organization revolving around the authority of the bishop was central to an emerging Anglo-Catholic missionary strategy. Unequivocal episcopal support for the movement, however, rested almost entirely among Scottish, American, colonial, and missionary bishops. As Scots had a disproportionate impact in British colonial emigration and imperial service, so too they disproportionately served as clergy overseas, and in the British Isles they helped to drive the movement forward.[56] This led Evangelical opponents to complain that without accountability to Parliament or to any English parish, Anglo-Catholic bishops with un-English associations aggressively supported ceremonial Ritualism. And supporters of some of the most radical formulations of Anglo-Catholicism did exist within the episcopacy, as the membership by 1868 of the bishops of Honolulu, Nassau, and Dunedin in the advanced Ritualist organization, the Society of the Holy Cross, demonstrates.[57]

But the developing commitment to missionary bishops was not simply attractive to advanced Anglo-Catholics. For High Churchmen of all persuasions, missionary bishops could be seen as reinforcing the traditional ideal of the ordered Church as advocated by the Anglican divines of the seventeenth and eighteenth centuries. Increasingly, appreciation for the apparent sacrifices of missionary bishops was normalized as a powerful example of reverence for the visible church. This recognition demanded, in the words of Bishop Christopher Wordsworth, reassessment of "principles and practice" in the mission field, where a broad view of the Church overcame "narrow prejudices" with "masculine vigor . . . and sober logic . . . exempt from the influence of sudden gusts of impulse, and passionate excitements of fanatical enthusiasm."[58] The linkage of missions and commerce, as advocated by Bishop Wilberforce and David Livingstone alike, was problematized in the following decades, as Anglo-Catholics argued that only under a significant transformation in the morality of English international conduct could the Church expect blessings and advancement.[59] However, advanced Anglo-Catholics also provided a path forward by which High Churchmen could reaffirm the Church's traditional mission of purifying human society and institutions, not by what was understood as emotional

56. Kevin Ward, *A History of Global Anglicanism* (Cambridge: Cambridge University Press, 2006), 31.

57. Reed, *Glorious Battle,* 147. The bishops were T. N. Staley (Honolulu, 1861-70), Addington Venables (1863-76, Nassau, Bahamas), and Henry Lacellus Jenner (Dunedin, New Zealand, consecrated but not enthroned due to evangelical opposition culminating in rejection by the local Diocesan Synod).

58. Christopher Wordsworth, "Introduction," in *Edward Steere: Notes of Sermons,* ed. R. M. Heanley (London: Bell, 1884), viii-x.

59. Porter, "Commerce and Christianity," 597, 617-20.

radicalism but rather by advancing sober and refined behavior as definitive to traditional Church extension.

Thus, despite the setback of the Mackenzie imbroglio, the missionary (and colonial) bishop remained the cornerstone of overseas Church extension among High Churchmen. The position was advocated continuously throughout the 1860s by the supporters of Mackenzie's African mission. This was true even when retrenchment was led by his successor Bishop Tozer, and it was extended in the 1870s under the inspiration created by the martyrdom of Mackenzie's brother missionary bishop, John Coleridge Patteson, missionary chaplain in Melanesia to Bishop Selwyn from 1856 and consecrated in Auckland as bishop of Melanesia in 1861. Patteson carried on Selwyn's Melanesian mission (founded 1849), which took as its core strategy the creation of an indigenous Melanesian ministry that would produce a self-extending church. To achieve this end in the island environment, Selwyn created a boarding school model in which boys (and later girls) were transported by mission ship to a central school for a portion of the year, educated in Melanesian languages, and returned home to teach in their communities.[60]

From the start Selwyn instructed Patteson that the Melanesian Mission was to operate on new lines. Rather than being subject to pressures from contributors who "want to see their money's worth in the shape of rapid conversion, speedy results, &c.," which forced missionaries to "minister to this mistaken craving for some hasty fulfilment of a no less hastily conceived wish," a mission that was run under the direction of a bishop would be "freed from the temptation to act incompetently and prematurely."[61] Envisioning themselves as educated professionals immune from the unrealistic expectations created by evangelicalism, Selwyn, Patteson, and other progressive High Church missionaries believed that a solid foundation for indigenous Christianity could be built under the guidance of a reverent, transcultural, historically malleable church. Selwyn was driven by a desire "to try what the actual system of the Church of England can do, when disencumbered of its earthly load of seats in Parliament, Erastian compromises, corruption of patronage, confusion of orders, synodless bishops, and an unorganized clergy."[62] Drawing on the work of sixteenth- through eighteenth-century Anglican divines such as Richard Hooker and Joseph Butler, Selwyn and Patteson emphasized the authority of the Church, led by its inspired bishops, to translate the substance of Scripture through changing practice appropriate to successive generations.

60. Sara H. Sohmer, "Christianity Without Civilization: Anglican Sources for an Alternative Nineteenth-Century Mission Methodology," *Journal of Religious History* 18, no. 2 (1994): 176.
61. J. C. Patteson to C. M. Yonge, 27 Apr. 1864, quoted in Yonge, *Patteson*, 2:93.
62. H. W. Tucker, *Memoir of the Life and Episcopate of George Augustus Selwyn* (New York: Pott, Young, 1879), 200.

In the Melanesian mission, then, strategy rested on Hooker's developmental view of morality and insisted on Melanesian culture as the foundation for Christianization and Church growth.[63] Rather than seeing potential converts as shackled in sin, the Melanesian missionaries emphasized their potential for rational moral development, sowing seeds for the later spread of an influential "fulfilment" theology. This was a theology that flowed through the Christian Socialism of F. D. Maurice, one inspiration for Anglo-Catholic inner-city slum missions. Maurice also advocated for a missionary outreach to "the heathen," whom he understood in broad terms as "partakers of the self-same Spirit" as Christians. This was a set of ideas further developed in the missionary thinking of B. F. Westcott, with significant impact in Higher Church and university missionary circles.[64]

It was in this spirit that the earlier Anglo-Catholic mission of the "Hawaiian Reformed Catholic Church" of T. N. Staley had explicitly challenged the "Puritan" evangelicalism of American Congregationalists and its uncompromising condemnation of "savage" Hawaiian culture in its totality. Rather than having raised the fundamental morality of Hawaiians, and thus their core aptitude for indigenized forms of civilized behavior, Puritanism had fetishized the superficial proclamation of the Bible, resulting in "a fearful amount of unreality and hypocrisy." Destructive strictures on traditional cultural expression were unsuited not only to Hawai'i and its "laughing children of the sun" but also to any modern civilization where "the old Puritan principle, if carried out, would put an end to the athletic pursuits and recreations of every Christian country in Europe." Ultimately, Staley and other Anglo-Catholics argued, "[i]t is not needful to denationalize a country in order to Christianize it," for it was the function of Christianity "to leaven and hallow all the instincts of our nature not to crush them." This prescription applied equally to England, where traditional sports and healthy community entertainments were to be encouraged among the working classes. It also applied to places like Hawai'i, where "old manly exercises, wrestling, running, throwing the spear, sliding on boards down deep descents, surf-riding, etc." were vehicles for, rather than obstacles to, the spread of a Christianity influenced by a deepening public school ethos of "playing the game."[65]

Significantly, then, Anglo-Catholics developed a missionary theory dedicated

63. Sohmer, "Christianity Without Civilization," 182-85.

64. F. D. Maurice, *The Religions of the World and Their Relations to Christianity*, 6th ed. (London: Macmillan, 1886), 199, 246-50. On the comparative religious and missionary theology of Maurice and Westcott, see Kenneth Cracknell, *Justice, Courtesy and Love: Theologians and Missionaries Encountering World Religions, 1846-1914* (London: Epworth, 1995), 35-71.

65. Staley, *A Pastoral Address*, 13-14, 40-41.

explicitly to the idea of the spiritual equality of the races that inhabited the social empire and the classes that made up nation which assumed a common human intellectual, moral, and religious potential. In this it mirrored core evangelical assumptions, but in contrast it rested on a professed respect for local traditions. This respect was seen as valuable, not least because it highlighted "the unlovely austerities of Congregational Puritanism" that were imagined to make Anglo-Catholicism comparatively attractive to common people at home and abroad.[66] Thus, parallel to Anglo-Catholic vision in English slum missions, innovating High Church missionaries who sympathized with Tractarianism, such as J. C. Patteson, followed Bishop Selwyn in insisting on narrowing the cultural gap between missionary and proselyte through shared observance of religious ritual and Christianized communal activities. Through understanding, sympathy, and evolutionary transformation, rather than through a "civilizing" replacement of indigenous society akin to instantaneous conversion, common humanity would be cultivated through the religious "capacity latent in every man, because he *is a man,* and not a fallen angel nor a brute beast." Patteson toured Australian colonial society, standing self-consciously, in his own words, "as the apologist of the despised Australian black, and the Chinese gold-digger, and the Melanesian islander" as spiritual and intellectual equals whose own forms of culture provided the natural and appropriate vehicles for Christianization.[67]

Standing as defenders of indigenous peoples against settler depredations was nothing new to the missionary self-construction of position in the South Seas, as LMS missionaries demonstrated in the 1820s.[68] But the progressive High Church attitude to indigenous culture was new. As Patteson made clear, and as Tractarian-influenced High Church missionaries in the Pacific emphasized, there was no inherent moral superiority in European peoples or cultures. "It is strange to be living so peacefully among nations accounted savage and fighting each other," Patteson wrote to his sister, "while you highly educated and civilized individuals act your barbarism on a more exalted scale. . . . It is very savage indeed to spear 3 or 4 men, but exceedingly valiant to leave about 3,000 dead on a field slain by the Enfield rifle. . . . What scene in Melanesia ever exceeded the horrors of the sack of a town by British troops."[69]

Much of Patteson's attitude grew from his and Selwyn's experience of the Maori wars in New Zealand in 1859 and 1860. Observing violent settler and colonial government responses to Maori land claims solidified Patteson's sense

66. Staley, *A Pastoral Address*, 14.
67. Yonge, *Patteson*, 2:89.
68. Twells, *Civilising Mission*, 192-98.
69. J. C. Patteson to his sister, 27 Aug. 1859, quoted in Sohmer, "Christianity Without Civilization," 187.

that the "intolerable Pride of Race & covetousness of the white man" required some means of atoning for imperial excesses in Africa, India, and other areas.[70] While the missionary encounter in Melanesia did not proceed smoothly according to any single set of blueprints, and while Anglicans in Melanesia fairly ineffectively faced the challenge of transferring control to indigenous Christians, Patteson's vision was an extension of more general Tractarian and Anglo-Catholic attitudes that had a lasting influence not only in the Melanesian mission but also in other areas of Anglican missionary expansion, such as Papua New Guinea. Although all South Pacific missionaries shared the Pauline scriptural emphasis on "one blood," articulated in Acts 17:26, and thus an ultimate commitment to human unity, the High Churchmen of the Melanesian mission focused less than Nonconformists on "the curse of Ham," under which darker-skinned humans supposedly labored, and viewed the culture and potential of islanders far more generously.[71] By insisting on the common cultural boundedness of human experience, activist High Church missionaries thus contested white settler discourses that regularly emphasized the defining and defeating power of indigenous "heathen" depravity.[72]

Patteson was murdered by inhabitants of Nukapu island in September 1871, in revenge, it was widely and repeatedly reported by missionary sources, for deadly raids conducted by unscrupulous labor recruiters who were supplying the Queensland and Fiji sugar plantations. The story of his "selfless sacrifice" raised him into the panoply of late Victorian Christian martyrs; Patteson became the rallying image around which support for High Church missions was built.[73] In two particular ways, Patteson's death changed the debate surrounding High Church missions. It neutralized the negative commentary and soul-searching that had surrounded Mackenzie's failed Zambezi mission. And it

70. Quoted in John Garrett, *To Live Among the Stars: Christian Origins in Oceania* (Geneva: World Council of Churches, 1982), 184.

71. Jane Samson, "Ethnology and Theology: Nineteenth-Century Mission Dilemmas in the South Pacific," in *Christian Missions and the Enlightenment,* ed. Brian Stanley (Grand Rapids: Eerdmans, 2001), 113-16.

72. On Patteson's missionary strategy, see Darrell Whiteman, *Melanesians and Missionaries: An Ethnohistorical Study of Social and Religious Change in the Southwest Pacific* (Pasadena, CA: William Carey Library, 1983), 116-25, 144-50; on the expansion of these ideals into a set Anglo-Catholic pattern of mission in Papua New Guinea, see David Wetherell, *Reluctant Mission: The Anglican Church in Papua New Guinea* (St. Lucia: University of Queensland Press, 1978), 46-48, 122-31.

73. See for example, Edwin Palmer, *Bishop Patteson, Missionary Bishop and Martyr* (London: Christian Knowledge Society, n.d., ca. 1872); H.A.S. [pseud.], *A Martyr-Bishop of Our Own Day* (London: Wells Gardner, 1881); Elizabeth Charles, *Three Martyrs of the Nineteenth Century: Studies from the Lives of Livingstone, Gordon, and Patteson* (London: SPCK, 1885); Jesse Page, *Bishop Patteson: The Martyr of Melanesia* (London: Partridge, n.d., ca. 1888).

**Commemorative engraving of Bishop John Coleridge Patteson, with Bible
and war canoe, following his murder by the inhabitants of Nukapu island
(Solomon Islands), 1871.** Lithograph by Gibbs, Shallard & Co., Sydney.
National Library of Australia, PIC S4463 LOC 7835.

provided a counterexample to the deeply controversial actions of interventionist missionaries, such as the LMS's J. G. Paton, whose active participation in the shelling by the Royal Navy of the island of Tanna, in retribution for murders of British subjects and destruction of mission property, had brought both censure and enthusiastic support in Australia for such blatant complicity with imperial power.[74] Here was an illustration of gentle, self-denying, tolerant missionary temperament that helped justify missions, the moral exercise of empire, and Christian internationalism within the wide and influential circles of the public school and Oxbridge connection. Patteson's death was ably converted for the consumption of a hero-worshipping public by his cousin, the extremely successful Anglo-Catholic novelist and children's author Charlotte Yonge, and as such it served as a new inspiration in progressive Anglican circles of all types for support of foreign missions and colonial Church extension.[75]

Yonge and other Anglo-Catholic writers on missions began shifting public perceptions of missionary work through a literary construction of the "gentleman missionary," helping to transform positively the profile of missionary work among the upper-middle and professional classes sustained by university networks. This was a project that had begun with the founding of the UMCA. For example, from the beginning the popular representation of High Church missions pioneered by Anne Mackenzie in the 1860s emphasized the need to establish a deeper and more sophisticated understanding of the history, culture, and social realities of mission fields in order for mission to be effective. In the opening number of her missionary magazine *The Net Cast in Many Waters,* for example, Mackenzie suggested that oversimplified, decontextualized extracts of mission work that appeared in many publications had led to misunderstanding. The real need, she wrote, was for supporters to understand "the manners and customs of the people, the nature of the country, &c."[76] This approach had a twofold appeal: it resonated more fully with a university-based clerical culture that was increasingly influenced by the detailed critical methods employed in biblical and orientalist scholarship, and it also served to differentiate Anglo-Catholic missions from the presumed simplistic crudity of evangelical proselytizing, which paralleled Anglo-Catholic claims regarding the shortcomings of evangelical theology and evangelical social practice toward the poor in England.

74. Garrett, *To Live Among the Stars,* 176-78.

75. Charlotte M. Yonge, *In Memoriam: Bishop Patteson* (London: Skeffington, 1872). The proceeds of Yonge's most successful novel, *The Heir of Redclyffe* (1853), went to fund Selwyn's mission ship the *Southern Cross,* £2000 from the influential *The Daisy Chain* (1856) went to building Selwyn's St. Andrew's College, Kohimarama, and the profits of the novel *The Ground* (1868) were dedicated to the "Mackenzie Mission" to Zululand established by Anne Mackenzie.

76. *The Net* 1, no. 1 (Jan. 1866): 1-2.

While Anglo-Catholic missions never matched the volume of support achieved by Evangelical missions, their fundamental claim to represent a more scholarly, more thorough, and ultimately a more culturally liberal vision of missionary work had a powerful leavening influence in the movement. For new constituencies of support, missions could be represented as more than senseless action by enthusiasts or attempts to buttress racial hierarchies by the privileged. Instead, missions could be represented as a response to colonial social evils of a nature that was also attracting parallel attention in Britain through inner-city slum settlements, whether influenced by high Anglo-Catholic piety, broad Christian Socialist concern, or a mixture of both.[77]

The saccharine furor that surrounded Patteson's death had significant outcomes for the Anglican missionary cause. High Church people had a hero — Patteson was an intimate and follower of Pusey and Keble — and the SPG now championed the mission cause with its proposal for a "Day of Intercession for Foreign Missions," which was designed to bring the cause prominently before every Anglican congregation in the British Isles, high, low, and broad alike. Anglo-Catholic missions thus came to be associated with a progressive imperial vision focused on defending indigenous interests. In Jane Samson's phrase, it was an extension of "imperial benevolence." In combination with political pressure exerted by the LMS and other influences, it resulted in a series of imperial actions that changed the face of the Western Pacific: the passage of the Pacific Islanders' Protection Act (1872 and 1875) and the annexation of Fiji (1873-74).[78] High Church missions seemed to be coming of age. And despite their frequent linkage in England with the work of moralizing empire, they were doing so in a Pacific environment that had incubated the development of an independent Anglican ideal of expansion beyond empire.

University Historicism and Elite High Church Missionary Strategy

The glow of the bishop of Melanesia's martyrdom fired interest in a growing range of Churchmen, some enthusiastically Anglo-Catholic, some leaning toward more orthodox High Churchism, some strongly influenced by Broad

77. Yonge, *Patteson*, 1:404-5; 2:92-93. Yonge, a Wantage sister (Community of St. Mary the Virgin) and protégé of Keble, was one of the most active supporters of Anglo-Catholic missions and defenders of Tractarianism.

78. Samson, *Imperial Benevolence*, 124-29, 158-59, 166-69. Notably, at the center of much of the activity in England was Bishop Selwyn, formerly of New Zealand, but translated to become bishop of Lichfield in 1868, who championed the passage of the Pacific Islander Protection Act in the House of Lords.

Church historicism. Virtually all were motivated in some measure by the budding Christian Socialism of F. D. Maurice and Charles Kingsley as it was put into practice in English urban slum work by Churchmen across the theological spectrum and strongly supported by Oxford-based Anglo-Catholics.[79] In the universities controversies generated by theological modernism — stimulated by historical and critical reading of scripture as featured in the controversial *Essays and Reviews* (1860) as well as the stridency of high-profile public advocacy for Darwinian evolution — stirred Anglican thinking. In missionary circles the controversy was notably tied to the contest from 1863 onward in the African church between Bishop Colenso of Natal, who espoused a liberal concern to make the gospel intelligible to the Zulu, and Bishop Gray of Cape Town, who determined on Tractarian foundations to root out what he saw as Colenso's heresy in renouncing the literal interpretation and authority of scripture.[80] As challenges to the faith and authority of the Church proceeded, so too did enhanced interest in the history and interpretation of the Church as an ancient, comprehensive foundation of accumulated wisdom and practice.

In this environment the universities became crucibles where interest in antiquity, both of the church and of other world religions, became avenues along which to respond to perceived burgeoning social and imperial challenges to the Church's legitimacy and effectiveness. Particularly within the clerical, university-oriented culture in which emerging Anglo-Catholicism flourished, pietistic religious practice melded with new thinking and creative, responsive attempts to formulate defensible positions vis-à-vis modern thought and modern social and imperial realities. These issues were of deep interest not only in England but also among reforming High Church missionaries in the field.[81] Connecting the new attention to antiquity and biblical and orientalist scholarship with a commitment to Anglican missions was a particular concern of another university figure, Brooke Foss Westcott, who presented a deeply pietistic and even mystical — but also scholarly — alternative to the fervent, combative pietisms of both advanced Anglo-Catholics and revivalistic

79. One central source for this interest was the new Keble College (1870) endowed and opened following John Keble's death in 1866. On the urban settlement work pursued by Anglo-Catholics through Oxford House (founded 1884) in London's East End, see Seth Koven, *Slumming: Sexual and Social Politics in Victorian London* (Princeton: Princeton University Press, 2004), chap. 5.

80. Chadwick, *Victorian Church: Part Two: 1860-1901*, 90-97. On Colenso's missionary practice as an extension of F. D. Maurice's Broad Church theology, see Gerald Parsons, "Rethinking the Missionary Position: Bishop Colenso of Natal," in *Culture and Empire*, ed. John Wolffe, vol. 5 of *Religion in Victorian Britain* (Manchester: Manchester University Press, 1997), 139-58.

81. This is evident, for example, in the letters and reading of J. C. Patteson in the Melanesian mission. See Yonge, *Patteson*, 2:20-21, 51-53, 74-75, 116-18 and passim.

Evangelicals.[82] Fully connected into the public school and university world, Westcott was first and foremost a biblical scholar who, with J. B. Lightfoot and F. J. A. Hort, revolutionized English-language biblical criticism. The three produced careful, precise, yet ultimately orthodox commentaries (launched in the 1860s in response to *Essays and Reviews*) and a critical edition of the New Testament in Greek, the foundation for the Revised Standard version of the Bible.[83] Less well recognized, however, are Westcott's deep and abiding interest in foreign missions and his critical role in the establishment of university-based brotherhoods as a variant method in the High Church missionary tradition. His role as historian and advocate of the "Alexandrian school" of the ancient church as a model for missions was significant and formed a major part of the inspiration for the Oxford and Cambridge Brotherhoods to India.[84] His influence also spread through close friendship with E. W. Benson, the archbishop of Canterbury (1884-96), whose interest in missionary matters and the historical, continuing relationship of Anglicanism to the Eastern Churches significantly exceeded that of his predecessors.[85]

Westcott's interests in biblical criticism, the ancient church, and foreign missions developed in the context of the critical debates between theological modernists such as Benjamin Jowett and the *Essays and Reviews* authors and both High Church and Evangelical critics determined to defend orthodoxy by returning to the ideally imagined purity of the primitive church and its missions. The Anglo-Catholic missionary ideal did not die with Bishop Mackenzie in Africa, but not until Bishop Patteson's high-profile martyrdom was the ideal, nurtured in the close circles surrounding supporters such as Mackenzie's sister Anne and the novelist Charlotte Yonge, reanimated as an attractive means of spreading Christianity. In High Church circles the 1870s saw the emergence of interest in new strategies modeled in the early church as a way forward for Anglican missions. Two such strategies were notable. One was the initiation of missions by brotherhoods. The first stable modern Anglican brotherhood was the Society of St. John the Evangelist (known colloquially as the Cowley Fathers), which was founded in 1866 by Father R. M. Benson and sent brothers to India as early as 1874. The other was the creation of explicitly missionary

82. On the mixed theology and party associations of the "Cambridge triumvirate" of Westcott, J. B. Lightfoot, F. J. A. Hort, as well as their friend (and future archbishop) E. W. Benson, see Hinchliff, *God and History*, 77-81.

83. Stephen Neill, *The Interpretation of the New Testament, 1861-1961* (London: Oxford University Press, 1964), 33-58, 69-75, 95-102.

84. Cox, "Independent English Women," 166-67.

85. J. F. Coakley, *The Church of the East and the Church of England: A History of the Archbishop of Canterbury's Assyrian Mission* (Oxford: Clarendon Press, 1992), 98-99.

brotherhoods, or "community missions," that were launched with the founding of the Cambridge Mission to Delhi (1877) by Edward Bickersteth (1850-97) and B. F. Westcott.[86] Bickersteth, a member of one of the most prominent evangelical Anglican families, was the son of influential CMS Committee member Edward H. Bickersteth of Hampstead (later bishop of Exeter) and grandson of Edward Bickersteth, one of the first CMS secretaries. But as a student he had come under the sway of the broader and higher Church views of Westcott and the ecumenical evangelicalism of Thomas Valpy French (founder of St. John's College, Agra, and bishop of Lahore, 1877-83). He proposed forming a "Cambridge Brotherhood," which while it would not insist on vows, would compel celibacy. This requirement, however, smacked too heavily of the feared trend toward Romanist influence and was thus unacceptable to many CMS supporters.[87] Instead the Cambridge Mission to Delhi, although exhorted by French to sympathize as fully as possible with CMS missionaries (who were not as narrow-minded in practice as their publications might suggest), proceeded with Westcott as its chairman, supported by Lightfoot and Hort, and sponsored, but not controlled, by the SPG.[88] It represented a missionary and imperial expression of High Church Anglican engagement with modernism and the university, designed to turn critical scholarship and Anglican idealism to the service of Christian extension.

At the heart of the Cambridge Mission to Delhi were several ideas and assumptions: that the university had a special call and ability to minister to the educated classes of "oriental" India; that in India both Anglicans and Hindus might profit from the exchange of cultural influence; that the incarnational emphasis on Christ's lived life would allow deep sympathy and collaboration with Indian subjects. These were all ideas drawn from High Church theology and scholarship on the early church, but they shared a Liberal Anglican insistence on the universality of human moral nature and a vision of ultimate human unity that transcended nationality.[89] Westcott, like Bishop Patteson and

86. W. T. Bullock to E. Hill, 31 Oct. 1876, Cambridge Mission to Delhi Archives, CMD 91, Bodleian Library of Commonwealth and African History, Rhodes House, Oxford (hereafter cited as CMD Archives); Gibbs, *Anglican Church in India*, 297-98.

87. In the event, negotiations with the CMS broke down over Westcott, Lightfoot, and other Cambridge leaders' insistence that a Cambridge Committee choose the members of the brotherhood. The CMS, resolute on complete control over the selection and posting of its missionaries, refused. Stock, *History of the CMS*, 3:151-52.

88. Thomas Valpy French, *The Proposed Cambridge University Mission in North India* (Private circulation, 1876), 14-17. SPG Secretary W. T. Bullock convinced Bickersteth, despite his "thirst for novelty" and independence, that attachment to "one of the great societies" was logistically wise. W. T. Bullock to E. Hill, 15 March 1876, CMD 91, CMD Archives.

89. On Liberal Anglican attitudes, see Mandler, "Race and Nation," 228.

exponents of the progressive High Church missionary impulse, believed that the early church — particularly the work of the church fathers in Alexandria in Hellenizing early Judaic Christianity — was a critically important model in envisioning missionary work and a missionary future beyond empire.[90] Westcott based his advocacy of foreign missions in his scholarly interests in the early church, thus reinforcing the emphases of the earlier pioneering missionary bishops and advancing the mission cause among High Churchmen who could imagine a re-creation of the successes of the early church as the destiny of the developing High Church ideal.

The basis of this vision was "a missionary-oriented ecclesiastical orientalism" in which, as in the early church with regard to the Greeks and Jews of the classical world, Hindus and Muslims would be engaged on their own ground with the goal of creating a new Christian synthesis from which missionary success and Anglican evolution would emerge.[91] While this appeal was profoundly orientalist and historicist, based in substantial ignorance of contemporary Hinduism and Indian society, it had a powerful appeal to those inclining toward a High Church position. Westcott inspired the Cambridge Mission to Delhi and restated the importance of missionary activity to the health of the Church of England, which was endorsed by Westcott's friend and academic collaborator J. B. Lightfoot, bishop of Durham from 1879. This vision led the Cambridge Brothers, and later the priests staffing the Oxford Mission to Calcutta — founded by Marsham Argles and Westcott's adoring student, as well as later influential Anglo-Catholic modernist, Charles Gore — to theorize that a mission of deeply educated ascetics could break through the veils of misunderstanding and reclaim the unity of Christianity, Islam, and Hinduism, conceived of as historically intertwined "Oriental religions."[92] While the Oxford Mission to Calcutta — also inspired by the Cowley Fathers and closely associated with the high, Anglo-Catholic leaning Cuddesdon College[93] — had a deeper Anglo-Catholic ecclesiology than the Cambridge Brotherhood, ulti-

90. Patteson to C. M. Yonge, n.d. [1865], quoted in Yonge, *Patteson*, 2:150-51; Westcott, *Religious Office*, chap. 2.

91. Jeffrey Cox, "George Alfred Lefroy 1854-1919: A Bishop in Search of a Church," in *After the Victorians: Private Conscience and Public Duty in Modern Britain; Essays in Memory of John Clive*, ed. Susan Pedersen and Peter Mandler (London: Routledge, 1994), 59-60.

92. Martin Maw, *Visions of India: Fulfilment Theology, the Aryan Race Theory and the Work of British Protestant Missionaries in Victorian India* (Frankfurt am Main: Lang, 1990), 142.

93. George Longridge and W. H. Hutton, *A History of the Oxford Mission to Calcutta*, 2nd ed. (London: Mowbray, 1910), 1-4, 12. Of the twenty-seven priests who staffed the Oxford Mission prior to 1904, ten were Cuddesdon graduates, as were several priests with the UMCA and Anglo-Catholic dioceses throughout the world. *Cuddesdon College, 1854-1904; a Record and Memorial* (London: Longmans, Green, 1904), 82-90.

mately both were influenced by a Cambridge Platonism that was traceable back to Samuel Taylor Coleridge. In connection with the deep faith and the impulses of Anglo-Catholicism, this created a synthetic mixture of liberal theology and orthodox faith convinced of the essential unity of universal truths. In this vein Bickersteth pursued the self-sacrifice emphasized in his evangelical heritage in a new formulation. He conceived a brotherhood without vows, but bound by friendship and devotion, as a means to funnel overseas the activist piety of Oxbridge undergraduates socialized into the public school ideal of dutiful masculine common action.[94]

By the late 1870s, then, a distinctive High Church foreign missionary culture associated with the universities had begun to emerge. This culture was tied to missionary brotherhoods that sprang up in Africa, India, and the South Seas, allied with the SPG and its emphasis on developing distinctively Anglican missions. It drew much of its energy from continuing the self-conscious High Church response to what was seen as Evangelical shallowness, arrogance, and ill-considered activity born of the narrowness of lower-middle-class culture.[95] The growing emphasis on the theology of the incarnation was advanced specifically as a counter to what was argued to be a dangerously unbalanced evangelical obsession with the atonement. Westcott, Lightfoot, and Hort were important influences in a process whereby, as Boyd Hilton notes, the emphasis on human agency in ameliorating the sins of the world, in emulation of Christ's earthly life, began to erode the overwhelming early Victorian emphasis on the atonement with its zero-sum logic of salvation and damnation. These ideas had far-reaching effects as habits of mind with regard to economic and social policy.[96] They were also profoundly influential in maintaining within the Church a tradition of liberal-minded trusteeship in the face of increasingly widespread deterministic race theory. As Catherine Hall has suggested, it was just at this point that some Anglicans like Charles Kingsley were turning to profoundly racial understandings of foreign peoples in the wake of the Morant Bay uprising (not to mention continuing self-examination forced by the 1857 rebellion in India). However, the tendency of mid-Victorian thinkers to reject deter-

94. Within a decade Bickersteth was consecrated bishop of South Tokyo (1886-97). Samuel Bickersteth, *Life and Letters of Edward Bickersteth, Bishop of South Tokyo* (London: Sampson Low, Marston, 1899), 26-39. The Mission to Chota Nagpur, supported by Trinity College, Dublin, was another emergent university brotherhood.

95. This condescending attitude toward evangelical cultural deficiency characterized the higher church spectrum from Ritualist controversialists such as R. F. Littledale to progressive High Church bishops like J. C. Patteson. Littledale, "Ritualism," 32-33; Yonge, *Patteson,* 1:404-5. See also Westcott, *Religious Office,* 38-39.

96. Hilton, *Age of Atonement,* 292-96.

ministic race consciousness and instead focus on a "civilizational approach" to understanding difference, which Peter Mandler has emphasized, remained strongly in force, buttressed now by influential strains of Anglo-Catholicism and modernism growing in university culture.[97] This environmental approach to cultural difference continued to be widely insisted upon within the generally robust and extensive missionary culture of the mid-Victorian era, which demonstrated a resilient commitment to older forms of Christian universalism and environmental explanations for human behavior, even in the face of emerging theories positing essentialist racial difference.[98] In Anglican circles incarnationalist theology was one expression of this, undoubtedly most peculiarly evident among Anglican Christian Socialists and modernists with their growing insistence on universal brotherhood as the basis of society, but also influencing High Churchmen to varying degrees as they pursued their program of developing the corporate church as an expression of faith.[99]

Incarnationalism was even more important in the larger missionary movement, however, through the indirect impact it had on the changing atmosphere in which evangelical revivalism developed. These transformations had a subtle, long-term impact on Evangelicals who confronted the results of spreading incarnational theology in the parishes and in the universities.[100] As evangelical revivalism developed in this era, Anglican evangelical missionary theology, while never abandoning justification by faith, came to highlight more willingly the life of sanctification that followed conversion. In the pattern of High Church missions, it shifted from a predominant emphasis on preaching and conversion (already under growing criticism as mass conversion failed to materialize in so many mission fields) to the strategies of the socially reforming ministry: education, medicine, and training delivered through established institutions. At the same time, even though strongly Anglo-Catholic missions expressed real suspicion of individualist models of westernization (preferring collectivist visions of an organic church), the Westcottian model also had the power to construct empire as sacred — to imagine it a consecrated vehicle for the incar-

97. Hall, *Civilising Subjects*, 438-40; Mandler, "Race and Nation," 231-33.

98. Twells, *Civilising Mission*, 13-15, 174-75, 214-15.

99. Alan Wilkinson, *Christian Socialism: Scott Holland to Tony Blair* (London: SCM Press, 1998), 12, 20, 37-39.

100. On the influence of the theology of F. D. Maurice on budding Christian Socialism both among higher church Anglicans and progressive Nonconformists, with suggestions of an impact that spread more broadly through the evangelical connection, see David M. Thompson, "The Christian Socialist Revival in Britain: A Reappraisal," in *Revival and Religion Since 1700: Essays for John Walsh,* ed. John Walsh, Jane Garnett, and H. C. G. Matthew (London: Hambledon, 1993), 273-95.

national power of a socially active Church. The potential of this language, particularly in the universities, was such that Christian Socialists and modernists of High Church predilections as well as moderate Evangelicals were affected by this shifting vision of the active religious life. Even though the theology and experience of radical Evangelicals were significantly different from those in High Church lines of influence, the "higher life" holiness that drove a parallel and larger Evangelical missionary regrowth also embraced a new emphasis on the post-conversion process of becoming more Christ-like. While retaining holiness-oriented evangelical confidence in the transformative powers of gospel preaching in the expectation of the millennium, even the most deeply evangelical of the new missionary agencies were drawn into institution building in the sponsorship of hospitals, schools, and mission houses, as they increasingly accepted that the Christian life should follow examples of service and duty.[101]

Revivalism, "Holiness," and Evangelical Missions

Evangelical missions, in parallel with those supported by High Churchmen, saw a significant impact from the pietism that characterized an age of deep religious challenges and changes. Arguably, however, pietism's influence within evangelical culture was even more profound. Because the CMS was larger than the SPG, supported by more Britons with a deeper commitment to missions, and linked into the pan-evangelical missionary network, its adoption of the spiritual enthusiasm of revivalism and the methods of faith missions proved widely influential. Faith missions grew with the spread of the second evangelical revival, influenced from the late 1850s by Americans such as Dwight L. Moody and Ira D. Sankey who cultivated an impatient desire for large-scale, instantaneous Christian conversion.[102] The missionary analogue to American-style English revivalism was developed in the CIM, founded in 1865 by J. Hudson Taylor, the first of a rapidly expanding number of "faith" missions. By 1899, with over 800 missionaries, the CIM had grown to rival the largest denominational societies and inspired a proliferation of faith missions in the 1880s that sent out, without assured financial support, all willing missionary candidates, female or male. Emphasizing itinerant preaching, the adoption of indigenous dress and language, and an apparent fiscal efficiency (the CIM, while fielding large num-

101. On this process in even the most advanced of the evangelical faith missions, the CIM, see Semple, *Missionary Women*, chap. 5.

102. On the revivalism of Dwight L. Moody, see George M. Marsden, *Fundamentalism and American Culture: The Shaping of Twentieth Century Evangelicalism, 1870-1925* (New York: Oxford University Press, 1980), 32-39.

bers of missionaries, compared poorly in contribution levels with the major societies), faith missions flooded missionary fields with enthusiasts. This example was followed by other revivalistic agencies, most notably the Salvation Army, which from the 1880s often sent lower-class, lay missionaries overseas in comparatively enormous numbers.[103] Because of the large numbers of evangelical Anglicans who supported the CIM and other faith missions, and the challenge that their methods and assumptions represented to the established, bureaucratic missionary societies, these developments ultimately became a phenomenon of critical influence at the CMS.

The revivalistic urge in Protestant Christianity was central to English evangelical missions from their inception and, for most Nonconformist missionaries and their supporters, it continued to be the core source of evangelical missionary enthusiasm through the century. Evangelical Anglicans, however, had always held themselves somewhat aloof from revivalistic populism, seeing their own marks of grace rather in their persecution and marginalization within the Church of England. Revivalism and its relationship to CMS missions began to shift from the 1870s onward, however, under the influence of two factors: growing conflict within the Church over Anglo-Catholicism and associated Ritualistic "aggressions," and imported American revivalist methods that fueled a fevered holiness culture that emphasized the powers of a sanctified life. Revivalism drew on many traditions, including Methodist perfectionism, Quaker spirituality, and the teachings of the United Brethren; like them, revivalists emphasized the transformative potential of the Holy Spirit working through individual religious experience. Nineteenth-century American revivalism of the Second Great Awakening dated from the early 1800s and drew heavily on what developed as Charles Finney's essential idea: that men could organize — through the use of tents, hymns, affecting stories, and exhortations — for successful mass conversion by revivalists, who would "expostulate with sinners with a warmth . . . which cannot be resisted."[104] American revivalism, based on a theology of assurance that grace would descend on any who sincerely offered themselves to Christ, gave birth to the modern professional revivalist.[105]

---

103. By the turn of the century the CIM supported 811 missionaries overseas, and the Salvation Army 2,728, with annual incomes of £53,197 and £26,847, respectively. Dennis, *Centennial Survey*, 22-23. Differences in method, types of missionaries, and terms of service, however, make comparisons problematic. But this did not stop polemical negative comparisons to the established societies made by those committed to faith-based missions.

104. Quoted in William R. Hutchison, *Errand to the World: American Protestant Thought and Foreign Missions* (Chicago: University of Chicago Press, 1987), 67.

105. Revivalism owed much to Finney's 1835 *Lectures on Revivals in Religion* (1839, in En-

Holiness teaching, however, which came to underpin late Victorian revivalism and its impact in the Church of England, focused on the life of sanctification beyond conversion, and in its more advanced forms it asserted that Christians could have a spiritual experience that would elevate them immediately to a sanctified life above the sinful world. This "higher life" teaching had wide currency in CMS circles in the 1870s, and it had obvious missionary potential in the way it envisioned the emergence of a cadre of particularly gifted and saintly Christian workers.[106] Over time more and more of these "higher life" converts saw missionary work as the ultimate, sanctified Christian life, but emotional religion of this particular type was still on the periphery of mainline denominational practice, and practically impotent within Anglicanism in the 1850s. By the 1860s, however, a series of popular conferences and orchestrated revivals channeled "higher life" evangelicalism into conventional devotional life and the denominational missionary societies. As the battles over Ritualism intensified in the 1870s, the ongoing power of sectarianism and party controversy to fire activity within Anglicanism became apparent in the emergence of what were in effect dueling revivalisms between Anglo-Catholic parochial missions and organized holiness revivals.

Anglican evangelicals were intensely suspicious of early "Methodistical" revivalism and were only brought along slowly, ultimately driven to enthusiastic support by rising fears of "Romanism." Most notable of the early holiness leaders was William Pennefather, Anglican curate of Christ Church, Barnet, Hertfordshire, who organized the Mildmay conferences. The first was held at Barnet in 1856, but it later moved (along with the pioneering Deaconess Institution founded and run by William and his wife, Catherine) to North London in 1864, when he became vicar of St. Jude's, Mildmay Park. Pennefather was a characteristic product of the particularly fervent evangelicalism of Ulster, and in his conferences he combined devotional intensity, ecumenism, premillennial expectation, and commitment to home and foreign missions into an enthusiastic new form of Churchmanship.[107] Pennefather's conferences were an important early influence, not least because emotional revivalistic religion was particularly attractive to women, due to both the spiritual authority it could lend them and to the sanction for new forms of women's work it provided. The Mildmay Deaconess Institution, for example, and a whole range of parish-based women's work constructed by Catherine Pennefather (who had begun these activities in

---

gland). But as John Kent has noted, Finney's influence can be overstated given the parallel influence of Wesleyan revivalism. *Holding the Fort*, 25.

106. Stock, *Recollections*, 199. Particularly influential was W. E. Boardman's *The Christian Higher Life* (1858).

107. On Ulster-based evangelicalism, see Hempton, *Religion and Political Culture*, 101-16.

1856 and vigorously extended them at home and overseas after her husband's death in 1873), were critical in pointing the way to the institutional integration of unmarried women into Evangelical charitable and missionary activity. Rapidly growing numbers of trained English female missionaries from 1860 onward, a large proportion employed in evangelical Anglican missions, were one result of the feminine spirituality cultivated at Mildmay. Drawing many of its participants from the revivalist world and owing much to the heightened spiritual atmosphere following the 1859-61 revival, which had started in the United States and then spread to Ireland and England under the direction of the professional American revivalists Charles Finney, James Caughey, and Phoebe Palmer, the movement caught up several very influential figures at the CMS. Most notable among these was prominent Anglican premillennarian Stevenson Blackwood, cousin to CMS Secretary Henry Wright (1872-80), who was invited to chair Mildmay conferences and institutes from 1873.[108]

Larger and larger Anglican evangelical circles were drawn into the movement through the influence of the Keswick Convention, held annually in the Lake District from 1875. The conferences were born both in the context of the desire of evangelicals to extend the results of the 1874-75 evangelistic tour of Moody and Sankey and in the evangelical outrage over Ritualistic innovations, including the defiant preaching of the confessional by advanced Anglo-Catholics during the second Twelve Days' Mission to London in 1874, which stoked the fires that led to the passage of the anti-Ritualist Public Worship Regulation Act.[109] Notable for providing a more "respectable" expression of revivalistic religious enthusiasm, which had been questioned by old-style Evangelicals as too Methodistically emotional, perfectionist, cross-denominational, and implicitly democratic during and after the 1859 revivals, Keswick and "higher life" culture emerged as enormously significant to Evangelical missions for two reasons: first, speakers at Keswick increasingly embraced missionary work as an ultimate act of sanctification (not unlike the calling that drew Ritualist priests into English slums), and second, Keswick authorized women as equal participants in the "blessings of the spirit" and thus encouraged more independent female roles ranging from expanding leadership in charitable organization to proclamatory preaching itself.[110] These orientations were further

108. Stock, *History of the CMS*, 2:31, 3:22.

109. For more on the conflicts that led ultimately to the attempt to curb Ritualism by legal prosecution under the (ineffectual) Public Worship Regulation Act of 1874, see Peter T. Marsh, *The Victorian Church in Decline: Archbishop Tait and the Church of England, 1868-1882* (London: Routledge & K. Paul, 1969), 111-57.

110. The most radical formulations of these ideas developed outside the denominations, as in the work of Catherine and William Booth, founders of the Salvation Army. On the expansion

Assembled China missionaries — ninety-five women, thirty-nine men —
at the Keswick Convention, ca. 1890. From Presbyterian Church of England
Mission Archives, South Fujian/Amoy, Photographs, Box 1, File 1.
Courtesy of the United Reformed Church.

reinforced in the movement by premillennialist convictions that impending divine judgment required immediate evangelistic action by every spiritually able worker. Although holiness and its associated revivalism remained widely suspect through the 1860s, holiness culture in the 1870s began to make significant inroads among the Evangelical clergy.

While traditionalist Evangelicals opposed holiness for diluting the idea of Christian life as a never-ending struggle against evil, the tide was turning by the mid-1870s, and by the early 1880s a large proportion of workers at holiness conferences were Anglicans.[111] Among those who feared for the future of Evangelicalism in competition with Anglo-Catholicism, the apparent effect of insisting on strict observance of older Evangelical traditions was to drive away the young. Grudging acquiescence resulted as holiness practices grew in appeal to young evangelicals.[112] At the CMS, always sensitive to shifting opinion within its core constituencies, the proportion of those on staff who frequented holiness

and professionalization of women's public religious work, see Pamela J. Walker, *Pulling the Devil's Kingdom Down: The Salvation Army in Victorian Britain* (Berkeley: University of California Press, 2001), 109-17, 130-74; on parallel expansions of women's roles in overseas missionary work, see Semple, *Missionary Women,* 190-206.

111. Stock, *Recollections,* 196, 264. On traditionalist reservations, see Bishop J. C. Ryle, *Holiness: Its Nature, Hindrances, Difficulties, and Roots,* reprint, 1877 (Grand Rapids: Kregel, 1962).

112. Lash diary, 24 June 1874, Birmingham, Lash Papers, CMS Archives, Acc 348 F 1/5A, fol. 89.

circles grew steadily. Wright himself sympathized with revivalist religion, and other CMS stalwarts such as the influential A. M. W. Christopher, Rector of St. Aldate's, Oxford came to see in holiness a way to reverse the spiritual decline of the 1860s, which he believed was responsible for the slump in missionary work.[113] Through family connections and creeping acceptance the holiness movement gradually gained respectability and influence at the CMS.

Evangelical Anglicanism and the "New Era" of Foreign Missions

Despite High Church accusations that the "faith" enthusiasms of many Evangelicals undermined the "authority" embodied in the Anglican episcopacy, the CMS became the primary vehicle for institutionalizing holiness within the Church. Acceptance of holiness at the CMS significantly enhanced both missionary recruiting — not least from coveted university circles — and income growth. Association with "higher life" evangelical culture provided not only a means to expand missions but also a weapon to fight what was feared as a new breed of Anglo-Catholic — the avowed Ritualist — whom many Evangelicals suspected of luring the gullible youth of the Church ever closer to Romanism. To Evangelicals Ritualism represented an egregious disloyalty to the Reformation principles that had providentially redefined the Church of England and the English nation in the sixteenth century. Religious party driven by theological fashion had emerged in yet another variation that proved crucial to the conceptualization and conduct of foreign missions.

Holiness, Charisma, and the Reorganization of the CMS

The 1880s proved to be a critical decade of change at the CMS. Despite an efficiency drive in the 1870s designed to support expansion in the mission field in Rupertsland, Palestine, Persia, India, and especially Africa that had occurred by 1876, heavy deficits, disasters in the Africa missions, and an involved dispute with the Ritualist bishop of Colombo all caused considerable strain in the offices of the CMS in the closing years of the 1870s.[114] To some leaders at the CMS the vigor of holiness culture, as demonstrated by the dramatic spirituality witnessed annually at the Keswick Convention, seemed an answer to perceived malaise.

113. J. S. Reynolds, *Canon Christopher of St. Aldate's, Oxford, 1820-1913* (Abington, UK: Abbey Press, 1967), 179-84.

114. Stock, *Recollections*, 137.

In the vividly beautiful setting at the heart of the Lake District, the conferences enhanced the feeling of the roughly 2,000 middle-class participants that they were inhaling a particularly rarefied spiritual air. At Keswick the exceptional was prized, and faith missions, particularly the CIM with its rejection of the worldly constraint of bookkeeping and its reliance on the premise of revivalism — that those who appealed to God could count on conversion, sanctification, and support — rapidly grew in popularity.[115] Increasingly, the CIM found its "worldly" support both among those affluent middle-class evangelicals of the Keswick connection and among the extended network of holiness enthusiasts that radiated out from it through a number of Protestant denominations.[116]

Although Keswick operated as a nondenominational evangelical fellowship, no group had as much enthusiasm or wealth to contribute to the cause as evangelical Anglicans. With financial crises in the late 1870s and reorganizations in the early 1880s, leaders at the CMS, even those outside holiness circles, turned hopefully to the Keswick movement as a potential boon. But traditional missionary societies, with their emphasis on the worldly machinery of mission work, found it hard to penetrate the world of Keswick. The critical figure in converting the CMS to a holiness-oriented strategy was Eugene Stock. A former City clerk, Stock became editor of the Society's publications in 1874, despite some opposition on the CMS Committee from members that took a dim view of his former editorship of the revivalistically evangelical *Church Bells*.[117] The holiness sympathies of both Stock and Wright clearly worried traditional Evangelicals such as CMS Home Secretary Samuel Hasell who, as Stock recalled, "used to boast that he had never been inside the Mildmay Conference Hall, *nor* at an S.P.G. meeting." But the CMS shed two old-fashioned evangelicals highly suspicious of holiness when Hasell died in 1879 and influential lay secretary Edward Hutchinson departed in 1881 under a cloud of hushed financial scandal.[118] The August 1880 drowning in the Lake District of Secretary Henry Wright, holiness enthusiast and major CMS benefactor, stunned the Secretariat and forced

---

115. J. C. Pollock, *The Keswick Story: The Authorized History of the Keswick Convention* (London: Hodder and Stoughton, 1964).

116. On the connection of Hudson Taylor, the CIM, revivalism, and Keswick spirituality, see Alvyn Austin, *China's Millions: The China Inland Mission and Late Qing Society, 1832-1905* (Grand Rapids: Eerdmans, 2007), 185-88.

117. Stock, *Recollections*, 130-33.

118. Robert Needham Cust, *Essay on the Prevailing Methods of the Evangelization of the Non-Christian World* (London: Luzac, 1894), 134. Hutchinson, a heavy-handed manager of growing influence following Venn's retirement, was forced to resign upon discovery of a private profit-making scheme he had organized utilizing CMS trading stations in the Niger mission. Williams, *Self-Governing Church*, 96-100.

reorganization of the now substantially expanded work. Rather than select a new secretary of undeniable talent, such as the principal of the CMS College at Islington, William Barlow, the CMS Committee, in a choice of finance and family connection, appointed Henry Wright's brother-in-law, Rev. Frederick E. Wigram, "an equally wealthy clergyman" who was linked to the same family and holiness circles as Wright. In the turmoil caused by Wright's death, Eugene Stock was raised to the position of Editorial Secretary and emerged as a major force at the CMS.[119]

While many of the members of the CMS General Committee continued to be deeply suspicious of holiness enthusiasm, not so the secretaries surrounding Wigram and Stock. Trade and agricultural depression, combined with the spread of Anglo-Catholicism, had resulted in "a heavy falling off in the funds in many parts of the country." While missionary interest had grown in holiness circles, many evangelical Anglicans supported nondenominational societies rather than the CMS. Only "strenuous efforts made by the House staff both to maintain and animate existing organization and to create and develop new agencies" had, by 1888, saved the CMS from disastrous reversals and maintained an income that had "at least kept up."[120] Central to this was the tapping of holiness culture, which allowed the CMS to maintain its position as it struggled to compete both with lower-class Nonconformist holiness initiatives, such as those launched by the Salvation Army, and with higher-class Anglo-Catholic resurgence in England and in Anglican missions. At stake in the minds of CMS secretaries and leaders who backed the holiness initiatives was the continued vitality and influence of Evangelicalism as a force within the Church and within English society.

Holiness initiatives, however, were not an obvious panacea, and they did not show clear results in volume of income and missionaries until the 1890s. During that most jingoistic of decades, however, income and recruiting accelerated as holiness, reinforced in its emotional intensity by imperial enthusiasm, paid dividends. Underlying that success was the way holiness authorized the laity, most particularly women, to activist public roles in its support; substantial expansion of CMS home organization in the 1880s also underpinned the advances of the 1890s. The basic machinery of local missionary associations, that of organizing collections and circulating printed materials, had emerged by the 1840s, but the association network only matured into a systematically worked,

119. Barlow had the nearly unique achievement among Evangelicals of having taken a double first at Cambridge, but he would have required a salary. Barlow, *Barlow*, 101; Robert Cust to "My dear sir," 28 Mar. 1882, CMS Archives, G/AC 4/3/457.

120. "Memorandum by the Secretaries on the Report of the Sub-Committee on Home Expenditure," 12 Dec. 1888, signed by all 7 CMS Secretaries, CMS Archives, G/CCb 7/2.

By 1902 Eugene Stock had risen to the position of preeminent "missionary statesman" as the influential Editorial Secretary of the CMS. From this position he was instrumental in crafting the society's new initiatives to recruit university students, men and women alike. Georgina A. Gollock, *Eugene Stock: A Biographical Study* (London: CMS, 1929).

intensive national system in the 1870s.[121] By that time, as Anglican diocesan revival progressed, virtually every country parish or city center had the benefit of at least one annual missionary appeal from one society or another, and most local areas saw competition between associations that were attached to different congregations, with local clergy acting as the gatekeepers and wielding the power of access to missionary deputations.[122]

While the structures and methods were in place by the mid-Victorian era, only late in the century did the CMS strongly press the potential of this system, resulting in fully national coverage. Thus, in 1881 the CMS established a Lantern and Loan Department (to coordinate limelight lectures and the loan of mission curios and costumes), created Honorary District Secretaries (a new cadre of voluntary clerical organizers), and instituted County Unions. In 1882 it organized its first Missionary Exhibition, its first Lay Workers' Union and Missionary Study Band, and its first systematic national program for addressing Sunday schools. The creation of the first Ladies Union followed in 1883, the formation of the Younger Clergy Union in 1885, and the launching of a scheme for hundreds of simultaneous missionary meetings (the February Simultaneous Meetings) and an organized cycle of prayer for all Anglican churches in 1886.[123] All of these developments were designed to supplement traditional parochial work and to provide new niches for enthusiasts within its bureaucracy. When in 1885 representatives of the long-standing local associations rejected a plan for a nationwide Church Missionary League, complaining that there was now already too much local organization, the London secretaries launched the Gleaners Union, and by 1897 they had signed up 112,000 members in 858 branches all across the country.[124]

Behind all the schemes, which necessitated intensive coordination from London, lay the advocacy of Stock and Wigram, the enthusiastic spirit of holiness, and the activist support of women. Bypassing the local association structure controlled by the parochial clergy, the CMS was able to utilize young, enthusiastic, mostly female supporters to engage with a rapidly evolving entertainment culture, organizing them into largely autonomous organizations.[125] In the 1880s the CMS wrested a good deal of control and responsibility away

121. Stanley, "Home Support," chaps. 5 and 6.

122. On the role of societies in the processes of diocesan reform, see Burns, *Diocesan Revival,* 114-30.

123. Stock, *History of the CMS,* 3:65, 305-8, 324.

124. Minutes of the General Committee, Funds and Home Organisation Committee, 2 June 1885, CMS Archives, G/C 1, vol. 50; Stock, *History of the CMS,* 3:328, 663.

125. Pierre B. de Lom (Eastern Yorkshire), *Association Secretaries' Reports, 1895,* p. 14, CMS Archives, G/AZ 1/7, no. 52.

from local associations in favor of this youthful missionary activism. This was a strategy specifically targeting for new initiatives and leadership groups that clerically dominated local associations too often neglected: women, young adults, laymen, and children. As urban consumerism undermined the traditional lines of patriarchal parish cultures, the CMS emerged as one of the first national charities to respond effectively to the opportunities of mass society. These methods, which all broke with past practice, sought to popularize, commodify, and democratize the missionary package in an age awash in a rising tide of popular entertainment, which itself was deeply influenced by a burgeoning mass market of religious publication and religious commodities particularly targeted to women.[126] Innovation at the CMS was thus tied to a further democratization of religious life through the growth of local organizations no longer dependent on clerical organization. This change gave power to constituencies in the missionary movement that had previously operated under the benign neglect of most of the clergy, many of them young and enthusiastic, most of them pious and female. As the societies began using popular entertainment-based methods — such as traveling missionary exhibitions, massive missionary prayer meetings, missionary weeks, and special children's gatherings — the growth of new organizations, staffed with new activists, provided all the increased support of the 1880s and 1890s. By the 1890s new organization had become crucial to the CMS home structure. Nearly all the CMS's salaried organizing secretaries complained of the difficulty of getting beneficed clergy, and even the specially appointed Honorary District Secretaries, to perform more than the most basic and trivial of duties. The activity of young enthusiasts — women, clergy, and students — now drove development at the CMS as new agencies, especially the Gleaners Union, held together CMS national organization.[127]

Organizing Enthusiasms: New Workers for God

New workers were critical to the re-organization at the CMS that characterized the 1880s, and these new activists were broadly animated by the revivalistic enthusiasms of the holiness movement. The CIM had provided an important example of how methods emphasizing faith and devotional life could be used to tap into a cause that offered spiritual power, activism, and monetary resources.

---

126. Mary Wilson Carpenter, *Imperial Bibles, Domestic Bodies: Women, Sexuality, and Religion in the Victorian Market* (Athens: Ohio University Press, 2003), xvi and passim.

127. Stock to "My dear friend," 24 July 1888, CMS Archives, G/AC 4/5/997; Stock to Wigram, 27 July 1890, G/AC 4/6/1188; W. Hatt Noble to Wigram, 25 Feb. 1892, G/AC 4/9/1603.

However, while women and unbeneficed clergy brought energy, they did not bring respectability. Thus, the significant effort the CMS made to connect particularly with holiness circles that developed within the universities had the potential not only to energize Anglican evangelicals but also to boost the respectability of new cadres of missionary workers.

Cambridge University rapidly emerged as a critical focal point in the CMS effort to launch its "revivalistic" program, not least because success seemed to show that Evangelicalism could compete in the perceived stronghold of Anglo-Catholic culture, the Oxbridge universities. When Dwight L. Moody returned to England in 1882, his tour focused on the universities, particularly Cambridge. John Barton, former CMS missionary and vicar of Holy Trinity, Cambridge, did his utmost to advance the CMS's interests in the Evangelical undergraduate subculture.[128] Soon after Moody's appearance, the CMS was given a memorable object lesson in the missionary power of holiness, when the "Cambridge Seven," a group of popular undergraduate athletes who had been inspired by Moody, responded to a wave of missionary enthusiasm at the University and offered themselves in 1884 as China missionaries under the CIM.[129] Following the declaration of the Cambridge Seven, Barton urged CMS officials to strike while the iron was hot. J. B. Whiting, untiring CMS organizer and ally of Barton, urged Wigram and Stock to action, as he was "sure many [students] are quite ready to join the CMS." Whiting argued that, should the CMS accept the sudden offers of students determined immediately to leave for the mission field, "they will bring many others after them." "What the men see in Hudson Taylor," he continued, "is progress and enterprise. His so called 'Faith' is captivating and they fear that the cold and calculating CMS will not give them opportunity."[130] This was a turning point. By accepting offers unconditionally from university students to enter the mission field, the CMS became committed to a "faith mission" program of disregarding both financial prudence and the rectitude of older evangelical behaviors in favor of "following the spirit" to new fields.

It is not difficult to appreciate the appeal to Evangelicals of enthusiasts such as the Cambridge Seven. Their message fit colorfully into the language of holiness, piety, and Christian sacrifice. As Stanley Smith preached to a university audience shortly before his departure: "We have become new creatures. We have been born again, and these things are true of us — we overcome the devil; we overcome the world — its fashions, its maxims, and its opinions. . . .

---

128. Memoir of Emily Barton, MS (hereafter cited as Emily Barton memoir), 89-90, Emily Eugenia Barton Papers, CMS Archives, Acc 137 F/1; Porter, "Cambridge, Keswick and Africa," 18-19.

129. Cecil Edward Barton, *John Barton: A Memoir* (London: Hodder and Stoughton, 1910), 107.

130. J. B. Whiting, Ridley Hall, to Wigram, 20 Nov. 1884, CMS Archives, G/AC 4/3/556.

[V]ictory over all forms of sin is our constant experience." And those with the greatest commitment, Smith intimated, could not avoid "the heart-wail of Christless millions in India, China, and Africa."[131] Traditionalist Evangelicals, such as many among the CMS's Organizing Secretaries, resisted this enthusiasm, wondering why the CMS should "stoop to imitate the methods of the C.I.M." and, by extension, the Salvation Army. However, when the YMCA, also influenced by Studd and Smith, proposed a joint meeting with the CMS, Wigram weathered criticism in the press, authorized CMS participation, and made sure the meeting was organized to appeal broadly, with speakers from the Evangelical old guard and university dons as well as enthusiastic student missionaries. The meeting's success led to the organization of several February Simultaneous Meetings, which were conducted on similar lines. Those held in the counties in 1886 were a mixed success, but in London, in 1887, they were a triumph.[132]

Experience with holiness in the universities led to the organization of home operations around the energy of the growing revivalist evangelical community, both to secure missionary candidates and home organizers. Revivals were in large part a reaction to urban problems, and the spinoff into activism, whether in the Salvation Army and Church Army or in the work of Anglo-Catholic slum priests and settlements, demonstrated significant potential. Tapping into this potential meant accommodating its values and embracing its ostensibly less-worldly foci more effectively than could traditional parish sermons and meetings. The Church Missionary Cambridge Association stressed, for example, that the primary goal of the February Simultaneous Meetings "is not the raising of money, or the advocacy of the special interests of the Church Missionary Society, but the urging on all Christian people of the great cause of the world's evangelization."[133] Particularly in university culture, cultivating evangelical manliness as a means to direct holiness more fully into support of foreign work was achieved by disparaging obstacles and dangers in the service of missions. A wave of CMS-organized "Missionary Missions," which took the form of simple, local revival-style meetings to advocate prayer for evangelization without appeals for money, were one manifestation of the new temper.[134]

131. Stanley P. Smith, "Address of Stanley P. Smith, Edinburgh, 23 Jan. 1885," in Stanley P. Smith, Charles T. Studd, and Reginald Radcliff, *The Evangelization of the World: A Three-Fold Appeal* (London: Hodder & Stoughton, 1885), 2, 6.

132. Stock, *Recollections*, 143-45.

133. *C.M.S. February Simultaneous Meetings . . . 25 Jan 1886*, inserted in Minutes of the Cambridge Association of the Church Missionary Society, 1815-1918, CMS Archives, Acc 216 O/1/1.

134. H. Newton to [D. H.] Wilkinson, 1 Apr. 1897, CMS Archives, G/AC 4/21/4168; Christian manliness, as constructed in the popular evangelical press, revolved around spiritual development,

So too was a heated new atmosphere centering on the millenarian hope of the Second Coming of Christ, which had long been a part of missionary ideology but now assumed a renewed centrality. Millenarian interpretations of history that predicted the imminence of final judgment proliferated in CMS circles. Evangelical theorists often disputed the proper mixture of missionary agencies overseas — that is, whether itinerant evangelism or settled mission communities should be used and what their relationship should be to Western influences. But the belief that missionaries would convert an accelerating percentage of the world's population, and that this would hasten an imminent millennium, was never far from the surface. Enthusiasts now emphasized that missions, once the cause of early Victorian pariahs, had assumed an established, legitimate place in British overseas activity, with the implication that as enthusiasm for conversion was sweeping England, so conversions themselves would sweep the world. This belief that the English nation and the British Empire provided providential vehicles that had only just come into their own had two formulations. On the one hand was the worldly argument that missions were "the salt of our extending civilization" where "commercial and scientific advance" were "essential to the permanent and elevating self-government which is the ideal of the English-speaking peoples"; and on the other hand was the spiritual assertion that missions would "hasten that time" when the Second Coming of Christ would end all sin with the destruction of all nations, all empires, and the world itself in a Pentecostal season of final judgment.[135] That both formulations operated parallel to each other only strengthened the appeal of holiness as a vehicle for both worldly reform and the hastening a divine ultimate solution to human misery.

Riding on the expectation of feats unmatched since the acts of the Apostles, the CMS in 1887 launched the "Policy of Faith" under which, in obvious mimicry of the CIM's recruiting ethos, the Society pledged to send abroad any volunteer regardless of finance. Many traditional supporters found this intensifying holiness orientation deeply troubling. Rev. C. V. Childe, for example, insisted that the CMS must encompass the full breadth of Evangelical opinion to help hold the party together. Evangelical unity would be harmed "if the teaching, phraseology, and methods of special schools of Evangelical thought such as Keswick and Mildmay become dominant in the committee

---

good deeds, and obedience to duty (unlike the more individualist tones of aristocratic command favored in popular secular boys stories). Kelly Boyd, *Manliness and the Boys' Story Paper in Britain: A Cultural History, 1855-1940* (Basingstoke, UK: Palgrave Macmillan, 2003), 49-51.

135. *Protestant Missions Conference, 1888*, 1:151; Graham Wilmot Brooke, "Outline of an Address on the Heathen mission field: To Cambridge Undergraduates," 1886, notebook, Brooke Papers, CMS Archives, Acc 82 F 2/5.

and publications of the Society."[136] CMS secretaries, however, embraced a formula that promised both growth in numbers of missionary candidates and financial support. In 1888 the organizers of Keswick allowed the convention to be "for the first time officially missionary," sponsoring missionary prayer meetings. This resulted from the initiatives of CMS secretaries, led by Eugene Stock, C. C. Fenn, and Frederick Wigram. Within two years missionary prayer meetings, missionary society information sessions and appeals, and missionary testimonials were a recognized part of the Keswick Convention. Despite increasing feelings of marginalization, older-fashioned Evangelicals had little choice. While High Churchmen had a variety of options, from the SPG to the UMCA and the various missionary brotherhoods, the CMS had become the chief national organ of evangelical Anglicanism. And the swelling number of well-educated missionary candidates volunteering for the mission field through Keswick connections had particular weight in status-conscious CMS circles. In the 1880s the CMS, to its great profit, built support among the enthusiasts of the holiness movement, and in the 1890s it experienced its greatest decade of missionary growth. As the expansion of the society accelerated, critics of growing expenditure demanded a review, and the Policy of Faith was vindicated, at least as measured by the statistics valued in the English churches. In seven years clerical missionaries had increased from 247 to 344, laymen from 40 to 82, women from 22 to 193, a total increase of 100 percent from 309 to 619. Of these missionaries, over 70 were self-supporting. By contrast only four self-financed honorary missionaries had gone out prior to 1887. Furthermore, home expenditures had declined from 13.5 percent of total income in 1887 to 10.8 percent in 1894, while income had risen from £200,777 to £237,797. A feared deficit for 1894, after the CMS launched a special appeal campaign, failed to materialize.[137] Critics could not argue effectively against such success.

Managing the "Keswick Effect": Unifying Anglican Evangelicalism

Keswick-style holiness spirituality was a form of evangelical enthusiasm that promised great advances for foreign missions. But it also proved potentially dangerous to Church order and missionary institutions; that is, it was challenging to the unique claims of Anglicanism and Anglican forms of authority and to the missionary stations, schools, dispensaries, hospitals, and other institutions

136. Childe to Frederick Wigram, 23 Dec. 1887 and 19 Nov. 1890, CMS Archives, G/AC 4/6/1001 and G/AC 4/7/1223.
137. *Church Missionary Society: 1887 and 1894*, CMS Archives, G/AZ 1/7, no. 3.

that had registered the missionary presence even in unpromising fields. Revivalism in general was a religiously unsettling phenomenon that brought the benefit of church growth, but it did so at the expense of the order and respectability that was so valued among middle-class Victorian churchgoers. Evangelicals faced their own youthful enthusiasts in the 1880s, much as in the 1860s High Churchmen had faced Ritualism, in part, as a countercultural, youth-oriented movement. The CMS, however, confronted a group of holiness enthusiasts who, for a variety of reasons, were disposed to accept CMS missions as providentially prepared spiritual paths. Because the CMS, with its careful deference to family responsibilities and authority, had preserved its reputation among Evangelicals as proper and respectful, it was well placed to draw many from the "respectable classes" in holiness ranks into its missionary networks. In the past, in the 1850s and 1870s respectively, waves of revivalism and their wilder manifestations had passed rather quickly, without profound effects for the CMS. Later CMS leaders, however, confronting the more institutionalized revivalism of Keswick, saw greater potential both to be cultivated and managed, making the long-term benefits of associating with a newer, more genteel pietism seem to outweigh any potential shorter-term embarrassments.

In the missionary movement, undiluted holiness attitudes were dangerous to the operations of the denominational missionary societies because holiness enthusiasts defined themselves against "lifeless" churches. Satisfying the enthusiasts and protecting the Society from the anti-authoritarian, anti-institutional, and anti-organizational urges unleashed by the movement required careful channeling. In this the CMS also had a significant advantage over the SPG. Whereas the youthful idealism of Anglo-Catholic holiness was often expressed under the protection or toleration of church authorities, against whom the SPG had little recourse, the youthful idealism of evangelical holiness produced young missionaries who ultimately could be manipulated through the complex systems of control that the CMS had evolved over decades of operation in order to manage their "men on the spot," primarily to prevent the explosion of scandals in the mission field that were so damaging to home support.[138] Those who could not be contained, however, operated as competitors. In the 1880s they established, alongside the already established CIM, several small independent faith missions that were tied tightly to burgeoning interest in prophetic eschatology. These included Henry Grattan Guinness's Livingstone Inland Mission of 1878 (supported by his East London Training Institute), followed by the North

---

138. Peter Hinchliff, "Voluntary Absolutism: British Missionary Societies in the Nineteenth Century," in *Voluntary Religion,* ed. W. J. Sheils and Diana Wood, vol. 23 of Studies in Church History (Oxford: Blackwell, 1986), 370-76.

Africa Mission in 1881, the Congo Balolo Mission in 1889, the Sudan Interior
Mission in 1893, the South American Evangelical Mission in 1895, and the Be-
har (Bengal) Mission in 1900.[139] They added to a growing congestion in the
philanthropic world and presented a direct challenge to established societies.

The experience of mainline missionary societies demonstrated that the spiritual superiority and the separatist inclinations of "higher life" enthusiasts could
be extremely divisive.[140] Enthusiasm was valuable when it could be safely channeled, but holiness also generated excesses and eccentricities. These could be
relatively innocuous, such as "one old lady [who] caused a sensation by calling
out in a loud voice [at the Keswick Convention] 'We are of the Circumcision!'",
to the significantly damaging, as when holiness enthusiasts created disruption
and scandal in the West African mission field.[141] Difficulties existed both at
the theological and practical levels. Bishop J. C. Ryle continued to remind
Evangelicals of his original strictures in the 1870s against perfectionist heresies inherent in holiness, while disenchanted CMS committee member Robert
Cust savagely blasted "faddist" enthusiasms at the CMS as a "goodness without
wisdom" that reinforced anew old racial and gender prejudices, marginalizing
Africans and women in mission work.[142] At its worst, traditional Evangelicals
feared holiness separatism as a weakening influence on Churchmanship, and
progressives insinuated that holiness operated as an excuse for racism when
indigenous churches did not conform to "higher life" standards of spirituality.[143] And holiness offended against Anglican snobbery, seeming repugnantly

139. Many of these amalgamated in 1899 with Grattan Guinness's Regions Beyond Missionary
Union (1872). Activist coteries of the revivalistically oriented eventually began to cohere into other
cooperative ventures as well, such as the Worldwide Evangelical Crusade, designed in 1910 to
channel the energies of undenominational enthusiasts. Norman P. Grubb, *C. T. Studd: Cricketer
and Pioneer* (London: RTS, 1933), 134-35. On premillennialist eschatological interests, see, among
many, Henry Grattan Guinness, *The Approaching End of the Age Viewed in the Light of History,
Prophecy and Science* (London: Frome, 1878).

140. The Congregationalist LMS's failure to emulate successfully the CMS's "Policy of Faith"
in the 1890s lay primarily in the animosity it created between old and young supporters. A[lbert].
Spicer to Basil Mathews, [ca. 1894], CWM Archives (LMS), Home: Personal, Box 2, folder 9; E. A.
Wareham deputation report, 31 Dec. 1899, CWM Archives (LMS), Home: Odds, Box 9, folder 1.

141. Memoir of Rev. A[rthur] B. Fisher, with notes and annotations by H. B. Thomas, MS,
(hereafter cited as Fisher memoir), A. B. Fisher Papers, CMS Archives, Acc 84 F 3/2, book 8, p. 10;
on the troubles and transformation in the CMS Niger Mission, see J. F. Ade Ajayi, *Christian Missions in Nigeria, 1841-1891: The Making of a New Élite* (Evanston, IL: Northwestern University
Press, 1965), 250-73.

142. J. C. Ryle, *More Prayer and Work! Being Thoughts on Missions,* 7th ed. (London: Hunt,
1886), 14; Cust, *Prevailing Methods,* 128, 139 and passim.

143. M. Langley Hall to J. Padfield, 5 July 1896, CMS Archives, G/CCb 8/3; William Wallace to
Henry Fox, 2 Jan. 1897, CMS Archives, G/AC 4/23/4484.

shallow, enthusiastic, and lower class, smacking of ranting Methodism or a Salvation Army band.

Radical holiness practitioners tended to exclusivity, and leaders at the CMS witnessed in the 1880s the impact of the dangerous attitude that Evangelicals who practiced a different standard of faith might be judged not truly Christian. The most damaging CMS encounter with this idea occurred in 1887, when it accepted the proposals of Graham Wilmot Brooke to found a new mission on the Upper Niger. The effect that Brooke and his party had on the Niger Mission — the disgracing and dismissal of Africa's only black bishop, Samuel Crowther, and the precipitation of a major local mission crisis — has received considerable attention from historians who have traced much of the trouble to Brooke's particularly radical brand of holiness enthusiasm as well as to rising race consciousness.[144] In Brooke's thinking only a few were truly spiritual enough to receive God's blessing, and his radical, fundamentally sectarian premillennialism led him to believe that wandering, unsupported preachers should simply proclaim the gospel to all nations, ushering in the Advent that would sweep away those "chains as had never been known before, Popery, Islam, Modern Skepticism." He insisted that the biblical methods he drew from the Acts of the Apostles would be successful, unlike those of the denominational missionary societies, with their wasteful and misguided structures of home support and worldly bureaucracies.[145] As Andrew Porter has noted, this was "a simple-minded message delivered with single-minded intensity"; but because of its intensity the message appealed to just that class of enthusiast the CMS was targeting.[146]

Dealing with men like Brooke was a dangerous gamble that reinforced a late Victorian tendency at the CMS to withdraw from Henry Venn's strategy of building independent, self-governing indigenous churches. In its place grew a more exclusivist policy reinforcing local European leadership in missions. This shift partly issued from a growing insistence on European standards of holiness, partly from solidifying systems of missionary professionalism, and partly from hardening theories of imperial control and racism. It led African Christians, frustrated with missionary refusals to transfer local control to local congregations, to create a growing number of ultimately flourishing indepen-

144. See, for example, Porter, "Evangelical Enthusiasm," 29-32; Andrew C. Ross, "Christian Missions and the Mid-Nineteenth Century Change in Attitude to Race: The African Experience," in *The Imperial Horizons of British Protestant Missions, 1880-1914*, ed. Andrew Porter (Grand Rapids: Eerdmans, 2003), 93-96.

145. G. W. Brooke, "Outline of an Address on the Heathen Mission Field: To Cambridge Undergraduates," notebook, Brooke Papers, CMS Archives, Acc 82 F 2/5.

146. Porter, "Evangelical Enthusiasm," 40.

dent African churches.[147] It also proved dangerous to the Society's carefully guarded reputation at home. As soon as Brooke joined the CMS, he set about constructing, as he put it, a "plan for reconciling the simplicity of apostolic organization with the necessities of the age of religious impostors and bogus charities."[148] Upon his return to the Niger mission in 1888, he quickly branded the indigenous Christians as "a den of thieves" and pronounced that "[i]f the C.M.S. do not revolutionize their work . . . they deserve to be put on the Charity Organization Society's list of swindlers for the lying and robbery going on out there is shameful."[149] Brooke's charges petrified the CMS Committee, not because black converts and Bishop Crowther were being slandered but because they feared damage to CMS's reputation in the universities; the danger finally receded only with Brooke's death from blackwater fever in 1892.[150]

The criticisms coming from holiness radicals were a critical challenge to the CMS's missionary strategy, but they were not isolated. They were tied in with a multifaceted debate in the late 1880s over the efficiency and efficacy of the missionary project.[151] The CMS found itself balancing the value of enthusiasm, which brought missionary candidates and organizers, against its identity as an evangelical organization loyal to the Church of England and a missionary agency committed to settled civilizational strategies. Adopting the holiness movement and adapting it to established missionary society practice was perhaps Eugene Stock's greatest achievement at the CMS. Stock was by no means an "undenominationalist," and, while he sympathized with and admired holiness practice, he remained a strong and loyal Churchman, professing a pragmatic latitude of belief that allowed sympathy with the pietism of Anglo-Catholicism and its project of integrating revivalistic activism into urban parochial structures.[152] Stock was involved early in the campaign to enlist evangelical Cambridge undergraduates, and the CMS had considerably more success than any other society among Oxbridge graduates. Similarly, Stock was one of the founders of the Gleaners' Union movement, which provided a legitimate structure for the energies of young activist women, often inspired by holiness, within

147. Edgar, "New Religious Movements," 216-19.

148. G. W. Brooke, Stanley Pool, to "My dearest pappy" [Lt. Colonel R. Wilmot Brooke], 10 Oct 1887, Brooke Papers, CMS Archives, Acc 82 F 2/5, part 1, 1884-85.

149. Brooke, Niger Delta, to "My Dearest Father," 24 Feb. 1888, Brooke Papers, CMS Archives, Acc 82 F 2/5, part 1, 1884-85.

150. For the most recent full account of the controversy in the Niger mission and its effect on the CMS Secretariat, see Williams, Self-Governing Church, chap. 4.

151. Thomas Prasch, "Which God for Africa: The Islamic-Christian Missionary Debate in Late-Victorian England," Victorian Studies 33 (Autumn 1989): 51-73.

152. Stock, Recollections, 130, 184, 188.

the missionary movement. By accepting holiness, but not without reservation, the CMS created a space for respectable spiritual radicalism. Stock and CMS Secretary Frederick Wigram became omnipresent figures at missionary society conferences and meetings in the 1880s and 1890s, consistently hammering home a central message: evangelization was complex and depended on the direct evangelism provided by itinerant preaching of the gospel, but also on the more diffuse culturally transformative efforts provided by educational work, medical missions, literary work, and the like.[153] By drawing heavily on Women's Depart-ment Secretary Georgina Gollock and her holiness background, the CMS was able to reinforce the development of service-oriented ministries that appealed to women who were motivated by holiness and willing to both volunteer for the mission field and organize for its support. To the very large degree that the CMS became the leader of the late-nineteenth-century missionary movement, it was because of success in generating a gendered strategy of spiritual enthusiasm that appealed to affluent evangelical Anglican women, whose spirituality was more significant in recruiting potential than that of men and less dangerous to the organized work.

The most important holiness initiative pursued by the CMS's central office arose out of the "Keswick Letter" of July 1890, which advocated issuing an appeal for one thousand new volunteers for the mission field. It also suggested the creation of roving bands of foreign preachers, greater use of lay evangelists from the working classes, and the development of overseas industrial work initiatives. This was, in essence, a call to draw the CMS even closer in attitude and strategy to the CIM. Several of the CMS Committee were uneasy with the enthusiasm, and perhaps rashness, of the proposals. But the success of Eugene Stock in bringing "our mission field before the earnest young people" won the Committee, despite fears that a large influx of European missionaries would relegate "native work" in the field to secondary importance.[154] Traditionalist criticism was quickly forthcoming. Robert Cust, voicing the objections of many, opposed action on the Keswick Letter on the grounds that the CMS should avoid an indiscriminate expansion of missionaries, especially laity from the working classes, because too many enthusiasts were unreliable both in theology and character. His conclusion was that the call for one thousand new

153. See, for example, both the speeches of Eugene Stock and Georgina Gollock (CMS Women's Department secretary) to the highly spiritual 1896 Students' Missionary Conference. *"Make Jesus King": The Report of the International Students' Missionary Conference; Liverpool, January 1-5, 1896* (London: SVMU, n.d.), 92-95, 233-34.

154. F[rederick]. W[igram]., "Notes of Comm[itt]ee of July 29," [1890], (William Barlow's comments), CMS Archives, G/AK 1. Only one of nine members mentioned as present at the meeting voiced reservations about the negative impact on indigenous workers.

missionaries "reads like a joke or an idle boast or a Salvation Army cry" when the CMS already had more work to do than it could effectively handle.[155] More importantly, it was evident to many that the policy of the primacy of cultivating native agency in missions, forged by revered honorary secretary Henry Venn, was being overthrown. The experienced West Africa missionary W. Salter Price warned how dangerous it would be to encourage the idea that "we foreigners are going to evangelize the world" when what was needed was indigenous missionaries trained up by leaders with culture and education.[156]

Such objections, however, were brushed aside as the CMS saw immediate results in its competition with Henry Grattan Guinness's East London Training Institute and its associated "faith" missions for "suitable" candidates.[157] While recommendations for industrial work projects contained within the original letter were rejected — Stock had argued that the Keswick Letter was not really about a desire "to herd out Working people" but rather to capture the attention of university students interested in slum settlements and working-class poverty — the CMS expanded use of lay missionaries in the form of bands of Lay Evangelists trained under "short courses" at the Church Missionary College at Islington, and of women of "deficient background," now to be provided training courses at Highbury.[158] This was primarily a drive to attract a wider pool of missionary candidates and supporters, enthusiastic, yet also respectable enough to appease traditionalist Evangelicals. Anglicans, unlike Methodists and Baptists, were never known as having relative strength of support in the working classes, although Churchmen made serious efforts to adjust to urban society from the 1860s onward, and many successful urban working-class parishes existed.[159] The working classes, much like indigenous peoples, were understood primarily to be targets of proselytizing, not agents of it, and this core prejudice, stronger at the CMS and SPG than in Nonconformist missions, was linked firmly to a class prejudice characteristic of Anglican attitudes.

155. Cust to Frederick Wigram, 12 [Nov. 18]90, CMS Archives, G/AK 1; "To the Secretaries and Committee of the CMS" (the Keswick Letter), 25 July 1890, CMS Archives, G/AC 4/6/1184.

156. W. Salter Price to [Henry] Morris, 12 Mar. 1891, CMS Archives, G/AK 1. He also shared Cust's doubts on the suitability of "mechanics & working men & women" as missionaries because they were "more inclined to kick over the traces than men of gentle birth and breeding."

157. F[rederick]. W[igram]., "Nov. 3/90 A Subc[ommi]ttee," MS notes, [1890], CMS Archives, G/AK 1.

158. W[igram]., "Nov. 3/90 A Subc[ommi]ttee"; "Report of Sub-Committee (B) on Industrial Work . . . ," 20 Jan. 1891, "[Report of] The Sub-Committee (C) . . . ," 19 Jan. 1891, and "Report of Sub-Committee (A) . . . ," 14 Apr. 1891, CMS Archives, G/AK.

159. McLeod, *Religion and the Working Class*, 22, 24, 39-45.

The engagement at the CMS with holiness, however, demonstrates not only the strong middle-class social base of missionary religion but also the ways that it transcended social class. Charity organizers knew that the nation was made up of discrete religious communities; and if these communities were to be reached effectively for specific purposes they needed to be analyzed systematically and approached rationally. One important resource that holiness enthusiasm provided was a new cadre of workers to staff new initiatives in the crowded late Victorian charitable market.[160] In a society ever more affected by suburbanization and the commercialization of leisure and entertainment, organized religion and especially Anglicanism showed considerable resilience through the Victorian and Edwardian periods and into the 1920s, particularly through effective control of institutions like the Sunday school, influence in the state education network, and organization of philanthropy.[161] However, the encouragement of styles of religion inspired by revivalism, and deeply appealing to women, also provided means of maintaining cross-class contact within the charitable environment. Missions paralleled the more general observance of religion in Victorian Britain and received substantial support from individual parishes and congregations in widely diverse areas, from secluded agricultural regions and northern industrial areas to affluent southern suburbs and inner-city slums in Bethnal Green and Bermondsey.[162] Holiness activism supported the maintenance and extension of these successful practices.

For an institution as large as the CMS, the most threatening aspect of holiness enthusiasm and revivalism was its reassertion of the ancient notion that worldly things — even the institutions of the church itself — were anathema. Criticisms of "worldly" methods inspired by this idea caused societies to reevaluate the "spirituality" of educational strategies and the use of settled mission stations in the field.[163] The CMS effectively responded to this criticism because as a large society with many mission fields it could advocate itinerant methods in new missions and retain the continuation of education, medicine, and institution-building in older ones. The CMS in the

---

160. Maughan, "Regions Beyond," 142-73.

161. Jeffrey Cox, *The English Churches in a Secular Society: Lambeth, 1870-1930* (New York: Oxford University Press, 1982), 268-69.

162. See, for example, the contribution lists of the CMS for the year 1895; lists of other societies demonstrate similar diversity. *Proceedings of the CMS* (London: 1895). On class and Victorian religion, see McLeod, *Religion and Society*, 62-66.

163. For this process in Scottish missions, see Andrew Porter, "Scottish Missions and Education in Nineteenth Century India: The Changing Face of Trusteeship," *Journal of Imperial and Commonwealth History* 16, no. 3 (1988): 33-57.

1890s, emphasizing that evangelization encompassed both open-air preaching and classroom teaching (if not maintaining highest priority for engineering native church independence), was able to draw in revivalistically oriented activists and safeguard traditional mission practice. Despite their high profiles and their appeal to activists, "faith"-style missions gathered only 10 percent of English missionary revenue compared to the over 70 percent maintained by the denominational societies (see Appendix I, Figure 5). The challenge presented by the practices of societies such as the CIM operated much akin to the challenge presented by Anglo-Catholicism: Evangelicals were driven, like High Churchmen, to innovation and activism in defense of their Anglican identity.

Anglo-Catholicism and the Fragmentation of High Church Missionary Vision

The challenge of the 1880s was to tap reserves of holiness-inspired Christian missionary enthusiasm and new interest in the British Empire. Under a new chief secretary, Henry W. Tucker, the SPG embarked on a program to create an efficient Church society that more accurately represented the views of its supporters. However, the SPG faced formidable obstacles, and while it increased efficiency it failed in the more crucial task of building loyalty, enthusiasm, and generosity in a unified constituency of supporters. This failure had a number of causes. Perhaps most fundamental was the insistence of advanced High Church controversialists that the SPG, or any voluntary society, offended against the principle of diocesan and parish organization centered around the holy clerical office. This attitude, of course, made accommodation difficult, and as the CMS lost Anglican supporters to the nondenominational faith missions, which were seen as more keenly embodying evangelical principles, the SPG lost supporters to the independent Anglo-Catholic dioceses that emerged in Central and South Africa, New Zealand and Melanesia, Hawai'i, North China, Colombo, and elsewhere. Even those High Churchmen who did not embrace advanced ritual, but still advocated for the creation of independent diocesan mission boards as the appropriate corporatist replacement of the individualist voluntarism upon which the societies existed, challenged support for the SPG. While the situation itself was difficult, SPG Secretary Henry Tucker made it more so. Tucker, a fiery controversialist, had little success negotiating the theological extremism of the High Church party. He alienated many supporters with a tactless authoritarian style and engaged the SPG in destructive public controversies.

Anglo-Catholic Ambitions and the SPG

At the heart of SPG strategy lay an appeal to the concept of Church duty, rather than the active, enthusiastic faith that evangelicals stressed. Linked to this was a constitutional reliance upon English bishops for governance and leadership, bishops too often distracted by the manifold problems of a rapidly growing and troubled Victorian society. In these two realities, the SPG remained a society yoked to older forms of religious faith and organization that were being rapidly superseded by voluntary religion. Wrestling with significant impediments to accommodating and co-opting the vision and energy of Anglo-Catholicism, the SPG experienced two decades of comparative stagnation; reliance upon the claim to the duty of Churchmen was simply insufficient. Attempts to unify missionary enthusiasm with the dynamics of the high imperial age were thwarted by intraparty controversy and infighting.

In the 1870s, the heyday of Ritualist controversies, the SPG shied from endorsing any particular High Church party. Serving a more divergent constituency than the CMS, as well as operating under episcopal leadership and an inclusive charter, meant that embracing a particular party identity was a perilous and perhaps impossible task, especially given the divide over support for establishment that split Anglo-Catholic enthusiasts from most other Churchmen. Instead, under the leadership of Secretary W. T. Bullock (1865-79), the SPG highlighted independent special mission funds, providing a variety of projects for people within its varied constituencies to support. Growing special missions, however, largely represented waxing interest in independent Anglo-Catholic missions, such as the UMCA, that were home to many who questioned the very existence of the SPG. The SPG's role vis-à-vis these special funds was that of paymaster to a bishop, and while this function in itself was not insupportable, when these bishops frequently returned to England and canvassed support directly from "SPG parishes," turf wars over cash and church authority resulted. Enthusiasm for High Church missions increased, then, as the SPG took advantage of growing interest in Africa and the Pacific. In contrast to the developments at the CMS, however, the SPG strategy relied on decentralizing control, rather than on defending enduring party identities, to take advantage of episodic imperial interest.

Continuation of this policy in the longer term would have required extreme tact and a delicate touch, as well as committed support from the English bishops or episcopal leadership of the SPG itself. Instead the SPG came to be dominated by a group ill-suited to generating missionary enthusiasm, innovation, or comity. Led by the coterie surrounding the Tractarian leader R. W. Church, Dean of St. Paul's Cathedral (1871-90) and his canons, most notably Robert Gregory (who rose to particular influence on the SPG Committee), the SPG came to represent defense of independent religious conscience, historically pragmatic Anglican breadth, toleration of gradualist Ritualism, and evolution of independent Church governance through the Convocations of Canterbury and York. Operating within this fold, and in parallel to the financial and liturgical reorganization of St. Paul's Cathedral, SPG Secretary Henry Tucker acted to bring the logic of diocesan re-form and bureaucratic efficiency characteristic of the age to the Society; he also defended the practice of High Churchmanship and Ritualism, not under exclu-sivist principles, but as part of a complex, historically evolving church.[164]

Henry Tucker's era (1879-1901) at the SPG began with changes designed to improve efficiency, the involvement of active contributors, and the formal con-nection of the society to the Church. Organizational efficiency, however, could not relieve the SPG of party controversy. Without the autocratic control that the CMS could exercise over its missionaries — that is, by simply terminating their appointments — the SPG could not limit the damage caused to its reputation in England by extreme Ritualists, who worked in the dioceses it supported with block grants or in special missions over which it had no control. Frequent troubles and scandals — usually involving provocative Ritualist activities and organized "Puritan" protests — alienated the SPG from respectable, moderate supporters by tending "to foster the growth of divers popular fallacies and mis-conceptions." Further, the SPG's image problems were compounded because its finances were vulnerable. Its limited collecting system depended heavily on once-yearly parish missionary sermons that were too often preempted or undermined by collections for Special Funds that supported the UMCA or Anglo-Catholic overseas dioceses. The SPG central office argued that, having served their original purpose of boosting enthusiasm in the 1860s and 1870s, when secular opinion was far less favorable to foreign missions, Special Funds should now be absorbed into the traditional system.[165] Tucker hoped to achieve loyal support such as that enjoyed by the CMS, which did not "divide the inter-est" and with a united "wonderful sweep" rallied its friends to "a strong centre."[166]

164. Henry Tucker and Richard William Church — both connected to Oriel College, the early Tractarians, and the *Guardian* — had a long, close association. In 1881 Tucker was made a Prebendary of St. Paul's, and Canon Robert Gregory, an SPG Committee stalwart, ultimately succeeded Church as Dean of St. Paul's (1890-1911). On R. W. Church's defense of Ritualism and opposition to legislative attempts to quash it, see Marsh, *Victorian Church in Decline*, 127, 156, 214, 235-34, 267-72, 285.

165. "S.P.G. Appropriated and Special Funds. Memorandum by Mr. Kemp. Private & Confi-dential," 9 June 1882, Edward White Benson Papers, vol. 17, fols. 139-42, Lambeth Palace Library, London (hereafter cited as Benson Papers).

166. Henry Tucker to "Dear Madam," 15 May 1890, USPG Archives, X 367.

Moderate High Churchmen, however, seemed to be incapable of providing that strong center. In the 1870s R. W. Church's circle had operated in the name of "Church defense" to help frustrate Archbishop Tait and his allies in the prosecution of Ritualists under the ill-fated Public Worship Regulation Act of 1874. But that did not mean they aggressively supported advanced Ritualism. Rather, like Pusey, they felt "'the extremes' have brought the whole army into a defile . . . [and] have missed such a glorious opportunity of concentrating the High Church party in a way that might have gone far to turn the tide!"[167] The "righteous cause" of fighting the Act, however, lay in undermining its foundation of "pure Erastianism." And as unsavory as defending the hubristic grandstanding of enthusiastic Ritualists might be, the defense of the Church as an independent "divinely constituted body" in control of its own litergy, ritual, and practice was the chief goal of the party. This goal was only practically achieved, after nearly twenty years of struggle, in 1892 through the Lincoln Judgment, by which Archbishop Benson's acquittal of Bishop Edward King of Lincoln for ritual excesses was upheld by the Judicial Committee of the Privy Council.[168] In this era of rapid changes in relationship between church and state, Tucker sought to throw the SPG's lot in with the efficiency of Church bureaucracy as a sure foundation for independent Anglican conscience and for the diocesan reform movements that had been transforming the place of the Church in society, hopefully strengthening Anglican unity.

When in 1881 the SPG sought to centralize administration with a new Royal charter allowing it to impose greater control on all the funds it handled, defenders of ecclesiastical independence — many of whom were decided Anglo-Catholics — saw the policy as symptomatic of continuing Erastian compromises that undermined the authority and independence of the Church. In effect, the continuing issue here was voluntarism versus organization through church structures, but with the twist that, in the name of greater bureaucratic efficiency, an essentially voluntary society was seen to be treading on the diocesan prerogatives of overseas Anglican bishops. While the SPG conceded the authority of a bishop in his own diocese, the question was really about a bishop's authority outside of it — more particularly, his authority over money raised in the English Church. This was a matter both of church party and finance. The most furious response to the SPG's efficiency drive came from Edward Steere, the UMCA missionary bishop in Zanzibar, whose aggressive public attack in the *Guardian* in 1881, pronouncing that the SPG had "gone to war" over Special Missions,

167. Berdmore Compton, *Edward Meyrick Goulburn, D.D., D.C.L., Dean of Norwich: A Memoir* (London: Murray, 1899), 124-25.

168. Compton, *Goulburn*, 126-27; Chadwick, *Victorian Church: Part Two: 1860-1901*, 353-54.

portended an ugly public battle. His essential argument, following that of his predecessor Bishop Tozer, was that bishops and experienced missionaries should have unassailable authority over strategy and finance in their own mission fields and independent colonial churches. He attacked the legitimacy of the SPG and the CMS, suggesting that the only true societies were those that operated in the field with apostolic directness, that the only legitimate Anglican activity was that organized under a bishop, and that the time had passed for missionaries such as himself — "a superior set of men" — to "allow themselves to be dictated to by a secretary and his clerks."[169] The SPG maintained, however, that it operated under the imprimatur of the English bishops and should control the money it collected and was commissioned to manage. This was a matter of imperial control — center versus periphery — writ small, but also an issue of growing importance, as the worldwide scope of the Church created deepening tensions between the national, imperial, and international character of the communion.

The support of the English bishops eventually fell not to Steere as a brother bishop but to organizers at home, who were intimately connected with the collection of the funds that sustained overseas work. A special subcommittee at the SPG supported by the new archbishop of Canterbury, E. W. Benson, chaired by the centrist Bishop Goodwin of Carlisle and filled with SPG Committee heavyweights, issued a report in July of 1882 upholding the centralization of SPG finance and closure or expulsion of 156 of its 198 special funds.[170] The English bishops were sensitive to issues of episcopal prerogative, but also to mitigating the public disputes of the Church. Ultimately they acted to protect the traditional functions of the SPG from being undermined by innovating Anglo-Catholics or enthusiasts with plans for creating missionary duchies supported from England. But this action was not without cost. When the special funds were expelled, the society saw nearly all its income gains of the previous decade wiped out. Bishop C. P. Scott of North China thought Special Funds in the 1870s had operated on the theory "that only by interesting them [potential supporters] in one definite work, in which they could take a proper interest" could support be built. Although the funds had served that purpose, the price in the long term had been division and bad blood.[171] In addition, this bureaucratic contest had

169. Pamphlet reprint of 8 June 1881 *Guardian* letter, Benson Papers, vol. 17, fol. 177; Edmund Steere to E. W. Benson, 12 Jan. 1882, Benson Papers, vol. 17, fols. 133-34.

170. Of these 198 special fund accounts, 135 averaged less than £33, 36 less than £5, and of the £39,643 total in the account, £21,877 went to 14 large missions that had their own administration. "Report of a sub-committee on the relations of the Society to Special Funds, adopted by the Standing Committee on July 13, 1882," Benson Papers, vol. 17, fols. 143-50, and "Central Agency for Foreign Missions (Special Funds)," 5 Feb. 1883, Benson Papers, vol. 7, fols. 359-60.

171. Scott to Henry H. Montgomery, Aug. 1903, USPG Archives, H 37.

much broader consequences when, five years later, Steere's arguments formed the basis of a furious attack against the society system by Canon Isaac Taylor of York, who held up the UMCA as "a type of the old apostolic method" against the profligacy and bureaucratized ineffectiveness of the traditional missionary societies, particularly the CMS, where London staff costs were equal to "the salaries of two English diocesan bishops."[172] This launched a wide-ranging controversy over missionary methods, with Henry Tucker drawn in as a vocal supporter of the maligned society system and, implicitly, of the CMS itself.

Henry Tucker had a penchant for efficiency, but he did not match it with a warmth of spirituality or tolerance of emotionalism. He conceived of the society's role as that of a business house, the spiritual side to be advanced by beneficed clergy, who should demonstrate "statesmanlike gifts of administration, to the suppression of the impetuous and selfish individualism which too often monopolizes the name of Enthusiasm."[173] The SPG merely tolerated lay involvement, and in this it was out of step with fundamental developments in the Church. By the end of the decade Tucker came to symbolize for many supporters the range of problems that a bureaucratic church model had brought to the SPG in the 1880s. Tucker clashed with a number of Anglo-Catholic bishops in the mission field, and he had a disconcerting talent for quenching enthusiasm in the ranks of SPG supporters while simultaneously embroiling the SPG in public disputes. By claiming aggressively that all Anglicans had a duty to support the SPG as a traditional organ of the Church, Tucker alienated Anglo-Catholics who accused him of creeping Erastianism, Evangelicals who accused him of High Church exclusivity, and all Anglicans who held an enthusiastic style of religion and who accused him of cold formalism. The SPG was by charter a Church organ, but it operated as a voluntary society. Its constitution tied it to the archbishop of Canterbury and thus to his unenviable task of mediating the conflicts between various shades of extremism in the Church of England. But the constitution also competed with Anglican missions that unashamedly appealed to party principles. While staunchly defending voluntarism, Tucker seemed unable to enter into its spirit. As he tightened his grip on the Society, the Standing Committee rose to almost unassailable control, with Robert Cust dubbing it "[t]he Venetian Council of Nine," which presided over meetings where "[o]ld Clergy come in, sit round, and grin, while idle forms are gone through, followed, however, by an admirable address by a Missionary from the

172. Isaac Taylor, "Missionary Finance," *Fortnightly Review* 50 (Nov. 1888): 581, 586. Taylor's comprehensive case can be found in "The Great Missionary Failure," *Fortnightly Review* 50 (Oct. 1888): 488-500.

173. H. W. Tucker, *The English Church in Other Lands; or, The Spiritual Expansion of England* (London: Longmans, Green, 1891), v-vi.

field, which is most enjoyable, and worth the trouble of a long walk."[174] Tucker's vision of a moderate High Church middle ground between the extremes of Ritualism and "enthusiastic" evangelicalism was only capable of consolidating the Society's interests in the shrinking number of traditional "high and dry" parishes and circles of moderate, aging Tractarian High Churchmen, such as R. W. Church, who commanded great respect but were not particularly notable for missionary enthusiasm.

The SPG in the 1880s was marked, then, by controversies that swirled around Tucker, who sought to justify SPG policy with a divisive legalistic strategy. After Tucker, with support of the CMS, made an especially strongly stated attack on diocesan Boards of Mission and the special missions that had left the SPG at the 1884 Carlisle Church Congress, Harvey Goodwin, the bishop of Carlisle, who had helped mediate the 1882 conflict, exclaimed: "I could scarcely have believed without proof that a man in his position would be so indiscreet." Tucker's reopening of the wounds of controversy led to the formation of another SPG subcommittee on special missions, which Goodwin suggested should force Tucker's resignation in the interests of reconciliation.[175] But the fact that Tucker was not compelled to resign is indicative of the kinds of church politics in which the SPG had become embroiled. Tucker doubtless saw the very existence of the SPG at stake in these questions: if its constitutional powers of "receiving, managing, disposing" of funds as laid out in its charter were destroyed, no redoubt would be left to defend the Anglican middle ground. Independent missionary funds might then become a means by which Ritualists could seize entire pre-existing missionary networks, controlling pulpits and public discourse. Unable to control bishops or even missionaries, the SPG had to control its organizational networks. But the defense of this bureaucracy formed a key reason why, despite its significant institutional connections, it was unable to match the CMS in cultivating missionary enthusiasm. In particular, the SPG under Tucker did little to take advantage of the expanding influence of the laity in the final decades of the century. This was evident in the SPG's failure to cultivate a younger constituency — particularly among women — that could help to revitalize the society. In the words of Tucker's successor, "[h]e looked down upon emotion or sentiment as contemptible."[176]

But the SPG's plight was also a result of the prevailing view of the English bishops, who understood that foreign missions, while a duty laid upon

---

174. Cust, *Prevailing Methods*, 138.

175. Goodwin to "My dear Bishop," 10 Nov. 1884, Benson Papers, vol. 17, fols. 151-54.

176. Henry H. Montgomery, "My S.P.G. Career. Jan. 1902–Feb. 1919," MS, Henry Hutchison Montgomery Papers, vol. 4540, fol. 331, Lambeth Palace Library, London (hereafter cited as Montgomery Papers).

the Church, were not its only, or even its most pressing, duty. Among liberal Churchmen this perspective was strengthened when under Archbishop Benson's leadership missions to the Eastern churches — particularly to the Assyrian church — were conducted not as an exercise in conversion to Anglicanism but as an offering of aid and support. They were "missions of maintenance," an approach that Benson saw, along with "missions to the learned," and the formation of independent churches, as "the very office of the English Church above all others."[177] This more careful, measured approach had many traditionalist clerical supporters, whose position was traceable back to the long-standing Anglican assertion, rearticulated by "orthodox" High Churchmen in the 1840s, that the English church, along with the ancient Eastern churches, had suffered under the schismatic actions of an error-prone Rome, not the reverse.[178] Tucker's crucial base of support among dominant SPG committee members, such as Canon Robert Gregory, Rev. Berdmore Compton, Sir Charles Turner, and Lord Stanmore (Arthur Hamilton-Gordon), rested in part on his acceptance of the importance of English Church priorities. That he was the biographer of Bishop Selwyn, that energetic campaigner for the independence of the Church in New Zealand, must have seemed an irony to bishops like Steere, who were attempting to work out what they saw as the logical conclusion to Selwyn's work: independence from the constraints of non-diocesan church organizations like the SPG. It also demonstrated that for an SPG administrator it was easier to support the independence of bishops in theory than in practice.

Defending the Middle Ground:
The SPG and Moderate High Churchmanship

Henry Tucker was loyal, outspoken, and devoted to the SPG as a Church institution. He was a loud and persistent defender of sober Churchmanship in a religious world of extremes. But his was not a style that attracted missionary supporters. Instead of renovating the SPG and making it a worthy rival of the CMS, Tucker and the party in power seemed to many to be undermining its support. As one friend of Tucker's recalled years later, his "views on Church questions did not help forward Missionary zeal."[179] Neither did closed, autocratic governance.

177. Edward White Benson, "Missions," in *The Anglican Pulpit of Today: Forty Short Biographies and Forty Sermons of Distinguished Preachers of the Church of England* (London: Hodder and Stoughton, 1886), 7-10.

178. Nockles, *Oxford Movement*, 180-83.

179. Michael R. Ransome to Henry H. Montgomery, 9 Nov. 1904, USPG Archives, H 37.

The atmosphere at the SPG, rather than being opened by the new Charter, allowed handpicked subcommittees to operate without oversight. W. R. Churton, complaining of the SPG's operation, insisted, "[t]his evidently calls for reform: but such apathy prevails on the subject of the foreign work of the Church, that it seems useless to attempt anything. Very few of our Vice-Presidents are ever present in the Board Room. The Bishops we never see. Yet measures of great moment to the Church at large are submitted to us, involving grave principles of Church order." Clashes with bishops such as Edward R. Johnson of Calcutta over jurisdiction were common, but the unrivaled control of the SPG by a small group led by Canon Robert Gregory meant that little could be done.[180] The SPG's open membership allowed its general meetings to operate as a forum for the discussion of larger Church issues, but it proved inefficient for daily management. This legitimized Tucker's decision to create inner systems of control. Debates over contentious issues, such as how to deal with the "heretical" bishop of Natal, John Henry Colenso, could lead to "rowdy brawling . . . [making] SPG a bear garden." But the real cause of the trouble at SPG, according to Churton, was neither politics nor personalities (including the "waspish disposition of the Secretary"); the real problem was "indifference" to the missionary work in favor of domestic controversies.[181] This was the world of masculine clericalism — the cut and thrust of doctrinal controversy, point-scoring debating, display of professional expertise, and the assumption of the weight and importance of the matters at hand. But it was not an effective means of drawing in the energy of the laity in a voluntary age.

Continuing problems led Archbishop Benson to appoint a committee of five bishops in July of 1887 to investigate the reasonable anxieties about falling revenues and widespread reports of the decrease in the SPG's influence. The Society's problems were clear enough. Despite a 7.5 percent increase in the English population, from 1882 to 1887 contributions had fallen from £92,459 to £90,780. This was a deeply embarrassing decline, and Victorian missionary commentators assumed that if missions were not "advancing" they must be "lifeless." However, in fairness the bishops could not condemn the SPG home staff or its local workers when episcopal leadership, their own responsibility, had so largely failed the Society. The report that the bishops issued in 1888 only confirmed the authority of Tucker and his supporters, pointing once again to the seemingly intractable position that the SPG was placed in by its Royal Charter.[182]

180. W. R. Churton to "My dear Bishop," 30 June 1887, Benson Papers, vol. 62, fols. 190-91.
181. Note, undated, initialed RTD [Randall T. Davidson], Benson Papers, vol. 62, fols. 194-95; W. R. Churton to "My dear Bishop," 30 June 1887, Benson Papers, vol. 62, fols. 190-91.
182. "The Committee appointed . . . to enquire into an alleged Diminution of the Funds of the Society, & into other Matters affecting its interests," [1888], Benson Papers, vol. 77, fols. 287-302.

Pushed into the world of voluntary religion by Church reform in the 1840s, the SPG had flourished at mid-century in the first decades of the Tractarian movement, functioning as a vehicle of High Church organizational and liturgical revival. By the 1870s, however, it found itself drawn into the complex divisions that advanced Ritualism caused in High Church ranks. The report reminded readers that the SPG had special claims on the Church of England, especially as the Society embraced comprehensively Anglican interests and about a quarter of its funds went to colonists, while five-eighths of its income went to those working with the "heathen" within the empire. Based on this loyalist interpretation of the SPG's mission — national, colonial, imperial — the bishops suggested that the Society try to poach support from CMS parishes by emphasizing its special character, while also expanding out into the churches that contributed neither to the CMS nor to the SPG. In effect the bishops, by admitting their insufficient support and thus shouldering the blame, declined to take on the powerful High Church group surrounding St. Paul's Cathedral, including R. W. Church and Robert Gregory, and they refused to force the SPG to operate in the character of a popular voluntary society.[183] Like the independent Ritualist priests who had defied the bishops and the Public Worship Regulation Act, Tucker followed an established pattern of independent priestly initiative within the Church and prevailed. The SPG was, for the time being, allowed to continue advancing a doctrinally sound, beautifully dignified, pragmatically subdued form of Anglicanism that appealed to moderate High Churchmen loyal to the ideal of the eighteenth-century Anglican divines. To Tucker's coterie the maintenance of this identity and its extension were far more important than any unseemly enthusiasm.

The SPG had no distinctive message except the duty to support missions within a Church with historic claims to authority, and therefore it could not capitalize on the unmistakable trend in the Church of England away from evangelicalism.[184] By the early 1890s it was becoming a commonplace among CMS organizing secretaries that their largest challenge lay in the battle against

183. Harvey Goodwin, bishop of Carlisle, to E. W. Benson, 29 Nov. 1888, Benson Papers, vol. 77, fols. 282-83. On Gregory's work at St. Paul's, see Robert Gregory, *Robert Gregory, 1819-1911: Being the Autobiography of Robert Gregory, D.D., Dean of St. Paul's* (London: Longmans, Green, 1912), 155-225.

184. CMS home workers were deeply troubled by a perception of high numbers of clergy associated with "High Churchism" being promoted to important parishes and canonries and to the bench. See *Association Secretaries' Reports, 1892* (London: private printing, n.d.), CMS Archives, G/AZ 1/4, no. 123A, and similar emphases in the reports of 1895 and 1896. On the gradual marginalization of Anglican evangelicalism, see John Kent, *The Unacceptable Face: The Modern Church in the Eyes of the Historian* (London: SCM, 1987), 87-88.

a rising tide of High Churchmanship. As Rev. W. Clayton, CMS association secretary for the South-east and Dorset, noted, "[t]here is a wave of Ritualism, or excessive Churchism, passing over the district. It is the *fashionable* religion of the day. Evangelicals are looked upon with disdain or pity! . . . In one rural deanery the H.D.S. [Honorary District Secretary] told me the clergy laughed when he mentioned the C.M.S.!"[185] But SPG officers did not laugh when they compared their financial results with those of the CMS, which had always out-performed the SPG in contributions. While Evangelicalism was losing influence in the Church hierarchy, it retained considerable popular force. Thus, while the CMS in the early 1890s rose quickly in support, the SPG was stagnant, and it was actually declining in such crucial districts as the London metropolitan area and Essex, where higher church contributions frequently flowed into divided collections.[186] This was the legacy of the SPG Special Mission rift: the Society found itself in competition for High Church donors with not only the UMCA but also the twenty-four smaller missionary organizations that owed their exis-tence to the SPG, all of which appealed to traditionally "SPG Churches." Henry Tucker, when under attack, commented that probably fewer than 10 percent of SPG parishes contributed solely to the SPG, while conversely he doubted that fewer than 10 percent of CMS parishes contributed to any other society.[187] Zeal had its uses, particularly when it bound together an embattled subculture such as that of evangelical Anglicanism. While the SPG had been involved in internecine strife and barren reorganization, the CMS had engaged in a new departure. By responding to changes in British evangelicalism and society, the CMS had cultivated new sources of missionary support that fueled the unprec-edented growth of the "new era."

Conclusion

The difficulty of encouraging sectarian identities in organizations formally tied to a "comprehensive" Church was that of balancing emotional, often absolutist spirituality with institutional loyalty. The CMS was challenged with incorporating holiness activism in such a way that the benefits of attracting young, ambitious,

185. W. Clayton (South-east and Dorset), *Association Secretaries' Reports, 1892*, p. 8, CMS Ar-chives, G/AZ 1/4, no. 123A.

186. Report of H. Percy Grubb (Metropolitan District, Essex, and Channel Islands), *Associ-ation Secretaries' Reports, 1892*, p. 1; H. Percy Grubb (Metropolitan District), "Centenary Review Section XII: Home Organisation &c. Replies to enquiries . . . ," [1898], CMS Archives, G/CCb 11/2.

187. "Memorandum on Bishop Anson's Circular and Letter," 11 Oct. 1894, Benson Papers, vol. 131, fols. 394-97.

Henry Tucker, photographed here in 1879, aimed to bring efficiency to the SPG
and evoke a sense of duty in Anglicans in the support of missions. His formal manner
and difficult position as the director of a society caught in the middle of Anglican party
politics led the SPG into a period of troubling controversies and stagnant support.
From SPG Photo Album 55a, Bodleian Library of Commonwealth and
African History, Rhodes House, Oxford. Courtesy of the United
Society for the Propagation of the Gospel.

women and men from the prestigious university and respectable Anglican suburban worlds was balanced against the preservation of authority and good repute, both of the missionary society and the Church. CMS success at achieving this balance made the 1890s the decade of its greatest growth and most extensive influence. Leadership in missions became a mark of pride among Evangelicals and an object of emulation for High Church Anglicans. Although the SPG never matched this success, response to the Evangelical missionary challenge reshaped the society, as did the work of Anglo-Catholics, not only through recognized missionary societies like the UMCA, but also through the scattered yet substantial efforts in Anglo-Catholic dioceses throughout the world, which incorporated the work of high-profile Anglican brotherhoods as well as the largely unrecognized and significantly greater work of Anglican sisterhoods.

The "new era" in British and American foreign missions that followed the anxious years of the late 1870s unleashed a flood of missionaries on the "heathen" world unprecedented in modern times. However, the missions of English "old Dissent" — Congregationalists, Wesleyan Methodists, and Presbyterians — and of the High Church were less fully affected than those associated in intimate ways with holiness charisma.[188] The contribution of the Anglican evangelicals to this "new era" was critical, drawing the "enthusiastic" methods and dubious class associations of popular evangelicalism into the realm of respectability over which an ostensibly authoritative national church presided. The experience of the SPG in the 1880s is instructive in highlighting the contrast between the higher and lower wings of the Church, their relatively higher and lower class associations, and the constraints placed on High Church missions by the more formal conventions of respectability and deference to Anglican Church organizational structure and bureaucracy. Evangelicals, on the other hand, molded the new style of revivalistic evangelicalism that dated from the 1860s into an instrument of missionary advance within Anglicanism that allowed it to compete with nonconformist spiritual radicalism embodied in the CIM and the Salvation Army. In order to capitalize on the zealous supporters these approaches drew, Anglican evangelicals, however, were torn over how far to emulate such fervency, for emulation that was too closely associated with such vulgar "enthusiasm" risked their acceptability within the core base of upper-middle-class support. These were not ungrounded fears, as a substantial part of late Victorian Anglican resurgence was based on advances made in the "respectable" suburbs in relation to Nonconformity, where a parallel process of Conservative growth

---

188. On parallel sluggish support for traditional Scottish missions in contrast to rising enthusiasm among "hotter" evangelicals, see Andrew C. Ross, "Scottish Missionary Concern 1874-1914: A Golden Era?" *Scottish History Review* 51 (1972): 51-72.

through "Villa Toryism" vis-à-vis the Liberal Party was underway.[189] Concern for social respectability was paralleled by linked worries over theology, for many older Evangelicals believed holiness revivalism was potentially, if not actually, heretical, and thus a dangerous solvent on the already fragile denominational loyalties of evangelical Anglicans. Handling charismatic spiritual radicalism required continuous, delicate management.

The 1890s were a remarkable decade for the CMS. Enthusiasm transformed itself into increased numbers of missionaries and then increased revenues in the run-up to the great Evangelical celebration of 1899, the CMS Centenary. By the turn of the century, the Policy of Faith adopted at the CMS thirteen years before had become "an old CMS principle," confirmed in its success by the CMS's special Centenary-year income, an unprecedented £404,905. Holiness-inspired recruits, both men and women, more than any other factor (CMS propagandists were adamant on this point) were responsible for the emergence of a "new era." In the whole of the nineteenth century the CMS sent out 2,003 missionaries, 999 in the 80 years before 1880, 1,004 in the 20 years after. Significantly, 200 of the 400 university graduates sent out in the nineteenth century sailed after 1887.[190] Advances at the CMS were dependent on the adoption of the methods and personnel of revivalism, and a strong case can be made that the "new era" of late Victorian missions was achieved by capturing the energy of an established revivalistic cycle and, in this particular case, the energy of women released by revivalistic culture. Alan Gilbert has identified general revivals in England in 1849, 1859-60, 1874-76, 1881-83, and 1904-06, each coinciding with periods of church growth among the various Methodist connections and Baptists. Statistics from the Anglican and Free Church of Scotland after 1900 suggest the same type of cyclical growth and periodization in these churches as well.[191] Notably, the frequency of occurrence of Victorian revivals suggests that sometime between 1889 and 1896 a revival was due. This period, of course, corresponds instead with the greatest period of missionary growth, when societies inspired by revivalism took up popular mass methods common to revivals and experienced a "new era," perhaps more aptly termed a "missionary revival."

---

189. The phrase is Lord Salisbury's. J. P. Cornford, "The Transformation of Conservatism in the Late Nineteenth Century," *Victorian Studies* 7 (Sept. 1963): 51-53, 65-66.

190. Fox to Lay Workers Union, 9 Jan. 1900, CMS Archives, G/AZ 2/2; Stock, *History of the CMS*, 3:465, 705. Peter Williams has calculated trends for CMS recruitment: 1800-50, 8.5 percent total increase; 1851-60, 17.5 percent increase; 1861-70, 28.5 percent decrease; 1871-80, 17.5 percent increase; 1881-90, 75 percent increase; 1891-1900, 133.5 percent increase. "Recruitment and Training," 6-9.

191. Alan D. Gilbert, *Religion and Society in Industrial England: Church, Chapel and Social Change, 1740-1914* (London: Longman, 1976), 187-92.

While attempting to retain their relevance in English culture, Evangelicals used their considerable successes in foreign missions to buttress their position in the Church. If, as Doreen Rosman has argued, evangelicals began withdrawing into a biblically defended, separatist subculture as early as the 1830s, the late Victorian period saw an attempt by moderate evangelicals to re-enter the world of activity and experience primarily through the foreign missionary enterprise.[192] Continuing evangelical missionary commitment spurred High Church and Anglo-Catholic clergy to sponsor missions in competitive response. When action motivated by party conflict was combined with growing anxiety that Protestantism was being effectively challenged abroad by other faiths and systems of belief — from Roman Catholicism and Islam to modernism and materialism — the result was a Church focused to support foreign missions to a degree unequaled in its previous history.

To a considerable extent, CMS expansion was dependent on activity by a committed core of organizers and missionaries who were in methods and temperament revivalists. Like revivalists, they were motivated by the sense that a crisis existed; in this case, in the missionary project. Critiques both inside and outside the missionary community regarding the stage that foreign missionary activity had reached fuelled this feeling. Internal criticisms, often linked to millennial expectations and to a reading of the quickening signs of the times, were also connected to an emerging critical assessment of future mission prospects, the product of interchanges between critics of missions and their defenders. From the 1860s these debates increasingly focused around arguments regarding the nature of Islam as a religious rival, but they also grew as an important part of the contest between Evangelicals and Anglo-Catholics over the shape that missionary practice and the churches it sought to found, as well as the society that surrounded them, should take.[193] A pious community struggling with mounting affluence and the rigorous claims of Protestant ethics was open to self-examination and to the suggestion that missionary enthusiasm provided some antidote to the spiritual deadening that prosperity could bring. While many felt, along with CMS missionary James Johnson, "that Protestant missionaries have, in a hundred years, accomplished as much as could reasonably be expected from the methods employed," the awareness of the extraordinary advances in wealth and power in Britain and its empire brought anxiety and

192. Doreen M. Rosman, *Evangelicals and Culture* (London: Croom Helm, 1984), 31-37.

193. Prasch, "Missionary Debate," 55-63 focuses on debates over Islam and the waning influence of evangelicalism, but it entirely neglects the central dynamic of intra-Anglican conflict implicit in Canon Isaac Taylor's championing of the Anglo-Catholic mission model through the UMCA and his denigration of Evangelical culture and methods in London's Islington district. Taylor, "Great Missionary Failure," 495, 497.

the sense that a new departure, a "new era" of consecration and sacrifice, was required, for the number of "heathen" and "Mohammedans" in the world in 1886 was immeasurably greater than in 1786.[194]

Imperial anxiety aside, other considerations also affected missionary strategies and enthusiasms in the late Victorian era. Developments at the CMS were driven by the dream among holiness enthusiasts that by transforming foreign missions they could come to control the Evangelical party, the Church, the nation, and even the world. Among mainstream Evangelicals, however, the clear understanding of their diminished national influence, compared to the early Victorian decades, meant that a focus on missions provided one sphere in which the evangelical party could still demonstrate its commitment to a cause neglected by the less godly. While the individualism and otherworldliness of Keswick challenged traditional bureaucratic missions and their methods, the CMS led the way in successfully synthesizing the new enthusiasms generated by this movement with long-held commitments to the importance of "civilizing" and institution building. Furthermore, the recruitment of new cadres of enthusiasts at home allowed systematic organization, with the goal of reaching beyond the committed few and the dutiful to the uninspired many. Following this pattern many societies launched or dedicated new resources to separate medical and women's auxiliaries in the 1890s. The goal, here, was to broaden the support base by appealing to those who had little sympathy for missionary aims per se, but who did have other connections to mission fields, an approach that the SPG also profitably pursued after the turn of the century.[195] Positive results were evident in CMS local Association income after 1894, wherein all the substantial growth in funds in the next twenty years came from specially earmarked ("appropriated") funds (see Appendix I, Figure 7).

It has been characteristic to see the holiness movement as inward-looking and sectarian in tendency, leading to a narrowing of the social and political concerns of evangelicalism in a secularizing society.[196] But holiness also led to a new activism that, while shifting interest from domestic relief work and social policy, nevertheless channeled evangelical energy into a liberal vision for overseas Christian expansion. In this way, if it is possible to see holiness in some ways as profoundly antimodern in temperament and approach to domestic social problems, it also effectively directed much evangelical enthusiasm into foreign missions and the imperial realm. Ultimately the "faith" ideal of holiness

194. James Johnson, *A Century of Missions and Increase of the Heathen,* 2nd ed. (London: Nisbet, 1886), 3-36.

195. Henry H. Montgomery, "Report on a meeting of an unofficial character with Secretaries of Special Mission Associations" [ca. 1904], USPG Archives, H 37.

196. Kent, *Holding the Fort,* 350 and passim.

missions proved to be the most important development in foreign missions since the founding of the denominational societies in the 1790s.

Holiness and enthusiasm affected both High Church support (through Anglo-Catholicism) and Evangelical congregations (through revivalism). The SPG, while it could embrace the more modest, establishmentarian High Churchism appreciative of the unique apostolic authority and antiquity of the Church, had difficulties absorbing the full measure of Anglo-Catholicism. Neither defending the Reformation settlement as normative (as the CMS did) nor embracing a rich medievalism and fully independent Ritualism as the Church's future (as advanced Anglo-Catholics did), the SPG opted for restraint and comprehensiveness. Appearing as an old-fashioned clerical preserve unresponsive to the potential and demands of an increasingly active laity — despite the fact that leaders like Tucker and Gregory imagined it as a rock of moderation and thoughtful, measured Churchmanship in a sea of emotional extremism washing from both the high and low ends of the Church's pool of support — meant the SPG languished in defending an older pattern of social deference and reserved respect for duty. This position may have retained its appeal to the old-fashioned squirearchy and to an emerging group of learned, historically oriented moderate High Churchmen, but it was not responsive to the potential and the expectations of a growing urban and suburban middle class that demanded enthusiasm and entertainment as it increasingly dominated late Victorian culture.

Evangelicals, on the other hand, focused more narrowly on missions as the century progressed. The movement within the Church of England, stretching back to the Clapham Sect, had always derived considerable energy from its sense of opposition to the sinful worldliness of both the poor and the rich alike.[197] Later in the century Evangelicalism also found itself stimulated to action by the sense of a potent new evil at the heart of the Church: the aggressive crypto-Papist idolatry of Anglo-Catholicism, which, when combined with fears of Islam and Rome resurgent in the international realm, fed a burgeoning evangelical millenarianism that spilled out into foreign missions. Because holiness evangelicalism was a cultural style particularly patronized by the younger generations of suburban, middle-class Evangelicals who were against old forms of behavior, and because Anglo-Catholicism was similarly countercultural in its appeal and delivered — in a much smaller but still influential way — religious enthusiasm to High Church Anglican cultures that were deeply entrenched in educated, metropolitan, and county elite establishments, both were productive of new departures in English missionary activity. That enthusiastic new ap-

197. Susan Pedersen, "Hannah More Meets Simple Simon: Tracts, Chapbooks, and Popular Culture in Late-Eighteenth Century England," *Journal of British Studies* 25, no. 1 (Jan. 1986): 109-11.

proaches spread so widely by the late nineteenth century was a testimony to the embeddedness of the missionary enterprise in Anglicanism. By the Edwardian period foreign missions within the Church had developed a more comprehensive appeal, for a variety of reasons, but none was more important than the increased recruitment of women and the penetration of the university world — both among High and Low Churchmen. While missionary support was never widespread among the aristocracy or professional classes, the embrace of missionary goals among High Churchmen and their spread particularly into the Oxbridge universities enhanced the social standing of missionaries and the legitimacy of missions.[198] One of the consequences was increased acceptability and respectability of missionary pursuits within the Church, especially among women, including by century's end, rapidly growing numbers of unmarried women. Another consequence was the growing influence of university culture and university dynamics in the Anglican missionary movement.

Within this late Victorian ferment, domestic issues of religious style, Church and charitable principle, bureaucratic strategy, and religious party were as important as questions of missionary strategy and imperial engagement. Missionary societies had to negotiate complex cultural and theological courses in Britain and adjust to circumstances to maximize their support. The CMS solution to the problem of retaining support in the late nineteenth century was to co-opt the energies of its most activist supporters and diversify its operations to appeal to a broader public. To enthusiasts at the CMS, it seemed apparent by the end of the 1890s that the missionary world had entered a glorious new age of Providential expansion. To propagandists such as Stock, the reason for the change was clear: the unleashing of the power of the Holy Spirit through the holiness movement. And at the core of the holiness movement, Stock emphasized, was the unleashing of women's activism. Even if most clerics and secretaries at the societies only grudgingly acknowledged this fact, there is no doubt that women were the real linchpin of the much-touted missionary revival of the late nineteenth century and that their energy drove the wave of growth that Anglican foreign mission experienced in the late Victorian and Edwardian Church of England.

---

198. "The Committee appointed . . . to Enquire into an Alleged Diminution of the Funds of the [SPG] . . . ," signed F. [Frederick Temple, bishop of] London, Benson Papers, vol. 77, fol. 293. On failed attempts to develop missionary support among these groups, see Maughan, "Regions Beyond," 235-42.

CHAPTER 4

Women's Work: Expanding the Home
in the Kingdom of God

*We know that home is the centre and fountain of social life; and woman is
the centre of home. Such as the women are, such are the homes, and such
the civilisation and the Christianity of society. To reach that centre, to purify it and consecrate it for the Kingdom of GOD, is woman's special work.*

Allan Becher Webb, 1883

*While people in England are looking with impatience for the day "when
the men will pull down the shutters of their zenanas and throw open the
doors of their inner apartments," ours is the more difficult task of educating
the women for a brighter future.*

Priscilla Winter, 1878[1]

In 1888, speaking to the Centenary Conference on Protestant Missions on "The
Place of Female Agency in Mission Work," Christina Rainy felt compelled to
provide a deep history of women's activism within the church, beginning with
the obligation laid upon women by the sins of Eve, followed by an examination
of the role of women as spiritual guides in the New Testament, particularly in
the recognized office of deaconess, and ending with the destruction of this apostolic office of public responsibility with the rise of the cloistered nun, one of

---

1. Allan Becher Webb, *Sisterhood Life and Woman's Work, in Mission-Field of the Church* (London: Skeffington, 1883), 3; Priscilla Winter, *On Woman's Work in India* (London: Clay, n.d., ca. 1878),
8. Winter was the wife of SPG missionary to Delhi, Richard R. Winter.

the many corruptions ostensibly introduced by Roman Catholicism. Overlaid on this narrative was another narrative, that of nineteenth-century Protestant missions, which emphasized that from the beginning of the movement women ("especially unmarried women") made up an "immense majority" of supporters but were relegated to prayer and "collecting and contributing money." Women were passive, isolated from the work, continued victims of medieval tyrannies even as evangelical religion was freeing men from the bonds of superstition. Rainy gloried that at this pass "it is becoming plainer every day that the Lord has need of women, and especially unmarried women in the foreign field itself." Along with expanded roles for women throughout the world of religious work, women in foreign missions were finally gaining that Protestant liberation to do good — to reinvent Eve — that missionaries preached was the gift of Christian society. This was a message that grew among advocates of women's missions, both outside and inside the Church of England.[2]

The transformation that Rainy described was a source of wonder, and in clerical circles, some consternation, as women's work rapidly grew as a source of gendered lay power. It was generally known that from its earliest inception the British Protestant missionary movement depended heavily upon the support of women at home and the work of married female missionaries in the field, although they were seldom acknowledged or tabulated as individual agents.[3] Yet, by the turn of the century, according to figures that almost certainly under-represent the numbers of missionary women — particularly wives, female family members, and indigenous "Bible women" — perhaps as many as 70 percent of Anglican missionaries, and certainly well over half of the total of British missionaries, were women. And women continued to do the overwhelming majority of home-organizing work.[4] It remains difficult to quantify precisely women's contribution, as well as that of non-Western work-

---

2. Christina Rainy, "The Place of Female Agency in Mission Work," in *Report of the Centenary Conference on the Protestant Missions of the World,* 2 vols., ed. James Johnson (London: Nisbet, 1888), 2:141-43. See parallel comments by Mrs. Bannister of the CEZMS committee, Spottiswoode, *Anglican Missionary Conference, 1894,* 580-83.

3. Deborah Kirkwood, "Protestant Missionary Women: Wives and Spinsters," in *Women and Mission: Past and Present; Anthropological and Historical Perceptions,* ed. Fiona Bowie, Deborah Kirkwood, and Shirley Ardener (Providence, RI: Berg, 1993), 23-42. On the parallel neglect of women's contribution to the foreign missions of the Protestant Episcopal Church in the United States of America, see Mary Sudman Donovan, "Women as Foreign Missionaries in the Episcopal Church, 1830-1920," *Anglican and Episcopal History* 62 (1992): 16-39.

4. See Appendix I, Figure 6. On the crucial mediating role of poorly recognized Bible women in Indian zenana missions, see Eliza F. Kent, "Tamil Bible Women and the Zenana Missions of Colonial South India," *History of Religions* 39, no. 2 (Nov. 1999): 117-49.

ers, however, because missionary records emphasize European male agency.[5] Anecdotal records suggest that women provided a critical, majority support for missions, particularly in the collection of funds and local organization, but also as liberal contributors. In the process of growing to this stature in the movement, women, while relying on particular lines of biblical sanction to secure general acceptance, came to define their work in energetically gendered terms as they labored against persistent clerical resistance to the expansion of their autonomy and authority. The Crimean War, beginning in 1854, and the Indian rebellion of 1857 proved to be critical turning points, after which women's roles in missions expanded rapidly, as an intersection of theology, imperial opportunity, and social change (including the growth of female professional roles, particularly surrounding nursing) allowed women to define the needs of empire and world as lying within the civilizing realm of feminine domesticity. In this process of transformation, the mission field, already containing large numbers of female missionaries in the form of wives and dependent family members, was affected by burgeoning numbers of a new and important addition to the missionary force: the unmarried missionary woman.

Women were critical to the support of foreign missions from their inception, but in the eyes of the predominantly middle-class male clerics that controlled denominational Christianity and its missionary societies, women — as wives and daughters — had a specific and subordinate part to play. The Victorian ideology of home life, characterized most fundamentally by a hierarchy of complementary male and female roles — female domestically focused and subservient — permeated the culture of middle-class affluence that grew rapidly in the second quarter of the nineteenth century.[6] Women, who had publicly supported the early denominational societies through local women's associations, were by the 1830s subordinated under local or parochial organization led by clerics, as the ideal of separate male and female spheres and an increasing emphasis on ministerial authority and philanthropic professionalism undermined initially independent organizations. The missionary standard to be achieved was respectability, associated with independent means and the adequate maintenance of a household under patriarchal controls. Evangelical men predominantly directed this missionary enterprise, but women and the networks of feminine sociability that underpinned women's religious life largely sustained it.[7]

---

5. Jeffrey Cox notes that in 1889, 22,422 "native" workers amounted to 84 percent of overseas mission staff, a proportion maintained into the interwar period. *British Missionary Enterprise*, 200, 230.

6. Davidoff and Hall, *Family Fortunes*, 71-192.

7. See for example, Piggin, *Making Evangelical Missionaries*, 128-31; Sue Morgan, "Introduction:

Rather than assaulting ecclesiastical or organizational structures of power, women within the Church, and within mission organization, built what Joan Gundersen has called a "parallel church," through which they were able to extend sororal networks of community activism, the weight of which substantially influenced male-dominated church structures and strategy for church extension.[8] As women and their kin increasingly organized missionary work and support networks and took advantage of widening opportunities in training and higher education, the second half of the nineteenth century saw a shift away from domination of the missionary movement by clergymen in the parish. In the context of these developments, the place of women in the foreign missionary movement altered as a new generation of female missionaries built on the earlier missionary culture formulated by mothers and aunts to shape new forms of religious pietism with which to justify and catalyze rapidly expanding work, both at home and abroad. The Church of England emerged over the Victorian era as a critical locus of women's voluntary activity, with women creating, staffing, and administering much of the parish-based philanthropy that supported Sunday schools, home visitations, and charitable institutions of dizzying variety.[9] Women within the church also grew to utilize a form of "civic maternalism." This was a body of ideas and approaches that emphasized, as Mary (Mrs. Humphrey) Ward insisted, both the maternal powers of social improvement, with which women were imbued, and the responsibilities women carried to engage in politics and public reform movements, not as voters in national politics but as volunteers focused on social improvement through charity organization, local government, and the eschewal of force.[10] A parallel "missionary maternalism" — one that could operate as a species of imperial maternalism and as the beginnings of a humanist maternalism — also grew within the missionary movement, affecting both Evangelicals and Anglo-Catholics, and drawing the attention of women within the Church. As it happened, this included Ward's sister-in-law Gertrude, who became first an Anglican sister

Women, Religion and Feminism; Past, Present and Future Perspectives," in *Women, Religion, and Feminism in Britain, 1750-1900*, ed. Sue Morgan (Basingstoke, UK: Palgrave Macmillan, 2002), 9-11.

8. Gundersen examines American Episcopalian experience, but her approach can equally be applied to the English experience. Joan R. Gundersen, "Women and the Parallel Church: A View from Congregations," in *Episcopal Women: Gender, Spirituality, and Commitment in an American Mainline Denomination,* ed. Catherine M. Prelinger (New York: Oxford University Press, 1992), 111-32.

9. Brian Heeney, *The Women's Movement in the Church of England, 1850-1930* (Oxford: Clarendon Press, 1988), 20-24.

10. Seth Koven, "Borderlands: Women, Voluntary Action, and Child Welfare in Britain, 1840 to 1914," in *Mothers of a New World: Maternalist Politics and the Origins of Welfare States* (New York: Routledge, 1993), 107-9.

in India, ultimately a nursing sister under the UMCA in Africa.[11] In the final decades of the nineteenth century this movement resulted in women (including the wives of missionaries) rising to become the single largest English group in the mission field, with single women as the fastest-growing section of new missionaries employed by the denominational societies.

The expansion of women's roles in missionary societies paralleled the broader expansion of their roles in English society. At the CMS administrators were eventually forced to credit women with the bulk of the advance in the 1880s and 1890s, and they furthermore tended to consider women the best hope for continued expansion of the cause because experience showed that "[w]here women have been stirred of God to active effort, matters have gone forward; where practical cooperation from them has not been evoked, matters have been either stationary or retrograde."[12] However, the considerably different concerns of male administrators and female activists in constructing women's missions led to friction within the societies. Both evangelical and Anglo-Catholic holiness ideologies gave women new license to act in the world of conservative religious cultures, as deaconesses and as sisters of charity, roles that were transferred to the missionary field.[13] Over time, they also effectively promoted a strategy for the cultural transformation of both indigenous and colonial societies that stressed the importance of independent female agency, which also had the potential to challenge patriarchal and imperial systems of control in the name of universalist Christian values.[14] This strategy legitimized the activity of British women in foreign service, drawing on British assumptions about feminine influence in the family, and enabling female missionary advocates to expand their roles as experts on social and imperial policy.

Women who theorized an extended set of female public roles that drew on the lessons provided by both religious and imperial experience led all of the major denominational missionary societies to establish popular and successful women's branches. The "new era" of missions after 1880 relied significantly on the rise of

11. Gertrude Ward, *The Life of Charles Alan Smythies, Bishop of the Universities' Mission to Central Africa*, 2nd ed. (London: UMCA, 1899), vi. On the missionary religious origins of internationalist human rights, see Kevin Grant, "Human Rights and Sovereign Abolitions of Slavery, c. 1885-1956," in *Beyond Sovereignty: Britain, Empire and Transnationalism, c. 1880-1950*, ed. Kevin Grant, Frank Trentmann, and Philippa Levine (Basingstoke, UK: Palgrave Macmillan, 2007), 82-83.

12. Georgina A. Gollock, "Women's Work and the Three Years' Enterprise," *The Church Missionary Intelligencer*, n.s., 21 (Oct. 1896): 733.

13. For a general view of Anglican sisters and deaconesses, see Gill, *Women and the Church*, 147-68.

14. For the development of such critiques, particularly following WW I, see Prevost, *Communion of Women*, chap. 5.

women to prominence in the movement. This makes understanding the overt feminization of the missionary endeavor critical, not least because of the impact that feminized missionary activity had on the civic life and imperial imagination of the late nineteenth century. For in the expansion of women's missions lay relative independence and access to public culture that allowed women's parallel church structures and activities to bleed over into clerically dominated realms, at first subtly, but by the turn of the century more insistently. The missionary movement, by cultivating feminine networks of sociability with increasing levels of professionalizing voluntarism, had the effect of bridging denominational subcultures, and female missionaries and their supporters, despite formal subordination in official church structures, assumed enhanced roles as legitimate participants in both religious and civil society.[15] By advancing a missionary maternalism that opened the mission field to women in rapidly expanding numbers, women set many of the terms of debate regarding the nature of indigenous societies and the "civilizing" processes operating through the family.[16] This debate was expanded not only by missionary theorists; colonial reformers of all sorts and nationalist movements in the many mission fields also took it up. In this way missions provided a theoretical field for the expansion of "spiritual womanhood" that extended the boundaries of acceptable domestic work, providing new sets of practical opportunities in public, colonial realms in the final decades of the century.[17]

The Origins of Independent Women's Missions

In the late Victorian age, in conjunction with the trend to popularize missions and draw in new constituencies of support, foreign missions came to depend heavily on the visible use of women as missionaries and home organizers. This transformation had deep roots. Women had been involved in the organization of Protestant missions since the eighteenth century, but when women went overseas they did so almost exclusively as missionary wives and immediate family dependents of male missionaries.[18] From the earliest stages of orga-

15. On the power of missionary wives and women to negotiate public and private realms better than status-conscious male missionaries, and thus carry missionary emotionalism more effectively to home audiences, see Semple, *Missionary Women*, 224, 227.

16. Patricia Grimshaw, "Faith, Missionary Life and the Family," in *Gender and Empire*, ed. Philippa Levine, The Oxford History of the British Empire Companion Series (Oxford: Oxford University Press, 2004), 263-65.

17. Jenny Daggers, "The Victorian Female Civilising Mission and Women's Aspirations Towards Priesthood in the Church of England," *Women's History Review* 10, no. 4 (2001): 652-53.

18. Rhonda Anne Semple, "Professionalizing Their Faith: Women, Religion and the Cultures

nization, women had collected both penny-a-week and guinea subscriptions, organized ladies associations and run local organizations, marshaled the support of children and the poor, organized innumerable sales of work, missionary teas, and Sunday school lectures.[19] Yet, in the male-dominated clerical world of early-nineteenth-century denominational Christianity, the essential support of women in England went largely unacknowledged, as did the continuously important part played by the wives of missionaries — as well as daughters, sisters, and aunts — in sustaining the overseas operations of a movement that had grown to formidable proportions by the 1840s.

Thus by the Victorian era, solidification of the middle-class codes of respectability that evangelical religion endorsed increasingly shut women out of formal public political life. At the same time, ideas about the "nature and mission" of women encouraged them to extend the private domestic sphere beyond the home into an expanding realm of social concern, both in England and in the world.[20] Because of this cultural formation and its inherent fissures and contradictions, women became engaged with social problems through charitable voluntary action, exploiting an inconsistency in Victorian gender ideology by embracing and expanding, both in Britain and overseas, the set of opportunities that could be defined as "domestic." Voluntary religious and philanthropic associations provided the primary opportunity for women, particularly middle-class women, to play growing roles in public life and, as women also expanded their overseas presence as missionaries, engage questions of imperial expansion and morality.[21] Women's voluntarism was wrapped up in issues of familial social concern both at home and overseas. Therefore it is not surprising that it was through imperial reform movements — antislavery, missionary settlements, colonial social and legal reform — that many women first entered into debates surrounding public policy.[22] Evoking both religious and imperial enthusiasms,

of Mission and Empire," in *Women, Gender and Religious Cultures in Britain, 1800-1940*, ed. Sue Morgan and Jacqueline deVries (London: Routledge, 2010), 127-30.

19. Stock, *History of the CMS*, 4:517. On the intensive use of children, see F. K. Prochaska, "Little Vessels: Children in the Nineteenth-Century English Missionary Movement," *The Journal of Imperial and Commonwealth History* 6, no. 2 (Jan. 1978): 103-18.

20. On the network of local and global concerns that created middle-class culture in Sheffield early in the century, see Alison Twells, "'Happy English Children': Class, Ethnicity, and the Making of Missionary Women in the Early Nineteenth Century," *Women's Studies International Forum* 21, no. 3 (May 1998): 235-45.

21. F. K. Prochaska, *Women and Philanthropy in Nineteenth-Century England* (Oxford: Clarendon Press, 1980), 8-17 and passim; Billie Melman, *Women's Orients: English Women and the Middle East, 1718-1918: Sexuality, Religion and Work* (London: Macmillan, 1992), 46-48, 166-67.

22. See Clare Midgley, *Feminism and Empire*, chap. 1; for later in the century, when attention shifted to women in India, see Antoinette M. Burton, *Burdens of History: British Feminists, Indian*

advocacy for foreign missions, and more specifically for indigenous female education, played an important role in extending women's domestic duty beyond the home and beyond the voluntary, local English realm of part-time activity endorsed in more restrictive formulations of domesticity.[23]

The development of women's public voice on missionary subjects was, however, a slow and uneven process. Institutionally, women's support for missions was associated with and legitimized by denominational societies and their slow growth through the first three decades of the nineteenth century. The actual experience of women in the field and the gradual growth in the number of missionary biographies featuring females undoubtedly normalized expanding women's roles in missionary work in the minds of increasing numbers of readers.[24] Following these leads, women assumed a growing role in instituting and defining foreign missions, both as active European agents in the field and as specific targets of Christian proselytizing whose family influence was theorized as central to effecting social change. Missionary societies, operating at the center of English religious associational life, were quite naturally deeply concerned about imperial and international matters. Missionary activity thus provided an important rationale for women's interest in British overseas activity. As the doctrine of evangelical Protestantism more insistently emphasized the freedom that Christianity gave Western women to improve manners, morals, and civilization, missions resonated with the socially conservative British women that dominated the religious associational networks of the Anglican church.

As advocates for the destruction of "native" barbarism at the hands of feminine philanthropic voluntarism, religious women, a growing proportion Anglican by the mid-Victorian period, entered public debates with a prescription for extending civil society to the empire and to "backwards" societies throughout the world. Nineteenth-century missionaries, in addition to spreading religious belief and dogma, broadcast British assumptions about liberal, progressive "civilization," and women drew Anglican missions beyond simple endorsements of the colonial status quo to more visionary concepts of imperial regeneration. As missionaries defined their own culture against the evocative examples of foreign cultures, they found in the comparative condition of English women the proof of the superiority of Christian liberalism and the English nation.[25] At the heart

---

Women, and Imperial Culture, 1865-1915 (Chapel Hill: University of North Carolina Press, 1994), 63-125.

23. David Savage, "Missionaries and the Development of a Colonial Ideology of Female Education in India," *Gender and History* 9, no. 2 (1997): 208-11.

24. Clare Midgley, "Can Women Be Missionaries? Envisioning Female Agency in the Early Nineteenth-Century British Empire," *Journal of British Studies* 45, no. 2 (April 2006): 340-49.

25. On later parallel strategies among Victorian feminists, see Burton, *Burdens of History*, 6-8.

of this project, however, remained the larger continuous tension within the broader missionary movement between a fundamental commitment to universal human rights and the disdainful arrogance and reflex to subordination produced by assumption of Western cultural and racial superiority.[26]

Yet missionary ideology was not simply a product of British religious doctrine and cultural beliefs. Over the course of the nineteenth century, British Protestants responded to the deeply foreign conditions and cultures that missions brought to their attention and the imperial means used to establish hegemony overseas. They were particularly troubled by the resistance to Christian transformation that they experienced in the majority of mission fields, but also by the invidious impact of European commercial and settler communities on the welfare of indigenous peoples and communities. Crucial to support for projects to transform indigenous societies were the "domestic" concerns of female supporters in education, child care, and household economy. By the 1840s a dominant modernization strategy had emerged in British missions, founded in education, training, and a patriarchal gender order that would rely on the building of Christian families, churches, schools, hospitals, and printing houses. At its heart was a reflexive assumption of the superiority of Western culture and European economic, social, and political organization as standards of "civilization."[27] Along with other evangelicals, Anglicans in the "Protestant" fold also threw their weight in the 1840s behind civilizational schemes such as West Indian "free labour" villages and the Niger Expedition, designed to drive Western commercial development and social change as a proof against the continuation of slavery. Missions that linked Christianity and commerce had come to participate in the reforged national identity of the reform age. These ambitious civilizational strategies, however, were destined for disappointment, and their failures both forced reassessment of missionary strategy in the next generation and opened missions to alternative gendered strategies revolving around the concept of "women's mission to women."

Protestant Missionary Theory: An Expanding Domestic Sphere

Because the missionary movement matured at the same time and in the same places as early Victorian, family-based capitalism, male-dominated civic elites that defined urban public life also controlled the missionary enterprise. In the

26. Grimshaw, "Missionary Life," 261-62.
27. On Baptist efforts to transform West Indian slave communities in the 1830s and 40s, see Hall, *Civilising Subjects*, 124-25, 134-39.

early period the figure of the missionary wife was ideologically central, even though actual missionary wives were largely relegated to background roles and written out of the heroic narratives of male missionary sacrifice produced by the societies. Missionary wives provided critical labor to the missionary task, but moreover married women were seen as anchoring the monogamous moral center and bourgeois respectability of missions in foreign, unfamiliar societies, where men might fall prey to sexual temptation and domestic impropriety.[28] In addition to establishing the respectable credentials of missionary settlements, women and families were also of considerable importance to the way social transformation in indigenous communities was theorized. Baptist missionaries in Jamaica, for example, argued that missionary wives, through the education and positive domestic examples they provided to "heathen" women, would encourage the morality, free association, and free labor destroyed by the slave system. Families were imagined as the fundamental units of society and social change as well as the crucial agency of spiritual and cultural change. The major denominations all used similar arguments to construct a special, although dependent, sphere for women in the mission field, especially married women.[29]

Evangelical culture could be prescriptive and puritanical. But it also held within it styles of charisma that allowed for the construction of innovative female roles in both religious and secular society.[30] In particular, it assumed that women were specially suited for ministering to women and children, especially young girls. This assumption provided an argument for female work outside of the home, but tension remained between the evangelical insistence on the spiritual equality of the converted and the demand that believers defer to established social hierarchies and the clear gender roles presumed to be demonstrated by Scripture. While spiritual equality was seldom imagined to imply gender equality, the ambiguity about what it did authorize allowed women to contest more restrictive definitions of the feminine sphere in order to encourage useful, serious, spiritual work for women outside the home.

28. Jocelyn Murray, "The Role of Women in the Church Missionary Society, 1799-1917," in *The Church Mission Society and World Christianity, 1799-1999*, ed. Kevin Ward and Brian Stanley (Grand Rapids: Eerdmans, 1999), 69-70; Julia C. Wells, "The Suppression of Mixed Marriages Among LMS Missionaries in South Africa Before 1820," *South African Historical Journal* 44 (May 2001): 1-20.

29. On the LMS, see Rosemary E. Seton, "'Open Doors for Female Labourers': Women Candidates of the London Missionary Society, 1875-1914," in *Missionary Encounters: Sources and Issues*, ed. Robert A. Bickers and Rosemary E. Seton (Richmond, UK: Curzon, 1995), 51 and Midgley, *Women Against Slavery*, chap. 5.

30. For an earlier but, by 1850, waning tradition authorizing popular prophesying and preaching by women, see Deborah M. Valenze, *Prophetic Sons and Daughters: Female Preaching and Popular Religion in Industrial England* (Princeton: Princeton University Press, 1985), 274-81.

Drawing on the presumption of authority over the instruction of children, English women launched new efforts to reach Indian women in the 1820s. These concentrated almost exclusively on the instruction of young "native" girls and were constructed in Britain as an essential component in the larger campaign to abolish *sati,* or widow burning. Focusing particularly on orphans and Eurasians, these efforts expanded quickly and relied on employing unmarried women.[31] Orientalist discourses on India had long constructed a vision of victimized women as an indicator of a degenerate Hinduism, and missionaries developed this discourse by the 1840s into a coherent strategy for female education. The degradation of women, which was premised upon the insistence that Christianity was the only basis for social progress, became the central image of a new evangelization strategy that encouraged British women to extend their domestic talents outside their own homes and into the zenana — the separate women's apartments in upper-class Indian homes — constructed as "the hidden center of Hindu domestic life."[32]

Women's missionary societies were initially founded with the limited goal of supporting female mission teachers for girls' schools, but by mid-century were more forcefully developing the zenana as a target of special feminine mission. The earliest were the Society for Promoting Female Education in the East (commonly known as the Female Education Society, or FES), in 1834, followed in England by the Indian Female Normal School and Instruction Society (IFNS) in 1851.[33] Both operated primarily as interdenominational auxiliaries to the major evangelical missionary societies, supplying teachers and submitting to clerical oversight in the field.[34] Within the denominational societies the envi-

31. Midgley, *Feminism and Empire,* 70-86; Eugene Stock, *An Historical Survey of Women's Work in C.M.S. at Home and Abroad* (London, 1907), 12.

32. Savage, "Female Education in India," 208-9. On CMS-generated images of Indian culture in the early nineteenth century, see Brian K. Pennington, *Was Hinduism Invented? Britons, Indians, and the Colonial Construction of Religion* (Oxford: Oxford University Press, 2005), chap. 3.

33. Originally known as the Calcutta Female Normal School Society, supporting from 1852 the Calcutta Female Normal School, its Board adopted in 1861 the new name (commonly abbreviated to IFNS) when it reorganized to tap domestic British support. Minutes of the London Committee of the Calcutta Female Normal School, 15 July 1861, Indian Female Normal School and Instruction Society/Zenana Bible Medical Mission/Interserve Archives, Home File List, General Committee minutes, 1859–Mar. 1865, School of Oriental and African Studies, London, Eng. (hereafter IFNS/ZBMM Archives). The Society changed its name to the Zenana Bible and Medical Mission (ZBMM) shortly after 1880, then to the Bible and Medical Missionary Fellowship in 1957, and then to the International Service Fellowship (Interserve) in 1987.

34. The FES supported women employed in Anglican, Congregational, and Baptist missions, among others. Minutes of the Committee of the Female Education Society, 1871-78, passim, FES Archives, AM 4, University of Birmingham, Birmingham, Eng. (hereafter cited as

sioned roles for women were those of the modest dependent missionary wife and the girls' school instructor or, ideally, a combination of the two.[35] In effect, the early Victorian missionary imagination defined civilization, and women's roles within its civic life, in the classical liberal terms of the eighteenth century: women were denied equal status in public affairs, although assigned theoretically crucial supporting roles in maintaining the families upon which the fortunes of free, rational, independent, middle-class men were presumed to depend. Nevertheless, at the IFNS independent female authority under only nominal male oversight eventually emerged, despite resulting friction with mission and Church authorities as the work expanded.

At Arm's Length: Anglicans and Women's Missionary Work

The institutional solidification of clearly subordinate women's roles, and the growing emphasis on clerical authority within Anglicanism through the era of Church reform, meant that early independent Ladies' Associations, which had been the visible organizational basis of the CMS from the time it was founded in 1799, saw their leadership roles progressively usurped in the 1840s by the parochial clergy. As clerical support for the CMS increased, local parochial or town associations absorbed women's organizations and placed them under the authority of the parish priest. This operated in parallel with the emergence of city missions such as the London Mission, where the rising use of paid male agents professionalized charity, displacing the women and voluntary parish visiting that had earlier defined urban philanthropy.[36] While at the foreign missionary societies women continued to be responsible for the bulk of the hard work of collecting, independent female organizations folded until fewer than a dozen CMS Ladies Associations existed in 1873, and the independent societies and the work of women "got little countenance from General Boards or Committees."[37] The rise to prominence that women, and especially single women, eventually assumed by the 1890s developed instead outside the structures of the denominational societies in the work of separate women's missionary societies and the independent initiative taken by the wives of missionaries in the foreign field.

FES Archives). Scottish women saw earlier organization, beginning in 1837 with the Church of Scotland Ladies' Association. Cox, *British Missionary Enterprise*, 189.

35. J. N. Murdoch, "Women's Work in the Mission Field," in *Protestant Missions Conference, 1888*, 1:165.

36. Donald M. Lewis, *Lighten Their Darkness: The Evangelical Mission to Working-Class London, 1828-1860* (New York: Greenwood, 1986), 220-22.

37. Rainy, "Female Agency," in *Protestant Missions Conference, 1888*, 2:145.

In overseas missions the societies structured women's roles as supplementary and subordinate to clerical efforts. Thus in 1821 the British and Foreign Schools Society sent Miss Cooke to Calcutta (Kolkata) to establish a girls' school, an effort that quickly expanded to twenty-two schools, prompting the formation of the Ladies' Society for Native Female Education in 1824.[38] When the work outgrew local Indian financial support, the CMS took her up as one of its agents. This pattern — a haphazard growth of female agency relying heavily on local initiative by missionary wives — provided an opportunity for the denominational societies to support useful work, but it did not induce them to organize and expand a relatively limited effort that had little exposure in England. That Cooke's first day schools were run by Eurasian girls from the Female Orphan Asylum, understood to be the innocent victims of sinful European male lust, was one peculiarly resonant aspect of the early history of women's missions, but it also pressed the bounds of respectable subjects.

Due to sensitivity to the proper relations between men and women at home and abroad, denominational societies were reluctant to accept women as candidates for missions. The CMS received its first offers from women in 1815. Despite its approval of male missionaries in India, the CMS Committee insisted that unmarried women not be sent into the field unless they were sisters accompanying or joining brothers who could ensure respectable living conditions and conduct. In 1819 the CMS sent out its first unmarried female missionaries, two "school mistresses," to Sierra Leone, to fill institutional educational posts. By 1887 the CMS had sent out a mere 103 single women, of whom roughly 40 percent were widows or daughters of missionaries and 95 percent were girls' school teachers in well-supervised mission stations. Nevertheless, they came to be known as particularly unreliable agents because they often quickly married in the mission field; of the first fifty women sent out by the CMS, 50 percent had married within three years of arrival.[39]

Early and mid-century women's work was left primarily to independent auxiliaries. Despite the nominal independence of these auxiliaries, the demands of marriage, sexual respectability, and dependence on men set parameters for the entire undertaking. The FES, derisively labeled "The Bachelors Aid Society," had to weather criticism that it provided little more than a marriage service for male missionaries and Anglo-Indians.[40] And indeed, in the experience of many of the women associated with the FES and IFNS, this expectation was borne

---

38. C. Harding, "Origins of the Church of England Zenana Society," TS, CEZMS Archives, CEZ/G EA 5A.

39. Stock, *Women's Work*, 12; Murray, "Role of Women," 72.

40. William Arthur, *Woman's Work in India* (London: Woolmer, 1882), 12.

out. Cooke's association with the CMS led eventually to her marriage to CMS missionary Isaac Wilson; Miss Suter, the superintendent of the Calcutta Normal School, married CMS missionary, and later CMS Home Secretary, Samuel Hasell.[41] The frequent decision of female agents to "change their circumstances" very soon after arriving in the field caused problems for the FES, but even more so it created anxiety that the "change" would occur in a way that suggested sexual impropriety on the part of an organization already operating in the boundary regions of acceptable gender behavior.[42] And as Anglican female celibate orders were founded in the 1840s, with all the controversy and opposition they aroused in evangelical circles, efforts to maintain a standard of family-based respectability redoubled among Anglican evangelicals.[43] For evangelical women, who had no recourse to the independence of a celibate vocation, it remained very difficult for those who chose the respectability of a married role also to secure the respect attached to a professional one.

Yet marriage in the mission field was the most reasonable of decisions for early independent female missionaries because it eradicated the debilitating sexual ambiguity involved in the position of the single woman worker. For this reason, the idea of female missionary work developed conceptually as a type of marriage, with all the duties and restraints implied in that institution. In the words of William Arthur, women had to be found who would embrace women's mission "and who, wedding that cause, should make it their life-work."[44] In effect, evangelical women were counseled to become members of a religious order without the binding vows that evangelicals found so abhorrent in Catholic and Anglican orders. But this set of ideas, subject to private interpretation, was always highly unstable and liable to criticism. Single missionaries who opted for marriage, despite the familial domestic duties incurred in respectable Victorian marriage, often proved better able to carry out their missionary educational duties, and particularly public advocacy of their cause, as married women. Such marriages also helped to solidify women's institutional connections to the mainline denominational missionary societies, with all of their influence and resources.

41. Irene H. Barnes, *Behind the Pardah: The Story of C.E.Z.M.S. Work in India* (London: Marshall, 1897), 3.

42. Margaret Donaldson, "'The Cultivation of the Heart and the Moulding of the Will . . .': The Missionary Contribution of the Society for Promoting Female Education in China, India, and the East," in *Women in the Church*, ed. W. J. Sheils and Diana Wood, vol. 27 of *Studies in Church History* (Oxford: Blackwell, 1990), 436-37.

43. Martha Vicinus, *Independent Women: Work and Community for Single Women, 1850-1920* (London: Virago, 1985), 47, 68-69.

44. Arthur, *Women's Work*, 11.

For up to the 1860s, separate female missionary work had a very low profile and a very small place in the overall program of the Anglican missionary societies. Maria Charlesworth, popular children's author and stern Evangelical, a second-generation product of the influential circle surrounding the Clapham Sect, lamented in 1860 that while the "improvement" of Eastern women had become a familiar subject, still only a very few earnest workers and supporters were involved. Until 1866 the SPG declined to send a single female missionary into the field.[45] The CMS was interested only in staffing the mission schools run by its male missionaries with female teachers for girls. However, new realms of women's activity were beginning to develop around new forms of women's Christian work and organization — sisterhoods and deaconess work most significantly — as well as around the subject of the Indian household. When zealous, reforming Christian women, empowered through new conceptions of women's pious organization, increasingly encountered the foreign and forbidden world of the Indian zenana — the exclusively female apartments of high caste Hindu and Islamic households where men outside the immediate family were not allowed — by imaginative extension they ideologically constructed all "heathen" homes as sites of resistance. Because of the inaccessibility of the zenana to men, only feminine power, it was argued, could penetrate them. As Janaki Nair has shown, although the zenana as an institution was far from widespread in India (occurring primarily in the north, northwest, and east), it took on a powerful, multifaceted life as a general representation of Indian home life and assumed an important place in a colonial discourse that sought explanation and justification for British rule in the subcontinent.[46] Missionary supporters, also seeking reasons for the slow progress of conversion, built a clearly conceived vision of "heathen homes" that harbored "isolated" communities of women, victimized by male abuse of power. Along these lines emerged a new pattern of mission, defined by women's gendered assumptions and concerns.

Women and the Building of "New Era" Missions

By the 1880s women's missions were routinely considered a crucial component of missionary work. Public advocacy for exclusively female missions using unmarried women dates from the mid-Victorian period with the foundation of

45. Maria Louisa Charlesworth, *India and the East; or, a Voice from the Zenana* (London: Seeley, Jackson and Halliday, 1860), 3; Thompson, *History of the SPG*, 235.

46. Janaki Nair, "Uncovering the Zenana: Visions of Indian Womanhood in Englishwomen's Writings, 1813-1940," *Journal of Women's History* 2, no. 1 (Spring 1990): 9, 11, 25-26.

women's branches at the major denominational societies.[47] Missionary societies
supported the creation of women's branches by drawing on arguments about the
supposed deleterious effect that indigenous women had on their own families.
Removing the "corrupt" ideas held by "heathen mothers" and thus regenerating
"native" families rapidly became a central concern and resulted in new strategies
designed to change religious and moral instruction within the indigenous family.[48] In the process of defining this new mission, the public roles and freedoms
of English women were explicitly defined in opposition to what Western commentators argued were the debilitating conditions suffered by the non-Western
wife and mother. Mary Weitbrecht, CMS missionary, widow of influential missionary to Bengal J. J. Weitbrecht, and prolific writer on missions and India,
insisted on "the greater liberty" of Western women compared to those of "the
East," a liberty that was dependent upon Christian influence.[49] Thus, as early
as the 1860s the shift that Anna Davin has seen in the later nineteenth century
surrounding imperial and eugenic themes — that is, the shift from defining
women as wives to defining them as mothers — was taking place. In this way
the image of Indian women as objects of rescue was displaced by a vision of
their critical power to transform the religious and moral basis of Indian society.[50]

Three interlocking developments in the 1860s led to these rapid and radical
changes in the position and expectations of women's missionary activity. One
of these was the rise of a new spiritual radicalism among both Anglo-Catholics
— leading to expanding numbers and acceptance of Anglican sisters within
High Church charitable networks — and evangelicals — leading to the growth
of the deaconess movement. Both provided a stronger religious support for the
spiritual equality of women, an equality that helped undermine older, more restrictive religious definitions of the "female" sphere. Independent communities
for women emerged both in association with the holiness enthusiasm advanced
by William Pennefather and his Mildmay conferences, institute, and deaconess
home, and in the Tractarian enthusiasm of E. B. Pusey and John Mason Neale

47. The WMMS was the first to form a Ladies Committee (1858), followed by the SPG (1866),
the BMS (1867), and the LMS (1875). The CMS did not form its own independent Women's Committee until 1895; however, it was intimately involved in the work of the IFNS and its offshoots
from the time it reorganized as a London-based society in 1861.

48. Charlesworth, *India and the East*, 4-5; Mary Weitbrecht, *The Women of India and Christian
Work in the Zenana* (London: Nisbet, 1875), 47-48.

49. Weitbrecht, *Women of India*, 1.

50. Anna Davin, "Imperialism and Motherhood," *History Workshop Journal* 5, no. 1 (1978):
12-14. This transformation began with the emergence of a coherent strategy for female education
by the 1840s. Savage, "Female Education in India," 205-9, 214-15. Only in the 1860s, however, did
this ideology become a basis for systematic propagandizing in Britain designed to draw focused
support for women's missions.

and the sisterhoods they patronized and championed. Another of these inter-locking developments was a new focus on reforming the Indian home. It was sparked both by the failure of missions to produce accelerating numbers of conversions and by the growth of imperial anxiety following the 1857 Indian rebellion. This approach provided a unique realm for women's activity and a reinvigorated desire within the missionary community to rebuild Indian society particularly, and "heathen" societies more generally, from the family level up-wards.[51] The third of these developments was the rapid expansion in accepted public roles for women in England itself. Driven by demographic pressure as the proportion of women in the population grew, it transformed the realms of charity and social reform and provided a rationale for the semi-professionalized expansion of the work of "independent" women overseas.[52] The combination of these three forces allowed missionaries to open paths of opportunity for the development of women's work beyond the relatively restricted levels of the early Victorian period.

Sisterhoods and Anglican Gender Roles

New departures in later Victorian missions were nearly all linked to the new forms of behavior authorized by theologies of personal and corporate holi-ness. The rise of relatively independent female missions was no exception. The new waves of holiness practice within Anglicanism had two sources. On the one hand was the development by High Church Anglicans of Anglo-Catholic forms of personal and corporate piety, notably advanced by sisterhoods and brotherhoods, gaining real momentum in the 1850s. On the other hand was the effect of North American–inspired revivals on evangelical Anglicans in the British Isles, particularly the second wave of revivals beginning in 1859 and 1860. Holiness pietism first generated a series of city and social mission strat-egies incorporating new, militant use of female evangelists and workers that were then extended into foreign mission work. The innovations represented in Anglo-Catholic practice catalyzed changes in the entire Anglican framework of religious gender understanding.

The legacy of rising female spirituality channeled through the re-foundation of sisterhoods proved central, and it was an undoubted spur in following years

51. Emancipation in the United States and the backlash following the 1865 Morant Bay revolt in Jamaica helped shift attention away from the Americas. Clare Midgley, "Ethnicity, 'Race' and Em-pire," in *Women's History: Britain, 1850-1945*, ed. June Purvis (London: UCL Press, 1995), 259, 263.

52. On independent women in religion, see Vicinus, *Independent Women*, 3-5, 46-84, 294; on the professionalization of women's work in missions, see Semple, *Missionary Women*, 197-206.

to an energetic evangelical response. From the foundation of the first sister-hood (1845) early in the development of the Oxford Movement, the creation of women's religious communities drew ferocious opposition from evangelicals and other social conservatives who feared them as a threat to the patriarchal home. Nevertheless, as communal religious life under vows expanded with the rapid foundation of new sisterhoods, so too did acceptance, even if slowly and primarily among High Churchmen, influenced positively by the celebration of Florence Nightingale during the Crimean War and her use of several volunteer nursing sisters.[53] Sisterhoods began as a deeply contested element in Victorian religious practice because they seemed to embody the worst popish, priestly excesses aimed at the most vulnerable victims that populated the evangelical imagination: young girls and women. In addition, women's religious commu-nities represented a burgeoning area of Church life that proved surprisingly resistant to male clerical and episcopal power.[54] They particularly became a center of controversy in the 1850s, as evangelical allegations that they violated patriarchal rights over dependent daughters blossomed to reinforce the ongo-ing controversy over Tractarianism and the emergent Ritualism of the Anglo-Catholic connection.

Plans for the missionary use of sisters had clearly been developing prior to the founding of the UMCA. Bishop Robert Gray of Cape Town, for exam-ple, was writing home about the need for sisterhoods as early as 1850, and he discussed the subject in 1856 with Pusey.[55] Sisterhoods were incorporated into Anglo-Catholic missions proper beginning with the arrival in 1864 of three sisters (Crimean War nursing veterans drawn from Ascot Priory) in the Diocese of Honolulu, on the invitation of Hawaiian Queen Emma. Visiting England in 1865 Emma sought the counsel of Bishop Samuel Wilberforce of Oxford, who assisted her fundraising for a Gothic-style Anglican cathedral and guided her acquaintance with Tractarian luminaries such as Keble and Pusey. She also visited Ascot Priory, where she asked Mother Lydia Sellon to send additional sisters to reinforce the three sisters who had arrived the previous year. Under the oversight of fire-brand, Anglo-Catholic Bishop T. N. Staley, the additional nuns operated from 1867 as Sisters of Mercy (Society of the Most Holy Trinity) out of an independent house, embodying one particularly defiant Anglo-Catholic countercultural practice.[56]

53. J. M. Ludlow, *Woman's Work in the Church: Historical Notes on Deaconesses and Sisterhoods* (London: Strahan, 1866), vii-ix.

54. Susan Mumm, *Stolen Daughters, Virgin Mothers: Anglican Sisterhoods in Victorian Britain* (London: Leicester University Press, 1999), 140-46.

55. Lear, *Gray*, 1:268-70, 280.

56. Kanahele, *Emma*, 194-98, 219-20; A. M. Allchin, *The Silent Rebellion: Anglican Religious*

Organized and largely funded by the influential Lydia Sellon — one of the most controversial and commanding women of the day — the Sisters worked in close cooperation with Queen Emma to establish boarding schools and multiply girls' education and thereby, it was believed, combat the decline of the Hawaiian people and their culture.[57] With this promising beginning, Gray then established the first sisterhood in South Africa following his visit to England in 1867 for the Lambeth Conference, making the rounds of several new Anglo-Catholic religious communities (including the community of St. Mary at the Cross in Shoreditch) and recruiting a small band of women who became the Sisters of St. George.[58] For Anglo-Catholic bishops like Staley, as well as for bishops, such as Wilberforce and Gray, who were supportive of such higher church initiatives, sisterhoods were part of the drive to create autonomous churches which, even if they continued the High Church ideal of partnership with government, would be assuredly separated from any Erastian control by the state. Bishop Wilberforce contributed to the process of normalization of sisterhoods, and he was known as the only English bishop not to harass them.[59]

Within the culture of advanced Anglo-Catholicism sisterhoods operated as an example of pious, godly independence. While only two specifically missionary-oriented sisterhoods were founded in the nineteenth century — the Missionary Community of St. Denys, established as a female missionary training school in the 1870s and evolving into a missionary sisterhood, and The Servants of Christ, founded in 1897 also as a missionary training center — the establishment of three sisterhoods in South Africa by British women, and the significant overseas activity of several English sisterhoods in British imperial possessions, meant that by the 1880s, sisterhoods were an established pres-

---

Communities, 1845-1900 (London: SCM, 1958), 119-20; "Hawaiian Mission," *The Net* 2, no. 5 (May 1867): 70.

57. Sellon travelled to Hawai'i and oversaw the creation of St. Andrew's Priory on land gifted by the Hawaiian royal family in 1867. Thomas N. Staley, *Five Years' Church Work in the Kingdom of Hawaii* (London: Rivingtons, 1868), 57-61; Kanahele, *Emma*, 155-56, 230-37. For a broader view of Sellon's contentious life and work, see Sean Gill, "The Power of Christian Ladyhood: Priscilla Lydia Sellon and the Creation of Anglican Sisterhoods," in *Modern Religious Rebels*, ed. Stuart Mews and John Kent (London: Epworth Press, 1993), 144-65.

58. Rowell, *Vision Glorious*, 169, 171.

59. Only two English bishops were willing to defend women's communities, Wilberforce and A. C. Tait, bishop of London (1856-68) and archbishop of Canterbury (1868-82). In 1866 virtually all English bishops consulted on the matter were vigorously opposed to the approximately thirty sisterhoods that had been founded by that time. These attitudes persisted among many bishops for the next several decades. Susan Mumm, "'A Peril to the Bench of Bishops': Sisterhoods and Episcopal Authority in the Church of England, 1845-1908," *Journal of Ecclesiastical History* 59, no. 1 (2008): 65-66.

ence in the field, primarily in South Africa, India, Canada, Australia, and New Zealand, but also in Persia, Korea, and the United States.[60] As in the case of St. Andrew's Priory in Honolulu, the primary approach to mission generated out of the sisterhood experience, and which was subsequently generalized to many High Church missions, was guided by what Elizabeth Prevost has called an "ideology of female protectionism." In this model the sisterhood operated as a closed charitable community supporting the founding of girls' educational systems based on boarding schools capable of sheltering vulnerable women. In this environment training an indigenized Christian womanhood that would serve as the foundation for evangelization and the reformation of colonial society could proceed.[61] Women were aided in the creation of such novel agencies by the Anglo-Catholic tradition of interpretation, which downplayed literal readings of the Bible (with their presumed injunctions against women's activism) in favor of a broader historical appreciation of Christian diversity and a strong predisposition to looser poetic interpretations of what faith might authorize.[62]

However, justifying the use of these "popish" sisterhoods to English constituents came in the longer run to involve emphasizing that they were not detrimental to "respectable" conceptions of femininity and domesticity in order to overcome the suspicion and obstruction of missionaries and mission administrators of more traditional High Church sympathies. The cultural and theological divide between moderate High Churchmen, with their characteristic support of the colonial project and strong backing for cooperative establishmentarian connection of national church and imperial state, and Anglo-Catholics, with their emphasis on building Church-based Anglican communities under the independent rule of bishops and synods, set the context for debate over introducing increased female missionary activity into High Church mission fields. The highly controversial reintroduction of Anglican sisterhoods in the 1840s seemed to both anti-Catholic evangelicals and traditional High Church bishops to challenge core assumptions of patriarchy and domesticity, under which women's activities in the parish and in the mission field had been

60. Mumm, *Anglican Sisterhoods*, 129-30.

61. For the development of this model in the 1870s in Madagascar, see Prevost, *Communion of Women*, chap. 1. See also Eleanor Joy Frith, "Pseudonuns: Anglican Sisterhoods and the Politics of Victorian Identity" (Ph.D. diss., Queen's University, 2004), chap. 6, which details the founding and development in British Columbia of female boarding school education in the 1880s by the Community of All Hallows, an extension of the Anglican sisters' work in Norfolk rehabilitating "fallen women" in a community-based penitentiary system.

62. Julie Melnyk, "Women, Writing and the Creation of Theological Cultures," in *Women, Gender and Religious Cultures in Britain, 1800-1940*, ed. Sue Morgan and Jacqueline deVries (London: Routledge, 2010), 39-41.

justified in the past. High Church bishops, even those supportive of sisterhoods in concept, were troubled by the independent female governance and autonomy that Anglican Church order, which had no formal place for sisters in a hierarchy of control, allowed to sisterhoods.[63] This remained a serious disability for the advocacy of sisterhoods in missions.

In the 1860s the SPG cautiously supported a few female missionaries, and from the 1880s it sent out single female missionaries. These women, however, served as employees in established mission institutions: schools for girls, dispensaries, and hospitals. Behind these practices lay the expectation of close male clerical supervision and, ideally, direction under the many missionary wives in the field. This had also been the approach of the SPG's Ladies' Association, founded in 1866. From its earliest work, the Ladies' Association placed all women strictly under the control of the SPG missionary-in-charge in the field. Through it the SPG entered into the growing practice of sending single women into the mission field but, even after four decades, only if they were sisters or daughters of responsible men or special precautions were taken to provide for a controlled, "civilized" atmosphere, such as membership in a sisterhood. As Rev. James Phillips insisted at the Bristol Church Congress in 1864, while it may be desirable to send out women, either deaconesses or sisters, all must certainly be under discipline, preferably under the authority of a bishop.[64] Such clerical insistence was only reinforced when even the most Anglo-Catholic of bishops, like T. N. Staley of Honolulu, found themselves at odds with independent female governance in the sisterhoods they endorsed. Thus a clash between Staley and Lydia Sellon led him simultaneously to praise the "great success" of the sisters in their schools while denouncing the principles of their rule as "radically unsound, and mischievous in their result on human character" because of the way Mothers Superior were led to prideful unfeminine tyranny, "lording it over God's heritage."[65]

In many ways, then, the institution of sisterhoods in Anglo-Catholic missions and missionary dioceses challenged, both implicitly and directly, the institutional rule of male missionaries and clerics. Anglo-Catholic assumptions

63. Carmen M. Mangion, "Women, Religious Ministry and Female Institution Building," in *Women, Gender and Religious Cultures in Britain, 1800-1940*, ed. Sue Morgan and Jacqueline deVries (London: Routledge, 2010), 81-85.

64. "Report of the Special Committee on the Relations between the W.M.A. and the S.P.G.," 2 Apr. 1903, in Minutes of the Women's Home Organisation Advisory Group, USPG Archives, CWW 71; James Erasmus Phillips, *Woman's Work in Foreign Missions: A Paper Read at the Church Congress Held at Bristol, October 11th, 1864* (London: Rivingtons, n.d.), 6-9.

65. T. N. Staley to John Jackson, bishop of London, 23 Aug. 1871, reprinted in Henry Codman Potter, *Sisterhoods and Deaconesses: At Home and Abroad* (New York: Dutton, 1873), 60-67.

Captioned "Lady Workers at Delhi," this group portrait of High Church women
workers in uniform (without their standard bonnets) presents a mix of married and
single female missionaries, operating as both deaconesses and sisters, and includes a
"native" Bible woman in the background, ca. 1885. United Society for the Propagation of the
Gospel Archives, SPG Photo Album 101, Bodleian Library of Commonwealth and African History,
Rhodes House, Oxford. Courtesy of the United Society
for the Propagation of the Gospel.

undermined Victorian family ideology. As John Shelton Reed has noted, in its
provision of independent work for women, celebration of celibacy, and disregard for conventional "manliness," Anglo-Catholicism "issued a series of subtle
but continual challenges to received patrimonial values."[66] The famous case of
the death of Anglican sister Amy Scobell in 1857 from scarlet fever, just two
months after defying her Evangelical clerical father to join the Society of St.
Margaret, led to the highly publicized Lewes riot, just one of several popular
actions against Anglo-Catholic practices. The cultural politics of employing
women in Church work, including foreign missions, was to be more complex

66. John Shelton Reed, "'A Female Movement': The Feminization of Nineteenth-Century
Anglo-Catholicism," *Anglican and Episcopal History* 57 (1988): 201, 213. The Anglo-Catholic movement was routinely stereotyped as effeminate and implicitly charged with encouraging and har-
boring homosexuality. David Hilliard, "Unenglish and Unmanly: Anglo-Catholicism and Homosexuality," *Victorian Studies* 25, no. 2 (January 1982): 187-91.

and contested for Anglicans than for any other denomination, bound up as it also was with the Protestant anti-Catholicism of the day.[67] The SPG directly supported women's missions earlier than any other society but studiously downplayed their role in mission work, likely to insulate itself from the scandals so publicly swirling around domestic sisterhoods and the fraught diocesan politics entailed by the attempts of bishops to govern independent women's foundations.

Sisters were controversial primarily because they represented to moderates in the Church the aggressions of Ritualists entering the realms of gender relations. Anglo-Catholic missions and sisterhoods seemed to many to contradict the Victorian ideology of home life, characterized most fundamentally by a hierarchy of male and female roles that permeated the culture of middle-class affluence. Sisterhoods also appeared to undermine the religious liberty of action and conscience that English Protestants believed Roman Catholicism destroyed, and for this reason even the most supportive Anglican bishops denounced any use of binding vows within the sisterhood movement.[68] Evangelicals responded in the 1860s by attempting to establish an Anglican diaconate, empowering trained, single women to engage in charitable action as recognized deaconesses.[69] Evangelical deaconesses, in deference to fears of papal-style authoritarianism, were never required to take vows, were always free to leave their calling at any time, and usually worked in their own parishes directly under the supervision of local clergymen. Sisters, in keeping with the ethos of reforming medievalism that characterized Anglo-Catholicism, sought to emulate and restore pre-Reformation English Church practice; they tied themselves to the communal life of prayer and regulated routine — bound to this calling by vows — and worked under a mother superior to create a virtuous atmosphere separate from worldly society.[70] Regardless of organization, however, both deaconesses and sisters encountered opposition from conservative Anglicans of both High Church and Evangelical sympathies. Similarly, on the fringes of Anglican missionary practice, the first attempts to use single female missionaries by the CIM foundered in the late 1860s in the face of hostility from a European community in China that revolved around the same objection that sisterhoods, and

---

67. Mumm, *Anglican Sisterhoods,* 175-76, 186-88. On the contemporaneous agitations over Catholic convents as seats of supposed tyranny over women, see Arnstein, *Protestant vs. Catholic,* 62-73, 125-39 and passim.

68. Gill, *Women and the Church,* 151-52.

69. Catherine M. Prelinger, "The Female Diaconate in the Anglican Church: What Kind of Ministry for Women," in *Religion in the Lives of English Women, 1760-1930,* ed. Gail Malmgreen (London: Croom Helm, 1986), 164-69.

70. Vicinus, *Independent Women,* 48-51.

by extension deaconesses, faced: vulnerable, unattached young women might become easy prey to the unscrupulous influence of charismatic male leaders.[71]

Despite available models for independent women's work, then, the large institutional Anglican missionary societies saw in their embrace considerable peril. This was particularly true at the SPG. Enthusiasm among High Church women and the obvious advantage of co-opting local female organizers spurred the SPG to acknowledge women's missionary desires in 1866, with the formation of a Ladies' Association. However, it then marginalized the Association while largely ignoring its own women's missions until the late 1890s. Virtually everyone concerned with SPG work acknowledged the coldness with which women's missions were treated. What accounts for this contradictory behavior? Two factors stand out. One was a social conservatism that led many High Church clerics to see female missionaries primarily as a source of marriageable women for missionaries and other men in the field and therefore not an agency to be seriously advanced. The other was a theological caution that led the SPG to calculate the possible cost of alienating moderate Anglican opinion by directly endorsing the use of independent women.[72]

Because of the Anglo-Catholic sisterhood example, Evangelical recruiting success through the 1880s at CMS-affiliated women's auxiliary societies, and a general expansion of public service lives for women, pressure grew on the SPG in the final decades of the century to more fully and sympathetically incorporate women. However, leaders at the SPG, most notably Secretary Henry Tucker, were presented with only two problematic models for the organization of women's work: the deaconess and the sister. Both were potential trouble for a very broadly supported missionary society. Deaconesses seemed to many High Churchmen to challenge church order and discipline with innovating enthusiasm, and sisterhoods were associated with multiplying conflicts over controversial ritual practices introduced by Anglo-Catholic priests. In order to appease traditionalist supporters, Tucker chose through the 1880s and 1890s to avoid controversy by distancing the SPG from the work of its Ladies' Association and Anglo-Catholic "special missions" such as the UMCA, although this did not prevent the SPG from quietly operating a deaconess training house and supporting the establishment of sisterhoods in the mission field through the block grant system.[73]

---

71. C. Peter Williams, "'The Missing Link': The Recruitment of Women Missionaries in Some English Evangelical Missionary Societies in the Nineteenth Century," in *Women and Mission: Past and Present; Anthropological and Historical Perceptions,* ed. Fiona Bowie, Deborah Kirkwood, and Shirley Ardener (Providence, RI: Berg, 1993), 48-49.

72. Henry H. Montgomery, "Survey of My Stewardship, 1902-1918," TS, p. 3, USPG Archives, H 3, box 2.

73. The SPG supported sisterhoods, for example in Bombay (Mumbai) from 1877, St. Stephen's

The SPG Ladies' Association, in fact, had always had a close association with the radicalism of Anglo-Catholic missions, being founded in the midst of the Universities' Mission excitement of the 1860s and closely associating itself with the circles supporting the UMCA, Melanesian Mission, Hawaiian mission, and several reforming High Church colonial bishoprics. Although the SPG had acquiesced to the formation of the Ladies' Association, it required completely separate accounts and administration, and its conservative policies meant that its women were progressively alienated. Originally envisioned as operating in close connection, SPG practices quickly subverted good intentions, despite the fact that Louisa Bullock, secretary of the Association for twenty-six years, was the daughter of SPG Secretary William Bullock (1865-79). The SPG had nothing to do with choosing Ladies' Association candidates, and from the beginning there was little sympathy between the two organizations. In 1902 E. P. Sketchley, the long-time SPG assistant secretary, recalled that prior to 1866 women sent out in association with the SPG had first come before its Board of Examiners. After that time, officially, the SPG no longer sent any women into the field.[74] In 1867, the year after the formation of the Ladies' Association, the leading periodical of the SPG had only one notice of the activity of the Association over the course of twelve months: a report on a soirée held in the SPG House during the SPG London Anniversary. By contrast, the Ladies' Association had multiple notices in the newly launched Anglo-Catholic missionary magazine *The Net Cast in Many Waters*, demonstrating its close relationship with Anne Mackenzie and Anglo-Catholic missionary networks.[75]

Thus, while the SPG provided block grants to a number of areas that supported sisterhoods, it remained aloof and institutionally separate from them. The most notable of these were various dioceses in South Africa: in Cape Town, where Bishop Gray in 1868 brought eight English women to found St. George's Sisterhood; and in Bishop A. B. Webb's two dioceses, first Bloemfontein, where he invited the Sisterhood of St. Thomas at Oxford to found the Community of St. Michael and All Angels in 1874, and subsequently Grahamstown, where after his translation he founded the Community of the Resurrection in 1883. South Africa became notorious as a high Anglo-Catholic environment where not only female but also male religious orders flourished, including the Soci-

---

Community in Delhi, and Inhambame, South West Africa, among others. Pascoe, *Two Hundred Years of the SPG*, 346d-346e, 577, 626-28d.

74. "An Informal Conference between S.P.G. & W.M.A. re. Future Relations . . . ," 4 July 1902, Special Sub-Committees and Reports of Conferences, 1898-1930, Committee of Women's Work, USPG Archives, CWW 90.

75. *Mission Field* (Aug. 1867): 345; "Ladies' Association for the Promotion of Female Education Among the Heathen [SPG]," *The Net* 1, no. 8 (Sept. 1866): 141-44.

ety of St. Augustine, the Society of St. John the Baptist, the Society of St. John the Evangelist (the Cowley Fathers), the Community of the Resurrection (the Mirfield Fathers), and the Society of the Sacred Mission (the Kelham Fathers). But others were also important, as sisterhoods were established in the Diocese of Honolulu, the Dioceses of Bombay and Calcutta (where Bishops Henry Alexander Douglas [1868-76] and Robert Milman [1866-76] introduced the Cowley Fathers in 1874 and the Wantage Sisters and All Saints Sisters in 1876), and in several other overseas dioceses, generally catalyzed by invitations from bishops to the various religious communities in England. Here they often worked alongside former deaconesses, or out of women's missions organized more closely on the model of the deaconess home in England.[76] But ongoing controversies surrounding the founding of Anglican sisterhoods abroad, which recurred for decades — such as the furor raised in the strongly Evangelical Diocese of Sydney with the arrival of the Kilburn Sisters in 1892 — surely reconfirmed the SPG London administration's caution in staying frostily formal in its connection to missionary sisterhoods in order to remain above the dangerous fray.[77]

In the mission field the seemingly radical threat of the sisterhood model — that of ungoverned women outside of a clerically controlled home environment committing themselves to devotional excesses — rapidly dissipated as sisters took up the same missionary function as other women. Uniformly, the work of sisters was to assume the operation of schools, hospitals, orphanages, and programs of local visitation that had previously been carried out by missionary wives and casually employed female mission workers.[78] Most women associated with the SPG in the early years taught girls, and in later years many were drawn from the ranks of deaconesses and did not necessarily enter sisterhoods abroad.[79] High Church champions of sisterhoods had worked persistently since the 1850s to differentiate themselves from Roman Catholics by constructing Anglican sisters not as convented nuns but as committed bands of charity workers, as Eleanor Frith calls "pseudonuns," whose liminal status as publicly valuable

76. Thompson, *History of the SPG*, 293, 298, 315, 354, 435, 454; Lear, *Gray*, 2:447-61; Eyre Chatterton, *A History of the Church of England in India* (London: SPCK, 1924), 208-10.

77. T. W. Campbell, "The Sisters of the Church and the Anglican Diocese of Sydney, 1892-1893: A Controversy," *Journal of Religious History* 25, no. 2 (June 2001): 188-206.

78. Thompson, *History of the SPG*, 315, 435.

79. Of the 312 SPG women missionaries who went out to Delhi and Lahore between 1860 and 1947, 81 had training in a Church of England deaconess home, 113 mentioned some type of secondary education, 40 had B.A.s or medical degrees. In Lahore, in 1899, the women's community of St. Hilda's under Bishop Lefroy operated as a deaconess home and cathedral school. Cox, "Independent English Women," 174-75.

"Sisters of Mercy" provided them unusual freedoms and a widening sphere of activity.[80] Acceptance of sisters grew in parallel with the expanding use of single female missionaries, as it became apparent that in colonial society the arrival on the scene of any religious, charitable women able to provide educational services was generally met with approval. Nevertheless, High Church bishops still felt it necessary to provide special justification and careful organization so as to defend sisterhoods in the mission field against charges that they undermined the authority of fathers in Christian homes and by extension weakened Western society itself.

Bishops such as A. B. Webb of Grahamstown, who was on notably uncomfortable terms with SPG House over issues of episcopal independence, recruited women in England to staff sisterhoods in their dioceses. However, since sisterhoods represented a volatile mix of some of the most sensitive subjects in Victorian life, it seemed necessary to reassure the fearful. When Webb published an appeal for sisters in 1883, he carefully set his aim, as the presiding bishop, to protect vigilantly against: (1) "Undisciplined devotion," (2) "Arbitrary government by a woman," and (3) "Narrowness of sympathy and intellect." The role of the bishop was to ensure "orthodoxy and continuity" as women, both missionary wives and missionary sisters, carried English civilization to colonial homes. "Sisterhood life," Webb declared, "is not antagonistic to the idea of the sacredness of Home and married life, though it is often supposed to be so. It is, in fact, for the sake of this idea, that we ask Sisters to help us to establish Christian homes."[81]

Thus Webb argued in a manner that turned evangelical criticisms on their head: sisterhoods were necessary in the mission field if only because of the tendency of single women who traveled to British colonies to marry rapidly, thus being lost as active reformers of "native families."[82] Sisters were the best agents for ensuring the building up of Western family life in the colonies, and they offered a defense against the successful strategies of Roman Catholics using "glitzy convents" and continental-style education to tempt young girls. Ultimately, Webb suggested, reforming indigenous women and families was a matter of imperial utility, a means of bringing "peace and progress" in a colonial realm bedeviled with "Kafir wars and chronic native restlessness."[83] Under Webb's oversight in Bloemfontein, sisterhoods and other forms of women's work had grown rapidly to deliver a wide range of options for female missionary activity directed toward

80. Frith, "Pseudonuns," 64-67, 77-80.
81. Webb, *Sisterhood Life*, 3, 54.
82. This, similarly, was the bishop of New Westminster, Acton W. Sillitoe's justification for funding from the SPCK in 1884 to set up a sisterhood in his diocese to provide girls' education. Frith, "Pseudonuns," 363.
83. Webb, *Sisterhood Life*, 34, 39, 42-43.

white, African, and mixed-race populations, a pattern he hoped to replicate in Grahamstown.[84] Nevertheless, in England the questions of allegiance and authority raised by sisterhoods so troubled moderate bishops such as Davidson of Rochester that they were careful to establish deaconess work instead of sisterhoods, and on clear lines that emphasized episcopal authority.[85] The SPG at home seems to have taken the view, despite endorsements by Convocation of the work done by sisters and their lifestyle (in 1878 and 1891 respectively), that the less they had to do with women's missionary activity, the less they would have to deal with the problems adventurous women raised. On a more practical level, shifting the burden of women's work allowed society secretaries also to exclude meddlesome activist women from the clerical preserve of SPG decision making.

Holiness, Women, and Anglican Evangelicalism

The sisterhood model that spread rapidly on the English domestic scene from the early 1850s clearly had a catalyzing effect on evangelical thinking about the acceptable roles of women at home and overseas. The opportunity to develop a response that resonated with evangelical cultures of belief appeared in the form of a new revivalism reminiscent of the eighteenth-century Methodist movement, but it developed in a style of delivery fitted to urban conditions. The message of American revivalists such as Phoebe Palmer and Hannah and Robert Pearsall Smith, who brought the second wave of nineteenth-century revivalism to England in the 1860s and 70s, was that an earnest presentation of Christian truth would miraculously infuse recipients with the power of the Holy Spirit without regard to gender.[86] While largely dismissed by mainline clergy, this message found a warm reception in holiness conferences, beginning in 1856 with the annual ecumenical gatherings at Barnet organized by evangelical Anglican William Pennefather, who was also involved in the early organization of the IFNS and later founded with his wife, Catherine, the Mildmay Deaconess Institution, a critical center of English theory and practice in deaconess work.[87]

---

84. Deborah Gaitskell, "Rethinking Gender Roles: The Field Experience of Women Missionaries in South Africa," in *The Imperial Horizons of British Protestant Missions, 1880-1914*, ed. Andrew Porter (Grand Rapids: Eerdmans, 2003), 144.

85. Bell, *Davidson*, 1:212. Davidson was also one of the most influential bishops with an interest in the SPG. See Bell, *Davidson*, 1:46.

86. Bebbington, *Evangelicalism*, 151, 155, 157-67.

87. Minutes of the London Committee of the Calcutta Female Normal School, 7 May 1862, IFNS/ZBMM Archives, Home File List, General Committee minutes, 1859–Mar. 1865; Robert Braithwaite, ed., *The Life and Letters of Rev. William Pennefather* (London: Shaw, 1878), 305-20.

From 1875 the annual Keswick Convention also became particularly in-fluential among Anglican women and men alike. One of the most significant elements of the new spirituality associated with Keswick was the important role it gave to the laity and, as members of the laity, to women. As incarna-tionalist attitudes — which modeled church life on the charitable, lived life of Christ — spread, so too did increased emphasis on callings for men and women fired by the Holy Spirit: lay preaching, platform speaking, visible and often autonomous public charity work, and, with ever greater frequency, for-eign missions. Much of the expanded role that women assumed in the world of foreign missions could thus be religiously justified — and religious justification was immensely important to the pious communities of Victorian England. This, however, was a dangerous area of contested norms which, if handled carelessly, could alienate a significant portion of mainstream Evangelical sup-port, particularly among traditional clerics who controlled access to English parishes. At the center of the uneasiness of conservatives was the concern that holiness license undermined traditional belief in the power of sin, particularly among the uneducated and weak, which seemed to necessitate deferential hu-mility from the poor and compliant silence from women. The abhorrence of ungovernable Nonconformity remained strong in the Church of England, even among many Evangelical clerics who were, like higher Churchmen, repelled by the loose interdenominationalism of early women's work and the enthusiasm of revivalism. Such supporters felt that Anglicans should avoid the deaconess training and holiness conferences sponsored by the Pennefathers, "lest they should become Methodists."[88]

Nevertheless, from the 1880s single female missionaries, in particular, grew in numbers and influence, the most significant contribution coming from evangelical Anglicans. This growth was largely carried out in the face of gen-eral clerical resistance, while interdenominationalism, which had little regard for clerical theological scruples, was a strong supporting commitment that among evangelical Anglicans fuelled women's activism. The IFNS, despite its close Anglican connections, remained committed to interdenominational co-operation, and the determination of those running its Female Normal School in Calcutta (Kolkata) to develop a support base in England was focused on drawing in any available source of interest, largely among evangelical Angli-can women, but also in other pietist communities. In India the IFNS received solid support from the Evangelical bishop of Calcutta, Daniel Wilson, and it took on Evangelical James Stuart and his wife as treasurer and secretary of the Calcutta Normal School, but also had the endorsement of the SPG mission-

---

88. Braithwaite, *Pennefather*, 324.

Photograph labeled "A[nnie]. P[erry]. H[owlett]. and the Biblewomen, Khurja 1910," **Upper Doab, Uttar Pradesh.** From Photographs & Slides, 1910s-1980,Small Albums, A. P. Howlett, "Early Days," North India, Khurja, 1910-15, IFNS/ZBMM Archives, School of Oriental and African Studies. Courtesy of Interserve England and Wales.

aries in the city.[89] Additionally, as early as 1851 the philanthropic evangelical Scotch Presbyterian Kinnaird family circulated letters to solicit female workers for the School, and after several years' connection Mary Jane Kinnaird (née Hoare, of the London banking family with close connections to the CMS) was appointed secretary in 1859 to the new London Committee of the Calcutta Female Normal School. By rapidly expanding its brief from candidate vetting to forming local British auxiliaries, by negotiating cooperative arrangements with the CMS, and by printing papers and annual reports, the IFNS's "large

89. Braithwaite, *Pennefather,* 6.

influence" grew larger as it became the de facto women's department for the CMS.[90] The IFNS generated support by appealing to all CMS female collectors and to select Nonconformists, drawing on the anxiety and fascination with India generated by the 1857 Indian insurrection. Operating as a drawing-room society convening home meetings of friends who read letters received from missionaries in the field, it fed on the excitement and power connected to dispensing privileged information within a coterie convinced that momentous work, at a critical time, was under way in the empire in India.[91] The many connections of Evangelicals in India were reemphasized at this time which drew support from many Anglo-Indian connected families motivated, like Henry Carre Tucker, by the notion of missions "as a species of 'Christian revenge'" for the rebellion. Tucker's brother Robert, judge in Futteypore, was killed in the Indian uprising; within a year Henry devoted himself to missionary work and later became one of the most influential members of the CMS General Committee. Charlotte Tucker, the sister of Henry and Robert and a widely known children's author writing under the pseudonym A.L.O.E. (A Lady of England), at age 54 also travelled to India as a missionary.[92]

The environment in the wake of 1857 created new ambitions, and rapidly growing momentum led the IFNS to expand its work to all of India. In a meeting on 15 July 1861 with influential representatives of evangelical Anglicanism — including CMS Secretary Henry Venn, Edward Auriol, A. M. W. Christopher, and Andrew Lang — the Indian Female Normal School and Instruction Society was formally chartered as a British national charity, including appointment of a male clerical traveling secretary. The IFNS thus received the stamp of approval of the Evangelical clerics who were most involved in the foreign missions of the Church, and while the Committee remained almost entirely the preserve of women it also acquired in Anglican parishes influence that only a male clerical secretary could wield with other clerics. The group rejected the first new name suggested for the Society — "The Society for the Evangelization of the Women of India" — after remarks by Henry Venn raised fears that the name implied women might transcend clerical limitations placed on female preaching. Thus it had its brief clearly limited to female education, under the supervision of male CMS missionaries, rejecting any suggestion that women might engage

90. Minutes of the London Committee of the Calcutta Female Normal School, 3 Jan. 1859, 7 Dec. 1859, 3 Jan. 1860, and 7 Feb. 1860, IFNS/ZBMM Archives, Home File List, General Committee minutes, 1859–Mar. 1865.

91. Minutes of the IFNS General Committee, 5 Dec. 1865, IFNS/ZBMM Archives, Home File List, General Committee minutes, Apr. 1865–Mar. 1870.

92. Agnes Giberne, *A Lady of England: The Life and Letters of Charlotte Maria Tucker* (London: Hodder and Stoughton, 1895), 111; *Proceedings of the CMS*, 1869-70, iv.

in gender-busting public preaching.[93] Emerging women's missions were part of a more general set of women's charitable initiatives from the 1850s, creating largely autonomous domestic organizations such as the YWCA (1855), Ranyard Mission (1858), the Salvation Army (1878), and its Church of England imitator, the Church Army (1882). Innovating missionary coteries, drawing heavily on new attitudes, enthusiasms, and an implicit democratization of religious life that holiness-based religious practice legitimized, operated on the assumption that the times were quickening.

But reassuring doubting Evangelical clerics and ensuring respectable control of women's agencies was an ever-present challenge, given the deeply emotional debates Anglo-Catholicism unleashed. The Nonconformist missionary societies — reacting to appeals from missionary wives and mindful not only of the IFNS's expansion but also of the launching of the CIM in the 1860s, with its aggressive interdenominational recruiting of single female missionaries — rapidly formed female agencies within society frameworks. Anglicans, who, if anything, had a stronger reflex to assert clerical authority, rather surprisingly did not follow the Nonconformist pattern. Why did the CMS fail to establish a women's committee until 1895, and why did the SPG, while forming a Ladies Association in 1866, marginalize it until after the turn of the century? The more complex Anglican pattern can be accounted for in the more tangled interaction of party, clerical prerogative, theological fashion, and organizational overlap characteristic of the Church of England. Both the CMS and SPG viewed the growth of women's home support and women's missionary societies with relative detachment. However, the CMS, more dependent on voluntarism and more open to enthusiasm, was forced to grapple with the issue of women's missions earlier. The SPG, more tightly in the grip of socially conservative clerics, persistently ignored women until obvious, striking success at the CMS in incorporating women's work compelled reorganization, but only after the turn of the century.

The CMS, while dependent in Britain on voluntary female workers, rested content for decades working them quietly through the traditional parochial structures of its clerically dominated local associations. The independence of Anglican clergy made it necessary for the CMS to adopt a strategy of reassuring parish priests that their right to local governance (including control over lay workers) would be respected. Societies were understood to stand as symbols

93. Minutes of the London Committee of the Calcutta Female Normal School, 15 July 1861, IFNS/ZBMM Archives, Home File List, General Committee minutes, 1859–Mar. 1865. For a similar venture launched by the British Syrian Schools and Bible Mission, see H. B. Tristram, *The Daughters of Syria*, 2nd ed. (London: Seeley, Jackson & Halliday, 1872), 60-77.

of apostolic Church governance. Indicative of this attitude at the CMS was the refusal by its Secretary Henry Wright to appear on the platform at the 1878 Mildmay Missionary Conference with a woman, in order to avoid the wrath of socially conservative supporters.[94] Anglican societies demanded greater deference from women, and this attitude produced an atmosphere in which obsequious pleas for even a bare acknowledgement of women's services became the norm.[95] The CMS, because of its desire to protect its legitimacy as a Church society, deferred to the jealous professionalism of Anglican clerics and refused for three decades, despite offers from women volunteering for the mission field, to form a Women's Department.[96] When the CMS received William Pennefather's offer to train female missionaries under his deaconess training scheme at Barnet during the escalating excitement of revival in 1859, the CMS agreed to send candidates to him for instruction, but only for subsequent placement with the IFNS or FES.

Throughout their history the Barnet and (later) Mildmay conferences run by Pennefather were constant objects of criticism.[97] However, Evangelical women's work, both in England and overseas, was intimately linked to the Mildmay Institute and its training of deaconesses. The deaconess movement drew on similar ideologies and constituencies as female missions, and it encountered even greater opposition from conservative Anglican clerics and laymen, who saw in the diaconate (in parallel to the sisterhood movement) a dangerous undermining of traditional patriarchal authority. Suspicion of any agency that potentially undermined the "sacred" structure of the family became the single most pervasive obstacle to the growth of the work of evangelical deaconesses, Anglo-Catholic sisterhoods, and unmarried female missionaries. Despite the explicit construction of the Deaconess House at Mildmay on the model of the patriarchal family, and despite the strong emphasis on the orthodox historicity of the office of the deaconess, many Evangelicals detected "popery," particularly in the uniforms worn by deaconesses.[98] The CMS, largely because of fears about offending sensitive "Puritan" supporters, waited longer formally to incorporate women into foreign missions than any other major society. But it also was more successful at it once begun than any other religious group.

Because of the fraught gender politics presented by the diaconate, the clergy of the Church of England could not settle the relationship of deaconesses to the

94. Stock, *History of the CMS*, 4:556n*.
95. E.g., Catherine Webb to "Dear Sir," 20 Apr. 1880, CMS Archives, G/AC 4/2/371.
96. Stock, *Women's Work*, 13-14.
97. Braithwaite, *Pennefather*, 419; Vicinus, *Independent Women*, 47.
98. Stock, *Recollections*, 197.

Church, sending a burgeoning movement into a frustrating state of limbo. The impasse instead channeled many potential deaconesses in the English Church into the foreign mission field. Clerical territoriality was a serious obstacle to the development of deaconess work in the Church of England, and Catherine Prelinger has suggested that Evangelical women's missions benefited from this opposition, evidenced in the growing percentage of female missionaries being trained in deaconess institutes. Around the turn of the century English Anglican deaconesses numbered somewhere between 180 and 200. The Mildmay Institution, which Prelinger identifies as "ecumenical," but which was strongly influenced by holiness-oriented evangelical Anglicans, supported an additional 220 deaconesses.[99] In contrast, sisterhoods had expanded in England to at least sixty-six communities with nearly 10,000 women in their employ spanning the sixty years prior to the turn of the century.[100]

The fully independent nature of sisterhoods, as well as the support they received from Anglo-Catholics, seems to have provided much stiffer competition for High Church missions seeking female agents, as well as considerable competition among overseas bishops for English sisters to perform missionary duties. The relative success of the Nonconformists in developing a working diaconate and relatively high levels of acceptance among High Church Anglicans for sisterhoods at home correspond to their employing lower numbers of single female missionaries than the CMS and its allied women's societies. In 1899 single female missionaries (excluding doctors) at the CMS made up 26 percent of its missionary staff of 1,238. When the women sent out by the Church of England Zenana Missionary Society (CEZMS) and the Zenana Bible and Medical Mission (ZBMM) — successor societies to the IFNS that continued working closely with the CMS — are added, the figure jumps to 41 percent of 1,567 missionaries. Holiness-inspired missionary culture, which always had considerable support in Anglican holiness circles, delivered similar numbers at the CIM: 287 of the CIM's 811 missionaries (35 percent) were single women. In contrast, at the SPG the same data set shows that unmarried women made up 6 percent of 1,174 fully and partially supported missionaries (the compiler estimated an SPG equivalent total of about 850 full-time missionaries, giving a figure of 8 percent), and Nonconformist missions also employed fewer single female agents (see Appendix I, Figure 6).[101] Determined Anglo-Catholics, of course, embraced

99. Prelinger, "Female Diaconate," 178-84. For a similar effect in Australia in the 1890s, Patricia Grimshaw, "In Pursuit of True Anglican Womanhood in Victoria, 1880-1914," *Women's History Review* 2, no. 3 (1993): 343.

100. Mumm, *Anglican Sisterhoods,* 152-53, 209, and appendix 1.

101. Thompson, on the other hand, indicates that at the turn of the century (1901) the SPG's Women's Association was supporting 128 women (with no indication of marital status) and the

missionary sisterhoods, and the most well-known Anglo-Catholic mission, the UMCA, employed a similarly high number of single women, at over 40 percent; however, while other overseas Anglo-Catholic dioceses clearly employed large numbers of local women, few appear to have achieved this proportion of unmarried British women.

The mainstream Anglican missionary societies remained cautious about employing single female agents, fearing conservative backlash against women's agencies. However, in constructing a profitable affiliation with women, the CMS, which was in complete control of its missionary agents, had a significant advantage over the SPG. By maintaining nominally independent women's agencies the CMS could play both games, drawing on women's resources while also maintaining a distance that assuaged clerical anxieties. The care with which such balances needed to be maintained demonstrates the high levels of ambiguity that Anglican women's missions experienced regarding their relationship to clerical and institutional authority. But the even greater questions raised by the diaconate meant for Evangelical women that Anglican foreign missions ultimately provided a channel of relatively greater opportunity. Still, the early phases of the growth of evangelical Anglican women's missions were slow and discouraging, in large part due to the refusal of the CMS to establish its own women's missions. Despite pressure from growing numbers of women offering themselves for missionary service and a resolution in committee in 1867 (backed by the influential Anglo-Indian Sir Herbert Edwardes) to absorb the FES and IFNS and engage in women's work on a larger scale, the CMS General Committee failed to act and continued to refer virtually all offers from women to the independent auxiliary societies. In retrospect, it appeared to Eugene Stock that the CMS had opted to suffer a slump in support and activism in the 1870s, rather than offend conservative clerical sensibilities.[102]

The repeated occurrence of revivals, however, and particularly their success in bringing converts into the evangelical fold, aided a slow change of attitudes toward women's public roles. Major revivals of one to two years recurred about once per decade from the 1850s to the 1900s, normalizing the behaviors associated with this form of popular religion.[103] While even in the late 1880s traditional evangelicals could write to the CMS to protest about the impropriety of women appearing on CMS public platforms, the CMS by this time had

---

SPG, 753 clergy, or 20 percent female missionaries. *History of the SPG,* 241. For more nuance on missionary statistics, see Appendix II.

102. Henry Wright to C. J. Down, 10 Dec. 1872, CMS Archives, G/AC 1/18; Stock, *Women's Work,* 13.

103. Gilbert, *Religion and Society,* 187-92.

firmly placed itself in the more enthusiastic camp of Keswick.[104] This environment brewed a potent evangelical ethos, founded primarily on the experience of conversion but also on expectations of service from the sanctified. In this atmosphere, women such as Fanny Woodman, who in 1888 was inspired by attendance at Keswick to missionary ambition and a career in China, found a new language and perspective that allowed them to subvert traditional prohibitions on women's work and preaching.[105]

Clerical Prerogative and the Reworking of Evangelical Women's Missions

Through the 1880s Evangelical women's missions continued to grow, buttressed by an active female public presence at the Keswick Convention that demonstrated expanded social roles possible to women empowered by holiness attitudes. Keswick, far more mainstream than the earlier Mildmay conferences, provided a space in which more establishment-oriented Evangelicals came in contact with adventurous spiritual behavior. Young women came to share the spectacle of the public platform at Keswick with men in a way that was quite unprecedented in older Anglican circles. By the 1890s, one CMS missionary, with evident appreciation, commented on the crowds drawn by the daughter of General Booth (founder of the Salvation Army), as well as the "beautiful eloquent daughters of Dr. Henry Grattan Guinness" (founder of the East London Missionary Training Institute) and the "two tall stately Miss Gollocks" (new staff members at the CMS).[106] Many men and women testified to the intoxicating and paradoxical sense of both freedom and duty that holiness evangelicalism imbued, and from the late 1880s onward such "spiritual power" flowed strongly into the CMS, the IFNS, and other CMS-affiliated women's societies.[107] In the context of Keswick, activist middle-class young women came to lead much missionary organization, and here they found themselves encouraged to organize freely and to influence their coreligionists and colleagues.[108]

---

104. C. Blake to Frederick Wigram, 7 Nov. [1887], CMS Archives, G/AC 4/5/945.

105. Gill, *Women and the Church*, 183-84.

106. Fisher memoir, [July 1897], Fisher Papers, CMS Archives, Acc 84 F 3/2, book 8, pp. 10-11.

107. See, for example, the testimony of Emily Kinnaird regarding both the IFNS and the YWCA, and how they fed on this feminine sense of "liberating duty," contrasting with "the horror with which the claim for the equality of men and women was hailed" among traditional evangelicals. Emily Kinnaird, *Reminiscences* (London: Murray, 1925), 25-26, 38-40.

108. The organizing rosters of the CEZMS show of its fifty-two voluntary Association Secretaries, 73 percent were unmarried, 25 percent married, with only one man listed. *Purpose, Principles, Progress, with Monthly Cycle of Prayer* (London, 1898), 3, CMS Archives, CEZ/G/EL 1/5A.

Only by slow degrees, however, under the influence of denominational rivalry and concern to safeguard clerical power in national and worldwide Anglican networks, did the CMS reappraise its policy on women's work. Rather than act to incorporate the work, as had the largest of the Nonconformist societies, Secretary Henry Wright and other members of the CMS Committee in 1880 took a smaller step: they encouraged a splinter group of Anglican women on the IFNS Board to break off and form the independent CEZMS.[109] The CEZMS was to operate in close connection with the CMS on the same evangelical Church of England principles, although it was to maintain a separate committee and home operation run predominantly by women.[110] The split in the interdenominational IFNS ostensibly began over a dispute about the baptism of converts in India. Anglicans were disturbed by the reluctance of some Baptist IFNS missionaries to allow the early baptism of women and children, which they claimed undermined the work of proselytizing and militated against the baseline sacramentalism that even Evangelicals observed. It was tied in the London committee rooms, however, with the feeling of Lord and Lady Kinnaird and other Nonconformist members of the Board that the IFNS was coming to associate too exclusively with the CMS, and by implication with Anglicanism's complicity with national and imperial power.[111] When Anglicans broke off to pursue separate, distinctive female missionary activity, it was primarily a move to defend Anglican position and identity in a context of denominational jealousy. The CMS still, however, remained less willing than Nonconformist societies to embrace women's work, largely because of the way Anglo-Catholicism had so deeply politicized women's place within the Church of England.

Schism at the IFNS proved to be a messy and unpleasant, but also a revealing, affair.[112] The controversy revolved around the legitimacy of Anglican withdrawal and continued dedication to "catholic and not denominational" women's missions. Anglicans at the IFNS believed that since the 1860s the real life and support in the society issued from "zeal" for work run on "distinctly Church of

109. Henry Wright to General Sir William Hill, 13 Apr. 1880, CEZMS Archives, CEZ/AP 2; "Indian Female Normal School and Instruction Society: In Cooperation with the Church Missionary Society, and Other Protestant Missionary Societies in India," Circular, [ca. May 1880], CMS Archives, G/AC 4/24/4718.

110. Letter from Miss E. G. Sandys, reprinted in *The Church of England Zenana Missionary Society Jubilee Souvenir, 1880-1930* (London, n.d.), 35.

111. Minutes of the IFNS General Committee, 6 Nov. 1878 and 3 Mar. 1880, IFNS/ZBMM Archives, Home File List, General Committee minutes, Oct. 1878–July 1886; C. Harding, "Origins of the Church of England Zenana Society," TS, p. 3, CEZMS Archives, CEZ/G EA 5A.

112. A full collection of the CEZMS circulars on the matter is to be found in the CEZMS Archives, CEZ/AP 2.

England principles." The CMS had used the IFNS for twenty years as its primary channel for women's work and had slowly impressed on it an Anglican identity. This arrangement had the advantage of masking CMS involvement in women's work from conservative clerics while allowing its quiet development. By 1880 Anglicans had become such involved supporters of the IFNS that the Society raised a substantial majority of its £16,500 income from them.[113] But the IFNS, as well as the YWCA in Britain, were also strongly influenced by Mary Jane Kinnaird and the Kinnaird family, who, while Presbyterians, insisted that the primary identity of the IFNS should be tied to a particularly enthusiastic undenominational evangelicalism. Deeply influenced by the new revivalism and the rise of interdenominational Christian life exemplified in organizations like the YWCA, the Kinnairds and their supporters attempted to reverse Anglican dominance at the IFNS, only to see the disintegration of the Society.

Battles over women's work in the Church of England had raised high the issue of respectability among Evangelicals who struggled to craft a response to sisterhood life. When pressed, their vision of women's religious place did not extend to the visionary undenominationalism expressed by the more enthusiastic. For the Anglican members of the IFNS committee, the defense of respectable denominational evangelicalism became the driving force behind their withdrawal. The Kinnairds, a Scottish Presbyterian banking family deeply bred into the interdenominational enthusiasm of American-style revivalism, dominated the IFNS committee.[114] The entire family organized "evangelistic meetings" during the 1859-61 revival led by Arthur Stevenson Blackwood, Reginald Radcliffe, Lord Radstock, and others. They were habitual attenders of holiness conferences, and did a good deal of the organizing for the 1874 revivalistic tour of Moody and Sankey.[115] Mary Jane Kinnaird was, in addition to her work for the IFNS, one of the earliest organizers of the YWCA in England and had a strong influence on its development. As her daughter Emily recalled, Mary Jane, who had herself hoped to be a missionary, instead founded a missionary society which "would answer the missionary call to carry the Gospel to India fettered by no ecclesiastical or imperial connection."[116] She was a passionate interdenominationalist, which in her mind meant, in part, creating a movement with the power to transcend church hierarchies, empire, and other worldly power

---

113. W. Hill and James Stuart, "Church of England Zenana Missionary Society," 23 Apr. 1880, CEZMS Archives, CEZ/AP 2.

114. "Indian Female Normal School and Instruction Society: In cooperation with the Church Missionary Society, and Other Protestant Missionary Societies in India," Circular, [ca. May 1880], CMS Archives, G/AC 4/24/4718; Kent, *Holding the Fort*, 156.

115. Kinnaird, *Reminiscences*, 38-39, 87-88.

116. Kinnaird, *Reminiscences*, 54.

structures while at the same time, with little sense of contradiction, particularly focusing attention "in the Eastern Empire of the Queen."[117] Revivalistic fervor likely fired her determination in the late 1870s to assure "spiritual" equality at the IFNS, which included equality across gender lines and the cultivation of what Susan Mumm calls a "civil Christianity" that de-emphasized the boundaries of denominationalism and shifted the society towards active Christian social reform.[118] In the end this program proved too strong for the Anglican Committee members to suffer, especially when the work had become large and consequential enough — including zenana evangelizers as well as school teachers — to draw the attention of Church bureaucrats.

The issue that instigated the crisis at the IFNS was significant. In 1877 Lady Kinnaird introduced a measure to create denominationally mixed local committees of control in India, displacing CMS local clerical Corresponding Committees. This proposal provoked a vigorous reaction, for it presented a challenge to the clerical authority of CMS missionaries and to the denominational interests of the Church of England in India.[119] Kinnaird's proposal drew a threat of mass resignation from the Anglican members on the Committee and was withdrawn, but continued attempts to institutionalize interdenominationalism paralyzed the IFNS. One crux of the dispute seems to have been a disproportionate number of Indian female converts entering the Church of England. John Barton, former CMS missionary to India, argued that the "so-called undenominationalism" of the Kinnairds "appears to have a very distinct colour of its own," and those who sought to spread it were stung, as their ambitions for expansion, denominational in all but name, were thwarted by Anglican successes in India.[120] Ultimately thirteen of the Anglicans, just over a third of the committee, tendered their resignations, "reserving to ourselves full liberty to establish a new Society & appeal to the Associations throughout the country."[121]

117. Her interdenominationalism, however, had evangelical limits: she vigorously supported missions not only to "heathen" women but also to European Catholics. "Editorial Paragraphs," *Life and Light for Woman* 21, no. 3 (Mar. 1891): 105.

118. Susan Mumm, "Women and Philanthropic Cultures," in *Women, Gender and Religious Cultures in Britain, 1800-1940*, ed. Sue Morgan and Jacqueline deVries (London: Routledge, 2010), 63-64.

119. CMS committees had directed the work since 1865, when CMS missionary John Barton had been appointed the IFNS Corresponding Secretary for Calcutta. W. Hill and James Stuart, "Church of England Zenana Missionary Society," 23 Apr. 1880, CEZMS Archives, CEZ/AP 2.

120. "Church of England Zenana Missionary Society," circular, reprint of a letter from John Barton to the Editor of the *Record*, 29 Apr. 1880, CEZMS Archives, CEZ/AP 2.

121. Letter to Lady Kinnaird, Vice-President and Chairwoman of the IFNS Committee, 10 Apr. [1880] read to the 13 Apr. 1880 meeting, IFNS Committee Minutes, IFNS/ZBMM Archives, Home File List, General Committee minutes, Oct. 1878–July 1886.

Their power quickly became apparent as three-quarters of the missionaries and 170 of the 200 local British secretaries went with them, leaving those remaining at the IFNS feeling that the Society had been mortally wounded.[122]

Notably, the same issue that split the IFNS also bedeviled the YWCA, leading to direct competition with the Girls' Friendly Society (GFS) of the Church of England (founded 1875).[123] Reflecting ruefully on the foundation of the GFS, Emily Kinnaird believed that "[s]ome Churchwomen found the Y.W.C.A. too wide; to meet on an equality with Dissenters was distasteful; to introduce girls into interdenominational company was harmful." The GFS also had a more exacting moral code than the YWCA, banning any girls who had "sinned according to the moral and legal code of the country," suggesting a more stringent insistence on respectability reigning in the Church of England, but it also found itself, perhaps because of this stringency, largely confined to charitable provision for domestic servants and unable to expand membership to more respectable working women in other industries.[124] The simple fact was that the growing weight of women's work and the prestige it brought were becoming too important to ignore. As long as only educational work was in question, CMS officials remained noncommittal; but serious reassessment seemed necessary, as IFNS work "passed into a new phase, and became far more of an evangelistic than a school agency."[125] For evangelization meant conversions, and conversions meant a choice of one church or another. When problems of church growth and discipline arose out of the relative success of zenana work in claiming converts, women's activities roused denominational clerical interest and determination. John Barton was certain that "English Episcopalians" would rally to a society that promoted the appropriate form of Church government. By 1880 the CMS had forced evangelical Anglican women's missions not only into the denominational mold but also into the intensive, systematic organization that characterized the CMS.

---

122. W. Hill, circular letter, "Church of England Zenana Missionary Society," 7 July 1880, CEZMS Archives, CEZ/AP 2. Twenty committee members remained, fifteen Anglicans and five Presbyterians. Loose table clipped in the front of IFNS Committee Minutes, IFNS/ZBMM Archives, Home File List, General Committee minutes, Oct. 1878–July 1886.

123. In just over a decade of operation the GFS boasted over 1 million members, 24,000 "associates," 850 branches, and sister societies in Scotland, Ireland, America, and "the Colonies" (including one in Lahore, India). *Official Year-Book of the Church of England* (London: SPCK, 1887), 90.

124. Kinnaird, *Reminiscences*, 29-30, 65. On the GFS constituency among domestic servants, see Mumm, "Philanthropic Cultures," 58-60.

125. "Church of England Zenana Missionary Society," circular, reprint of a letter from J. Barton to the Editor of the *Record*, 29 Apr. 1880, CEZMS Archives, CEZ/AP 2.

Imperial Opportunity and the Ideology of Home

Party dynamics and the struggle to define acceptable gender roles within the Church formed essential context that conditioned the development of women's roles in the Church and its missions. As critical, however, was the environment of imperial and social opportunity that provided models and rationales for the development of female spirituality and church work. The size and popularity of women's foreign missionary work grew slowly prior to 1860; thereafter, catalyzed by events in the empire and the changing position of women in England, interest grew much more rapidly. Women's foreign missions to women were justified through an ideology of work drawing on Western ideas of domesticity and gender hierarchy. By the 1880s the movement had constructed a range of visions of foreign families that neatly located the condition of women in England in an imagined range of development that emphasized the presumed superior nature of English womanhood. In developing a distinctive new vision of women's mission, one that focused on relieving the conditions of "suffering sisters" throughout the world, Anglican women constructed a durable set of gendered imperial rationales for overseas women's work.[126]

Women's work became important in the missionary world partly because of the way it both drew on and helped to shape English middle-class domestic ideals. Certainly, women were attracted to female missions because, by highlighting and attempting to reform foreign domestic arrangements, they stressed the superiority of the Western and specifically the English domestic model, a strategy that dated back to the debates over *sati* (widow-burning) and female infanticide in India in the 1820s and 1830s.[127] The idealization of the English home and the ideal of a distinctive separate sphere of female action had reached a mature form by the late Victorian period, and statements about women's special domestic mission in the world of foreign missions, such as Emma Pitman's, abounded:

> It is only in Christian lands that women occupy their proper place. In all other countries they are drudges, slaves, or victims; but equals or companions, *never!* . . . [Christ] took the bitterness out of the woman's lot by honouring and adopting motherhood. From that time, all

126. For a detailed study of these processes in the CEZMS, see Jennifer A Morawiecki, "'The Peculiar Mission of Christian Womanhood': The Selection and Preparation of Women Missionaries of the Church of England Zenana Missionary Society, 1880-1920" (Ph.D. diss., Sussex University, 1998), chap. 2.

127. Midgley, *Feminism and Empire*, 73-86.

motherhood became brighter and holier, and all womanhood grander yet tenderer.[128]

If the extension of domesticity to the foreign sphere was the means of ideologically justifying women's foreign mission work, however, elaboration of the vision of the Christian home occurred through constant juxtaposition with the imagined foreign (or "heathen") home.

Emerging ideologies of women's missionary work in the mid-Victorian era were deeply conditioned, in particular, by changing attitudes toward India. In the wake of the Indian rebellion of 1857, Anglicans, and in particular Evangelicals, struggled to assess the reasons for continued Indian resistance to Christian proselytizing. The Indian rebellion unleashed imperial anxieties of a magnitude unseen since the Napoleonic wars, and it reinforced fears raised generally among missionaries that the strategies for transforming indigenous societies — building new Christian communities around missionary families, as in the West Indies, New South Wales, South Africa, and elsewhere — were failing to make the rapid progress toward "new Jerusalems" that had been optimistically projected.[129] If the leadings of the Holy Spirit toward Christian homes were being ignored, there must be a particular site of resistance. Besides the obvious argument that God was chastising the English for withholding the gospel from Indians, increasingly, missionary theorists found this resistance in the presumed nature of the Indian home and the plight of women within it.

Domesticating the Rebellious Indian Home

Following the 1857 Indian rebellion, evangelical religious commentators focused with renewed intensity on Indian home life, emphasizing that the presumed conditions of the zenana — the exclusively female apartments of many high-caste Hindu and Islamic households — essentially defined its nature. The zenana had long been an object of fascination to European observers of India, but systematic attention in missionary circles centering it theoretically as fundamental to the nature of Indian society dates from the 1860s. Inaccessible to male missionaries, zenanas were occasionally opened to enterprising missionary wives, who persuaded householders to permit entry by offering to teach the occupants useful

128. Emma Raymond Pitman, *Lady Missionaries in Foreign Lands* (London: Partridge, n.d., ca. 1889), vi.

129. Catherine Hall, "Of Gender and Empire: Reflections on the Nineteenth Century," in *Gender and Empire,* ed. Philippa Levine, The Oxford History of the British Empire Companion Series (Oxford: Oxford University Press, 2004), 59-66.

needlework skills and basic education. This model was one taken directly from domestic social and moral theories of charity, where it was assumed that transference of the English "working party" and its feminine culture of communal needlework to India would allow the Indian woman to "[prove] that she has learned 'the moral power of the needle.'"[130] This was work, female supporters emphasized, that only women could do — a sphere God had opened specially and exclusively for their talents.[131] While it was too much to claim that men had absolutely no part in this work, Maria Charlesworth nevertheless asserted that men "cannot rise to the calm home endurance of self-sacrifice in order to achieve the liberation of countless women and children," not least because the experience of the zenana had led "millions of women [to] now believe the heart of man to be destitute of all sympathy for women."[132] Thus the development of work for single women in the mission field followed the pattern in home charity work, where women claimed the home and the remediation of its problems through visitation and education as a calling fundamental to women's contribution to social reform.[133] As William Arthur noted, in the earliest period of Indian missionary work, supporters hoped that the conversion of Indian men would lead to the opening of the zenanas as well. The clear failure of this strategy led to new approaches and complementary forms of assault; and with the time of missionaries' wives tied up by other duties, employment of single women was more frequently considered a necessary agency to influence Indian families.[134]

In the late 1850s the lack of success in India along with the perceived potential in the new forms of revivalism growing in America gave impetus to plans for women's work. Holiness-oriented evangelical culture turned to the power of women within family life as a panacea for the reversal of sin in English and "heathen" homes. Actively advanced in the Pennefathers' Mildmay conferences, this belief in the profound power of women to minister holiness to men and salvation through the family was strongly linked to foreign mission ideology. Tied from the outset to slum evangelization carried out by militant, often anticlerical women like Ellen Ranyard, female missionary activists applied this core

130. Charlesworth, *India and the East*, 12. On the culture of needlework, the working party, and the mothers' meeting in England, see F. K. Prochaska, "A Mother's Country: Mothers' Meetings and Family Welfare in Britain, 1850-1950," *History* 74 (Oct. 1989): 382-87.

131. *How the Zenana Missions Began* (n.p., n.d., ca. 1890), 4-5.

132. Charlesworth, *India and the East*, 9-10.

133. Prochaska, *Women and Philanthropy*, 97-110.

134. Arthur, *Women's Work*, 11, 31. This was a pattern that repeated itself afterward, as in Yale, British Columbia, where twenty years of failure to substantially influence the Interior Salish catalyzed the establishment of Anglican missionary sisters in the Fraser Valley. Frith, "Pseudonuns," 352-56.

concept to the salvation of India through Indian homes, as did Hudson Taylor in his call for missionaries to China at Mildmay in 1878.[135] Rising faith in domestic evangelism within holiness circles supported the sudden rise of women's activity in the area of zenana visitation in the 1850s and 1860s.

Attitudes toward women's work were changing rapidly, and part of this change was manifested in the increasing appeal of zenana work to English women, reinforced after 1857, because it meshed closely with evangelical assessments of the Indian rebellion. While most civilian officials in India, like the official classes in England, interpreted what they invariably called the "Indian Mutiny" as a reaction against rapid Western imperial cultural transformation, the evangelical community preached that the shirking of religious duty in India had led to chastisement by God.[136] After 1857, missionaries redoubled their arguments that religious proselytizing and imperial stability would go hand in hand.[137] The CMS, for example, sent a memorial to Queen Victoria suggesting that a means of preventing future outbreaks would be to end British government "neutrality" toward Hinduism, introduce the Bible into the curriculum of all government schools, and end all government revenue subsidies to "the Mohammedan, Hindu, or other false religions."[138] George Smith recalled that after 1857 "[t]he Churches awoke, and the cry for vengeance took another form — not for more soldiers, more blowing from guns, more hanging, but for missionaries . . . , [as] a splendid missionary revival began."[139] Despite the fact that the evangelical initiative (led by the CMS) to advance broadly mission education in India in the aftermath of 1857 failed — in the face of ministerial fears of reigniting Indian opposition and Nonconformist insistence on voluntarism as the basis of English religious policy in Britain and the empire — missionary societies themselves gained considerable new, short-term momentum in recruiting and fundraising.[140] As post-rebellion imperial government withdrew from westernization strategies, in the absence of any immediate hope for cooperation from the Colonial government to Christianize through education or preaching, the alluring idea of

135. Williams, "Women Missionaries," 47-48, 50-53.
136. Stanley, "Commerce and Christianity," 86-89. See also Sugirtharajah, *The Bible and Empire*, 64-66, 73-75.
137. *The Indian Crisis: A Special Meeting of the Church Missionary Society at Exeter Hall* ([London], 1858), 18-20, 31; James M'Kee, *Obstacles to the Progress of Christianity in India* (Belfast: News-Letter Office, 1858), 3-5.
138. *The Indian Crisis: A Memorial to the Queen from the Church Missionary Society, on the Religious Policy of the Government of India* ([London], 1857), 4.
139. "The Shaking of the Nation," Speech of 3 Jan. 1896, in *Students' Missionary Conference, 1896*, 88.
140. David Savage, "Evangelical Educational Policy in Britain and India, 1857-60," *Journal of Imperial and Commonwealth History* 22, no. 3 (1994): 432-33, 450-52.

pacifying and elevating a rebellious population through a reformation of family life went hand in hand with the notion of converting the next generation of men and reclaiming the loyalty of India through the agency Indian mothers.[141]

Evangelicals always emphasized that social change would come by focusing on individuals and their moral development, conversion by conversion. In India the lesson of experience seemed to be, in the words of Maria Charlesworth, that "until we raise the women of India, but little can be done in morally elevating the men." This was logical if, using the moral and individual model of causation so dear to the evangelically minded, observers appreciated that

> the heathen mother corrupts the mind of her child in its infancy; the evil infection so prevailing over them, that the government professor and the Christian missionary, alike find "the whole head sick, the whole heart faint, the intellectual and moral intelligence polluted and defiled."[142]

This defamatory analysis, articulated at a time of crisis, reversed the top-down theory of early Christian missions that assumed the power and influence of the upper strata of society to shape and remake society as a whole and resulted in a program of attempting to reach the most influential classes in India through higher education.[143] Significantly, in the wake of 1857, the IFNS began to emphasize its zenana work and took steps to move to a closer cooperation with the largest and most influential of the societies involved in India, the CMS. The attempts of missionary wives to proselytize "native" women in the context of the anxieties that created the Raj progressively transformed the style and ideology of missionary work. At the heart of this transformation was a common belief in the critical role Indian women played in defining national character.

Thus, when the IFNS adopted its new name in 1861, it also clarified the purposes of the society: support of normal schools and vernacular boarding schools providing English education; support for Christian instruction delivered through indigenous "Bible women"; and "zenana work . . . [as its] peculiar though not exclusive object."[144] The committee made these ambitious

---

141. On the response of imperial officials after 1857, see Bernard S. Cohn, "Representing Authority in Victorian India," in *The Invention of Tradition*, ed. Eric Hobsbawm and Terence Ranger (Cambridge: Cambridge University Press, 1983), 165-209.

142. Charlesworth, *India and the East*, 4.

143. On the influential educational work from the 1830s of Scottish missionary Alexander Duff, and that of his emulators and critics, see Porter, "Scottish Missions," 38-51.

144. Letter to Henry Venn, 4 Feb. 1861, copy, Minutes of the London Committee of the Calcutta Female Normal School, 15 July 1861, IFNS/ZBMM Archives, Home File List, General Committee minutes, 1859–Mar. 1865.

changes in the context of energetic public discussions of women's position in society that encompassed, among others, the debates over nursing, marriage, and prostitution.[145] They also formulated their expectations in the context of the celebrated "surplus woman" debate. In England and Wales in the year 1861 there were 513,706 (5.25 percent) more women than men in a population of 20,066,224.[146] In 1862 in the *National Review*, W. R. Greg offered the famous and invidious solution of colonial transportation of these women for marriage.[147] For Greg and many others the problem was a pressing one, particularly since the mid-Victorian construction of femininity allowed few options for women outside of marriage and narrowly defined domestic work. Anglican sisterhoods (domestic and foreign), the IFNS, and other female missions that sprang up in the 1850s sought to capitalize on the situation. As Mary Weitbrecht, pioneer CMS missionary wife and founding member of the IFNS phrased her appeal for women, "Oh may the Lord so pour out of His Spirit in these last days, that *maidens, daughters, widows,* may rise up in adequate numbers and say, 'I can be spared here; I am wanted there; and though I may suffer, I will go.'"[148]

Motivating women to suffering service was a common strategy for Evangelical commentators such as Mary Weitbrecht and Maria Charlesworth, and in the missionary context they asserted that the women of the zenana, parallel to the Christian middle-class women of Britain, exemplified the condition and potential of the women and the families of the entire society. The idea that the mothers and women of India were the key to the conversion of India grew in importance as influential men, such as Oxford orientalist linguist Sir Monier Monier-Williams and many others, asserted that Christianity would make little progress in India until female missionaries had free access to Indian women.[149] And the cause received increasing publicity as more women volunteered. Propagandists for women's work constructed the image of the Indian zenana in particular as an example of the state that resulted when a gendered separate-

145. Florence Nightingale and the debate over nursing receive valuable treatment in both Poovey, *Uneven Developments,* chap. 6, and Vicinus, *Independent Women,* chap. 3.

146. Figures in Vicinus, *Independent Women,* 293, Appendix A. Matters remained much the same through to the end of the century. In 1901 there were 1,070,617 (6.8 percent) more women than men in a population of 32,527,843. As John Shelton Reed has further noted, at any time in the second half of the nineteenth century, nearly a third of women aged twenty-five to thirty-five were unmarried, and nearly 10 percent of the female population aged over forty-five were widows. Reed, "Female Movement," 211-12.

147. Poovey, *Uneven Developments,* 1-6.

148. Mary Weitbrecht, "Christian Work among the Women of India," Speech of 23 Oct. 1878, in *Proceedings of the General Conference on Foreign Missions, Held at the Conference Hall in Mildmay Park, London, October, 1878* (London: Shaw, 1879), 188. Italics in original.

149. Pitman, *Lady Missionaries,* vii.

spheres ideology was put into practice without allowing for woman's moral influence within the domestic sphere. In the minds of English missionaries, upper-class Indian zenana women lay in dissipated isolation, so despised as to be unable to influence husbands and brothers, and lost to the world of purposeful caring public service to which growing numbers of English middle-class women were devoting their lives.[150] In the wake of the Indian rebellion, the argument grew in volume that girls' and women's education was crucial, and that it was time to "advocate the agency of female missionaries in India."[151] In this context the zenana emerged as a "crucial narrative device" around which discussions of race, gender, and formulations of the domestic revolved, not least because the ambiguity of parallel gender ordering between Eastern and Western systems that the zenana seemed to represent allowed for a range of responses at a time of rapid transformation in religious gender roles.[152]

The growth of an exclusive female sphere of missionary activity paralleled the growing role of independent women in domestic charity in Britain. While the manuals for spinsters and other "surplus women" in the period counseled "religion and restraint," female foreign missions operated in the same idiom employed by the female "war hero" Florence Nightingale and in the slum visitations of Ellen Ranyard's Bible women. These lives provided the examples that transformed the virginal, self-sacrificing, but passive woman into the spiritually and socially active single female nurse and charity worker. Thus, when evangelical theology, imperial opportunity, and the incipient drive toward active and professional identities for women in England combined in the 1860s, women's missions became an avenue for religiously conservative women legitimately to claim an independent, public missionary role in the name of "womanhood" and "home." Notably, while holiness enthusiast Hudson Taylor carried out the first radically innovative use of single female missionaries, catalyzing a rapid transformation in the understanding of women's missionary roles, he actually did little to construct that transformation as positive and acceptable in mainstream religious culture. Within the denominations, justifications for women's missions operated on a different plane, largely in reference to the need for success and stability — for a source of feminine purity and power — that would

150. Rainy, "Female Agency," 2:141. For an examination of parallel constructions of zenana ideology among American missionaries, see Leslie A. Flemming, ed., *Women's Work for Women: Missionaries and Social Change in Asia* (Boulder, CO: Westview, 1989), 38, 40, 118-21. On the supposed existence of zenana abuses as a reason to withhold Indian political rights, see Sinha, *Colonial Masculinity*, 44-46.

151. C. B. Leupolt (CMS missionary, Benares), *Conference on Missions Held in 1860 at Liverpool*, ed. The Secretaries to the Conference (London: Nisbet, 1860), 112.

152. Johnston, *Missionary Writing*, 74, 95.

lay the foundations of virtuous homes. While family and domestic issues had been central to the evangelical missionary agenda since its inception, a focus on inaccessible foreign feminine spaces such as the zenana allowed the construction of some forms of mission as exclusively the province of women. In this way, evangelical prescriptions for English social reform became the foundation of independent women's mission abroad, as both slum-visiting Bible women in England and zenana missionaries in India assumed the power to reverse sinful degradation in the homes of the English poor and of the foreign heathen. This, the Sanskrit scholar and Chairman of the CEZMS Sir Monier-Williams asserted, was "the key to our national greatness and prosperity," and became the core ideology of zenana missionary work.[153]

The cult of the exalted spiritual nature of woman had had currency since the writings of Hannah More in the 1790s, but only in the 1860s did this set of ideas begin to have real significance in encouraging independent organization of women's foreign missionary work, as zenana visitation and female home visitation in British slums reinforced each other. In India, as a veteran missionary wife recalled, the most rewarding aspects of female missionary work arose out of "house-to-house visitation among . . . [Indian] women. Their horizon is bounded by the four walls of the Zenana, and dreary, monotonous and dull are all their lives."[154] The description of the state of zenana women presented an antipodean vision to what committed, charitable, activist Christian women in Britain asserted should be their role. Rather than being frivolous, superstitious, and useless — the example ostensibly presented by the zenana — women should be serious, Christian, and useful — the example presented by the zenana missionary and the English parish visitor. These qualities were, of course, already part of the discourse on women and respectability in England, but the prerogatives of charity mandated their extension to the public realm outside the home, and the prerogatives of zenana work compelled a coherent and concrete imperial role. As women's charitable activity increased in the Church over the course of the century, women's public speaking roles, verging on preaching, were particularly advanced by philanthropic advocacy early in the century, particularly in connection with the abolition cause, and later in the century in support of foreign missionary work.[155] In the world of conservative religious

153. Monier-Williams quoted in John Murdoch, *The Women of India and What Can Be Done for Them,* 2nd ed. (Madras: Christian Vernacular Education Society, 1891), 3; Ellen Henrietta Ranyard, *Life Work; or, The Link and the Rivet* (London: Nisbet, 1861), 5-6, 38-40.

154. Mrs. Ferguson, address to a public meeting, 25 Oct. 1878, in *Mildmay Conference, 1878,* 309. For parallel portrayals of Indian women in feminist periodicals, see Burton, *Burdens of History,* 66-67.

155. On women and abolitionism, see Clare Midgley, "Anti-Slavery and the Roots of 'Imperial

belief this formulation, when coupled with the sanction for the pious action that holiness practice delivered, proved to be both persuasive and capable of neutralizing the worst fears of improper female behavior.

Class, Gender, and the Missionary Social Imagination

The most desirable target audience for female missionary recruiting was obvious. As Lord Kinnaird, patron of the IFNS suggested, there was "a wide field . . . presented to ladies who have no specific home ties, and who possess a moderate income," adding, "[w]hat could be a more interesting work, for an English lady prepared to master a native language than to be located near some European Missionary, and to superintend the working of a band of native Bible-readers . . . ?"[156] Zenana work, like most Victorian charity, was conceived of as a field for certain kinds of women. The high social position of Indian zenana women was the constant backdrop in writings about missions to them, and accounts of zenanas were designed to maximize empathy in target audiences. The constant implication of such writings was that zenana women occupied an analogous social position to English women in "respectable" homes, building affinity with women who had embraced the middle-class ethos of Victorian culture. By constructing an imaginary sisterhood of common interest between English and Indian women, these accounts contributed to popularizing the cause through the projection of supporters' own identities on their subjects of interest.

Upper-class Indian women were the primary focus of zenana work, and early supporters painted detailed pictures of how zenana women were relegated to an exclusively private, idle, monotonous, and oppressive existence, devoid of even the modest physical comforts enjoyed by English ladies.[157] This existence denied Indian women the pleasures and benefits that Western arts, commodities, and true religion brought to the English household, an existence akin to "the home-bred canary . . . never [knowing] how to stretch their wings into open air," and one that destroyed the natural kinship that women should feel with each other, because of the unnatural jealousies that polygamy bred. Perhaps

---

Feminism,'" in *Gender and Imperialism*, ed. Clare Midgley (Manchester: Manchester University Press, 1998), 164-66; on public addresses and missionary advocacy, see Gill, *Women and the Church*, 138-39.

156. Arthur F. Kinnaird, Speech to a public meeting. 25 Oct. 1878, in *Mildmay Conference, 1878*, 276. See also, Edward Bickersteth, bishop of Exeter, "The Church's Duty and a New Departure in Missionary Enterprise," Opening comments for the 18 June 1888 meeting, in *Protestant Missions Conference, 1888*, 1:420.

157. C. B. Lewis, *A Plea for Zenanas* (n.p., n.d., ca. 1866), 1-3.

worst of all, Indian women were entirely dependent on the capricious whims of a single man rather than on the generalized norms of civilized behavior that, missionaries argued, had issued from the historic Christian appreciation of the strengths and limitations of women themselves.[158] This image of the zenana had the power — because it was believed to be a widespread institution in both Hindu and Islamic homes — to bind together orientalized visions of home life across two major cultural fields. The source of this degradation was often constructed as "[t]he Mahommedan religion . . . carried into India by the sword," responsible for "the now abject social position of women in India . . . regarded almost as a different species of being from man, having no friendly intercourse with him."[159] It was the appreciation of women's true nature, supporters of women's missions maintained, that had liberated Western women within the domestic sphere and allowed their influence to extend beyond it where public needs corresponded with private vocations.

Seen in this way, the zenana represented more than just a primitive holdover from the past. It also served as a cautionary example. In the zenana, English middle-class men and women could imagine the results of a rigid ideology that rigorously limited women to a physical private space rather than allowing domestic economy and philanthropy to flow into the public realm.[160] The theme of women as "prisoners innocent" yet "still the commander of Indian life" suggested both that women needed to be drawn into the public realm so that their "superstition" could be assailed and that they could then provide the key to constructing a moralized Christian society that would convert and "civilize."[161] Underlying the developing ideology was a theme of fear: fear of the uncontrolled power of men. This was mutually constituted with strong feminist arguments against the Contagious Diseases Acts that underpinned the campaigns of Josephine Butler against the state control of prostitution, at first in Britain from the 1870s, later in the empire, and the furor raised by the child-prostitution and white-slavery scandals of the 1880s.[162] Missionary narratives

---

158. J. C. Parry, *What Is a Zenana?* (London: Yates & Alexander, 1872), 5-6.

159. "Ladies' Association for the Promotion of Female Education Among the Heathen [SPG]," *The Net* 1, no. 8 (Sept. 1866): 141.

160. Cf. Nair, "Uncovering the Zenana," 16-18.

161. George Ensor, *"Help These Women": A Plea for the Work of the Church of England Zenana Missionary Society* (London: Hunt, 1894), 4-7.

162. Judith Walkowitz, *Prostitution and Victorian Society: Women, Class and the State* (Cambridge: Cambridge University Press, 1980), 90-147, 246-56; Philippa Levine, *Prostitution, Race, and Politics: Policing Venereal Disease in the British Empire* (New York: Routledge, 2003), chap. 4; Judith Walkowitz, *City of Dreadful Delight: Narratives of Sexual Danger in Late Victorian London* (Chicago: University of Chicago Press, 1992), chaps. 3 and 4.

TABLEAU OF THE INDIAN ZENANA FROM THE OPEN WINDOW."

Dramatic re-creation of an "Indian Zenana" for the SPG Westminster
Missionary Exhibition, a popular London missionary event staged in June 1912.
From SPG Photo Album 98, Bodleian Library of Commonwealth and African History, Rhodes
House, Oxford. Courtesy of the United Society for the Propagation of the Gospel.

of the lives of Indian women relied heavily on themes of enforced ignorance
and sexual slavery that had strong contemporary resonance.

Throughout the major mission fields similar rhetorical strategies came to
support arguments for girls' education and women's work. Social transformation
through the evangelization of women and education for girls was bound up with
efforts at social amelioration such as medical missions, which paralleled developments in the late Victorian domestic response to urban poverty. Anglican women
developed a sense of international responsibility for non-Western women and children in an age of rising imperialistic fervor, emphasizing a maternalist strategy for
"civilizing" foreign cultures through the domestic transformation of women, families, manners, and morality. And increasingly in missions British women found
considerable freedom to teach, preach, and engage in professionalizing social service — for instance, in medicine — as strategic emphasis at societies such as the
CMS shifted from conversionary tactics that focused on salvation to socially ame-
liorative strategies that focused on educational and medical service.[163] As Rhonda

163. Guli Francis-Dehquani, "Medical Missions and the History of Feminism: Emmeline Stuart of the CMS Persia Mission," in *Women, Religion and Feminism in Britain, 1750-1900*, ed. Sue
Morgan (Basingstoke, UK: Palgrave Macmillan, 2002), 197-98.

Semple has noted, this transformation was possible because of the success women had within the missionary movement "in conflating the professional and the private in mission practice" while expanding the definition of valid mission work using the vocabularies of emotional, revivalistic religion, rather than traditional masculine theological languages.[164] As these roles and the numbers of women in the mission field grew, a change in the representation of Protestant female missionaries occurred. Instead of focusing exclusively on traditional womanly work — education and child care requiring kindness and a tender touch — women were more frequently depicted as soldiers, if soldiers of civilization, adopting the older powerful trope of Christian militarism in support of an expanding women's work.[165] Such soldiers remained necessary because, even if medicine and education were expanding as mission agencies, the underlying vision of foreign women as enslaved to superstition and male power — as in the zenana — remained the central image projected in order to maintain the sense of urgent missionary need.

By the final decades of the century, the range of cultures encompassed by women's foreign missionary work — and thus both the explanatory and the emotional range of the exotic degradations it purported to expose — had expanded significantly. The image of the zenana pressed heavily in the 1860s exemplified the dangerous seclusion of women from public life, implying that purely private lives consigned women to domestic ornamentation and sexual slavery. New missionary initiatives in the 1870s in Africa and China in particular allowed the elaboration of a more comprehensive imagined map of foreign family life.[166] The zenana and the "imprisoning" of all non-Western women that it implied operated at the core of missionary constructions of "heathen" women in the second half of the nineteenth century.[167] The rhetoric was refined, however, as women's missions grew rapidly into the 1890s and missionaries multiplied the images of African and Chinese domestic life available for comparison to the British home. African homes purportedly demonstrated what happened when women were thrown into public life as laborers and drudges. Thus, rather than the private seclusion seen in India, in Africa powerless women suffered the unmediated horrors of male exploitation in an unregulated public market

164. Semple, *Missionary Women*, 2-3, 43-50.

165. Judith Rowbotham, "'Soldiers of Christ'? Images of Female Missionaries in Late Nineteenth-Century Britain: Issues of Heroism and Martyrdom," *Gender and History* 12, no. 1 (Apr. 2000): 96-98; Olive Anderson, "The Growth of Christian Militarism in Mid-Victorian Britain," *English Historical Review* 86 (Jan. 1971): 46-72.

166. For CMS expansions in Africa and China including the extended use of women, see Stock, *History of the CMS*, 3:226, 363, 368-71, 431-32, 559, 562-63, 568-70, 735-37.

167. "'Daybreak Workers' Union leaflet," CEZ Girls leaflets, ca. 1900, CEZMS Archives, CEZ G/EC1/5C.

where they were "in fact slaves, bought & sold at the caprice of the husband." Constructing African women as "contemporary ancestors" gave force to these images. As Dr. G. R. M. Wright, CMS missionary to Uganda, emphasized in his fundraising speeches, "England was a heathen country 1000 years ago. If there had been no missionaries we should be no better than Uganda."[168] The imagery of women in Africa was strongly influenced by its connection to earlier abolition efforts and the attention drawn by David Livingstone to the continuation of slavery in East Africa under the direction of "Mohammendans," in which commodified personal relationships supposedly destroyed family solidarity.[169]

Similarly, the plight of Chinese women was constructed to suggest the problems arising when women were treated as mere commodities, "piece[s] of goods bought and sold" as chattels.[170] This was the extreme of an unregulated market defined by male appetites where women lived in blind and resentful obedience to men, devoid of the love and respect believed to characterize Christian marriages in Britain.[171] Such representations formed the ideological foundation for the movement. From the origin of the SPG's Ladies' Association in 1866, for example, the "honour and respect" accorded Western Christian women was the standard against which women in "heathen lands" were constructed as objects of pity and horror: mere "playthings" in the harems and zenanas Islam had produced in the East, property and "a slave all her life" in Africa.[172] In addition, such narratives also had particular resonance because they directly paralleled popular anti-Catholicism; in Anglican rhetoric, among both Evangelicals and orthodox High Churchmen, it is often difficult to differentiate between the venomous denunciations of the supposed tyranny over ignorant, idolatrous female victims that was exercised by Catholic, Brahmin, and African pagan priests.[173] These standard motifs of missionary rhetoric and the vision of the

---

168. G. R. M. Wright, 1893 "Uganda" notebook, pp. 50-52, Dr. Gaskoin Richard Morden Wright Papers, CMS Archives, Acc 134 F/2. For a broader discussion of the usage of the idea of Africans as "contemporary ancestors," see Cairns, *Prelude to Imperialism*, chap. 3.

169. Emma Raymond Pitman, *Central Africa, Japan and Fiji: A Story of Missionary Enterprise, Trials, and Triumphs* (London: Hodder and Stoughton, 1882), 16; Minna C. Gollock and Georgina A. Gollock, *Half Done: Some Thoughts for Women* (London: United Council for Missionary Education, 1916), 49.

170. W. S. Swanson, comments at 14 June 1888 "Women's Work to Women" session, *Protestant Missions Conference, 1888*, 1:400; Harriet Warner Ellis, *Our Eastern Sisters and Their Missionary Helpers* (London: RTS, n.d, ca. 1883), 120.

171. Charles G. Sparham, *Christianity and the Religions of China: A Brief Study in Comparative Religions* (London: Snow, 1896), 21.

172. "Ladies' Association for the Promotion of Female Education Among the Heathen [SPG]," *The Net* 1, no. 8 (Sept. 1866): 141-42.

173. On parallels between anti-Catholicism and opposition to Indian "idolatry," see Pen-

home as the repository of virtue saturated the movement's propaganda as it was extended to mass audiences in the late Victorian era. Woman was constructed as the anchor around which family and Christian stability were to be built, and this formulation came to have a powerful, long-lasting resonance not only in missionary rhetoric but also in a very broad range of colonial civilization-building projects.[174]

Using African and Chinese examples of women's domestic plight, as well as originating Indian ones, missionaries and their supporters imagined a range of extremes bracketing the British domestic norm. Rather than constructing a single "other" against which to compare British women, missionary supporters imagined a range of domestic arrangements that molded women through environmental as well as religious conditions.[175] To one side of the civilized Christian mean, excesses of the private led to female seclusion, as in Indian zenanas and Islamic harems, extinguishing women's familial genius and destroying the domestic sphere as a location for social and political reform. To the other side, the influence of public commercial relations and the unfettered power of men destroyed domesticity entirely, as in African and Chinese society, where exploitation of women as unprotected labor reduced them to chattel. Under both the extremes, missionary enthusiasts implied, the crucial civilizing effect of domestic influence was lost on male public society. Furthermore, this linear conceptualization of male and female relations suggested that on one side of the proper balance of feminine social and religious activism achieved in Victorian England lay exploitation under the influence of brutalizing male market relations, and on the other lay torpor and uselessness, as women's natural "genius" was destructively channeled inward in domestic seclusion.[176] Theorists advancing women's missions constructed a cross-cultural sisterhood that would raise foreign women and reform their conditions of existence, matching

nington, *Was Hinduism Invented?* 67-68; on early Anglican associations of paganism and popery, see Peter Harrison, *"Religion" and the Religions in the English Enlightenment* (Cambridge: Cambridge University Press, 1990), 143-45; on the association of various forms of "idolatry" in Anglo-American Protestant popular culture, see David Morgan, *Protestants and Pictures: Religion, Visual Culture and the Age of American Mass Production* (New York: Oxford University Press, 1999), 220-28.

174. Deborah Gaitskell, "At Home with Hegemony? Coercion and Consent in African Girls' Education for Domesticity in South Africa Before 1910," in *Contesting Colonial Hegemony: State and Society in Africa and India,* ed. Dagmar Engels and Shula Marks (London: British Academic Press, 1994), 114-18.

175. On parallel comparisons in earlier antislavery discourse involving colonial slavery, African polygamy, and Oriental harems as comparative points in the development of British feminism, see Midgley, "Imperial Feminism," 167-77.

176. Charlesworth, *India and the East,* 5.

the benefits achieved for women in England. At the same time, however, this model indicated that conservation of these benefits required the shielding of the "weaker sex" from the brutal world of market forces. Having been secured from the tyranny of ungoverned fathers and husbands, women should thankfully accept as their greatest attainable public position the unequal and "nonpolitical" roles that had delivered Western women the greatest possible comparative advantages in the public realm.[177]

Missionary feminist arguments paralleled those of British and colonial feminists who championed an evolutionary change in civil society away from primitive male force and toward morality as a basis for order.[178] Yet arguably the message, spread through conservative religious channels, reached more broadly and deeply than that voiced by more secular feminists, not least because missionary ideology operated within the confines and controls of regulated, respectable official religion.[179] Operating with clerical sanction provided modest new opportunity while simultaneously reducing the threat of further, more radical feminist demands. In virtually all the rhetoric of the times, the role of the Western woman was to raise "heathen" women to her own level as part of a developmental schema whereby historical forces begun in the West would sweep the world. "Woman has always been the slave and drudge of man," Mrs. Thompson explained at the London 1888 centenary conference, "but now through the influence of the Gospel she is raised to be man's helper and equal."[180] In the missionary vision, however, the implicit contradiction between being both an "equal" and a "helper" remained in deep tension. The insistence on urgent, rapid action masked this tension, emphasizing instead the superior state of womanhood in Western countries and the activist place it had in the missionary program. Increasingly this became a program for reshaping not only the spiritual but also the social aspects of a world perceived as critically tipping in a time of radically shifting secular, material, and governmental forces. As the founders of the CEZMS stated, the special concern of female missions was not simply that of "false religion," but also "the way in which false religion affects social habits, and has moulded the entire constitution of Hindu society." Social

177. See, for example, comments at the Public Meeting on 25 Oct. 1878, *Mildmay Conference, 1878*, 302-3.

178. Burton, *Burdens of History*, 79-80; Grimshaw, "Anglican Womanhood," 333.

179. For a parallel assertion regarding the relative impact of evangelical and feminist experience in widening women's opportunities in Northern Ireland, see David Hempton and Myrtle Hill, "Born to Serve: Women and Evangelical Religion," in *The Irish Women's History Reader*, ed. Alan Hayes and Diane Urquhart (London: Routledge, 2001), 119-24.

180. Mrs. Thompson, LMS Matabeleland Mission, quoted in *Protestant Missions Conference, 1888*, 1:446.

reform necessary to "alleviate the misery" of Indian women and thus stabilize colonial society rested at the center of concern.[181] Ideas about the "equal" but limited place of women in society, as well as the conviction that Protestant women had a distinct role in bringing change to the world through public activity, were part of a heroic missionary outlook — focused on both England and overseas regions — that accelerated from the late 1870s, transforming missions in their greatest phase of expansion.

Conclusion

By the late Victorian era, High Church experiments with women's community, evangelical cultural change, imperial concerns, and changing social conditions had combined to increase the role of women in both the home support and the overseas operations of foreign missions to a level of overwhelming importance. Advocates of expanding women's responsibility in mission administration indicated that in most English parishes women did most of the work and nearly all the door-to-door collecting. The CMS Gleaners' Union, whose 70,000 members had spearheaded the much-vaunted, late Victorian expansion of the society, was almost entirely the preserve of women. By 1910, 970 of its 1,128 secretaries (86 percent) were women, and these figures held in local missionary unions of all sorts, which women staffed almost without exception. To missionary organizers like Georgina Gollock, women, "as a rule untied by business restriction," were the natural foot soldiers of home organization because "concentration of devotion and energy in a restricted sphere are more akin to the genius of women than of men." Furthermore, not only did widespread female voluntary service affect massive economies, but women's administrative proficiency exceeded that of men. Thus, "in a large majority of parishes, even where women do not hold nominal office, they carry on the work for the busy clergy whose names appear in the lists, and . . . as collectors the women have practically a clear field."[182] Levels of women's interest in and support of the foreign missionary enterprise had always been very high; with the advent of single female missionaries and women's missions, their support — both financial and logistical — grew even greater.

181. M. Weitbrecht, circular, "India's Women. To Our Friends," reprint from the first issue of *India's Women*, [1880], CEZMS Archives, CEZ/AP 2.
182. Georgina A. Gollock, *The Contribution of Women to Home Work of the C.M.S.* (London, n.d., ca. 1912), 5-8. Throughout England at least 75 percent of financial contributions can be plausibly ascribed to women. Susan Thorne, "Missionary-Imperial Feminism," in *Gendered Missions: Women and Men in Missionary Discourse and Practice*, ed. Mary Taylor Huber and Nancy C. Lutkehaus (Ann Arbor: University of Michigan Press, 1999), 41.

Women were equally crucial abroad. The "new era" in late Victorian missionary recruitment rested heavily on successfully enlisting single female missionaries. Between 1880 and 1900, the total number of CMS missionaries in the field increased from 252 to 889; of the 637 new missionaries, 331 (or 52 percent of the increase) were single women.[183] When both single women and missionary wives are considered, the numbers at the turn of the century are striking. In the BMS women made up 56 percent of missionaries in the field; in the CMS and the LMS, 55 percent; and in the WMMS, 45 percent. When the numbers of agents employed by the CEZMS and the ZBMM — both were independent societies closely associated with the CMS — are added to its figures, women account for at least 64 percent of the CMS's agents in the field, exceeding even women's numbers on the CIM's missionary staff, where female agents made up 60 percent of the total. Among High Church missions, figures can be more difficult to calculate because of the block grant system used by the SPG and the even greater propensity at the SPG to ignore missionary wives and female workers. Nevertheless, SPG missions registered 48 percent female workers, and Anglo-Catholic mission fields were also strongly affected, such as in East Africa, where 41 percent of the UMCA's mission staff was composed of unmarried women. By 1900 women clearly made up substantially more than 50 percent of British Protestant missionaries overseas and, given the persistent undercounting of women, perhaps over 70 percent, particularly among evangelical Anglicans (see Appendix I, Figure 6).[184]

Burgeoning concern among English women to empathize with and transform the home lives of foreign women, channeled through holiness-oriented revivalism of both evangelical and Anglo-Catholic varieties, was largely responsible for the resurgence of Anglican missions. This was particularly true at the CMS where fundraising was revolutionized through popular methods that engaged the public in new ways. In conjunction with this growth, women and university professionals increasingly shifted the gendered construction and strategy of missions away from an earlier emphasis on building model families around a strong patriarchal center to new approaches resting on reaching foreign women through strategies to serve children, family life, and health.[185] As

183. *Proceedings of the CMS . . . 1879-80*, xii-xiii; Stock, *History of the CMS,* 4:465. These figures do not include missionary wives, since their numbers were not tabulated in 1880. In 1900 the total CMS missionary force, including wives, was 1,238.

184. The standard comprehensive history of Christian missions for years, Stephen Neill and Owen Chadwick, *A History of Christian Missions,* 2nd ed. (Harmondsworth, UK: Penguin, 1986), makes virtually no mention of women's contribution. This omission has been redressed in Cox, *British Missionary Enterprise,* 196-98 and passim.

185. Rosemary Fitzgerald, "A 'Peculiar and Exceptional Measure': The Call for Women Medical

important as the growing women's numbers in the mission field were, so also were the advocates for women's missions, who effectively promoted a strategy for the cultural transformation of indigenous societies that stressed the centrality of female agency and the necessity of new and independent missionary identities for women, institutionalized in education and health provision overseas. As English women developed a more fully socialized vision of missionary engagement — often pioneered by missionary wives and widows — they also reinforced trends toward professionalism within the missionary movement. Emphasis on professionalized service also supported another long-cherished goal of Anglican missionary leaders: building a place for missions in the British universities.

By developing informal communities of interest through which shared ideals and goals were established and communicated at the grassroots level of religious culture, women transformed the missionary movement in the late Victorian era, both in the field and in England. Relying on a strong sense of cultural superiority over foreign women to advance their domestic programs (just as British feminists advanced their authority as protectors of women in the empire), women in the British missionary movement constructed a unique mission of "women's work for women," advancing their own influence and autonomy.[186] The extension of domestic models and stereotypes was crucial to justifying women's claims to represent a socially improving force, both inside and outside empire, and the work of women gained momentum in the final decade of the century, reinforced as it was by the rise of university-based student missionary professionalism. Debate over the proper role of female missionaries, as part of the larger debate over the proper outlines of the feminine sphere, had been developing since the 1830s, but general expansion of women's work in the field and the achievement of substantial support had to wait decades to unfold. The formal subordination of women within church hierarchies and institutions, however, did not ultimately prevent them from making critical contributions to most areas of Anglican religion.

This suggests that a history of women in conservative denominational contexts can illuminate how they, short of embracing overt forms of feminism, nevertheless advanced and transformed their roles and authority, slowly at first, more rapidly in the waning decades of the century, to achieve an effective "feminist practice" within what remained a set of patriarchal religious institutions.[187] Foreign missions were critical to the process, for the middle ground established

Missionaries for India in the Later Nineteenth Century," in *Missionary Encounters: Sources and Issues,* ed. Robert A. Bickers and Rosemary E. Seton (Richmond, UK: Curzon, 1995), 174-76, 194-96.
  186. Burton, *Burdens of History,* 63-74.
  187. Mangion, "Female Institution Building," 87-89.

between suffragist feminism and restrictive domestic patriarchy in women's missions was ideologically located through the lessons constructed around the Indian zenana and African and Chinese families. While women's missions drew heavily upon ideas of a divinely ordained domestic hierarchy and celebrated the presumed differences between the sexes, they were also open to those increasingly professionalized pursuits outside the home that could be defined as appropriate for women and modeled by women's independent public activity carried out by both Anglo-Catholic sisters and Evangelical deaconesses. For the women of mid-Victorian evangelical subcultures, holiness theology provided the license that was a crucial opening to public space; for Anglo-Catholics the sisterhood delineated a realm and opportunity for independent action and the transgression of conventional Victorian gender ideology. In turn, these openings reinforced the sense of imperial and international need and the broader growth of women's roles in secular society, as the models became avenues for the expansion of women's activity overseas. Although women did not enter missionary work with the expectation of greater autonomy and authority — rather, they entered voicing ideologies of sacrifice and altruism — the nature of their work in the field drew them into expanded, demanding careers. These were often at odds with traditional views of appropriate domestic duties and attitudes, and they demonstrated in clear ways women's own capacities, particularly upon their return to Britain, when the limitations that characterized home churches and society became obvious in contrast.[188]

This situation, however, was fraught with complexities and contradictions. Women utilized ideologies of service and maternalist authority in support of missions, Christian communities, and empire; although they seldom openly criticized the unequal power inherent in the ideology of separate gender spheres, they consistently exploited opportunities within the mission endeavor to subvert established hierarchies and advance both individual and collective boundaries within the missionary project.[189] That is, pragmatic strategies for expanding work and authority, even in the face of conservative religious patriarchal institutional arrangements, had the potential to shift practice, especially as women's indispensability to the movement grew.

---

188. T. O. Beidelman, "Altruism and Domesticity: Images of Missionizing Women Among the Church Missionary Society in Nineteenth-Century East Africa," in *Gendered Missions: Women and Men in Missionary Discourse and Practice*, ed. Mary Taylor Huber and Nancy C. Lutkehaus (Ann Arbor: University of Michigan Press, 1999), 113-14, 133-36.

189. Many studies of women's missions demonstrate this. Brouwer, *New Women*, 188; Melman, *Women's Orients*, 166-68; Rutherdale, *Canadian Mission Field*, 54-72, 113-17. This effect was particularly demonstrated in the case of female mission medical doctors. Francis-Dehquani, "Medical Missions," 199-200, 203-5.

Women in traditional English religious cultures found in the missionary cause opportunity to become agents of a wider interpretation of religious, national, and imperial life, tied in particular to education and social service. These approaches operated parallel to, but in a far less threatening fashion than, the social purity and suffrage movements of the same era. By emphasizing self-sacrifice rather than self-assertion they drew in large numbers of Victorian women, personally and ideologically sheltered within the strong family networks of fathers, mothers, aunts, brothers, and sisters that were the crucial axis of the entire movement.[190] While the continuance of deeply conservative attitudes toward respectable gender behavior at the missionary societies and in evangelical culture more generally remained a significant stumbling block to expansion of women's roles in mission, and undoubtedly repelled many talented and privileged women with other open possibilities, foreign missions operated as a sphere of expanding opportunity and social vision for many women, from the most conservative religious cultures.[191] As Jennifer Morawiecki points out, the missionary goal of raising indigenous women to be equals in marriage, as effective wives and mothers, was the same aim espoused for English women by many feminist reformers.[192] Women involved in social reform utilized parallel arguments about the need to contain unregulated male power, in support of both social purity movements and foreign missions. Yet it is difficult to see support for missions at this stage as part of any comprehensive "missionary feminist" campaign explicitly questioning the fundamental legitimacy of male power in both Eastern and Western settings, given the clear absence of any critique of women's subordination in Anglo-American culture in the missionary literature. Nevertheless, speakers did increasingly question male depravity and patriarchal tyranny, and in the most enthusiastic circles, such as the revivalistically fired annual evangelical Mildmay Conference that was inspired by the Pennefathers and their deaconess work, missionaries such as C. H. Judd of the CIM could and did emphasize the legitimate prophetic and ministerial powers of women, when properly regulated under the "token of subjection" represented by husbands and, by implication, more generally of men.[193] Missionary visions of social transformation, revolving as they did

190. As Brian Harrison notes, most women opposing suffrage nevertheless were deeply involved in the progressive expansion of women's social role, and these conservative "Antis" shared many general attitudes with Anglican missionary communities. Brian Harrison, *Separate Spheres: The Opposition to Women's Suffrage in Britain* (London: Croom Helm, 1978), 55-85. On the family nexus and informal networks of female missionaries, see Semple, *Missionary Women*, 38-39, 110-12.

191. Williams, "Women Missionaries," 66-67.

192. Morawiecki, "Women Missionaries, CEZMS," 69.

193. C. H. Judd, "Woman's Ministry," in *Proceedings of the Conference on Foreign Missions*

around the need to neutralize unbridled male power, thus advanced the explicit role of active philanthropic feminine action in ameliorating social evils, transforming in the process Victorian assumptions about the nature of social action.[194]

Women's work in the missionary movement, like most women's work within the churches, pressed women's roles beyond traditional, limited definitions of domesticity and propriety. Outspoken proponents of mission did not shrink from the feminine professionalism that was expanding in nursing, education, and charity more generally. The case of Charlotte Maria Tucker is illuminating in this respect. Held back by a conservative father's resistance to her aspiration for useful public work, she immediately began parish and workhouse visitation upon his death in 1851; and following her mother's death in 1869, she left for India within five years as a self-supporting Evangelical missionary whose publishing profits went to support the cause.[195] Similarly, for the Anglo-Catholic author Charlotte Yonge, work with the Wantage sisterhood and support of foreign missions — she was a founding member of the SPG Ladies' Association, and all profits from her successful novel *The Daisy Chain* (1864) went to support Bishop Patteson's Melanesian Mission — created an imperative justifying a widening sphere of activity.[196]

By the 1880s, missions to women by women were widely accepted by the boards of missionary societies because they offered a maternalist strategy for "civilizing" that did not fundamentally challenge the belief in female subordination held dear by traditionalist clerics. The path of cleaving loyally to the Church of England in the split from the IFNS, which was taken by the majority of Anglican women, arguably provided greater opportunity for the expansion of women's work than a more independent line would have allowed, precisely because it did not rouse opposition from clerics within the majority culture. Ironically, within the world of evangelicalism, claiming less proved to be a recipe for women to gain more chances for work in the mission field. For it was within evangelical Anglicanism, including that Anglican fringe patronizing the IFNS

Held at the Conference Hall, Mildmay Park, London, October 5th to 7th, 1886 (London: Shaw, 1886), 32-33.

194. On "missionary feminism," see Sarah Caroline Potter, "The Social Origins and Recruitment of English Protestant Missionaries in the Nineteenth Century" (Ph.D. diss., University of London, 1974), 220-26; cf. on the projection in missionary rhetoric of women's oppression outside the boundaries of Britain, Thorne, "Missionary-Imperial Feminism," 45-47.

195. Margaret Nancy Cutt, *Ministering Angels: A Study of Nineteenth-Century Evangelical Writing for Children* (Wormley, UK: Five Owls, 1979), 80-83.

196. Mumm, *Anglican Sisterhoods*, 75; Henry H. Montgomery, *The Light of Melanesia* (London: SPCK, 1896), 5.

and CIM, that missionary women, particularly single female missionaries, found their greatest opportunities despite Evangelical theological conservatism.[197]

By the 1890s missionary strategies focusing on women had widespread currency in Britain. Their popularity opened crucial areas of public debate to women residing within the most religiously conservative subcultures. Missionary activity directly affected more women than virtually any other single imperial or international issue. It also brought women to a position of indispensability in the massive Victorian missionary enterprise, and it legitimized women's voices in public discourses on empire and overseas social reform. As women's mission grew, women's appropriate public roles became an important issue in the shifting debates over how to define both the convert societies that missionaries attempted to construct and the changing nature of the English churches that were presumed to be their model. While women may have largely operated out of "parallel churches" in the organization of women's and missionary work more generally, the changing nature and scope of that work ensured that women could not be easily ignored.

The process by which women rose to this level of significance in the movement was the result of what was perhaps the greatest achievement of the foreign Protestant missionary movement in the second half of the nineteenth century: the transfer of a substantial portion of British women's pre-existing interest in community, child care, and women's welfare to foreign mission work. In the process, women of conservative Evangelical and High Church backgrounds claimed a place in public debates about society writ on a global scale, and they forged ideologies that idealized maternal contributions to the causes of empire, the expansion of "civilization," and the definition of international Christian community. In this way the charitable concerns of women formed the nucleus of the "civilizing" discourse about "progress" that the British world vision encompassed in the high imperial age. Foreign missions served to funnel these concerns into the empire and the "regions beyond" that made up the Protestant mission field. While the several Victorian religious denominations did not, in stated theory, endorse extending the public roles of women, competition between them and within them, operating within the context of evolving Victorian Protestant theology, shifting social attitudes to female public activity, and the anxieties produced by imperial challenges, provided a field of opportunity for the extension of women's roles in religion, in the professions, and in society at large.

---

197. Into the 1930s, at least half of the missionaries employed by the IFNS/ZBMM were Anglicans. J. C. Pollock, *Shadows Fall Apart: The Story of the Zenana Bible and Medical Mission* (London: Hodder and Stoughton, 1958), 171.

CHAPTER 5

Anglicans and Education: University Culture and the Professionalization of Conversion

There is need in [our missionary work] . . . of a clearer understanding of the old faiths, and of a livelier sympathy with the peculiar religious instincts to which they correspond. There is need of a more distinct apprehension of the social power of Christianity. There is need of a more systematic effort to evoke rather than to mould native pastorates. In all these respects, I cannot but believe that the Universities are able to take a characteristic share in foreign evangelization.

B. F. Westcott, 1872

This has been called a great missionary epoch, but we must see a much wider awakening in interest than we have seen yet. Our hope lies in the fact that the youngest of our ministers are the most alive on this subject.

Eugene Stock, 1896[1]

In 1892 hundreds of British university students, following a movement originating among American YMCA activists gathered in 1886 in Massachusetts, took the "missionary pledge," promising themselves as overseas missionaries. From this movement the Student Volunteer Missionary Union (SVMU) was formed, and the following year several British women, from Girton and Newnham Colleges, pledged to serve in India, forming the Missionary Settlement for University Women (MSUW). While modeled on East London settlement

---

1. Westcott, *Religious Office*, 30-31; *Students' Missionary Conference*, 1896, 253.

houses, the MSUW operated independently of male-dominated denominational missions, with the goal of evangelizing the future female leaders of India in what had become, under Parsi patronage, the most developed center of women's education: Bombay (Mumbai).[2] The Student Christian Movement (SCM) that rapidly developed out of this activity emerged largely from the subculture of evangelical holiness life, revivalism, and faith missions that had transformed the transatlantic evangelical world. The inspiration for the movement had been the galvanizing example of the "Cambridge Seven," university graduates who in 1884 had volunteered with the CIM.[3] The deeply ecumenical spirit of this student movement in many ways reflected the practical theology and interests of women, who became so central and integral to it, and who found, as in the MSUW, encouragement and opportunity for independent action.[4] Despite the fundamentally interdenominational spirit, certain denominational societies, particularly the CMS, were able to harness the new enthusiasms among students. This resulted in a wave of university-educated, middle- and upper-class missionaries who made their influence felt in late Victorian missions, through not only the SVMU but also the YMCA and YWCA, as well as intervarsity Christian fellowship organizations. As the missionary movement grew and changed in the final decade of the nineteenth century, no group was more influential among both Evangelicals and High Churchmen than the university students for whom both parties aggressively competed.

The student missionary movement provided not only one of the key channels through which women found access to larger organizational networks in foreign missions and influence in missionary counsels, but also the primary channel through which missionary practice was professionalized and the missionary transformed into a figure of respectability. The Oxbridge universities had been solid centers of Anglican learning and identity for centuries, but they underwent decades of anxious transformation following university reforms in the 1850s, the abolition of Anglican religious tests for admission in 1871, and

2. Symonds, *Oxford and Empire,* 223; Ruth Rouse and Stephen C. Neill, eds., *A History of the Ecumenical Movement, 1517-1948,* 2nd ed. (Philadelphia, PA: Westminster, 1967), 328-29.

3. Susan Billington Harper, *In the Shadow of the Mahatma: Bishop V. S. Azariah and the Travails of Christianity in British India* (Grand Rapids: Eerdmans, 2000), 39n12. By 1891 over 7,000 American students had pledged through what was then the Student Volunteer Movement, organized in 1888 under Cornell University YMCA Secretary John Mott. Extensive communication existed with British missionary leaders. Tissington Tatlow, *The Story of the Student Christian Movement of Great Britain and Ireland* (London: SCM Press, 1933), 22-23, 29-30.

4. From its origin the SVMU allowed women full rights of membership, and rapidly women, particularly the CMS's Georgina Gollock, rose to positions of influence. Tatlow, *Student Christian Movement,* 31, 56-58.

the addition of women's education starting in 1869. Frequently arenas of contested national and imperial identity,[5] the universities also saw disputes over
Anglican identity directly tied to missionary initiatives, as evangelicals worked
to establish missionary organization particularly at Oxford and Cambridge,
assaulting them as strongholds both of a higher and drier Anglicanism and
an emerging dangerous "Romanizing" Anglo-Catholicism. Concurrently, the
entry of Nonconformists challenged the ancient privileges associated with the
Church that the universities represented. With missionary societies desperate
to cultivate a university presence, from the 1870s women — educated at Girton
and Newnham Colleges, Cambridge (founded 1869 and 1871 respectively), and
Lady Margaret Hall (exclusively Anglican), Somerville, St. Hugh's and St. Hilda's,
Oxford (founded 1878, 1879, 1886, and 1893) — who had received a hostile reception from traditionalists like E. B. Pusey and many college heads, found allies on
missionary service matters among pious undergraduates of all Anglican persuasions.[6] By the 1890s, a growing international Christian student movement, born
of revivalism and the holiness movement but also progressively influenced by
ecumenism and social activism, focused on creating a unified and "scientific"
missionary project. Student leadership built on the legacy of international missionary conferences dating from the 1860s to manufacture a sense of momentum. Inspired by American student leaders like John Mott, the SVMU ambition
to achieve "The Evangelization of the World in This Generation" — its famous
"watchword" — seemed achievable to many British supporters in the 1890s,
who were also influenced by imperial enthusiasm peaking at the same time.

The growth of missionary recruiting in the universities had far-reaching
effects on the movement: first, shifting the cultural position of the missionary
to a considerably higher level of social respectability; second, significantly professionalizing missions; third, providing an important site of contact between
the official church and the professionalizing missionary women rising through
parallel church structures. The missionary — who had represented the outsider,
a "not quite gentleman" early in the century — began by the 1880s to have a
much more positive cultural presence within the denominations and "respectable" classes.[7] This transformation was linked to the Anglo-Catholic emphasis
on university and ecclesiastical training for missionaries, which drew a strong

5. Paul Deslandes, *Oxbridge Men: British Masculinity and the Undergraduate Experience, 1850-
1920* (Bloomington: Indiana University Press, 2005), 185-88, 211-13.

6. On resistance to women's colleges, see Antoinette M. Burton, *At the Heart of the Empire:
Indians and the Colonial Encounter in Late-Victorian Britain* (Berkeley: University of California
Press, 1998), 130-32.

7. C. Peter Williams, " 'Not Quite Gentlemen': An Examination of 'Middling Class' Protestant
Missionaries from Britain, c. 1850-1900," *Journal of Ecclesiastical History* 31, no. 3 (July 1980): 301-15.

Evangelical response, bringing Anglican missions into much closer contact with university-based imperial enthusiasm and associated ideals of social engineering and institution building. For reasons of both partisan advantage and social aspiration, High Churchmen and Evangelicals actively pursued new missionary initiatives in the universities in the 1870s. These projects — including the foundation of halls, prayer groups, and missionary associations — produced a dynamic missionary subculture not only in the Oxbridge universities but also in British universities as a whole, leading in the 1880s to new support and a rapid rise in the numbers of coveted university-educated missionaries. In the 1890s, the separate Evangelical and High Church subcultures of students that had characterized earlier missionary coteries began to erode as ecumenism and "scientific" organization were emphasized in the movement. But tendencies to sectarian exclusivity also remained, as High Church junior clerical leaders launched a separate, self-consciously competitive imperial program and as growing unease among "protofundamentalist" Evangelicals began to manifest itself in the creation of separate, exclusive evangelical undergraduate unions.[8] Despite ambitions to unite missionary effort, continuing diversity and intense competition to define missions in terms of faith, gender, nation, empire, and international Christianity were still of the essence of an expanding missionary enterprise.

The Universities and the Transformation of Mission

From the beginning Anglican missionary societies had coveted the support and service of graduates from the ancient English universities. In the early nineteenth century, however, such support was rare and often unenthusiastic when it existed, and thus the CMS found itself falling back on informal training of candidates by committee members in their homes and on recruitment of German pietists. Evangelicals strongly valued clerical status as foundational to social and religious respectability, but they also feared perceived corrupting influences in the universities and shrank from the high costs, leading the CMS to open the Church Missionary Institution in Islington in 1825 with the object of training missionary candidates for ordination.[9] Early circumstance dictated that the CMS took what few university recruits came to it and trained the bulk

8. For a more in-depth discussion of English protofundamentalism, see Chapter 8.

9. This meant providing them with the ability to pass the bishop of London's ordination examinations. Piggin, *Making Evangelical Missionaries,* 189-95. The CMS was the only society to establish its own training institution; other societies instead, from about mid-century, affiliated with independent missionary colleges. Stock, *History of the CMS,* 1:265.

of its missionaries itself.[10] By contrast, the SPG simply avoided the problems presented by ambitious recruitment and training; it paid scant attention to training, relying instead on the anemic supply of members of the "inferior clergy" prepared to offer for the foreign field. It also accepted referrals from Heads of Houses at Oxford and Cambridge and made some connections to King's College, London, for missionary training lectures. Yet on the whole the SPG undertook no dynamic measures to penetrate the English university world. From 1848 onward, St. Augustine's College, Canterbury, designed as a training school primarily for High Church missionary candidates, provided the chief supply of SPG missionaries.[11]

New patterns of party conflict, the imperial events of the late 1850s, and the linked foundation of the UMCA in 1859 changed the atmosphere, and by the 1870s, spurred on by the threat of a rout in party conflict in the universities, Evangelicals attempted to institutionalize their presence at Cambridge and Oxford, led by a small elite of graduates from the 1860s. It was the impact of the 1857 Indian rebellion, the University Lectures of David Livingstone, and the 1858-61 revivals that altered the thinking of a new generation of pietist evangelical students. This generation — which included John Barton, Henry Wright, and Frederick Wigram — was to have a profound influence on the more widespread "missionary revival" of the 1880s at Cambridge. Their work was to prove crucial, for when the holiness revivalism associated with Keswick and the American Dwight L. Moody swept over Cambridge in the 1880s, the CMS was well placed to encourage, shape, and control the movement for the benefit of its foreign missions. In this way the student missionary awakening formed one key ingredient of Evangelical missionary revival, and of a broader student movement that grew from these beginnings.

Missionary Evangelicalism in the Universities

Inspired by the visit of David Livingstone to Cambridge in 1857, the Cambridge University Church Missionary Union, formed in 1858 with ninety-five undergraduate members, proved to be a turning point in CMS fortunes in the universities. Under the direction of the devout young undergraduate John Barton, shortly after a CMS missionary to India himself, the Union solidified

---

10. Of the two hundred missionaries sent out by the CMS between 1824 and 1840, only sixteen were from a university background: seven from Cambridge, six from Oxford, three from Trinity College, Dublin. Stock, *History of the CMS*, 1:263-64.

11. Piggin, *Making Evangelical Missionaries*, 197-99; Bullock, *Ridley Hall*, 1:10.

the presence of the CMS at Cambridge. In many ways, the Church Missionary Union at Cambridge was an extension of the Cambridge University Prayer Union, founded in 1848 with sixty-four members, growing by 1875 to 1,028. The Prayer Union was a central gathering place for Evangelicals at Cambridge, and its rolls from the 1850s and 1860s contain the names of some of the most influential CMS Committee members of the following four decades: Sidney Gedge, John Barton, Frederick Wigram, Frank Wright (brother of Henry), William Barlow, H. W. Webb-Peploe, H. E. Fox, and H. C. G. Moule, among others. But the Missionary Union focused this energy by assigning undergraduates to the Cambridge countryside to hone their missionary speaking skills.[12]

In the 1870s Evangelicals, led by the CMS, launched a strategic program to increase their influence in the Church. Central to the project was a strengthening of the CMS itself, especially through university connections, as an institutional foundation for combating perceived advances by Ritualists and free thinkers. The struggle between the factions in the Church of England had involved clerical training from the earliest phases of the Tractarian movement when, with the founding of Chichester and Wells Theological Colleges in 1839 and 1840, and Cuddesdon, Lichfield, Salisbury, and several others after 1850, advanced High Churchmen sought to set new standards for clerical education that were based in the elevated definitions of Anglican orthodoxy that had emerged out of the storms of religious controversy centered in Oxford in the 1830s.[13] Within these colleges more moderate episcopal leaders sought to rein in enthusiasts, but to Evangelicals, all represented a dangerous challenge.[14] While Evangelicals intended the foundation of St. Aiden's College, Birkenhead, in 1846 and St. John's Hall, Highbury, in 1863 to buttress their reform tradition, the sense began to grow in the early 1870s that Evangelicalism was losing its grip on "the influential classes" and was beginning to alienate the average Churchman. Many thoughtful Evangelicals believed vituperative litigation to quash "illegal" Ritualism was tarnishing the Evangelical reputation, requiring more sophisticated action to advance "Protestant truth."[15] The paradox of the Evangelical position was that while their enemies asserted Evangelicals were more influential and powerful than they had ever been, operating outside of the established channels of Church life through voluntary societies undermined the Evangelical position

12. Minutes of the Cambridge Association of the CMS for the Town and University of Cambridge and the Archdeaconry of Ely, p. 6, CMS Archives, Acc 216 O 1/1; Barton, *Barton*, 11-17.

13. Bullock, *Ridley Hall*, 1:10-11.

14. For the struggle between Samuel Wilberforce, the bishop of Oxford, and H. P. Liddon (later the influential Ritualist Canon at St. Paul's Cathedral) to maintain at least an appearance of non-party Anglican instruction at Cuddesdon, see Meacham, *Wilberforce*, 197-203.

15. Porter, "Cambridge, Keswick and Africa," 10-12.

within the Establishment. One location for building Evangelical institutional power was in the universities, but evangelical "religion of the heart" had led the subculture to downplay learning.

Those associated with Evangelical missions, where issues of training, prestige, and ecclesiastical order were of continuing importance, had a particular interest in advancing a higher educational agenda, and it was the CMS that led the program to found the Evangelical Training Colleges at Oxford and Cambridge, both to produce mission leaders and to maintain the cohesion of Evangelicalism. As early as 1873 Henry Wright, the new honorary clerical secretary of the CMS, canvassed his wealthy industrialist father for the support of a "small college" for Evangelicals at Cambridge.[16] Plans circulating in CMS circles for launching a bricks-and-mortar assault on the Oxbridge universities materialized when in 1875 Edward H. Carr argued that the foundation of university halls could counter "the notorious distemper of Ritualism" that was represented in the open partisanship of some university colleges, notably Keble College (founded in honor of Tractarian leader John Keble in 1868). Carr quickly tapped into the support networks of the CMS. In 1875 he and Wright canvassed in Cambridge, and the following year, after a meeting at CMS House, they launched a full fundraising campaign.[17] Charles Perry, the former Evangelical bishop of Victoria (Melbourne), and William Barlow, a brilliant Cambridge graduate who had attempted to enlist the support of Oxford undergraduates in his slum work before being appointed the new Principal of the CMS College in late 1875, quickly rose to lead the initiative. For both Perry and Barlow, as well as other CMS supporters, the new theological colleges were conceived primarily as forces to counter both Ritualism and rationalism. Evangelicals feared "[t]he extremer men of the new [Ritualist] party [who] had made clear that their purpose was to go behind the Reformation and to assimilate both the doctrine and the ritual of the Church of England to those of Rome."[18] In the campaign to counter these forces Evangelicals saw Bishop Perry as a public competitor against progressive High Church bishops such as Selwyn (formerly of New Zealand, but translated to Lichfield in 1868),

16. The scheme seemed to require promises of at least £50,000. Frank Wright to Henry [Wright], 7 Feb. [1873], CMS Archives, G/AC 4/1/40.

17. An Evangelical vicar with connections to the CMS Committee and, like Henry Wright, the product of an affluent colliery family, Carr made his argument in two articles in *The Christian Observer and Advocate*. Council members of the resulting training halls read like a roll call of the most influential and active CMS supporters: Auriol, Barlow, Fremantle, Knox, Ryle, Tristram, Wright. Bullock, *Ridley Hall*, 1:80-82, 87-88, 112.

18. John Battersby Harford and Frederick Charles Macdonald, *Handley Carr Glyn Moule, Bishop of Durham: A Biography* (London: Hodder and Stoughton, n.d., ca. 1922), 91-92.

while Barlow, with his double first from St. John's, Cambridge, was a visible symbol of Evangelical scholarship.[19]

Continuing advanced High Church successes, such as the miscarriage in early 1876 of negotiations with the young Edward Bickersteth, son of a leading CMS family, to affiliate his scheme for a new Cambridge Mission to Delhi with the Society, reinforced the urgency of the Evangelical task. The Cambridge Mission's connection with the SPG represented another anxious failure to connect with the younger generation in the university battleground.[20] Yet for some Evangelicals — especially that emerging activist "neo-Evangelical" school that was determined to speak and compete in the new Church Congresses — the fear of Anglo-Catholics was mitigated by their common interests with them: opposition to "modern thought" and a rising level of foreign missionary interest. Thus, for E. A. Knox in the 1870s, possible rapprochement with Tractarians was grounded in "[a] common opposition to what we called 'neologianism,' that is to the teaching of Strauss and Renan, to the philosophy of Comte and John Stuart Mill, to Colenso's attack on the Pentateuch, and to the conclusions drawn from Darwinism."[21] Evangelical weakness meant that common cause with Anglo-Catholics was one of the only options within the Church. However, many Evangelicals still believed that the greatest modern evil was the threat to the Reformation that Ritualism posed, and Cambridge, historically more favorable to Evangelicals than Oxford, presented opportunities to challenge successfully the "Romanism" unleashed by the Oxford Movement. High Church encroachment upon the missionary movement, which had always been a hallmark of Evangelical power, was particularly ominous, and the seriousness of the threat that Ritualists might seize the leadership of the missionary movement seemed evident in the student-driven initiatives of both the Anglo-Catholic UMCA and, from 1876, the High Church Cambridge Mission to Delhi. Still, the battle lines in such conflicts were not always as clear-cut as controversialists made them out to be. For example, some considered Thomas Valpy French, one of the sponsors of the Cambridge Mission, to be an Evangelical, but others considered him a dangerous Ritualist. His fascination with the Baptist divine Charles Spurgeon and the American revivalist Dwight Moody, combined with a "romantic Medievalism" and an openness to High Church innovations such as brotherhoods and sisterhoods, confused the issue.[22] Ultimately appointed bishop of Lahore in 1877, he personified how university environments could

19. Bullock, *Ridley Hall*, 1:94, 101, 119-22.

20. Bickersteth, *Bickersteth*, 26, 33-37.

21. Edmund Arbuthnott Knox, *Reminiscences of an Octogenarian* (London: Hutchinson, 1935), 112-13.

22. Bickersteth, *Bickersteth*, 40-41.

break down binary divisions that were more easily drawn in public controversy than sustained in the more intimate worlds of university connection.

To those with strong convictions, however, foundational principles were at stake, and the ambition of the most powerful High Church bishop of the age, Samuel Wilberforce of Oxford, could not be mistaken. Wilberforce determinedly canvassed for the SPG throughout the country in the 1850s, and in 1858 he threw his weight behind the scheme for the UMCA, with its conscious opposition to emphasis on evangelization prior to episcopal church governance as practiced by the CMS. However, in avowing episcopal independence from the State, enthusiasts for the UMCA raised fears among Evangelicals that the mission could become a conduit for "papist" bishops, who would inaugurate ritual innovations overseas, free of the checks of English law.[23] The universities continued to be seen by Evangelicals as the ground from which assaults on the Reformation would issue — now critically linked to university-based missionary activity and the latitude for inaugurating new practices in overseas dioceses it enabled.

Driven by the anxieties of decline, Evangelicals saw dangers multiplying. While revivalism offered the benefits of enthusiasm and conversion, it raised concerns about unorthodoxy in the practice and theology of American revivalists. When combined with more general fears regarding the general spread of rationalism in the universities, and the alleged breakdown of civilization and rise of "neo-paganism" in the cities and mills of the nation, enthusiasm for the creation of defensible centers of Evangelical training grew. But Evangelical training colleges also drew criticism from moderate Churchmen, such as the Divinity Professors J. B. Lightfoot (Lady Margaret) and B. F. Westcott (Regius), who not only supported the Cambridge Brotherhood but also objected that the party exclusivity of the Evangelical halls would tend to build "a Church within a Church," compromising the theoretical comprehensiveness of Anglicanism.[24] Yet party leaders felt compelled to defend the "Reformation principles" upon which, as a most basic touchstone, they believed the Church of England, the English nation, and its empire should unapologetically depend. In 1877 Wycliffe Hall, Oxford was founded, followed by Ridley Hall, Cambridge in 1879.

On the one hand, while the foundation of Ridley and Wycliffe was to narrow further the sympathies of Evangelicalism and heighten the sense of heroic defense against the assaults of the modern world, on the other hand the creation of legitimate and outspoken centers of "evangelical truth" at the universities opened a completely new space for activity concerned with strengthening the

23. Stock, *History of the CMS*, 2:17-21.
24. Lightfoot quoted in Bullock, *Ridley Hall*, 1:185.

party. The leaders who stepped into this space, largely appropriating it for the CMS, were "Senior men" who filtered back to Cambridge in the late 1870s and 1880s and found an Evangelical community increasingly influenced by revivalists and holiness practitioners such as Arthur Stevenson Blackwood and Sholto Douglas and the Americans Dwight L. Moody and Robert Pearsall Smith. Drawing on the tradition of the Cambridge University Prayer Union and the Cambridge Church Missionary Union, Evangelicals founded the Cambridge Inter-Collegiate Christian Union (CICCU) in 1877 to encourage spiritual work by undergraduates to the general student population.[25]

These developments at Cambridge were paralleled in Oxford. In 1879 the Oxford Inter-Collegiate Christian Union was founded, but the influence of evangelicalism at Oxford was never as strong, and Wycliffe Hall, despite energetic efforts by its Principal and by CMS officials, never achieved the success of Ridley Hall. Stiff opposition from College authorities intent on training in diocesan colleges or providing for College ordination meant that years later Wycliffe still struggled to lodge even twenty students.[26] The university that had spawned the Oxford Movement, with its deep emotional and institutional loyalties to the Tractarian heritage, proved relatively inhospitable to evangelical missionary activity.

Students and Revivalism: The Origins of the Student Missionary Awakening

Aggressive American-style revivalism had a decisive influence at Cambridge, where the power of CMS insiders was conspicuous, particularly that of John Barton. Barton returned to Cambridge after a sixteen-year missionary tour in India to become, in 1877, vicar of Holy Trinity, the pulpit occupied for fifty-two years by the Evangelical preaching lion and founding member of the CMS, Charles Simeon. From this revered position Barton partnered with Handley Moule, first Principal of Ridley Hall, and both men emerged as pervasive influences reasserting the power of evangelicalism. Recalling the days of Livingstone's university lectures, and fired by the zeal derived from the growing style of English evangelical revivalism, Barton and Moule aimed to create an activist Evangelical network.[27] Barton, for example, inaugurated in 1877 a se-

25. After 1880, when personal invitations were made to freshmen, attendance of the yearly inaugural lecture stood at 800 to 1,000. Harford and Macdonald, *Moule,* 114-15.

26. Barton, *Barton,* 106-7; Stock, *Recollections,* 243.

27. Porter, "Cambridge, Keswick and Africa," 12-13, 17-19.

ries of missionary soirées, held two or three times per year. These featured holiness-influenced speakers, such as Sholto Douglas, Evan Hopkins, H. W. Webb-Peploe, and Hay Aitken, and well-known missionary leaders, such as Bishops James Hannington of Uganda, Arthur W. Poole of Japan, and Waite H. Stirling of the Falkland Islands. Such events placed exoticism and religious emotionalism on display. Emily Barton remembered that the inaugural soirée featured the first black African bishop, Samuel Crowther, whose complexion, she related, terrified her children.[28] Together John and Emily cultivated "a large and steadily increasing family of 'Sons in the University,' . . . never less than 200 on our books, introduced by parents, guardians or clergy," served with a weekly university Bible reading, a weekly afternoon "at home," and a Sunday open house with a regular attendance of twenty-five to thirty.[29] At Cambridge, missionary loan exhibitions and university-wide collections for the CMS became common, emulating the activities in well-worked parishes, and Barton made his presence felt at the weekly CMS Committee meeting in London.[30] In developing this network Barton was doing what Evangelicals had done for decades, but in a more systematic fashion, and the Cambridge and London Evangelical coteries he was a part of — a CMS ruling elite of Evangelical families that can be traced back to the circle of Henry Venn and the Clapham Sect — gathered around radiating circles of connection sustained by such freely intermarrying families as the Bickersteths, Moules, Harford-Battersbys, Wigrams, and Wrights (the balustrade of whose country residence, Osmaston Manor, was composed of four-foot-high stone letters, visible a mile away, reading "The works of our hands are vanity, but whatsoever God doeth it shall be forever").[31] The CMS formed the focal point for elaborating a national network, linked by family and religious association, reinforcing a sort of broadly dispersed middle-class tribe with its own rites and rituals.

Barton's credentials — graduate of Christ's College, veteran of the 1850s revivals, virtual founder of the Cambridge Church Missionary Union, experienced missionary to India, adviser to the late revered Henry Venn — combined with his activism to make him a critical player, along with Handley Moule, in the expansion of the intense evangelical subculture at Cambridge. Moule's influence in Cambridge was, if anything, more pervasive than Barton's. Scholarship was

28. Emily was Barton's second wife; his first, Henry Wright's sister, died of consumption after a year of marriage. Emily Barton memoir, pp. 82-84, Barton Papers, CMS Archives, Acc 137 F/1.

29. Emily Barton memoir, 84-85.

30. Barton, *Barton*, 103, 113.

31. The Wright fortune was based on the Butterly Iron Works, to whose five hundred workers Henry Wright acted as chaplain in the 1860s. Emily Barton memoir, 43-44. For more elaboration on CMS family and associational networks, see Maughan, "Regions Beyond," 173-213.

relatively rare among Evangelicals, and Moule's first in Classics, followed by a Fellowship at Trinity, made him seem the ideal candidate for the Principalship of Ridley, which allowed in addition an evening lectureship at Holy Trinity. Moule's renown soon spread beyond the University, so that by the 1890s Evangelicals generally recognized him as their most influential leader and clear successor to the towering figure of J. C. Ryle, the Evangelical bishop of Liverpool.[32] During his tenure at Ridley (1881-99), an unheard of 37 percent, or 190 of the 514 Ridley men, went out as missionaries or colonial chaplains, largely because in 1884 Moule became a champion of the theology and practice associated with the Keswick Convention. Alleviating the anxieties of older-style Evangelicals, encouraging enthusiastic students, and facilitating a shift in the broader Evangelical school was possible only because through Ridley Hall activists could begin advancing more ambitious formulations of holiness theology under careful tutelage.[33] As one missionary recalled, "[t]here was a tendency at this time for keen men to 'run off the lines,' and we owe it to Mr. Barton and Dr. Moule . . . that so much of the spiritual force of the time was kept within safe bounds and gained and preserved for the Church of England."[34]

Developing a thriving Evangelical subculture at Cambridge in an age of rapid change and secularization was rough business. When the CICCU invited Moody and Sankey to Cambridge in 1882, for example, Barton and other Evangelical leaders were forced to protect the evangelists from the mockery and even violence of rowdy undergraduates. At the first meeting in Cambridge in November, with 1,700 students present in the Corn Exchange, three hundred or more were "singing rowdy songs" and "prepared to mob Messrs. Moody & Sankey." Derisive shouts and jokes flew "until half a dozen Proctors and M.A.s present . . . [including Barton] walked down the Hall in cap and gown, and picking out the ring leaders, quietly ordered them out, & thus restored silence."[35] On the other hand, Moule and Barton also had to limit the influence of potentially heretical enthusiasms, such as those stirred by two CMS missionary candidates who had arrived in Cambridge in 1884, J. H. Pigott and W. E. Oliphant, who preached the possibility of the "eradication of sin" — that is, what many Anglicans considered the key Methodist error of worldly Christian perfection,

32. Handley Moule ultimately married Emily Barton's sister Mary. Barton, *Barton*, 101-2; Chadwick, *Victorian Church: Part Two, 1860-1901*, 471-72. On Moule's influence in Cambridge, see Harford and Macdonald, *Moule*, chaps. 9 and 10.

33. Alexander Smellie, *Evan Henry Hopkins: A Memoir* (London: Marshall, 1920), 122-24. Similarly in the sixteen years after Barton's arrival at Holy Trinity, 140 Cambridge University offers were made to the CMS, of which ninety-seven went out. Barton, *Barton*, 103.

34. Letter from A[rthur] J. S[hields]., quoted in Barton, *Barton*, 105-6.

35. Emily Barton memoir, 89.

which had driven the opposition to revivalism in the Church of England in the eighteenth century. Despite such dangers, Moule felt in later years that occasional aberrations — Pigott and Oliphant soon caused controversy as curates when they joined the Salvation Army — were an acceptable price to pay for the associated missionary enthusiasm.[36]

The fervor of the "higher life" encouraged at Keswick had always smacked of a sort of middle-class tribalism, and soon it was common for student enthusiasts to define the greatest sacrifices as being for the "voiceless millions" overseas. As the activist variants of Christian manliness embodied in "muscular Christianity" grew as an overall style of undergraduate piety — displacing the reverent but less enthusiastic "godliness and good learning" that had defined much of university culture at mid-century — the raw emotionalism of holiness grew.[37] The decision in 1884 by several undergraduates influenced by the Moody visit, the famous "Cambridge Seven," to offer themselves to Hudson Taylor's "faith" mission, the CIM, raised a furor. This was an event, evangelicals proclaimed, that the scoffing outside world could not write off, as it demonstrated how missionary revivalism had made a mark on worldly Cambridge and worldly England.[38] After the offer of the Cambridge Seven, evangelical devotees of public school athleticism could now look to C. T. Studd, one of the greatest cricketers of his generation, as a sacrifice for the mission field.[39] They could look to Stanley Smith, stroke oar of the Cambridge boat crew, and others of the group drawn from the Royal Artillery and Dragoon Guards, as examples of masculine missionary devotion and evangelical defense infiltrating areas of life not usually associated with Christian piety.[40] Entering more fully into the public school games' culture, Evangelical missionaries participated in the moralized ideology and practice of "manly" Christianity that the spread of imperial sports encouraged.[41] Perhaps as important as anything else, this quickening within the

36. Harford and Macdonald, *Moule*, 117-19; Stock, *History of the CMS*, 3:312-13.

37. On this transformation late in the nineteenth century, see David Newsome, *Godliness and Good Learning: Four Studies on a Victorian Ideal* (London: Murray, 1961), chap. 4.

38. For a sympathetic account of the Cambridge Seven and holiness influence at Cambridge, see J. C. Pollock, *The Cambridge Seven: A Call to Christian Service* (Chicago: Inter-Varsity, 1955).

39. When Studd volunteered, he was Captain of the Cambridge Eleven. He played on the England team which for the first time lost, then in the following year, regained, the Ashes from Australia. Charles Studd's brother, Kynaston (himself and another brother George also accomplished cricketers), was one of the organizers of the 1882 Moody mission. Grubb, *Studd*, 17, 28-32.

40. Porter, "Cambridge, Keswick and Africa," 20-21.

41. J. A. Mangan, *The Games Ethic and Imperialism: Aspects of the Diffusion of an Ideal* (New York: Viking, 1986), 177-91; Gerald Studdert-Kennedy, *British Christians, Indian Nationalists, and the Raj* (Delhi: Oxford University Press, 1991), 226-36.

undergraduate world reinforced the development of a missionary subculture at Cambridge and gave Evangelicals hope for continued growth.

Drawing on shifting Christian gender constructions and the enthusiastic service vision parallel to the social and imperial service encouraged in some universities, notably at Balliol College, Oxford, Trinity College, Dublin, and to a lesser degree Trinity College, Cambridge, Evangelicals were able to claim a share of this powerful late Victorian movement and direct it abroad.[42] Evangelical leaders in Cambridge actively cultivated the hothouse atmosphere thickening in the university, particularly because foreign missionary objectives featured prominently therein, and they built on a series of university tours by the leaders of the Cambridge Seven, supporting the CIM with a six-day Cambridge mission. These university candidates were not only a prestigious addition to the missionary rolls; they also often paid their own charges.[43] CMS organizers arranged meetings and movements in association with the YMCA, the CICCU, and the women's colleges of Girton and Newnham, with the result that university offers to the CMS skyrocketed. When the CMS was able to publicize its own "Cambridge Eight," sent out in 1889, Stock, Barton, and Moule celebrated the fruit of their efforts.[44] While higher and broader Church students were focusing on social problems in England's slums, Evangelicals were directing the same energies overseas, where the drama of expanding colonial churches, exemplified in the thrill and horror of Bishop Hannington's murder in Uganda in 1885, was increasingly attached to constructions of imperial duties and dangers.[45] Subsequently, probably no single episode in the history of the late Victorian CMS received more publicity than the story of how Uganda, after Hannington's shocking martyrdom, was "saved" at the urging of CMS supporters in the early 1890s, when the government of Liberal Imperialist Lord Rosebery formalized British control under an imperial protectorate.

However, the motivations underlying the late Victorian Evangelical missionary movement were not simple. Student-based evangelistic initiatives grew as a factional reaction to High Church expansion in the Oxbridge colleges, while at the same time "faith" missions typically operated as committed interdenominational, and even undenominational, exercises in evangelical unity.

42. David Gilmour, *The Ruling Caste: Imperial Lives in the Victorian Raj* (New York: Farrar, 2006), 45-54.

43. J. B. Whiting to Wigram, 20 Nov. 1884, CMS Archives, G/AC 4/3/556; Harford and Macdonald, *Moule*, 117-19.

44. Stock, *Recollections*, 251-55. By 1888, Moule noted that eighteen Ridley men had gone out to the mission field: two with the CIM, sixteen with the CMS. Bullock, *Ridley Hall*, 1:233.

45. Edwin C. Dawson, *James Hannington, First Bishop of Eastern Equatorial Africa* (London: Seeley, 1887), 465-71.

Diverse influences lay behind student missionary efforts, and party competition was a crucial mediator in their development. Student support for missions grew rapidly in the 1870s, most notably at Cambridge, and was characterized in its early stages by a vigorous competition between Anglo-Catholic, High Church, and Evangelical schemes for organized university support, at which Evangelicals once again proved to be the most successful, largely because missionary service formed such an important element in their party identity.[46]

By the 1880s, the most dynamic section of Cambridge support came from Evangelicals. However, as a new generation of student missionary leaders began to formulate more ambitious plans for an expansive university missionary movement in the 1890s, they found the holiness-based missionary revivalism of the CIM and CMS to be of limited appeal in the broader realms of a rapidly evolving Christian landscape. The particular culture engendered by the narrow circles of revivalism revolving around the Keswick Convention and Ridley Hall was not congenial to broader possible student audiences. The holiness-inspired student revivalism that the CMS drew on was, while highly activist in nature, as a phenomenon in the broader university culture comparatively exclusive in theology, marginal in social life, and few in numbers. Under the influence of new ambitions to broaden and expand the student movement, which came from a progressive party within the evangelical movement itself, the aims of the student missionary movement began to change. Yet this movement away from evangelical exclusivity caused troubling conflicts between those who sought to defend a traditional formulation of evangelicalism that emphasized its unique and separate identity, and those who embraced a new ecumenism and a desire to combine Christian resources in the interests of world evangelization. These conflicts prefigured the forces that were later to split the movement.

The SVMU: Enlarging the Student Missionary Movement

The pietist evangelical community in the Oxbridge universities and its organizations, such as the CICCU and Oxford Inter-Collegiate Christian Union (OICCU), had the capacity to marshal and energize young university men, mostly products of the leading Evangelical homes of England, and to forge their loyalty to the "Reformation" program within the Church of England. Cambridge University was never the only base of support for educated missionaries,

---

46. Symonds, *Oxford and Empire*, 209-10. The following university missionary recruiting figures from between 1860 and 1900 suggest relative Anglo-Catholic and Evangelical missionary success. UMCA: Oxford, 46; Cambridge 26. CMS: Oxford, 79; Cambridge 241.

although it was undoubtedly the most important in the late nineteenth century: of the 312 university men the CMS sent out prior to 1894, 180 came from Cambridge, 61 from Oxford, 48 from Trinity College, Dublin, and 23 from other institutions.[47] However, as the leaders of the missionary societies and the new generation of student leaders in the 1890s sought to expand the movement, particularly to include higher varieties of Churchmanship and more liberal opinion within Nonconformity, they found its original basis in evangelical holiness to be intellectually, denominationally, and socially constraining, particularly in the university atmosphere. With the emergence in the 1890s of the SVMU, which was a new organization dedicated to broad missionary cooperation among students, the CMS discovered a vehicle for widening the student movement to include not only an emerging liberal evangelical camp but also women with greater professional aspirations. Founded in 1892, and organically related to the American Student Volunteer Movement, the ambition of the SVMU to create a new world missionary era led to innovations designed to encompass as wide a range of missionary traditions as possible, including most notably, the High Church party. In seeking to achieve these goals, the SVMU championed a new approach incorporating "missionary science," designed to harmonize with the growing force of scientific academic culture in the universities and to facilitate cooperative schemes to rationalize the movement. Implicit in the program was a rejection of the exclusivity of Anglican evangelical holiness circles.

Exclusivity and Ecumenism: Evangelicalism at a Crossroads

The missionary revival of the 1880s in Cambridge was firmly rooted in the subculture of the CICCU, which operated both as a set of shared cultural assumptions about charismatic religious experience and as an expression of Evangelical social networks cultivated in the Oxbridge universities. To those with ambitions to continue the expansion of the student missionary movement beyond the bounds of holiness subculture, however, it became rapidly apparent that there were obvious problems with using the CICCU as a basis for a broad, university-based foreign missionary program. First, members of the subculture surrounding the CICCU tended to have specific types of evangelical background that provided the experience, particular vocabulary, and mental habits that upperclassmen used to identify recruits. Second, holiness as a movement was essentially experiential and rooted in shared culture; it was, at its core, anti-intellectual. Since many of the most influential religious leaders in the

47. A. H. Arden, *Objections to Foreign Missions* (London: CMS, 1902), 24.

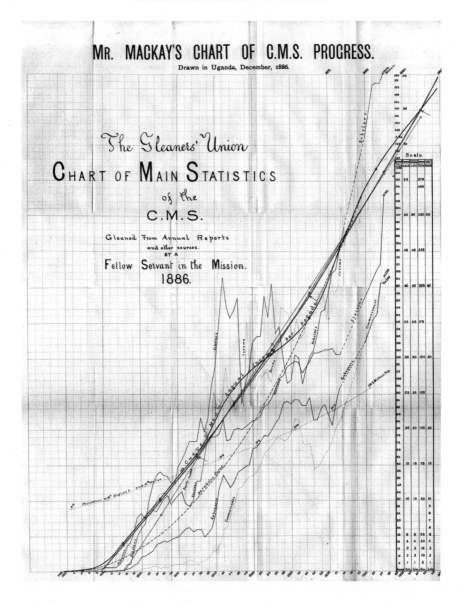

Chart of CMS statistics — ranging from income to stations, communicants, and workers, and including mathematical functions of income means and the like — compiled by CMS Uganda missionary Alexander Mackay, in the field. Such statistical compilations, which became something of a missionary fetish late in the century, illustrate one facet of the "science of missions" that emerged in tandem with the student missionary movement. From *Church Missionary Intelligencer and Record*, n.s., 12 (July, 1887). Special Collections, Yale Divinity School Library.

universities had striven since mid-century to incorporate modern and scientific approaches to religious faith — notably in the growing movement surrounding Westcott, Lightfoot, and Hort through the 1870s and 1880s, and Charles Gore and the contributors to *Lux Mundi* (1889) in the 1880s and 1890s — this was a fundamental problem. Evangelical efforts to build the prestige and membership of their halls, let alone expand the movement beyond them, were dogged by the reality that their students had a reputation, sometimes undeserved, but in many more cases well merited, for being poor scholars.

From its earliest years, Evangelicalism in the Church of England had developed a reputation for being without a real theology, and from the 1870s onward many outside the movement felt that it did not possess the resources to combat or assimilate modern thought.[48] Resistance to innovation and a reactionary approach to the challenges of evolution, biblical criticism, and scientific discovery led in the 1870s to "Evangelicalism passing under a cloud." The bitter spirit of partisan battle soured the subculture and generated a reputation for "slowness and exclusiveness" among its adherents. Yet the dominant response to these developments was to increase the emotional rather than the intellectual elements of the evangelical experience. Under the influence of holiness, Constance Maynard suggested, Evangelicalism encouraged

> loyalty to existing forms of government, the tenderness to bodily suffering, the taking up of causes not our own, the heartfelt enthusiasm of the missions to the heathen, the sunny outlook of hope and help for the woes of all the world, whether spiritual or physical, the steady basis of a well ordered church government, combined with varied and informal methods of presenting of the Gospel to the heart and will of the individual who chooses to remain outside, the recognition of Evangelical Nonconformity, and the willing and glad cooperation with it in all good works.[49]

Notably absent from this formulation — a formulation endorsed by Maynard, the foremost female Evangelical educator — is cultivation of study or the intellect. Education was important more for reasons of morale and status in a professionalizing Victorian society than as a means of better explicating the teachings of the Church. This was an attitude alien to the most influential circles of public school headmasters and scholars — individuals surrounding, for example, E. W. Benson, archbishop of Canterbury (1883-96), including B. F. Westcott, J. B. Lightfoot, F. J. A. Hort, Christopher Wordsworth, Frederick Temple, and a number of

48. Porter, "Cambridge, Keswick and Africa," 9.
49. Constance Maynard, "Westfield College (University of London)," in Barlow, *Barlow,* 118.

other university worthies who came to dominate the leadership of the Church in the final decades of the century.[50]

Ridley Hall displayed this central paradox of the Evangelical educational program. Among the qualities that made Handley Moule an academic leader at Ridley — separate from his sympathy with holiness-influenced religious styles — were his optimism and patience with relatively poor students. Reporting to the Ridley Council in 1886, Moule characterized his students as "a very nice earnest and diligent set of men." His vice-principal put it more directly: "Altogether, while there was great zeal for active religious work and a great desire to join frequently in devotional meetings, the intellectual side was disregarded," with the result that "in general University circles Ridley was deemed to be a resort of pious men indeed, but not of men of thought or learning."[51] As growth characterized the Cambridge missionary movement through the 1880s, transforming the CIM and the CMS with a flood of recruits, this narrowness and anti-intellectualism was not perceived as a problem.[52] Focusing on the immediate transfixing power of the Holy Spirit to change lives and save souls, impressionable undergraduates found it difficult to concentrate on studies. The emphasis was on evangelizing Cambridge, and later, if the mission field was chosen, "heathen" lands. Yet this emphasis gave the members of the CICCU the reputation, despite the much-touted example of the Cambridge Seven and the adulation of Evangelical clergy, of being outsiders, of being earnest buffoons "unfit for the river or cricket field . . . only good for Psalm-singing and pulling a long face."[53]

The difficulty of relying on the narrow base of Keswick to build university support was precisely that it was narrow. Only in the 1890s, when the manifest success of the culture of the CICCU in generating missionaries began to draw the notice and emulation of other denominations, did the failings of holiness evangelicalism become more apparent. The CICCU was a conservative organization, strongly reliant on the advice of "senior men" that insisted on fidelity to traditional evangelical theology and conservative tenets such as the verbal inspiration of the Bible and open opposition to High Church ritual practices.[54] The conservative evangelical commitment of the CICCU meant that over time it

50. Newsome, *Good Learning*, 20-25, and on the career of Westcott, Lightfoot, and Benson's influential headmaster, James Prince Lee, see chap. 2.

51. Moule and G. A. Schneider quoted in Bullock, *Ridley Hall*, 1:222-23.

52. The CIM's growth was striking: from 137 missionaries in 1885 to 825 by 1905. J. Hudson Taylor, ed., *China's Millions* (London: Morgan and Scott, 1885), 85; *The Land of Sinim: An Illustrated Report of the China Inland Mission* (London: CIM, 1905), 22.

53. Grubb, *Studd*, 45.

54. Tatlow, *Student Christian Movement*, 381.

came to represent intransigent opposition to the influence of groups outside the pale of traditional Evangelical leadership. For example, the CICCU seemingly had little room or sympathy for the rise of women's presence and activity at English universities, even in the face of the rising importance of women within Evangelical missionary societies such as the CMS. Conservative Evangelicalism also often stridently opposed the conclusions drawn from biblical criticism, liberal theology, and training in evolutionary sciences.[55] Yet in the age when *Lux Mundi* was legitimating advanced views of religion among the pious and when the rapid founding of University Colleges was advancing the claims of strong scientific curricula, some approach to these difficult subjects seemed necessary if the missionary movement was to attract the best Christian undergraduates.

The ethos generated by the CICCU in the 1880s, with the support and guidance of CMS leaders like Barton and Moule, was in many ways an echo of the Evangelical subculture of faith and revivalism that emerged at Cambridge in the 1860s. While this movement had seen opposition on the basis of its theology and temperament, in a university world that had not yet been stamped by the religious (though not ethical) skepticism of Matthew Arnold, Benjamin Jowett, Mark Pattison, and T. H. Green, its lack of critical impulse and broad synthetic sympathy was not an insuperable problem. By the 1890s this had changed. The limitations of anti-intellectualism and exclusivity were apparent to many leaders in the student missionary subculture, and the movement began to transform, primarily through the influence of the SVMU. Using the CICCU as its base for organization in the early 1890s, the SVMU rapidly evolved under the influence both of "progressive" Nonconformists and "neo-Evangelicals" toward a more "modern" and "scientific" approach to missions.[56]

Philosophically astute Evangelicals had always been aware of the nagging problems posed by anti-intellectualism, and a persistent minority sought to advance Evangelical educational standards. The views of progressive Evangelical educators were marked by a concern to enhance scholarship and advance missionary interest; these views are exemplified in the work of leading neo-Evangelical William Barlow, one of the founders of Ridley and the Principal of the CMS College in Islington from 1875 to 1882. Upon taking on the work at Islington, Barlow's ambition was to move the College to Cambridge, in the words of Stock, "to breathe there the freer air of university life."[57] The CMS Committee rejected this suggestion as unfeasible and perhaps undesirable, leaving Barlow to press for the foundation of Ridley and Wycliffe Halls, simultaneously plac-

55. Wellings, *Evangelicals Embattled*, 145-54, 206-21, 227-35.
56. Tatlow, *Student Christian Movement*, 381.
57. Stock, *History of the CMS*, 3:45.

ing a greater emphasis at the Islington training college on both the practice and appearance of academics. Aiming to make Islington graduates successful in the Preliminary Theological Examinations introduced in the mid-1870s for Oxford and Cambridge graduates, Barlow introduced academic rituals and regalia, seeking to reverse the social stigma attached to the missionary profession by raising Islington to a university standard, thus also raising morale at an institution plagued by the professional inferiority often ascribed to missionaries within the clerical world.[58] Barlow's hope was that Evangelicalism could shed its reputation for anti-intellectualism while at the same time retaining its spiritual enthusiasm. But the measures taken at Islington could never compensate for the prestige of an Oxbridge education, despite the very real accomplishments achieved there — by the mid-1880s, for example, Islington graduates were taking more first-class results in the Universities' Preliminary Theological Examinations than Oxbridge candidates.[59]

Evangelicals desperately pursued Oxbridge respectability, and by the late 1880s Frederick Wigram was doing everything possible to align the Society with Cambridge missionary revivalism.[60] By the late Victorian era the advantages of a university degree were self-evident to missionaries operating in a professionalizing English and imperial world dominated and structured by degree holders for whom the snobbery, assumptions, and manners of the university provided powerful codes of sociability and access.[61] With robust expansion and missions engaged with imperial and diplomatic officials throughout the world, the key issue was access and leadership, rather than theological purity, and that was only to be had, in John Barton's opinion, "through a University course."[62] How was the CMS to maintain enthusiasm while securing obedience? How was it to procure able and reliable university graduates amenable to direction from Salisbury Square in sufficient numbers? The lesson taught by the Niger crisis of the late 1880s, when the holiness-inspired Cambridge missionary G. W. Brooke attempted to seize control of the mission and discredit the Society's African agents, was that uncontrolled enthusiasm could very well become dangerous.[63]

The rise of the SVMU in the early 1890s, with its more balanced approach, came as a welcome alternative. Its earliest methods and message — enthusiastic evangelism pressed by motivational speakers — made it look like yet another manifestation of holiness revivalism. But the SVMU soon began to advance a

58. Lash diary, 29 Sept. [1875], London, Lash Papers, CMS Archives, Acc 348 F 1/5A, fol. 116.
59. Porter, "Cambridge, Keswick and Africa," 12.
60. Williams, *Self-Governing Church*, 156-57.
61. Symonds, *Oxford and Empire*, 300-301.
62. John Barton to "My Dear Brother," 1 Nov. 1890, CMS Archives, G/AK 1.
63. For details on this episode, see Chapter 3.

program designed to professionalize and systematize the practice of missionary study and integrate it more closely with the more open spirit of the universities. Eugene Stock, in close contact with early SVMU leaders, forwarded a parallel program at the CMS, and while the CMS continued to support the CICCU, it soon began to throw its considerable weight behind the more liberal SVMU.[64] The situation was a delicate one, because while the CMS, as influenced by Stock, supported missionary efficiency, study, and cooperation, under its new fire-breathing Evangelical secretary from 1895, H. E. Fox, it also sought to present a traditional image to supporters opposed to liberalism and "modernist threats." Conflict between the emerging positions of liberal and conservative evangelicalism was not yet so pointed as to produce a split between the SVMU and the CICCU, but tension was growing. In the 1890s the CMS supported a dual policy, recognizing, it appears, the conflicting paths that all Anglo-American Christians were facing with liberal modernism and protofundamentalist evangelicalism increasingly at war with each other.[65]

The Challenge of Denominationalism

The SVMU began its existence as an American organization — the Student Volunteer Movement (SVM) — drawing heavily on the same holiness influences that animated the missionary revival in the late Victorian English universities. It originated from the first student summer Bible conference in America, organized in 1886 by Dwight L. Moody, and by 1888, after a successful college tour by Princeton undergraduate Robert P. Wilder, it had pledged over 2,200 students to become foreign missionaries.[66] The early SVM drew heavily on premillennialist theology and a belief in the imminence of the Advent, parallel to the message preached in the halls of Keswick, the Bands of the Salvation Army, and the student missionary revival in Britain. Given the strong influence of Moody in Britain, this was natural. Graham Wilmot Brooke, along with numerous other holiness "missioners" to the British universities, emphasized

---

64. Prominent participation by Eugene Stock and Georgina Gollock at the 1896 and 1900 student movement conferences was one demonstration of CMS support for the movement. *Students' Missionary Conference, 1896*, 40-41, 92-95, 148, 223, 238-39, 253; *Ecumenical Missionary Conference, New York, 1900: Report of the Ecumenical Conference on Foreign Missions*, 2 vols. (London: RTS, 1900), 1:92-95, 111-12, 224-25, 329-31, 401-13.

65. Bebbington, *Evangelicalism*, chap. 6.

66. Clifton J. Phillips, "The Student Volunteer Movement and Its Role in China Missions, 1886-1920," in *The Missionary Enterprise in China and America*, ed. John K. Fairbank (Cambridge, MA: Harvard University Press, 1974), 92.

to students that there were three reasons to become a missionary: one might save many souls abroad, one could bring about evangelization at home, and one would "distinctly fulfill a condition of our King's return." While Christians could not by their own struggles bring in the millennium, sanctified believers — male and female — had the responsibility to open the door for Christ to do so.[67] This most extreme formulation of holiness millenarianism was one of the chief links between the North American SVM and the swelling English evangelical university movement.

The SVM had strong international ambitions, and the connections between the two movements developed rapidly.[68] The decision of the Cambridge Seven to choose a life of "missionary sacrifice" was hardly less influential in America than it was in Britain, reinforced by a tour of American universities undertaken in 1885 by J. E. K. Studd, Charles Studd's brother. In 1886, John N. Forman, an associate of Robert Wilder and future India missionary, visited England to give information on the American movement; and, as if in reciprocal trade, in 1887 the influential Edinburgh University evangelical Henry Drummond, who had joined the Scottish tour of Charles Studd and Stanley Smith in early 1885, toured American colleges.[69] Through the late 1880s extensive informal networks grew as the student movement developed independently through university unions and YMCA conferences, usually deeply involved with the Keswick Convention and holiness culture, but significantly drawing many students from Oxford, Edinburgh, Aberdeen, Glasgow, and Dublin and broadening the movement beyond intimate Cambridge evangelical circles.[70]

The student movement appealed to both professionalism and revivalism in an evangelical ethos trained to philanthropy. In the words of the experienced CMS missionary to Africa W. Salter Price, "[t]he demand of the present day in India and elsewhere is, more & more for men of culture and education."[71] This growing emphasis in the missionary movement was itself part of a broader development in the late Victorian period whereby the focus of an earlier gener-

67. G. W. Brooke, "Outline of an Address on the Heathen Mission Field: To Cambridge Undergraduates," (second address), notebook, Brooke Papers, CMS Archives, Acc 82 F 2/5.

68. On the transatlantic nature of evangelicalism, see Richard Carwardine, *Transatlantic Revivalism: Popular Evangelicalism in Britain and America, 1790-1865* (Westport, CT: Greenwood, 1978) and on growing Anglo-American missionary cooperation led by American students in the late nineteenth century, see Hutchison, *Errand to the World*, 91-136.

69. *The Student Volunteer Missionary Union: A Brief Statement of Its Origin and Growth, February, 1899* (n.p., n.d.), 1.

70. W. H. T. Gairdner, *D. M. Thornton: A Study in Missionary Ideals and Methods* (London: Hodder and Stoughton, 1908), 18.

71. Price to Morris, 12 Mar. 1891, CMS Archives, G/AK 1.

ation on spiritual individualism and private conscience, which had exalted the power of individual converts to spread conversion, gave way to a new attitude defined by an appreciation of organized collective effort and public duty. In Anglican circles it crossed party lines, being primarily associated with the initiatives of High Churchmen and Christian Socialists to engage domestic social problems, but it also had its influence on Evangelicals. Across the Anglican parties, however, the impulse remained enmeshed in a profoundly hierarchical vision of society.[72] Its adherents focused on creating institutional structures through which "educated" and "cultured" professionals could advance religious goals through both social service and individual example.[73] In the missionary movement this emphasis expressed itself in a growing support for church structure, educational efforts, cooperation, and settled missionary influence.

These goals matched those of the CMS, if not in the recruitment of missionaries, then in the implementation of mission itself. Eugene Stock therefore pressed aggressively for the foundation of a more efficient umbrella organization to facilitate greater student collaboration with the missionary societies. Chairing the 1889 gathering of London students at Exeter Hall to form a Students' Foreign Missionary Union, he participated widely in interdenominational student conventions, facilitated meetings of American and British student leaders, and oversaw the resulting formation of a nationwide British SVMU.[74] From its inception, fully in sympathy with the ethos of its American counterpart, the SVMU was steeped in the deepest-hued holiness of Cambridge and Keswick, led by Cambridge men, members of the CICCU, and members of Ridley Hall, many of them the rising Evangelicals of the 1890s, including Douglas Thornton, W. H. T. Gairdner, Donald Fraser, and G. T. Manley. Concurrently in Oxford a wave of OICCU enlistments followed amidst revivalistic demonstrations by evangelicals, including notable figures such as J. H. Oldham, W. E. S. Holland, and Alec Fraser. These men were "prigs and smugs" in Holland's recollection, puritanical but delirious with the spiritual excitement of the moment.[75] By May 1893, 491 students had signed the SVMU pledge: "It is my purpose, if God permit, to become a foreign missionary." By 1900 the number was 1,720: 1,339

72. The Christian Socialism of the 1880s did not advocate rearrangement of existing social and economic relations, and it operated primarily as a deeply moralized liberalism that pressed a voluntarist collectivism to ameliorate specific social evils. Edward R. Norman, *Church and Society in England, 1770-1970: A Historical Study* (Oxford: Clarendon Press, 1976), 176-86.

73. Exemplified in one particular case by G. A. Lefroy, bishop of Lahore, and his work in the university-based Cambridge Mission to Delhi. Cox, "Lefroy," 54-76.

74. *SVMU Origin*, 1; Stock, *Recollections*, 238; Tatlow, *Student Christian Movement*, 22-29.

75. Symonds, *Oxford and Empire*, 216-20; Constance E. Padwick, *Temple Gairdner of Cairo*, rev. ed. (London: SPCK, 1930), 28-31.

men and 381 women from dozens of denominations, of whom 566 had sailed (119 women).[76]

The approach of the CMS to the SVMU clearly had another key attraction in the 1890s: it provided a new route of access to the growing block of potential recruits among university women. By this time the expanding use of women by the CMS had become its most important innovation. In keeping with its class and educational biases regarding male candidates, the CMS sought to recruit as many university-educated women as possible. The first approach of the generally conservative Evangelical connection to women's education came once again through William Barlow and the neo-Evangelical connection. Women's higher education even remotely parallel to men's only became possible with the foundation of Oxbridge residential women's colleges in the 1860s and 1870s. In the 1880s, the London women's colleges Bedford, Royal Holloway, and Westfield extended higher education to women in the metropolis.[77] Barlow was connected to the early foundation of Girton and Newnham Colleges (Cambridge) and, in the recollection of one early student, represented the rare exception: he was an evangelical who rejected "much of the religious feeling of the time [which] was on the side of distrust and suspicion as to the issue of such a sudden intellectual enfranchisement of the young womanhood of our country." Opposition to women's education from traditionalist Evangelicals was related to the issues driving religious debate in the 1870s: evolution, literary studies, and philosophy, all of which "seemed directed against the fortress of the Christian faith." These subjects were judged particularly dangerous to the undisciplined minds of women.[78]

Conservative resistance was only slowly broken down. The foundation of Westfield College in 1882 was an Evangelical response to the growing demands among women for higher education and the sense that, without opportunity, Evangelical women's talents would shift from sacred to profane. Like the American influences that permeated the Oxbridge Evangelical Halls in the 1880s, Westfield College gained inspiration from the American religious example. Domestic and foreign missionary work inspired by Mount Holyoke and Wellesley Colleges proved to be the motivation behind the founding of Westfield. Its charter, at the cost of a good deal of "progressive" skepticism, proclaimed in familiar evangelical style that the New Testament was to be central to its teaching. Even this was not enough to win the official support of either the CMS or the

---

76. *Students' Missionary Conference, 1896*, 111; Address of H. C. Duncan, *Missionary Conference, 1900*, 109-10.

77. Vicinus, *Independent Women*, 124-27.

78. Quoted in Barlow, *Barlow*, 113-16.

Mildmay Conference, which still "rather looked askance at this excursion [by women] into other fields than those of spiritual and physical help."[79] Westfield hovered on the fringes of both educational "progressivism" and revivalistic evangelicalism (including ecumenical cooperation with Nonconformity) that alienated stronger Churchmen. Male-dominated evangelical undergraduate associations such as the conservative CICCU were not hospitable to the diversifying range of women's activity, nor were they well equipped to defend foreign missions in the secularizing university.

The SVMU, on the other hand, had both a foot in holiness culture and a more open attitude toward those groups excluded by practice or temperament from pietist evangelicalism. Abandoning the evangelical Anglican exclusiveness of the CICCU, when the SVMU accepted women and Nonconformists as full members, it rapidly became one of the leading forces in the British missionary movement, forcing Anglicans of all parties to adjust past practices of denominational exclusivity or risk marginalization in university life. The CMS embraced the new opportunity, and Georgina Gollock, then herself doing women's college tours for the Society to encourage and exploit missionary revivalism, successfully pressed the SVMU to recruit Oxbridge women actively, and also women at Westfield and all the London colleges. Organized around professional rather than revivalistic themes, these meetings drew into the movement later SVMU leaders such as Agnes de Selincourt and Ruth Rouse (both Girton students). In the quickening atmosphere women's branches and societies across the denominational spectrum competed furiously to develop a university presence and support new institutions such as the MSUW and the SVMU.[80] As a means of accommodating theological liberals, women, and evangelical Nonconformists, as well as defending the missionary project in the broadening secular environment of the late Victorian universities, the SVMU was shaping into an invaluable ally to a neo-Evangelical project for foreign missions.

With its openness to women, interdenominationalism, and internationalism — in 1894 national Christian movements were connected together into the World's Student Christian Federation — the SVMU rapidly expanded its membership

79. Major Malan first put forward the plan, which was subsequently taken up by T. P. Boultbee, first Principal of the Evangelical Training College, St. John's, Highbury, and one of the leaders of the CMS Committee. Barlow and some other London Evangelical clergy were also involved. Barlow, *Barlow,* 119, 121.

80. Minutes of the General Committee, 2 Oct. 1895, Zenana Bible and Medical Mission, IFNS/ZBMM Archives, Home File List, General Committee minutes, Oct. 1886–Oct. 1889. Tatlow reckoned that at the first SVMU conference, held in July 1893 in Keswick the week before the convention, 40 percent of the attendees were Church of England, 30 percent Presbyterian, and 30 percent Free Church (mostly Congregationalist). *Student Christian Movement,* 43, 56.

beyond exclusive evangelical coteries and the ancient universities, extending its reach into the newer university colleges, medical schools, theological colleges, and technical colleges.[81] In the first several years of rapid organization, there was little sense of strain, but as the SVMU began to approach High Churchmen and increasing numbers of Nonconformists, suspicion and uneasiness grew, exacerbated by renewed Ritualist conflicts following the 1898 campaigns of the ultra-evangelical John Kensit.[82] The problem resided in what were the essentially pro-tofundamentalist views of the CICCU, which insisted on simple veneration of the Bible, the "definite and drastic" dividing experience of conversion, and the eager categorization of all people simply into the saved or the damned. "[T]hey were not," E. T. Whittaker recalled, "as a rule highly esteemed" because of "a kind of spiritual bumptiousness, . . . their tendency . . . to belittle the intellectual element in religion . . . [and the fact that] to all that went on in the world outside, even the religious world, they were completely indifferent."[83] Christians outside the CICCU tended to see them as simplistic, arrogant, and destructive of efforts to build a wider fellowship. SVMU leaders also wanted to tap the growing interest in social reform in High Church and Nonconformist circles that was manifested in a developing Christian Socialist tradition, from the Christian Social Union of B. F. Westcott, Charles Gore, and Henry Scott Holland to the progressive social thinking of Nonconformists such as Hugh Price Hughes.[84]

The transition, however, was not sharp. The mid-1890s saw a complex mixture of progressive thinking and conservative theology developing within the movement. The SVMU had a broader platform than the Keswick Convention, but many of its members drew heavily on the holiness tradition for their own religious vision. Youthful enthusiasm clearly worried many at the CMS, and Oxford students believed that CMS Secretary Frederick Wigram did not quite approve of students' headlong rush to missionary volunteerism; yet Eugene Stock and Georgina Gollock were energetic supporters, as were Ralph Wardlaw Thompson at the LMS and Hudson Taylor at the CIM.[85] Stock and Gollock

81. Of the students enrolled in 1896, 416 were from universities, 79 university colleges, 98 medical schools, 268 theological colleges, and 177 other colleges and schools. Furthermore, only 577 were English, with 281 Scots, 111 Irish, and 66 Welsh, representing 26 denominations. "Report of the Executive of the SVMU," in *Students' Missionary Conference, 1896,* 111.

82. Tatlow, *Student Christian Movement,* 381. On Kensit, see Martin Wellings, "The First Protestant Martyr of the Twentieth Century: The Life and Significance of John Kensit (1853-1902)," in *Martyrs and Martyrologies,* ed. Diana Wood (Oxford: Blackwell, 1993), 347-58.

83. Whittaker, quoted in Edward S. Woods and Frederick B. Macnutt, *Theodore, Bishop of Winchester: Pastor, Prophet, Pilgrim* (London: SPCK, 1933), 15-16.

84. On the Christian Socialism of Westcott and Hughes, see Edward R. Norman, *The Victorian Christian Socialists* (Cambridge: Cambridge University Press, 1987), chaps. 8 and 9.

85. Tatlow, *Student Christian Movement,* 46-47.

clearly saw the SVMU as a means to educate and control the thrusting spirituality of Keswick in the student community. But uneasiness also arose out of
the friction that the SVMU produced with more traditional evangelicals, as
the career of "extreme left" SVMU leader Douglas Thornton demonstrates. An
emotional holiness devotee deeply involved in the CICCU, Thornton came to
embody "the clash of the Progressives and the Conservatives." In this context
his progressivism meant support for the broad ecumenism generated by new
strains of liberal evangelicalism in the Student Christian Movement, endorsed
by international leaders like John Mott.[86] Under the direction of Thornton, and
also of Theodore Woods (later bishop of Peterborough, 1916-23 and Winchester
to 1932), the CICCU launched broadening initiatives at its first Keswick summer conference in 1893, forming the British College Christian Union (BCCU),
extending also into other universities as a staging organization for the SVMU.
Conservatives, however, rapidly began to criticize the loss in the CICCU of a
traditional evangelical culture that leapt readily to the defense of "Protestant
truth," and problems were only smoothed over with difficulty.[87]

Thus when the SVMU held its first major British conference in 1896 in Liverpool, it had already begun to push toward ecumenical expansiveness, demonstrated in the role of the BCCU and the SVMU as 1894 founding members of
the World's Student Christian Federation.[88] To protofundamentalist evangelicals such ecumenism harbored the danger of Romanism on the one hand and
secularism on the other. Ironically, when earlier in the 1880s criticism had
arisen against interdenominationalism, it was generally registered by Anglicans
who objected to Church societies combining with nondenominational organizations such as the YMCA and stooping to sensational methods such as the
celebrations surrounding the Cambridge Seven.[89] By the mid-1890s, however,
the principal opposition to interdenominationalism came from pan-evangelical
conservatives, the enthusiasts of the 1880s, who now sallied forth to defend
biblical literalism and oppose the old enemies: Ritualism and modernism.

It took time, however, for divisions to surface clearly. The emotional fervor
of the early movement masked several realities. As theological and confessional
differences emerged they were only reinforced by another reality: despite the
international composition of student members and leaders, the movement was

86. Gairdner, *Thornton*, 19, 28-29.
87. Woods and Macnutt, *Theodore*, 26-27; Wellings, *Evangelicals Embattled*, 274-75, 278.
88. By 1901 the BCCU evolved into the umbrella organization under which the SVMU, two
college departments and local Christian unions collaborated to advance a range of activities that
slowly came to be known as the Student Christian Movement (SCM). Tatlow, *Student Christian
Movement*, 49-50, 63, 67-68, 209-10.
89. Stock, *Recollections*, 143-44.

not internationalist in ideology; rather, by demonstrating clear and deliberate impulses to maintain separate national identities among student delegates as one form of cohesion in the midst of diversity, the student movement was notable from its beginning for a tone of Anglo-American triumphalism.[90] In the early heady atmosphere, theological conservatives such as the rising young Anglican G. T. Manley could still easily cooperate with ecumenical visionaries such as Douglas Thornton. But already at the 1896 SVMU Liverpool conference, four short years after its founding, the heat of the early movement was beginning to cool. At the convention the executive warned that while the numbers of students offering to serve as missionaries through the SVMU continued to grow, financial difficulties loomed large, the problems of spiritual separatism and snobbery were becoming apparent, and the lure of home social work for those "quickened" by the movement was proving an increasing distraction.[91] Furthermore, student leaders, so ablaze with grand schemes for a rapid and unprecedented missionary advance, were disillusioned when the churches of England did not respond with immediacy to the growing college movement, blaming them as the bottleneck to continued growth. The enthusiasm and zealotry of a privileged religious subculture was facing the real challenge of organization that had always been at the heart of a materially ambitious missionary movement.

The beginnings of a more pragmatic policy grew out of the organized challenge to the churches that the SVMU launched at its 1896 conference. Here, after much debate, the delegates adopted the American "watchword" for the SVMU: "The Evangelization of the World in This Generation."[92] Despite criticisms that the "watchword" implied arrogance, undisciplined enthusiasm, too great a reliance on simple evangelism, and an unseemly judgment on past generations, the leaders of the movement resolved to take the new slogan to the churches for adoption. However, the movement's organizers quickly discovered mainstream English religious leaders remained extremely wary of holiness-style religious initiatives. "[T]he continual stream of polite refusals" from those outside Keswick and CICCU circles bred growing discouragement, forcing leaders to tone down emotionalism and discourage censorious Keswick-style attitudes toward the "rebellious unsaved."[93] Such experiences forced ambitious student leaders

90. Comments of J. Rutter Williamson in *Students' Missionary Conference, 1896*, 118. For more detail on the militant, even militarist, Anglo-American imperial tone of the SVMU by the end of the decade, see Clifton J. Phillips, "Changing Attitudes in the Student Volunteer Movement of Great Britain and North America, 1886-1928," in *Missionary Ideologies in the Imperialist Era, 1880-1920*, ed. Torben Christensen and William R. Hutchison ([Aarhus, Denmark]: Aros, 1982), 135-37.

91. "Report of the Executive," in *Students' Missionary Conference, 1896*, 114-16.

92. "Report of the Executive," in *Students' Missionary Conference, 1896*, 117.

93. Tatlow, *Student Christian Movement*, 63.

toward religious latitude. And as William Hutchison has noted, the happy ambiguities of a "watchword" in which the key term "evangelization" was not defined allowed both an elderly moderate, Stock, and a young conservative, Manley, to cooperate in "a liberal-premillennial collaboration" in which "cultural enthusiasms and promotional needs outweighed theological differences."[94]

Organizational ambition led the SVMU to create a large tent under which a variety of missionary schemes — from evangelistic to educational and medical — could be forwarded, not least by women. In the foreign missionary and allied Christian movements, Constance Maynard credited the student movement as bringing "the reversal of almost every hostile verdict" to women's Christian education, thus acting as a liberalizing force.[95] So too Nonconformists saw opportunity to crack the holiness exclusivism of the movement within the broader evangelical world through the SVMU, particularly Congregationalists, who had benefited little from Keswick.[96] But the results from canvassing all British churches demonstrated just how much opposition still existed, particularly within the Church of England. In an 1895 interview with Archbishop Benson, Anglican representatives of the SVMU sought an introduction to Anglican theological colleges. Benson declined for a number of reasons: the theological colleges were fiercely independent, the SVMU was itself rapidly changing, but most significantly, the SVMU disregarded the "ordinances" of the Church, and "[i]t was not possible that the Ch[urch] of E[ngland] c[oul]d agree with the Baptists e.g. as to their conception & teaching of [Chri]st."[97] Despite such discouragement from the leadership of the Church and from growing suspicion at the populist evangelical end, SVMU leaders decided to publish a memorial for distribution to the churches. It was written in the Cambridge rooms of G. T. Manley under the advice of Handley Moule, Eugene Stock, Georgina Gollock, and other "senior friends."[98]

The SVMU was anxious to enlist the higher realms of Anglicanism, but both the broad confessional membership of the Union and its known origins in extreme evangelicalism branded it for many as outside the pale. When Benson died in October 1896, SVMU leaders hoped for a new start at Lambeth Palace, and the new archbishop, Frederick Temple, proved more encouraging, but at the cost of the SVMU toning down what Temple saw as its ultra-Protestant rhetoric. The SVMU leadership, now more experienced with the episcopacy

94. Hutchison, *Errand to the World*, 118-19.

95. Maynard, "Westfield College," in Barlow, *Barlow*, 121.

96. Ralph Wardlaw Thompson, LMS secretary, in *Students' Missionary Conference, 1896*, 254-55.

97. The representatives were Frank Anderson and Douglas Thornton. Memo. on reverse, Frank Anderson to Benson, 15 Oct. 1895, Benson Papers, vol. 140, fols. 71-72.

98. Tatlow, *Student Christian Movement*, 94-95.

and more flexible, agreed to Temple's request to recast the opening paragraph of its "Memorial to the Churches," significantly changing its tone and content: references both to a "Degenerate" medieval Church and to "Visionary" eighteenth-century evangelicalism were struck, making the memorial far more acceptable to Anglicans of all outlooks. Temple agreed to present the revised document to the 1897 Lambeth Conference, but with the pessimistic remark, "I only hope you'll get the Bishops to take it up. I've been trying to move them for the past ten years, but they are hard to move."[99] The encounter with university liberalism, women's growing religious ambitions, Nonconformist anti-elitism, and High Church cultural distinctiveness led the SVMU away from narrow, evangelical theological definitions to pragmatic adjustments in strategy and a professionalizing identity that did not offend any of a broad range of religious sensibilities. The ecumenical movement that grew out of the student movement was fundamentally a product of professionalizing missionary ambition and the liberal theology that followed in its wake.

The bishops of the Church of England, however, were concerned with matters other than missionary ambition; Temple suggested they were too old and preoccupied to be roused, and he was reticent to press the matter too aggressively. While it was a "great disappointment" that the bishops at Lambeth declined to adopt the watchword, they were only following the same refusals delivered by the rest of the British churches and missionary societies.[100] Denominational identity and independence were not to be easily swept away by enthusiastic arguments such as those of G. T. Manley, who asserted that the evangelization of the world was indeed possible in one generation, especially if one considered the successes that followed upon concerted effort in Uganda under the CMS.[101] Most disappointing of all, then, was the CMS, which, despite its unanimous endorsement of the memorial, refused to endorse the watchword as "a present duty" of the Church. Religious politics, membership sensitivity, and the desire for freedom of action precluded the endorsement, but CMS staff continued to render full support to the organizing work of the Union.[102] From these perceived rebuffs to their "spiritual power" grew a new educational, professionalizing policy at the SVMU, which was forced to recognize that neither the churches nor the broader public were to be easily conscripted into a

99. "A Memorial of the Student Volunteer Missionary Union to the Church of Christ in Britain," two drafts, F. Temple Papers, vol. 7, fols. 44-45, 48-49; Douglas Thornton to Temple, 15 Feb. 1897, F. Temple Papers, vol. 7, fols. 42-43.

100. G. T. Manley and Douglas Thornton, quoted in Gairdner, *Thornton*, 39-40.

101. Tatlow, *Student Christian Movement*, 106.

102. Douglas Thornton to Fox, 21 Apr. 1897, and G. T. Manley to Fox, 11 Jan. 1898, CMS Archives, G/AC 4/22/4201 and G/AC 4/23/4494.

generic missionary project in the name of faith, religious triumphalism, or Anglo-American destiny.

"Mission Science" and the Professionalization of Missionary Practice

The educational program at the SVMU drew on evangelical student activity of previous generations, most notably exemplified in the popularity and success of the Children's Special Service Missions and in the strong history at the missionary societies of producing instructional material on foreign missions, though usually for a juvenile audience. Like the deaconess movement, the Children's Special Service Mission had originated in the 1860s out of the Mildmay Institution; Eugene Stock thought it brought boys "to a genuine and manly personal religion," with the added benefit of "training young University men in the practice of mission work." Since the mission catered exclusively to middle-class children at seaside resorts, however, it was mild training.[103] Its primary goal was to solidify the heated emotionalism of the revival environment by constructing a "stable basis" of concrete knowledge through educational programming. This was the work Douglas Thornton undertook when he initiated missionary study programs for the BCCU, writing one of the crucial early textbooks for the movement *(Africa Waiting)* and aggressively pressing for this strategy within the SVMU leadership.[104] However, the educational strategy that came to dominate the approach of the SVMU had greater pretensions than simple propaganda or storytelling. It absorbed and disseminated a contested idea that had been growing slowly among liberal missionary theorists and strategists since the mid-1880s: that foreign missions had to be placed on a "scientific" basis and prosecuted by rational and strategic means, including the development of sympathy for and understanding of foreign cultures and peoples, an approach that began to erode the uniformly defamatory approach to non-Christian religions of the past.[105]

---

103. Stock, *Recollections,* 192-93. This is confirmed in the account of Arthur Fisher, returned Uganda missionary, known on the beaches in 1898 as "the Pygmy & cannibal man." Fisher memoir, Fisher Papers, CMS Archives, Acc 84 F 3/2, book 9, p. 14.

104. Gairdner, *Thornton,* 47-48. Douglas M. Thornton, *Africa Waiting; or, The Problem of Africa's Evangelization* (London: SVMU, 1897). Thornton's was the first of dozens of publications, and was followed by others, including Harlan P. Beach, *Dawn on the Hills of T'Ang; or, China as a Mission Field* (London: SVMU, 1898); W. T. Gidney, *The Jews and Their Evangelization* (London: SVMU, 1899); Otis Cary, *Japan and Its Regeneration* (London: SVMU, 1900); William St. Clair Tisdall, *India: Its History, Darkness and Dawn* (London: SVMU, 1901).

105. On Temple Gairdner's vision of bridging the worlds of Christianity and Islam, see Cox, *British Missionary Enterprise,* 225-26.

In the late 1870s, the call for "clear Christian statistics on progress" did not fall on deaf ears.[106] Advocacy for the "scientific" study of foreign missions developed in the 1870s in parallel with the more general emphasis in the British universities of placing the study of theology itself on a more scientific basis.[107] And in the 1880s the compiling of ever more comprehensive sets of missionary statistics became something of a minor industry, which had the effect of projecting an image of professionalism and competence within a movement that had always relied heavily on spreading carefully selected information, allowing it to work on Christian consciences. Missionary advocates found systematic missionary study particularly useful because it constructed arguments out of statistics with which to counter an emerging new crop of critics, and it provided answers for uneasy supporters, as missionary societies faced an increasingly frequent question: Were foreign missions a success? The question became important for a variety of reasons. Abroad, the societies faced criticism from many in the growing force of professional imperial officials who doubted the usefulness of their presence. At home they encountered doubts generated by burgeoning scientific racism within anthropological circles as well as traditionalist religious criticisms of the popular entertainments they increasingly employed. And within missionary ranks Anglo-Catholics and enthusiasts associated with faith missions and the Salvation Army raised doubts regarding traditional evangelistic and westernizing strategies.[108] Particularly damaging were the pronouncements of the UMCA's combative Bishop Edward Steere on the destructive impact of denominational infighting, missionary commitment to ineffective Western cultural forms, the prevalence of English evangelical mores in the movement, and unnecessary missionary luxuries. These he asserted were critical stumbling blocks to missionary success. Similarly, the low-cost operations of the Salvation Army and other pietist organizations provided ammunition for critics.[109]

Ultimately, however, the societies were able to brush off these attacks, primarily by reference to detailed statistics, appeals to the complexity of the task, and reliance on the growing stature of missionary effort with the general public. In a decade flush with unprecedented success, the delegates at the 1888 London conference happily emphasized that virtually every public school and all the

106. Dr. MacGill in *Mildmay Conference, 1878,* 339.

107. Chadwick, *Victorian Church: Part Two: 1860-1901,* 450.

108. On official criticism of missions, see Greenlee and Johnston, *Good Citizens,* 10-13; on the professionalization and growing acceptance of biologically deterministic anthropological racism by the 1880s, see Douglas Lorimer, "Theoretical Racism in Late-Victorian Anthropology, 1870-1900," *Victorian Studies* 31, no. 3 (Spring 1988): 421-30.

109. Taylor, "Great Missionary Failure," 493, 495-97.

major British universities were engaged in some fashion with foreign missions. This change in situation, such that "no Christian minister would now dare to sneer at Missions," was attributed not to raw success in the field but to broader public acceptance and to the recognition that pragmatically varied strategies needed to be employed in vastly differing foreign fields. "The truth is," Anglo-Indian administrator and educational advocate William Wilson Hunter stated, "that with the introduction of a more scientific treatment of the question, we have gained the support of scientific thinkers and of the leaders of English education and of English thought."[110] This was, of course, an overstatement, for the open support of a Scottish scientist such as Henry Drummond or the acceptance of missionary bands at some of the public schools far from constituted committed support from the scientific or educational communities. But the more general point that missions were more widely supported outside the missionary world — and this largely because the societies worked vigorously to present them as running on an efficient basis appropriate to rationalizing imperial practice — was undeniable.

The SVMU, then, built on existing patterns of missionary education and statistics gathering, but dynamically extended them, initiating integrated study programs with purpose-written textbooks, reading schedules, and systematic coverage of the major mission fields, all drawing on carefully compiled statistics and corroborated histories.[111] Innovative programs created for organized Sunday school curricula and introduced by the CMS and other societies in the 1880s provided a platform for the movement to more effectively engage undergraduate supporters and contradict critics of missions, such as the infamous Canon Isaac Taylor, who in 1887 not only challenged missionary practice on quantitative and qualitative grounds but also went so far as to suggest that Islam may be a more fit religion for certain races than Christianity. Scrambling to defend Christianity as a universally "civilizing" religion while also debunking charges that the traditional societies, particularly the CMS, with so many resources and so few converts, must be guilty of extraordinary levels of ineptitude or self-delusion, the missionary societies fought back.[112] This was but one more chapter in an ongoing argument, launched by the notorious early-century articles of Sydney Smith, whose strictures against missions stood, amended only in details, throughout the century: first, missions rouse "native" opposition and

110. *Protestant Missions Conference, 1888*, 15.

111. By 1900 the SVMU had established sixty-nine directed study bands in fifty-eight colleges with 776 participants. By 1906 it had enrolled 2,078 in 211 bands (740 men and 1,338 women). Tatlow, *Student Christian Movement*, 270.

112. Prasch, "Missionary Debate," 52-57. For Eugene Stock's account of the many layers of a branching controversy, see Stock, *History of the CMS*, 3:345-52.

are thus a danger to empire, their only benefit to "gratify the puerile pride of a missionary"; second, "fanatical excess" makes missions ineffectual and their few dubious converts, made miserable by their alienation from their own societies, commonly "bring ridicule and disgrace upon the gospel"; and third, as long as immorality and impiety are rife in England's parishes, duty to charitable needs at home outweighs duty to missions.[113]

Thus when Taylor launched his attack on the missionary methods of the day at the Wolverhampton Church Congress, his criticisms owed much to Smith, but also to the emerging Aryan race-consciousness of the day.[114] Focusing on the failure of missions in particular to Muslims, Taylor suggested that Islam was in fact a religion better adapted than Christianity to the "lower races." At a fundamental level this argument drew on the same assumptions about cultural change that advanced Anglo-Catholic missionaries had made for two decades. As Taylor stated in his later *Fortnightly Review* article, "Islam succeeds better than Christianity largely because it leaves the people, Asiatics or Africans, undisturbed in all the outward circumstances of their lives." Similarly the Anglo-Catholic UMCA had long advocated indigenization and abandonment of Western cultural forms, as well as the use of ascetic missionary brotherhoods and sisterhoods, in order to transmit only essential core Christian rituals and beliefs. Furthermore, Taylor also strongly pressed the old High Church assertion that by creating diocesan missionary boards bureaucratic waste would be minimized and a broader range of Anglicanism brought to its missionary duty.[115] Taylor's criticisms were brusquely, and to all evidence effectively, rebuffed by CMS supporters, who found Taylor's assumptions deplorable, racist, and an affront to evangelistic universalism. To general Evangelical satisfaction the controversy resolved itself in the general periodical press in favor of support for continued, existing missionary work. This was a position eventually conceded by Taylor himself, but the controversy had the effect of further legitimizing specially designed, culturally sensitive developmental work in the varied mission fields, beyond the simple evangelization advocated by many in the charismatic holiness world. This thread of missionary thinking was further extended by student leaders, and particularly resonated in the 1890s among younger High Church clergy in the SPG's Junior Clergy Missionary Association (JCMA).[116]

113. Smith, "Indian Missions," 170-80.

114. Taylor was one of the leading Aryan ethnologists, famous for his theories on racial expressions of religion in Teutonic and Celtic peoples. Colin Kidd, *The Forging of Races: Race and Scripture in the Protestant Atlantic* (Cambridge: Cambridge University Press, 2006), 177, 194-95, 199.

115. Taylor, "Great Missionary Failure," 495, and "Missionary Finance," 591-92.

116. Prasch, "Missionary Debate," 71. Prasch divides the participants in the debate roughly into

At a time when many critics were suggesting that the missionary project needed to be seriously rethought, the advent of systematic missionary study helped minimize negative press by emphasizing the inherent complexity of the work while also providing a manageable forum for new ideas. However, missionary study also allowed young activists, whose inexperienced judgment old hands often suspected, to assert the authority of scientific professionalism within the movement. The student movement offered a new enthusiasm and breadth of vision that progressives hoped would shatter the complacency of missionary organizations they often characterized as over-bureaucratized and overly cautious. Even for the older critics such as Cust, the new attitudes represented a hope that the CMS — which he characterized as "very emotional, very conservative," and very narrow in view — was feeling "a shaking of its dead bones" by young professionals.[117] Raising intellectual standards also allowed young activists to inject the respectability of education into suspect popular events like missionary exhibitions. Godliness and good learning, once the preserve of private life and public schools, was invigorated and directed through missionary study to a broader popular audience in a manner often acceptable to even older traditionalist evangelicals, while at the same time an appeal could be made in the universities to new forms of masculinity that rested on the proficiencies, knowledge and intellectual fortitude of a new age of professionalism.[118] In addition, this new emphasis on missionary study offered a style of technical language embedded with Christian, rather than scientific, models of development. With such a language, mission supporters could confront apathy in support of the mission cause with a vision of the utilitarian developmental benefits that missions delivered and also make them more attractive to a broader range of potential supporters in the universities, cooling the heated discourse of party conflict between Evangelicals and High Churchmen, as well as between Nonconformists and Anglicans, with a more dispassionate rationalism. As such it created a language of ecumenism that advanced the cooperative missionary agenda of the SVMU, but it also further shifted the focus of missionary activity to a developmental social service model beyond that of simple faith-based Christian progressivism, which women and the university-trained found more appealing.

---

those accepting Islamist assumptions, with racist overtones, predicated on scientific developmentalism (such as Taylor) and missionary advocates supporting the CMS position (such as Stock). The debate was significantly complicated, however, by deep Anglican religious and cultural divisions within the Church of England. On the JCMA, see Chapter 6.

117. Cust, *Prevailing Methods*, 8.

118. On masculine forms of professionalism rooted in an emerging success-oriented university culture, see Deslandes, *Oxbridge Men*, 124-25, 152-53.

The creation and direction of study programs claimed a growing amount of student leaders' time, and after 1900, the resources of the missionary societies. The image of "scientific missions" projected in these study schemes represented the ambitious strategy of the student movement to create an area of legitimacy for missions within the wider university. The new missionary scientism — in which student theorists analyzed the social and cultural background of target populations in order to devise the most effective strategies for proselytizing — involved an appropriation of the social scientific language employed by urban reformers and ethnologists, but also the colonial state.[119] The underlying assumption of the new educational strategy was the same as that on which Indian missions (and inner-city English settlement houses) operated: by educating "the classes" to their religious and social duty, their services could be enlisted in reaching and saving "the masses."[120]

Following the lead set by the YMCA, the SVMU launched plans for university organization not only in Britain but throughout the mission field. The parallels between the vision at the SVMU of a highly educated cadre of 30,000 British students "settling" the colleges of the non-Western world to make them distribution centers of Christianity, and the vision of the University Settlement movement to colonize the "paganism" of British slums, are striking and significant.[121] Notably, the flush of SVMU pledge signing in Oxford in 1892 led university women, with Una Saunders and Agnes de Selincourt at their head, to form the MSUW, Bombay, in obvious emulation of Toynbee Hall and other East London settlements.[122] On one level, the language of missionary science enhanced the ability of mission apologists to effectively deploy statistics and speak the objective language of their critics. On a second level it represented the hope that through organized efficiency the missionary movement could be made central to new spiritual life in the Church at large. In the end, missionary statistics were used in similar ways to those for religious revivals themselves. Like Moody on evangelistic tour, missionary study circles deployed "objective"

---

119. George W. Stocking, *After Tylor: British Social Anthropology, 1888-1951* (Madison: University of Wisconsin Press, 1995), 15-46; Henrika Kuklick, *The Savage Within: The Social History of British Anthropology, 1885-1945* (Cambridge: Cambridge University Press, 1991), 41-49.

120. See for example, Mrs. Ashley Carus-Wilson, "A Call to the Colleges," [ca. 1905], p. 3, CEZMS Archives, CEZ G/EA 1/3.

121. "Memorial of the Student Volunteer Missionary Union to the Churches of Christ in Britain," F. Temple Papers, vol. 7, fols. 44-45. See also Koven, *Slumming*, 21, 236-37, 280-81 and passim for an examination of the mutual constitution of foreign and slum missions.

122. Symonds, *Oxford and Empire*, 223. Other women involved in slum settlements also pressed their experience outward into imperial service, such as Edith Langridge, who founded the Oxford Mission Sisterhood of the Epiphany in India in 1902. Koven, *Slumming*, 196.

statistics relating the numbers of potential converts reached, always supported by individual accounts of personal conversion and salvation. The personal testimonials acted as a visceral demonstration of truth delivered in rhetorical tropes familiar in evangelical culture.[123] Statistics, "objective" history, and strategic analysis gave modern reinforcement to these older forms of witness, designed to appeal to audiences that increasingly expected "scientific" evidence for the validation of truth claims. But as "mission science" advanced, it tended to leave behind the languages of faith that had formed the earlier vocabulary of the evangelical missionary movement.

These developments supported the pragmatic policy of mission technocrats at the CMS, who drew on the work of student activists and mission theorists (stressing the singularity of conditions across mission fields) to defend the mixed mission strategies that were forced on the CMS by the enormous variety of its cross-cultural work, from North America and Africa to Asia and the Pacific. Mission science had its roots in the "science of religion" practiced by Anglican orientalist scholars at Oxford and elsewhere, such as (the unorthodox) Friedrich Max Müller, but also the deeply evangelical Anglican orientalist Monier Monier-Williams.[124] Thus, it had the potential both to produce more open attitudes to religious value in non-Christian religions and to reinforce older exclusivist evangelical opinions. Stock and other CMS mission leaders leveraged particular value out of these developments because of the way they allowed the CMS to co-opt holiness theology, emphasizing that spiritual devotional practice was not incompatible with temporal agencies. As the debate over primitivism and "faith" methods developed in the 1880s and 1890s, a synthesis occurred at the CMS that took suspicions about the ambiguous benefits of westernization and turned them into a new optimism that faith and cooperation with temporal agencies, as in Uganda, could positively transform the mission field. The new emphasis on education in the missionary movement also meant that university leaders tended to focus sharply on both university and children's educational work as their special preserve. The attention to new forms of children's work seemed particularly necessary, as the Education Act of 1870 made the Sunday school a far less effective location for the dissemination of missionary and, more generally, religious learning.

The greatest challenge within the universities, as the SVMU leaders saw it, was reaching beyond the subculture of holiness evangelicalism. Suspicion ran high in higher church circles because observers could hardly help but recognize that the Anglicans who were members of the movement were "almost to a man

123. Kent, *Holding the Fort*, 367.
124. Sharpe, *Not to Destroy*, 43-54.

products of the Evangelical party."[125] When the SVMU held a conference in 1898 in Birmingham designed to attract theological college students, while Presbyterians and Nonconformists were well represented, of the twenty-three Anglican colleges, only eight, predominantly Evangelical in standing, were represented. The SVMU found itself shut out from one of the most attractive sources of earnest and respectable undergraduates, and their desire to engage Anglican college students spurred the progressives in the movement away from holiness roots. Douglas Thornton, with his broad Anglican evangelicalism, pressed to draw in High Churchmen, working on the influential bishop of London, Mandell Creighton, who gave his official opinion that since the SVMU championed only missionary work, not any form of church government, all Anglicans could conscientiously join it.[126] From 1898 onward, the SVMU substantially expanded its basis, abandoning the undenominational holiness attitude that presumed a uniform revivalistically oriented evangelicalism among "true Christians," and adopting an interdenominational approach, which allowed it to embrace a greater breadth of belief without pronouncing on what should constitute a common creed. The desire to enlist Anglicanism in all of its diversity and to engage with the broader range of theologically liberal positions existent in the university were chief forces driving the SVMU to leave behind the exclusive, largely evangelical Anglicanism of its origin.

Following the 1898 Birmingham conference, considered a failure regarding levels of Anglican involvement, the SVMU planned a London conference for 1900, and aware that growth in membership numbers was slowing, redoubled efforts to broaden the movement. Targeting High Churchmen, SVMU organizers made some headway in attracting members of the JCMA, representatives from the UMCA, and both the archbishop of Canterbury and the bishop of London as speakers.[127] Douglas Thornton continued to press forward expansion of the denominational breadth of the movement, based on his belief that those animated by personal holiness could easily work with others from different spiritual traditions. But a new attitude was also developing at the SVMU. One rising young SVMU leader in the late 1890s, the Congregationalist Frank Lenwood, voiced a growing theological liberalism. The new strategists reasoned that the emotional style and narrow theology of Keswick must be moderated if the SVMU was to meet the challenges of growing social and educational diversity in a rapidly transforming Britain.[128]

---

125. Tatlow, *Student Christian Movement*, 115.

126. Gairdner, *Thornton*, 56-57.

127. Tatlow, *Student Christian Movement*, 182-84.

128. Frank Lenwood's father, a Congregationalist minister raised as an evangelical Anglican, became a Baptist to avoid the compromises of the Prayer Book, and ultimately a Congregational-

As the first generation of leaders at the SVMU — including many evangelical Anglicans such as Thornton, Temple Gairdner, G. T. Manley — prepared to live the message of the movement by becoming missionaries, second generation leaders, such as Frank Lenwood and Tissington Tatlow, increasingly influenced the executive of the Union. Much more theologically liberal than either Temple Gairdner or Thornton, these men were inclined to regard the enthusiasm of Keswick with extreme skepticism. Saving the SVMU from falling recruiting seemed to Lenwood to mean saving it from the shallowness of evangelical holiness culture. Thus one of Lenwood's intimates, G. A. Johnson Ross, wrote to Lenwood that in the wake of the 1900 SVMU London conference, with its broad theology and wider attendance, "the redemption of the Student Movement" was underway, and "it is glorious to think that it is 'being saved' to make the synthesis of intellectuality & devotion." Half jokingly, Johnson Ross reported to an appreciative Lenwood that he and twelve other skeptics were to meet with J. B. Meyers, who was to give "a private exposition of Keswickism" in order to challenge "[t]he whole question of Keswick. . . . 'Are the expectations which it arouses <u>legitimate</u>?'"[129] The answer that Lenwood and a new breed of liberal evangelicals gave (echoing the views of older evangelicals like Bishop J. C. Ryle, who, it should be noted, had arrived at these through the more traditional evangelical emphasis on sin) was that to expect the gift of miraculous results without struggle and hard work was simplistic and unequal to the challenges of piety and belief in the modern world.

That the number of convinced evangelical undergraduates was on the decline was the underlying problem, and an even smaller number of "the best people in College" were in their diminishing ranks. On latitudinarian grounds Lenwood became the chief voice that argued for making allowances in the SVMU for doubt, but the rising influence of High Church Anglicans was also making the embrace of "personal" religion, which Anglo-Catholics saw as a shibboleth, less attractive as an emphasis in the movement.[130] Tatlow, himself in the liberal vanguard, justified this transformation of the SVMU by arguing that it had had to prepare itself "to meet the questionings of the modern mind and to offer something more than spiritual devoutness to the student body."[131]

ist after abandoning belief in eternal punishment. Lenwood absorbed and retained much of this background and on graduation from Corpus Christi, Oxford in 1897 became a tutor at the new Congregationalist college, Mansfield. Roger C. Wilson, *Frank Lenwood* (London: SCM, 1936), 15, 20-22, 25.

129. G. A. Johnson Ross to Lenwood, 1 Nov. 1900, CWM Archives (LMS), Home: Personal, Box 7, folder 4.

130. Tatlow, *Student Christian Movement*, 201-2, 207-8.

131. Tatlow, *Student Christian Movement*, 213-14.

For the young men of the SVMU, the mission field offered a productive arena in which one could bury doubt in practical activity.[132] In the atmosphere of increasing uncertainty that pervaded the SVMU after 1897, the approach to High Church Anglicanism fit the need for both new recruits and honest discussion of religious differences.

Conclusion

The student missionary movement and its origins and developments were crucial to the reformation of foreign missions and British Christianity in the Edwardian age. In its earliest phase, the student movement defined itself primarily by the imperatives of revivalism, drawing on the cultural power and expectations of the revivalist idiom to channel religious charisma into missions. Holiness styles of piety, and their associated Anglo-Catholic and evangelical revivalisms, were the primary influence that allowed the missionary societies to grow and, ultimately, to build successful organizations in the universities in the 1870s. The contest in the Church at large between "Catholic" and "Protestant" Anglicans replicated itself in the universities, and the heat created by that contest generated both the characteristic missionary brotherhoods of the Anglo-Catholic pattern — the Oxford and Cambridge Missions to Calcutta and Delhi, as well as the UMCA — and the even larger student "missionary awakening" in Cambridge among evangelicals, which drew its inspiration from American revivals. In this period, in direct competition with High Church initiatives kept alive by the recruiting and fundraising tours of returned missionary bishops such as Steere and Selwyn, the universities also became a new field for evangelical activity. However, the energetic and often unorthodox spirituality of revivalism not only proved difficult to control but also limited the appeal of missionary activity to a narrow constituency of students.

In the 1890s, as attempts were made to widen the movement, its basis in the university broadened and democratized as it spread to the wider range of city colleges, universities, and professional institutes that made up the multifaceted world of late Victorian higher education. The rise of a new generation of university-trained leaders, employing new sets of strategies advocating the professionalization of missionary theory and practice, particularly through the SVMU, allowed Anglican moderates to avoid the worst excesses of revivalistic emotionalism while continuing to cultivate the underlying spirituality that

132. G. A. Johnson Ross to Frank Lenwood, 24 Aug. 1901, CWM Archives (LMS), Home: Personal, Box 7, folder 4.

A group portrait of catechists and masters from the Cambridge Mission to Delhi, ca. 1885. Created in the Anglo-Catholic pattern, "community missions" such as the Cambridge Mission to Delhi sought to engage indigenous religious cultures with celibate missionaries committed to learning and culture. From United Society for the Propagation of the Gospel Archives, SPG Photo Album 101, Bodleian Library of Commonwealth and African History, Rhodes House, Oxford. Courtesy of the United Society for the Propagation of the Gospel.

drove missionary support. As the SVMU absorbed a wider set of religious traditions, the challenging enthusiasm of Keswick and other evangelical holiness movements was channeled into the "higher and drier" realms of the Anglican Church. The influence that students and young clerical leaders came to wield was based on activism and success within missions at a time when evangelical religion, at least within the Church of England, seemed elsewhere to face little but challenge.

At the CMS this success issued from the missionary Anglicanism of Keswick. More broadly, in a Church ever more influenced by a growing enthusiasm for High Church attitudes and more frequent acceptance of Broad Church sentiment, the student missionary movement also seemed to provide a way to bind the support of Evangelicals while simultaneously extending missionary enthusiasm to the Church and the nation at large. An increasingly marginalized radical evangelicalism had transmitted its missionary fervor, in an attenuated way, to the university world, and in the process it provided the means for High Church missions to begin to absorb and use the methods and spirit of holiness revivalism within the idiom of Church social activism. The way in which missionary organizers carried out the complicated and not always successful balancing act between conservative Evangelical enthusiasm and liberal Church professionalism forms the story of a movement building momentum but struggling to retain relevance in a rapidly changing world.

New cadres of leaders sought in the 1890s to transcend the exclusive sympathies of denominationalism and of holiness-oriented forms of piety to create a university movement that could appropriate both moderate evangelicalism and the High Church "Catholic modernism" associated with the followers of Charles Gore. Emphasizing a new openness to the intellectual and theological questions that defined an emerging Christian modernism driven by a perceived "crisis of faith" in university culture, student missionary leaders transformed the emphases of foreign missions by seeking to apply a new approach to Christianity and to the rationale and methods of foreign missions.[133] From this effort the new focus on education and social service — already pressed forward in missionary fields by the work of women — as well as systematic study and the creation of a "mission science," defined the student organizers who became the next generation of leaders in the denominational societies. The change in focus had two effects: a progressive alienation of the most militant evangelicals, who had driven the early movement and who objected to "liberal" strategies; and a progressive attraction of those High Church Anglicans who had once objected strenuously to the theological emphases of evangelical student circles but who now saw great potential in a successful movement that emphasized strategy and cooperation over conversion and evangelism.

As the air of revivalistic confidence in which the SVMU had been forged subsided after 1900, the Edwardian student movement, seeking to broaden beyond waning Evangelical support, increasingly drew on the missionary resources of the High Church wing of the Church of England. For the first time evangelicals, through the SVMU, began courting the SPG. This openness at the SVMU, and its earnest approaches to the Junior Clergy Missionary Association of the SPG, helped produce unprecedented cooperation between evangelicals and High Church Anglicans. Paradoxically, however, the JCMA became such an important target for the SVMU precisely because in the 1890s higher church students and younger clergy had begun reorganizing and reinvigorating High Church missions with the aim of emulating the successes of Evangelicals.

A variety of new stresses both in the world of English denominational religion and in the mission field had affected the foreign missionary movement. While some more traditional Anglicans would have preferred to ignore "mod-

---

133. The Victorian "crisis in faith" has generated much commentary. For a view that historicizes its oft presumed severity, see Timothy Larsen, *Crisis of Doubt: Honest Faith in Nineteenth-Century England* (Oxford: Oxford University Press, 2006).

ern" challenges, the progressivism of the student movement provided a crucial set of channels for adjustments to missionary strategy and discussions of what the relationship of foreign missions to national and imperial life should be. Most notably, the range of women's public actions and their acceptability was changing as women in the professions and the suffrage movement pushed the boundaries of gender roles. Not only did the student movement provide a forum for dialog between Anglicans of different parties and between Anglicans and Nonconformists, it also provided the first example of an influential missionary organization involving Anglicans in which women achieved visible positions of executive power and demonstrated that they had options, even within the missionary movement, outside the traditional societies.

In a number of areas that activists identified as containing the most crucial problems faced by "modern" Christian missions — questions of theological modernism, of social activism, of sympathetic cultural encounter, and of colonial nationalism — the student movement provided both respectable rationales for innovation and mechanisms for cooperation in a missionary world buffeted after the turn of the century by crises of confidence. This movement particularly influenced the Anglican missionary societies through their long tradition of linkage to the universities and strong desire to draw on the prestige and talent of undergraduates as missionaries and administrators. Both the CMS and the SPG also conceived of themselves as leading an important and necessary project of redefinition, as not only missions but also the Church, the nation, and the empire faced peculiarly insistent problems. The substantial new degree to which they found themselves cooperating after 1900 was largely the result of diplomacy and cajoling by student missionary leaders.

The story of the reinvigoration and recasting of High Church missions, and the subsequent revival of the SPG after 1900, shows that the student influence on the missionary movement extended beyond evangelical culture and that it was ultimately responsible for new growth in the higher realms of the Church. Out of this movement arose a broad and keenly supported set of pan-Anglican missionary initiatives in the Edwardian era which, while never to reach the spectacular successes of the CMS in the 1890s, nevertheless generated unity, initial strong support from the episcopacy, and new initiatives to achieve Church-wide comprehensiveness in the support of missions. It also produced, however, growing unease in traditionalist circles: both those of animated protofundamentalist evangelicals and those of staunchly exclusivist High Church Anglicans. Within a decade the missionary movement split again down old fault lines. Nothing represented the erosion of the ecumenical spirit of Keswick more than the decision by the CICCU in 1910-11 to break off affiliation with the SCM and SVMU. In the controversy that led to the breach, conservative evangelicals characterized the SVMU as a purveyor of evil modernism and the dangerous trend to liberalism within a faithless segment of the evangelical party now numbered along with Romanist sacerdotalists as enemies of "Protestant truth."[134] The divisions of modernism that came to characterize Protestantism in the twentieth century were to strike the missionary movement, but not before a brief age of Anglican unity in which missions were to reflect a final, ultimately impossible vision of unified empire and unified faith.

In the late Victorian period, student missionary involvement issuing from both the holiness and Anglo-Catholic movements came to have a decisive effect on the course and conduct of Anglican foreign missions. Student activism had the effect of reinforcing an underlying trend whereby professionalized missions, resonating particularly with progressive social-imperial ambitions in the universities, shifted the missionary movement to greater reliance on more respectable middle-class candidates. The university, however, presented significant challenges to missionary societies, both in how to generate zeal within the secularizing embrace of higher education and in how to promote a standard of theological and intellectual respectability despite the high levels of emotionalism upon which missionary advocacy traditionally relied. This was the task before the SVMU, but also of the organization that came into existence to rebuild the High Church missionary enterprise in the face of clear evangelical successes: the JCMA of the SPG. Both were dedicated not only to emulating the earlier successes of holiness-based revivalism and social reform but also to extending those successes beyond the shrinking world of limited holiness subcultures at both the evangelical and the Anglo-Catholic ends of the missionary spectrum.

The new initiatives launched by the SVMU and the JCMA had resonance and power not least because new pressures in the opening decade of the twentieth century exerted themselves on the evangelical missionary project. The massive celebration of the CMS Centenary, during which the society raised an unprecedented additional £212,297 on top of base annual income of about £300,000 and cleared all its debts,[135] had masked the effects of cooling evangelical ardor and waning evangelical strength. The CMS faced the new century with a growing sense that the emotion and success of the 1880s and 1890s were ebbing. The Edwardian period saw the dilution of many of the forces that characterized the late Victorian missionary movement. The SVMU stands as

---

134. Tatlow, *Student Christian Movement*, 381-85. The pressure on the CICCU to admit High Churchmen and liberal Evangelicals to its ranks (and thus countenance questioning biblical inspiration, millenarianism, and exclusivist atonement theology) led to the break. Ultimately, ultra-evangelicals formed the Inter-Varsity Fellowship of Evangelical Christians (IVF) in 1928. Wellings, *Evangelicals Embattled*, 278-81.

135. Stock, *History of the CMS*, 4:14, 476-80.

the primary example of this change: the real inspiration in its early history was the anti-intellectual emotionalism of Keswick-style holiness, but to appeal to "better minds" within the evangelical community and to a broader range of students in university culture, it found it must forsake its origins, including an exclusivity focused heavily on Cambridge University. While the SVMU moved rapidly into other institutions of higher education, Oxford University — with its stronger High Church heritage — also rose to a new prominence and zeal in the cause of foreign missions. Thus, when Arthur Fisher, traveling for the CMS in 1898, spoke at Oxford, he was struck by "the deep spiritual feeling as against Cambridge" and found that it was the work of the new bishop of London, Mandell Creighton, and of the archbishop of Canterbury, Frederick Temple, who had instilled this "burning zeal."[136] Creighton, himself associated with other Broad and High Church initiatives that sought to deepen Church life, was tied to Sidney and Beatrice Webb in their Fabian educational program, and he drew together many Churchmen, including Cosmo Gordon Lang and Edward Stewart Talbot, into support for "national reconstruction" based on "national communal aspirations."[137] Just as the fortunes of Anglican evangelical missions were cresting, a new interest in foreign missions within the episcopacy, associated with intellectual projects for national efficiency, and more closely connected to the SPG than the CMS, made missions, conceived of as a unified Church project, the focus of a new agenda in Anglican missionary enterprise.

136. Fisher memoir, Fisher Papers, CMS Archives, Acc 84 F 3/2, book 8, p. 28. Mandell Creighton's wife Louise rapidly became an important advocate for SPG women's missions.

137. Creighton quoted in G. R. Searle, *The Quest for National Efficiency: A Study in British Politics and Political Thought, 1899-1914* (Oxford: Blackwell, 1971), 98.

CHAPTER 6

Ideals of Church Revival: Christian Communalism and the High Church Bid for Anglican Unity

As we have looked at the fact of the empire to which we belong, we have begun to ask ourselves what is the meaning of these unique powers of colonization and expansion with which GOD has endowed the British people? If they are not given to us to enable us to promote GOD's cause in the world, what are they given to us for? We have begun to form a conception of a Missionary Empire whose contribution to the world's progress shall be the making permanent of those ideas of liberty, and truth, and justice, and love, which we ourselves have learned from Christ.

John H. Ellison, 1898

Slowly but surely, the English people, who are not easy to move, and who are a strange mixture of insularity and imperialism, have been brought to respect the Christianity which believes sufficiently in Christ to carry his name throughout the world.

Henry H. Montgomery, 1901[1]

In November 1890, as the student movement at Cambridge continued to gain ground and the CMS worked through the implications of significant increases in university interest, several clerics gathered in the rooms of Canon Henry

1. Ellison to the Federation of the JCMA, presidential address, 11 May 1898, in Minutes of JCMA Conferences, USPG Archives, X 540; Montgomery, *Foreign Missions* (London: Longmans, Green, 1902), 153.

Scott Holland of St. Paul's Cathedral. They met there to consider the appropriate response of High Churchmen to the needs of foreign missions and to discuss the duty of higher church Anglicans to respond to the quickening times in Church and empire. Holland, a follower of legendary Balliol College idealist T. H. Green, as well as friend and lifelong associate of Charles Gore (then principal of Pusey House, Oxford), pressed forward a visionary scheme designed to capture the next generation in the life of Christian service. B. F. Westcott, Gore, and Holland had been principals in the founding, one year earlier, of the Christian Social Union, an Anglican association designed to inspire Church-based social action, ameliorate urban and industrial poverty, and thereby stabilize English society.[2] Now, the assembled clergy, including Frederick Temple, bishop of London (and later archbishop of Canterbury), R. S. Hassard, and other High Churchmen, pressed forward a parallel initiative explicitly targeted to provide for Church programs, and particularly for larger numbers of clergy, in the British Empire. Voting to form an Association of Junior Clergy of London that aimed to raise awareness and support for missions, these founders saw the SPG act upon their petition and charter a nationwide Junior Clergy Missionary Association (JCMA).[3] Anglican Christian Socialism, defined by B. F. Westcott (from 1890 the bishop of Durham) as the claim of "Christian law" to "rule social practice," was not simply a response to the problems of industrial society but, in parallel to the imperial policies advanced by Imperial Federationists, the Fabians, and Tariff Reformers, it was constructed to support the project of moralizing not only English but also imperial society.[4]

Facing the successes of Evangelicals in missionary realms, High Churchmen in the "Alexandrian school" of Westcott, Lightfoot, and Archbishop Benson, as well as the "Catholic modernist" younger guard led by Gore and Holland, recognized the need to respond, and the parallel birth and growth of the JCMA and the SVMU fed off each other.[5] By 1900 when the SVMU had 1,720 who

2. The second wave of Christian Socialism of the 1880s included the founding of the Fabian Society in 1884 and the expansion of slum settlements (including Toynbee Hall, 1884), as well as the creation of the Christian Social Union. Wilkinson, *Christian Socialism*, 28-35, 42-47. By 1910 the CSU counted 6,000 members.

3. Pascoe, *Two Hundred Years of the SPG,* 828a. Gore and Holland had also been involved in the founding of the Oxford Mission to Calcutta in 1880. Notably, missionary brotherhoods and sisterhoods, as well as indigenizing missions such as the UMCA, preceded and presumably formed a model for the later Victorian London slum settlements such as Oxford House and Toynbee Hall, both founded in 1884.

4. Westcott quoted in Arthur V. Woodworth, *Christian Socialism in England* (London: Swan Sonnenschein, 1903), 150-51. On the imperial socialism of the Tariff Reformers and the Fabian Society and their fellow travelers, see Semmel, *Imperialism and Social Reform,* chaps. 3 and 5.

5. Anglican "Catholic modernism," or "Liberal Catholicism," was defined largely through the

had taken the missionary pledge, the JCMA had recruited over 2,000 members, and while the SVMU had sent out 566 missionaries, the JCMA could boast of over 150 who had taken up overseas work as colonial chaplains and missionaries.[6] Thus, while ultimately not as successful in producing missionaries, the JCMA represented a significant response to Evangelical initiatives. Supported by leading higher church Anglicans in the final decades of the century, leaders of the JCMA envisioned imperial enthusiasm as a counter to evangelical emotionalism, with the JCMA as a focal point of new High Church activities that changed the way the Church of England pursued missions and engaged with imperial questions.

Students and younger clergy from the High Church and Evangelical traditions of Anglicanism forged new cooperative ventures in the 1890s, having been inspired by the potential of the SVMU, the successful Younger Clergy Union founded in 1885 by the CMS, and the new ideas now being fronted by the JCMA. As a consequence, plans for a more completely national Anglican effort began to materialize, drawing the previously separatist High Church SPG into the mainstream of British foreign missions. This development amplified the influence of the SPG, along with its strong loyalty to national and imperial ideas and institutions. The JCMA's emphasis on Church unity, imperial engagement, and widespread activism generated new enthusiasm. With many of its activist leaders closely associated with Anglo-Catholicism, however, the JCMA presented a challenge to SPG ideals similar to that faced by the CMS in its encounter with holiness-based evangelicalism. The JCMA party gained considerable influence and was also softened as a Ritualist stronghold when with JCMA support the moderate High Churchman and imperial enthusiast Bishop Henry H. Montgomery, formerly of Tasmania, came to the secretariat of the SPG in 1901. The missionary culture prevalent among students and young clerical leaders shifted in emphasis under these influences from a missionary Anglicanism based on revivalist charisma to an Anglican world vision increasingly established around the idea of a national church with an imperial mission.

essays published in 1889 in the controversial *Lux Mundi: A Series of Studies in the Religion of the Incarnation*. Edited by Gore and with contributions from Henry Scott Holland, Edward Talbot, R. C. Moberly, Arthur Lyttelton, and J. R. Illingworth, among others, the book attempted to reconcile Anglo-Catholic faith with biblical criticism and evolutionary understandings of religion. It thus broke with "old Tractarian" attitudes subscribed to by E. B. Pusey and others who supported biblical inerrancy and the knowability of providential history.

6. Pascoe, *Two Hundred Years of the SPG*, 828a; *Official Year-Book of the Church of England* (London: SPCK, 1897), 247-48.

The High Church Vision: Historicizing Church and Empire

The intellectual father of late Victorian High Church missions was, as seen in Chapter 3, B. F. Westcott, who drew on a rising and prolific Platonist idealism informed not only by T. H. Green and his followers but also by the historical Church studies pursued by Westcott and his associates, the founders and supporters of the Oxford and Cambridge Brotherhoods to India. From early sermons on the religious duties of the universities to the founding of the university missionary brotherhoods, the result of Westcott's theorizing and fervent support of missions was to perform an idealistic intellectualizing of missions. This made them respectable, at least to many students, within a university rife with modernist challenges to faith. It also helped create, out of a deep interest in the early Alexandrian church fathers, a more widespread accommodationist school of missionary theory that sustained a clerical subculture emphasizing the need for sympathetic cultural understanding and a pragmatic approach to other faiths, both tempered with respect and appreciation. For Westcott, the promise of foreign missions was of expansive historio-religious proportions. Brushing aside "the commonplaces on English dominion, and commerce, and energy" as reasons for interest in missions, Westcott instead constructed a vision of scholarly missionary service in India that would repay "a clearer understanding of the old faiths, and a livelier sympathy with the peculiar religious instincts to which they correspond" with an organic emergence of Indian Christianity that could launch a new era of Christian understanding and devotionalism.[7]

At the heart of Westcott's vision was a profoundly romantic and orientalist vision of India that constructed its people as close in cultural reflex to the lost purity and potential of the Church in Alexandria in fourth-century Egypt. Westcott saw the Alexandrian church as providing a tradition that had, through its undogmatic universalism, unleashed a creative syncretism that, before the Alexandrian school was quashed, profitably combined Judaic and Hellenic influences.[8] India now held the latent power of the immanent spirit that would allow a new reformation of the Church along "the lines traced out by Origen and Athanasius, [rather] than along those of Augustine and Anselm, which we have followed."[9] Central to this vision was a fundamental rejection of evangelicalism and Roman Catholicism; both were presumed to represent a cramped, authoritarian theology and social vision. In their rejection lay a rationale for

---

7. Westcott, *Religious Office*, 27 and passim.
8. Maw, *Visions of India*, 153-54, 159.
9. Westcott, *Religious Office*, 33,

Broad and moderate High Churchman to embrace missionary endeavor of an alternative, generous, and historically constructed sort.

For Westcott, India had become a tableau upon which to project a revision of English theology and social vision, and Westcott's later full-blooded embrace of Christian Socialism was but another facet of this outlook. But as Jeffrey Cox has noted, the import of Westcott's message represented more than simply another orientalist fabrication; it held within it the germs of a culturally liberal vision of missionary agency with far-reaching implications.[10] Rather than aiming for "English clergy who may reflect to our eye faint and imperfect images of ourselves," Westcott emphasized the dangers of simply assuming that a message of presumed truth could overcome the resentment caused by imperial occupation, cautioning that

> [i]t is very difficult for us to appreciate the overpowering effect of a dominant class in enforcing their own beliefs. It is even more difficult to apprehend the relative shape which these beliefs assume in the minds of alien races. If then . . . we are ourselves in due time to draw from India — to speak only of that empire which GOD has committed to our charge . . . if we are to contribute to the establishment of an organisation of the Faith which shall preserve and not destroy all that is precious in the past experience of the native peoples; if we are to proclaim in its fullness a Gospel which is universal and not western; we must keep ourselves and our modes of thought studiously in the background.[11]

Like all other mission theorists Westcott relied in part on racial conceptions to ground his program, but he notably emphasized the potential of theorized racial communities to produce fruitful interchange rather than conflict. Similarly, mindful of the diversity of experience in the early church, and thus in many respects suspicious of crude westernization strategies for missions, Westcott and his followers instead embraced a cultural assimilationist model. However, both Anglo-Catholic and Westcottian supporters of High Church missions nevertheless tended to see empire as a providential and powerful aid to human development, rather than as a fundamentally exploitative system.[12] As Henry Scott Holland recalled, the ultimate goal in Westcott's vision was the emergence of a new internationalism that would defeat militarism and foster a peaceful "fellowship of free peoples" which, he believed, was "the ideal towards which

10. Cox, "Lefroy," 59-60.
11. Westcott, *Religious Office*, 38.
12. Maw, *Visions of India*, 147.

our British Empire, in spite of all that marred and disfigured its advance, was still heroically working."[13] Missionaries of all schools were profoundly troubled by the immorality and violence characteristic of settler and trader societies, Anglo-Catholics generally more so than others, but few in this era ever accepted that the empire could not be Christianized in the same way (and by the same methods) that were being applied to English society.

The general acceptance of empire as providing both providential opportunities for mission and avenues for worldly sinfulness characterized both Evangelicals and High Churchmen of all stripes throughout the century. Thus there were critical tensions in the "Westcottian school." On the one hand, an authentically liberal vision of Christian apologetics and encounter with other cultures was imagined as possible within a providentially appointed empire. The empire was accepted as an accomplished fact, and it was seen nearly universally in terms of trusteeship: the common missionary perception cast empire as entailing religious duty laid upon the English as a chosen people. On the other hand, fundamental inequalities of power structured by race, wealth, and access to resources of education and governmental power were an ineradicable component of the imperial system, and operated deeply at odds with the Christian vision of a spiritually egalitarian society and international religious system in which a federation of developmentally rich national and apostolic churches, paralleling the early centuries of Christian growth, fostered the development of humanity. Giving sermons in Cambridge was one thing, but in the field these contradictions became sites of struggle, where Anglican elitism operating in the context of local social practice could easily lead to the breakdown of theories that had such strong appeal in England.[14] In isolated missions such as Central Africa or Melanesia, it was easier to live by the growing Anglo-Catholic and Westcottian ideals of separation from Western culture; however, in a field as deeply penetrated by imperial power structures and interests as India, the task was significantly more difficult. Members of the missionary brotherhoods, such as Henry Whitehead and G. A. Lefroy, already a part of the same educational and social networks as those in the Indian Civil Service, found themselves progressively drawn into the authority network of imperial rule. Over time the university background of the "gentlemen missionaries" of the Anglo-Catholic connection militated against the emergence of indigenous pastorates, as the professional prejudices toward maintaining

13. Henry Scott Holland, *Personal Studies* (London: Wells Gardner, Darton, 1905), 135-36.

14. For a detailed analysis of precisely this phenomenon, as the Cambridge Mission to Delhi struggled to establish relations with untouchable Chamar Christians, see Cox, *Imperial Fault Lines*, 136-42.

English educational and clerical standards in "native" clergy prevented the rapid expansion of locally led churches.[15]

Within the English Church, however, this ideal had considerable power, both with Westcott's contemporaries — for example, Archbishop E. W. Benson, scholar; Bishop J. B. Lightfoot; liberal Anglican novelist and Dean of Westminster, Frederick W. Farrar — and with his pupils and protégés, notably Edward Bickersteth (bishop of South Tokyo, 1886-97); Charles Gore (influential Anglo-Catholic modernist); and Henry H. Montgomery (bishop of Tasmania and SPG episcopal secretary).[16] Showing significant overlap in personnel and ideological influence, these associations of similarly minded Churchmen formed the communities out of which two decades later both the Christian Social Union, with its strong social vision, and the JCMA of the SPG, with its strong imperial vision, were generated. Historicizing both Church (which had grown in identifiable, exemplary ways in antiquity) and empire (which had demonstrated both its transient nature and its potential to aid Church extension, as exemplified in the history of the Roman empire) allowed High Churchmen a new way into a missionary world previously dominated by the often more simple, direct assumptions and actions of evangelicals.

The JCMA and the Transformation of the SPG

For decades the example of the university missionary brotherhoods had presented a particular vision of High Church missionary inspiration. Based as they were on a program of serious study and gradualist educational missionary strategy, however, brotherhoods had not attracted as much support or enthusiasm as Evangelical programs for radical transformation through dramatic proclamatory preaching. As the SPG's seemingly dismal comparative growth raised more and more alarms, and as High Church visions of mission resonated more strongly with the burgeoning settlement movement and the professionalization

15. Porter, *Religion Versus Empire*, 231-37. On the more general imposition of Anglican imperial concerns on Indian congregations, see Robert Eric Frykenberg, "Christian Missions and the Raj," in *Missions and Empire*, ed. Norman Etherington, The Oxford History of the British Empire Companion Series (Oxford: Oxford University Press, 2005), 117-23.

16. For another measure of the weight of Westcott's circle upon the late Victorian and Edwardian Church, see the listing of influential Churchmen — archdeacons, canons, deans, and bishops — who passed through Lightfoot and Westcott's "Auckland Brotherhood," including particularly relevantly, George L. King, bishop of Madagascar (1899-1919) and Secretary of the SPG (1919-24), see George R. Eden and F. C. Macdonald, eds., *Lightfoot of Durham* (Cambridge: Cambridge University Press, 1933), 166-73.

of imperial bureaucracies of control, the appeal of a renovated High Church missionary effort, resting heavily on the Westcottian model of enlightened imperial service, grew rapidly in the higher realms of the Church.

Invigorated and challenged by evangelical student volunteer movements, higher church students and younger clergy redoubled efforts to change the SPG and its methods of operation. The High Church movement never generated student missionaries in numbers to rival evangelicals, but it did grow rapidly by drawing heavily on evangelical organizational practice while also fundamentally changing the conduct of High Church missions. Change was only achieved, however, as a complex struggle involving younger clergy, the SPG's women's association, and the secretariat of the SPG unfolded, each group possessing a diverse set of party and organizational agendas. Under the transformation High Church missions increasingly abandoned earlier isolationism as the student movement provided the first forum in which traditionally exclusive High Churchmen entered into dialog with Nonconformists on missionary subjects. The SPG moved through these channels into the mainstream of English foreign missions, culminating in the presence of official delegates from the SPG at the 1910 World Missionary Conference in Edinburgh. Here High Churchmen mingled officially for the first time with interdenominational evangelical enthusiasts from "faith" missions, such as the China Inland Mission, although distinctions in style and temper still differentiated the missionary movement. The SPG's secretary, Bishop Henry H. Montgomery, for instance, quipped that Edinburgh's evangelical bias led him to feel like "one of a very small band of lions in a large den of Daniels."[17] Edinburgh delivered an unprecedented show of cooperation in a missionary community that was more accustomed to the jealous preservation of independent action and acrimonious clashes in the mission field between high and low styles of English religion. The student movement also provided the impetus for pressing the SPG to an openly and aggressively "imperial" missionary strategy and provided an atmosphere in which some Anglicans could develop an unapologetic program for cooperation between foreign missions and the structures of formal empire.

The striking new successes of the CMS, trumpeted far and wide by society supporters, had a profound effect at the SPG, where the 1880s seemed to demonstrate the comparative failure of the foreign missions of the Society. The example of successful Evangelical missions kindled reforms at the SPG, including the formation of the activist JCMA. While never achieving the size or influence of the SVMU, the JCMA was nevertheless crucial in leading a

---

17. H.L., "The World Missionary Conference," *CMS Gazette* (1 Aug. 1910): 237.

missionary renovation at the SPG and in transforming the ideology of High Church missions. Because of a complicated interplay between the party politics of clerics, organizational tensions between men and women, and differing levels of willingness to emulate evangelicals, the transformation of the SPG in the 1890s involved a web of interests. When finally the younger clergy of the JCMA had triumphed, they had done so by relying on the one platform that seemed most to unify and animate enthusiasm: service to the empire. In this emphasis they also found a basis for cooperation with other missionary traditions that had previously been closed to them.

Old Brigade and New: The Struggle for the SPG

The late 1880s and after saw a growing chorus of complaints about a moribund SPG, but the hold of a conservative "old Tractarian" clique — centered around deans of St. Paul's Cathedral R. W. Church (1871-90) and Robert Gregory (1890-1911) — meant that Secretary Henry Tucker and his ideals of sober, business-like operation remained strongly entrenched. Many echoed the criticisms of Bishop Adelbert Anson, formerly of Qu'Appelle (1884-92), who sensed that the problems of the SPG, while reflected in what he believed was the disagree-able character of Henry Tucker, nevertheless had a deeper cause. As Anson asserted, "I have heard the . . . grumbling and complaints as to the lack of spir-itual fervour and enthusiasm in all connected with S.P.G. as contrasted with C.M.S. The letters that are constantly appearing in the Papers are but a very feeble indication of this wide-spread discontent."[18] And the discontent was sharpest among student and junior clerical supporters who as curates were often burdened with the duty of raising support for foreign missions and who bridled under Tucker's imperious temper. Among JCMA reformers, however, the opinion generally held that simply replacing Tucker would not solve the Society's deeper problems.

Henry Tucker's position was indicative of the growing divide between the old and the young at the SPG. Defending the SPG on grounds of religious style and philosophy, he insisted that if the SPG filled 8,488 pulpits year after year with sermonizers supporting the cause, the responsibility lay with loyal Churchmen to respond to legitimate calls on Anglican duty. Displaying the complacency of a professionalized establishment, Tucker asserted that he could not see how organizing secretaries "can hope to stir up zeal among the clergy

18. Adelbert Anson to the Members of the Standing Committee of the Society for the Propa-gation of the Gospel, circular, [ca. July 1894], Benson Papers, vol. 131, fols. 392-93.

if it does not exist."[19] Tucker continued to reject the logic and the aesthetics of evangelical revivalism, but also the claims of Anglo-Catholic activists. Friction had grown at the SPG between "old Tractarians," who accepted moderate Ritualist desires to make worship more attractive and who remained faithful to the theological conservatism of Pusey, and Anglo-Catholics, who were animated by engagement with social questions, inner-city settlements, and, with growing frequency, imperial service. Often accepting the writings of theological liberals such as Charles Gore and the contributors to *Lux Mundi* as legitimate explorations of faith, higher church progressives and modernist Anglo-Catholics stimulated debate, but also traditionalist opposition.

Responding to evangelical success in foreign missions in the 1870s, higher church Anglicans had, of course, had relatively modest successes in the work of the Cambridge Mission to Delhi, the Oxford Mission to Calcutta, and the UMCA under Bishops Steere (1874-82) and Smythies (1883-90). The new round of Evangelical missionary advances from the late 1880s led many of the younger clerical supporters of the SPG to imagine a further transformation of the Society under the progressive inspiration that was developing among the "Catholic modernist" followers of Charles Gore. Such a transformation would draw on the rising enthusiasm for social service in slum work that led to the foundation of famous settlements such as Oxford House in East London. Here men such as Henry Scott Holland encountered the exoticism of poverty and saw in their own dedicated lives of simple, manly religious benevolence and sensuously rich ritual worship the keys to engagement with poor and heathen populations and the foundations upon which to build social service in England and the empire alike.[20] The theology of incarnation, which tended toward a vision of God as an evolving, organic force, was conceived as the basis for a new pursuit of social justice and democratic participation, and it had the effect of inspiring a number of figures, such as George King, bishop of Madagascar, and Helen Hanson, who would come to embrace a new missionary progressivism that eschewed blatant racism and didactic proselytizing.[21]

The Anglican Missionary Conference of 1894 marked the next round of reformist spirit, starkly publicizing the comparative successes of the CMS and the SVMU against those of the SPG and JCMA. The infighting the conference precipitated at the SPG led the bishop of Jamaica, Enos Nuttall, to write to Archbishop Benson that something had to be done to smooth the waters and

19. H. W. Tucker, "Memorandum on Bishop Anson's Circular and Letter," 11 Oct. 1894, Benson Papers, vol. 131, fols. 394-97.
20. Koven, *Slumming*, 254.
21. Prevost, *Communion of Women*, 281-82.

open channels of communication, so that the rumors of Tucker's inordinate influence, whether true or false, could be dispelled and the SPG revivified.[22] For the first time in its nearly two-hundred-year history, the SPG saw a contest for appointment to seats on its Executive Committee in 1894 by two "reformers," and the following year the creation of a committee to consider revitalization in the Society's home organization.[23] By 1896 activist younger clergy were seeking to topple the old regime. But the old leadership — led by Tucker and supported by powerful Standing Committee members, including Sir Charles Turner and the recently retired colonial governor Arthur Hamilton-Gordon (created Baron Stanmore in 1893) — were not prepared to be toppled.

Tucker and the SPG staff had spent the 1880s centralizing authority and beating back challenges. The CMS model, by providing openings for activist women and younger clergy, suggested a clear avenue for new initiatives at the SPG that would connect with the lay power that was growing in the Church of England. The SPG, however, still wedded to presumptions of the sanctity and centrality of clerical authority, had never organized any coherent nationwide program of lay activism focusing on children or anything else. This refusal to develop systematically the work in one of the Church of England's great areas of strength, Sunday schools, left the neglected, resource-starved Ladies' Association to haphazard organization, with the women organizing children's deputations as best they could, most notably led by Fanny Patteson, the sister of martyred Bishop Patteson of Melanesia. At the conference of the SPG Ladies' Association in 1890 women pressed for a more organized approach, particularly spurred on by accounts of flourishing CMS children's organization.[24] In 1891 women's work with children received official sanction when the Guild of the Children of the Church was formed at a meeting of the SPG Ladies' Association. Though formally associated with the SPG, consultations with CMS Secretary Eugene Stock provided organizational expertise, and with his advice the Guild began publishing a magazine in January of 1892.[25] In response to Evangelical successes the SPG secretariat turned this important work over to the only body of supporters willing, and apparently able, to take it up. Children and their instruction were, after all, generally conceived of as the special preserve of women.

22. Enos Nuttall to Benson, 22 Oct. 1894, Benson Papers, vol. 131, fols. 401-4.

23. Cust, *Prevailing Methods*, 130; "Meeting of a Special Sub-Committee appointed 3 Jan. 1895 to Report on the Re-constitution of the Home Organisation Sub Committee," in Rough Minutes of the Home Organisation Committee, USPG Archives, H 137.

24. "Junior Work. SPG," memorandum, USPG Archives, X 557a.

25. Constance E. Bunyon, "Notes on Children's Work," memorandum; *Guild of the Children of the Church. Report, 1892*, USPG Archives, X 557a.

But the junior clergy who identified the SPG as a target of reform also viewed work among children as crucial, and one primary motivation in the founding of the JCMA was to emulate the growing work of the CMS Younger Clergy Union. Formed in 1885 under the leadership of CMS College Principal, T. W. Drury, the Younger Clergy Union delivered systematic Sunday school addresses, prayer meetings, and farewell services for outgoing missionaries.[26] A focus on children and young people would allow the JCMA to advance systematically the higher church vision of mission, but also lay the foundation for what was conceived as a complementary focus for the SPG: an ambitious, specifically imperial program.

To Henry Tucker, the JCMA must have appeared to present the same threat to established, responsible practice that the enthusiastic, independent action of Special Missions and even university brotherhoods had in the 1880s.[27] However, the JCMA was a threat of a different order. It represented "progressive" reform at the SPG that aimed to capture the Society rather than split from it. JCMA members began by organizing a more enthusiastic style of support for the SPG through Exeter Hall meetings and devotional services, most notably in St. Paul's Cathedral. Like the SVMU, it also came to advocate for the systemic study of missions and through new educational programs created alternate paths to missionary service. But at the JCMA, the label "progressive" came to have a complex meaning, mediated by Anglo-Catholic ideas about clerical authority, ecclesiastical practice, imperialism, and simple enthusiasm. Beginning with their program for educating children, from the mid-1890s the JCMA "Progressives" found themselves increasingly in conflict with an "old Brigade" at the SPG.[28]

One of the most prominent early JCMA leaders was Allen Bell, the young vicar of Pershore in Worcestershire, who organized all his local Sunday schools into an SPG Union known as the King's Messengers.[29] By expanding Bell's scheme, the JCMA sought to claim children's work as their own special preserve.

---

26. Stock, *History of the CMS*, 3:323, 667; Pascoe, *Two Hundred Years of the SPG*, 828a.

27. On the frictions raised in the SPG Delhi mission between the established missionary Robert Winter and the young university men of the Cambridge Mission, see Maw, *Visions of India*, 181-88.

28. These were the labels applied to the warring factions at the SPG by John H. Ellison, one leader of the "progressives." Ellison to Randall Davidson, 11 Apr. 1901, Davidson Papers, vol. 68, fols. 243-44.

29. The date of the origination of Bell's scheme is unclear and was vigorously disputed — younger clergy claimed 1891, SPG officials 1896 — and had relevance as a bitter struggle between the younger clergy and women at the SPG for precedence and control of children's work unfolded. "Junior Work. SPG," memorandum, USPG Archives, X 557a; Thompson, *History of the SPG*, 239.

But there was more to this than a simple attempt to reverse a lack of organization and zeal at the SPG. Tucker clearly saw the new initiative as a backdoor strategy to give independence to missionary bishops as well as influence to enthusiast supporters of the UMCA, university brotherhoods, and independent Diocesan Boards of Missions who had fought the battles over Special Funds in the 1870s and 1880s.[30] Aggressive stances taken by extreme Anglo-Catholics against the missionary societies themselves at Church congresses had raised alarms through the 1880s, and while moderate High Churchmen might support the evolution of modest ritual enhancements to public worship, they were also committed to defending traditional Church practices of the past century, including voluntary organization. Moderate Churchmen thus found themselves in a dilemma over the JCMA's initiatives. In the 1890s, in a revival of the controversies raised in the 1870s over Boards of Missions, champions of the societies such as Eugene Stock for the CMS and William Grey, the ninth Earl of Stamford, for the SPG, found themselves defending the missionary societies again against the charge brought by Anglo-Catholics that they interfered with legitimate independent diocesan Church authority.[31] In the context of these larger Church questions the cause of advancing missionary enthusiasm was at the SPG inseparable from broader questions of Church order and party program.

The cause of "progress" was complicated at the SPG. In this atmosphere the organizational work of "progressive" women developed at cross purposes with that of "progressive" younger clergy. This was because, for many of the most activist younger clergy, the desired end of the campaign to renovate the SPG was the ultimate supersession of the Society itself. Many JCMA activists were deeply anti-Erastian Anglo-Catholics, committed to a unified Church freed from the polluting "Protestant" shackles of the state, in which societies — the representatives of diversity of opinion — would ultimately be superfluous. Henry Tucker and his connection of "old Tractarians," while also defenders of clerical independence from state sanction — most clearly represented in their opposition to the Public Worship Regulation Act of 1874 — were nevertheless committed to the preservation of High Church societies and their centralized London administrative control. For this reason Tucker had long opposed the idea of diocesan Boards of Missions, which were too subject to control by enthusiasts ready to score party points at the expense of actual foreign mission support, and in this Tucker operated in agreement with the leadership of the CMS. But JCMA leaders hoped for the ultimate unity of Church of England missions as an ideal aspect of a larger program for cultural unification of the

30. For more detail, see Chapter 3.
31. Stock, *Recollections*, 151.

empire. The control of SPG children's work became a means of introducing principles of independent diocesan organization to the SPG, and from that stage Tucker feared a mounting takeover of the SPG itself.

In this program one of the most active JCMA members was John H. Ellison, from 1888 brother-in-law to Randall Davidson, Queen Victoria's favored dean of Windsor and Archbishop Benson's influential secretary.[32] In 1893 Ellison became the second chairman of the weighty JCMA London Association, the vicar of Windsor in 1894, and the first chairman of the nationwide Junior Clergy Missionary Federation from 1895 to 1898, which connected together the multiplying Associations.[33] In 1893, according to arch-opponent Constance Bunyon in the SPG Ladies' Association, Ellison launched "an elaborate scheme for incorporating all the children's missionary magazines" as the foundation for unifying all Anglican foreign mission work among children. His plan had the SPG, the CMS, and the UMCA all handing their children's magazines to him, including the publications of the Guild of the Children of the Church, which Bunyon edited. Incredulous at his presumption and naiveté, she referred him to Tucker, assuming correctly that JCMA ambitions would result in deeply strained relations between women workers, the SPG administration, and its younger clerical "supporters," particularly over issues of Church order and the future of the SPG.[34]

The aggression of the JCMA toward the SPG, and the resistance of Tucker — and SPG women, who had a stake in present institutional arrangements — grew rapidly over the 1890s. In correspondence with the editor of JCMA publications, Bunyon was informed "in confidence that 'their [the JCMA's] real object was to abolish the Society,'" which she "thought so traitorous that I reported it to Mr. Tucker."[35] And it is clear that the SPG secretariat viewed the JCMA as a disloyal fifth column.[36] The members of the JCMA were defining themselves, parallel to the self-construction of many Anglo-Catholic missionaries overseas, as a heroic camp of reformers storming the crumbling walls of a moribund

32. Bell, *Davidson*, 1:119. Although Ellison's wife died soon after the marriage, he maintained a lifelong intimate connection to the Davidson family. C. M[ary]. M[ills]., *Edith Davidson of Lambeth* (London: Murray, 1938), 68-69, 125. Davidson was made bishop of Rochester in 1891, of Winchester in 1895, and archbishop of Canterbury in 1903.

33. Diary of John Ellison, 1888-1935, John Henry Joshua Ellison Papers, SGC M.160/B/5/1, St. George's Chapel Archives, Windsor.

34. Constance E. Bunyon, "Notes on Children's Work," memorandum, USPG Archives, X 557a.

35. Bunyon, "Notes on Children's Work."

36. See for example marginal notes on "breach of confidence" and disloyalties committed by JCMA members in the document "Resumé of the Proceedings of the Conference of Delegates held at Leeds . . . 1896," Secretary's Correspondence, H. W. Tucker, 1898-1901, USPG Archives, H 2.

society. For his part Tucker believed the SPG to be under assault. Constance Bunyon understandably sided with Tucker, for in 1895 the first conference of the Federation of the JCMA passed a resolution asking that she be replaced as editor of the Children of the Church Magazine by a member of the JCMA. "Mr. Tucker shewed it to me in print," Bunyon recalled; "he laughed — it was war."[37]

In this war, however, the JCMA rapidly gained the upper hand because of its ability to marshal activist support among High Church clerics. While the SPG began the 1890s with falling revenue all along the line, by the middle of the decade CMS organizing secretaries noted that the SPG exhibited growing activity and an adoption of successful CMS methods. To a substantial degree, even biased observers had largely to credit the activism of the JCMA with these advances.[38] This performance intensified the conviction among members of the SPG's Standing Committee that the JCMA could not be ignored. In 1898, three years after federation, the JCMA claimed forty-eight Associations and 2,500 members; by 1900 the number had grown to seventy Associations with a membership of 3,800.[39] Under pressure the SPG Standing Committee agreed (much against Tucker's historical inclination) to a series of concessions: to set up the Junior Clergy's children's organization, the King's Messengers, on de-centralized diocesan lines and in cooperation with parochial Church work; to grant the JCMA a federation secretary, who would control their funds; and to establish organizational links between SPG Committees and the King's Messengers.[40] Shortly afterwards, at the second conference of the Federation of the JCMA, John Ellison triumphantly reported that under "steady *constitutional* pressure" and "loyal devotion to the venerable Society," the Standing Committee had consented to changes that amounted to "a great day for all of us who year after year have been working . . . for S.P.G. reform. . . . It was not merely that the resolutions were carried, but they were carried without any serious opposition."[41] The momentum of the JCMA was growing, and while it never made the mistake of public partisan attacks, its triumphal air sat poorly with the "old Brigade."[42]

---

37. Bunyon, "Notes on Children's Work."

38. H. Percy Grubb (Metropolitan District, Essex, and Channel Islands), *Association Secretaries' Reports, 1892*, p. 1, CMS Archives, G/AZ 1/4, no. 123A, and J. E. Brenan (Southern District), *Association Secretaries' Reports, 1896*, p. 8, CMS Archives, G/AZ 1/7, no. 68.

39. John Ellison to the Federation of the JCMA, presidential address, 11 May 1898, in Minutes of JCMA Conferences, USPG Archives, X 540; Aubrey B. Mynors to "Dear Sir," 2 May 1900, USPG Archives, H 2.

40. "Résumé of the Proceedings of the Sub-Committee . . . held at the S.P.G. House . . . ," [12 Nov. 1896], USPG Archives, H 2.

41. "Résumé of Proceeding of Conference of Delegates held at Leeds . . . ," 21 Nov. 1896, USPG Archives, H 2.

42. "Meeting of the Conference of Delegates," 16 Nov. 1898, in Minutes of JCMA Conferences,

One of the chief difficulties for the JCMA, however, was that its ideological emphasis on clerical precedence militated against an alliance between women and younger clerics. As the battle between "progressive" junior clergy and traditionalists at the SPG spread, women's activity within the SPG advanced along the lines of opportunity opened up by the party fissure. As the SPG "old Brigade" sought to fend off the younger clergy, the SPG Ladies Association — previously ignored and marginalized — was built up as a valuable auxiliary. As Ellison sought to absorb women's work under the JCMA, the act of defending the honor of underappreciated women became tactically useful; and as the women became valuable allies, Tucker strengthened their hand, adopting the magazine published by SPG women for children as the official children's magazine and stalling the organization of diocesan children's work.[43] Furthermore, SPG women gained clerical supporters, particularly in London, where contact with SPG home organization was more influenced by female voluntarism. E. N. Powell, Chairman of the London Junior Clergy, urged against displacing women, as this would do a "gross injustice" to the female pioneers of children's work who had poured substantial amounts of personal money into the effort. By 1897 a state of divided opinion reigned. Some wanted a coalition and a mixed committee of men and women. Others believed the claims made by women to equal governance over the work were too difficult to swallow and would result in intractable problems, believed inevitable on "mixed" committees.[44] The firm stance of the SPG women and the secretariat, as well as the position of the more cosmopolitan London JCMA, forced the JCMA Federation to agree to an amalgamation of children's work that embraced diocesan organization but gave women prominent positions of power, liberalizing gender politics within High Church organizations throughout the country.[45] In the clash of the new and old guards at SPG, women turned out to be unexpected beneficiaries, demonstrating the complex relationship of gender, belief, and party politics within the Church.

The issue of who controlled the children's work of the SPG was but a surface element of the deeper struggle for control of the SPG. The opposition to Tucker

---

USPG Archives, X 540; [Lord] S[tanmore]. (Arthur Hamilton-Gordon) to Tucker, n.d., USPG Archives, H 2.

43. Ellison to Tucker, 31 Mar. 1897, USPG Archives, H 2; "Junior Work. SPG," memorandum, USPG Archives, X 557a.

44. Minutes of the London Junior Clergy Missionary Association, 26 Mar. and 9 Apr. 1897, USPG Archives, X 539.

45. "Meeting of the Conference of Delegates," in Minutes of JCMA Conferences, 5 May 1897, USPG Archives, X 540. Named "The Children of the Church — King's Messengers," the new organization was staffed predominantly by female volunteers, led by Bunyon as editor. *Children of the Church — King's Messengers, Report 1899*, USPG Archives, X 557a.

was formidable because it included not only those activists at the JCMA who desired to oust Tucker in the name of advanced Anglo-Catholicism but also more mainstream High Churchmen who criticized the SPG for its coldness and inefficiency. In 1897 Henry H. Montgomery, the bishop of Tasmania, added his voice to that of Adelbert Anson and others and asserted that Tucker was so temperamentally unsuited to a position that required warmth and enthusiasm, as well as competence and resolve, that he must be ejected. Broad-based opposition to Tucker led to a petition sent to Archbishop Temple in 1897 asking for Tucker's removal, but the combination of Tucker's loyal supporters, Temple's well-known avoidance of difficult decisions, and the general observance in the Church of England of Archbishop Tait's maxim that "only time or death can mend some matters," worked to save Tucker one last time. Nevertheless, committed missionary supporters such as Montgomery — himself a public-school intimate of the inner-ecclesiastical circles surrounding Archbishops Benson and Temple as well as a vigorous advocate of missions in Australia and the Pacific — were increasingly feeling that "about S.P.G. — I groan — I lament — I despair."[46]

By the turn of the century JCMA members had come to dominate key areas of SPG operation, particularly home organization.[47] Even more galling for Tucker was the fact that JCMA men had come to have an uncontrollable influence on the Standing Committee and seemed to have secured the power to select Tucker's successor. Given this situation, Tucker felt it his duty to warn Randall Davidson, as one of the bishops demonstrating an interest in the SPG, of the state that he felt had come to characterize the SPG Standing Committee:

> There has been for the past five or six years a steady deterioration in the personnel of the Committee. Those come in to whom it is an advertisement to get on the Committee & they bring others in. They are not numerous but a compact body, always in attendance & keen just on their own designs. They get their way too often because the better class do not come to contend with them but only call them Vulgar.[48]

As Tucker approached retirement after twenty years as SPG secretary, an atmosphere of bitterness polarized the Society. But High Churchmen of a variety of persuasions were already constructing a new cloak for the SPG, and it was

46. Montgomery to Randall Davidson, 12 July 1899, Davidson Papers, vol. 519, fols. 244-47.
47. In 1900 half of the twelve members of the Home Organisation Sub-Committee of the SPG were among the most aggressive JCMA "progressives" of a few years before: Bell, Ellison, Hassard, Isaacs, Jackson, and Neligan. "Draft Report of the Home Organisation Sub-Committee," 21 Dec. 1899, in Rough Minutes of the Home Organisation Committee, USPG Archives, H 137.
48. Tucker to [Davidson], 15 Mar. 1901, Davidson Papers, vol. 68, fol. 221.

with the cloth woven by the JCMA that the revitalized SPG of the Edwardian period was to cover itself.

Imperial Service and the Bid for Anglican Unification

In the 1890s the plans of activist junior clergy to renovate the SPG were only partially successful, but they nevertheless animated a good deal of new High Church interest in the foreign missions of the Church. Both moderate High Churchmen and evangelicals witnessed the growth of JCMA activism with some alarm because of traditional Anglo-Catholic hostility to the operation of foreign missions through voluntary societies. But two developments transformed the atmosphere. One was the appropriation of the language of efficiency and "mission science" that characterized the SVMU by activists in the JCMA; the other was the embrace of an explicit and enthusiastic missionary imperialism by many High Church "progressives." The SPG had always more closely aligned its ideology with that of the formal British Empire than had the evangelical societies, playing heavily upon its contribution to "the spiritual side of the Imperial shield . . . [and] showing what has been done towards the building of the Empire 'on the best and surest foundations.'"[49] However, the imperialism that the JCMA adopted in the 1890s was unprecedented both in its vigor and in the positive program around which it was constructed. The particular advantage the JCMA had in adopting a strident imperial rhetoric was its capacity — with deep connections to the long-standing SPG message about its unique duty to colonists and the frontiers of the empire — to reconcile more traditionalist supporters to the JCMA program while also drawing on a rising popular enthusiasm to extend SPG support beyond its historic base.

The imperial tone adopted by the JCMA was not unique in the missionary movement of the 1890s and was echoed in the evangelical student movement represented by the SVMU. Missionary propaganda across the denominations embraced a core message that foreign peoples, not only those specially commissioned set of populations within the empire but also the rest of the world, needed the assistance of white, Anglo-Saxon missionary tutors for some stretch of time to achieve both salvation and the healthy societies necessary to deliver worldly advantages and general happiness.[50] The attitude of John Mott at the

---

49. Pascoe, *Two Hundred Years of the SPG*, ix.

50. On the specific missionary presentation of Africa as a site for colonial reform, see Annie E. Coombes, *Reinventing Africa: Museums, Material Culture, and Popular Imagination in Late Victorian and Edwardian England* (New Haven: Yale University Press, 1994), 176-78.

This 1920 cartoon from the *New York Tribune* inspired by the Quadrennial Conference at Des Moines, Iowa, of the international Student Volunteer Movement for Foreign Missions captures the ambition, tone, and vision of the mature Anglo-American Student Volunteer Movement. From Student Volunteer Movement Archives, Record Group No. 42, Special Collections, Yale Divinity School Library.

1902 Toronto Student Volunteer Movement conference is indicative of an easy acceptance of a general sort of Anglo-American missionary imperialism that saw the advance of Christianity as tied to "the great British Empire and the Republic of America." In this style of rhetoric, much in keeping with the ambitious and self-important temper of the student movement itself, the Anglo-Saxon nations particularly would introduce civilization to the "depressed and neglected races" to achieve the evangelization of the world.[51] Such rhetoric flowed easily in the late 1890s and meshed effortlessly with the older evangelical tendency to speak in military metaphors of assault, territorial conquest, and "triumphant warfare in these distant, difficult fields."[52] Thus SVMU leader Donald Fraser, a Scottish Free Churchman, could unselfconsciously proclaim at the 1906 Nashville SVM conference that "I am a loyal Briton, and I am proud of the high imperial destiny of our nation, for I see that the result of its occupation of Central Africa was the healing of Africa's open sore."[53] However, such attitudes were greeted with repugnance by many continental observers, especially German pietists such as Gustav Warneck, who emphasized sober assessment, moderate means, and Christian humility, and who for these reasons rejected the watchword of the Student Volunteer Movement.[54] The leaders of the SVMU were sensitive to such criticisms, and by 1906, Frank Lenwood on tour in China and India was expressing intense doubts about the beneficence of an empire that was clearly not operating on Christian lines.[55] The concept of racial and civilizational hierarchies structured missionary strategies for dealing with colonial governments — primarily in the form of ongoing demands in the name of international humanitarianism that governments fairly carry out the responsibilities of rule.[56] However, because of ongoing anxieties about imperial injustices, the evangelical language of empire and conquest, while used by many,

51. Quoted in Phillips, "China Missions," 102. Similarly Eugene Stock enjoined all students "in the British Empire and America" to rise in support of the movement. *Missionary Conference, 1900,* 1:58.

52. Basil Mathews, *John R. Mott: World Citizen* (London: SCM, 1934), 224.

53. Quoted in Phillips, "Changing Attitudes," 136.

54. As early as the 1888 London conference, Continental delegates complained that English-speaking missionary enthusiasts were obsessed with quick results, impressive statistics, and publicity. In 1897 and 1900 Warneck assaulted the SVM watchword as rash, exaggerated, self-righteous, and arrogant. Hutchison, *Errand to the World,* 134-35.

55. Frank and Gertrude Lenwood, Mission Tour Circulars, 26 Feb. 1908, Agra, CWM Archives (LMS), Home: Personal, Box 7, folder 6.

56. Brian Stanley, "Church, State, and the Hierarchy of 'Civilization': The Making of the 'Missions and Governments' Report at the World Missionary Conference, Edinburgh 1910," in *The Imperial Horizons of British Protestant Missions, 1880-1914,* ed. Andrew Porter (Grand Rapids: Eerdmans, 2003), 80-81.

was seldom extended to create concrete metropolitan programs for imperial engagement beyond lobbying for indigenous rights and educational provision.[57] The CMS, for example, never developed procedures in England to prepare its missionaries for imperial service and, while taking advantage of imperial rhetoric, it tended to act opportunistically in its relations with imperial authorities.

The SPG, however, under the influence of the JCMA, forged a new vision of "imperial Christianity" in its quest for motivation, purpose, and unity. The highly pointed rhetoric and concrete planning to achieve imperial engagement by the Church of England was a unique characteristic of the program of the JCMA in the missionary movement. While the evidence does not suggest that the JCMA began its organizational life with a particularly focused imperial program, and while earlier Anglo-Catholic mission theory leaned strongly towards indigenization, the presumption of the utility of imperial opportunity to mission had always been present in Westcott's thought. By 1897, when Bishop Henry H. Montgomery of Tasmania first addressed the Conference of the Federation of the JCMA, a coherent imperial vision was crystallizing in the JCMA.[58] High Church bishops in the mission field and in England were deeply involved in the life of elites and processes of governance and, like Bishop C. P. Scott of North China, were more apt than evangelicals to engage in enthusiastic imperial rhetoric regarding British naval expansion in places such as the Far East.[59] The emphasis of the JCMA on a strong and unified imperial Church combined easily with the growing sense that the empire required reform and reinvigoration. And perhaps most importantly, High Church missions seemed to need some cause to generate an enthusiasm comparable to that achieved by evangelicals through theology and partisanship.

In the mid-1890s the JCMA rapidly developed imperial rationales for missionary action. As early as 1896, JCMA members began plans for a foreign service order by which clergy, even if not committing to a life of missionary sacrifice, might serve the empire in colonial chaplaincies and other imperial appointments. By 1898 John Ellison based his presidential address to the JCMA delegates at the Federation conference on a vision of "a Missionary Empire," in which, as Bishop Henry H. Montgomery had articulated a few years earlier, a system of proselytizing at every level could turn even the imperial labor traffic into an opportunity for sanctifying the empire.[60] The goal

57. On the highwater of missionary imperial rhetoric in the 1890s, as well as reservation about it among many missionaries, see Greenlee and Johnston, *Good Citizens,* chap. 2.

58. Speech of Montgomery to the Federation of JCMA, 5 May 1897, in Minutes of JCMA Conferences, USPG Archives, X 540.

59. Greenlee and Johnston, *Good Citizens,* 104.

60. Montgomery, *Light of Melanesia,* 250-51.

was to extend "the missionary vocation" beyond "certain exceptional types of character," to regularize it as a part of Anglican ministry, and to extend imperial opportunity to larger and larger numbers of young clergy. Only then could progress toward "liberty, and truth, and justice, and love" as universal experience grow. For "[w]ith larger ideas of what the British Empire means," Ellison enjoined the delegates, "there have come larger ideas of what the work of the English Church in the Empire means, and what the commission of an English priest means."[61]

In part, this striking rhetoric was the reflection of a larger wave of imperial enthusiasm spreading through the Church of England. This was exemplified by the pronouncements of another returned Australian bishop, the liberal Low Church supporter of learned university Anglicanism, Alfred Barry, who argued the "unexampled expansion of commerce, dominion, intellectual and moral civilization which . . . has been granted to the English-speaking race" needed to be unified through ecclesiastical cooperation to create not a "spiritual Empire" but a "free spiritual Federation."[62] Ellison suggested that, as other professions were becoming less insular and more imperial, advancement of the Church's imperial duty required the clerical profession to follow suit. However, while such sentiments could also be heard in the environs of the evangelical missionary societies, most often they were articulated by lay supporters and local speakers, rather more seldom by society officials. While evangelicals certainly did not ignore imperial themes, they had other means in their repertoire for stimulating enthusiasm for foreign missions. In an important way Ellison's rhetoric operated as a means to appropriate the enthusiasm of holiness theology; in order to do so, High Churchmen had to have recourse to another ideology that could generate enthusiasm and interest, and the growing force of popular imperialism offered that opportunity.

The High Church style of Anglicanism focused on ecclesiastical authority. This suggests that the student movement, with its riot of individual initiative, represented an unlikely place for the origins of High Church imperial Christianity. Indeed, as indicated earlier in this chapter, the deeper source of High Church student enthusiasm, other than the imperial excitements of the 1890s, was B. F. Westcott's advocacy of foreign missions, based in scholarly interests in the early church, which gave missions a new basis of support among High Churchmen who could imagine a re-creation in the empire of ancient missionary success. Westcott was at the forefront of the movement to advance a High

61. Ellison to the Federation of the JCMA, presidential address, 11 May 1898, in Minutes of JCMA Conferences, USPG Archives, X 540.
62. *Ecclesiastical Expansion*, 8, 27.

Church missionary program, and in doing so he linked it to a regeneration of the imperial power of the British nation. Expressing extreme dissatisfaction with the levels of support for foreign missions in England, especially from the "wealthier classes," Westcott in 1888 proposed making foreign missions "central" to normal Church work rather than "supplemental." Insisting that every "progressive people" had been molded by Christianity, Westcott urged that Christian missions were the reparation for imperial sins against the peoples of the world. Furthermore, he asserted, "[t]he National Church is the spiritual organ of the Empire. It expresses the general religious history and character of the English people. . . . It brings to the National Church a responsibility which no other Christian communion can share."[63] This was the source and authority for the program of the JCMA, and when Westcott was elevated to Durham in 1890, he carried his enthusiasm for High Church missions to the episcopal bench, lending weight to the arguments of SPG "progressives."

The proof of the imperial program of the JCMA was that, unlike much other imperial rhetoric, the ideas of Ellison assumed concrete dimensions. In 1898, Ellison unveiled his plans for "Colonial Service," by which he hoped to make a period of work in the empire — particularly its "English-speaking Colonies" — as natural as a period of service in the slums of Leeds or East London. The influence of settlement work was far deeper among High Churchmen than Evangelicals, and the settlement ideology was easily transferred to the imperial sphere. As the cultural practice of "slumming" grew in the 1880s and 1890s among precisely the affluent classes that SPG progressives wanted to engage, the JCMA sought to define positively an imperial "descent" across global, racial, class, and gender boundaries parallel to the practices Seth Koven identifies as central to the transgressive descent urban charity and settlement work represented in this era.[64] Rather than returning from colonial work "empty" and damaged by association with socially suspect missionary evangelism, Ellison — at this time vicar of Windsor and chaplain to the Queen — assured his listeners they would come back, even after short terms of service, "full." This was because the SPG had always maintained an honorable connection to racial and imperial purpose, having "clung to the principle that to keep the white man Christian was just as important a part of the Missionary work of the Church as to convert the coloured man." Ellison insisted, much as those who supported Mission Boards insisted, that erasing the distinction between home and foreign missions was critical to service across colonial, class, and

63. B. F. Westcott, "Board of Missions of the Province of Canterbury. Memorandum on the Responsibility of Churchmen . . . ," 23 Apr. 1888, Benson Papers, vol. 74, fols. 327-28.
64. Koven, *Slumming*, 9-10.

racial boundaries in a world where "the work is one and the Church that is doing the work is one."[65]

The traditions of the SPG fit neatly into this developing set of beliefs, which emphasized the capacity of lay Christian philanthropists and imperialists to affect the world for good. For High Churchmen, the understanding that Western culture often incited evil in and against primitive cultures did not reflexively produce, as it did in ultra-evangelicals such as G. W. Brooke, a desire to create gathered churches safe from Western influence. Instead, it led to the recommendation that the inevitable presence of Western Europeans in the colonial sphere required that they too be properly Christianized to ensure a beneficial influence on the "heathen." This idea was also familiar to CMS leaders, but did not produce a strong program of promoting imperial Christianity. At the JCMA, however, the imperial idea became the heart of its program, resonating with other forms of pro-imperial thinking, most prominently, tariff reform, which argued the social condition of England was dependent on industry and imperial markets.[66] In these associations, which aimed not only at greater strength for England but also at the welfare of imperial subjects, the JCMA was following B. F. Westcott who, rallying students to support the SPG in 1884, enjoined them to share "the destiny of your Church" in taming a provocative heathen primitivism beyond England's shores.[67]

In 1898, following JCMA plans, the archbishops of Canterbury and York appointed a council which, under the guidance of the United Boards of Mission, was to make authoritative calls to young Anglicans for foreign missionary service. The principle of unified "Church Authority" was embodied in the call, and Ellison saw it as essential to the success of the scheme. But he also emphasized that "we want to bring much more into our foreign and missionary work the thought of the responsibility which we owe as patriotic Englishmen to the British Empire." In doing so, the Englishman would be walking in the steps of the apostles; as Paul was a missionary, but still gloried in his Roman citizenship, so too could Englishmen be the heirs of the Roman Empire. Just as importantly, the language of empire was designed to interest the general public more broadly in the work of the Church, a public that might otherwise turn a cold eye on both the Church and its foreign missions. "We must speak out naturally what every one of us believes," Ellison declared to the JCMA delegates, "that missionary work, instead of being the 'fad' of a few pious souls, is the only

65. Ellison to the Federation of the JCMA, presidential address, 11 May 1898, in Minutes of JCMA Conferences, USPG Archives, X 540.

66. Semmel, *Imperialism and Social Reform*, 14-16.

67. Quoted in John Ellison to the Federation of the JCMA, presidential address, 11 May 1898, in Minutes of JCMA Conferences, USPG Archives, X 540.

foundation on which a permanent Empire can be built up in the world."[68] In this way, the imperial bid of the JCMA became the means by which young "modern Tractarians" sought through foreign missions to stir zeal, expand interest, and push forward the interests of the Church and the empire.

Imperial Anglicans and the Church in Greater Britain

On 26 July 1901, Henry Hutchinson Montgomery, the bishop of Tasmania, sent a telegram from Hobart to the archbishop of Canterbury, Frederick Temple, that was composed of one word: Accept.[69] With this, Montgomery became the secretary of the SPG, signaling the victory of "progressives" at the Society and in the student movement, who had fought for a reforming leader. His blueprint called for the SPG to be cast on the efficient and enthusiastic lines of the CMS, and came at the end of a decade of vitality and growth for Evangelical foreign missions. Largely successful in emulating the CMS by reorganizing the publications and management of the Society on more efficient and popular lines, Montgomery saw substantial increases in the income and prestige of the SPG in his first five years. As many organizers and supporters warmly embraced his plan to infuse the Society with an ideal of imperial Christianity, the Society became a leading force in Anglican missions.

Changes at the SPG in the 1890s had led progressives to hope that the Society was entering a new period of growth, but the failure of the SPG Bicentenary in 1901 finally spurred the bishops to support reform. Despite the example of the strikingly successful 1899 CMS Centenary, Henry Tucker had largely ignored the progressives as he planned and executed the SPG Bicentenary. Shunning popular methods, however, meant that when the Society's "dignified" celebration largely failed to meet its fundraising targets, Tucker was again privately pilloried as the embodiment of all that was stale and unproductively traditional in High Church circles.

Bishop Montgomery, a leading critic, and a rising leader of ambitious High Church missions in Australia and the Pacific, where he championed the use of sisterhoods and stronger Western planning and oversight in missions, represented an alternative voice inspired by white colonial Anglicanism. He found natural allies in the JCMA, asserting to its 1897 Federation conference that the battle being fought in Australia between Anglicans and "bitter" Nonconformists

68. Ellison to the Federation of the JCMA, speech, 16 Nov. 1898, in Minutes of JCMA Conferences, USPG Archives, X 540.
69. Montgomery to F. Temple, telegram, 26 July [1901], F. Temple Papers, vol. 49, fol. 96.

demonstrated that those with definite Anglican convictions were desperately needed in the colonies to counter the work of the Salvation Army and other evangelical enthusiasts.[70] Also, the first speaker at the fourth Lambeth Conference, Montgomery lamented to the bishops, assembled from across the world, that when he had arrived in Australia in 1889 "the Church of England was expected to be last in looking after its own people in new mining fields and new settlements. It was not a question of argument, but a settled fact that it was necessary to shew a more eager missionary spirit among our own people." Sentiments such as these characterized a growing feeling of colonial Anglican resurgence, stirred by the 1894 Anglican Missionary Conference, at which Archbishop Temple "fairly blazed, and carried all before him" in a passionate speech advocating overseas missions.[71] But, again, the stumbling block remained the SPG, and in the aftermath of stirring events in England, Montgomery honed the edge of his criticism in correspondence with his old public school friend Randall Davidson, now the bishop of Winchester, to whom he asserted that High Churchmen at the SPG must emulate evangelical Anglicans, for whom foreign missions were "not duty . . . but love — *passion*." Tucker's manner, so stiff and formal, led Montgomery to predict that the SPG Bicentenary would suffer:

> I feel that the year-long festival for S.P.G. will be a grim, cold, virtual failure. Just to think of it! I do believe S.P.G. could now & at once burst its grave clothes, get £30,000 extra next year and rise to £100,000 extra income in 10 years. One expects instead to bear a paltry £10,000 addition next year — and the regular income increased by £1,000! and a report saying how thankful they are & how well they are doing! "Poor S.P.G." that is what one of my Clergy called her yesterday — and he is no C.M.S. man. . . . But what are you to do for a mother who seems to have become dull and heavy?[72]

For both Montgomery and Davidson, adoring students of B. F. Westcott at Harrow, the possibilities of charisma in High Church mission were evident, and Davidson, who had risen to nearly unprecedented influence as trusted secretary to Archbishops Benson and Temple, as well as being the beloved chaplain and confidant to Queen Victoria, became a champion of reform when Montgomery's prediction proved correct.

70. Montgomery to the Federation of the JCMA, speech, 5 May 1897, in Minutes of JCMA Conferences, USPG Archives, X 540.

71. "My Three Lambeth Conferences: 1897, 1908, 1920," Montgomery Papers, MS 4541, fols. 3, 60.

72. Montgomery to Davidson, 12 July 1899, Davidson Papers, vol. 519, fols. 244-47.

Henry Tucker, through steady competence, astute politics, and powerful supporters, had survived many years at the SPG. But the failure of the Bicentenary forced retirement on the seventy-one-year-old secretary, for the contrasting success of the CMS Centenary in nationwide impact and financial achievement was a humiliation. After a week of joyous celebration in April of 1899, the CMS counted its Centenary gifts and found itself £212,297 richer. In the twelve years between 1887 and 1899, CMS annual income had advanced from about £200,000 to over £300,000 and the Society cleared its debts as it entered the new century.[73] CMS propagandists painted the 1890s as a decade of glorious success, capped by a striking celebration portending a new century of unparalleled missionary advance. In contrast, the SPG could claim only modest gains. Between 1887 and 1900, the SPG increased its income by a mere £10,000, to a yearly total of about £100,000, and it was only able to raise one-fifth of the Bicentenary Fund target of £250,000.[74] Claims that the Boer War had harmed fundraising rang hollow as far away as Tasmania, from where Montgomery lamented that "the results of the Bicentenary effort have been a fiasco, and . . . a very strong effort must be made to bring in fresh blood and to put S.P.G. into its right position."[75]

The failure of the SPG Bicentenary was a pivotal moment, for it finally catalyzed action. In the wake of the Bicentenary the bishops commended Tucker for all his considerable past labors, but they insisted that he must now go. Following several antagonistic meetings, "full of painful things," Tucker tendered his resignation at a Standing Committee meeting on 14 March 1901.[76] But core tensions between younger progressive members and older established ones were still live, particularly over seemingly mundane local issues of cooperation in Manchester between the junior clergy and High Church women.[77] Traditionalists like Sir Charles Turner and Lord Stanmore, opposing cooperation as an insidious decentralization of power that benefited the JCMA, faced off against the reformers, who saw cooperation both as efficient and as a return to diocesan organization under the proper authority of a bishop. In the few weeks after Tucker's resignation, Turner and Stanmore used the Manchester controversy to

---

73. £65,616 was collected between 1896 and 1898, £146,681 in the Centenary year. Stock, *History of the CMS*, 4:14-16.

74. Pascoe, *Two Hundred Years of the SPG*, 832d and table p. 832.

75. Montgomery to F. Temple, 17 June 1900, F. Temple Papers, vol. 49, fols. 51-56.

76. Tucker to Randall Davidson, 15 Mar. 1901, Davidson Papers, vol. 68, fol. 221; J. F. Moor to Temple, 10 Mar. 1901, F. Temple Papers, vol. 49, fols. 4-5.

77. "Report of the Special Committee on the Relations between the W.M.A. and the S.P.G.," 2 Apr. 1903, in Minutes of the Women's Home Organisation Advisory Group, USPG Archives, CWW 71.

seize the initiative, leading the SPG Standing Committee to declare the cooperation "illegal," instead of putting the divisive issue on hold until the Society could appoint a new secretary, as the JCMA recommended. As JCMA members complained they had been unjustly "jockeyed" by a duplicitous clique, the bishops, led by Archbishop Frederick Temple, intervened, asserting their authority to choose the new secretary.[78]

The bishop of Newcastle, Edgar Jacob, a new episcopal supporter of foreign missions and outspoken in his approval of the SVMU, wrote enthusiastically to Archbishop Temple that Tucker's resignation presented prayed-for opportunities, but that past mistakes regarding the SPG, such as "the policy of promoting an undersecretary," must be avoided. "An ecclesiastical statesman who can inspire offers" was now needed, one "who will attract young men to the Mission field, & in sympathetic touch with the Church at home & abroad & in the confidence of the missionaries."[79] Temple agreed, and Bishop Davidson joined the cabal.[80] Episcopal control over the selection of the new SPG secretary was in reality the only solution, given the enormous rifts that had opened at the SPG. The Standing Committee had become so fractious that even old guard members and Henry Tucker himself, fearful of a JCMA coup that would place in power exactly those younger clergy whom he so despised, pleaded for a prudent episcopal committee to bring forward suitable candidates.[81]

The SPG's troubles drew the entire Church into a reconsideration of the importance of foreign missions and illustrated the polarization of forces that was to be at the center of Anglican missionary dynamics in the Edwardian age. The attempt of Lord Stanmore and the "old Brigade" to defend traditional attitudes against the determination of the leaders of the JCMA, who wanted to change the "high and dry" reputation of the SPG, led to a standoff.[82] Here in a nutshell was the conflict between older conservatives — with their emphasis

78. John Ellison to Randall Davidson, 30 Mar. 1901, Davidson Papers, vol. 68, fols. 235-38.

79. Jacob stated that if his friend John Selwyn, the second bishop of Melanesia, had in 1879 been appointed SPG secretary instead of Tucker, income would have been double its present level, and far more men in service. Temple commented, "I agree with him." Jacob to Temple, 9 Mar. 1901, F. Temple Papers, vol. 49, fols. 2-3.

80. Davidson to Temple, 6 Apr. 1901, F. Temple Papers, vol. 49, fols. 8-9; Jacob to Davidson, 21 Mar. 1901, Davidson Papers, vol. 68, fols. 225-26.

81. Tucker feared in particular Ellison's selection, who had been suggested by Anglo-Catholic Bishop Louis George Mylne, formerly of Bombay. With his aggressive church politics and loud imperial rhetoric Ellison had "made himself prominent on platforms" but was "ignorant & quite unfit to deal with the foreign work which is the chief duty of the Secretary." Tucker to [Davidson], 15 Mar. 1901, Davidson Papers, vol. 68, fol. 221; Edgar Jacob, bishop of Newcastle to Frederick Temple, 19 Mar. 1901, F. Temple Papers, vol. 49, fols. 6-7.

82. Ellison to Davidson, 9 Apr. 1901, Davidson Papers, vol. 68, fols. 241-42.

on authority, orthodoxy, and reserve — and younger progressives — with their zeal for inspiration, innovation, and enthusiasm — that would arise repeatedly in the coming decade across the missionary spectrum. On 18 April 1901, after a delicate backroom campaign in which both Ellison and Tucker, pressured by the bishops, rallied their supporters, the Standing Committee officially accepted an episcopal committee of selection unencumbered by representatives of either party. The road was open for a call to the best possible candidate.[83] But paranoia was so rife, especially among junior clergy that were not a part of the close-knit London clerical community, that some threatened to "transfer their allegiance to CMS" if an unsatisfactory choice resulted.[84]

The bishops considering the matter decided that one of their own number would be necessary to reunite a society so completely divided. Colonial bishops, in particular, had close links to missionary work and also possessed the episcopal authority to command respect among High Churchmen. Bishop Montgomery of Tasmania, with his known missionary zeal, his links to the junior SPG clergy, and his close friendship with Randall Davidson, was an obvious choice, especially considering the barrage of letters advocating reform that he sent to England following Tucker's resignation.[85] Montgomery's model for change was the CMS, and he praised the "living devotion" of the CMS to Randall Davidson, proclaiming it an exemplar that "our High Church certainly may well admire."[86] Such appreciation of evangelical feeling, and desire to infuse High Church circles with it, was natural in a man whose father had been a prominent, influential Evangelical lay supporter of the CMS. First educated in an evangelical boarding school, next trained at Harrow as a "Broad Church Evangelical" by F. W. Farrar, finally prepared for ordination by the pious, conservative High Church leader Dr. Charles Vaughan, Master of the Temple, Montgomery's diverse Anglican background, and his service in the 1870s as personal secretary to A. P. Stanley, led him to embrace Stanley's commitment to the ideal of a comprehensive national church and afterwards pursue unity in the Anglican Communion. But Montgomery had other useful associations too, both Anglo-Indian — he was

83. Tucker to Davidson, 31 Mar. 1901; Ellison to Davidson, 9 Apr. 1901; Samuel Bickersteth to Ellison, 10 Apr. 1901; E[llison]. to Davidson, 19 Apr. 1901, Davidson Papers, vol. 68, fols. 239-40, 241-42, 245-48, 252-53.

84. J[ohn]. H. E[llison]. to Davidson, 27 Apr. [1901], Davidson Papers, vol. 68, fols. 258-59. A gag order on the JCMA men on the SPG Standing Committee compounded paranoia. [M. R. Neligan to Ellison, 25 Apr. 1901; Ellison to Randall Davidson, 29 Apr. 1901, Davidson Papers, vol. 68, fols. 260-61 and 267-68.]

85. M[aud]. M[ontgomery]., *Bishop Montgomery: A Memoir* (Westminster, UK: SPG, 1933), 47-48.

86. Montgomery to Davidson, 12 July 1899, Davidson Papers, vol. 519, fols. 244-47.

born in India to Robert Montgomery, Indian Army officer and English hero of the 1857 rebellion who subsequently served as Lieutenant Governor of the Punjab — and progressive — he later worked through Harrow connections to assignment as a curate for Farrar, popular novelist and increasingly famous as a moderate Churchman of advanced but pious views.[87] And his analysis, which placed all the blame for the troubles of the SPG on Tucker, was beguiling, for it made the process of transformation seem elementary. Montgomery wrote to a number of bishops in this vein, advocating that someone of real enthusiasm should be appointed. These letters were evidence to the committee of six bishops that Montgomery himself was the perfect candidate for the difficult position.

The telegram Montgomery received in Tasmania on 6 June 1901, calling him to lead the SPG, gave him the commission to completely renovate the Society. He agreed, writing to Temple that he understood "[t]hat you do not wish the post of the new Secretary to be only what it has been — but to be something much more forceful and if possible more influential."[88] Montgomery had reservations about abandoning his colonial bishopric, but he was assured that the new post would be truly "episcopal work" with wide power, latitude, and support from the English bishops.[89] The position of SPG secretary, he concluded, "<u>may be made</u> a post of infinitely greater importance than work in Tasmania . . . but such a work has to be <u>created</u>."[90] With the encouragement of brother bishops, Montgomery became the willing architect of ambitious plans for the SPG.

For supporters on either side of the conflict, the character and program of the secretary determined the character of the Society. Not surprisingly, Montgomery was not Tucker's ideal choice. In a "full and frank" letter to Randall Davidson, Tucker expounded on necessary secretarial qualities and delineated the hopes of the "old Brigade": not a bishop called home from the field, as the SPG already had twenty-four retired colonial bishops on its books as vice-presidents

87. Montgomery married Farrar's daughter Maud in 1881. Geoffrey Stephens, *H. H. Montgomery — The Mutton Bird Bishop*, University of Tasmania Occasional Paper 39 (Hobart: University of Tasmania, 1985), 1-2; Henry H. Montgomery, "Robert Montgomery of the Punjab. From 1839 to 1857," TS, Robert Montgomery Family Correspondence, 1842-87, vol. 2, Asia, Pacific and Africa Collections, MS Eur.D.1019/2, British Library, London (hereafter cited as Robert Montgomery Family Papers). For details on Montgomery's early life, see the biography of his more famous son, Nigel Hamilton, *Monty: The Making of a General, 1887-1942* (London: Hamish Hamilton, 1981), 14-18.

88. Montgomery to Temple, 17 June 1901, F. Temple Papers, vol. 49, fols. 51-56.

89. Fearing criticism of abandoning difficult colonial work, Montgomery requested an "order" from the bishops. Montgomery to Temple, telegram, 6 June 1901, and Temple to Montgomery, telegram, n.d., F. Temple Papers, vol. 49, fols. 25-26.

90. Montgomery to Temple, 17 June 1901, F. Temple Papers, vol. 49, fols. 51-56.

and that fact had been used very effectively by evangelical controversialists against it in the past; a man who must focus assiduously on the foreign work and be reconciled to a vocation of routine, detail, and drudgery; an employee satisfied with a modest salary of around £600 per annum, as experience had shown supporters would allow no higher.[91] The traditionalists found the enthusiasm of the JCMA uncouth, and they rejected the idea of the integration of missionary activity with the concerns of the home church, as well as the principle of orchestrated, centralized organization. Tucker clung to an orthodox, respectable mid-Victorian vision of foreign mission.[92] Yet five days after his letter was written, the offer for the SPG secretaryship went to Montgomery.

John Ellison and the JCMA had won the battle, using the argument that matters were moving too quickly in the home church to return to Tucker's old sternly held principles. "In view of the present position," Ellison wrote to Davidson, "and the way in which things are coming together — CMS, SPG, Board of Missions, Council for Service Abroad &c., it seems to me that the main interest for the next year or two will be at home."[93] His emphasis was on renovating the domestic base of High Church missions and promoting unified action by the corporate Church. But a number of objections to the JCMA program emerged, reflected in the criticisms that met the announcement of the "call" to Montgomery. Some believed the secretary should be an unsalaried enthusiast of private means, others complained that any increase in the salary of the secretary was "misappropriation of Missionary Funds," still more objected to a colonial bishop being recalled to mundane home work. F. D. Cremer, Montgomery's own commissary, reported that he was "horrified" that Montgomery had not refused the appointment, because it was sure to destroy the bishop, a good and visionary man, and lead to other colonial bishops abandoning their posts. Yet Archbishop Temple insisted that enthusiasm was "priceless" when "persistently the missionary feeling is welling in the Church of England."[94] In the end, the Incorporated Members of the SPG, with the bishops appearing

91. Tucker explicitly recommended against John Ellison and Samuel Bickersteth, instead suggesting the solid T. H. Dodson, principal of St. Paul's College, Burgh, Lincs. Tucker to Davidson, 1 June 1901, Davidson Papers, vol. 68, fols. 279-81.

92. Tucker's obituary emphasizes his command of the SPG, commenting "in the great majority of cases under discussion Prebendary Tucker meant to have his way and had it." This authority meant he "had been not merely secretary, but a sort of incarnation of the society since 1879." "Prebendary Tucker," Times, 7 Jan. 1902.

93. Ellison to Davidson, 5 May 1901, Davidson Papers, vol. 68, fols. 273-74.

94. John Percival, bishop of Hereford to Temple, 14 Apr. 1901, R. S. Hassard to Temple, 27 Apr. 1901, Cremer to Temple, 10 July 1901, Herbert Macklin to Temple, 22 July 1901, Temple to Herbert Macklin, 14 Aug. 1901, F. Temple Papers, vol. 49, fols. 15-16, 19-20, 63-66, 78-79, 103-8.

in force, elected Montgomery with only minor objections — largely because the bishops had secured the loyalty of the most important group of potential dissenters, the junior clergy. When a critic — "who talked like a dissenting minister" — launched a campaign to reverse Montgomery's appointment by voting to slash his salary, it was easily defeated by an alliance of bishops and junior clergy.[95] The issue was really won by Archbishop Temple's strong presentation of the appropriateness of placing a bishop in the secretaryship: Montgomery was to "exercise 'quasi-episcopal' control," which would find great scope in "Government" of the worldwide Church.[96] The bishops had carried the day on the specific platform of using the SPG to unite the entire Church under Montgomery's reforming leadership.

Immediately upon his election, Montgomery announced that he had been commissioned to lead the SPG on a "new departure" designed to make it "a potent engine for developing the Church and for bringing its Branches into closer union." The Church as a whole was Montgomery's focus, and the SPG was a means of reviving strength at a time when many were coming to doubt the Church's resilience in the face of modern challenges. On a more mundane level, Montgomery had various practical agendas: to make SPG publications superior to those of the CMS and put them at the cutting edge of Church opinion; to emphasize spirituality at the SPG and make Delahay Street "the warmest spot in London"; to boost cooperation with High Church junior clergy and women and create a sophisticated SPG administration; to build a new headquarters building and attach it to Church House in Westminster.[97] But at the heart of his program for the unification of the Church was an overarching imperial principle.

The assertion that the SPG was a peculiarly imperial institution had a long history and was commonplace among its supporters certainly by the 1840s, while Anglo-Catholics who supported the "venerable society" cherished the idea of the SPG as an agency of Christian reunion in the empire.[98] Yet Montgomery's program transcended the simple reflex sentiments of attachment to

95. Ellison recalled that the vote was "200 & something to 140 or so." Ellison to Davidson, 15 Nov. 1901, Davidson Papers, vol. 68, fols. 310-11. In the pinch the "old Brigade," including Sir Charles Turner and Canon Stenning, rallied to support the bishops. John Wogan Festing, bishop of St. Albans to Davidson, 1 Nov. 1901, Davidson Papers, vol. 68, fols. 294-97.

96. Ellison to Davidson, 1 Nov. 1901, Davidson Papers, vol. 68, fols. 302-5.

97. Montgomery to the Deans, circular letter, [Autumn 1901], F. Temple Papers, vol. 49, fols. 115-16.

98. See, for example, the speech of the Marquess of Cholmondeley (George Horatio Cholmondeley) to the Chester SPG Association, 26 Sept. 1842, in Minutes of the Chester District SPG Association, USPG Archives, X 342, and the pamphlet, *Why Do We Support the S.P.G. as a Missionary Society of the Church of England?*, no. 3, enclosure in letter of 5 Dec. 1892, CMS Archives, G/AC 4/11/2083a.

empire that pervaded the SPG, casting it as an auxiliary force to the central powers of diocesan expansion. Montgomery's Anglo-Indian background and subsequent posting for twelve years of work in the white settlement colony of Tasmania led him to develop an elevated view of British imperial power.[99] His plan was for the SPG to become something like "a sort of Foreign Office" for the Church and establish first "the same course as that taken up in these days by England towards her Colonies — to give ungrudging praise, to claim the privilege of giving help, not calling for it," and thus binding "England . . . [to] her Colonies to herself by what seems to be an indestructible chain."[100] Montgomery had arrived with an ambitious vision for the Anglican Communion, writing in a letter to his father-in-law, F. W. Farrar, now the dean of Canterbury,

> I can truly say that there is no post in all the world I would rather hold. To create a sort of foreign secretaryship of Anglican missions with a bishop at its head, to be a referee and guide in all Greater Britain questions. The outlook is terrifying in its possibilities. Had one the gifts, one could almost transform the general ideals of the Church and make them actually embrace the world. It strikes me at times as more Pauline in scope than that of any bishop in the Anglican communion, and therefore most episcopal.[101]

Montgomery's ambitious plans for the SPG had been brewing at least since his appointment in 1889, by Archbishop Benson, as bishop of Tasmania, where Montgomery and his family took to the rough environment, intent on "civilizing" both settlers and indigenous peoples. His vision for the SPG was related to a personal family vision, especially involving his sons, whom he counseled "whatever professions they chose, to put God first in their lives and to strive to serve the empire."[102] His "dream" for his eldest son, a bluff and accomplished horseman, was that he "might enter some sort of African Civil Service under Rhodes & Co. The field is glorious."[103] The enthusiasm Montgomery showed both for missions and for empire was widely known and was not idiosyncratic. His imperial fervor came to maturity in the 1890s, when public support for

---

99. Henry H. Montgomery, "Robert Montgomery of the Punjab. From 1839 to 1857," TS, Robert Montgomery Family Papers.

100. Montgomery to the Deans, circular letter, [Autumn 1901], F. Temple Papers, vol. 49, fols. 115-16.

101. M[aud]. M[ontgomery]., *Montgomery*, 49.

102. M[aud]. M[ontgomery]., *Montgomery*, 28-33, 45. See also the family life of Montgomery from the point of view of his son Bernard Law Montgomery, *The Memoirs of Field-Marshal the Viscount Montgomery of Alamein, K.G.* (Cleveland, OH: World Publishing, 1958), chap. 1.

103. Montgomery to Davidson, 28 May 1899, Davidson Papers, vol. 519, fols. 240-43.

Henry Hutchinson and Maud Montgomery, outside the Lambeth Palace Library,
1908, at the time of the Pan-Anglican Congress, the crowning organizational
achievement of Montgomery's Secretariat at the SPG.
From the Montgomery Papers, vol. 4541, fol. 72.
Courtesy of the Trustees of Lambeth Palace Library.

imperial ideologies, both in England and in the white-settlement colonies, was arguably at a historic high point. The fulsome optimism that the imperial sphere could help relieve the social problems of an urban industrialized England was supported among the Liberal Imperialists of Lord Rosebery and the ranks of the radical conservative Tariff Reformers under Joseph Chamberlain. Montgomery transferred the assumptions of this "social imperialism" to the Church by arguing that missions could excite denominational unity, defuse party tensions at home, and encourage the acceptance of the status quo in matters of Church authority.[104] But Church leaders had to calculate whether an imperial program advocated by an elite would really elicit wide support in an era in which social elites were everywhere under attack.

At the turn of the century, the riot of patriotic imperial sentiment generated by the Boer War amplified the imperial enthusiasms of the 1890s.[105] In the midst of these passions Montgomery had launched an Australian missionary campaign which, he wrote, left audiences rapt in Adelaide and other Australian cities filled with a new imperial Christian feeling.[106] This enthusiasm, when conveyed to JCMA members, solidified their confidence in the decision of the bishops, and when Montgomery went on to enthuse about his dreams of a ten-year campaign of missionary visits by English delegates to Canada, Australia, and South Africa, the bishops at least knew that they had a leader who could confound charges of High Church missionary languor.

To the progressives of the 1890s, a new era at the SPG seemed at hand, hopefully comparable to the "new era" experienced by the CMS in the previous decade. Montgomery made these plans public with his book *Foreign Missions*, written on his England-bound steamer journey in 1902 from Tasmania. Stating his conviction that "[t]he clergy are officers in an imperial army," he tied his initiatives not just back to the early church but to clerical duty that should "date [its] imperial traditions back to Abraham, 'the father of missionaries.'"[107] Here he also declared that the primary obstacles to missionary success were "party spirit" and a "want of missionary zeal."[108] Both of these, he suggested, could be overcome by "men full of the Imperial spirit, not merely of the empire of

104. On social imperialism as a lens for understanding and prescription for domestic urban anxieties, see John Marriott, *The Other Empire: Metropolis, India and Progress in the Colonial Imagination* (Manchester: Manchester University Press, 2003), 176-81.

105. Eugene Stock remembered that as "the Queen's soldiers flocked to South Africa," missionary supporters also imagined that they might capture and harness similar passions for the empire of Christ. Stock, *History of the CMS*, 4:21.

106. Montgomery to Davidson, 24 May 1900, Davidson Papers, vol. 519, fols. 248-56.

107. Montgomery, *Foreign Missions*, 1-2.

108. Montgomery, *Foreign Missions*, 10.

England, but of something still greater, the empire of Christ."[109] Such attitudes were not isolated or even novel in this era of waxing imperial sentiment, but they held a new significance coming from Montgomery because he sought to institutionalize a reform program that would also be used as a springboard for the imperial idea in the Church.[110] He imagined himself an "Archbishop of Greater Britain," with the "dearest dream to make S.P.G. the 'centre of reconciliation'" in a Church where moderate Churchmen of all parties needed a common focus to strengthen it for expansion on all fronts.[111]

Montgomery instituted a thoroughgoing reform program when he took over the SPG office in January 1902. In one brief statement made to Archbishop Temple, Montgomery very neatly made the scope of his program explicit:

> The work of the new Secretary is practically to re-invent the Society at its headquarters — to give it more humanity, more tenderness, more emotional fervour in the Central Office — and also to adapt it more and more to the pace at which things go now — "telephone pace" in place of "letter pace" — also to realize the conditions of the world and to work more and more on Imperial lines. In fact to bring the S.P.G. up to the force and dimensions of the C.M.S. only upon its own lines.[112]

For Montgomery the theology of Keswick was not essential to missionary enthusiasm; instead, he sought to substitute Anglo-Catholic devotional intensity and imperial fervency in its place. This is evident in an account of his early encounter with the SPG Central office, in which, identifying a lack of "warmth" and "the human element," he determined "[t]o make people realise that nowhere in London could a warmer welcome be expected" and that "[t]he tone of the Office was to be something different from that of a business house: among ourselves a family, with our centre the Chapel."[113] Changing the spiritual culture also involved recognizing the critical role of women in transforming the CMS and the late-century culture of missions, resulting in his insistence

109. Montgomery, *Foreign Missions*, 145.

110. See for an example of the many Christian imperialist visions generated at the time of the Boer War, G. Robert Wynne, *The Church in Greater Britain: The Donnellan Lectures Delivered Before the University of Dublin, 1900-1901* (London: Kegan Paul, Trench, Trübner, 1901), and T. A. Gurney, "Modern Imperialism and Missions," *Church Missionary Intelligencer*, n.s., 27 (July 1902): 481-88.

111. Montgomery to Davidson, 27 May 1901 and 21 July 1901, Davidson Papers, vol. 151, fols. 284-87, 304-5.

112. Montgomery to Temple, 7 June 1901, F. Temple Papers, vol. 49, fols. 30-35.

113. Henry H. Montgomery, "Survey of My Stewardship, 1902-1918," TS, pp. 4-5, USPG Archives, H 3, box 2.

that the women's branch of the SPG be fully and completely integrated into the Society.[114] With the coming of Montgomery the SPG finally embraced the ideal of expanded roles for women that had grown at the CMS, and thus accepted a home strategy based heavily on feminine models of informal sociability.

Montgomery's changes at the SPG, like his election itself, were not effected without friction. When he took over at the SPG, he found a Standing Committee still deadlocked between the forces of Tucker and the forces of Ellison. "So painful were the scenes," Montgomery recalled, "that I began to wonder whether any blessing could come to our deliberations."[115] Montgomery requested assistance from Archbishop Temple to bring peace, but the decade of pressure from reformers and the unmistakable bias of Montgomery toward radical change evidently convinced the leaders of the "old Brigade" that their day had passed, and resignations followed, with reforms coming in their wake.[116] Montgomery changed operations at the SPG London office. Open communication between department heads and with the secretary became the rule, while modern business methods including the use of typewriters and telephones were introduced. He also led the transformation of the publications of the Society. An experienced manager from Spottiswoode publishers was recruited, the existing publications were reworked in more popular form, and a new, serious quarterly review — *The East and the West* — was established under the editorship of Canon Charles Robinson. Montgomery also insisted on reinvigorating the work of the local organizing secretaries. The group was transformed from one that "had no initiative, had no suggestions to offer" into one that was earnest, active, self-motivating, and self-critical. He also led a revolution in the relationship between the SPG and its Women's Mission Association. The WMA became the Committee for Women's Work at the SPG, with a substantial degree of autonomy and influence.[117]

New support registered itself in a rapidly rising level of income. When

114. For details on the negotiations that integrated women's work and Montgomery's role, see Chapter 7.

115. Two old personalities on the Committee "would not brook the leadership of the Secretary, and resented any move upon his own part": Lord Stanmore and Prebendary Berdmore Compton. Committee meetings became "dreadful occasions, not because the opposition was against myself but among different sections of the Committee." Henry H. Montgomery, "Survey of My Stewardship, 1902-1918," TS, pp. 1-2, USPG Archives, H 3, box 2.

116. Stanmore and Compton both resigned, alienated from the "new" SPG; Stanmore broke all connection with the Society in 1906. Henry H. Montgomery, "Survey of My Stewardship, 1902-1918," TS, p. 2, USPG Archives, H 3, box 2.; Montgomery to Lord Stanmore, 6 July and 21 July [190]6, USPG Archives, X 366.

117. Henry H. Montgomery, "Survey of My Stewardship, 1902-1918," TS, pp. 2-6, USPG Archives, H 3, box 2. See also M[aud]. M[ontgomery]., *Montgomery,* 51-57.

Montgomery came to the office in 1902 regular annual income at the SPG rested at £88,586; when he left in 1918 it had risen 68 percent to £148,381.[118] But not all of Montgomery's initiatives worked out smoothly, and many areas of SPG practice remained resistant to change. In 1899 Montgomery had predicted that an income of nearly £200,000 within a decade would be simple for the right leader to engineer. In pursuit of this he discovered the reality of difficulties that Henry Tucker had always emphasized: the problems of Special Funds and of dutiful but unenthusiastic supporters. Montgomery's solid achievement lay in reorganizing an inefficient office and increasing income in an era in which many missionary societies were overstretched and stagnant. With this transformation the Society's prestige and influence multiplied. However, while Montgomery helped the SPG to develop an ideal of "imperial Christianity," his larger project to unify the Church through an appeal to empire was far less successful.

Montgomery was good at articulating an ideal of imperial cooperation that appealed to the uncritical enthusiasm of young High Churchmen. His plans for imperial engagement, however, never took much concrete shape beyond successful agitation for a great Pan-Anglican Congress that would draw all the divisions of Anglicanism together. This vagueness about what his plan entailed in practice indicates the inherent problems sure to arise with any comprehensive or centrally directed "imperial" plan in a Church that had largely ceded independence to overseas bishops in their dioceses generations in the past.[119] Furthermore, Church unity under an imperial umbrella entailed cooperation between groups that were highly antagonistic: orthodox theological conservatives from both the High Church and Evangelical party and a modernist student movement, as well as historically exclusivist High Churchmen and an Evangelical party still prone to ultra-Protestant opposition to "Romanism." Montgomery wanted to direct the attention of a troubled home Church overseas, and in engaging its interest create an area of consensus. However, he had no means of compelling acceptance of his imperial rhetoric, and he faced the problem that any concrete plans to advance an irenic "imperial" program would draw fire from several directions. The struggles between the "old Brigade" and

118. This compares to an SPG regular annual income increase of £15,192 (21 percent) over the thirty years from 1872 to 1902 (regular income accounted for general donor support, and excluded legacies and special appeals). From 1902 to 1912 it increased by £34,405 (39 percent) to £122,991, supporting a total income of £218,031. Figures from Pascoe, *Two Hundred Years of the SPG*, 832, and Thompson, *History of the SPG*, 722.

119. For an overview of the beginning of this set of developments see Hans Jacob Cnattingius, *Bishops and Societies: A Study of Anglican Colonial and Missionary Expansion, 1698-1850* (London: SPCK, 1952), 188-91, 195-229. On the strains that relations between overseas bishops and missionary societies bred from early in the Victorian missionary movement, see Shenk, *Venn*, 35-37.

"Progressives" in 1901 portended a difficult road for Montgomery, who rapidly discovered that he had his hands full in simply holding the SPG together. Nevertheless, Montgomery's supporters saw his new leadership, his enthusiasm, and his ideals as a way to challenge the CMS and assume precedence in Church missions. The opening for such a program by High Church progressives also seemed available because the CMS suddenly found itself facing its own troubles, which spelled a perceptible weakening of its position. Just as some believed the SPG was entering its own "new era" after 1901, the CMS experienced a slump in growth, as if its Centenary were a final Victorian consummation before the more difficult years of doubt and retrenchment prior to the First World War.

Conclusion

By the late Victorian period, groups of High Church Anglicans, many influenced by Christian Socialist ideals and animated by public-school enthusiasms for duty and sacrifice in imperial service, sought to construct a new missionary culture that emulated the style, enthusiasm, and methods of evangelical holiness-driven missions. The imperial vision of the JCMA was on one level just one more manifestation of a more general ballooning of imperial enthusiasm in the 1890s in Britain.[120] On another level it represented a High Church attempt to popularize its missions among students and younger clergy, in emulation of a more successful evangelical effort, which was itself seeking new lines of contact with a changing undergraduate religious culture. In the 1890s the SVMU came to be a crucial adjunct to the CMS, while the JCMA and those supporting its program won the battle of control for the SPG, both movements gaining decisive influence by 1900. The sign of the influence and vision for the future that had come to be embodied in the JCMA by the turn of the century was its direct effect on the selection of the next secretary of the SPG. Montgomery and the leaders of the JCMA desired to reinvigorate the Church itself by directly linking the fortunes of Anglicanism with the British Empire. Through a missionary program relying heavily upon episcopal authority, they hoped to broker a reconciliation between the parties of the Church while marshalling party energy (employed in the past at cross purposes) against the religious doubts bred by the modern world. In pressing this vision of an imperial-missionary Church,

---

120. On the effect of the popular imperialism of the 1890s on Methodists, who similarly adopted the "jingo" attitude, see Stephen E. Koss, *Nonconformity in Modern British Politics* (Hamden, CT: Archon, 1975), 29-37. But note also Koss's indication of the far more ambivalent attitude to empire among other Nonconformist denominations.

the "Progressives" of the SPG sought to force the Anglican establishment to reconsider the role of the Church of England in the empire.

Montgomery's arrival at the SPG launched a new departure in High Church missions, building on the growing success of the JCMA, itself a reflection of the larger ambitious desire of the SVMU to move the missionary movement to a new phase of inclusive growth. SVMU leaders pressed unification of High and Low Church missionary Anglicanism, as well as that of Church and Nonconformity, under the big tent of a multidenominational missionary movement. From this program issued the driving force behind a new missionary ecumenism that catalyzed a whole series of collaborations drawing Christian unions and associations into the Student Christian Movement. One critical goal was reaching the Church of England in its entirety. This required an infiltration of the theological colleges, which their principals jealously protected as bastions of Anglican orthodoxy. Leaders at the SVMU saw the JCMA as the instrument to effect their opening.[121] Douglas Thornton launched the project to canvass High Church students, urging them to associate with the SVMU, with a Christmas address to the JCMA in 1897; Frank Lenwood and other second-generation leaders carried it on after Thornton's departure for Egypt.[122] The difficulty that barred any easy cooperation was a familiar one: the SVMU was "not a church movement but undenominational," which troubled High Churchmen accustomed to Anglican exclusivity.[123] Members of the JCMA were concerned to associate only with "Christian" men, as they understood that designation, and therefore desired that the Nicene Creed or a standard of baptism be adopted by the SVMU as a basis for the movement.[124] On the other hand, the power and influence of the SVMU were so obvious that the leaders of the JCMA felt that they could neither rudely dismiss nor disingenuously lead on the SVMU. Since they were "like ourselves, moved by the impulse of the Holy Ghost," it was legitimate to entertain the idea that "we may, under God, be allowed to sympathize with this vast body of Missionary enthusiasm."[125]

In the end, the burgeoning ambition and widening toleration of student

---

121. Wilson, *Lenwood*, 52.

122. Minutes of the General Meeting of the London JCMA, 10 Dec. 1897, USPG Archives, X 539; Tatlow, *Student Christian Movement*, 138-40.

123. These questions dogged negotiations when members of the SVMU and the JCMA met in roundtable discussion. Minutes of the General Meeting of the London JCMA, 10 Dec. 1897, USPG Archives, X 539.

124. John Ellison to W. H. Gairdner, 23 Feb. 1899, inserted between pp. 113-14, Minutes of JCMA Conferences, USPG Archives, X 540.

125. John Ellison, speech to the Federation of JCMA, 4 May 1899, Minutes of JCMA Conferences, USPG Archives, X 540.

leaders led to agreement between the JCMA and SVMU. The London JCMA inaugurated friendly relations with the SVMU when their members agreed to provide hospitality for delegates attending the 1900 London SVMU conference and Mandell Creighton, bishop of London, spoke to the group.[126] By 1910 the Student Christian Movement (SCM), to which the SVMU was affiliated, had successfully connected with High Churchmen, drawing Cuddesdon and many other High Church colleges into association and securing many High Churchmen and Anglo-Catholics — C. F. G. Masterman, C. H. Robinson, Henry Scott Holland, and Charles Gore, among others — as supporters and speakers at its summer conferences.[127] The initiative of JCMA members to respond to SCM advances showed an openness to missionary cooperation quite unlike earlier High Church practice, and it demonstrated a growing willingness to advocate greater unity with Anglican evangelical missions. An interdenominational organization such as the SVMU was more successful at reconciling differences within the Church of England than any partisan Anglican organization could have been. The legacy of embittered struggle between High Churchmen and Evangelicals left little room for compromise. Perhaps as important, however, the "progressive" thinkers of the SVMU and the "progressive" thinkers of the JCMA seem to have had more in common than the Church supporters of the old CMS and SPG, and thus a common belief in the empire as a providential structure of opportunity for social and religious advancement remained a powerful link of ecumenical bonding.

These changes reflected a more general transformation. British missions were forced ever more insistently, late in the nineteenth century, to accommodate or to confront the rising tides of economic, political, cultural, and popular imperialism. Growing missionary interest in the university can be traced partly to strengthening concepts of "muscular Christianity" advanced in the public schools and ideas of "England's mission" to the "younger races" articulated in university circles.[128] The responses among missionaries to the age of high imperialism were not, however, uniform or simple. Denominational societies, such as the CMS and SPG in particular, but also the WMMS, showed themselves willing in many circumstances to cooperate with and to urge forward imperial authorities in the construction of colonial webs of governance. Other societies, however, such as the UMCA and CIM, often found themselves, for varied reasons, in conflict with imperial culture and purposes.

126. St. Clair Donaldson, "London JCMA," circular letter, 8 Dec. 1899, in Minutes of the London JCMA, USPG Archives, X 405.

127. Wellings, *Evangelicals Embattled*, 272-73.

128. J. A. Mangan, *Athleticism in the Victorian and Edwardian Public School: The Emergence and Consolidation of an Educational Ideology* (Cambridge: Cambridge University Press, 1981), 135-39.

In the age of the "new imperialism," many missionary societies leaned more heavily toward advocating British imperial expansion, such as the annexation of Fiji as a Crown Colony in 1875 at the urging of WMMS missionaries and the declaration of a full protectorate over Uganda in 1894 at the urging of the CMS and its supporters. Central and East African missions in particular expanded in the context of the European scramble for territory in Africa; they fed on the reports of explorers such as Henry Morton Stanley and the example of sacrificial missionary deaths such as those of Bishop James Hannington and John Alexander Mackay.[129] Students were particularly attracted to the narratives of sacrifice and heroism generated in those recently opened fields that were connected to the new crusade against slavery, launched by David Livingstone, the greatest of the late Victorian missionary heroes.[130] As rivalry with the French and the Germans, as well as with Roman Catholics and Muslims, helped to drive missions to heartily pro-imperial stances, the initiative of the JCMA to link High Church missions under the direction of the SPG to a robust "missionary imperialism" and protectionism had a strong logic in the late 1890s. This was a logic reinforced by the rhetoric of mastery and destiny of the Anglo-Saxon race that was explicit in Sir John Seeley's *The Expansion of England* (1882) and explicated in clear Anglican ecclesiastical terms by the vigorous colonial imperial vision of the former bishop of Sydney Alfred Barry in his 1894 Hulsean lectures at Cambridge. Here he argued that "an elder brotherhood of protection and guidance . . . dependent largely on English teaching and authority and inspiration" was necessary to protect and tutor "the inferior races, more or less barbaric." At the core of much similar thinking that had developed out of earlier Westcottian themes was the presumption of clear racial hierarchies of character and ability, and while many still advocated the indigenization of churches, they now often did so in more or less hardening racial terms. While tending also to depend upon gendered languages of family ranking to justify the station of "mother" and "daughter" churches in an imperial "ecclesiastical federation," this ambitious, mutually constituted hierarchical program insisted on the need for structured systems of racial tutelage within a model of domestic care.[131] It was both strengthened and tempered by emphasis on the destructive influence of colonists and settlers, the devastating effects of colonial trade and labor practices, and a questioning of particularly exploitative imperial processes. Such

129. Among many contemporary hagiographies, see Edwin C. Dawson, *Lion-Hearted: The Story of Bishop Hannington's Life* (Seeley: London, 1890) and Andrew Melrose and T. C. Wilson, *Alexander Mackay, Missionary Hero of Uganda* (London: Sunday School Union, 1893).

130. On the cultivation of the Livingstone legend, keyed to his opposition to East African slaving, by the Anglican editor of his *Last Journals*, see Helly, *Livingstone's Legacy*, 193-215, 261-96.

131. Barry, *Ecclesiastical Expansion*, 5, 33-35.

imperial reformism thus reinforced the claim to legitimacy of religiously defined moral duty within the larger imperial frame.

The imperial context, then, became an important one for the growth of the student movement, and intellectual attitudes shared between student members strongly aided cooperation between the SVMU and JCMA and reinforced the optimistic openness practiced by Montgomery when he came to the SPG. Common missionary and imperial ambitions encouraged ecumenism. Despite social conventions that had previously barred interaction between High Church Anglicans and Nonconformists, conferences between the JCMA and SVMU revealed a common valuation of deep piety, intellectual adventurousness, and imperial opportunism. These values became features of later SPG culture when prayer, piety, and a reflex to interrogate past practices came to define the SPG home office, evident, for example, in the launch of the self-consciously progressive publication *The East and the West* in 1903, which quickly stirred trouble with more conservative supporters. Cooperation between Evangelicals and "modern Tractarians" was nearly unthinkable in some circles, given John Kensit's ultra-evangelical crusades of the late 1890s, yet Frank Lenwood got on very well with High Church Anglicans in conference because "he sympathized with people whose convictions were often taken for mere angularities."[132] Following these conferences, missionary gatherings in England saw the presence and influence of High Churchmen increase steadily, while the participation of strong Churchmen also rose at the SVMU. This participation was insurance, as Canon C. F. G. Masterman put it in 1906, of the continuing interdenominational nature of the SVMU precisely because, "from our very nature, we constitute a particularly indigestible element in any undenominational organization."[133] Anglicans were cautious, yet by 1910 the SVMU had gained the support of nearly all the Anglican theological colleges regardless of Church politics. The 1908 Liverpool conference of the SVMU even attracted the principal of Cuddesdon College and other eminent High Churchmen, prompting Eugene Stock to proclaim that "[t]he Student Movement has the high honour of uniting us all."[134] And, ultimately, when Bishop Montgomery and his band of SPG delegates arrived at Edinburgh in 1910 to attend the World Missionary Conference, which was planned and prosecuted on the ideals of the student movement, their presence indicated the development of missionary ecumenism and Anglican unity that would have been unthinkable twenty years previously.

132. Wilson, *Lenwood*, 53-56.

133. Masterman quoted in Tatlow, *Student Christian Movement*, 153. From 1903 the SPG, like the JCMA, began sending delegates to SVMU conferences. Rough Minutes of the Home Organisation Committee, 5 Nov. 1903, USPG Archives, H 137.

134. Stock, *Recollections*, 241-42.

In a similar reversal, under the influence of its younger clergy and its new secretary, the SPG from 1902 rose to a standard of practice and progressiveness that made it a model of missionary enterprise within the Church. Within five years some were beginning to argue that the SPG was eclipsing the CMS, which after the turn of the century experienced a series of crises that forced a rethinking of the assumptions of the 1890s. The way the CMS and the SPG adjusted to the new conditions of a new century depended in large part on the traditions of operation inherited from the past, the ideas of a new generation of activists groomed almost entirely in the student movement, and the evolving attitudes of episcopal leaders in a Church that for the first time was turning its eyes as a corporate body to the problems and challenges of the foreign mission field. The gold ring that student leaders, both young men and women, saw as the ultimate prize was a missionary movement that would draw a wave of idealists into active service, transcending sectarian, denominational, national, gender, and racial divisions. This was a heady vision, which faced increasing challenges as ideals met the realities of deep-seated beliefs and behaviors, particularly in those evangelical subcultures that had once formed the core of missionary advance. For the greatest of the Victorian societies, the CMS, those realities proved most troublingly to arise in the area in which institutionally committed Evangelicals had heretofore been so extraordinarily successful: the expansion and utilization of women and women's work in support of foreign missions. It is in the growing problems revolving around women and their place in the missionary movement that we can see the limitations of student culture to transform evangelicalism in the opening decade of the twentieth century.

CHAPTER 7

Women's Work: Leadership, Dependence, and the Limits of Change

Do you long for romance? to break away from conventional English life? to strike out for yourself, and, above all, in an utterly noble cause? We offer you the very noblest cause, and the completest romance, and the utmost self-sacrifice.

Henry H. Montgomery, 1915

Its members [The Women's Foreign Committee of the CMS] have mostly not been sufficiently educated up to the point of providing real help in some of its [The General Committee's] discussions. . . . As one member said to me "We soared so high that there was nothing for it but to fall down again."

Edith Baring-Gould, 1914[1]

In 1915 veteran CMS women's organizer Minna Gollock, speaking to an SPG training institute audience, revealed that after forty years of intensive organization and growth in women's missionary work it remained "specially difficult" to analyze the subject due to a poverty of data and the absence of any clear analysis of its substantial but highly varied impact across the mission field. Noting that there was "singularly little literature on the subject, and what there is is chiefly American," she lamented the lack of any great book that might make the work

---

1. *"With the Women," A Sermon Preached in Westminster Abbey on April 22nd, 1915, on the Occasion of the Commencement of the Jubilee Year of Women's Work of S.P.G.* (London: SPG, 1915), 11; "Memo. by Miss Baring-Gould," n.d. [1914], pp. 1, 3-4, CMS Archives, G/C 26A.

330

come "alive with the flame of God." Much of the problem, she suggested, was due first to the appeal to English women "on the ground of pity for our sisters," which masked the central strategic importance of the work to any progressive missionary policy and, second, to "some mystery of stupidity" that "women's work has been tacitly regarded as secondary in importance to work among men." Such stupidity had resulted in the Balkanization of women's missionary endeavor. A serious consideration of women's work from a theoretical position that could affect the most basic decisions made by the exclusively male hierarchy of control at CMS had, she implied, never been undertaken. The effect, she further suggested, was to dilute and squander the magnificent efforts of generations of women in support of the cause.[2]

Gollock's address suggests several critical facts about specifically targeted Anglican women's missionary effort and the use of unmarried female agents in the several decades prior to World War I: first, its importance and magnitude had been hidden by neglect; second, it had nevertheless come to pervade every mission field; third, proponents of women's work imagined it to be of critical, if not paramount, importance in the movement; and fourth, despite a half century of advocacy on behalf of women's missions, the male clerical domination of missionary strategy and leadership had never been cracked. While in the years since 1890 independent women's work had become central to missionary tactics, women nevertheless experienced increasing frustration that the clerical authorities who made ultimate decisions had refused to integrate women's work and leadership into the broader realm of missionary strategy. The expanding work of women in the field had clearly extended the boundaries of what respectable women could do overseas, where, despite their formal subordination within church and missionary structures, women often found a much wider sphere of opportunity, authority, and power than in Britain.[3] Women also often found upon return from the mission field that the home church had become, by comparison, a cramped, limiting environment, and that the cooperation, coordination, and partnership that were required in the mission field had little impact on the operation of the parallel churches of official men and volunteer women working in Britain.[4]

It is not surprising, then, that Gollock's speech is defined by its tone of frustration. Holiness styles of religiosity, among both enthusiastic evangelicals and

2. Minna C. Gollock, "Women's Work," in *The Church and the Empire: Addresses at the Summer School at Eastborne, June 19 to June 26, 1915* (London: SPG, 1915), 197-200.

3. For vignettes of two such women, Amy Carmichael of the CEZMS and Eva Swift of the American Board, see Kent, *Converting Women*, 102-20.

4. For Annie Small's shocked reaction to unyielding patriarchy in the Scottish Presbyterian church on her return, see Semple, *Missionary Women*, 144.

pietist Anglo-Catholics, had opened progressively wider spheres of legitimate activity for women precisely within the religious cultures most bound to conservative Victorian gender constructions. In the context of expanding imperial enthusiasms and anxieties alike — from the expansionary trustee model of mission embraced by the CMS in Uganda in the 1890s to the anxious reconsiderations of imperial need and opportunity occasioned at the SPG by the Boer War — holiness sanction widened women's opportunities. But as those vistas expanded, reactions from traditionalists — especially evangelical conservatives facing modernist challenges — saw a resurgence. Conservative male clerics, reacting to liberal theological developments, challenged further extensions of women's authority and autonomy. Progressive liberalization at other societies and in English society at large spurred, in particular, a series of conflicts at the CMS in the years prior to the Great War. In those conflicts women faced opposition from religious conservatives who saw in female independence a destruction of fundamental elements of evangelical belief. While ultimately the CMS gave women positions of executive control in the wake of the war, the relative slowness of women's empowerment in the CMS command structure can be traced, early on, to its conservative evangelical constituency. Within this constituency women's autonomy was seen as threatening by an influential minority of conservative clerics and, in the end, was unimportant enough to the many female supporters at the English local level that they never articulated demands for a different response from the Society. In the end, it appeared, the bulk of supporters remained content enough with the vision of a mission home, resting at the center of missionary practice, where the mission wife served in her traditional role of parochial support.

Notably, in Minna Gollock's case, she and her older sister Georgina had for a quarter century struggled to craft a position of relevance and cooperative reciprocity with the rest of the male, largely clerical staff at the CMS, and had manifestly failed. From acting in the 1880s as a force of inspiration on the platforms of Keswick and in the YWCA movement, the Gollocks had been drawn into administrative and organizational work for the CMS, bright with promise in the 1890s. When Minna spoke as she did from the SPG platform a quarter of a century later, she must have reflected on the surprising reversal of the relative position of Evangelical and of High Church women. In 1890 no one would have called the SPG's women's policy progressive; by 1910 no one doubted that SPG women had surpassed their Evangelical counterparts in leadership and opportunity. Gollock, of course, wrote at a time of crisis and extreme fluidity, as World War I threw European Christianity, empires, and mission fields into turmoil. But her criticisms, her charges of stupidity, were not new. Rather, they were the culmination of more than a decade of growing frustration at the CMS among independent women who remained marginalized while other Anglican societies, like the CEZMS, put women into positions of authority and command, and even witnessed the rise of High Church women into positions of missionary leadership. How had this reversal occurred? What was the relationship between the Anglican women who opted for the respectability and resources of the CMS and the women who chose instead alternate models of mission? And how progressive was the SPG policy in a larger English society that increasingly accepted new freedoms and new opportunities for the "New Woman" of the Edwardian age?

The backlash that manifested itself at the CMS, and the alternate trajectories of rapidly expanding women's autonomy at the CEZMS and SPG, had their origins in the final two decades of the nineteenth century, when evangelical Anglican women's missions grew so rapidly in activity and support that they could no longer be prudently marginalized or ignored by the mainline societies. At first, because of its less enthusiastic temperament and the controversial nature of the sisterhoods advanced by Anglo-Catholics, the SPG shied from any active development of women's work. Evangelical successes, however, were celebrated, which led the CMS, after refusal for four decades to employ independent female missionaries, to reverse this policy in 1887 and form a women's department in 1895 to manage the work. Such decisions and the rapid growth of the influence of student leaders in the movement also forced the SPG to come to grips with demands being made for greater use of women; after 1900 the SPG made significant strides in incorporating women's work into its public missionary system.

Thus, after 1880, as women's missions entered their decades of most dynamic growth, their very success began to generate both competition and criticism. From outside the movement, feminists, secular social reformers, and indigenous nationalists challenged missionaries for the role of legitimate defenders of "native" women.[5] Within the movement, traditionalist Evangelicals and conservative High Churchmen began to attack the public roles of female missionaries by defining women's leadership in civil and religious society as a dangerous symptom of "modernist" infidelity to Scripture. By the turn of the century, female missions began to evoke a multipronged reaction. While women had always been under tightly controlled reins of patriarchal oversight in the field, they nonetheless experienced relative freedom in what still remained exotic, exacting, and comparatively independent work. The lure of professional and

5. See for example, Antoinette M. Burton, "Contesting the Zenana: The Mission to Make 'Lady Doctors for India,' 1874-1885," *Journal of British Studies* 35, no. 3 (July 1996): 368-97, and Partha Chatterjee, "Colonialism, Nationalism and Colonialized Women: The Contest in India," *American Ethnologist* 16, no. 4 (Nov. 1989): 622-33.

quasi-professional opportunities outside the churches — predominantly in education, nursing, and public health — continued to grow in the opening decades of the twentieth century, and within this general expansion of women's employment, female missionaries represented one niche filled by the most religiously devout women with professional aspirations. Despite widening secular opportunities, and partially because of the postwar backlash against women's employment, enthusiasm and recruitment for women's missions continued to have substantial momentum into the interwar period, buttressed by the continuing decline of clerical social and professional authority.

The changes wrought at the SPG, and the impact of these relatively liberal innovations in their turn on the CMS, reveal a movement in rapid flux. Women influenced by the energetic spirituality of the age formed the core of the new and effective organizational structure that gave "worldly substance" to the ambitious new program of late Victorian missionary enthusiasts forwarded by the Student Volunteer Movement — in which educated women had a major impact — to quickly convert the world to Christianity. By 1910, however, an evangelical culture that had once provided routes to relative independence for women seemed to female activists cramped and restrictive. From being the invisible support structure for a male-led endeavor, women came to have a highly visible, if still largely subordinate, role in the profoundly influential nationwide network of one of Victorian England's largest centralized voluntary philanthropies. In the early twentieth century Evangelical theology and culture, which initially had provided a crucial rationale in the Victorian era for women's entrance into missions — and through missions authority in imperial and international debate — increasingly erected barriers to the further extension of women's leadership and authority in public life.

This restriction of opportunities for women, at least among Evangelicals, was a direct result of growing friction with the authority of clerics that ambition bred, leading to a reaction from conservatives within the clergy. From the 1880s, denominational conflict, followed by disagreement over the degree of independence to be accorded women, led to the fragmentation of Anglican women's work. Institutions through which female missionary activity was funded and controlled grew along different, uneasily coexisting lines. By 1890 three major independent female missionary societies supported in the main by evangelical Anglicans existed — the FES, the ZBMM, and the CEZMS — in addition to the women's work supported by the CMS, the SPG, the UMCA, and many independent higher church dioceses in Africa, India, the Pacific, and elsewhere. While foreign missions had always depended heavily on the missionary work done by wives of missionaries, after 1890, as all missions drew increasing numbers of unmarried women, women strove for greater responsibility, often helped by mothers and aunts with long records of missionary service and support. While reformist religious ideologies (both evangelical and Anglo-Catholic) gave women a new license to act in the world of Anglican culture, there remained, in systems wedded strongly to conservative forms of religiosity and gender roles, deeply frustrating limits of change that during the Edwardian age ultimately undermined the rapid growth of women's mission in a world of expanding opportunities for women outside the churches and their missions.

Evangelical Women:
Opportunity and Dependence in the Imperial 1890s

As the strength of holiness culture grew in the 1880s among Anglicans, and as the Student Volunteer Movement expanded — notably including educated, activist women in its organizational structure and leadership — women's missions led by the CEZMS, the ZBMM, and the FES also grew. Considerable support also flowed to the CIM, notable for its adventurous use of women. The degree of autonomy to be accorded women, however, became a significant issue, leading to skirmishes between mission agencies. The CMS ultimately incorporated women's work in the 1890s by insisting on complete cooperation between men and women, with leadership firmly in the hands of men, in opposition to the philosophy of separate "women's work for women" pursued by the ZBMM and CEZMS. Although the women's movement within the Church of England had found women's work separate from men's to be the most logical course in the 1880s, the imperatives of an aroused male clericalism, and the desire of many evangelical Anglican women to unify women's work, led to a CMS women's missionary initiative in which the Society used its considerable resources to ensure continued clerical control in its missions.

Dependence and Independence in Anglican Women's Missions

In the early 1880s, friction quickly developed between the newly formed CEZMS and the CMS around local fundraising competition, as complaints arose from some parochial supporters that the CEZMS poached CMS supporters. James Stuart, lay secretary of the CEZMS, responded to these criticisms by reminding new CMS Secretary Frederick Wigram that the CEZMS "distinctly . . . had the confidence of the [CMS] Committee" and that in almost every case CEZMS committee members and office bearers were either officially connected to the CMS or were the wives or widows of officials or missionaries, and that CEZMS missionaries in the field worked directly under CMS mission clergy, ensuring defense of "Protestant & Evangelical principles."[6] Concerns over cash collections, however, rapidly became secondary to calculations by CMS officials such as Eugene Stock that the CMS might be able to leverage a greater expansion of Anglican missionary work as a whole by engaging with women's enthusiasm unleashed by holiness culture. Stock and others had long believed that Anglican missionary societies could much more effectively harness the energies of young middle-class women, who since the 1860s had steadily increased their involvement in urban philanthropy. The growth of the Ranyard Missions, Missions to Sailors, and inner-city charities demonstrated their potential.[7] The desire to introduce an alternative model of women's work that contrasted with the "exclusivism" of "women's work for women" advanced as the independent CEZMS also persuaded CMS leaders finally to engage female missionaries directly.[8]

Just as denominational jealousy had been aroused by the IFNS's interdenominational activism in the 1870s, institutional jealousy seems to have been aroused by the success of the CEZMS, which by 1887 supported eighty-seven single women in the field.[9] But this was not the only factor. As engagement with Keswick and the holiness activists it generated advanced, a turning point came in 1887 when a series of women offered themselves, at their own expense, as missionaries to the CMS — including the daughter of the revered late CMS Secretary Henry Wright. Agnes Wright volunteered for China at the same time as her brother Harry, and she deliberately applied to the CMS, despite the fact that her mother was a leading member of the CEZMS Committee; undoubtedly, she volunteered with the collusion of supporters of women's work such as Stock. She applied at roughly the same time as the receipt of an appeal from Bishop Parker of Uganda for female missionaries, as well as the announcement of an appeal for women for Palestine at the Keswick Convention and nearly simultaneous offers from four other women, including Westfield College mathematical lecturer Katherine Tristram, daughter of influential CMS supporter and naturalist Canon Henry Tristram of Durham. Shortly afterward, Agnes Wright's two younger sisters also volunteered as CMS missionaries.

Significantly, Henry Wright had been one of the key CMS Committee figures encouraging the formation of the CEZMS to uphold Anglican principles in women's work, and the coordinated campaign had all the marks of a bid by influential insiders to unify the work of the two Anglican societies. Coinciding with the CMS

6. Stuart to Wigram, 1 Nov. 1881, CMS Archives, G/AC 4/3/436.

7. Stock, *History of the CMS*, 2:31.

8. On the exclusive recruiting of middle-class missionary candidates at the CEZMS, see Morawiecki, "Women Missionaries, CEZMS," 159-65.

9. "Proposed Resolution on Women's Work, in Connection with C.M.S. Committee of Correspondence," 22 Jan. 1895, CMS Archives, G/AZ 2/1, fol. 43.

adoption of the Policy of Faith, the weight of holiness culture forced the hand of the CMS Committee, which endorsed employing single female missionaries not only in India but also in China, Japan, and other fields.[10] On the one hand, the CMS's change in policy was the mark of progressive thinking among members on the CMS staff, but it met opposition, especially from conservative rural clerical members of the General Committee.[11] Yet as the CMS secretaries would have it, God was clearly leading them into a glorious new age of missionary activity, and the rise of women's work was but part and parcel of a larger institutional expansion and shift in strategy the CMS had begun at home in the 1880s.

On the other hand, CMS policy looked decidedly less progressive from the point of view of leaders at the seven-year-old CEZMS, who saw in the move danger to the status of the society as a closely allied but independent "handmaid" working freely "under the shadow, among the women" of the CMS.[12] A possible shift in CMS policy as early as 1885 alarmed supporters who feared absorption was planned as a matter of course. H. P. Parker, a friend from Calcutta (Kolkata) of CEZMS Lay Secretary James Stuart, and later the second bishop of Equatorial Africa, wrote to deplore the dissolution of CEZMS, as the momentum and quality of women's work was likely to suffer.[13] Early in 1887 the CMS had assured the CEZMS Committee that it was not engaging in women's work. So when subsequently the CMS began sending out female missionaries — a break from its past policy of employing only school teachers — on the pretext that CEZMS was exclusively an Indian zenana society and women were needed in the Far East, a feeling of betrayal grew. A conference representing both societies, called to deal with questions raised by the new CMS practice, took as its greatest task the prevention of a second schism in the women's work supported by evangelical Anglicans. While CEZMS delegates argued that the new CMS policy was a break with valuable precedent, and even a breach of faith, CMS delegates emphasized first, that the continued independent work of the CEZMS threatened to sap women's support for the general work of the CMS, and second, that as the most powerful missionary society in England, the CMS had a responsibility to extend the work according "to what were believed to be clear leadings of God's Providence."[14]

10. Stock, *Women's Work*, 16-20.

11. Robert Needham Cust, *Memoirs of Past Years of a Septuagenarian* (Private circulation, 1899), 117, 193.

12. [Jane Mulvany], "C.E.Z.M.S. and C.M.S. Conference of Assoc. Secs.," MS paper read at the Conference of Association Secretaries, 27 Apr. 1895, CEZMS Archives, CEZ G/AP 1.

13. Parker to Stuart, private, Oct. 1885, TS precis in "C.M.S. and C.E.Z.M.S. Correspondence &c, on the relations between the two Societies. 1885-1895," Feb. 1911, CMS Archives, W/A 4.

14. "1887," MS sheet, CEZMS Archives, CEZ G/AP 1; "Final Report of the Conference," 6 Feb. 1889, labeled "Only copy. J. Mulvany," CEZMS Archives, CEZ G/AP 1.

Amalgamation seemed the obvious solution to those ambitious leaders at the CMS who emphasized that the two societies had identical religious and ecclesiastical principles, the same supporters, "lady" missionaries drawn "from exactly the same class of society and the same section of the Church," and a common interest in the bureaucratic efficiencies to be gained.[15] But the issue of maintaining the autonomy and control women had achieved at the CEZMS ultimately derailed every attempt at amalgamation.

Several amalgamation conferences followed in the next decade, and each failed due to opposition from the CEZMS side. Despite an 1888 proposal from CMS secretaries to make the CEZMS "the Female Branch of C.M.S." and to allow it to maintain "its identity & independence," suspicion ran too high to allow passage of any proposal with large enough support to prevent schism.[16] In actual debate pro-amalgamation factions argued that union would be best overall for the work and that competition between the societies was destructive and exhausting. They were unable to carry the day against those believing that independent women's work held a special power, and competition between CEZMS and CMS in fact leveraged greater overall missionary support from a greater diversity of parishes.[17] Fear of harming established home structures that had been laboriously built up in distinct communities with a particular ideology was undoubtedly a concern, but in the end the issue of who was to control the foreign operations of women was the deepest root of opposition to amalgamation. Thus, when the issue of amalgamation came up again in 1893 and intermittently thereafter, much the same conclusion was reached: mutual assurances of good will, practical arrangements for dividing the work abroad, and continuation of separate operations.[18] The secretaries of the CEZMS, notably Home Secretary Jane Mulvany, continued to hope for amalgamation on advantageous terms, because of the growing problems caused by parochial competition between the two societies.[19] But by 1895 the CMS had been so successful recruiting women that it would not consider turning its own two

15. "Church of England Zenana Missionary Society . . . 3 Jan. 1894. To the Secretaries of the Church Missionary Society," CEZMS Archives, CEZ/G AP1.

16. "Scheme submitted by Messrs Karney and Stock in 1888 . . . ," in TS, "C.M.S. and C.E.Z.M.S. Correspondence &c, on the relations between the two Societies. 1885-1895," private, Feb. 1911, CMS Archives, W/A 4.

17. Printed proposals, "A" and "B," private, with pencil notes on the opinions of Edward Hoare and William Grey, CEZMS Archives, CEZ/G AP 1; G[eorgina] A G[ollock], "Memo. re. C.E.Z. Question. Private," 27 Feb. 1911, CMS Archives, W/A4.

18. "Sub-Committee. July 1, 1895," and "Resolutions adopted unanimously at the General Committee. July 9, 1895," in TS, "C.M.S. and C.E.Z.M.S. Correspondence &c, on the relations between the two Societies. 1885-1895," private, Feb. 1911, CMS Archives, W/A 4.

19. Mulvany to Mrs. Sandys, 12 Dec. 1892, CEZMS Archives, CEZ/G AP 1.

hundred female agents over to another society or absorbing a separate admin-istration.[20] Control of the foreign work was the point on which neither side would compromise.

Opposition to amalgamation did not come, despite some reservations, from the London staff of the CEZMS. Rather, the resistance came from countryside supporters and missionaries, demonstrating high levels of local engagement with the Society and loyalty to the idea of distinct and autonomous women's work within the Church. Local association secretaries, workers, and foreign missionaries feared that amalgamation would strip away their autonomy and distinctive identity as a society employing single women to engage in women's work. Georgina Gollock recalled that "the real difficulty lay in the fact that the C.E.Z. workers at home & abroad had always administered their own affairs" and that in England the strongest opposition came from "the wisest & strongest C.E.Z. workers in the country," who were repelled by the size and bureaucracy of the CMS. To these women, whose religious experience was tied up in the networks of feminine sociability and charity that made up the parallel church, "amalgamation would spell defeat & be the triumph of a big organization over a small one," with all that implied in a clerically dominated church. Further-more, Gollock felt that CEZMS supporters were deeply imbued with "a spirit of controversy," no doubt derived both from the more radical Protestant circles, to which CEZMS supporters were attracted, and from the continuing anti-popery agitations animating this group in the 1890s under the leadership of John Ken-sit and the Protestant Truth Society. Consequently, CEZMS supporters were likely to react against a CMS increasingly moderate in its stance toward ritual prosecutions in the wake of the Lincoln Judgment. Gollock further noted that rather than having a professional tone, the CEZMS Committee was defined by "undue domination" by leading members. Independence and the tendency toward strong influence by charismatic individuals were characteristic of the smaller "faith" missions of the age. So too was a tendency to use female agents freely and extensively. Holiness-oriented evangelicalism provided strong justifi-cation for independent action among women, despite the traditional evangelical tendency to encourage gender hierarchies. One result was the resistance of CEZMS missionaries in the field (who prized their autonomy) to working under "local bodies of [CMS] men."[21] For more independent, professional-minded Evangelical women both the CEZMS and the ZBMM provided a more prom-

20. "C.M.S. & C.E.Z.M.S," TS, signed CMS Salisbury Square, 5 Apr. 1895, CEZMS Archives, CEZ/G AP 1.

21. G[eorgina] A G[ollock], "Memo. re. C.E.Z. Question. Private," 27 Feb. 1911, CMS Archives, W/A 4.

ising prospect, as the substantially higher proportion of women doctors at the CEZMS and ZBMM compared to the CMS seems to suggest.[22]

The deeper issues of contention between the CMS and CEZMS were thus of style and ideology. The formal clerical efficiency of the CMS and its moderate evangelicalism repelled women who were passionately committed to personal service. In evangelical circles, advanced argument about the radical expansion of the women's sphere was tied to ultra-Protestant denunciations of popery. Even more important, the CEZMS rejected the CMS philosophy of women's work. Specifically, secretaries at the CMS emphasized that man and woman should toil as one in Christ, but with man as the head. The CMS stressed that its philosophy was different from many other societies, and particularly from that of the ZBMM, the CEZMS, and women's missionary societies in America: CMS women were to stand visibly on the same level with men and work cooperatively while being enjoined to support the whole of mission work, not just women's work.[23] But women's roles were to be strictly defined and unequal. Women were to have a consultative role, and enlightened men, who understood the special nature of women's capacities, were to use such insights when exercising executive power. This, essentially, was the offer for partnership that was tendered to the CEZMS and rejected. Following that rejection the CMS formed its Women's Department in 1895 on precisely these lines.[24] For those who pressed at the CMS for full membership rights and responsibilities for women, this outcome was disgraceful. Robert Cust, for example, advocated that women "must have precisely the same allowances, be provided with similar accommodation, and placed on the same footing as the male Missionary." Likewise, women must be given real power and authority within the societies. If missions were attractive to ambitious, professional women they would induce that "sweet superfluity of women, to whom a vocation is not marked out," to choose a missionary career.[25]

Having supported all, and more, that the CEZMS proposed throughout the amalgamation negotiations, Cust resigned from the CMS Committee in 1892 when it refused to allow women to sit as equals on its General Committee.[26] In recalling his last Committee meeting at the CMS, Cust portrayed the event with

22. The proportion of female medical doctors at the CEZMS in 1899 was 4.3 percent, at the ZBMM 6.3 percent, and at the CMS .4 percent. See Appendix I, Figure 6.

23. "Miss G. A. Gollock," TS committee resolution, n.d., Papers of Rev. Gordon Hewitt, 1937-77, CMS Archives, Acc 318 Z/5.

24. "Meeting of Sub-Committee. June 21 1895," and "Secretaries C.E.Z.M.S. to Secretaries C.M.S. April 1895," in TS, "C.M.S. and C.E.Z.M.S. Correspondence &c, on the relations between the two Societies. 1885-1895," private, Feb. 1911, CMS Archives, W/A 4.

25. Robert Needham Cust, *The Female Evangelist* (Hertford, UK, n.d., ca. 1891), 6-7.

26. Cust, *Female Evangelist,* 7.

characteristic acerbity. Arguing that women in local government boards and in the professions had been successfully tested at home and now made up the majority of missionaries in the field, Cust moved their admission to the CMS General Committee. The motion, wrote Cust,

> was met by a fat old clergyman, who knew as much about Mission-work as he did of Astronomy or Chemistry, and who evidently had more of the conventional old woman in him than the thoughtful male, moving the previous question, which was carried by a forty-parson power of ten-and-sixpenny clergymen. And yet we all know, that this measure must very soon be carried. I rose from my seat, and have never darkened the door of Salisbury Square since.[27]

Clerical conservatism at the CMS, and the Society's cold bureaucratic nature, thus caused wariness among CEZMS supporters. Strict deference and decorum were expected of female staff members in Church Missionary House; for example, in the period after her appointment in 1891 to the Editorial Department, the daughter of CMS Secretary Baring-Gould recalled that "the women would don their hats and gloves if they left their rooms, walk the corridors with their eyes cast down; and when later they were allowed to attend prayers in the headquarters it was never alone but in pairs that they took their places in Chapel."[28] In contrast, the CEZMS Committee carried out its work primarily from the home of Sir William Hill, in an informal family atmosphere, where the leading members of the Committee, James Stuart, his wife, and his sister, Mrs. Sandys, were part of a well-connected former Calcutta (Kolkata) merchant family that included Bishop Edward C. Stuart of Waiapu, New Zealand.[29] The female missionaries knew Mrs. Stuart as their "Missionary Mother," and the homes of the committee members acted as boarding houses for the furloughed missionaries.[30] As the CMS organized its women's work, the independent-minded suspicions of CEZMS supporters about the place to which women would be relegated in the large clerically dominated CMS bureaucracy must have been amply confirmed.

At the CMS, however, women's work demanded direction if only because of its burgeoning size. From 1887 to 1894 the CMS added 218 single women workers

27. *Prevailing Methods*, 140.
28. Obituary of Miss Edith Baring-Gould, *Times*, 5 July 1961.
29. Eugene Stock, "The Men of the Past," in *Records of Missionary Secretaries: An Account of the Celebration of the Centenary of the London Secretaries' Association* (London: United Council for Missionary Education, 1920), 20.
30. E. G. Sandys, "Memories from the Home Side," letter printed in *CEZMS Jubilee Souvenir*, 35.

Annie Perry Howlett, with driver, bullocks, and pointer, at a Zenana
Bible and Medical Mission station, Upper Doab, Uttar Pradesh, ca. 1910.
From Photographs & Slides, 1910s-1980, Small Albums, A. P. Howlett, "Early Days,"
North India, Khurja, 1910-15, IFNS/ZBMM Archives, School of Oriental
and African Studies. Courtesy of Interserve England and Wales.

to its rolls and began expanding training for women at Mildmay and in Highbury.[31] The Gleaners' Union, directed centrally, freed ladies from local parochial
organization and provided "closer rapprochement between individual workers
& the . . . Centre with its Missionary life and fresh plans." The new Department
promised greater use of "so many upper class girls . . . who have speaking, writing,
or organising power but who are not being developed as workers by C.M.S."[32]
Thus the CMS, despite its difficulties with CEZMS, tapped into the parallel church
to mobilize Evangelical women throughout the country. Calling on two holiness
stalwarts specifically to organize women's work, the CMS hired YWCA veteran
Georgina Gollock in 1890 as an editorial assistant, the first "lady full member of
staff," and, in 1895, appointed her the CMS's first Women's Department secretary.
Her sister Minna, working as a volunteer alongside her for years, succeeded to
the position in 1905.[33] In the early years of promise, two Ladies Consultative

31. "Proposed Resolution on Women's Work, in Connection with C.M.S. Committee of Correspondence," 22 Jan. 1895, CMS Archives, G/AZ 2/1, fol. 43.

32. L. G. Handley, Clifton to "Dear Sir," 26 Jan. [1895], and S. Stebes, Southampton to Mrs.
Grubb, 16 May [1895], CMS Archives, W/A 1.

33. Stock, *History of the CMS*, 3:660, 662, 695; 4:441, 453.

Committees were created to advise on home organization and the foreign work. While the Home Consultative Committee found itself busy organizing women's support for the CMS, the Foreign Consultative Committee languished. Despite engaging in extensive research into the condition of female missionary work, the CMS Area Committees that ran the foreign work neither called upon nor committed work to the committee, and it withered away by 1901 because "month after month the Secretaries of the Foreign Department had nothing to propose for the [women's] Agenda." While never an advocate of giving women executive powers at the CMS, Georgina Gollock was deeply troubled by the fact that CMS secretaries did not remotely honor the ideal on which the CMS Women's Department had been formed: that women would perform a vital consultative role.[34] She could hardly fail to reflect that the fears of CEZMS amalgamation skeptics had come to pass at the CMS in six short years, a demonstration that, at least in English administration, the beautiful ideal of men's and women's cooperation had little power to change deeply set patterns of privilege and authority between the official male church and its parallel female counterpart.

"Puritan" Anglican Patterns of Women's Mission

By the turn of the century, support for women's missionary activity within the Evangelical wing of the Church of England had divided into three primary streams. The IFNS represented the first and weakest of these currents. Shortly after the split with the CEZMS in 1880, the IFNS renamed itself the Zenana Bible and Medical Mission (ZBMM) and worked to claim support from those in the Church of England who had a strong loyalty to cooperative "undenominational" missionary efforts, vigorous support for faith missions, deep suspicion of popery within and without the Church, and full commitment to independent women's missions. Excepting the last of these points, the ZBMM's culture of mission paralleled that of the CIM, which all observers acknowledged garnered a strong minority of its support from those uncompromising evangelical Anglicans often styled "Puritans." The ZBMM remained a predominantly Anglican-supported society with a strong link to radical holiness subcultures and a continued commitment to undenominational militancy reinforced by the determination of the Kinnaird family.[35] The CEZMS represented a second, stronger current that

---

34. "Memo. re. the Ladies' Foreign Consultative Committee," G[eorgina] A G[ollock], Dec. 1902, CMS Archives, W/A 1.

35. In 1894 the secretaries of the CMS noted that of the sixty-three women the ZBMM had sent out in the previous seven years, two-thirds were Anglicans. "Proposed Resolution on Women's

drew in those who wanted to emphasize a distinct Anglican identity but who, like ZBMM supporters, embraced separate and independent "women's work for women" and the more radical holiness-based pietism and "Puritan" suspicion of Ritualism that supported this position. The CMS represented the third and strongest current. Supporters dedicated to the CMS as the traditional organ of Evangelical missions — most comfortable with its moderating neo-Evangelicalism, establishment connections, and conservative philosophy of women's work — fed this current.[36] This philosophy of cooperative male and female work was based on the model of male governance within marriage and had considerable appeal within respectable Evangelical communities.

Despite the CMS's more restrictive policy toward women's roles in mission activity at home and abroad, or rather perhaps because of it, the Society had the most striking success among Anglicans in its development of women's work, much more so than the ZBMM and CEZMS, and it closely rivaled the interdenominational CIM in overall use of women. Anglican women who gave their time and energy to the missionary cause, it seems, tended to conservative religion, or were deeply enmeshed in patriarchal male family structures, and preferred associating with the CMS, a central rock on which respectable evangelical identity in the Church of England rested. In an age when many felt that evangelicalism in the parish and on the episcopal bench was under progressive threat from "High Churchism," the CMS played heavily on its position as a bastion of Evangelical strength, and it also used its already finely developed system for home support to advance its women's missions. This was, of course, one of the key reasons for the continuing attempts at the CEZMS to negotiate amalgamation, for no one could doubt the success of the CMS: it was in fact the most successful of the denominational missionary societies in recruiting single female missionaries, peaking in 1909 with 439 in the field. When mission wives were added to this number, 825 CMS women considerably outnumbered men in the mission field.[37]

When the CMS began employing female agents, and especially after it organized its Women's Work Department in 1895, the ZBMM and the CEZMS came under growing competitive pressure. The confusion and damage caused at both the CEZMS and the ZBMM by CMS women's policy were evident in the 1880s,

---

Work, in Connection with C.M.S. Committee of Correspondence," 22 Jan. 1895, CMS Archives, G/AZ 2/1, fol. 43.

36. A relative view of the strengths of those strands can be seen in their recruiting successes: from 1887 to 1894 the IFNS/ZBMM grew from 32 to 63 missionaries, the CEZMS from 87 to 157, and the CMS from none to 218. "Proposed Resolution on Women's Work, in Connection with C.M.S. Committee of Correspondence," 22 Jan. 1895, CMS Archives, G/AZ 2/1, fol. 43.

37. The number of clergy was 405, the number of laymen 154, and the total number of missionaries 1384. Stock, *History of the CMS*, 4:465.

and became acute in the 1890s. The CEZMS experienced cash crises, for example, that repeatedly forced it to consider retrenchment in the field.[38] In the mid-1880s a spirit of common cause led most of the leaders of women's missions in the denominational missionary societies to participate in united prayer meetings, but by the early 1890s that spirit had evaporated.[39] At the CMS and the CEZMS, Georgina Gollock and Jane Mulvany made active efforts to maintain cordial relations between the two societies by establishing common prayer meetings for evangelical Anglicans, and they reminded supporters that contributions to both societies were to be encouraged, since CMS Women's Department contributions went to support all CMS work, while CEZMS donations supported "women's work for women" alone. But friction continued, requiring repeated reminders to local secretaries "of the close and friendly relationship" between the two societies.[40]

The ideal of "women's work for women" was, in fact, one of the key attractions that CEZMS organizers built on to develop women's support for the society. In this, the CEZMS operated in an idiom much closer to the broad pattern of independence and separation characteristic of American women's missions. Those at the CEZMS who consistently opposed amalgamation with the CMS over the years partially did so on the grounds "that the plea of 'Women's Work for Women' is essential to their cause." But the CEZMS also closely associated itself with the spirituality and exclusivity of the more radical, or Puritan, wings of Anglican evangelicalism, and Georgina Gollock noted that on such grounds "the C.E.Z. gets into many parishes where C.M.S. would not be welcomed." Clearly these were the same parishes where faith missions and their more advanced ideals of independent women's work, from the RBMU to the CIM, were also greeted favorably. But Gollock also noted that many parishes backed both the CMS and CEZMS, indicating that support was certainly not exclusive within Anglicanism based on theological or gender considerations.[41] Because of this distinctiveness in its cause and identity, the CEZMS jealously guarded its independence, chastising the CMS for moves that it considered as impinging on its

---

38. Minutes of the Home Organisation Committee, 24 Nov. 1898 and 5 May 1902, CEZMS Archives, CEZ H/C 1/1.

39. United Prayer Meetings begun in 1886 were attended by the FES, the Baptist Zenana Mission, the LMS Zenana branch, the ZBMM, the CEZMS, and the Women's Missionary Association of the Presbyterian Church of England. In Nov. 1893 the meetings were cancelled, and denominational prayer meetings held in Mission Houses were substituted. Minutes of the CEZMS Union Committee, 1886-1893, CEZMS Archives, CEZ/G C11.

40. G[eorgina]. Gollock, M[inna]. C. Gollock, and Jane Mulvany, draft circular letters, Nov. 1903 and Jan. 1904, CMS Archives, W/A 4.

41. G[eorgina] A G[ollock], "Memo. re. C.E.Z. Question," private, 27 Feb. 1911, CMS Archives, W/A 4.

freedom of action.[42] Despite friction, the CMS and the CEZMS did continue co-operative organization, such as the sharing of travelling missionary exhibitions. But the CMS did not extend this courtesy to the interdenominational ZBMM, even though both organizations continued to cooperate in India.[43]

Growing Anglican exclusivity on the part of the CMS caused even greater problems for the ZBMM. After the Anglican members split from the IFNS in the early 1880s, survival was its primary focus. In the immediate aftermath of the split, the secretaries at the IFNS scrambled to retain as much support as possible, not, however, in "places like Oxford and Cambridge where Church influences would be very strong."[44] Seeking to update its image in 1881 the IFNS changed its name to the Zenana Bible and Medical Mission (ZBMM), although for years afterward it was routinely referred to in publications as the IFNS.[45] Its budget shrank from £13,000 in 1879 to £6,000 in 1881. Despite the gloomy prognosis, however, outside observers considered the society's success in rebuilding support impressive. By 1892, receipts had returned to £16,000 and a £20,000 goal seemed realistic.[46]

In large part the ZBMM based its new success, after losing so many of its officers and supporters, on pressing its association with radical ultra-Protestantism. Through the Kinnairds the ZBMM was on intimate terms with the most charismatic elements in the English holiness movement, and its committee rooms were more often frequented by holiness dignitaries such as John Paton, Henry Grattan Guinness, and the influential Anglican holiness preacher H. W. Webb-Peploe. In 1890, to further tap this vein of support, the ZBMM appointed the zealous evangelical Rev. A. R. Cavalier so that "he should be to our Society what Mr. Hudson Taylor is to the China Inland Mis-

42. George Tonge to H. E. Fox, 5 Apr. 1898, CMS Archives, G/AC 4/24/4624a. Despite persistent financial hardship the CEZMS resisted amalgamation with the CMS in 1919, 1939, 1940, 1944, and 1951, but finally merged in 1957. These negotiations are detailed in CMS Archives, G/AP 1.

43. Minutes of the Home Organisation Committee, 23 Feb. 1899 and 22 Apr. 1903, CEZMS Archives, CEZ H/C 1/1.

44. Minutes of the IFNS General Committee, 7 Apr. 1880, 19 Apr. 1880, and 5 Jan. 1881, IFNS/ZBMM Archives, Home File List, General Committee minutes, Oct. 1878–July 1886.

45. On 6 April 1881, the Committee adopted a new name: the Indian Female Normal School and Instruction Society, or Zenana Bible and Medical Mission. On 21 Sept. 1881 the Society officially began using the short title: The Zenana Bible and Medical Mission. Only in 1915 did it drop entirely "Indian Female Normal School and Instruction Society." Minutes of the IFNS/ZBMM General Committee, 5 Nov. 1873, 6 Apr. 1881, 21 Sept. 1881, and 6 Jan. 1915, IFNS/ZBMM Archives, Home File List, General Committee minutes, May 1870–Apr. 1875, Oct. 1878–July 1886, and May 1911–Apr. 1915.

46. Minutes of the IFNS General Committee, 2 June 1880 and 20 Feb. 1880, IFNS/ZBMM Archives, Home File List, General Committee minutes, Oct. 1878–July 1886; Minutes of the ZBMM Finance Committee, 5 May 1892, IFNS/ZBMM Archives, Home File List, Finance Committee minutes, Jan. 1882-Oct. 1909.

sion."[47] The ZBMM also benefited from its close connection to the rapidly growing YWCA, with its influential London secretary Emily Kinnaird and slate of past secretaries, all returned missionary wives. Also, the vogue for foreign missions had swept up the YWCA when in 1886 it began organizing Missionary Missions in England and the following year held "A Conference for the deepening of our interest in Foreign Missions." Inspired by the example of Hudson Taylor, Moody and Sankey, and the Cambridge Seven, the YWCA "became rather a hunting-ground for all the missionary societies," leading it to begin sending secretaries abroad to form foreign YWCA Branches.[48]

Yet, like the CEZMS, the ZBMM found itself suffering, relatively at least, as CMS women's work expanded, and even more so as the CMS excluded it from its support network.[49] The ZBMM had much the same relationship to the CEZMS as the CIM had to the CMS. Both the ZBMM and the CIM, despite their interdenominational holiness basis, drew heavily on the ultra-Protestant "Puritan" wing of the Church of England, whose loyalty to the episcopacy was most tenuous. Given its interdenominational and "enthusiastic" background, and its competitive troubles with the CMS, the ZBMM naturally considered amalgamation with one of the most dynamic of the "faith" missions of the age, Henry Grattan Guinness's RBMU. In 1899 the RBMU had absorbed a number of other smaller regional faith missions to form a more general "faith" society second only to Hudson Taylor's CIM.[50] But the strength of Anglican support continued to exert a powerful influence at the ZBMM: the opposition of Anglican supporters and the difficulties that would be raised in India concerning cooperation with the CMS scotched the plan for amalgamation.[51]

Women's foreign missionary work in England had strong popular support. But the forms that women's mission work took among Evangelicals varied

47. Minutes of the ZBMM General Committee, 2 Jan. 1890, IFNS/ZBMM Archives, Home File List, General Committee minutes, Oct. 1886–Oct. 1890. Cavalier, an Islington College–trained CMS missionary, served in the Tamil Coolie Mission through the divisive Ceylon Controversy with Ritualist Bishop Copleston. Clerical secretary for the CEZMS from 1881 to 1883, he also worked in Tinnevelly from 1883 to 1887. On the illuminating, ferocious controversy that ensued when one of Cavalier's six sons embraced Anglo-Catholicism while studying at St. Paul's School, see Martin Wellings, "Anglo-Catholicism, the 'Crisis in the Church' and the Cavalier Case of 1899," *Journal of Ecclesiastical History* 42, no. 2 (Apr. 1991): 239-58.

48. Kinnaird, *Reminiscences*, 57-61.

49. A. R. Cavalier to H. E. Fox, 25 May 1898, CMS Archives, G/AC 4/24/4718.

50. "Memorandum regarding proposed Union between the Regions Beyond Missionary Union and the Zenana Bible & Medical Mission," CMS Archives, G/AC 4/28/5560.

51. The threat of union and thus the closing out of CMS from several parishes did, however, lead to re-establishment of joint fundraising with the ZBMM. Gertrude Kinnaird to H. E. Fox, 20 June 1899, CMS Archives, G/AC 4/28/5559.

because organizers, missionaries, and supporters disagreed over how deep denominational loyalties should be and how far theology sanctioned the autonomy of women. After a struggle, the interdenominational ZBMM retained its principles and secured for itself a solid but distant orbit around the evangelical foreign missions of the Church of England. The Anglican CEZMS maintained a closer connection, but it resisted an absorption into the CMS that would mean the annihilation of its separate identity and purpose. Focused strongly on women's work for women, and the only society to support exclusively single female missionaries, the CEZMS engaged women who had a deep Anglican identity, but also a committed vision of autonomous women's mission agency. At the center, the more traditional CMS attracted strong Anglicans who accepted its claims of authority and patriarchy, and by the century's end the CMS proved the most successful agency supporting Evangelical women's work.

Evangelical Anglican women's missions were the most rapidly expanding sector of a growing late Victorian foreign missionary campaign, and the enthusiasm surrounding them had the capacity to support a number of different groups that held significantly different ideas about the proper organization and governance of women's work. Just as the Church of England was broad, so was the range of the female foreign missions generated within the Church, even its evangelical wing. Yet evangelical Anglicans were not the only members of the Church who succeeded in encouraging women's missions; they were just the most prolific and productive. The advances Evangelicals made using women were too consequential to be ignored in the higher church wings of Anglicanism, despite the rather different types of problems they posed for organizations with different constituencies within the Church.

High Church Women: Expanding Authority in a Progressive Empire

While Evangelicals rapidly succeeded in recruiting and organizing women for foreign missions, the SPG sheltered itself from the difficulties raised by the use of women, keeping its Ladies' Association at arm's length and tepidly supporting sisterhoods in foreign dioceses. As much as possible, the SPG downplayed connections to its separately organized female supporters. The Ladies' Association in connection with the SPG had been formed early, in 1866, to promote women's work — supporting female teachers, scholars, and schools, but also "zenana teaching & practice of medicine"[52] — and to relieve the General Fund

---

52. Minutes of the Ladies' Association of the SPG, 11 May, 11 July, and 14 Nov. 1866, USPG Archives, CWW 59.

of the SPG from this "new and expensive undertaking."[53] The work of the Ladies' Association rapidly settled into a standard pattern of fundraising through cooperative working and needlework parties held regularly by local women. Within ten years the Association had five hundred Branch Associations raising £3,500 and supporting fifty-nine teachers (twenty-nine "European," thirty "Native"), but at the same time it was chafing at the "lack of definite recognition . . . by S.P.G."[54] The neglect experienced by the Ladies' Association set the pattern for the next three decades.

Like every other missionary society, however, the SPG ultimately was dependent on the grassroots organizing power of women, and the acutely developed clerical resistance to women's influence at the SPG is central to understanding its relatively poor performance at garnering missionary support. Even at the SPG insiders, looking back, recognized that what success the society had had was due to women's energies, "as the men were not considered half as keen over the work as the women."[55] Thus, despite a conservative reflex to distance itself from the potentially suspect cause of female missionary work, the SPG nevertheless could not allow the Ladies' Association, a potentially dangerous rival, independence from the Society, and thus women supported by the Ladies' Association were to be strictly controlled by the SPG missionary-in-charge in the field.[56]

This awkward positioning of women's work in the chief organization supporting High Church missions was a persistent drag on the cause, retarding professionalization of female mission and reproducing the patriarchal subordination of power relations between fathers and daughters: the secretary of the Ladies' Association for twenty-six years, Louisa Bullock, was the daughter of SPG Secretary William Bullock (1865-79). The Ladies' Association operated quietly and independently, the SPG maintaining deniability regarding the control of women's work, but still within the SPG orbit. Women's work was also supported completely separately through a parallel local Association structure, reinforcing the segregation of the two organizations.[57] Only with the

---

53. "Female Education in India," *The Mission Field* (Feb. 1866): 37-38.

54. Minutes of the Ladies' Association of the SPG, Dec. 1875 and Nov. 1876, USPG Archives, CWW 59.

55. "Special Organisation Sub-Committee Meeting," TS, 12 Mar. 1907, in Minutes of the Women's Home Organisation Advisory Group, USPG Archives, CWW 71.

56. "Report of the Special Committee on the Relations between the W.M.A. and the S.P.G.," 2 Apr. 1903, in Minutes of the Women's Home Organisation Advisory Group, USPG Archives, CWW 71.

57. "An Informal Conference between S.P.G. & W.M.A. re. Future Relations . . . ," 4 July 1902, Special Sub-Committees and Reports of Conferences, 1898-1930, Committee of Women's Work, USPG Archives, CWW 90.

quickening of imperial enthusiasm in the 1890s did a new generation of High Churchmen inspired by student-driven progressivism — linked to the rise of the Christian Social Union, sisterhoods, and settlements — create the pressure necessary to crack the pattern and draw women more fully and influentially into High Church missionary planning and execution.

Imperial Extension and High Church Women's Missions

When Bishop Montgomery took the SPG secretaryship in 1902 and implemented the sweeping reforms that were to transform the SPG into a more serious rival to CMS, he recalled that "the Women's Department was not much more than tolerated . . . a sort of disagreeable necessity." What few innovations might have been brewing at SPG in the 1890s arose from the pressure of students, the JCMA (which coldly orthodox secretary Henry Tucker greatly resented), and the Women's Department (which Montgomery noted had secretly conveyed a typewriter into the House "in terror of discovery").[58] In an attempt to emulate the rapid extension of women's work among evangelical Anglicans, the Ladies' Association in the early 1890s worked systematically to reach children and adolescents and through this to extend networks of support for women's missions. In 1895 it adopted the more "modern" name of the Women's Mission Association (WMA) and began collaborating with the "progressive" JCMA on children's work. But the efforts of the WMA had little noticeable effect on the stolid SPG and, like the junior clergy and many enthusiastic supporters, the women associated with the SPG, despite all their good faith efforts, were coldly rebuffed by the Society.[59]

Certainly the SPG did not place the same emphasis on women's work as the CMS or Anglo-Catholic missions such as the UMCA. While women's work expanded rapidly with encouragement and institutional support at the CMS from about 1885 onward, and Anglo-Catholic colonial and missionary bishops heartily encouraged the creation of missionary sisterhoods, the SPG resisted the trend toward developing women's missions. Simple clerical arrogance was one of the most basic obstacles to harnessing the potential of women's enthusiasm throughout the Church of England, but it was particularly pronounced at the SPG, where both old guard leaders and progressive younger clergy alike

58. Henry H. Montgomery, "Survey of My Stewardship, 1902-1918," TS, USPG Archives, H 3, box 2.

59. Rough Minutes of the Home Organisation Committee, 21 Mar. 1901, and comments attached to p. 199, USPG Archives, H 137.

patronized and obstructed women's workers who sought to carve out a niche of responsible work. Constance Bunyon, for example, fiercely resented the clerical manipulations of the mixed men's and women's committee assigned to organize the children's work that JCMA leader F. W. Isaacs attempted, but she received little validation from the SPG secretariat and even less support for her work to incorporate popular methods, such as exhibitions and public children's meetings, into the Society's work. Instead she experienced only a growing frustration and sense of grievance over how local organization was arrogantly foisted on overworked female volunteers, and at the end of 1898, in disgust, withdrew the salary she had personally contributed to support the Secretary for Children's Work.[60] Such seemed the experience of too many talented, energetic High Church women within the structures of the formal Church.

Yet to those who observed the progress made at the CMS, the critical role played by engaging the women's parallel church was clear. SPG efforts to harmonize women's work into its structures in Tucker's final years all failed, however, due to criticisms that the separate work of women and men was mandated by its traditional constitution.[61] The deadlock was only broken when in 1902 Bishop Montgomery, a staunch advocate of colonial sisterhoods, succeeded Henry Tucker.[62] Following the lead of clerical progressives, Montgomery endorsed the complete renovation of women's organization as one way to pursue the JCMA imperative of enhancing efficiency and imperial linkages at the SPG. The JCMA's animating ideas, heightened by the anxieties raised by the Boer War, now were able to overcome conservative clerical obduracy.[63] Direct sympathetic cooperation with women followed, including provision of SPG grant money to WMA, relocation of WMA offices to SPG House, and negotiations to rearrange their constitutional relationship.[64]

However, transforming a thirty-five-year pattern presented a deep challenge because, as SPG organizing secretaries related, throughout the country SPG and WMA were considered separate, rival organizations. The situation varied

60. Bunyon to Henry Tucker, 24 Feb., 15 Mar., 19 Apr., 21 Apr., and 6 Dec. 1898, USPG Archives, X 557a.

61. Nicholas Mannisty to Tucker, 4 Mar. 1901, L. Fletcher to W. F. Kemp, 18 Mar. 1901, and L. Fletcher to Tucker, 21 July 1901, Ladies Association and Committee for Women's Work, Letters Sent (Home), 1901-1908, USPG Archives, CWW 304.

62. On Montgomery's committed support of sisterhoods as bishop of Tasmania, in the face of controversy from the Evangelical diocese of Sydney, see Campbell, "Sisters of the Church," 195-97.

63. Cecil Stanton to [Montgomery], 18 Feb. 1902, USPG Archives, X 557a.

64. Ethel F. Mackenzie (WMA secretary) to Montgomery, 15 July 1902, and Marion H. Bickersteth to Montgomery, 13 Nov. 1902, Ladies Association and Committee for Women's Work, Letters Sent (Home), 1901-1908, USPG Archives, CWW 304.

widely. In some parishes the WMA was so zealous that the SPG collected practically nothing. On the other hand, twenty-one of sixty-five voluntary organizing secretaries had little difficulty with the WMA largely because there was practically no activity to support women's work in the areas under their supervision. WMA workers often experienced cold resistance and prohibitions on parish activity by clergy who saw competition from multiplying organizations outside their control as a threat to the SPG and to their own authority, particularly where newer WMA branches, generally run by enthusiastic younger women, were viewed as unwelcome interlopers.[65]

Bishop Montgomery, upon arrival at the Society, insisted that a solution be hammered out, and he acted as referee at the negotiations. Old arguments and justifications boiled quickly to the surface, but clearly leaders of the WMA and SPG had never spoken openly on the subject before and operated in completely different worlds. The central issue was the same as that faced by the CMS seven years previously: Was the WMA to remain an independent entity or was it to be completely amalgamated, gain a measure of influence in the operation of the SPG, and combine women's work with men's in a unified Church effort?[66] Parallel to the prevailing opinion expressed at the CMS, some higher church Anglicans wanted to fully unite women's and men's work, a reflection of a strong vision in a communion based on the ideal of a unified national church. Responding to a questionnaire on the matter, 68 percent of SPG organizing secretaries supported amalgamation, paralleled by 56 percent of WMA organizers.[67] The women, while coveting greater financial resources, feared a loss of position and autonomy. A Miss Phillimore, for instance, noted that a restrictive amalgamation plan frightened women in the countryside who were nevertheless hopeful of a looser cooperative scheme.[68] The uncertainties of WMA supporters proved powerful, for under the leadership of Montgomery the staff at the SPG were determined to co-opt women's energy as fully as possible, to which end they were willing to concede considerable autonomy. By 1902, in the wake of a

65. "Report of the Special Committee on the Relations between the W.M.A. and the S.P.G.," 2 Apr. 1903, pp. 5-8, in Minutes of the Women's Home Organisation Advisory Group, USPG Archives, CWW 71. Results tabulated from the replies of 59 of the 104 WMA Diocesan Presidents and correspondents.

66. Special Sub-Committees and Reports of Conferences, 1898-1930, Committee of Women's Work, USPG Archives, CWW 90.

67. "Report of the Special Committee on the Relations between the W.M.A. and the S.P.G.," 2 Apr. 1903, in Minutes of the Women's Home Organisation Advisory Group, USPG Archives, CWW 71. The numbers were twenty-four organizing secretaries in favor, eleven against; thirty-three WMA workers were in favor, ten were doubtful, and sixteen were against.

68. "Notes of a Conference between S.P.G. & W.M.A. re. Future Relations," 15 Dec. 1902, in Minutes of Special Sub-Committees and Reports of Conferences, Committee of Women's Work, USPG Archives, CWW 90.

failed bicentenary collection campaign, the chief desire at the SPG was to raise energy and support, an impossible task without women's activism.

The decision to provide a large measure of autonomy for women at the conservative SPG was facilitated by strong leadership on the women's side, particularly that of Louise Creighton. Popular author, noted social activist, and advocate of women's education and advancement tied to the maternalist Oxford educational circles of Lady Margaret and Somerville Halls, Creighton had been recently widowed in January 1901, with the death of husband Mandell Creighton (influential historian and bishop of London).[69] Just beginning a decade of high-profile public advocacy, Louise Creighton was dedicated to promoting women's influence in national life outside of formal politics, and the SPG proved at this point to be one of the first such causes she supported.[70] Creighton brushed aside the objections of one of Henry Tucker's old allies, Sir Charles Turner, that the fragile financial network of WMA might be disturbed by amalgamation, that the women were angling for easy money, and that the prejudices of SPG Committee clerics who "disapprove of Zenana work" would be inflamed. She countered these objections with the forceful argument that any problems caused by zenana work that was not "entirely judicious" were best corrected by guidance from the SPG, saying also that for too many years "Sir Charles Turner ignored all the difficulties felt in the country which have been brought before us as to the present arrangement of two funds."[71]

Articulate, well-connected, and determined, Creighton carried the day, not least because progressives at the SPG hoped, along with the aggressive amalgamation advocate Samuel Bickersteth (himself of a weighty Anglican family), "that by the scheme of complete amalgamation SPG would share in the enthusiasm of the ladies."[72] To any who observed the undeniable changes in society, Bickersteth argued, opposition must be seen as foolish and futile:

69. Julia Bush, *Women Against the Vote: Female Anti-Suffragism in Britain* (Oxford: Oxford University Press, 2007), 35-46, 51-53.

70. Creighton, along with Mary (Mrs. Humphrey) Ward, had been a prominent opponent of women's suffrage. Never believing women incompetent to vote, she thought it desirable for the country "to have a large body of intelligent & influential opinion which was outside party politics." As women nevertheless "increasingly took part in politics in a decidedly party manner," she came to believe that "they had better have full responsibility" and reversed her position in 1906 and began to support women's suffrage. Louise Creighton, *Memoir of a Victorian Woman: Reflections of Louise Creighton, 1850-1936*, ed. James Thayne Covert (Bloomington: Indiana University Press, 1994), 89.

71. "Notes of a Conference between the S.P.G. & W.M.A.," 27 Jan. 1903, in Minutes of Special Sub-Committees and Reports of Conferences, Committee of Women's Work, USPG Archives, CWW 90.

72. "Notes of a Conference between S.P.G. & W.M.A. re Future Relations," 15 Dec. 1902, in Minutes of Special Sub-Committees and Reports of Conferences, Committee of Women's Work, USPG Archives, CWW 90.

Here in England we have seen in all other departments of social and charitable work, women working with men, and the question is not raised, Do the women raise more money than the men, or work harder than the men or vice versa? Their work is felt to be one work, and it is the recognition of this feeling, which many men and women wish to see in the support of Missionary work at home.[73]

The WMA ratified union with the SPG on 7 May 1903, "believing it to be for the good of the work entrusted to them," and henceforth it became the Committee for Women's Work (CWW) under the direction of the Standing Committee of the SPG.[74] Amalgamation established a unified fund, retained all the personnel and machinery of the WMA, acknowledged women's work by earmarking all their funds, provided for additional SPG grants for women's work, and directed parochial cooperation throughout the country.[75]

This was a relatively liberal accommodation for SPG women, but what made sense in London aroused considerable skepticism in local women's networks.[76] At the following SPG Women's Annual Conference, Lady Frederick Cavendish conceded that after thirty-seven years of independence the WMA had made a sacrifice, but she urged her listeners that the SPG "was no alien society into which we were being absorbed." Miss Phillimore emphasized "that by its acceptance an enormous dignity & support had been added to the W.M.A."[77] But palpable skepticism meant that an SPG that was desperate for positive, progressive relations felt it necessary to leave independent women's local practices in place for fear of harming lucrative channels of contribution. Whereas the strength of the CMS meant it had been able to dictate the shape of women's work, the weakness of the SPG, and the more positive High Church vision of independent women's work associated with sisterhoods, meant that for years to come the WMA would continue to function as a *de facto* independent society.[78]

73. "Memorandum on Relations of S.P.G. and W.M.A. by the Rev. Samuel Bickersteth," 27 Jan. 1903, in Minutes of Special Sub-Committees and Reports of Conferences, Committee of Women's Work, USPG Archives, CWW 90.

74. Ethel F. Mackenzie to Montgomery, 7 May 1903, USPG Archives, CWW 304.

75. "Report of the Special Committee on the Relations between the W.M.A. and the S.P.G.," 2 Apr. 1903, in Minutes of the Women's Home Organisation Advisory Group, USPG Archives, CWW 71.

76. Ethel F. Mackenzie to Montgomery, 15 June 1903, USPG Archives, H 149.

77. Report, Annual Conference, 30 Apr. 1903, in Minutes of Special Sub-Committees and Reports of Conferences, USPG Archives, CWW 90.

78. "Secretary's Report, Jan. 1910"; and the Monthly Summaries, Jan. 1910-Apr. 1918, Committee for Women's Work Secretary, Monthly Summaries and Reviews, 1910-1918, USPG Archives, CWW 1.

Central to this outcome was the fact that while the SPG, like the CMS, adopted and emphasized the idea that all God's mission work was one, it did not insist that control of women's work should be exercised by male-dominated committees.[79] The SPG had waited to absorb women's work, and as a result it encountered a women's organization that was both too important and too independent to be bullied, particularly when championed by influential, high-profile Churchwomen such as Louise Creighton and Edith Temple, widow of the late archbishop. The agreement that resulted from negotiating with the WMA left the SPG Standing Committee holding final power, but in practice women's work was to be carried out "by the agency and under the management of women in every detail so far as it is possible," and thus female subscribers elected Committee members, the Women's Committee could initiate plans for new work, and the CWW supervised all women's work.[80] The results were impressive, with a rapid expansion of unmarried female workers in High Church overseas dioceses, particularly those deeply influenced by Anglo-Catholic culture such as South Africa.[81]

As in the case of High Church junior clergy, the driving force behind this transformation was a new vision of imperial efficiency and enhanced opportunities for women to contribute as imperial citizens. Progressives at the SPG, especially younger clerical supporters in the 1890s, argued that shutting out women wasted an obvious and potentially enormous source of High Church enthusiasm. Despite the fact that the SPG had continued to support women's work piecemeal — as advocacy of women at the 1894 Anglican Missionary Conference for a whole range of missionary agencies shows — other societies placed far greater emphasis on women's work. Yet the records of the 1894 conference indicate strong general levels of support for women's missions in the Anglican Communion, and a particular advocacy for the focused discipline of sisterhoods directed to address the problems created by scattered efforts to advance a family-focused civilizing effort. While the SPG supported these efforts by degrees, it still did not press women's work forcefully as a central strategy in foreign missions. But the appeal of advertising the social services advanced through schools and hospitals as an imperial support was growing, while at the same time the poor preparation of SPG women, who lacked female

79. Notes on a speech by Mrs. Sunderland, in Minutes of the Women's Diocesan SPG Committee, 2 Nov. 1909, USPG Archives, X 281.

80. "Report of the Special Committee on the Relations between the W.M.A. and the S.P.G.," 2 Apr. 1903, in Minutes of the Women's Home Organisation Advisory Group, USPG Archives, CWW 71.

81. In South Africa, for example, by 1914 single women had increased nearly fivefold over their numbers in the 1880s. Gaitskell, "Rethinking Gender Roles," 150-51.

training homes, increasingly forced the SPG to rely on English sisterhoods to carry out this work.[82]

So when the organization and strategy of women's work shifted rapidly at the SPG after the turn of the century, there were several causes: the obvious success of evangelicals; the important place of women in an emerging student missionary movement; the now longstanding, successful, and largely normalized sisterhoods in High Church dioceses and missions; and the arrival of a progressive, imperially oriented secretary at the SPG. Anglican sisterhoods were recognized by the late 1880s as a particularly successful option for women's work precisely because they offered high levels of independence and, as SPG Committee member Rev. Berdmore Compton allowed, "ladies like independence as much as men do."[83] Similarly, the significant growth in the student missionary movement by the early 1890s raised the profile of the growing numbers of women with college educations and pressured missionary societies to provide them with expanding opportunities. "Mission science" and "progressive missions" became slogans for a new style of missionary leadership that was simultaneously technocratic, enthusiastic, and largely open to women.

British female missionaries had always had a noticeable affinity for empire and its structures. American women, however, emphasized that their experience of political democracy produced a superior missionary egalitarianism, in contrast with what they saw as the hierarchy and snobbery inherent in British imperialism and missions.[84] At the SPG Montgomery's program to develop the Anglican Communion as an "imperial church" rested heavily on English pride in gentility, breeding, and the more ordered culture and society they were presumed to generate. It provoked a wide-ranging discussion of the purposes and strategies of Anglican missions. Often at the heart of these discussions was the role of female missionaries, because of both the power that idealized conceptions of feminine power had in constructing a "civilizing" imperial project and the fact that enhanced use of women's missions was imagined as providing a way forward for missions that faced increasing difficulties in a field transformed by indigenous nationalisms.[85] This project included enhancing the civilizing mission ascribed to women that was so prevalent in the evangelical world as well as using women to bring a new "sympathy" to missions that would mollify indigenous anger in increasingly contested imperial realms, most notably

---

82. Spottiswoode, *Anglican Missionary Conference, 1894*, 597-600. On the poor preparation of SPG female missionaries, see Gill, *Women and the Church*, 180.

83. Quoted in Prelinger, "Female Diaconate," 184.

84. Hunter, *Gospel of Gentility*, 152-55.

85. On the challenges presented by rising Indian, Chinese, and Japanese nationalisms, see Greenlee and Johnston, *Good Citizens*, 148-49.

"tropical and semi-tropical lands." The SPG's concession of considerable autonomy to High Church women over women's work was designed to secure
their confidence and cooperation. For Montgomery, appealing to women by
emphasizing the crucial cross-cultural powers of feminine sympathy — "gra-
ciousness, dignity, gentleness" — would provide the example of true morality
and an attractive future to indigenous societies that chafed under crude forms
of imperial rule. This program, Montgomery suggested, was essential to revi-
talizing High Church missions.[86] And in at least some fields, as with the case
of Gertrude King in Madagascar, it was supportive of revitalized approaches
to evangelization that vigorously pressed leadership and proselytizing by indigenous women, colored by a commitment to the preservation of traditional
culture, in this case Malagasy.[87]

Shifting social attitudes to women's public work strongly reinforced rapid
changes in the treatment of High Church women's missions, from mere toleration to acceptance as a necessary aspect of mission work. By the 1900s even
traditionalist High Church mission supporters no longer considered women's
missions a tainted Anglo-Catholic agency because in the mission field there was
realistically little difference between the operation of High Church and Evangelical women's foreign missionary communities, despite earlier fears many
had held of the dangerous precedents toward feminine license that sisterhoods
might ostensibly set. Furthermore, conditions in the mission field had changed
sufficiently to make the high-profile use of women, in and out of sisterhoods,
seem more necessary. This was most notable in the rapid expansion of the
Mothers' Union following the Boer War, an organization designed to pull together British and colonial society around the commonality of motherhood
and to create an educated Christian womanhood the world over, as part of an
expanding Christian internationalist vision intent on social and moral reform.
This movement linked white and indigenous colonial societies, and after 1910 in
Madagascar, for example, under the leadership of Gertrude King, it pressed for
an enactment of equality between the linked branches, including the MU's first
"Black Branch."[88] Additionally, by the final decades of the nineteenth century,
settled mission strategies had normalized in what had earlier been reformist
High Church experimental mission fields such as East Africa and Melanesia.
In these, European women were now increasingly conceived of as essential to a
settlement of indigenous communities that was designed to protect them from

86. Montgomery, *With the Women*, 11-12.

87. This program was reflective at least in part of her embrace of Anglo-Catholics' modes of
thought and training with the All Saints Sisters at Wantage prior to her arrival in 1900. Prevost,
Communion of Women, 77-82.

88. Prevost, *Communion of Women*, 267-69.

backsliding into "pagan" practices and to provide an edge as mission fields saw rising competition between rival faith traditions.[89] Significantly, by 1900 the UMCA, thirty-five years in the field, had grown to employ forty-two single women in East Africa, or 40 percent of its staff.[90] In missions that were moving away from earlier ideals of rapid indigenization, the growth of rhetoric regarding the use of women reinforced the trend toward professionalism that strengthened European control, but a European control that could be used either to further or to thwart indigenization practices.

In England, advocates of the use of High Church women's missions emphasized the professionalizing aspect of women's work, most notably Louise Creighton. After 1900 Creighton became a growing force in the movement to extend women's power and influence in the Church of England as a whole; part of this larger program was to advocate vigorously for the enhanced use of women in SPG missions in order to maximize the "civilizing influence" women had on indigenous societies. Creighton was a leading female figure in the Church of England in the first two decades of the twentieth century, and her moderate Anglican feminism represents one of the most advanced positions adopted by female missionary supporters with any level of influence. Creighton, who after her involvement in the SPG women's amalgamation negotiations became the president of the National Council of Women Workers, was one of the first female members of the SPG Standing Committee. Unlike Anglican radicals such as Maude Royden, who chose to preach in the face of Anglican clerical condemnation, Creighton worked within Church structures, and while she advocated independence and individuality for women, she also maintained a strong advocacy for traditional domestic arrangements and family life.[91] She was also an ardent supporter of the empire, touting, in parallel to Montgomery, the deepened "sympathy" women could bring to the movement in order to stabilize an empire shaken by rising nationalist movements of those "alienated" from imperial progress and rule. In her comments at the 1908 Pan-Anglican Congress she matched the responsibilities of "citizens of a great empire" to the need for "a real and sympathetic understanding of the characteristics of . . . other races" and called for "missionaries to . . . recognize all that is beautiful in the native customs with which they come in contact." Such comments operated in the context of discussions with missionaries from the field that emphasized the need to placate "natives" who were agitated with nationalist emotions and

<hr>

89. E.g., for changes in the High Church Melanesian Mission after 1900, see Whiteman, *Melanesians and Missionaries*, 171-86, and in Central Africa, Porter, "UMCA," 95-96.

90. Dennis, *Centennial Survey*, 23.

91. For a discussion of Creighton and Royden, see Heeney, *Women's Movement*, 92-93.

angry at the cold arrogance of many Europeans involved in trade and imperial governance.[92] She also resonated with a growing emphasis on racial duties in an imperial context. As she related to her sister in the midst of her preparations for the congress, "the whole subject is so absorbing and interesting . . . when the opportunities are so great . . . to educate & develop the backward races, as well as help the women of India & China to get a chance of being educated and come out of their seclusion."[93]

Rapidly the SPG, previously seen as the least progressive and least enthusiastic of the English missionary societies, surpassed evangelical agencies in the advanced nature of its women's work. CMS women, in comparison, were to complain, especially after the 1910 World Missionary Conference, that the SPG had so rapidly developed its women's work since 1903, and particularly after the 1908 Pan-Anglican Church Congress, that the High Church society now showed up the CMS. Even old hands at the CMS began to warn that the Society's unenlightened stance toward the women who kept the entire edifice afloat threatened CMS precedence in the mission world. Georgina Gollock commented in 1914, in support of criticisms voiced by her sister Minna against CMS women's policy, that while the CMS still had the largest women's operation in the British missionary world, it was no longer the leader: "It used to be in the fore-front. At the time of the Pan Anglican Conference the S.P.G. ladies used to envy us, and we were the means of starting them on freer lines. Now they are far ahead of us."[94] While resistance to the expansion of women's roles persisted, in the wake of the 1910 World Missionary Conference, the prominent position of women on its Continuation Committee, and in its new periodical, *The International Review of Missions,* wherein women argued the case for their admission to the highest levels of decision making in the missionary movement, allowed them now to see past the conservative stonewalling of traditionalists to a new missionary world.[95] Women's support at the CMS, especially in developing and maintaining local support networks, was absolutely crucial to success. Yet despite this fact, by 1910 women at the CMS were complaining bitterly that the CMS still seemed openly to despise the aid of the women upon which its prosperity rested.

92. Louise Creighton, "The Claim of Non-Christian Womanhood" in *The Church's Mission to Non-Christian Lands,* vol. 5, Sect. D of [Report of the] Pan-Anglican Congress, 1908 (London: SPCK, 1908), 9-10.

93. Louise Creighton to Ida Koch, 13 June 1908, Louise Creighton Papers, MS 3678/110/1, Lambeth Palace Library, London.

94. "Memorandum Submitted by Miss G. A. Gollock," 22 May 1914, CMS Archives, G/C 26 A.

95. See, for example, Minna C. Gollock, "The Share of Women in the Administration of Missions," *International Review of Missions* 1 (Oct. 1912): 674-87.

Clerical Culture and the Backlash of "Ultra-Protestantism"

The 1910 World Missionary Conference in Edinburgh, with its emphasis on the most effective use of all missionary resources and its placing of women in positions of executive power, stirred women and progressive men at the CMS to challenge the long-standing conservatism of the Society's gender practice.[96] Impatience had been building, and the gathering of Anglican women at the 1908 Pan-Anglican Church Congress spurred demands, especially at the CMS, for a larger share of the work. At the meetings of the Pan-Anglican Women's Sub-Committee on Missions, SPG women advertised the great strides they had achieved. Possessing a separate committee with powers of administration and initiation, as well as financial independence through block grants, SPG women expressed a satisfaction that contrasted starkly with the impotence that women at the CMS felt. While the CMS had never developed a functioning women's committee with oversight powers, women at the SPG had been able to leverage influence and authority by emphasizing the crucial role of women in advancing an imperial civilizing mission through special agencies directed toward advancing the welfare of indigenous women. Despite these changes, however, the World Missionary Conference ended with a deep note of dissatisfaction even from Louise Creighton, leader of negotiations on the part of women at the SPG. Creighton closed the session on women in the administration of missions with the observation that in no Anglican society — not even the CEZMS — were the administrative powers of women equal to those of men. "Are the women not fitted," she asked, "or are the men unwilling to admit them to an equal share in the government?"[97]

Dissatisfaction with the relative powerlessness of women that the rhetoric of "unified work" had produced at the CMS led to agitation for change by women secretaries, activists, and their young clerical allies. These were consistently thwarted, however, by the CMS secretariat. An attempt to alter CMS procedure to allow women to sit on the Foreign Group Committees that oversaw overseas work produced an impasse and was shelved. A special committee followed, which revived the original arrangements for women's work of 1895: formation of both a Women's Home and a Women's Foreign Committee.[98] Once

96. "E[xecutive]. C[ommittee]. 12.12.45 Miss E. M. Baring-Gould — resignation," Hewitt papers, 1937-77, CMS Archives, Acc 318 Z/1.

97. "Notes of a Missionary Conference. . . . The Share of Women in Government and Administration of Missions," 12 Mar. 1908, in Minutes of the Pan-Anglican Congress, Women's Committee: Missionary Sub-Committee, USPG Archives, CWW 11.

98. "The Special Committee of Representatives of the Three Group Committees to Consider Proposals for Admitting Women to a Share in the Administration of the Foreign Work of the Society," 3 Nov. 1911, in Minutes of Sub-Committees, CMS Archives, G/CS 4.

again ignored by the foreign group secretaries, these two committees by 1914 had failed. Minna Gollock stated that "decisive action is imperative if the past as well as the future are not to be lost. . . . [T]he danger is lest by indeterminate action they fail to hold the women who are ready but who will not indefinitely wait." Years of feminine "moral influence" had little effect, and rising frustration, Gollock reported, meant that women were transferring their support to rival charitable organizations. Disillusion arose from the fact that the women's "demands" were really quite modest: some level of decentralization giving slightly more autonomy to local Associations and a share for women in the London office of the executive work, which was being done by the exclusively male Home Organization and Area Group committees.[99] Yet CMS secretaries refused to give women any work of responsibility or substance, and they argued that it was "very difficult to see what foreign work there was that could anything like occupy the whole time of an able woman."[100] The only duty that CMS officials assigned to the Women's Foreign Committee, for example, was consideration of furlough scheduling. This led Minna Gollock to note bitterly that the woman serving as assistant secretary over the committee, with nothing to do, felt that "the post became gradually and finally untenable being a waste of the Society's money and of the woman's life."[101] To another prominent home worker, Edith Baring-Gould, it was also evident that the Committee had failed: "The W.F.C. has through lack of means by which to gain information, not had a fair chance at gaining the knowledge necessary for its work." Given the extraordinary growth of women's work over the past twenty-five years, Baring-Gould was more sanguine about the immediate future of women's work at the CMS than the Gollock sisters; she believed that with more quiet influence women would prove their value and be invited to sit on CMS Committees, but that they had currently overreached their grasp.[102]

The Women's Department at the CMS was the victim of two converging forces: a professionalizing world of male missionary endeavor that fed on the territorial instincts of traditional clerical privilege, and a rising protofundamentalist reaction that identified women's equality as one more challenge to biblical truths. In general, women at the CMS accepted the professionalizing claims of the new "science of missions" advocated by the student missionary movement and female supporters in women's colleges that emphasized exper-

99. Minna C. Gollock, "Memo. on the C.M.S. Women's Department" [1914], CMS Archives, G/C 26 A.

100. [Herbert Lankester], "Memo. by the Lay Secretary" [1914], CMS Archives, G/C 26 A.

101. Minna C. Gollock, "Memo. on the C.M.S. Women's Department" [1914], CMS Archives, G/C 26 A.

102. "Memo. by Miss Baring-Gould" [1914], CMS Archives, G/C 26 A.

tise and training. But CMS secretaries, busy and insensitive to women's aspirations, preached internal cooperation while failing to build any meaningful integration of women into missionary power structures. "We are theoretically 'out' for the ideal of true co-operation between men and women instead of for separate women's work," Georgina Gollock stated, "but I am being driven to take the position that either would be better than neither, and that if the former is not possible the latter would be better than what has come to exist."[103] Revealingly, in past years the Women's Department had worked very well when it met in conference annually with female missionaries apart from the men. But once male and female missionaries met together in the name of unified work, the situation rapidly deteriorated, leaving women little autonomy and less responsibility. Contradicting the sitting secretaries, Minna Gollock insisted on the "overwhelming claim" of women's leadership, the "magnificent work waiting to be done," and that it was no longer enough to rely on "a mere desire for co-operation."[104]

Progressives insisted that a crisis had arisen at the CMS between women and men in the wake of the Edinburgh conference due to "a discouraging lack of co-operation and fellowship" that led to a "confusion of relationships throughout the country." Minna Gollock argued that the CMS was losing the support of the most talented women and that the simplest way to reverse the problem was "at once to place a suitable number of selected women on C.M.S. committees. They expect it, they are worthy of it. Other Societies are giving them freely what C.M.S. withhold as yet."[105] In support of her sister's position, Georgina lectured the CMS that her work on the Continuation Committee of the World Missionary Conference showed that cooperative work on executive committees "answers perfectly." But after twenty years of loyal service Georgina Gollock now felt forced to publicize the disagreeable reality that the CMS had actually retrogressed in its relations with women, making known that the CMS, in refusing to allow even a "small number of competent" women voting status, defended an insulting position that bordered on the irrational. Furthermore, because the CMS's unparalleled size and influence gave it enormous "potential for good or evil," its policy was damaging throughout the international missionary movement.[106] With the intent of immediate reforms, progressives at the CMS initiated a subcommittee to implement recommendations recently

103. "Memorandum Submitted by Miss G. A. Gollock," 22 May 1914, CMS Archives, G/C 26 A.
104. Minna C. Gollock, "Memo. on the C.M.S. Women's Department" [1914], CMS Archives, G/C 26 A.
105. Minna C. Gollock, "Memo. on the C.M.S. Women's Department" [1914], CMS Archives, G/C 26 A.
106. "Memorandum Submitted by Miss G. A. Gollock," 22 May 1914, CMS Archives, G/C 26 A.

made at the 1912 Swanwick Conference that advocated extending real power to women in mission administration. The subcommittee concluded that as a matter of efficiency, not justice, women should be admitted to all committees, including the General Committee.[107]

For the most part the secretariat, essentially pragmatic, relented once the progressives impressed the danger of a public revolt against the Society by its most articulate and highly educated female friends.[108] As Eugene Stock, now the venerable "missionary statesman," argued, the example of the SPG showed that women's administration under male supervision was safe and effective — due to "the immense advance in the education of women, their increasing knowledge of the work, &c." — and, unlike at the CEZMS, reforming at the CMS would tie them to the "whole work," rather than to women's work alone.[109] But the extreme Protestant defenders of male command fought tooth and nail to prevent "biblical principles" from being reversed.

Ever since the formation of the Women's Committee in 1895, traditional evangelicals had challenged CMS policy on women. While after 1902 at the SPG those opposing women's ambitions for greater influence had been openly engaged and routed, conservative evangelical attitudes had never been clearly challenged at the CMS. They re-emerged with new force after 1910, with Rev. G. T. Manley and other conservatives insisting that the Bible offered no principle to support the introduction of women to executive power. Christ had chosen twelve male apostles; the New Testament taught a reciprocal but not identical relation between the sexes, such that "[t]he function of government and leadership is committed to the male; that of dependence to the female." The early history of the CMS, they further argued, showed that its founders understood these truths.[110] The subcommittee appointed to consider the question split, and while the arguments of the more liberal secretaries won the day, they did not do so unanimously. This caused the liberal majority to remain decidedly cautious. While recommending full voting membership for women on the most important CMS Committees, it did so with the proviso that committees should never be over one-third female and that only a limited number of

107. "Report of Joint Sub-Committee to Review the Conditions under which the Home Work of Women for C.M.S. Is Done" [1913], CMS Archives, G/AZ 2/4 (part 1).

108. "Statement by Rev. F[rederick]. Baylis," in "Report of Joint Sub-Committee to Review the Conditions under which the Home Work of Women for C.M.S. Is Done" [1913], CMS Archives, G/AZ 2/4 (part 1).

109. Address by Stock, Minutes of the Sub-Committee on the Representation of Women on Committees, 16 Jan. 1914, CMS Archives, G/CS 4.

110. G. T. Manley, "The Sub-Committee on the Representation of Women on Committee," 1 Dec. 1913, in Minutes of Sub-Committees, CMS Archives, G/CS 4.

Annie Perry Howlett and pupils at the entrance to the Zenana and Bible Medical Mission girls' school at Khurja, North India, ca. 1910. From Photographs & Slides, 1910s-1980, Small Albums, A. P. Howlett, "Early Days," North India, Khurja, 1910-15, IFNS/ZBMM Archives, School of Oriental and African Studies. Courtesy of Interserve England and Wales.

women should sit on the General Committee.[111] The presentation of a majority and a minority report to the General Committee in March led to a decision to postpone appointing women to the General Committee, but to appoint women to the Funds and Home Organisation Committee immediately. In November of 1914, the General Committee began appointing women to the Correspondence Committee. And in February of 1917, the CMS appointed twenty-four women to a General Committee, which had a regular attendance of fifty to sixty and potentially hundreds.[112] In the face of conservative opposition, the

111. The minority report, signed by four of the twelve members of the subcommittee, echoed the objections of Manley. "Report I. Representation of Women on Committees," Feb. 1914, and "Report II. Representation of Women on Committees," 28 Feb. 1914, CMS Archives, G/AP 2.

112. Irene H. Barnes, *In Salisbury Square* (London: CMS, 1906), 22.

CMS tentatively implemented a policy that, while repugnant to an important minority, was too dangerous to the health of the CMS and too important to the "progressives" at the CMS, including Cyril Bardsley, its new honorary clerical secretary, to postpone.[113]

The extraordinary convulsions caused by a seemingly obvious decision, which every other major missionary society had already taken, reveal deeper divisions within the Evangelical connection. Significantly, the campaign by women at the CMS to advance their position coincided with the most radical phase of the suffragette campaign to obtain the vote.[114] In this way, the campaign paralleled cultural and political changes that also had an impact on the broader evangelical party, for the cause of women at the CMS had become enmeshed in the theological battle between liberal and conservative factions of evangelicals that grew after the turn of the century. Rooted in controversy over the literal authority of the Bible, biblical criticism, and presumption of the active operation of the Holy Spirit in the world, this broader theological division within the evangelical world led conservatives to insist on the biblically ordained, subordinate position of women as an article of faith.[115] Protofundamentalist evangelicals sought to reforge the CMS as a "traditional" conservative evangelical organization; but Georgina Gollock, who had long been in CMS House, urged that the CMS had always been broadly evangelical and that the Society could not allow itself to be narrowed to "one type or school of evangelicalism" or "bound within new definitions or self-imposed creeds." Its very life and leadership were at stake, for experience had shown that "the lingering of unsympathetic tone and attitude" and the abandonment of "a young and growing attitude" had always proven hurtful to recruitment and broader influence.[116] However, progressive arguments that "[t]he whole trend of modern life is towards self respect and mutual respect" had little force with conservatives, who were fighting precisely against the whole trend of modern life.[117]

Why had the society that was so often seen as among the most progressive

113. "Women on Committees," MS, CMS Archives, G/AP 2; Joan Bayldon, *Cyril Bardsley, Evangelist* (London: SPCK, 1942), 34-35.

114. Notably, the sentiments of the minority report of the subcommittee on women's representation parallel those of the opposition to the votes for women campaign. "Report II. Representation of Women on Committees," 28 Feb. 1914, CMS Archives, G/AP 2.

115. On the split between liberals and conservatives and the fissures it caused in evangelicalism, see Bebbington, *Evangelicalism*, chap. 5.

116. "Memorandum Submitted by Miss G. A. Gollock," 22 May 1914, CMS Archives, G/C 26 A.

117. Minna C. Gollock, "Memo. on the C.M.S. Women's Department" [1914], CMS Archives, G/C 26 A.

in the 1880s proven to be the most reactionary regarding the expansion of responsibility and leadership for women after the turn of the century? The strength of the conservative position rested on its many vocal clerical supporters. At the same time, the reformers lacked vigorous support at the grassroots for their demand for change, which the conservatives used to their advantage. G. T. Manley alleged that in six years of mission study work throughout the country, meeting hundreds of women workers, he had never once heard a demand for more representation of women's views and that in the field the majority of women workers, and nearly all married women, favored government by men. Furthermore, had not the success of the CMS in the past with women, greater than at any other society, already been magnificently fostered by the government of men?[118] The demands of missionary progressives clearly were not echoed very loudly among supporters at large, again demonstrating the fundamental conservatism of the CMS's core local constituencies. Female activists were exposed to liberal ideas generated in missionary councils, the charitable world, and the public life of the metropolis, where since the turn of the century women had been appointed on equal terms in great numbers on royal commissions, university senates, and boards of education.[119] But these were not significant concerns in the localities. This was a problem for reformers at the CMS, not just with their English supporters but also among female missionaries overseas, who had carved out relatively autonomous realms and preferred not to be disturbed.[120]

The tendency of Evangelical women to remain well enmeshed in the older formulations for women's work ran on parallel lines to those of many female missionaries in the field. Religiously minded conservatives formed the bulk of support that the CMS received. Even activists such as the Gollock sisters wanted no more than a workable advisory capacity (which was the only thing that a slim minority position on a large committee amounted to), public recognition of the worth of their work, meaningful labor, and limited autonomy within the particular sphere that they claimed. Those who wanted a greater sense of freedom and a more exclusive women's community were free to support the

118. Statement by G. T. Manley, 1 Dec. 1913, and statement by G. Furness Smith, 22 Dec. 1913, in "The Sub-Committee on the Representation of Women on Committees," TS, in Minutes of Sub-Committees, inserted between pp. 255-56, CMS Archives, G/CS 4.

119. Stock, *History of the CMS*, 4:454.

120. One missionary, for example, noted that "some of the older female missionaries have said they would prefer to be under the Men's Conference, as the men interfere very little with their work and women would probably be more strict." "Statement by Miss Brownlow, Palestine," 22 Dec. 1913, in "The Sub-Committee on the Representation of Women on Committees," TS, in Minutes of Sub-Committees, inserted between pp. 255-56, CMS Archives, G/CS 4.

CEZMS, ZBMM, or overseas missionary sisterhoods. That this issue raised so little heat in the country at large demonstrates that while missionary work may have opened opportunities for women's work in the field, and the student movement may have provided a model of feminine leadership, the missionary enterprise remained deeply rooted in fundamentally conservative English local religious cultures.

Conclusion

The relations between men, women, and missionary work in the later CMS were in many ways indicative of general attitudes that characterized evangelical missions as a whole. The most significant changes that affected the organization of English female foreign missions after the 1860s were closely linked to the concerns of male clerics to fit women's work into the existing structures of churches and denominational societies. When male-dominated General Committees absorbed the activism of women workers in the 1880s, they did so in ways that maintained their control over policy making. With amalgamation, female staff either dealt almost exclusively with other women — candidates, supporters, and missionaries — acting as liaisons to a support base whose sensitivities brusque male secretaries often offended, or filled support positions as voluntary laborers or low-wage staff. Long-term CMS home staffer Edith Baring-Gould argued that the most essential function of a woman secretary was to maintain a personal link with the women in the field, and Georgina Gollock concurred that it was constantly necessary to widen female missionaries' contacts to prevent them from becoming narrow and lift them "out of a tendency to individualism."[121] Women were essential to maintain the culture and social networks through which the women's parallel church functioned and upon which women's missions depended for emotional and financial sustenance.

The growing support that missionary societies received from women, especially young activist evangelical women, had a good deal to do with the pressures exerted by a combination of outside factors: the rise of the single female population and the "surplus women" problem, the broadening opportunities and attitudes toward women's public work in general, and the particular roles that holiness approaches to piety offered to women in both the evangelical and

---

121. "Memo. by Miss Baring-Gould" [1914], and "Memorandum Submitted by Miss G. A. Gollock," 22 May 1914, CMS Archives, G/C 26 A. On complaints about consistently lower salaries for female secretaries, paid less than even the lowest level of CMS male clerk, see Edith Baring-Gould to [S. H.] Gladstone, 24 Mar. 1920, CMS Archives, G/AS 3/4.

the Anglo-Catholic subcultures. The relationship of women's missionary work to late Victorian feminism is ambiguous, not least because of the range and varied intensity of feminist positions taken by women in the period. Women who supported foreign missions and who offered themselves for the field certainly did not consider themselves as proto- (or crypto-) feminists, but they did have a significantly expanded notion of what roles women were competent to fill, whether through service or evangelism.[122] Because feminist advances outside of the churches were far greater than those achieved within them, the pressure of an expanding feminine sphere into professionalized positions of leadership increased, gaining a response first at the SPG, but at the CMS only during and after World War I. After the turn of the century Evangelicals, resistant to changing attitudes, were compelled to recruit women by focusing more intensively further down within the middle classes than in previous decades.[123] Support for foreign missions, it appears, operated in part as a socially conservative alternative to more advanced feminist programs. Missionary societies could, nevertheless, operate in advance of practice within the denominations that they represented. In the Anglican church, in combination with the inspiration that imperial opportunity and anxiety provided, women's roles rapidly expanded in High Church missions precisely at the time that growing battles over theological modernism in Evangelical circles slowed the growth of women's roles and autonomy, at least for the decade prior to 1914. Overall, after the turn of the century the Anglican women's missionary impulse flowed outward not only into the traditional channels but also into parallel forms of missionary activism more fully controlled by women, such as the Mothers' Union and, after WWI, the League of the Church Militant.[124]

As long as women's missionary endeavors were limited or peripheral, they operated easily outside of the control of the mainline denominational missionary societies. However, as specifically targeted women's issues raised more money and supported more missionary activity in the field, the situation changed. The position of women in the denominational societies had been more

122. The determination of whether women's foreign missions were inherently "feminist" seems to depend on which of the shifting historical definitions of feminism is used: if feminism entails advocating for women's education and training while opposing sex discrimination, positive parallels exist; if feminism must involve demands for formal economic, social, and political gender equality, then virtually no female missionary qualifies. Cf. Sarah Potter's positive argument for "missionary feminism" and Peter Williams' more cautious assessment. Potter, "Social Origins," 220-29, and Williams, "Women Missionaries," 64-67.

123. On this phenomenon in the CEZMS, see Morawiecki, "Women Missionaries, CEZMS," 163-67.

124. Prevost, *Communion of Women*, chap. 5.

or less regularized by the 1890s: women were visible and active but effectively subordinated members of mission staffs and committees.[125] It is notable that the situation among Episcopal missionary societies in England worked itself out quite differently than among their sister societies in North America. In the CMS, the SPG, and the UMCA, women's work was, in varying degrees, dependent upon and amalgamated with the work of the larger society. The Women's Association in connection with Canadian Episcopal missions was, on the other hand, completely independent with separate meetings, finances, and administration. Female and male societies never exchanged funds. In America the Women's Association had no central structure; it was, instead, composed of widely dispersed independent diocesan branches raising special gifts for women's missions. Mrs. Patterson Hall of Montreal related that these North American Women's Associations emphatically "Don't want men."[126]

The much stronger ecclesiastical structures and loyalties in England, where the established Church jealously guarded its prerogatives, successfully resisted disestablishment, and imprinted its followers with a horror of schism, help explain the difference. Even as Minna Gollock at the CMS fought for greater responsibility for women, she asserted that "Women's Work for Women" — a motto dear to Americans — was the most invidious slogan in the whole movement. The ideal within the Church of England, at both the CMS and the SPG, was close cooperation, for women's activities were conceived of as essential to the success of men's work and thus to a broader civilizing mission project. Women's work was integral to strategies for effecting the social transformation necessary for the Christian message to gain sympathetic responses throughout the empire and the world.[127] This ideal of cross-gender unity had broader implications for reformulating missionary relationships, as the support in 1912 of Bishop Montgomery's wife, Maud, for the Mothers' Union suggests. In imagining the MU as a universal communion of mothers cutting across cultural and racial categories of colonial difference, Maud Montgomery extended the High Church ideal of corporate Anglican community building as a universal bond. It was this potential that progressive women such as Mrs. Ashley Carus-Wilson and Gertrude King built into a model of universal Christian womanhood as

125. The exceptions were the BMS, where women's independence rested on greater Nonconformist egalitarianism and on the Society's much smaller budget and bureaucracy, and the SPG, where persistently illiberal attitudes maintained a longer marginalization of women. Maughan, "Regions Beyond," 281-84.

126. SPG Home Organisation Sub-committee members advised against allowing such a situation to develop in England. Rough Minutes of the Home Organisation Committee, 26 June 1908, USPG Archives, H 137.

127. Minna C. Gollock, "Women's Work," 197-200.

the constituent of a non-temporal "spiritual empire," extending beyond a limiting nationally defined concept of European femininity, in the decades that followed WWI.[128]

In England, the experience of greater female subordination to clerical power ultimately set the context in which women's activity in foreign missions would be played out.[129] The demise of the FES in the 1890s exemplifies the fate of female missions that did not develop strong denominational identity, aggressive local organization, and workable religious alliances. From the 1830s onward the FES did not change its character as a modest auxiliary society to the CMS. It did not leverage denominational connections or develop a particular ideological niche for its existence. Instead, it relied largely on the loyalty of the supporters it recruited in its early stages and on the zeal of Rosamund Anne Webb, its chief secretary of fifty-eight years. In competition with the denominational societies, the extent of its work consistently shrank; and in 1899, when Webb died, the Society was disbanded and the bulk of its work was handed over to the CMS.[130] In the world of late Victorian missions, the FES had ceased to have a place, and the pioneer English female missionary society fell victim to professionalizing and denominational forces in English religion.

The difficulties that missionary women found in expanding their roles, both overseas and at home, issued from one source: defense of clerical privilege. The weight of tradition and heightened defensiveness in the face of the continuing threat of disestablishment made this difficulty greater in England than in the mission field. Developing women's work in England was a particularly delicate business, for if a clergyman was not disposed to have women's organizations in his parish he could effectively banish them. Even organizing secretaries within the CMS itself complained of the independent operations of women's organizations like the Gleaners' Union, which they often felt should be under their direction.[131] But the growing consequence and resources of the women's church lured progressives to new innovations, and the degree of success missionary societies had in the late Victorian era was in nearly direct proportion to their

128. Prevost, *Communion of Women*, 269-71, 282-88.

129. Cf. the experience of American women, despite some exceptions, of generally greater independence, Patricia Hill, *The World Their Household: The American Woman's Foreign Mission Movement and Cultural Transformation, 1870-1920* (Ann Arbor: University of Michigan Press, 1985), 45-60.

130. The small number of remaining supporters were encouraged to continue to raise funds for the CMS, and FES working parties continued to exist until 1915. Minutes of the FES General Committee, 1895-99, FES/AM 6 and Circulars, FES Archives, FES/Z 4/1.

131. T. T. Smith (Leeds), "Centenary Review Section XII: Home Organisation &c. Replies to enquiries . . ." [ca. 1897], CMS Archives, G/CCb 11/2.

ability to tap women's enthusiasm, voluntarism, and support. Once in the field, as Elizabeth Prevost has suggested, women often experienced advanced levels of practical, independent action, an independence that ultimately produced questioning of both the depth and nature of the cultural transformation and westernization supposedly necessary to advance the gospel, and the subordination of women within the hierarchy of the Church. This was demonstrated in East African mission fields where over time women came to question the necessity of replicating the European home, Western cultural forms, and colonial institutions more generally. Furthermore, Church feminists such as Helen Hanson and Maude Royden saw the flow of female talent into overseas evangelism and service as one of the chief arguments for the extension of women's influence in imperial policy making. Overseas maternalist social reformation and the expansion of women's leadership in the Church would ultimately become one of the chief arguments for the ordination of women.[132]

As the upper classes in Victorian and Edwardian England experienced religious crisis, the missionary movement, particularly its most active Anglican evangelical wing, tied its fortunes to the growth of enthusiastic piety, which appealed particularly to women. Thus the missionary societies tapped a source of support that allowed them to expand at a time when English institutional religion as a whole was stationary in growth.[133] On the broadest level the ethos of holiness and the increased women's involvement it brought contributed to a change in organizational style at home in the foreign missionary societies: a new family-oriented philosophy arose which turned mission houses into centers of religious sociability and personal networks of feminine religiosity, none more so than the SPG after 1902. The core of female community that underpinned domestic missionary practice throughout the nineteenth century expanded by late in the century to create a new tone to missionary practice, an expanded national organization, and a more sophisticated local strategy.

As the CMS grew in size, bureaucracy, and impersonality, it risked losing women to whom personal interaction was essential to social and religious life. It solved this problem by allowing women, at least in autonomous local organizations, to develop new public networks, authorized by evangelical enthusiasm. However, the official structuring of women's work from the 1860s showed just how enmeshed were models of organization in the domestic ideology of the patriarchal family. Even High Churchmen who advocated for missionary sisterhoods did so by emphasizing their role in supporting family life through

---

132. Prevost, *Communion of Women*, 230-39, 250-54, 290-93.

133. For general trends in institutionally measured indicators of religious growth in late Victorian and Edwardian England, see Gilbert, *Religion and Society*, part 3.

the education of Christian wives and mothers. And the difficulties at the CMS that involved the thwarted ambitions of women in the Edwardian period and afterward showed the clear limits that existed in so many conservative evangelicals' minds regarding the future of women in the movement.

The theory of women's missions at its most radical never transcended a separate-spheres ideology providing autonomy for women within their sphere. But such transcendence was never a goal within the women's movement. The relationship of evangelical theology, gender, and social service through missions in the British Empire and the wider world led to significant expansion of women's roles, but in a way that tied them into the restrictions of literalist interpretations of the Bible. In this way the growth of women's foreign missions operated in the familiar groove that characterized so much of the experience of English women over the course of the nineteenth century: by building on the definition of a separate and idealized female nature, Victorian female missionaries sought to transform society; but in embracing the idea of female purity, they also embraced the very definitions that ultimately limited the power and independence they could achieve.

> Woman is pre-eminent above man in her sentimental, emotional, and religious nature; so it is that she holds the very keys of the domestic sanctuary in the opportunity to form the youthful character. She has marvelous capacity for teaching and endurance. She is especially fitted to care for, sympathize with, and reach her own sex.[134]

Embodied in this characteristic view are the boundaries of action that both enabled and limited women's foreign missionary activity.

The lineaments of the movement were fundamentally conservative. Respectability and propriety were constant goals. In the words of the WMA's rules for female missionaries, they were "[t]o cultivate at all times a quiet, modest and unobtrusive manner, avoiding all that would bring discredit on their calling."[135] The expectations of even the most advanced home workers were sharply bounded by class and culture. In the midst of the most progressive women's conference yet held in the Anglican Communion, Louise Creighton, while energetically advocating toleration of racial difference, also inquired of missionaries whether housekeeping in mission homes and institutions was good, "as she felt that in England any household of women are not particular enough & that the

---

134. Quote from the *Missionary Review of the World* in Pitman, *Lady Missionaries*, viii.

135. Minutes of Special Sub-Committees and Reports of Conferences, 16 Feb. 1898, USPG Archives, CWW 90.

constant criticism of men is needed to keep women up to good housekeeping."[136] For Georgina Gollock, caught up in the most rapid expansion of Western missionary activity in modern history, a key concern lay in discouraging male missionaries going into the field from forming "early and irresponsible engagements with girls of an inferior social class, who are not really suited to be the wives of our young clerical missionaries."[137] The women who organized foreign missionary work were obviously products of their environment, which was rich with rigorous gender- and class-based systems of belief and social convention. In the religious subculture that formed their setting, women, like their male counterparts, saw themselves as engaged in a titanic struggle for the salvation of the world from the heresies of modernism, for "Sacerdotalism, Universalism, Perfectionism, Theosophism, are only samples of systems numberless, whereby unstable souls are led astray at home and abroad."[138] In this world, acceptable options for women were limited, but the options women did have were broader than in the past because of new theologies and changing social practices.

The most far-reaching changes were driven by cultures of holiness in both the Evangelical and Anglo-Catholic wings of the communion, and they facilitated the widening of women's activity within the most conservative sections of English Christianity. In the missionary movement, as in the broader church, women found that the most persistent obstacles to greater participation were linked to their exclusion from the ordination necessary to preach. Within the Church, holiness license for women's evangelistic activity was thus correspondingly more important than in other realms of English society, and the allowable path of evangelization through education drew women ever closer to functional public preaching, as schools, hospitals, and Bible instruction expanded as missionary agencies. The conservative evangelical section of the Church offered the greatest missionary activism, and holiness was essential to opening women's work within this subculture. But as the experience of women in the CMS showed, there was a paradox in the influence that holiness-oriented evangelicalism had on women's missions. While a close and spiritual reading of the Bible justified expanding women's work in the 1860s, the same tradition of "Puritan" Christianity in the 1900s, tempered by its experience with modern latitudinarianism, produced the most staunch opposition to further extension of women's authority (although not their activity) in foreign missions.

Prior to the twentieth century, as experience at the SPG showed, women in

136. "Report of a Missionary Conference . . . Payment," 10 Feb. 1908, Minutes of the Pan-Anglican Congress, Women's Committee: Missionary Sub-Committee, USPG Archives, CWW 11.

137. Georgina A. Gollock, "Outfit Allowances for Finances," memorandum, 23 Jan. 1903, CMS Archives, G/CR 1/3 (part).

138. Barnes, *Story of CEZMS*, 10.

the respectable higher realms of the Church had lower profiles as missionary agents and fewer administrative opportunities than did women in the various Evangelical subcultures. But once those in higher church circles accepted the principle of women's independent leadership there was a more rapid and pro-found expansion of the responsibilities accorded, at least in theory, to female workers after the turn of the century. The speed of this change may be related to the familiarity and acceptability in High Church circles of the more indepen-dent sisterhood model and to the fact that higher Churchmen had less bruising, internal theological debates than Evangelicals, as an earlier Tractarianism and Ritualism shaded over into the Catholic modernism of Charles Gore, the Chris-tian Social Union, and the JCMA. Regardless of theological tradition, however, the flow of women into the mission field grew from the 1880s onward, and An-glican women increasingly supported the expanding social service orientation in foreign missions, a trend reinforced from the 1890s by a redoubled emphasis on service to imperial subjects. A shifting of focus to an overtly imperial civ-ilizing mission for women's work helped, however, to erode the commitment to indigenized churches implicit in earlier Anglo-Catholic missions, as women progressively took up "civilizing" activities.[139] Ultimately the limitations on evangelism that were placed on women reinforced their commitment to the so-cial service ideals so integral to their family-based maternalist social reformism, with the result that women's slowly expanding support for humanitarian work in foreign missions was intensified by imperial circumstance and emerged as a strong rationale for extending women's work.

Under these conditions within the realms of High Church missions, con-servative forces hoping to avoid conceding relative independence for women's work were defeated early in the twentieth century at the SPG, and in the pro-cess of drawing women in, gender values focusing on the purported civilizing powers of domesticity to advance the empire became an ideological mainstay. Once women's work had been redefined to minimize the potentially radical independency of sisterhood organization, and given the support of the more openly pro-imperial SPG, the work could be aggressively advanced. As com-mentary at the 1908 Pan-Anglican Congress shows, the call for "sympathy" with indigenous cultures and indigenization of missionary churches had been largely co-opted for imperial "civilizing" purposes. This call to sympathize with "native races" multiplied as descriptions of the rising discomfort and anger of

---

139. The same general transformation can be seen in evangelical Anglican missions, where a variety of shifts of ideology — theological, imperial, and racial — eroded the original theory of indigenizing churches set earlier by Henry Venn. For one account of this transformation see Williams, *Self-Governing Church*, 146-257.

indigenous populations animated by a growing nationalism, including within indigenous Christian communities, formed an essential background for the Edwardian missionary discourse.[140] In these ways the ideal of women's work was expanded in High Church missions, but it was also homogenized and contained in its imperial function of defusing conflict between European and indigenous communities.

From the 1890s onward, the influence of college-educated women and men was crucial to the changing agendas of the foreign missionary movement. When in 1882, despite early skepticism from Evangelical conservatives, Westfield College was founded to provide an evangelical Anglican alternative to Girton, Newnham, and other women's colleges, the missionary movement obtained access to a new generation of female leaders who desired to take their place alongside the men of the student missionary movement. This movement animated a new attitude toward foreign missions that mixed evangelical enthusiasm, technical expertise, and a growing appreciation of the British Empire as a structurally advantaged environment for foreign missions. With their sense of power to effect national regenerations in the mission field growing in the 1890s, educated female missionaries joined with their male counterparts, often driven by the sense that they were "the mission of the daughters of a ruling race."[141] After the turn of the century, the influence of growing numbers of women with college educations and experience in the student missionary movement generated pressure on the missionary societies to provide expanding opportunities to women.

While the expansion of women's missionary work in the late nineteenth century was a critical component supporting the "new age" of British missionary activity, it also created rising tensions over questions of clerical authority and church government. The series of contests that occurred between female missionaries and missionary bureaucrats resulted, on the whole, in the subordination of women's missions to male clerical authority. However, the ensuing more complete incorporation of women's missions into the bureaucratic structure of the mainline societies only partially solved the problem of maintaining the support of higher class, highly educated women in the movement. Many women found it difficult to swallow the resistance to

140. See for example the comments of Louise Creighton (p. 10), Dr. Whitehead, bishop of Madras (p. 21), Rev. E. A. Douglas (CMS missionary in Tinnevelly) (p. 27), Mr. James Pereira (missionary in Colombo) (p. 40), and Dr. Mary Scharlieb (p. 48) among many more. Similarly, the Pan-Anglican Congress featured several expressions of affronted impatience at persisting European control of missions from the bishops of West Africa and repeated references to the rising feeling of nationalist emotion in India. *Pan-Anglican Congress Report, 1908*, Vol. 5.

141. T. A. Gurney, "Introduction," in Barnes, *Story of CEZMS*, v.

women's agency and the questioning of social service in the mission field voiced by evangelical conservatives who advocated old-fashioned gospel preaching. With the shift in evangelical discourse brought by a new wave of ultra-Protestant reaction to modern challenges in the 1890s, the power given to women through radical evangelical practice in previous decades rapidly ebbed, as conservative clerics fought what they saw as larger battles over literalist scriptural interpretation and biblical infallibility. The result was that women remained barred from the CMS General Committee until 1917.[142] These conflicts were part of a greater set of divisions between liberal and conservative evangelicals after 1900 that eventually led to a schism in the CMS, with the formation of the traditionalist Bible Churchman's Missionary Society in 1922, publicly endorsed by the immediate past CMS honorary clerical secretary (1895-1910), H. E. Fox.[143]

Outside of the religious dynamics of evangelicalism, larger social transformations also presented new challenges. Not only did other professional voices challenge the social authority of missionary women to speak to the condition of Indian and other indigenous women; nationalists in the mission field claimed indigenous women as their own special responsibility, and in India they attempted to remove women from Western contact and the authority of the colonial regime, thus insulating Indian culture and buttressing their own political and social authority.[144] The challenges presented by this ideological contest were compounded by competing professional opportunities for potential missionary recruits. Both the claims of groups outside the missionary subculture to represent indigenous women and rapidly changing imperial opportunities meant that by the Edwardian era a movement which at one point had promised women the unique opportunity to express deep religious commitment and considerable freedom overseas began to pale in comparison to other openings for women in the professions and in the workforce. Evidence from the CMS shows that after 1900 the society had increasing difficulty recruiting the university women it most coveted, because of a prevalent idea that the CMS was "very old-fashioned and narrow in its views."[145] Even in its training homes for women of "deficient background," the CMS found itself faced with demands for more sophisticated academic treatment of subjects such as Christian apologetics, eschatology, and comparative religious study, all

142. Bayldon, *Bardsley*, 34-35.

143. Kenneth Hylson-Smith, *Evangelicals in the Church of England, 1734-1984* (Edinburgh: Clark, 1989), 252-55.

144. Chatterjee, "Colonialized Women," 627-31.

145. "Special Committee to Consider the Ladies' Training Homes' Curriculum, &c.," interview of Agnes de Selincourt, 12 Nov. 1906, in Minutes of Sub-Committees, CMS Archives, G/CS 4.

of which were poorly served by the evangelical emphasis on emotional rather than intellectual spirituality.[146]

Holiness-based evangelical religion had legitimized women's role in the missionary movement for decades, but the actual work performed by women and their expanding public roles eventually challenged the moral and social boundaries that traditionalist religious doctrines and institutions had sought to uphold. Female students at Oxford and Cambridge, for example, engaged in more vigorous intellectual questioning of Christianity than men, a fact no doubt known to those conservatives within the societies who opposed on biblical grounds the expansion of women's authority.[147] As controversies over women's authority developed, the emancipatory potential embodied in holiness-oriented forms of piety reached its limits. Thus, evangelical religion had an ambiguous function in the history of women within the missionary movement. Initially, when operating in an atmosphere of largely uncontested imperial opportunity and restricted public roles for women outside of charitable voluntarism, zealous evangelicalism played a crucial part in the expansion of women's public missionary roles. Mobilization of interest in empire as a justification for feminine activism was one crucial feature of evangelical missionary enthusiasm, but as other forces — professionalism, feminism, indigenous nationalism, liberal Christianity — came to challenge the social authority of revealed religion, revivalistically oriented Anglican holiness culture fragmented, producing conservative and protofundamentalist variants that resisted further expansion of missionary and public authority for women. By the end of the Edwardian era, the High Church vision of feminine imperial service had become the leading edge of Anglican formulations of women's mission, and it drew much of the ideology of the movement along with it. The efforts of conservative Evangelicals to hold back the tide of English missionary women ultimately failed, and in the interwar period, as the British missionary force continued to grow, its increase was due entirely to the continued flow of women into the missionary field.

146. "Special Committee to Consider the Ladies' Training Homes' Curriculum, &c.," interview of Miss Outram, 5 Nov. 1906, in Minutes of Sub-Committees, CMS Archives, G/CS 4.
147. Tatlow, *Student Christian Movement*, 217, 226, 230, 294.

CHAPTER 8

Edwardian Challenges and the Collapse
of an Anglican Greater Britain

The expansion of SPG which is to be the new factor in this century is in a sense to revolutionize Church ideals and make the ancient Church of England more completely an Imperial Church — the unit being the world and not the United Kingdom.

Henry H. Montgomery, 1901

From the muscular Christianity of the last generation to the imperial Christianity of the present day is but a single step; the temper of growing sacerdotalism and the doctrine of authority in the established churches well accord with militarism and political autocracy.

J. A. Hobson, 1901[1]

"These are great times and one feels the stir of an Imperial [Christ]ianity. Thank God it is good to live in these days." Henry Hutchinson Montgomery, bishop of Tasmania, writing six days after the relief of Mafeking in the Boer War to his friend Randall Davidson, bishop of Winchester, expressed an imperial fervor common to the time. Soon to receive appointment to lead the SPG, Montgomery was voicing a sentiment that resonated with the cresting wave of popular imperialism in the 1890s: that there was an organic connection between the

---

1. Montgomery to the Standing Committee of the SPG, 17 Aug. 1901, Davidson Papers, vol. 151, fols. 322-23; J. A. Hobson, *Imperialism: A Study* (London: Nisbet, 1902), 228.

religion of Britain and the success of its empire.[2] When elevated to the leadership of the SPG fourteen months later, in 1901, Montgomery avowed that he would work to reorder High Church, and indeed all, Anglican missions. In many ways this was a romantic and enthusiastic plan, redolent with the sentiments of Kipling and other popularizers of empire. The SPG would be transformed into a popular organization leading the Church consciously into a program of imperial duty. While for decades the SPG had languished in comparison to mainstream evangelical missionary societies, especially the CMS, Montgomery aimed to draw the higher varieties of Anglicanism back into the world of missions. He also aimed to make explicit the connection between British religion and British empire, define a loyal, core Churchmanship as lying at the center of national life, and establish the Church of England as the leader of British missions. Ultimately, Montgomery failed in his efforts to weld Christianity and empire into a single popular program, and his story might be considered no more than a quixotic episode in the history of Anglicanism and popular imperialism. The history of the SPG in this era, however, illuminates several deeper dynamics in the complex history and interrelationship of Christian missions and the British Empire.

New challenges faced Anglican missionary societies after the anxieties unleashed by the Boer War.[3] By 1902 the flood of missionary and imperial enthusiasm characteristic of the 1890s began to wane just as demands for domestic social improvement began to rise. Further challenges posed by theological modernism, revived partisan warfare over Ritualism, and declining levels of worship encouraged many Anglican missionary theorists, especially higher church students and younger clergy, to endorse the SPG program for "imperial Christianity." Within the SPG this strategy was designed to replace evangelical enthusiasm for revivals — repugnant to many High Churchmen — with a new enthusiasm for the British Empire. Leaders such as Montgomery and John Ellison hoped this program would also allow imperial sentiment to heal the rifts between Church parties and channel their energies into a unified project to eradicate essentially theoretical modernist religious doubts through a robust practical dedication to world Anglican mission. Similarly the CMS — troubled by the waning influence of evangelicalism within the Church, the sectarian fragmentation of evangelicalism under the influence of theological modernism, the continued division over how to respond to Ritualism, and a stagnation in

2. Montgomery to Davidson, 24 May 1900, Davidson Papers, vol. 519, fols. 248-56; Wolffe, *God and Greater Britain*, 222-25.

3. For the "ambivalences of war" unleashed in Britain, see Denis Judd and Keith Surridge, *The Boer War* (London: Murray, 2002), 221-56, and Searle, *Quest for National Efficiency*, chap. 2.

fundraising — increasingly articulated an imperial vision for the Society within the Church.

But Montgomery, arriving just as the fortunes of the foreign missionary movement were shifting, was confronted with unexpected challenges. Leaders at both the SPG and CMS had to adjust to the waning flood of enthusiasm that marked the 1890s, but more importantly, they had to respond to complications raised by renewed Anglican party confrontation and growing challenges in the religious and secular worlds to the morality of imperial practice.[4] Initially it appeared as if both the SPG and the CMS would meet these challenges head-on. Both made new efforts to cooperate with each other directly and through the bishops. Both also showed greater sympathy toward students and younger clergy who were concerned with the challenges of biblical criticism and science that formed the core of the modernist "threat." And both attempted to stand aloof from partisan battles over Ritualism. In addition, Anglican missionary leaders turned more frequently to imperialism to provide a new framework for missionary activity, to spur giving, and to inspire a Church of England struggling with the old problem of competition with Nonconformity and the new problem of declining standards and levels of worship.

Within a decade, however, the imperial-missionary bid to unify the Church and infiltrate the empire had collapsed, and student-driven "imperial Christianity" had not united but instead further divided Anglicanism. This collapse had a number of causes: traditionalist resistance to the "modernist" theology associated with many student leaders, opposition to direct engagement with troubled questions of imperial rule, and, perhaps most important, the dearth of evidence that this strategy had the popularity to increase funding or recruiting of missionaries. These realities had become evident by the time Bishop Montgomery's great Anglican conclave, the 1908 Pan-Anglican Congress, convened; here the participants focused their attention not on foreign missions, as Montgomery had intended, but on the problems facing domestic congregations. Similarly, while High Churchmen participated in the great ecumenical World Missionary Conference held in Edinburgh in 1910, the conference demonstrated clearly the continuing predominance of evangelical influence in the missionary world both inside and outside the Anglican Communion, troubling many in the SPG fold who feared the destruction of their distinctive identity. While the SPG was home to the most ardent missionary imperialists at the turn of the century, the disappointments suffered by Montgomery demonstrate that the equation between support of empire and support of missions was not an auto-

---

4. On contemporary Congo reform agitations and South African Chinese slavery controversy, see Grant, *Civilized Savagery*, chaps. 2 and 3.

matic one and that the conversion of diffuse imperial enthusiasm into concrete support and action proved to be unexpectedly difficult. Bishop Montgomery and his followers discovered that the construction of clear and proactive imperial policies in missions was unsustainable precisely because discourses on empire, nationality, and race were contested, further complicating and stimulating conflict over theology, religious authority, and religious identity both in Britain and in the empire.

Evangelicals faced similar problems. The CMS encountered unexpected challenges following the striking success of its massive centenary celebration in 1899. As the imperial anxieties unleashed by the Boer War and Boxer Rebellion in China destabilized the assumptions of the previous decade, divisions within the Evangelical party grew as extremist ultra-Protestants again took on Anglo-Catholics and the CMS faced an emerging financial crisis. One result was an extension of the accommodationist attitude of moderate Evangelicals, which had grown following the Lincoln Judgment, and a new willingness to cooperate with the SPG — haven for moderate and nonpartisan forms of High Church belief. As the overseas costs of Victorian success outstripped the Edwardian ability to pay, optimists rationalized that divine guidance was leading to wise consolidation of earlier gains. Stagnation of income growth was obvious, not only at the CMS but also among the Nonconformist societies, which were even more severely hit; the state of Edwardian income figures led an anonymous correspondent to the Evangelical *Record* to deduce a "pause in missionary progress."[5] As early as the mid-1890s anxieties had been rising because the real problem in its most elementary form was that the enthusiasm of supporters had not risen as fast as that of activists; the growth of energetic coteries outstripped economic and charitable growth. When the secretaries made special appeals to supporters, they increasingly received responses that pled poverty of time and money.[6] At the CMS the perception of crisis led to a reassessment of past policy, a new sympathy with cooperative Pan-Anglican missionary ventures, and a new willingness to consider openly an imperial vision for the Society. Openness to Anglican cooperation led to a major realignment of CMS policy and new levels of unity in Anglican missions, under a diffuse imperial rationale, at a time when arguably the influence of foreign missions overseas was at its peak. Ironically, however, public pronouncements of resonance with the imperial ideal in England corresponded to rising private doubts about the workability of cooperation with empire in the field, on the part of both politicians

---

5. E. Graham Ingham, "Why Should There Be a 'Pause'?" *Church Missionary Review* 60 (May 1909): 257. On Nonconformist societies, see Greenlee and Johnston, *Good Citizens,* 128-40.

6. E.g., Martin Hope Sutton to Frederick Wigram, 23 Apr. 1894, CMS Archives, G/AC 4/15/2947.

and missionary theorists, demonstrating a new fluidity in missionary ideology in this troubled era.[7]

Anglican missionary experience following the death of Queen Victoria was marked by anxiety in the face of a world changing so rapidly that the successful evangelical formulations of the late Victorian era, while not failing catastrophically, no longer seemed to provide a way forward. The bid for Anglican leadership launched by Bishop Montgomery transformed the SPG. No longer was it to be an organ of old-fashioned "high and dry" Anglican conservatism; rather, it was to be a progressive home for "Imperial Anglicans" searching for a solution in the face of seemingly rampant secularization in England and the empire. The most important asset that Montgomery had in 1901 was an unprecedented level of support from the English bishops, and in 1903, with the elevation of Randall Davidson to the See of Canterbury, backing from the most missionary-minded archbishop yet to occupy Lambeth Palace. SPG efforts to create broad Anglican cooperation in missions were reinforced by pressures that led the English bishops to endorse connecting the formal empire and its semi-autonomous colonies on the level of Church policy. The 1908 Pan-Anglican Congress and plans for the 1910 World Missionary Conference vividly exemplified a new commitment to worldwide Anglican solidarity. Yet Bishop Montgomery confessed after the Pan-Anglican Congress that a "sense of bewilderment" gripped the leaders of the Church about their future corporate responsibility. And an even deeper pessimism was evident two years later at Edinburgh about the adequacy of the English churches to sustain the world missionary project.[8]

Despite all the optimism of Montgomery and the student movement, by the onset of World War I hopes for Anglican unity of the sort envisioned by SPG progressives in 1901 had been shattered, and the two societies had fallen back into old patterns of sectarian strife. Most indicative of the failure of cooperation was the partisan feeling unleashed anew in 1913 by the Kikuyu Controversy, in which the Anglo-Catholic bishop of Zanzibar accused the Evangelical bishops of Mombassa and Uganda of heretically ecumenical associations with Nonconformists. As cooperation faded, it became evident that the two crucial momentums of the new strategy — greater sympathy toward the concerns of students and younger clergy and a new imperial rhetoric — had failed to generate yet another "new era." Both approaches were problematic because they distanced the societies from their most fundamental base of support: local English communities of the faithful that reflexively condemned scholarly modernism and were troubled by the responsibilities of rule implied in formal imperial coop-

7. Greenlee and Johnston, *Good Citizens*, 113, 118-20.
8. "The Pan-Anglican Congress, and After," *The East and the West* 6 (Oct. 1908): 361.

eration. With the collapse of the progressive program and growing polarization in the movement, the foreign missions of the Church entered an era of global war fraught with challenges unmatched since the Napoleonic conflicts of a century earlier.

The CMS and Missionary Overstretch in the Edwardian Age

In the early 1900s with Bishop Montgomery the SPG acquired a vigorous new leader and launched a reform program based heavily on an ideal of imperial engagement. Simultaneously the CMS entered a period of financial difficulty when the Evangelical party declined and fragmented, resulting in doubts about its reliance on older holiness-inspired policies. The CMS, previously the undisputed leader of Church missions, now experienced financial deficits brought on by its rapid extension of overseas work, and it weathered a new wave of attacks by evangelical "Puritan" radicals, who condemned it for tolerating Ritualism in the Church. The crisis of confidence that resulted led the CMS to bind itself more tightly to the Church Establishment by openly emphasizing its moderate Anglican identity, expanding cooperative work with the SPG, and experimenting with a new openly imperial identity.

Thus the CMS crisis reinforced a new sympathy with cooperative Anglican missionary ventures within the higher reaches of the Church that had been growing through the 1890s, and it articulated a Pan-Anglican missionary effort more united and fervently imperial than ever before. A cooperative imperial spirit had already been strengthened late in the century through the experience of substantial successes in Uganda under imperial protection, and Eugene Stock had voiced this general enthusiasm for the opportunities provided by imperial expansion in his monumental *The History of the Church Missionary Society: Its Environment, Its Men, and Its Work,* published in celebration of the CMS Centenary.[9] This new attitude received direct articulation by T. A. Gurney in a groundbreaking article in the CMS's "serious" magazine, which for the first time approached "imperialism" as a topic in itself for consideration in relation to foreign missions.[10] In a time of rising anxiety, it appears that, to many, the old evangelical formulas for determining missionary direction seemed unequal to new challenges. The CMS paradox was that, despite troubling new concerns, it remained virtually the only Anglican evangelical organization that had shown

9. This is most evident in volume three, especially *History of the CMS,* 3:428-54, 800-803.

10. T. A. Gurney, "Modern Imperialism and Missions," *Church Missionary Intelligencer,* n.s., 27 (July 1902): 485-86.

robust growth and promise of continued strength. In the context of exultant assertions by Anglo-Catholic partisans that they had supplanted evangelicalism, Anglican evangelicals held firmly to the CMS as an anchor. But retrenchments forced on the CMS by troubled times following its triumphal Centenary amplified fears in a besieged evangelical subculture.

Decline and Division: Edwardian Evangelical Fortunes

The evangelical party in the Church of England suffered from a general decline in influence that contemporaries believed had two primary facets: failure in their contest with the High Church party to maintain influence among the laity, and failure to secure positions of influence in the Church hierarchy. Virtually every member of the Anglican ecclesiastical network believed that "High Churchism" was triumphing, not necessarily because of any dramatically increasing strength in the High Church party, but because overall the Evangelical cause seemed to be weakening. By the late 1880s Archbishop Benson "recognized that the Evangelical movement was, for some cause little understood, dying out in England," and anxious Evangelicals accused the Conservative government of Lord Salisbury of unfairly passing them over in appointments to the ecclesiastical bench.[11] Also, the charged atmosphere generated by the prosecution of Bishop Edward King of Lincoln for illegal ritual in 1888, which dragged out to the upholding of his acquittal in 1892, further deepened ultra-Protestant evangelical paranoia.

However, the explanation by Church authorities that the problem was not prejudice, but a dearth of suitable Evangelical candidates had force because of its ring of truth.[12] The Evangelical party, for example, no longer seemed to offer the home church many men qualified to hold episcopal office. Two major reasons lay behind this: the anti-intellectualism of holiness did not encourage the academic success necessary to the bench, and those Evangelicals who seemed to have episcopal promise all too often volunteered for the mission field. Critics and supporters alike acknowledged that Evangelical strongholds such as Ridley Hall lacked intellectual accomplishments, even if they produced enthusiasts adept at preaching "simple Gospel truths," and few could fail to notice the numbers of foreign missionaries flowing through their doors. And the problem grew worse in the Edwardian period. Even the influential home secretary of the

11. Benson, *Benson*, 1:234.
12. Davidson to Frederick Gell, bishop of Madras, 11 Mar. 1890, quoted in Bell, *Davidson*, 1:178-79.

CMS, Bishop Ernest Graham Ingham — formerly of Sierra Leone (1883-93) and an early Keswick supporter — had to admit, when consulted by Archbishop Davidson in 1911, "that there really are so few leaders in what are known as the Evangelical ranks" that he was only able to forward about six names for appointment.[13] The "fashionable" religion in the Church remained Ritualistic, especially in the south of England. But the real dilemma of the Evangelical party lay in the common impression that the mission field, so strong a rallying point for the faithful, also damagingly drained talent as Evangelicals focused so exclusively on obedience to Christ's command to spread the word throughout the world. This led propagandists at the CMS to defensive arguments, for relatively high levels of missionary recruiting had an ominous overtone in a subculture racked by the anxiety of decline. That the anxiety had a real basis is underscored by the fact that twelve of the nineteen bishops that Ridley had produced by 1920 were overseas.[14]

Holiness theology at Keswick and Cambridge had constructed an Evangelical position whose strength for the missionary cause was encapsulated in the idea that "it was a higher and holier vocation to go to the heathen than to work at home."[15] Foreign work excited loyal enthusiasm but weakened the home position, particularly as success in university missionary recruiting meant that the best ordinands often went abroad. In addition, as growing numbers of commentators inside and outside the Evangelical fold argued, foreign missionary preoccupations encouraged avoidance of difficult issues of domestic social reform with which Evangelicals had engaged early in the century, but which were now too often left to higher Churchmen. E. T. Whittaker recalled that within this subculture an "apathy reigned with regard to social questions — the sweating system, housing conditions, unemployment, and temperance reform, which were then receiving much attention, both in High Church and in Nonconformist circles."[16] And holiness in Cambridge in the 1890s was also linked to the evolution of two movements, later at odds with each other: modern ecumenism and what subsequently became known as fundamentalism. A large part of the difficulty experienced by the CMS after 1900 arose from the split in Evangelicalism between liberals sympathetic with ecumenism, mod-

13. Evangelicals continued to hold a majority of the bishoprics in the north of England through 1920. But in the more populous and influential south they were considerably outnumbered, despite Evangelical efforts to secure appointments. Ingham to Davidson, 7 Oct. 1911, quoted in Bell, *Davidson*, 2:241-42.

14. Henry Sutton, "The Alleged Drain of Men to the Foreign Field," *Church Missionary Intelligencer*, n.s., 20 (Feb. 1895); Harford and Macdonald, *Moule*, 108-9.

15. Bullock, *Ridley Hall*, 1:216.

16. Quoted in Woods and Macnutt, *Theodore*, 21-22.

ernism, and growing concerns for social justice and conservatives who rejected these preoccupations. Protofundamentalism stressed a complete reliance on a narrow interpretation of biblical authority that, while easily reconciled with the foreign missionary project, only reinforced the Evangelical tendency to anti-intellectualism and apathy on domestic social questions.[17] Thus, when the future liberal Evangelical bishop of Winchester, Theodore Woods, became embroiled in holiness culture in 1890s Cambridge, his father sent him a warning which summarized the dilemma of Evangelicalism:

> [do] not be led aside by the fallacy which wrecks the after usefulness of some earnest undergraduates, viz.: so to fill up your time with external works for God, meetings, etc., as to neglect your studies. They come first, for our great need in the Church is a learned and spiritual Ministry, not an ignorant and spiritual one.[18]

When new controversies over Church ritual re-erupted in the late 1890s, Evangelicals were even more diverted from what one of their number called the "old crusade against public evils."[19] The continuing sense that Evangelicalism within the Church was under assault from two sides — "Romanism" and modernism — reinforced anxieties about decline. The central problem of the CMS is suggested in the fact that yet another outburst of vocal "Puritan" Evangelical horror at the dangers of Ritualism ran parallel to its Centenary preparations. Led by John Kensit, president of the Protestant Truth Society (a more radical version of the Church Association), this last of the great public anti-ritual campaigns protested the growth of ritual practices in the wake of the Lincoln Judgment (after which litigation largely failed to halt "high" innovations in Church services). The loud, direct-action program of public disturbances at Ritualist services was supported by only a tiny minority of evangelical Anglicans, but was virulent, and the fires stoked by evangelical radicals following Kensit swept up both the CMS and the SPG when in 1898 Sir William Harcourt took up the issue and legitimized it by turning it into a parliamentary question.[20]

---

17. While full-blown, American-style fundamentalism and its wide-ranging cultural effects never developed in England, Edwardian "extreme Protestants" shared many responses with American fundamentalist evangelicals, particularly with regard to a common unshakable insistence upon divine biblical inspiration and authority as well as the efficacy of supernatural agency in conversion and spiritual life. George M. Marsden, "Fundamentalism as an American Phenomenon: A Comparison with English Evangelicalism," *Church History* 46, no. 2 (June 1977): 216-24.

18. Quoted in Woods and Macnutt, *Theodore*, 22.

19. Samuel Garrat quoted in Bebbington, *Evangelicalism*, 147.

20. Chadwick, *Victorian Church: Part Two: 1860-1901*, 355-57.

In this atmosphere, student-driven cooperation between the CMS and the SPG came under sharp attack in 1899 over a joint meeting planned by the CMS Younger Clergy Union with the members of the JCMA and other High Church London clergy. Denouncing CMS association with "each and every clerical Romanizer in and near London," radical Protestants threatened to split the society, as the matter was taken up by the High Church *English Churchman* and the radical evangelical *Rock*. Protests flooded the CMS suggesting that it was "more tolerant of error than is acceptable to many lovers of the Word," and the editor of the *Rock* defended its series of articles on the matter by saying that it was airing widely held feelings.[21] The younger clergy supporting the CMS braved the protests, and E. N. Coulthard, president of the CMS Younger Clergy Union, in his opening speech to the joint meeting argued that cooperation was justified because "the real, the standing crisis of the Church, is the appalling religious indifference of the masses at home, and the great extent of the lands yet unoccupied for Christ in the regions abroad."[22] But foreign missions were clearly not a simple means to unify Church factions when party controversies flared. The idea that missions should provide a location to preserve a purer strain of evangelical Protestantism had long been current among some Evangelicals, and after 1900 extremists renewed the call.

In the face of renewed party conflict, the CMS opted to stay with its previously charted moderate course and began to distance itself further from radicals.[23] Emphasizing the importance of education in sound Reformation principles, rather than controversy prosecuted with "too little prayer and sense of responsibility," CMS leaders directed attention to more important controversies "with the non-Christian religions of the world."[24] The decision to continue moderate policies was not difficult, for even though new CMS Secretary H. E. Fox was a well-known Northern "Puritan" controversialist, he could not support the outrageousness of the actions of Kensit when ever more frequently the CMS was publicly put on trial with all the rest of the so-called "willful accommodators

21. T. J. Gaster to J. C. Ryle, open letter and attached note, n.d.; Handley Moule to H. E. Fox, 24 Jan. 1899, CMS Archives, G/AC 4/26/5117; Editor of the Rock to H. E. Fox, 26 Jan. 1899, CMS Archives, G/AC 4/26/5118, 5125 and 5126.

22. Ernest N. Coulthard, TS speech, 7 Feb. 1899, CMS Archives, G/AC 4/5175.

23. Many Evangelicals, such as Bishop J. C. Ryle of Liverpool, wanted the most egregious Ritualists prosecuted, but the bishops as a whole barred all prosecutions by veto power, providing instead for private admonitions by the archbishops of York and Canterbury. Ryle believed this "a most lame and impotent conclusion," but he stood alone, for "the great majority of all the bishops present seemed to think it a very wise arrangement." J. C. Ryle to H. E. Fox, 18 Jan. 1899, CMS Archives, G/AC 4/26/5175.

24. H[enry]. E. F[ox]., "Missionary Work and Church Controversy," *Church Missionary Intelligencer*, n.s. 24 (Mar. 1899): 162-63.

of Rome."[25] What was to be done when ultra-Protestant Kensitites denounced the CMS in rabid pamphlets for holding its Centenary in St. Paul's because they believed the national cathedral to be "a hot-bed of Ritualistic treason"? What was to be done when they castigated the primate, Archbishop Temple, and moderate bishops, such as Davidson of Winchester, as anti-Christian traitors, supporting public protests at CMS meetings that were led by vociferous YMCA-based "Puritan" youth? What the Kensitites were asking for, in a style of extremist polemic from which the CMS had long fought to dissociate itself, was nothing less than that the CMS join radical millenarian Nonconformity and leave the Church.[26] When the crusaders began forging documents and distributing them in the name of the CMS — pamphlets that with savage humor invited Evangelical Churchmen to join forces with Papists, Rationalists, and Socialists to form a Church with no principles at all — the secretaries were willing not only to denounce such cheap tactics but also to embrace the Church all the tighter.[27] This validation of Stock's earlier pro-Church policy and desire to correct errors by patient discussion advocated in the name of "missionary cooperation" was to become crucial to the hopes for a new Edwardian Church missionary project.[28]

Eugene Stock, who had been so central to forging CMS policy in the 1880s, emerged again as a leader of CMS home strategy after 1900, for Stock, like Montgomery, believed that home divisions were destructive and that true Christian union based on "the Historic Episcopate" was the only legitimate goal for Churchmen.[29] The traditional non-Anglican sources of Evangelical zeal — enthusiasm for the Bible, anti-Ritualism, and deference to evangelical cultural norms, including a private gender sphere for women — were increasingly problematic because of the growing influence of biblical criticism, the irreversible spread of ritual, and the loosening social practices that characterized Edwardian England. Many Evangelicals, accustomed to voluntary means of advancing the faith, began to turn to the institutional powers of their Church, now holding

25. T. J. Gaster to H. E. Fox, 10 Mar. 1899, CMS Archives, G/AC 4/27/5252.

26. James Mortimer Sangar, *Old Paths and New: Thoughts on the Centenary of the Church Missionary Society* (London: Wileman, 1899), 2-3; Randall Davidson to F. Baldey, 20 Apr. 1899, CMS Archives, G/AC 4/27/5318 and 5175.

27. See for example the forged pamphlet "The Church Missionary Society and the Reunion of Christendom" [Jan. 1899], CMS Archives, G/AC 4/26/5175. Some observers saw Kensitite radicalism as an amplified version of the excesses of early Keswick. Kensitite Anglicans were believed mostly to support the CIM, as indicated by the number of people in hotbeds of anti-Ritualism ("especially in Somerset") who read the CIM's *China's Millions* instead of the *Intelligencer*. See H. Bothamly to H. E. Fox, 27 Apr. 1899, CMS Archives, G/AC 4/271/5318.

28. Handley Moule to Fox, 26 Jan. 1899, CMS Archives, G/AC 4/26/5129; Stock, *Recollections,* 393-94.

29. Stock, *Recollections,* 394.

holiness as a personal, though not necessarily institutional, ideal; and moderates on questions of ritual diversity such as Stock and P. V. Smith grew in numbers.[30] While the fallout over the turn-of-the-century Ritualist controversy continued to plague the CMS, its secretaries stoutly defended their loyalty to episcopacy and advanced policies that drew them further into the Church.[31] At the same time new names such as "moderate Churchman" and "central Churchman" were coming into usage to identify High Churchmen who similarly wanted to dissociate themselves from the extremism of aggressive Ritualists.[32] These developments at the CMS combined with Montgomery's initiatives to produce a new atmosphere in which the mainstream parties of the Church could cooperate to address more pressing problems — perceived irreligion in the working classes, modern skepticism, paralysis within the Church over doctrinal matters — by using missionary cooperation as a basis for collaboration.

Edwardian Anxieties and the Rise of Missionary-Imperial Cooperation

The Evangelical public viewed the CMS Centenary as the high point of Evangelical missionary history, but immediately following the Centenary, circumstances forced the CMS to reconsider the basis and extent of its foreign missionary work. Overseas costs incident upon the massive growth in missionary numbers in the 1890s skyrocketed, and although the CMS Centenary did achieve an overall increase in income and maintained this higher level of income through the Edwardian period, it did so only by progressively more desperate appeals. CMS income in 1890 had been approximately £250,000, where it stubbornly remained until 1896, when the kickoff of the Three Years' Campaign pushed income by 1899 to £400,000. In the decade following, income stabilized at a new high-water mark, fluctuating between £350,000 and £400,000. However, this impressive new level of income was difficult to maintain and, somewhat ironically, was not sufficient to please the ambitions of a generation fed on the giant advances of the 1890s. Perception was critical, for no society had ever attained such elevated levels of absolute income, but, in the face of disappointed rising expectations, confidence simultaneously ebbed at the CMS.

Continuing to advance the Society's income stretched its home staff to the breaking point, and fear of failure defined the Edwardian ethos at the CMS. The

30. Wellings, *Evangelicals Embattled*, 115.

31. E[ugene]. S[tock]., "Concerning Some Misconceptions," *Church Missionary Intelligencer*, n.s., 27 (Apr. 1902): 307-10; "On 'Joint Meetings,'" *Church Missionary Intelligencer*, n.s., 29 (Jan. 1904): 31-37.

32. Chadwick, *Victorian Church: Part Two: 1860-1901*, 357.

frenetic organizing that had characterized fundraising in the heady days of the 1890s became problematic by 1900. The massive campaign leading up to the Centenary had overworked the localities and the Boer War distracted public interest in overseas activities outside the war zone.[33] By 1903 expanding costs of overseas operations outstripped income gains, a difficult reality that secretaries scrambled to explain to supporters:

> The number of missionaries — clergymen, laymen, single women (not including wives) — has risen to 977, more than three times the 309 of 1887, nearly four times the 256 of 1880. All the agencies, the native teachers and evangelists, the schools, the hospitals, the dispensaries, have multiplied in corresponding degree.[34]

In November 1906 "A Plain Statement" laid out the real basis of CMS advance: over twenty-five years the number of missionaries had quadrupled while the income had not quite doubled. This feat had been achieved largely through the use of unmarried men, who "cost less," and women, who "cost still less."[35] The eggs set to incubating by the Policy of Faith of the late 1880s had hatched and begun to demand feed. The secretaries who had exultantly justified the policy in 1894, when critics had questioned the wisdom of sending out missionaries without money to support them, were now forced to face the problem. Deficits, cleared only by emergency appeals, were the Society's reality from 1893 to 1903.[36] Donor fatigue under Edwardian conditions made sustaining the advances generated by Victorian holiness impossible.

The CMS had to find an honorable way to break with that cornerstone of the "new era," the Policy of Faith, which dictated that any qualified missionary be sent abroad regardless of Society finances. Since the 1890s, however, the secretaries had claimed that despite criticisms from ultra-Protestants the success of the Policy of Faith proved God's continued favor. Abandoning the Policy of Faith would seem to corroborate the charges of faithlessness put by Kensitites and, it was feared, could burst the bubble of contributor confidence.[37] As Bishop

---

33. For a similar set of problems among Baptists, see Brian Stanley, *The History of the Baptist Missionary Society, 1792-1992* (Edinburgh: Clark, 1992), 220-27.

34. E[ugene]. S[tock]., "The Position of the Society," *Church Missionary Intelligencer,* n.s., 28 (Dec. 1903): 883.

35. "A Plain Statement," circular letter, 13 Nov. 1906, CMS Archives, G/AZ 2/2.

36. Between 1893 and 1903 the CMS registered an aggregate of £210,452 in deficits. G[eorge]. F[urness]. S[mith]., "The Society's Financial Position," *Church Missionary Intelligencer,* n.s., 28 (July 1903): 482.

37. Kensit's "martyrdom" in 1902 from injuries inflicted by a hostile Roman Catholic crowd

Montgomery at the SPG put it, "[t]he heads want to modify. But the policy has become a fetish with others, & with many of the red hot ones, with money. To them it is doubting the promises of God . . . [b]ut they are now whipping a tired horse." He revealed that most of the secretaries were now for dropping the policy, but saving face was a delicate matter.[38] The last expedient in the face of a £70,000 deficit in 1905 was to canvass each Anglican communicant, and the failure of the appeal to cover the entire deficit the following year led to several developments: drastic retrenchments in the field, quiet abandonment of the Policy of Faith, severe curtailment of lay evangelistic work, and the end of an era.[39] The symbolic end of the Victorian missionary movement came the same year when the CMS held its last Anniversary Celebration in Exeter Hall. With the legendary evangelical venue slated for demolition — tied as it was back to the first generations of successful public anti-slavery and missionary agitation in the 1830s and 1840s — few could doubt the passing of a grand era.[40]

These difficulties at the CMS, combined with new initiatives at the SPG, led to a reassessment of the Societies' public orientation toward formal empire. After 1900 the CMS embraced the empire more directly and ardently than before. The immediate goal does not seem to have been to wrangle greater cooperation with imperial governance. In the wake of the Chinese Boxer Rebellion, pronouncements by Prime Minister Salisbury (at no less an event than the SPG Anniversary) regarding the unpopularity of missionaries at the Foreign Office suggested a decided cooling in that relationship.[41] But the Society did work to associate itself with a broader secular ethos of imperial enthusiasm. One of the key factors in shifting the CMS toward a more openly imperial posture in the 1900s, a posture that the Society and its supporters had been more reticent about adopting in earlier decades, was the experience of the CMS in the 1890s in Uganda. In this missionary field the CMS pursued close cooperation with imperial authorities after a vigorous campaign to secure imperial annexation that allowed for a consolidation of missions in an area of acute competition with both economic imperialists and Roman Catholics. With this aid, the CMS by 1895 was experiencing unrivaled success in Uganda.[42] Ugandan advances

raised further furious emotionalism in the most extreme ranks of popular Protestantism. Wellings, "Kensit," 347-58.

38. "Memorandum for the Archbishop. C.M.S. Private," 20 Feb. 1904, Davidson Papers, vol. 92, fol. 240.

39. John Kennaway to "Dear Friends," circular letter, 24 May 1905, CMS Archives, G/AZ 2/2; "Review Sub-Committee (Third) Interim Report," 16 July 1907, CMS Archives, G/CR 1.

40. *Proceedings of the CMS, 1906-7,* 165-67.

41. Greenlee and Johnston, *Good Citizens,* 113-19.

42. For more detail on this mission field, see the brief description in Stanley, *Bible and Flag,*

under strong European leadership contrasted with trouble and schism in the CMS mission on the Niger, which CMS leaders, including Eugene Stock and Frederick Wigram, believed had been weakened by independent indigenous control under the Church's first black bishop, Samuel Crowther.[43] The result of such crucial experiences in the mission field, as well as a shifting political and cultural climate that gave increasing emphasis to aggressive "tropical"-style imperialism, was a CMS organization that, while not uncritically imperialist in the 1890s, nevertheless showed a distinct willingness to reverse earlier policies that had been designed to encourage "native self-government" by enhancing control of missions from the metropolis on an imperial model.[44] In this it received support from the highest authorities in the Church.[45]

The change was palpable and now led the fervently critical Robert Cust to assert that "we can expect no blessing on Gospel-teaching, when in close contact with Calico-bales, and Rifles, not to say tons of Liquor, cases of firearms, barrels of gunpowder, and Maxim-guns, as at U-Ganda."[46] While Stock and Wigram were far from strident, racist imperialists — Stock envisioned generous cooperation in the mission field between European missionaries and indigenous converts — they did firmly insist that the work to be done and the standards of leadership for that work be defined in European terms. This partly emerged out of eagerness at the CMS to cultivate positive relationships with young, activist supporters, which encouraged extension of European standards of religiosity normalized in the holiness subculture to the mission field. A growing reluctance to advance indigenous control and independent "native" Church development resulted.[47] The reaction of Cust, inspired by Henry Venn's vision of independent, self-propagating "daughter" churches, was to question whether the CMS had not grown too fast and lost its soul to the secular world.[48] Stronger brands of missionary paternalism, more in line with the ideology and expectations of colonial officials, nevertheless reigned at the CMS, eliciting

---

127-32, and the much greater detail of Holger Bernt Hansen, *Mission, Church, and State in a Colonial Setting: Uganda, 1890-1925* (New York: St. Martin's, 1984).

43. For the classic treatment of the eventual ousting of Crowther and African control in the mission, see Ajayi, *Christian Missions*, 250-73.

44. Peter Williams has commented perceptively on the complicated and changing nature of missionary attitudes at the CMS in the 1890s and the importance of theological and ecclesiastical attitudes in addition to racial and imperial ones to shifting attitudes and policies. Williams, *Self-Governing Church*, 226-27, 232.

45. "Memorandum: Niger," 3 Mar. 1893, signed E. W. Benson, F. Temple Papers, vol. 8, fols. 105-7.

46. Cust, *Prevailing Methods*, 144.

47. E. A. Ayandele, *The Missionary Impact on Modern Nigeria, 1842-1914* (London: Longman, 1966), 212-17, 222-26.

48. Cust, *Prevailing Methods*, 141.

uneasy warnings from those doubtful about the shift, such as Bishop E. C. Stuart of Waiapu (New Zealand), that the CMS not be "beguiled by any dream of Imperialism."[49]

Despite warnings of critics, imperial models of operation were applied more frequently in the establishment of CMS policy, and imperial fantasies populated the rhetoric of the most successful of CMS missionaries on deputation.[50] CMS Uganda missionary Arthur Fisher related that his deputation tour of 1897 saw incredible receptions from audiences fascinated by "'The Mountains of the Moon', The Pigmies [*sic*], The cannibals, Darkest Africa, Elephants, lions, leopards, mighty lakes & rivers, extinct Volcanoes, a land just beginning to claim attention in every department of human society." Fisher encountered banners proclaiming him to be "Our Stanley," and he described his listeners as "all Christian Imperialists, whose love & interest surround the world & they are all encouraged in their difficult home work by the triumph of the Gospel over sin & Satan in the dark & gloomy places of the world."[51] This style of rhetoric had not been foreign to the CMS in the past, but it moved from the mouths of local speakers into the pronouncements from London in the 1890s and 1900s.

Experimentation with the idea of "Christian Imperialism" grew at the CMS, which T. A. Gurney, writing in the *Church Missionary Intelligencer,* insisted was not "the rule by conquest of the Roman Empire, or the absolutism of the Holy Roman Empire, or of the Czar." The ideal was inspired by Seeley and by Froude's *Oceana,* and strengthened by the Queen's Jubilees. The CMS produced a vision of empire designed to appeal to those whose motives for supporting foreign missions were presumed to be pious and charitable, in which the empire was "a federation of freedom-loving peoples, united by common ideals, common sentiments, common interests, linked powerfully together by the forces of modern civilization," which were, of course, presumed to include Christianity. Regardless of the distance that existed between this vision of empire and its operation on the ground, the CMS, which certainly was home to many imperial enthusiasts, was now for the first time openly and publicly appealing to imperial motivations as such to support its missions.[52] As with most Christian imperialists, Gurney asserted that the ultimate goal of empire had to be

49. Quoted in Williams, *Self-Governing Church,* 227. The end result of these changes was reduced freedom for CMS-affiliated independent indigenous churches (p. 249).

50. R. G. MacDonald, "Memo for Consideration of B VII Sub-Committee," 30 Nov. 1896, CMS Archives, G/CCb 7/2.

51. Fisher memoir, Fisher Papers, CMS Archives, Acc 84 F 3/2, book 9, pp. 6, 9-10.

52. Gurney, "Modern Imperialism," 485-86. See also Gurney's similarly imperialist preface to Irene Barnes's 1897 history of the CEZMS, lauding "the Pax Britannica and all its untold blessings, and our British administration of the country [India]." Barnes, *Story of CEZMS,* iii.

the transformation of the world into the empire of Christ, and the tone of the CMS's imperialism remained libertarian and pan-racial. The CMS as an institution had never been stridently anti-imperialist, and it had deep personal and institutional connections with all the British colonial possessions.[53] Yet, in the mid-Victorian era of Henry Venn, the Society had undoubtedly, and in significant contrast to the SPG, been more wary of close contact with the official arms of empire; and it distrusted programs to westernize indigenous peoples under strong European control.[54] These early suspicions were related to the closeness that Anglican evangelicals had previously had to Nonconformists, with their developed suspicions of establishments of all kinds. However, as the CMS experienced difficulties at home and challenges to its leadership in the world of missions, it embraced more deeply the Church and rationales for supporting secular imperial power. This had begun in the 1890s with Eugene Stock and Frederick Wigram's growing appreciation of imperial opportunities and cautious endorsement of the more vigorous expression of race-based arguments for Anglican imperial expansion and unification that were issuing from the higher realms of the Church, and with Gurney it reached full and open expression.[55]

By 1902 few at the CMS could doubt that the period of advance from the 1870s had been interrupted. In this environment, experience in the mission field, the challenges of Edwardian missionary finance, and the abandonment of the CMS by "Puritan" evangelicals led the Society to much closer collaboration within the Church of England and fuller acknowledgement of the formal role of the national church in the empire. It also led to a greater openness to cooperation with the SPG and favorable consideration of the new Pan-Anglican and pan-imperial plans of Bishop Montgomery, now closely consulting with the new archbishop of Canterbury, Randall Davidson, to create a concrete missionary-imperial program within the Church. The identity of the CMS was, of course, not severed from Keswick or from holiness-based evangelicalism, with its otherworldly, often oppositional cultural style, but the Edwardian period with all its troubles intensified a strategy of emphasizing moderate loyal Churchmanship. This would become a central defining element in CMS identity after 1900, as a more definitively positive attitude toward imperial ideals offered the potential to help support the overextended missions of the Society, and it led to historically

53. In particular, Evangelical Anglo-Indians formed a significant component of the membership of the CMS inner circle, with numbers that no other society matched. In 1869 and 1899 alike, one third of the CMS Committee members had held army ranks, nearly all from service in India.

54. Williams, *Self-Governing Church*, 2-21.

55. Kevin Ward, "'Taking Stock': The Church Missionary Society and Its Historians," in *The Church Mission Society and World Christianity, 1799-1999*, ed. Kevin Ward and Brian Stanley (Grand Rapids: Eerdmans, 1999), 28-29.

high levels of unified Anglican missionary activity. However, with the series of imperial debacles that opened the new century — the Boxer Rebellion, the Boer War, agitations over atrocities in the Congo, and Chinese labor scandals in Africa — reliance on empire simultaneously became more problematic as struggle developed in both religious and political circles over what kind of nation with what kind of empire England was to be.

The Imperial-Missionary Bid in the Edwardian Church

When Bishop Montgomery accepted the secretaryship of the SPG in 1901, he aimed to draw the Church into a newfound sense of responsibility and support for foreign missions. When Randall Davidson was appointed archbishop of Canterbury in 1903, Lambeth Palace saw for the first time a primate with long and demonstrated support for foreign missions. Both the potential and the need seemed to exist for new missionary initiatives within a Church facing troubling domestic and foreign challenges: at home, widely perceived problems of growing apathy and internal divisions; abroad, growing competition with Roman Catholic missions, Islam, and emerging nationalist movements. Especially troubling were the internal problems of the Church, which seemed to be eating away at the lineaments of basic loyalty that held together not only the Anglican Communion but Christianity itself. Thus, problems at home and abroad combined to make attractive schemes for the unification of Anglican missionary effort and its elaboration as the touchstone in a reconfigured Anglican identity. For a number of reasons this missionary bid in the Church of England failed; nevertheless, it had a crucial impact on the ethos of Protestant missions in an era when the overall resources of the movement were unmatched.

Missionary Imperialism and the Perception of Religious Decline

Fears about the state of religion had been growing for decades in the English clerical world. At the 1888 London missionary conference a Canadian Anglican identified the chief tasks for the churches: conquering apathy and the checking of the schemes of Jesuits, atheists, agnostics, and materialist scientists.[56] The prescription of missionary interest and organization as a cure for domestic ills, which had long been characteristic of evangelicalism, also became a focus of

---

56. A. Sutherland, "Development and Results of the Missionary Idea, Especially during the Last 100 Years," in *Protestant Missions Conference, 1888*, 1:145.

Anglican moderates in the 1890s. As the Kensitite campaigns reignited party combat, the influence of those who saw in popular support of empire a means to channel enthusiasm and promote unity grew. In the final decades of the nineteenth century, moderate Churchmen, both High and Low, began to agree that two destructive forces must be defeated in the Church: party faction, which sowed discord, and theological modernism, which sowed heterodoxy. Neither was new to the Church, but the perception that each contributed to a more serious problem — declining levels of piety and religious observance — encouraged enthusiasm for a unifying missionary offensive. Church leaders were particularly sensitive to the problem. Archbishop Benson believed the charges of excessive Ritualism in the 1890s led the laity to "divide the Clergy into Romanizers and Puritans and they are angry with both." What Randall Davidson believed was needed was a program that would "open the eyes of the laity as to the existence of the broad plateau of central sensible clergy."[57] These perceptions made a missionary *via media* look more and more attractive.

More distressing, however, was the growing conviction that old orthodoxies were crumbling, leading to drift in the Church, an unraveling of the fabric of English society, and a weakening of nation and empire. The threat of what was styled as modernism — both theological and secular — threw High and Low Church traditionalists into a shared conservative activism. Fear of secular critical thought had its roots in the mid-Victorian period, and by the 1870s Victorian commentators who talked about "secularization" seemed to mean by this a perceptible loosening of institutionally committed religious behavior and loss of deference to religious expectations on the part of both the affluent and the working poor.[58] But the problem for the churches was not simply one of a turning away from traditional religious behavior; it was also a weakening sense of relevance and vigor in dealing with the secular world. In 1889, Randall Davidson wryly noted the contrast between the energy with which T. H. Huxley attacked Christian dogma and the self-absorption of the Church in its Ritualist controversies.[59]

Anglican modernism, like university-based missionary activism, was on one level an attempt to make religion relevant to a new, educated generation. By bringing Anglican belief into sympathy with biblical criticism and scientific understandings of the world, however, Anglican modernists earned the enmity of traditionalist Anglo-Catholics and Evangelicals alike. All the Anglican parties developed modernist wings and extremist camps with regard to ritual innova-

57. Bell, *Davidson*, 1:136.
58. Chadwick, *Victorian Church: Part Two: 1860-1901*, 423-25.
59. Bell, *Davidson*, 1:153.

tion; however, as a broad middle group of clergy came to accept moderate High Church ritual as the common ground that could draw temperate Churchmen together, more and more Evangelicals also accepted moderate ritual, allowing them to contemplate alliances with higher Churchmen in order to oppose doctrinal modernism.[60] Old issues of ritual seemed less important than in the past. As long as ritual display was divorced from any open "Romanist" theological significance, both moderate Evangelicals and progressive High Churchmen could agree on a rising standard of Churchmanship. And for a growing body of bishops, the protection of the heritage of the early Victorian Church fathers, whether of the school of the Earl of Shaftesbury or of E. B. Pusey, was bound up in this collaboration across party lines.[61]

The reaction of traditionalist Anglo-Catholics and Evangelicals alike to the rise of Anglican modernism was merely a facet of a broader set of anxieties generated by a growing belief that urban religious observance was declining and that in educated circles the relevance of religion was receding. In an English culture in which both professionalism and the rise of commercialized leisure confronted religion with competing interests, the problems of the Church both in the cities and in the universities grew from the 1880s forward into a dominant perception of a national church in crisis.[62] The problem was neither uniform nor catastrophic. As Alan Gilbert has pointed out, in the thirty-five years leading up to 1914, Anglicans steadily increased the number of communicants relative to British population.[63] It may therefore seem strange that Anglican clerics were so preoccupied with what they often termed "crises." Leading clerics, however, were products of the universities. And in the universities, and in late Victorian consciousness more generally, problems in the city — and increasingly in the empire — loomed large as indicators of spreading degeneracy. The evidence seemed to suggest that in major metropolitan areas such as London, as well as among intellectuals and politicians, Anglicanism was declining.[64]

In addition to rising domestic uncertainty, Anglican leadership and laity

60. This process of "leveling up" in public worship practices was one cause of the emergence of a "Liberal Evangelical" group within the Church in the early 1900s. Wellings, *Evangelicals Embattled*, 115-19.

61. Roger Lloyd, *The Church of England, 1900-1965* (London: SCM, 1966), 70, 120-21; Hylson-Smith, *Evangelicals*, 230-31.

62. Bell, *Davidson*, 1:190-91; Cox, *English Churches*, chap. 3; Chadwick, *Victorian Church: Part Two: 1860-1901*, 439-62.

63. Gilbert, *Religion and Society*, 29.

64. Informal but well-known late Victorian religious censuses in London of 1886 and 1902-03 seemed to indicate a clear decline of religious observance, and Charles Booth's disturbing studies of irreligious London life were widely cited. R. C. K. Ensor, *England, 1870-1914* (Oxford: Clarendon Press, 1936), 308-9.

alike became more concerned that the Church was under attack overseas. The Anglican position abroad faced two primary challenges in the late Victorian period: competition from Roman Catholic missions and the growth and revitalization of Islam.[65] Concern about the competition posed by Nonconformity had always troubled High Churchmen, but apprehension at the success of Catholic missions, linked in often historical ways to the even more alarming growth of Islam in Africa, the Near East, and India, was an anxiety liable to unite all Churchmen.[66] The expansion of Islam forced many Anglicans out of the complacent sense of superiority with which they were accustomed to regard "paganism" or "lesser faiths" and drove them to mount more sophisticated missionary efforts. English supporters of Islam argued for its virtues and its suitability to certain "degraded" races, and in 1891 Archbishop Benson on a tour of North Africa was impressed by the power, devotion, dignity, and growth of Islam.[67] The revival of Islam in the context of empire also provided fuel for jingoistic pronouncements in an age of imperial enthusiasm. When Kitchener retook Khartoum in 1898 many Churchmen found that missions had a renewed appeal, as evidenced in newspaper clippings collected for the archbishop of Canterbury, one of which pronounced: "[i]t cannot be too clearly recognised that Islam, the hereditary foe of Europe, is contending for every inch of Africa . . . and that in their ineradicable hatred of the European and . . . determination to rule the negro in their own way, the Arabs form a vast confederacy. . . ."[68] Chauvinistic generalities of this sort received varied responses, but many Churchmen — such as Bishop George Blyth, who argued that the extension of British influence in Egypt under Kitchener was a golden opportunity to launch an Anglican mission in the Sudan — saw the power of such emotions, and they worked to redirect back into religion the deep feelings that nationalism and imperialism could evoke.[69] This was a religious version of the late Victorian secular urge to empire, which argued that salvation from national malaise and class conflict would come with the creation of "a national purpose with a high moral content."[70]

The British evangelical missionary movement had always been strongly influenced by strains of internationalism and interdenominationalism. This

65. Porter, "Anglican Missionary Expansion," 354-60.

66. Comments of Bishop G. F. P. Blyth, in "Notes of the Lambeth Conference, July 1897," Lambeth Conference, MS 1397, fol. 46, Lambeth Palace Library, London.

67. Benson, *Benson*, 2:413, 419, 459-60. See also Prasch, "Missionary Debate," 53-64.

68. F. Chenevix Trench, "Christian Mission in the Nile Valley," *Church Times*, 6 May 1898, press clipping in F. Temple Papers, vol. 18, fol. 434.

69. G. F. Popham Blyth to Frederick Temple, 24 May 1898, and Blyth to Secretary of the UMCA, 24 May 1898, F. Temple Papers, vol. 18, fols. 396-99.

70. MacKenzie, *Propaganda and Empire*, 2.

influence provided an internal logic that militated against any simple or complete immersion of missionary activity in an ideology of crude and jingoistic
imperialism.[71] Yet led by circumstance and the example of higher Churchmen,
evangelicals in the Church of England — who had always been strongly disposed toward seeing empire as a providential reward for England's staunch
fidelity to Reformation teachings — were more willing to embrace national
and imperial sentiments, which seemed to offer a foundation for putting down
evil practices, understood as particularly associated in imperial borderlands
with Islam and Roman Catholicism.[72] And as the imperial urge grew among
Evangelicals, it did so even more among High Churchmen.

Still, neither SPG missionaries nor their evangelical counterparts uncritically espoused empire. Just as after 1875 a growing number of younger enthusiasts at the CMS questioned its earlier secretary Henry Venn's assumption
that close contact with Western culture was beneficial to convert communities,
activists within the SPG also voiced criticisms of harsher unregulated forms
of economic imperialism. Thus in an 1897 meeting of the London JCMA one
SPG supporter, Canon Scott, emphasized the influence of British "white men,"
saying "[w]e act as solvent wherever we go, shattering creeds & customs & now
we stand face to face with a problem wh[ich] we have ourselves created."[73] This
was an old missionary impulse: to act as conscience of empire, as missionaries
had in South Africa and the West Indies in the 1820s, and in the South Seas
and Africa in the 1860s and 70s.[74] The SPG, so long generally allied to landed
colonial interests, was still to be avowedly imperialist, but younger, modernist
clergy imagined it to be a corrective to the unscrupulous and unspiritual European influence that was "making a very hell" of places like Masonaland. "The
Empire is in the making now," Scott emphasized, and asked, "Is it to be another
of our huge failures?"[75] The imperial idea had a long incubation, as one succinct
subheading in the Report of the 1888 London missionary conference suggests:
"Foreign Missions, like colonies, a defense."[76] But after the turn of the century
the almost unanimous proclamation among Anglicans of foreign missionary
activity as vital to the life and health of churches in nation and empire is striking. Extending these ideas throughout the home Church, however, required
new commitment by the English bishops and concrete efforts by the societies.

71. Porter, *Religion Versus Empire*, 324-29.

72. Bebbington, "Atonement and Empire," 19, 23, 27-29.

73. Minutes of the London JCMA, 26 March 1897, USPG Archives, X 539.

74. Stanley, *Bible and Flag*, 85-98, 112-32.

75. Minutes of the London JCMA, 26 March 1897, USPG Archives, X 539.

76. "The Church's Duty and a New Departure in Missionary Enterprise," in *Protestant Missions Conference, 1888,* 1:435.

Evangelical bishops — Ryle, Bickersteth, Thorold, Moule — had always energetically championed foreign missions by making the common evangelical argument that missions brought "reflex benefits" of deeper piety, stronger churches, and divine favor to nation and empire. The greater visibility of higher church bishops advocating missions as a central concern of the national church, especially B. F. Westcott of Durham (1890-1901), provided support for a missionary program drawing on English episcopal leadership. Foreign mission had in the past, however, been largely peripheral to the concerns of the archbishops of Canterbury. Archbishop Benson (1884-96) had feared that radical Protestantism could lead to an exodus of Evangelicals from the Church, destroying its position as the established church. Praise and support of missions was a way of placating Evangelicals, but Benson's primary interest lay in preserving Church unity through attention to domestic social problems: poverty, working-class alienation, and the challenge of socialism. His primary goal was to moderate party conflicts and ensure Anglican cohesion. Recalling the speech he made at the 1891 CMS London Anniversary, he commented: "No worse evil could befall the Church than a rupture in the C.M.S. It is the power that keeps the Puritan party faithful to the Church of England."[77] He did not see the interests of the Church being advanced by bringing its missionary societies together, which experience showed were explosively quarrelsome when forced into proximity.

Yet by the 1900s the SPG and the CMS had developed surprisingly cordial relations, contrasting sharply with their stormy rivalry in the Tractarian age, which had carried well into the 1880s. Compromises on ritual matters brokered by the bishops in the 1890s brought closer cooperation, the crucial turning point being the Lincoln Judgment, by which Bishop King of Lincoln was acquitted in the court of the archbishop of Canterbury of practicing illegal ritual. While extreme evangelicals believed failure to censure Bishop King's ritual practices had revived the "Romanism" of seventeenth-century Archbishop Laud himself, moderate Evangelicals had angrily opposed the Church Association's prosecution of the bishop. They accepted the Judgment, with its limitations on ritual, as a decision that curbed the worst abuses, and as technically Protestant — an eirenicon rather than a betrayal. Similarly, Lord Stanmore (Arthur Hamilton-Gordon), weather vane of Ritualist opinion and powerful patron of the SPG, also reported general satisfaction with the Judgment.[78] Cooperative attitudes were also facilitated by the waxing influence of the SVMU, which was grappling with radical Protestantism in its own sphere,

77. Benson, *Benson*, 2:398-99.
78. Wellings, *Evangelicals Embattled*, 102-4; Benson, *Benson*, 2:253, 369-70.

and by the Younger Clergy Unions of both the CMS and the SPG, with their emphasis on cooperative Church organization.[79] Student-driven collaboration spilled over to official society relations in 1900 when the CMS formed an Association of Church of England Secretaries and invited all the major societies involved in overseas missions to join.[80] Thus, while ultra-Protestant Evangelicals balked at associating with High Churchmen because High Churchmen balked at associating with Nonconformists, ultimately in 1903 the CMS General Committee voted to endorse cooperation with diocesan Mission Boards, and eventually leaders at the SPG and CMS began meeting periodically to regularize missionary policies and compare notes on recruiting, propagandizing, and field policy.[81]

"Archbishop of Greater Britain": The Anglican Missionary Gambit

The elevation of Randall Davidson to the archbishopric of Canterbury in February 1903 meant the arrival of a committed and experienced "missionary archbishop." Davidson, as Archbishop Tait's Chaplain from 1878, pioneered an "active . . . daily administration of missionary questions" and continued this role during the primacy of Archbishop Benson, for whom he also served as chaplain and chief adviser on missionary work, the Colonial Church, and the effect of missionary activity on the English Church.[82] Growing rapprochement between the CMS and SPG had as early as the 1890s opened an opportunity for the archbishop of Canterbury, rising in leadership within the communion through the Lambeth conferences, to champion plans for union of the CMS and the SPG through missionary effort. But the successor at Canterbury in 1896 upon Benson's death, Frederick Temple, was 75 years old, of failing sight, and not well suited to this task. Despite speaking positively on support for mis-

79. Despite protests by the radicals, joint meetings continued, supported by SVMU commitment to engaging with higher church Anglicans. Minutes of the London JCMA, 13 Dec. 1901, USPG Archives, X 405.

80. The Societies invited were the Religious Tract Society, the London Jews Society, the SPG, the Zenana Bible and Medical Mission, the Spanish and Portuguese Church Aid Society, the UMCA, the Colonial and Continental Church Society, the South American Missionary Society, the Society for the Promotion of Christian Knowledge, the Church of England Zenana Missionary Society, the Parochial and Foreign Jews Society, and the British and Foreign Bible Society. "Letters Regarding the Formation of Association of Ch[urch] of Eng[land] Secretaries," CMS Archives, G/AC 4/30/5847a.

81. George Tonge, CEZMS to H. E. Fox, 24 Jan. 1900, CMS Archives, G/AC 4/30/5847a; Henry H. Montgomery to Bishop [Herbert] Tugwell, 21 Mar. [190]6, USPG Archives, X 366.

82. Bell, *Davidson*, 1:46; Benson, *Benson*, 2:468-73.

sions, he neglected correspondence with overseas bishops and failed to broker compromises as in the past.[83] Davidson, however, elevated to the bishopric of Rochester in 1891 and translated to Winchester in 1895, developed his ideas on missions in association with the JCMA and correspondence with his old and close friend Bishop Montgomery. Once appointed archbishop he was strongly predisposed to leverage the authority of Lambeth Palace, placing himself as chief counselor on matters of common concern throughout the worldwide Anglican Communion.

Montgomery saw Davidson as his most crucial collaborator, sympathizer, and co-architect of plans to reorient the vision of the Church and effect unification in the Anglican Communion, with the SPG as the center from which moderate Evangelicals and High Churchmen would heal Anglican rifts.[84] The bishops had recruited Montgomery to generate enthusiasm, but he believed his success or failure lay with the English clergy, who could only be effectively moved by the bishops. The linkage of empire and social reform was not uncommon in the late Victorian period, including plans for encouraging emigration and establishing industrial colonies for the poor as a means of solving social problems rooted in unemployment and pauperism.[85] For Montgomery, the importance of a parallel linkage of empire and church reform seemed obvious. In the context of rising religious difficulties — as both Anglo-Catholics and Nonconformists argued that traditional High and Low Churchmen were not adequately serving England's urban poor — many Anglicans accustomed to thinking of colonies as a defense of nation came to imagine foreign missions as a potential defense of the Church.[86]

Montgomery designed his program both to emulate Evangelical enthusiasm for foreign missions and to make the SPG the instrument for broadening that enthusiasm and channeling it back into the Church. Writing to Randall Davidson in 1899, after praising CMS enthusiasm, Montgomery commented,

83. Temple was selected largely because of the calculation that he was one of the few men who could secure the confidence of both Evangelical and High Church parties. Bell, *Davidson*, 1:283, 290-92.

84. Montgomery to Davidson, 27 May, 21 July, 4 Oct. and 13 Dec. 1901, Davidson Papers, vol. 151, fols. 284-87, 304-5, 335-44 and 348-51.

85. On voluntary charities, including well-known activities of the Salvation Army and Dr. Barnardo's Homes, see Stephen Constantine, "Empire Migration and Social Reform, 1880-1950," in *Migrants, Emigrants, and Immigrants: A Social History of Migration*, ed. Colin G. Pooley and Ian D. Whyte (London: Routledge, 1991), 62-70. The plans of L. Parry (Sister Beatrice) to inaugurate colonial training institutes for waifs and strays demonstrate that such ideas extended to higher Church Anglicans. L. Parry to Benson, 15 Dec. [1890], Benson Papers, vol. 92, fols. 338-47.

86. For an early example, see "The Church's Duty and a New Departure in Missionary Enterprise," in *Protestant Missions Conference, 1888*, 1:435.

"How interesting it is too to see how the devotion of the CMS party is in one channel & <u>does not touch</u> great <u>social questions</u>. It doesn't come into their horizon." Montgomery's conclusion, natural in a man with his preoccupations, was "[t]ruly the marriage of High & Low is needful."[87] Through such a marriage the enthusiasm of Evangelicalism could be absorbed and redirected to benefit Church projects at home and abroad. But one of the chief difficulties with Montgomery's scheme, which Davidson realized from the beginning, was that a vision of unity achieved through an engagement with empire raised alarms with many in the Church, moderates as well as radicals, who prized the independence that the historically broad Anglican Communion provided. Montgomery's early visionary statements on the creation of an "Imperial Church" were suppressed by Davidson.[88] Many of Montgomery's ambitions had to remain under cover, shared only by an internal coterie of enthusiasts in the JCMA, for fear of setting off a furious reaction.

Significantly, the primary purpose of Montgomery's plans was not to advance evangelistic conversion. Much as secular imperialists looked to empire as a realm of salvation for England,[89] success at the SPG meant that the Society "might help to check the falling off in men in Holy Orders in England as well as supplying the world." Furthermore, he hoped to shift the focus of Anglican missions away from the simple evangelistic enthusiasms touted by Keswick. Montgomery's goal was the creation of a "Pax Evangelica," in which the officers and the supporters of the missionary societies would be "indirectly banded together against the E[nglish] C[hurch] U[nion], C[onfraternity of the] B[lessed] S[acrament] and Ch[urch] Association."[90] These were ideas likely to gain sympathy from moderate leaders at the CMS, who were coming more fully to embrace the idea of using missionary societies to ameliorate party strife. Thus Montgomery's imperial program was, on an important level, an attempt to move the SPG to claim a broad Anglican middle ground opening between advanced Anglo-Catholicism, of both ritual and doctrinal kinds, and the extreme Protestantism of the staunchest Evangelicals.

87. Montgomery to Davidson, 12 July 1899, Davidson Papers, vol. 519, fols. 244-47.

88. Montgomery to the Standing Committee of the SPG, 17 Aug. 1901, Davidson Papers, vol. 151, fols. 322-23, with handwritten note at top: "Not sent by RTW [Randall T. (bishop of) Winchester]."

89. Duncan Bell, *The Idea of Greater Britain: Empire and the Future of World Order, 1860-1900* (Princeton: Princeton University Press, 2007), 33-40.

90. That is to say, the highest and the lowest realms of the Church. Montgomery to Davidson, 13 Dec. 1901, Davidson Papers, vol. 151, fols. 348-51.

The Failure of the Missionary Gambit, 1901-1914

Bishop Henry H. Montgomery successfully articulated an ideal of imperial co-operation that appealed to the enthusiasm of young High Churchmen. How-ever, while Montgomery developed an SPG ideal of "imperial Christianity," his larger project to unify the Church through an appeal to empire was less successful. In fact, very little materialized out of Montgomery's program beyond the undoubted revitalization of the SPG and his successful agitation for the international and comprehensive Pan-Anglican Congress of 1908. Montgomery wanted to direct the attention of a troubled home Church to the overseas prob-lems of the communion, including continued expansion of foreign missions, which he believed could be solved by focusing Churchmen on the "natural" connection between religion and empire. The attempt to construct even the most rudimentary platform to advance this program, however, rapidly broke down. Montgomery had, in the end, no means of compelling acceptance of his imperial rhetoric, especially in a Church that was home to historically an-tagonistic, independent parties. Moderate High Churchmen and Evangelicals alike desired a more unified communion, but there was no explicit agreement on the basis of this union. Montgomery implied something close to imperial federation; Eugene Stock of the CMS advocated something nearer to coopera-tive evangelization; Archbishop Davidson favored worldwide Anglican concord through consultation. All hoped for a Christian community in which deep in-volvement with foreign evangelization would erase domestic controversy. Their fellow Churchmen, trained in an individualist and often confrontational com-munion, remained wary. Montgomery's broad agenda of unifying and energiz-ing the Church of England through an imperial program failed to catch hold because of vagueness in conception and the complications of implementation in a Church of widely varied interests.

Launching the Missionary Gambit

In 1901 a combined sense of crisis in the Church and new imperial preoccupa-tions bred by the Boer War made attractive Montgomery's plans for remaking the SPG. Energy in the JCMA was high, and its leaders pursued long-incubated plans. Samuel Bickersteth suggested, for example, that the SPG should make a bold public claim on Westminster Abbey, "which has, if any building has, an Imperial outlook," and transform it into "the Foreign Office of the Church of England." The suggestion of the Abbey also had overtones of moving the SPG closer to advanced modernist views, since in contrast to St. Paul's, known for traditionalism in its High Church curates, Westminster Abbey was noted as a home of Broad Churchmen.[91] John Ellison launched a rededication of the Council for Service Abroad, hoping to minister to the colonies and the "heathen" with new vigor.[92] The passions and self-conscious imperialism unleashed by the Boer War provided a broad source of emotional energy, vividly embodied in the message of the touring bishop of Quebec, A. H. Dunn, who asserted, "[j]ust now there is a spirit of Imperialism in the air" because the war led men "to see the marvelous possibilities underlying the active union of Great Britain with her Colonies, and indeed, the further possibilities underlying the united action of the whole Anglo-Saxon Race." This was a reinvigorated, turn-of-the-century statement of an old theme: "The expansion of our Empire has in God's providence helped forward the expansion of the great Spiritual Kingdom." The apostolic Church of England was to provide the basis for reuniting Christianity, first within the Church, then throughout the world.[93] A new claim of comprehensiveness for the SPG emerged in which the most ambitious writers in support of the Society claimed that its work, through the empire, was broader than the work of the Church of England alone.[94]

Randall Davidson's call to Canterbury in 1903, and his close association with Conservative Prime Minister Arthur Balfour, lent immediate weight to Montgomery's agenda. Montgomery advised Davidson on missions, and the archbishop used Montgomery to establish personal contact with as many overseas bishops as possible, with the intention of establishing a worldwide network of episcopal correspondence.[95] Also, Montgomery convinced Davidson that a great act of symbolism was in order: relocating and expanding the SPG London headquarters by attaching it to Church House in Dean's Yard next to Westminster Abbey, which according to Montgomery was "the only position worthy of S.P.G." When that move was achieved in 1907, the dedication of the new headquarters by the Prince of Wales allowed Montgomery to proclaim the SPG's mission to be the "strengthening of the religious and moral life of the

91. Samuel Bickersteth to Randall Davidson, 19 Apr. 1901, Davidson Papers, vol. 68, fols. 254-57; Chadwick, *Victorian Church: Part Two: 1860-1901*, 393.

92. Ellison to Randall Davidson, 26 Mar. 1901, Davidson Papers, vol. 68, fols. 227-30.

93. *The British Empire and Its Spiritual Expansion. An Illustrated Address Delivered at Several Centres by the Bishop of Quebec in View of the Bicentenary of the Society for the Propagation of the Gospel* (n.p., n.d., ca. 1901), USPG Archives, H 69.

94. "The C.M.S. & the S.P.G.: Does Their Work Dovetail?" *The Church Family Newspaper*, ca. 1902, press clipping, USPG Archives, H 96.

95. Bell, *Davidson*, 1:715-16. After Feb. 1903 Montgomery also sent Davidson regular reports on overseas Church matters. Montgomery to Davidson, 7 Feb. 1903, Davidson Papers, vol. 87, fols. 207-11.

Collage group portrait of the major participants at the 1908 Lambeth Conference, including female leaders Constance Bunyon, Georgina Gollock, and Louise Creighton, set in an artist's rendition of St. Paul's Cathedral, from the Lambeth Conference Papers, LC 104a.

Courtesy of the Trustees of Lambeth Palace Library

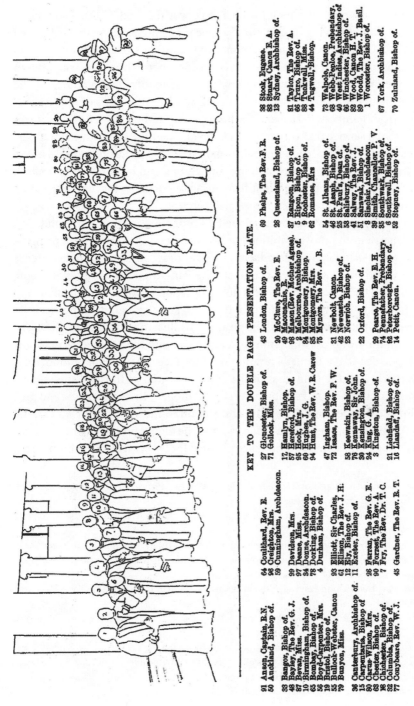

KEY TO THE DOUBLE PAGE PRESENTATION PLATE.

91 Anson, Captain, R.N.
50 Auckland, Bishop of.
38 Bangor, Bishop of.
48 Bayley, The Rev. G. J.
87 Bevan, Miss.
10 Birmingham, Bishop of.
65 Bombay, Bishop of.
56 Boyd-Carpenter, Mrs.
19 Bristol, Bishop of.
55 Bullock-Webster, Canon
79 Bunyon, Miss.
36 Canterbury, Archbishop of.
15 Carpentaria, Archbishop of
80 Carus-Wilson, Mrs.
68 Chester, Bishop of.
32 Chichester, Bishop of.
77 Conybeare, Rev. W. J.

64 Coulthard, Rev. E.
96 Creighton, Mrs.
59 Cunningham, Archdeacon.
99 Davidson, Mrs.
97 Deane, Miss.
34 Donne, Archdeacon.
78 Dorking, Bishop of.
4 Durham, Bishop of.
93 Elliott, Sir Charles.
61 Ellison, The Rev. J. H.
12 Ely, Bishop of.
11 Exeter, Bishop of.
26 Farran, The Rev. G. E.
90 Forrest, The Rev. A. C.
7 Fry, The Rev. Dr. T. C.
45 Gardner, The Rev. R. T.

27 Gloucester, Bishop of.
71 Gollock, Miss.
17 Hamlyn, Bishop.
57 Hereford, Bishop of.
95 Hook, Mrs.
60 Hughes, J. G.
94 Hunt, The Rev. W. E. Carew
47 Ingham, Bishop.
73 Isaacs, The Rev. F. W.
58 Keewatin, Bishop of.
76 Kennaway, Sir John.
30 Kensington, Bishop of.
24 King, G. A.
3 Kingston, Bishop of.
21 Lichfield, Bishop of.
10 Llandaff, Bishop of.

43 London, Bishop of.
20 McClure, The Rev. E.
49 Maconachie, R.
98 Mason (Rev. Mother Agnes).
2 Melbourne, Archbishop of.
84 Montgomery, Bishop.
85 Montgomery, Mrs.
75 Mynors, The Rev. A. B.
31 Newbolt, Canon.
42 Newcastle, Bishop of.
23 Norwich, Bishop of.
22 Oxford, Bishop of.
29 Pearce, The Rev. E. H.
74 Pennefather, Prebendary.
92 Peterborough, Bishop of.
14 Petit, Canon.

69 Phelps, The Rev. F. R.
28 Queensland, Bishop of.
87 Rangoon, Bishop of.
5 Ripon, Bishop of.
9 Rochester, Bishop of.
62 Romanes, Mrs
54 St. Albans, Bishop of.
46 St. Asaph, Bishop of.
25 St. Paul's, Dean of.
33 Salisbury, Bishop of.
41 Salwey, The Rev. J.
51 Sarawak, Bishop of.
8 Sinclair, Archdeacon.
39 Smith, Chancellor. P. V.
35 Southwark, Bishop of.
6 Southwell, Bishop of.
53 Stepney, Bishop of.

38 Stock, Eugene.
83 Stuart, Canon E. A.
13 Sydney, Archbishop of.
81 Taylor, The Rev. A.
66 Truro, Bishop of.
88 Tunkwell, Miss.
44 Tugwell, Bishop.
73 Walpole, Canon.
68 Webb-Peploe, Prebendary.
40 West Indies, Archbishop of.
66 Winchester, Bishop of.
82 Wood, Canon H. T.
89 Woodd, The Rev. J. Basil.
1 Worcester, Bishop of.
67 York, Archbishop of.
70 Zululand, Bishop of.

Key to the 1908 Lambeth Conference portrait, from the Lambeth Conference Papers, LC 104a. Courtesy of the Trustees of Lambeth Palace Library.

407

Empire as may make it potent for the whole world's good."[96] Davidson fell in with the plan, involving himself for example in the public campaign generated by the JCMA to raise scholarship money to Oxford or Cambridge designed to encourage promising public school boys "to offer themselves as Missionaries in the Imperial work of the Church of England" and in turn "give a fillip in public school life to the ordination idea."[97] The JCMA also, after years of requests, received from Lambeth Palace and the bishops the "authoritative call" to foreign and colonial service that was designed to break prejudice against what was perceived as professionally inferior missionary work.[98] Davidson hoped to efface the distinction of the Church at home and abroad and by doing so to "enlist a wider measure of support while still giving an opportunity for the enthusiasms of those to whom foreign service specially appeals."[99]

Montgomery most clearly developed his program for Church consolidation and defense in the most ambitious of his schemes: advocating for a comprehensive Pan-Anglican conference that would draw all the national churches of the world into sympathetic contact. The Pan-Anglican Congress of 1908, Montgomery's "special 'child,'" was not to be a purely High Church affair, and Montgomery sought fully to involve the CMS and through it Evangelicals.[100] CMS participation represented the growing disillusionment of some Evangelicals with the world of Nonconformity, as well as with the acceptance of Montgomery's idea that a unified communion must face the problem of modernity by gathering all the Churches of the empire, as well as those of the regions beyond, in common and sympathetic consultation.[101] In its systematic and professional character and in its close connection to the student movement, the Pan-Anglican Congress was a predecessor to the higher profile, interdenominational World Missionary Conference planned for two years later in Edinburgh.

96. Davidson to "Your Royal Highness" [George Windsor, Prince of Wales], copy, [Mar. 1907], Davidson Papers, vol. 135, fol. 401.

97. Davidson to C. H. Turner, bishop of Islington, 16 Mar. 1905, Davidson Papers, vol. 106, fols. 217-18.

98. John Ellison, letter read to the Federation of the JCMA, in *Federation of the Junior Clergy Missionary Association . . . Resumé of Proceedings at the 23rd Conference of Delegates . . . Nov., 1905*, p. 7, Davidson Papers, vol. 115, fols. 316-23.

99. Davidson to John Percival, bishop of Hereford, 22 Mar. 1905, Davidson Papers, vol. 106, fols. 224-25.

100. Montgomery to Frederick Temple, 5 Aug. 1902, F. Temple Papers, vol. 55, fols. 103-6; Stock, *Recollections*, 218.

101. Montgomery noted that Eugene Stock had found the 1900 New York Missionary Conference "almost wholly what we call Nonconformist," thus diminishing the influence of Anglicans despite their leadership in world missions. Montgomery to George Howard Wilkinson, bishop of St. Andrews, 25 Mar. [190]7, USPG Archives, X 366.

Its organizers judged the Pan-Anglican Congress a triumph primarily because "the Anglican Church had arrived at the psychological moment when any effort to deepen the sense of corporate life throughout the world would meet with success."[102] But, as Eugene Stock openly acknowledged, the Congress, which was originally conceived of as advancing foreign missions, came to focus primarily on the internal order of the communion and the home problems of the Church. "Other questions," which Montgomery had originally cast as peripheral, particularly the social issues and local diocesan challenges addressed in the session on "human society," dominated the Congress.[103]

Montgomery discovered through the Pan-Anglican Congress the true weight of imperial rhetoric: while it roused gatherings at the JCMA, it was a difficult sell to those preoccupied with pressing English problems. The concerns of the Congress, revolving as they did around continuing social challenges and the declining power of the Church at home, suggested that a program for building enthusiasm for foreign missions had come by 1908 to be seen by many clerics as a largely inadequate solution to Church problems. Henry Scott Holland, one of the founders of the JCMA, reflected the wonder of many Anglicans at the expanse and exoticism of a communion that had "planted its feet on every shore that ocean washes" but also the seeming incongruity that it was "this English church, snug and smug among the hedgerows, that has done it." "Who would have dreamed it of her?" he continued, "She hardly believes it herself."[104] Like Holland, many felt pride at Church growth overseas, but they perceived no substantial, focused program lying behind it, nor any pressing need for one. The continuing preoccupation with social questions and concern with religious competition that registered itself at the Pan-Anglican Congress indicated the chief challenge that any institutionally led missionary bid faced: attracting the support of the hard-toiling parish priest who was struggling to keep religion relevant in the localities.

The difficulties Montgomery's ambitious imperial project faced at the Pan-Anglican six short years after his arrival at the SPG were evidence that securing the success of his program to make Church missions the center of Anglican

---

102. Like Edinburgh, the Pan-Anglican Congress involved detailed preparation including the solicitation of topics from around the world, formation of specialist panels, the distribution of thirty-eight papers produced by these panels, and discussions on the responses to the papers, all prior to the Congress. M[aud]. M[ontgomery]., *Montgomery*, 58. It drew at least 4,500 people to whom tickets were issued, and the six evening public meetings were continuously full, representing about 13,000 in attendance for each of eight successive days. *General Report*, vol. 1 of [Report of the] Pan-Anglican Congress, 1908 (London: SPCK, 1908), 1, 5-6, 11.

103. Stock, *History of the CMS*, 4:549; *Pan-Anglican Congress Report, 1908, Vol. 1*, 30-31.

104. Henry Scott Holland, *A Bundle of Memories* (London: Wells Gardner, Darton, 1915), 231-33.

life, devotion, and dedication was going to be far more challenging than his confident early rhetoric had suggested. Three major areas of conflict emerged to thwart his plans. First, the old divisions between Evangelicals, Anglo-Catholics, and "rigid" High Churchmen flared, despite their common abhorrence of the threat of liberal theological modernism; at the same time, within each of these groupings emergent modernist attitudes also caused tensions. Second, the Anglican clergy remained concerned predominantly with domestic problems. Third, Churchmen disagreed over the proper basis that should constitute meaningful Christian imperial engagement. Montgomery's program was visionary, but the world in which the SPG operated — especially as conditioned by the limitations imposed by Church parties, local preoccupations, and the imperatives of missionaries in the field — redirected his program and diluted his efforts. The most obvious reason for the ultimate failure of Montgomery's program is easy to identify: in an age of defensiveness in both the High Church and Evangelical parties, foreign activity, itself contested on many levels, had only a limited ability to displace the local concerns that grounded the social reality of religiosity in England.

Romanism, Modernism, and the Tyranny of the Home Church

One of the greatest obstacles to any program for Anglican Church unity resulted from the stubborn persistence of party divisions within the communion. While missions tended among evangelicals to encourage strategic ecumenical cooperation, for generations competition and sectarian identity had been a primary factor in generating missionary support. As doubtful as Montgomery's original premise was, that missionary preoccupations could heal party rifts within the Church, even more doubtful was the idea that unity within the Church would increase levels of support for foreign missions. Long experience suggested instead that it was precisely competition and sectarian identity that most strongly animated missionary supporters. Because so much of the Victorian missionary ethos had been based on this competition, it was risky to dilute the core of individualist evangelicalism that had underpinned the Victorian missionary movement.

The JCMA tactic of using the authority of the episcopate to revitalize missions was picked up at the CMS, which, following the SPG, in 1904 appointed E. G. Ingham, formerly of Sierra Leone, as the home secretary of the Society. In reality, however, the change was but a small concession to the new ideal of Anglican unity: Ingham was a bishop, but he was also closely associated with the famous Keswick Letter, and the Society remained under the control of an independent honorary secretary, still allowing it to defend itself as staunchly evangelical.[105] Many Evangelicals were becoming more comfortable within the Church, but the ever closer relations between the CMS and the SPG also re-irritated old wounds originally inflicted in the battles over ritual. Strikingly, the chief opposition that arose to Montgomery's "Archbishop of Greater Britain" rhetoric came not from anti-imperialists but from three different religious quarters: Evangelicals, who imagined that he had been "appointed by a set of Ritualists to advocate Ritualism all round the world"; Anglo-Catholics associated with the *Church Times,* who opposed any move perceived to centralize any power in the Church over that of the bishop in diocese; and exclusivist supporters of the SPG itself, who resisted cooperation and association with evangelicals and Nonconformists.[106] It was this kind of party identity that the system of independent voluntary missionary societies served.

While cooperation and ecumenism among missionary students and an emerging Liberal Evangelical group were on the rise, so too were ultra-Protestant forms of evangelicalism. Consistently, Montgomery discovered that the "narrowness" of many of his Evangelical collaborators caused problems.[107] Significantly, one of the narrowest of Evangelicals was H. E. Fox, the honorary secretary of the CMS, who had been appointed in the 1890s precisely to reassure northern Evangelicals that the CMS would not fall prey to Ritualism. Fox's inability to work constructively with the student movement because of his deeply partisan style of evangelicalism added to the uncertainty at the CMS about its fundamental identity.[108] And the CMS ultimately gave only lukewarm support to Archbishop Davidson's plan to provide scholarship support to missionary students, vowing that the Society would pay back any money accepted from the fund by students who subsequently became CMS missionaries, fearing charges of complicity with Romanizers.[109] It was undoubtedly disconcerting for progressives at the CMS that not only their honorary secretary but often the General Committee itself displayed attitudes characteristic of radical "Puritans." And on the High Church side, bishops still had to acknowledge these delicate realities and restrain Anglo-Catholic enthusiasts, who wanted to "undermine the independence of the Societies" to engineer a unified church missionary structure, or-

105. H. E. Fox to Davidson, 28 Oct 1904, Davidson Papers, vol. 92, fols. 241-42.

106. Montgomery to Davidson, 21 Aug. 1901, 8 Sept., and 4 Oct., Davidson Papers, vol. 151, fols. 324-25, 333-34, 335-44.

107. Montgomery to Davidson, 10 Oct. 1905, Davidson Papers, vol. 106, fols. 250-52.

108. Tatlow, *Student Christian Movement,* 406-7.

109. "The Special Sub-Committee appointed to consider the Archbishop of Canterbury's proposals for Exhibitions for Missionary Students," 4 Apr. 1905, in Minutes of Sub-Committees, CMS Archives, G/CS 4.

ganized through the Boards of Mission, to serve a unitary Church and empire.[110] In the end bowing to the realities of a divided Anglican support base dominated by Evangelicals "really aglow with belief in Foreign Missions" — reckoned by Davidson to outnumber similarly enthusiastic High Churchmen by ten or twenty to one — meant quietly abandoning the dream of unified Mission Boards, and stripping them of all but promotional and consultative functions.[111]

Continuing religious divisions thus manifested themselves in familiar ways. "Rigid Churchmen" at the SPG, for example, despite Montgomery's pleading, resisted ecumenical cooperation outside of the communion. Precisely at the time that Montgomery was organizing the Pan-Anglican Congress, he was also warning the organizers of the ecumenical World Missionary Conference, scheduled for 1910, that "I don't think anything will make us go in for Undenominational Congresses. Rightly or wrongly we won't! I feel that is the universal feeling here."[112] These attitudes increased tensions with Evangelicals, particularly when the most unbending of High Churchmen accused them of fostering "Pan-Protestantism" and Anglo-Catholics criticized them for hindering progress toward achieving reunification with the Eastern Churches and Rome.[113] Notably, only by both persuasion and threats was the secretary of the SVMU, Tissington Tatlow, able to secure SPG participation, first in his own conferences, then in the World Missionary Conference. The SPG had, along with the other societies, become dependent on the student movement for its best recruits, yet only after Tatlow threatened to "wash my hands of the S.P.G." if delegates were not sent to the 1907 SVMU conference, was Montgomery able to convince the Standing Committee to acquiesce.[114] The Standing Committee did not, however, abandon its more traditional reticence toward contact with Nonconformists. In December 1908 the attitude of "the more rigid Churchmen" reasserted itself when the Standing Committee refused the invitation to be officially represented at Edinburgh, although, ultimately, under intense pressure, the SPG reversed this decision.[115]

110. A. W. Bedford, Chairman, London JCMA, to Davidson, 10 Oct. 1901, Davidson Papers, vol. 68, fols. 298-99.

111. Davidson to Bedford, 15 Oct. 1901, Davidson Papers, vol. 68, fols. 300-301; E. G. Ingham, Honorary Secretary, Board of Missions of the Province of Canterbury to Frederick Temple, 29 Oct. 1902, F. Temple Papers, vol. 59, fols. 188-89; Stock, *Recollections*, 234.

112. Montgomery to George Howard Wilkinson, bishop of St. Andrews, 25 Mar. [190]7, USPG Archives, X 366.

113. Stock, *History of the CMS*, 4:26.

114. Tatlow, *Student Christian Movement*, 308-9; Montgomery to Tatlow, 12 June [190]7, USPG Archives, X 366.

115. Bell, *Davidson*, 1:573. The SPG Standing Committee only relented in April 1910, the last-minute preparations causing considerable difficulties. "Monthly Summary. May 24, 1910," Com-

Party identities also took on new meaning in the age of theological modernism. The burgeoning student missionary movement was ironically involved in the reemergence of party strife because, although it emphasized ecumenical cooperation through its program of advocating "scientific" missions, it rejected earlier styles of holiness-based evangelicalism that had initially driven the evangelical student movement. This rejection served to highlight the fiery controversies ignited by the advance of theological modernism. The original intent of the evangelical student movement had been, like Montgomery's imperial program, to dissolve party difference in the work of mission. But instead, student activity served to publicize the new set of fault lines emerging in British religious culture. As systematic examination of foreign mission grew through the educational program of the SVMU, problems inherent in the movement overseas — negative indigenous reactions to missionary presumptions of Western cultural superiority, evangelical disregard of social and material obstacles to conversion, missionary complicity with dominant imperial powers — all became more evident. In effect, within the movement "scientific" mission study shifted the debate about missions to limitations in the field, rather than limitations of the home church. This removed much of the crisis-minded immediacy of missionary activity and the expectation of miraculous missionary transformations.

Modernism posed one critical question to foreign missions: Could they survive without reliance on the inerrancy of biblical faith, unquestioning obedience to Christ's command to evangelize, and the belief that conversion could overcome all material and cultural obstacles? Had the encounter of evangelical spirituality with rationalism and professionalism in the university sapped evangelicalism's vitality by making simpleminded faith unacceptable? After the 1890s the assertions of the next generation of revivalists that science revealed the greatness of God became far more problematic as the majority of undergraduates, drawn into scholarly, scientific, and professional tropes of investigation, examined such claims with an ever more critical eye.[116] The student movement, the great hope for missionary advance and strategic sophistication in the 1890s, became a center of dispute after the turn of the century. While student leaders could proclaim that "the blaze of Western science has exposed the superstitions and absurdities of the non-Christian religions," the very real danger embedded

---

mittee for Women's Work Secretary, Monthly Summaries and Reviews, 1910-1918, USPG Archives, CWW 1. See also Brian Stanley, *The World Missionary Conference, Edinburgh 1910* (Grand Rapids: Eerdmans, 2009), 68-70.

116. Chadwick, *Victorian Church: Part Two: 1860-1901*, 457. CMS evangelicals still claimed that the vastness of nature demonstrated God's existence. "Our Monthly Message," *CMS Home Gazette* 3 (Mar. 1905): 25. On Evangelical accommodations to, as well as rejection of, much evolutionary and liberal critical thought, see Wellings, *Evangelicals Embattled,* chaps. 4-6.

in modernism and the concept of "mission science," a danger that some evangelicals perceived clearly, was that the same cold, scientific analysis that was being directed toward "heathen" religions could be, and had been, applied to Christianity, questioning whether it was possible to "harmonize the teachings of their religious books with modern scientific truth."[117]

Problems of this sort became particularly acute at the CMS, where Secretary H. E. Fox was undeniably out of sympathy with liberal university Christianity, and visibly so, as a public supporter and later president of the Bible League, with its strident defense of verbal inspiration and biblical literalism. "Bible conservatism," originally confined to the Baptist and undenominational evangelical fringes, was increasingly embraced by Anglican evangelicals of strong Keswick persuasion.[118] From the turn of the century SVMU leaders at Cambridge University had sought to broaden the membership and the conservative theology of the CICCU. Its members responded by spreading rumors that the SVMU had entirely rejected biblical inspiration and the divinity of Christ. In 1910, shortly after a Bible League meeting held in Cambridge and Fox's departure as CMS secretary, the CICCU voted to sever all ties with the student movement, primarily over SVMU sponsorship of advanced biblical critics as speakers. As tensions grew in the student movement, they were mirrored at the CMS. While the Bible League had Fox's support, Eugene Stock was a close and sympathetic adviser to the SVMU secretary.[119] When H. E. Fox was succeeded by the young, dynamic, and progressive Cyril Bardsley, a "broadening" Anglican, it confirmed the liberal drift at the CMS.[120]

Bardsley's appointment was the culmination of a decade-long growing storm. The CMS found itself straddling antagonistic conservative and liberal positions. Evangelical conservatives saw Ritualism and modernism as two sides of a single debased coin, and believed liberals too willing to pass this currency. This split Evangelicals into competitive wings. These controversies threatened the uneasy but extremely fruitful balancing act at the CMS between evangelical enthusiasm and Church organization — the very basis of its unparalleled Victorian success. By 1907 conservative opposition to liberal drift at the CMS expressed itself as a reaction to a large London bureaucracy characterized as too unresponsive to grassroots evangelical interests.[121] On one level this strand of

117. Mott, *Home Ministry*, 19-20.

118. Fox poured significant amounts of his personal fortune into the Bible League; other important CMS officials, such as C. M. Waller, CMS Tutor at its Highbury Training Home, were also members. Bebbington, *Evangelicalism*, 182-88, 217-18, 224.

119. Tatlow, *Student Christian Movement*, 383-86; Wellings, *Evangelicals Embattled*, 280.

120. Bayldon, *Bardsley*, 32.

121. *A Series of Papers concerning the Home Organisation of the Church Missionary Society*, 26 Nov. 1907, CMS Archives, G/CR 1/3 (part).

criticism was a reaction to the immense professional bureaucracy — the "mini-empire" — that the CMS had become by the Edwardian age.[122] On another level the debate over inadequate "democratic" control at the CMS was a reflection of the contest between liberal and conservative forces seeking to capture the CMS and through it to influence the identity of Evangelicalism, England, and its empire. Were these to be defined by the spiritual libertarianism that Evangelicals imagined would allow godly transformation through charismatic Bible preaching? The high public profile of the 1910 Edinburgh World Missionary Conference, with its strong support of ecumenism and the presence of High Churchmen who emphasized reliance on Church organization and organic community, reopened the question of what level of comprehensiveness and cooperation was acceptable in the CMS. The elevating heat of this debate marked Bardsley's secretariat as a troubled one. Early skirmishing did not become public controversy until 1917, largely because of the war, but conservative Evangelicals, failing in their attempts to limit "heresies" surrounding disputes at the CMS over biblical authority, were encouraged by H. E. Fox, and they withdrew in 1922 to form the rival Bible Churchmen's Missionary Society.[123]

Modernism also proved to be an equally divisive issue for the SPG. One of Bishop Montgomery's primary goals was for the SPG to integrate as many "advanced" students as possible and thereby reconstruct the Society as modern, progressive, and imperial. This meant taking an open and even an adventurous approach to missionary problems. The SPG launched *The East and the West*, a new "issues and problems" publication, with the aim of engaging the Society with the concerns that drove the student missionary movement. Instead, it brought the wrath of traditional constituencies against the Society.[124] Two articles — "The Teaching of the Higher Criticism Incompatible with Missionary Work" and "The Higher Criticism Considered as an Aid to Missionary Work" — engaged the most theologically sensitive of subjects. The response was an immediate denunciation of the SPG for promulgating "sceptical theories."[125]

122. CMS figures for the year 1906 illustrate this: 256 committees, 3,600 incoming letters, 975 missionaries and 8,850 "native" spiritual agents, 37 colleges, 92 boarding schools, 12 industrial institutions, 2,400 elementary schools, 40 hospitals, 73 dispensaries, 21 leper homes, 6 homes for the blind, 18 orphanages, and 17 presses and publishing offices. Barnes, *Salisbury Square*, 18, 27, 77-80.

123. For an examination of this controversy, see Wellings, *Evangelicals Embattled*, 281-89.

124. Montgomery's plan was to supersede the CMS *Intelligencer*, recognized as the "first [missionary] magazine in the world." [Montgomery], MS document labeled "S.P.G." [ca. July 1901], Davidson Papers, vol. 151, fols. 309-15.

125. James Monroe, "The Teaching of the Higher Criticism Incompatible with Missionary Work," 1 (Oct. 1903): 413-420, and X. P. , "The Higher Criticism Considered as an Aid to Missionary Work," 1 (Oct. 1903): 426-37. Critics assumed X. P. to be the editor, Charles Robinson. See also J. C. Sharpe, "The 'Higher Criticism' and the S.P.G.," *Church Times*, 18 Nov. 1904, USPG Archives, H 37,

Montgomery was forced to back down, and a public expression of regret by the SPG "settled" the matter.[126] A serious obstacle had arisen to Montgomery's missionary program, as he suggested in a circular letter explaining the SPG position:

> We found ourselves met by two very strong parties: in one sense these parties represented the old and the young — surely a very interesting fact. . . . there are a great many of the older men who have been made very unhappy . . . [and] their letters showed me that their alienation would lead to a large withdrawal of money from the Society unless some means could be discovered to comfort them without in any way compromising our position, which of course is as broad as the Church.[127]

The whole scandal was a testimony to how older issues of party had been transformed by modernism, and how they operated on a plane separate from, but connected to, imperial issues. The youthful imperial enthusiasms of university-based Christians were essential to any Anglican imperial program, yet the concerns of those same Christians to engage "modern" subjects, both theological and imperial, were increasingly at odds with the anxieties felt by the deeply orthodox lay and clerical supporters of the traditional missionary societies. Montgomery, as he commented to the bishop of London, after working to defend the SPG in northern England against "the High Church Stick," now feared "the Broad Church Stick in London," despite all the reforms that had resulted in the SPG's new "warmth & spirituality."[128]

Besides controversies swirling around Ritualist and modernist theological disputes, Montgomery's program also faced the challenge of breaking through the continuing preoccupation of the majority of the clergy and episcopacy with the domestic problems of the Church. From the beginning, many had doubted the realism of Montgomery's plans, none more so than Montgomery's own commissary of thirteen years while he was stationed in Tasmania, F. D. Cremer. Objecting to Montgomery accepting the post of SPG secretary, Cremer argued Montgomery was destined to fail. "Have you weighed up the exact value of my

---

folder 1. The SPG archives contain about forty letters of opposition to the article, and about seventy signed preprinted forms supporting a joint letter of protest sent in March 1903.

126. A special SPG session produced "a most dramatic scene" where the objectors demanded among other things a disavowal of modernism in all forms. They had to be satisfied with a resolution expressing the regret of the Society over the controversy. Despite the trouble, the majority present supported the apologetic Society. Montgomery to Davidson, 3 Nov. 1904, Davidson Papers, vol. 98, fols. 22-25.

127. Circular letter, 15 Dec. 1904, USPG Archives, H 37, folder 1.

128. Montgomery to Arthur Winnington-Ingram, 11 Oct. 1904, USPG Archives, X 382.

friend's high-sounding phrases," he asked Archbishop Temple, "'Archbishop of the World of Missions,' 'Worldwide oversight'? Are they not a trifle inflated? Is the office of Secretary to <u>one</u> of our great Mission Societies anything of the sort?? Ought it to be?"[129] Cremer questioned the visionary nature of Montgomery's ambitions, but he also hinted at a deeper problem: clerics were unlikely to focus so closely on missions when the Church was facing important domestic challenges. This became rapidly evident to Davidson upon his elevation to the See of Canterbury in 1903. English problems demanded immediate attention, including the need to reconcile orthodox conservatives (both High and Low) to theological modernism, to attract qualified clergy and laity alike to the Church, and to engage with newly militant Nonconformity, roused by educational reforms seen as favoring the Church of England.[130]

In the context of these unsettled politics occasioned by the resurgent Nonconformity and Liberal Party that the Church under Davidson faced, Montgomery attempted to strengthen the appeal of the SPG to Anglo-Catholics by linking foreign missionary commitment into more general Anglican concerns with the "social question." Davidson, however, had evidence of the continuing primacy of home mission work among Anglo-Catholics, who continued to denigrate Evangelicals and High Churchmen alike for preoccupation with the foreign field. The simultaneous reflex among the bulk of Evangelicals, particularly those associated with the anti-modernist camp, was just the opposite: to withdraw from calls to social duty, emphasizing instead the primacy of individual spiritual experience, evangelization, and conversion.[131] While over time an eventually dominant "modernist" group of younger Evangelicals emerged — attempting after 1905 to respond to the growing strength of Anglo-Catholicism by rejecting renunciation of the world and attempting to inscribe religion with social relevance — in the Edwardian period emergent fundamentalist and modernist variants of Evangelicalism only made the task of advancing Church unity more difficult. Just as Montgomery launched his imperial program, English Church leaders faced new frictions that led them to resist championing missionary unity, for despite the early expectations of "imperial Anglicans," their program in practice appeared to increase rather than decrease difficulties at home.[132]

---

129. F. D. Cremer to F. Temple, 10 July 1901, F. Temple Papers, vol. 49, fols. 63-66.

130. On Nonconformist politics and the 1902 Education Bill, see Bebbington, *Nonconformist Conscience,* 141-52.

131. The withdrawal from a "social gospel" was particularly notable among those associated with the "Keswick School." Bebbington, *Evangelicalism,* 214.

132. Liberal Evangelicalism still embraced an essentially conservative set of beliefs, and only slowly came to dominate Evangelical higher education by the 1920s. Bebbington, *Evangelicalism,* 199, 203, 221. On its still generally conservative nature, see Wellings, *Evangelicals Embattled,* 256-64.

When the promised waves of new Anglican enthusiasm and unity did not issue from SPG efforts, Davidson's support waned. In the course of commenting on the 1905 Church Congress, John Ellison suggested that a core problem was that the communion was increasingly made up of "[n]othing but parsons and women," with negative implications for JCMA programs.[133] Women, evidently, were not animated by exhortations to imperial gallantry, and the majority of the parish clergy had more immediate concerns to preoccupy their time. Davidson and the bishops could see that a problem existed, and by 1905 they regarded aggressively pro-imperial plans with growing skepticism. When the JCMA requested from Davidson and from the individual bishops another "authoritative" call for foreign missionaries, Davidson resisted. He asked John Ellison to imagine what might happen if he were to comply:

> What would occur if I as Archbishop were to send, say, to the Bishop of Worcester, or Hereford, or Norwich, a definite request for, say 10 or 12 of his best younger men to be sent up within a year for me to dispatch them over the world. . . . [Or] let us say that [a] committee is to make a claim on England now for say 60 men, who must be young and keen and presumably unmarried. . . . Are the Colonial members of this committee to take into account or to disregard English needs and English conditions? Or is England simply to be a region whereon they draw, leaving the home authorities to arrange the details for meeting the demand?[134]

As a pragmatic leader of a Church that was governed largely through consent and good will, Davidson now questioned the grandiose imperial rhetoric of both the JCMA and Montgomery. Ultimately if the young men of England were largely unmoved by such calls, what could the hierarchy of the Church do "unless we are to attempt arrangements corresponding to those of the Papacy"?

Looking backwards, Davidson also had to assess how successful the imperial strategy at the SPG had ever been. A program launched by the JCMA in 1898 to rotate curates through an imperial appointment was a case in point: "I rather gather," Davidson wrote, "that the Council for Service Abroad, which we used to believe was going to do so much, is now regarded by the junior clergy generally as a self-assertive interloping authority which ought to be snubbed or abolished."[135] What Davidson understood was exactly that principle which Evangelicals had asserted throughout the nineteenth century: in a broad Angli-

---

133. Ellison to Davidson, 7 Oct. 1905, Davidson Papers, vol. 106, fols. 235-36.
134. Davidson to Ellison, 17 Oct. 1905, copy, Davidson Papers, vol. 106, fols. 237-39.
135. Davidson to Ellison, 17 Oct. 1905, copy, Davidson Papers, vol. 106, fols. 237-39.

can Communion concerned first and foremost with local affairs, the prosecution of foreign missions had to operate as an act of persuasion rather than an act of compulsion. At the heart of much missionary persuasion was a distinctive, individualist, libertarian evangelistic spirituality that militated against any narrow programmatic imperial vision. Reversing his earlier position, in 1905 John Ellison reported to the JCMA that plans for an "authoritative" Anglican missionary program were "unworkable" and "unEnglish."[136] Yet, as Ellison had noted, the same difficulties were not experienced by women, who rallied not only to missionary activity but also to rapidly growing support for the Mothers' Union. Conceived of by many women as an instrument of reformation of homes and family life throughout the world, service-oriented educational missions and the MU were dedicated, in the words of Mary Sumner, to support imperial expansion not as "a call to national aggrandizement, acquiring riches, worshipping the golden image" but rather as support for "the duty demanded of all British citizens in the Home."[137]

Regardless of either expansive imperial rhetoric or the welling of women's interest, the attention of the home episcopate, which largely controlled the training and assignments of non-Evangelical clergy, was never deeply or consistently engaged with imperial or missionary concerns. This did not change with Montgomery's arrival and prosecution of a self-important program at the SPG. The matters that the English bishops dealt with were overwhelmingly domestic, as the Agenda Sheets of Lambeth Palace bishops' meetings show.[138] The systematic programs of the late 1890s, designed to "kill missionary sentimentalism" and destroy "mere armchair enthusiasm" through study, had not produced appreciably larger levels of missionary commitment. By 1905 the impressive-sounding initiatives of Montgomery and the JCMA had clearly begun to wear thin, and critics within the JCMA itself noted the lack of action. The association, with 5,524 members in 1906, had sent only fifty-six abroad, roughly 1 percent of its members, in the previous year, and at most of its meetings, Edgar Rogers complained that "the only inspiration was tea and a pipe, with clerical gossip afterwards."[139] The young visionary C. F. Andrews, himself increasingly troubled by the racism and missionary complicity with colonial

---

136. Ellison to Davidson, 24 Oct. 1905, Davidson Papers, vol. 106, fol. 242.

137. Quoted in Prevost, *Communion of Women*, 264-65.

138. Between 1897 and 1902, the monthly assembly of English bishops typically considered one item of significance to foreign missions on a docket of fifteen to thirty items. From 1902 onward, however, even this level of attention diminished. Bishops' Meetings, 1897-1907, BM 4, Lambeth Palace Library, London.

139. "The Junior Clergy Missionary Associations: A Plea for Development," *The East and the West* 4 (Oct. 1906): 403.

society that he had experienced in his first years in India, presented it as a problem of complacence: "I cannot adequately describe how distressed and pained I was, when in England on sick leave, at the easy-going and indolent clerical life I met with in many quarters."[140] In many communities a once-yearly missionary sermon was all that country vicars and congregations, reluctant to disrupt local routines, would support, a reality that exhortations to support empire proved unable to shift.

Missionary Imperialism: Race, Nation, and Collapsing Consensus

The problem of how precisely to define the nature of imperial-missionary engagement — in the face of both conflict in British politics and the rise of colonial nationalisms — proved to be the final intractable difficulty that derailed High Church imperial-missionary programs. The nature of the British Empire was becoming a topic for debate and division in the missionary world. The SVMU was again implicated in the disturbance of British imperial practice through criticisms made by some of its prominent leaders. Such criticism divided student leaders from many at the SPG, and is perhaps best exemplified by the evolving ideas of Frank Lenwood, the Congregationalist student leader who keenly pushed the SVMU in the "modernist" direction, became a missionary, and then, in 1912, foreign secretary of the London Missionary Society.[141] From his missionary experience in India Lenwood came to believe that the operation of the British Empire was deeply flawed due to a lack of sympathy with indigenous peoples. Although Lenwood was no anti-imperialist, and was not above criticizing harshly the "Indian character" and Indian culture, he developed an equally harsh assessment of the cold, hierarchical, and bureaucratic operation of the Raj in India. While many missionaries were at fault, their attitudes were only a small part of a larger problem among Indian civil servants and English "sahibs" in general. Unless this attitude was conquered, he and progressive student leaders suggested, in tones presaging the more famous formulations of E. M. Forster in *A Passage to India* fifteen years later, a fundamentally alien and immoral empire would be misgoverned, and inevitably lost on the worst possible terms.[142]

This critique was developed in its fullest form by C. F. Andrews, a JCMA leader who left the Cambridge Mission to Delhi in 1914 and ultimately aban-

---

140. "The Junior Clergy Missionary Associations," *The East and the West* 5 (Apr. 1907): 168-69.

141. Tatlow, *Student Christian Movement*, 202, 220 and passim.

142. Frank Lenwood, circular letter, 26 Feb. 1908, Agra, CWM Archives (LMS), Home: Personal, Box 7, folder 6.

doned all hope for justice for India via the empire. He assessed the missionary movement in India as a failure for several reasons: its association with oppressive imperial rule, its failure to engage sympathetically with Indians, its inability to find worth in Indian culture and religion, and its failure to create indigenous Churches.[143] In this way a younger generation of missionary leaders came to reiterate the classical liberal ideal that a "downtrodden" people could be raised by education, but they insisted the process must be tempered by Christian sympathy fully and truly applied.[144] Thus, liberal student leaders forwarded a criticism of the cold, formal, distant imperial policy of colonial rulers, emphasizing instead the need for "a Christianized world with a juster and nobler order of society."[145] While Lenwood's missionary liberalism retained social Darwinist assumptions about presumed racial hierarchies, racial difference was not his primary emphasis.[146] Instead, he called for a missionary encounter based on sympathetic friendship with indigenous Christians. These ideas were to develop in the interwar decades into the critique of imperial exploitation voiced by progressive Anglican leaders such as J. H. Oldham and Bishop Frank Weston who denounced the forced labor and race laws that were increasingly resorted to by African settler societies, and in the process eroded the presumption of compatibility between Christian and imperial ideals.[147]

However, the criticisms of liberal students seemed dangerously naive to the more committed imperialists at the JCMA and the older stalwarts at the SPG offices. Imperial sympathizers emphasized the "responsibilities" of rule and the "backwards" nature of colonial subjects.[148] Firmness and morality at home were

143. O'Connor, *Gospel, Raj and Swaraj,* 32-33 and passim; Jeffrey Cox, "C. F. Andrews and the Failure of the Modern Missionary Movement," in *Modern Religious Rebels: Presented to John Kent,* ed. Stuart Mews (London: Epworth, 1993), 233-39.

144. For an overview of this liberal ideal and its development see Susan Pedersen and Peter Mandler, "The British Intelligentsia After the Victorians," in *After the Victorians: Private Conscience and Public Duty in Modern Britain; Essays in Memory of John Clive,* ed. Susan Pedersen and Peter Mandler (London: Routledge, 1994), 1-24.

145. Tatlow, *Student Christian Movement,* 250.

146. For more on Lenwood's "Protestant missionary liberalism" see Brian Stanley, "Manliness and Mission: Frank Lenwood and the London Missionary Society," *Journal of the United Reformed Church History Society* 5, no. 8 (May 1996): 465-69.

147. Adrian Hastings, *A History of English Christianity, 1920-2000* (London: Collins, 1986), 60-62, including Oldham's importance as an advisor to Archbishop Davidson.

148. See, for example, the emphases of former JCMA member, later bishop of Auckland, M. R. Neligan, "New Zealand. An Ill-Constructed Quadrilateral," in *Church and Empire: A Series of Essays on the Responsibilities of Empire,* ed. John Ellison and G. H. S. Walpole (London: Longmans, Green, 1907), 180 and passim.

paralleled by the assertion that firmness and Christianity were the backbone of imperial rule and missionary activity.[149] These divisions over how to conceptualize imperial relations were reinforced by political agendas as well. For missionary progressives such as Lenwood, the rejection of unpalatable forms of imperial control was implied by the Liberalism swept into office by the 1906 Election. This Liberalism reacted against "the doctrine of efficiency which Rosebery and other such had been preaching"; rejected "Toryism, by its very essence, always considering the system, the machine, their efficiency"; and embraced a "real Liberalism always . . . thinking first of the well being and above all the free development of the individual."[150] While these styles of "liberal imperialism" were hardly the stuff of anti-imperial radicalism, they did recall the long-established division between libertarian and authoritarian styles of empire. The well-known predilection of mainstream Anglicans for Conservative politics did not mesh well with liberal trends among student missionary leaders.

Evangelicals also harbored a tendency to regard imperial power with suspicion. Those who spurned the social gospel as being inherently socialistic often argued against social agencies associated with colonial rule in favor of direct evangelism, although they often avoided overt criticism of British imperial policy.[151] The more influenced by holiness pietism Evangelicals were, the greater was their tendency to advocate for evangelistic action to be as separate as possible from worldly structures and powers. In parallel, deep distrust of westernization strategies was common among Anglo-Catholic enthusiasts, such as those at the UMCA, who — following the zealous Christian Socialist Frank Weston, UMCA missionary from 1898 and bishop of Zanzibar (1908-1924) — were deeply dismayed by European race consciousness. Anglo-Catholic pietists, who embraced the notion of missionaries adopting African customs and ideals (when not in direct contradiction of Scripture), and who expressed deep suspicions about the usefulness of supposed "civilizing" influences, such as trade and association with settler populations, also consistently expressed doubts about the beneficence of imperial structures.[152]

Yet among High Churchmen, in contrast, the so-called progressive ideals of Anglican imperialists, such as Bishop Montgomery, gained in stature as they envisioned the elaboration of a moral empire that would transform "native"

149. W. T. Gaul, "South Africa. The Anglican Church and Imperialism," in Ellison and Walpole, *Church and Empire*, 239.

150. [Frank Lenwood], "The British Government of India," 22 Mar. 1911, TS, CWM Archives (LMS), Home: Personal, Box 7, folder 10.

151. On the attitude of pronounced hostility of Anglican Evangelicals to socialism, including their primary support of the Anti-Socialist Union of Churches, see Bebbington, *Evangelicalism*, 215.

152. Porter, "UMCA," 86-88.

populations through kind, yet firm application of Western education under the direction of religious professionals. To such thinkers, such as the SPG's Charles Robinson, Eastern Christianity, developing under the invidious influences of colonial nationalism, had the potential (if it ran to heresies old and new) to shatter what slender consensus continued to exist in traditional European understandings of the faith. In this context, imperial theologies of missionary tutelage were imagined also as defending traditional understandings of Anglican theology and identity from alien redefinition.[153] The simple dynamics of "new era" missionary success also led moderate Evangelicals to greater sympathy with imperial institutions. The unprecedented flow of missionaries into the field that the CMS engineered from the 1890s onward had by its very volume impeded the process of cultivating indigenous church leadership and independence, drawing the Society into more frequent contact with the colonial state.[154] These developments placed institutional moderates at increasing odds with the radical wings of the Church. On the high and low extremes of Anglicanism, the tendency remained to emphasize the development of independent Christian internationalism: Anglo-Catholics emphasizing world Anglicanism; Evangelicals, pan-Protestant international alliances. Among moderates, however, the tendency to pursue institutional and ideological alliances with empire prevailed, although these were progressively challenged by the younger generation of missionaries associated with C. F. Andrews, Frank Lenwood, and from 1910, Cyril Bardsley, the new CMS chief secretary.

Missionary progressives from both the high and low ranges within the Church were on a fundamental level reacting to the challenge of the non-Western nationalisms that grew rapidly after the turn of the century, strengthened by the astounding victory of the Japanese over the Russians in 1905, until by 1910 many perceived colonial nationalism as the primary problem in the mission field.[155] The triumphalist tone of British missions of the 1890s rapidly waned in the wake of the Chinese Boxer Rebellion of 1899, with its violent anti-foreign sentiment, the difficult South African War of 1899-1902, and the rapidly increasing colonial nationalisms that generated strong feelings of imperial anxiety in European populations of all kinds. The student movement responded by reinforcing its emphasis on professionalization, continuing to advance the academic study of missions — missiology — and advocating for more sophisticated training of missionaries in the language and culture of receiving societies

153. Greenlee and Johnston, *Good Citizens,* 149.

154. Gordon Hewitt, *The Problems of Success: A History of the Church Missionary Society, 1910-1942,* 2 vols. (London: SCM, 1971), 1:xiv-xv.

155. "The Renaissance of the Non-Christian World," meeting notes, 27 Oct. 1910, CMS Cambridge Association, Letter Book, CMS Archives, Acc 216 O/2/1.

in order to cultivate "sympathy."[156] With a focus on the ecumenical potential existing in transnational evangelistic Christianity and the social conscience of the emergent social gospel, student leaders tended to embrace a "fulfillment" theology, which saw non-Christian religions as vehicles through which dialog with Christianity would fulfill divine purposes in the evolution of faiths.[157] Critical to these changes was the perception that colonial nationalisms presented a new key challenge that had to be faced, so that the "great basis of Indian Nationalism" (and other nationalisms) could be grounded in Christianity and the bonds of sympathy built through education that focused on the ideal of social service.[158]

Meeting the challenge of colonial nationalisms, students argued, required a fresh attitude and perspective. This was an approach that many overt imperialists were unwilling to consider. For a small but vocal and influential group in the new generation, foreign missions had to frankly disavow their connivance with imperial structures and seek to embrace a new open partnership in faith; otherwise, the growing tendency to dismiss missions as a weak, superfluous, and ultimately negative force in national life would continue among the "influential class" of educated "natives" that traditional missionary policy had often targeted. Yet this strategy questioned the authoritarian spirit that had so often defined relations between Western and indigenous Christians in Anglican foreign missions. It represented a strong minority opinion in the movement, growing through the 1890s and demonstrated in 1899 in the answers to questions posed by the CMS Centenary Review Committee: here a significant minority of missionaries judged that the failure of "native" churches to grow lay not with the converts but with the rigidity in the Anglican ecclesiastical structure, and moreover in European bigotry, not least registered in "prejudice against native Bishops on the part of the Dominant Race."[159]

As broader political conditions changed, Church leaders in positions of

156. In 1906 the most important tool in the movement was missionary study (one-third of its members were attracted through organized study bands), and most of the energy of the movement went into advancing this strategy. Tatlow, *Student Christian Movement*, 230, 258-63.

157. Sharpe, *Not to Destroy*, 165-71; Chandra Mallampalli, "British Missions and Indian Nationalism, 1880-1908: Imitation and Autonomy in Calcutta and Madras," in *The Imperial Horizons of British Protestant Missions, 1880-1914*, ed. Andrew Porter (Grand Rapids: Eerdmans, 2003), 177-80; on Anglicans, see Sachs, *Transformation of Anglicanism*, 243-54, 299-300, and O'Connor and others, *Three Centuries*, chap. 11.

158. J. P. Haythornthwaite, in *Report of Commission III: Education in Relation to the Christianization of National Life*, vol. 3 of *[Report of the] World Missionary Conference, 1910* (Edinburgh: Oliphant, Anderson and Ferrier, n.d.), 413; W. H. T. Gairdner, *Echoes from Edinburgh, 1910: An Account and Interpretation of the World Missionary Conference* (London: Revell, 1910), 118-22, 130-33.

159. G. Baskerville, quoted in Williams, *Self-Governing Church*, 205, 256.

power came to realize that more strident forms of jingoistic imperialism, as opposed to vague support for the idea of empire, often proved a dividing rather than a unifying force — at home as well as in the mission field. John Ellison's enthusiasm for joining a rising Tory bandwagon of support for Lord Meath's "Empire Day" received a cautious response from Archbishop Davidson for precisely this reason. The propaganda that developed around Empire Day echoed many themes common in the missionary movement: the empire, Meath argued in tones of Kipling, was far more in danger from internal moral decay — the increase in luxury and selfish personal and class interest, and the domination of the empire by unscrupulous profiteers — than from outside shocks. Despite the apparently reinforcing ideologies, Davidson only reluctantly circularized Cathedral Deans about Empire Day.[160] To Meath's own urging that the Church should heartily support the celebration, Davidson replied that changes in the political situation could turn such Church support into a weapon for its enemies. He agreed, nevertheless, to circularize the foreign bishops to help make a decision, but he commented on the far more staunch imperial sentiment in white settlement colonies than at home: "I suppose there is no question that in a matter of this sort England at home is likely to lag behind England in the Colonies, and that it would be very much harder to stimulate Somerset or Norfolk than it is to stimulate Toronto or Auckland or Capetown."[161] And enquiries overseas revealed that while Empire Day in Montreal, Melbourne, and Rupertsland had rapidly become a popular "Public Holiday," Empire Day in colonies less heavily influenced by English immigration and settlement, such as Jamaica and particularly India, was less popular. Anglican leaders also reported that glorification of empire raised vigorously indignant responses from local populations, which made the celebration positively detrimental to the interests of the Church.[162] Davidson ruled that the Church would not officially support Empire Day. Protecting the neutrality of the Church proved sound policy when, in the wake of the Liberal election landslide in 1906, attempts to pass formal recognition of Empire Day in the House of Commons failed, to loud cheers

---

160. Lord Meath, "Empire Day," printed address, 24 May 1904, Davidson Papers, vol. 115, fols. 187-88. Ellison wrote advocating that the Church "seize the opportunity of growing national sentiment." Ellison to Davidson, 28 May 1905, Davidson Papers, vol. 115, fols. 180-81. Davidson instead emphasized that moderation would be prudent. Davidson to "My Dear Dean of _____," circular letter, 18 Apr. 1905, Davidson Papers, vol. 115, fol. 198.

161. Davidson to Lord Meath (Reginald Brabazon), 8 Dec. and 15 Dec. 1905, Davidson Papers, vol. 115, fols. 207-8.

162. Replies of W. B. Montreal (Bond), S. P. Rupertsland (Matheson), H. L. Melbourne (Clarke), E. Jamaica (Nuttall), R. S. Calcutta (Copleston), and others, Davidson Papers, vol. 115, fols. 217-19, 222-28, 239, 243.

from Irish Nationalists and Labour MPs.[163] While criticism of "Imperial Christianity" from pro-Boer critics of the South African War could be safely ignored
prior to 1906 — J. A. Hobson excoriated "Christianity in Khaki" as the shameless
reflex of "the State Church" supporting "the passions of race-lust, passion and
revenge" — only at their peril could Anglican leaders do so after.[164]

Davidson's reticence over one of those popular imperialist rituals that became so common in the early twentieth century indicates that for a broad and
comprehensive institution such as the Church an empty rhetoric of empire was
far safer than any concrete imperial policy. The unfolding lesson of how Tariff
Reform was rending the Conservative Party lay before him, and the emerging
danger of emotional imperial controversies, such as the growing South African
"Chinese Slavery" scandal, demonstrated how uncertain imperial waters could
be. Davidson, of course, was not unwilling to maintain existing pro-imperial
structures within the Church, and in 1905 he recommended Montgomery as the
Prelate of the Order of St. Michael and St. George, with all the opportunities it
presented to commemorate and popularize the idea of colonial and imperial
service. In his address in St. Paul's Cathedral at the Inaugural Service of the
Order in 1906, Montgomery sounded grandiose tones, asserting that "in many a
land dark faces look gratefully toward [the men of the Empire], mindful of their
unselfish work . . . [who] typify the flood of our race rolling westward mightily,
till it returns to us again from the East, bearing on its bosom the sheaves, we
trust, of no selfish harvest."[165] But fulsome imperial sentiments did little to
confront the growing challenges to the Church as a whole.

In a worldwide Church, the Edwardian era increasingly revealed, open support of empire exacerbated the problems faced by missions. This was true even
in the "white settlement" colonies, where the rhetoric of an imperial Church
raised hackles as independent national identity grew alongside the churches,
Anglican and Nonconformist alike. It was an even more critical problem elsewhere, producing positive hostility in other imperial holdings, particularly
India.[166] Bishop G. A. Lefroy wrote frankly in preparation for the 1908 Pan-
Anglican Congress that educated Indian sentiment found "the very word and
thought of Imperialism . . . in the highest degree obnoxious," adding that widespread fears existed among Anglo-Indian Christian thinkers regarding the fu-

163. J. O. Springhall, "Lord Meath, Youth, and Empire," *Journal of Contemporary History* 5, no.
4 (1970): 105.

164. J. A. Hobson, *The Psychology of Jingoism* (London: Richards, 1901), 41, 56.

165. M[aud]. M[ontgomery]., *Montgomery*, 64-67, 106-9.

166. On colonial nationalism in settlement colonies, see S. C. Donaldson, the archbishop of
Brisbane, "Australia," and Neligan, "New Zealand," in Ellison and Walpole, *Church and Empire*,
152-68 and 169-91.

ture for the Church if ideas associated with "Empire and Imperialism" spread within it. The Indians, Lefroy also commented, "resented bitterly the claim of racial superiority" and "coldness" in English manners.[167] In this respect, the greatest long-term weakness in Montgomery's position was its openly racist basis; while he encouraged "sympathy" toward other races, he also insisted upon each race occupying "the place reserved from the beginning for it" — implying a clearly subordinate position for all outside the "Anglo-Saxon" race.[168] In these ideas Montgomery followed the racial views of his more famous father-in-law, the liberal Dean F. W. Farrar, whose philological interpretation of religion drew on orientalist scholarship and rested on the assumption of complementary race characteristics existing between "Aryans and Semites." Farrar maintained Christian universalist attitudes by asserting the positive contributions of the different races to the past development of civilization, and he envisioned future contributions from the world's other races, a view which Montgomery shared.[169]

Montgomery's understanding of race was often contradictory, ranging from a deeply held conviction that the global variety of racial churches would all contribute to a divine evolution of the Christian faith, to his expression of horror at the prospect of miscegenation, going so far as to propose a "new Table of Prohibited Degrees" in the Prayer-book that would police marriages between "races too far apart."[170] Like Farrar, his vocabulary of race remained a jumbled and confused mixing of imprecise notions based in language group, national characteristics, ethnicity, and religion, as well as biology.[171] Montgomery, as one of the most profoundly race-oriented missionary figures of the age, and surely one of the most influential, expressed a deep racial consciousness that was rooted primarily in a climatological understanding of racial difference. Seeing Anglo-Saxons as having been formed by a common environmental background, Montgomery assumed continuing mutual affinities and abilities in the "Teutonic" peoples. His views, however, represented an overlaying, or melding, of the newer race consciousness arising at mid-century on the older Christian

---

167. G. A. Lefroy, "Our Indian Empire," in Ellison and Walpole, *Church and Empire*, 66-68. For further background on Lefroy's attitude toward British racism and empire, see O'Connor, *Gospel, Raj and Swaraj*, 76-79.

168. Henry H. Montgomery, "Introduction," in *Mankind and the Church*, xii.

169. Kidd, *Forging of Races*, 187-88.

170. Henry H. Montgomery, *Service Abroad: Lectures Delivered in the Divinity School of the University of Cambridge* (London: Longmans, Green, 1910), 9-10.

171. See for example, Montgomery, "The Aliens Question," *The East and the West* 2 (July 1904): 267-77, in the course of which Montgomery uses the term "race" sixty-five times to denote differences (among others) of skin color, geography, nation, temperament, technological advancement, cultural preference, biological resilience, and religious affiliation, as well as to emphasize the unity of "the human race."

and Enlightenment assumptions of a common humanity. In this Montgomery was a product both of his early years and of the subsequent social Darwinian thinking associated with Benjamin Kidd's *Social Evolution* (1898), which emphasized the continuation of biological racial development into intellectual and ethical systems. As Peter Mandler has argued, even in the midst of advancing biological race thinking, however, in Britain the civilizational perspective — which accepted some level of racial differentiation but did not hold that it operated in historic time, emphasizing rather the notion of "social evolution" to construct a ladder of civilizations — stubbornly remained the dominant understanding for national and other forms of human difference.[172] Montgomery reflexively assumed a hierarchical ordering of civilizations, which was tempered by the social evolutionism that he had learned at the hands of Anglican liberals such as Farrar, but also E. W. Benson, B. F. Westcott, and the larger circle of university scholarship and public school culture that he had risen through. He easily deployed geographically defined racial assumptions — thus, equatorial peoples, more spiritual, less rational in nature, could more easily "see God"; northern peoples, more competitive, display a "rough thoughtlessness" that "offends sensibilities" — but he consistently argued for Christian unity, asking "[w]hy should colour and climate separate us in this world morally?"[173]

For Montgomery, somewhat counterintuitively, the language of race allowed an ethical assault upon European arrogance and contemptuousness toward colonized peoples, which he understood deeply alienated them from the missionary message. He was at pains to emphasize that "[w]e cannot say that in God's sight one race is more important than another," following the older logic of Westcott and other liberal Anglicans that millennia of history produced unexpected results in the fates of nations and religions. Thus, in keeping with the assumptions of "gentlemanly" mission forged earlier among Anglo-Catholics (and which he also developed to support his arguments for the expansion of women's missions), he advocated for tolerance, understanding, sympathy, and "manners" when dealing with "gentler and more naturally polite races," who felt such pain at "our rough behavior." At the same time, however, he often expressed considerable uncertainty about the limits of racial potential — wondering, for example, whether some races in Africa "will perpetually live in the nursery." And he fully embraced the assumption of Western cultural and religious superiority, arguing primarily for magnanimity and paternal understand-

---

172. Peter Mandler, *The English National Character: The History of an Idea from Edmund Burke to Tony Blair* (New Haven: Yale University Press, 2006), 59-60, 76-77, 119-22.

173. Montgomery, "Introduction," in *Mankind and the Church*, xv; "The Attitude of the White Man Towards Darker Races," *The East and the West* 1 (Jan. 1903): 22; "The Passing of the Colour Line," *The East and the West* 3 (1905): 150.

ing on the part of the Anglo-Saxon. While ultimately Montgomery remained dismissive of essentializing biological racism, contemptuous of those who "seek merely their own advantage and talk of the survival of the fittest," he nevertheless envisioned a virtually perpetual separation of races maintained under the leadership of various "ruling races." It was upon these rulers — and after 1905 this included the Japanese, who had proven the power of their victorious "character and civilization" in the Russo-Japanese war — that he believed the fate of missions, the Church, and the human race lay.[174] Thus, as in the case of the Anglican feminist Maude Royden, the impact of racial understandings was complicated, and characterized by both exclusivist and universalist potential. Royden, for example, shared with Montgomery a hierarchical understanding of human culture and development, an acute awareness of race, and a vigorous opposition to European arrogance, which discounted the value of each nation to the evolution of a more just global order. Such understandings supported continuing hierarchical race thinking, but also could and were built through the evolution of mission Christianity into new forms of internationalism in the decades following WWI.[175]

Despite his appeal for sympathy between peoples, Montgomery was undoubtedly aware of the problems of resentment that emphasizing clear constructs of racial hierarchy produced in the mission field among non-European peoples. But capitalizing on a language of race allowed Montgomery to pursue one of his chief priorities, the shaping of a strong rationale for Church unity. For Montgomery, in addition to demonstrating the spiritual unity of humanity, foreign missions also illuminated racial hierarchies within Christianity at large. With this emphasis, Montgomery could begin to explain sectarianism in the history of Christianity as a manifestation of racial temperament. While Montgomery imagined the "imperial Church" to be an expression of Christian unity through worldwide Anglicanism, he also imagined this union to be racially divided, with the British "Church of the race" analogous to the Church of England. Anglicanism could embrace many races but, at least for the time being, could be led by only one race. Once the "Church of the race," the Church of England, was educated to the essential reality of its Anglo-Saxon unity, internal divisions could be vanquished, the Church could fully embrace its fated duty to lead, and division within the world Anglican Communion could be diffused by a patronizing tolerance of racial difference on the part of the Church's civilizational leaders.[176] Awareness of racial hierarchy, then, formed the basis of an

---

174. Montgomery, "Attitude of the White Man," 55, 58 and "The Colour Line," 150, 155.

175. Prevost, *Communion of Women*, 214-16.

176. Montgomery, "Introduction," in *Mankind and the Church*, xxvii-xxviii.

understanding that could unify the Church, strengthen the empire, and brace the loyalty of its subjects. These were Montgomery's most cherished goals, and they reflected a very particular missionary imperialism that faced multiplying challenges in the new century.

The open theorizing about the characteristics of different races and the hierarchy of functions that it set for the various Anglican "racial" churches of the world was not unique to Bishop Montgomery, and not unusual at this time.[177] It was, however, much more characteristic of mainstream High Church than of evangelical mission theorists. The CMS's Eugene Stock, for example, used the term "race" far less frequently than Montgomery, and almost always in connection with religious affiliation or the level of civilization, referring thus to the "Jewish race," "Mohommedan races," and "uncivilised tribes or races," and Stock almost never made distinctions based on complexion or appearance. Much like Montgomery, however, Stock did emphasize the civilizational advantages brought by Christianity, claiming that missions had "cultivated industry and frugality . . . restrained anti-social customs . . . introduced Western medicines and medical science . . . promoted cleanliness and sanitation and checked war."[178] While for the most part Evangelicals only inconsistently employed race as a keystone for conceptualizing mission, nevertheless at this time an increasing number did adopt a more specifically racial language and point of view. Thus Eugene Stock and many moderate Evangelicals did believe that Keswick-style faith, and its message that "sin can be overcome," could be integrated with "the Visible Church as an organized body," leading to a flexible "great Federation of national or racial Churches in full communion with each other."[179] Missionary fantasies of this sort came to their peak in the first years of the twentieth century. Rapid changes in the mission field, however, ensured that racialized understandings of the Church, even if appealing to English Anglicans, would suit neither indigenous Christians, whose legitimacy in places such as India was contested by nationalists, nor missionaries in the field who, like G. A. Lefroy, embraced the wisdom of crafting missionary ideologies that would not unnecessarily antagonize the ethnic, racial, or national identities of the proselytized.

177. See for example parallel emphasis on the importance of developing "an Imperial Christian Race" by the president of the Mothers' Union, the Dowager Countess of Chichester, in 1912. Prevost, *Communion of Women*, 263.

178. Eugene Stock, *A Short Handbook of Missions,* 2nd ed. (London: Longmans, Green, 1905), 155; "An Early Anglican Mission to the Eastern Churches," *The East and the West* 3 (July 1905): 283; "Thirty Years' Work in the Non-Christian World: A Brief Survey of Protestant Missions, 1872-1902," *The East and the West* 1 (Oct. 1903): 450, 455.

179. Stock, *Recollections*, 394.

Conclusion

Bishop Montgomery's imperial vision was attractive to many in 1899, but it had grown out of Australian conditions. His primary assumption was that the reflexive support of empire characteristic of Australian Anglicans could be easily extended throughout England and the empire. As the debate over what sort of empire the British should have unfolded in the Edwardian period, Montgomery advanced an ideal of imperial federation in which colonies would be tied with the bonds of Anglican spiritual loyalty and English culture to the mother country. This was an old idea, dating back to the origins of the SPG in the eighteenth century, and as it had failed in the previous century, so it did again.[180] But he miscalculated the appeal of this program because of his misperception, in part as a result of his colonial experience, that "Mighty England" could operate as a powerful metropolitan engine of imperial good if only its people could be educated to their duty. Other returned bishops shared this misperception, and it was reinforced at the SPG, which, supporting comparatively fewer missionaries in tropical Africa and India, worked more than other societies in areas thoroughly dominated by settler populations.[181] The SPG's relative underexposure to non-Western peoples and Montgomery's colonial experience combined to support an imperial vision that concentrated on common cultural, national, and racial identities. Evangelicals, on the other hand, had a greater propensity to think about mission and empire as parallel, but ultimately separate, processes.

In 1908, following the Pan-Anglican Congress, Montgomery retreated from agitating for an "imperial Church." In 1910, following the World Missionary Conference, Montgomery and Davidson pulled back from the pan-denominational missionary cooperation advocated by its Continuation Committee, fearing the independent power to compel policy that was implied in its ambitious programs. Thus the SPG refused to engage in joint educational ventures overseas, despite pleas from the CMS that these would multiply the force of failing missionary finance; and Davidson also refused to lead joint lobbying of government by coalitions of missionary societies (in this case, against French policy in Madagascar).[182] After 1910 the SPG attempted to reclaim the successful Victorian strategies of the past, and the CMS soon followed suit. Disagreement over the relationship that Christian missions should have to imperialism and racialist thinking, particularly the more jingoistic forms, which

180. Strong, *Anglicanism and the British Empire*, 111-17, 218-21.
181. E.g., the vigorous, racialist Anglican expansionism endorsed by the returned bishop of Sydney, Barry, *Ecclesiastical Expansion*, 25-37.
182. Greenlee and Johnston, *Good Citizens*, 153-54.

to many students seemed counter to the ideal of Christian humility, rendered it critically difficult to construct a meaningful, unifying Anglican imperial program. Hopes that Anglican unity would be achieved through the actions of university students, ecumenical cooperation, and imperial progress were thwarted by university heterodoxy, reemerging party factionalism, and discomfiture with contending imperial models. While the core ideologies of the Victorian Anglican missionary movement, rooted heavily in an enthusiastic evangelical impulse and a parallel High Church reaction, continued to have a force and resilience through the Edwardian period (which ultimately meant stability in income and even modest growth), by 1911 the bid to unify foreign missions in the shape of heroic imperial Anglicanism had failed.

Quite simply, in the Edwardian era the problems of empire became more acute. High Churchmen had always tended to demonstrate a more energetic missionary-imperial enthusiasm than Evangelicals, partly because of the closer association of evangelicalism with Nonconformity and Liberalism, partly because the CMS operated far more substantially outside the boundaries of "Greater Britain" than did High Church missions.[183] As explicitly imperial strategies became a key area of missionary theorizing, especially among High Church enthusiasts, missions and missionaries were forced to define their relationship to empire. This development had a strong connection from the 1870s to growing interchange within the Church between the colonies and metropole, as colonial bishops, Churchmen, and missionaries influenced attitudes and policies as imperial communication networks, particularly steamship lines, and imperial associational webs rapidly expanded.[184] But even in an age of rapidly expanding popular imperialism and enhanced imperial communication, imperial enthusiasts within a national church with deep ties to Englishness, Tory sensibilities, and established authority could not parlay imperial interest into successful missionary programs, as a series of largely failed initiatives to encourage "imperial service" among the younger clergy seemed to demonstrate.

In the Edwardian period the SPG emerged as a major force in the missionary world just as that world was entering a period of significant instability and

183. On the spectrum of attitudes from "spiritual free trade" to support for "God's Greater Britain," see Greenlee and Johnston, *Good Citizens*, 6-68. In their analysis of new missionary initiatives in the context of growing imperial anxiety in the 1880s, however, Greenlee and Johnston ignore domestic religious sources of growth, in particular the holiness movements of the era, assuming an eschatological response to a rising tide of imperial sentiment and opportunity as the critical determinant in missionary growth (pp. 42-44).

184. Daniel R. Headrick, *The Tools of Empire: Technology and European Imperialism in the Nineteenth Century* (New York: Oxford University Press, 1981), 130, 166-72.

retrenchment. Edwardian Anglican foreign missions operated in a Church that enjoyed the highest level of unity on missionary issues in the long nineteenth century, but it was also a Church that had achieved that unity largely because the strength of Evangelicalism appeared to be rapidly waning, and fears of Anglican infirmity inspired a fortress mentality. The Evangelical party, in the tradition of moderate "neo-Evangelicals" such as Eugene Stock, was willing to strengthen ties to the Church establishment, although it never totally abandoned the ecumenism traditional in the evangelical connection. The early Edwardian period therefore produced two major Church parties that embraced the imperial idea to achieve independent goals: the High Church party hoped to seize leadership in the Church and quell discord; the Evangelicals hoped to stave off a distressing decline of influence and growing factionalism within their own ranks.

The failure of the Anglican missionary bid can ultimately be traced to problems raised by the student movement, which the mission strategists of the 1890s had seen as the force that would save and remake foreign missions. Through the student movement the denominational societies gained access to coveted university subcultures, but in the process university attitudes forced the societies to engage with theological modernism and critiques of empire. This engagement did nothing to reassure the solid core of missionary support found in communities of older traditional Protestants, while at the same time it did little to legitimate foreign mission in the minds of those government officials, academicians, business leaders, and students who were not already a part of the shrinking subcultures of activist, middle-class Christian piety in England. Cooperation with students and extension into the prestigious university world slowly eroded essential bases of support in the communities of insular sectarianism that gave such devoted attention to the cause, but which demanded uncomplicated, direct action in the mission field.

The change in direction back to Victorian strategies for building active support from sectarian loyalties helps explain a revealing address that Bishop Montgomery gave in June 1915 to the SPG home workers. Reasoning that the Anglo-Saxons were an impatient race from a temperate climate advancing through the lethargic tropics, he argued that, understandably, as they progressed they were constantly diverted by the internecine squabbles of a people ruthlessly critical not only of others but of themselves. This critical British nature expressed itself nowhere more virulently than in the most important project the race was undertaking: the planting of churches in every land. Furthermore, church conflict, he suggested, expressed itself most forcefully among Anglicans, who had to contend with a broad and diverse communion overlaid with the necessity of church order. While Montgomery had not abandoned his racial and imperial paradigms for explaining missions, he had reversed his rhetoric on imperial Church unity, suggesting instead that restless, critical, individualistic chauvinism was the foundation of British strength.[185]

The CMS plotted a similar course as the advanced thinking of university progressives began to cause widening rifts in its Evangelical constituency. The problem was that reforms which included strong imperial linkages, introduced both by Montgomery and by student enthusiasts at the CMS, were not popular. The slowness of change at both the SPG and the CMS discomfited activists. Following the methods of the student movement, both the CMS and the SPG embarked on significant educational programs: summer schools (begun in 1904 at the CMS), a growing set of reading and study group sessions aimed at the young, and innovative new approaches to education, such as "travelling mission-ary study vans" staffed by university students. By drawing on the voluntarism of committed supporters, mostly women, the societies were able to organize a regular series of large, popular missionary exhibitions that served the dual pur-pose of usefully employing thousands of enthusiasts and carrying the message to a wider public.[186] Despite hopes that the launching of educational programs would dispel ignorance, significantly improved levels of interest and giving did not materialize. When the SPG launched a new "Forward Movement" based on the educational methods advocated at the World Missionary Conference in 1910, its income actually decreased. The personal motivation of local organizers was the crucial determinant in society success, and their most constant motiva-tion was religious, expressed as party loyalty or spiritual enthusiasm. Religious motivation was open to influence by imperial ideas, but only when those ideas did not erode spiritual inspiration or party identity. As one commentator on the lackluster performance of the SPG's Forward Movement put it, "the reason for our not getting an increase in our funds . . . [is] we are not a praying society, and compared to the workers in other societies . . . we are not in earnest." Given this reality, the plan to turn the Forward Movement into a "sweeping movement of purely educational nature" missed the mark.[187]

Bishop Montgomery had achieved substantial growth at the SPG by empha-

185. Henry H. Montgomery, *The S.P.G.: Its Principles and Ideals* (London: SPG, 1915), 3-6.

186. Large organized missionary exhibitions existed alongside the activities of "Loan Depart-ments." At the CMS the Loan Department in 1914 provided slides for 2,648 gatherings and loaned out 2,709 "native" costumes. The CMS's 1909 "Exhibition on a colossal scale in London . . . Africa and the East" was attended by nearly 250,000 visitors, and toured throughout England. Stock, *History of the CMS,* 4:503-5. Emulation followed at the SPG, its 1912 Westminster Exhibition at-tracting 26,000. "Monthly Summary: July 1912," Committee for Women's Work Secretary, Monthly Summaries and Reviews, 1910-1918, USPG Archives, CWW 1.

187. "Monthly Summary: October 1912," Committee for Women's Work Secretary, Monthly Summaries and Reviews, 1910-1918, USPG Archives, CWW 1.

sizing efficiency. His program can be seen as a microcosm of the broader model of missionary society centralization and organizational change that most of the societies had gone through in the previous forty years. He came to the most backward society and focused it on spiritual practice and standards of organization comparable to other national societies of the day. But he was unable to secure a new departure in support and funding primarily because he was unable to infuse the SPG with the spiritual energy that had characterized Victorian evangelicalism. Ultimately, Montgomery's missionary bid was an attempt to generalize interest in foreign missions, expressed through the societies, to the corporate Church as a whole. In this it differed little from earlier schemes to form diocesan Mission Boards that would express unified Anglican missionary will. While foreign missions organized and supported through the CMS and SPG continued to grow in this period, the bid to unify these efforts, and to use the enthusiasm they generated to help solve problems in the home church, failed largely because of the resilience of religious identities tied to the essential sectarianism of English popular Protestantism and the historic divisions within Anglicanism. By 1915, in the midst of an unprecedented war, no one could doubt the failure of Montgomery's hopes for worldwide Anglican unity cut from the cloth of a new imperial missionary paradigm.

In a fundamental way Bishop Montgomery's imperial program represented an attempt to draw the experience of holiness-inspired activism and enthusiasm outside the subculture that produced it. Anglican missionary leaders tried to shift from a missionary movement that focused on religious identity to one that focused on the wider role of missions in imperial and national life. However, removing foreign missions from the important place that they had assumed in the debate over Anglican identity, spirituality, and theology, thus disconnecting them from party passions, ran counter to the defining role played by party in the Victorian church. Missionary strategists, focusing on the leadership supplied by university recruits, allowed the concerns of the university — most prominently religious innovation and imperial efficiency — to redefine missionary goals. Yet the event that in 1913 finally saved the financial situation of the CMS, after years of growing deficits, was not a manifestation of programs for Anglican unity, imperialism, or missionary cooperation, but a return to the style and language of Victorian revivalism. For in that year, with the CMS in the midst of crisis, the Society organized a meeting of local Association officers, conducted on the model of a holiness prayer meeting, and appealed to its supporters to provide direction for the Society. The appeal within the revivalist idiom worked. Evangelicals rallied at the 1913 Swanwick conference to promise immediately one thousand gifts of £100 each, clearing the accumulated deficit and placing the CMS on a new financial footing.[188] Only by focusing on the pan-evangelical vision of a charismatic spirituality that transcended church, nation, and empire did the CMS rally supporters to the levels of generosity necessary to put an end to the accumulating crisis.

The claims of the CMS secretaries that Swanwick vindicated the Society's spirituality and that it finally opened the door to the promise of advance in the turbulent "regions beyond" of the twentieth century were never to be tested. Circumstances had altered radically by the end of the First World War, but throughout the war, despite fears of debilitating crisis, CMS income held steady. This last CMS missionary "revival" did not operate on the methods and ideals of progressives; rather, it reclaimed the ethos and methods of Keswick and the 1880s. This was widely understood, and even the *Times* commented that Swanwick was a "Derbyshire township . . . from which a good half of the Anglican missionary enthusiasts at home and abroad lately received a Pentecostal inspiration."[189] The spirit among the three hundred delegates at Swanwick — "the spirit of prayer and absolute dependency on God" — represented not an embrace of the "scientific" ethos of Edinburgh, but rather a nostalgic return to revivalism, spirituality, and the hopes of an older generation.[190]

Similarly the SPG, experiencing scant success with its "Forward Movement," pulled back from the objectives of the student movement in the years following Edinburgh. In Africa, India, China, and Japan conferences and federations on the model of Edinburgh had appeared, prompting Montgomery in 1915 to complain: "I think I foresaw this tendency after Edinburgh. . . . I am to-day among those who are alarmed. I could not go to an Edinburgh Conference to-day."[191] In stating that he believed that "[t]he pendulum has swung of late years towards the extreme left," he did not mean socialist syndicalism but ecumenism (although some religious conservatives saw in them a similarly insidious collectivism). Like the CMS leadership, Montgomery advocated a return to the old loyalties, a reversal of policy solidified by the final controversy between Evangelicals and Anglo-Catholics of the prewar period, the 1913 Kikuyu Controversy in East Africa.

The issue at the center of Kikuyu was ecumenism and the willingness of the Evangelical Anglican bishops of Mombasa (J. W. Peel) and Uganda (J. J. Willis) to foster cooperation and some type of "federation" with the missions of the Church of Scotland, the American Presbyterian Africa Inland Mission,

188. Stock, *History of the CMS,* 4:481-85.
189. Quoted in Stock, *History of the CMS,* 4:409.
190. Bayldon, *Bardsley,* 40-41.
191. Montgomery, *Principles and Ideals,* 12.

and the United Methodist Mission in East Africa. The Anglo-Catholic bishop of Zanzibar, Frank Weston, and the "advanced Churchmen" at the UMCA who supported him, argued that ecumenism would betray the "Catholic inheritance" of the Church. Appealing to Archbishop Davidson to put Peel and Willis on trial for "grievous faults of propagating heresy and of committing schism," the resulting public controversy turned the clock back forty years, replicating the Ceylon controversy of the 1870s, in which the bishop of Colombo refused preaching licenses to CMS missionaries because of their cooperation with Non-conformists.[192] This reemergence of old disputes between High Churchmen and Evangelicals after 1910 forced the SPG to draw back from commitment to cooperation and ecumenism — to reassert its traditional principles and ideals — for fear of losing the support of "eager, fervent, convinced Churchmen." This, in terms of Montgomery's ambitious imperial dreams, constituted an admission of failure. The SPG was now to adjust its policy to accommodate "those who . . . are deeply and fervently true to what they know of Church life here at home, with its old battle fields of controversy."[193] Recoiling from the Protestant ecumenism of the age, Montgomery emphasized the importance of maintaining an identifiable and distinctive religious identity at the SPG, not least because cooperation with evangelicals increasingly appeared incompatible with holding the allegiance of the SPG's Anglo-Catholic constituency. With this last prewar controversy, Montgomery's hope for building Church unity through imperial enthusiasm was finally and irrevocably dashed.[194] More than any other event, the Kikuyu Controversy demonstrated the degree to which the Anglican missionary societies had returned to Victorian passions and strategies and had abandoned hope of the unity of missions through a shared ideology of empire.

It was the Pan-Anglican Congress of 1908 that had fully revealed the weak-

---

192. The Kikuyu Controversy was widely perceived to be the most important debate over Church principles and doctrine in generations, and it generated an extraordinary amount of print. Stock, *History of the CMS*, 4:409-24; Harford and Macdonald, *Moule*, 250-55; Bell, *Davidson*, 1:690-708; Herbert Maynard Smith, *Frank, Bishop of Zanzibar: The Life of Frank Weston* (London: SPCK, 1926), 145-70. In the end Archbishop Davidson convened the Consultative Committee of the Lambeth Conference, which ruled that while a federation of missionary societies had been proposed, it had not been effected, and that because the ecumenical communion service held at Kikuyu was pure in Christian motive it was not to be judged; however, to habitually repeat it would be inconsistent with Anglican principles. This was a compromise and a dodging of the issues that pleased neither side, but in the context of the war was bound to be accepted.

193. *Principles and Ideals*, 3-6.

194. Following Montgomery's retirement in 1919, under the influence of Charles Gore's advocacy of greater accommodation to ecumenism, the SPG under its new secretary, Bishop George L. King (formerly of Madagascar), did once again more fully embrace ecumenical bodies such as the Conference of British Missionary Societies. Stanley, *World Missionary Conference*, 319-20.

nesses of the High Church Edwardian missionary bid, as it demonstrated that foreign missions could not form the focal point of Church renewal. Quite to the contrary, the Pan-Anglican demonstrated that domestic issues of worship and religious observance remained paramount within the Church. The plan to implement a student-driven "imperial Christianity" had not united the Church but had further divided it. Traditional communities of the faithful were distressed by the issues of theology that Church unity raised. Additionally, direct engagement with troubled questions of imperial rule raised fears that missions would be implicated in the worldly doings of traders, secular officials, and the military. The new strategy, in the end, failed on the most important level: it did not significantly increase missionary recruitment or funding. Yet this was not a failure on any quantitative level; rather, it was an imagined crisis caused by checked momentum experienced in the context of the inflated expectations produced by the "new era" mission culture of the 1890s. In absolute monetary terms, the movement far from failed.[195]

Imperial ideas proved to be useful when they were general and amorphous, but an imperial missionary initiative could not bear the weight of a concrete program capable of generating new growth. Just as Victorian Christians could not agree on dogma, they could not agree on what "imperial Christianity" should entail, making the creation of a unifying program built around the imperial ideal extremely problematic. The attempt from the mid-1890s to redefine an essentially evangelical missionary movement along pro-imperial lines for Pan-Anglican purposes instead generated even more sectarian feeling and activity within the Church, returning the movement to its Victorian footings on the eve of the great social and theological changes that would emerge from the experience of the First World War.

---

195. As Eugene Stock pointed out in 1916, in the sixteen years following its Centenary, the CMS averaged an annual income of £390,193, whereas income had averaged only £270,130 in the sixteen years before. Stock, *History of the CMS*, 4:486.

CHAPTER 9

Conclusion

Foreign missionary societies were organized to encourage and gather the philanthropy of the religious in Victorian and Edwardian England. To do so they mirrored the concerns of their constituents. These concerns, however, were characterized by ambivalence and tension. What should be the priority of local, national, imperial, and universal commitments in Christian life? What loyalty should an Anglican feel to sectarian as opposed to Church identity? What should be the relationship of faith to regional, racial, and universalist identities? What license should piety and virtuous religious practice give to women and to indigenous Christians? Just as missionary ideologies were capable of constructing unitary visions of English cultural superiority, sacrificial duty, and national and imperial destiny, so too they created division over the precise nature that English influence in the empire and the world beyond it should take. As eminently sure as most missionaries were that English influence in the world was providentially beneficent, they were often bitterly divided over how beneficence should be achieved in relation to worldly power. Attitudes ranged from slavish deference to colonial and imperial prerogatives, which were often tied strongly to traditionalist and establishmentarian forms of both Evangelicalism and High Churchmanship, to contempt for earthly rule, which was generally associated with forms of holiness-oriented pietism in the zealous wings of Evangelicalism and Anglo-Catholicism. But missionary engagement in a world in which Western hegemonic powers functioned in formal and informal networks of cultural, military, and economic control meant that it was always necessary to engage with imperial realities.

In order to untangle these tensions, Anglican missions must be approached through the language and assumptions of religion and religious institutions because these were the forces that structured understandings of race, gender, nationalism, imperial policy, and Christian universalism within the religious cultures that provided the support for missionary activity. Religious languages associated with the Low, High, Anglo-Catholic, and Broad (liberal or modernist) Church parties and the attitudes that characterized them set the parameters of missionary discussion. This was not only because party issues were a sort of "professional" interest of the clergymen who organized foreign missions and controlled the pulpits from which the proselytizing message was spread, but also because party identity had the capacity to solidify loyalties within the laity and to spur activists and contributors alike by appealing to future visions of a reformed nation, empire, and world. Debate often swirled around which of these realms should receive the greatest commitment of Churchmen, but foreign missions always operated to legitimize the existence and display the vitality of different parties and different denominations; they focused the attention of adherents on heroic religious expansion, not only within the empire but also beyond it, in the context of intense religious competition. The struggle between Anglo-Catholics, Evangelicals, and High Church institutional moderates (led largely by the episcopal bench) to define precisely what the term "Anglican" was going to mean, and what relationships Anglicans should cultivate with state and imperial power, accelerated in the late Victorian period. In this battle Anglican party combatants consistently used the foreign missionary movement as a potent weapon to define Anglicanism in a rapidly expanding and increasingly worldwide Church.

The struggle between those Anglicans who supported interdenominational missions such as the CIM or ZBMM, those who backed the Evangelical CMS or CEZMS, those who endorsed the High Church SPG, and those who sustained Anglo-Catholic efforts, such as the UMCA and Melanesian Mission, was intertwined with a confusing variety of theological, ecclesiastical, regional, social, and temperamental motivations. Religious heterodoxy within British Christianity had a striking impact on the nature of foreign missionary organization and strategy; as groups sought to distinguish themselves, they used foreign missions to shape belief, institutions, and religious practice in both the Anglo-American and the wider world. For mainstream missionary leaders at the CMS and SPG maintaining the enthusiastic support that sectarianism bred conveyed considerable advantages. Simultaneously, however, they needed to discourage the more radical varieties of party that threatened the Anglican Communion with schism. This was a precarious balance. Outlying groups on the Evangelical and High Church sides of the communion — from the interdenominational evangelical supporters of the CIM to the ecclesiastical exclusivists throwing their weight behind the UMCA — generated new energy and vision.

The CMS and the SPG grew in weight and success in the missionary movement by channeling this energy, but of necessity they had to resist radical programs of change in church and society that were destructive of the society system. By becoming bases of support for moderate "neo-Evangelicals" and the Anglican bishops respectively, the CMS and SPG by century's end drove toward greater unity within the communion and greater cooperation with both ecclesiastical and imperial "establishments." At the same time they also softened — at least briefly in the Edwardian period and also over the longer run — traditional Anglican resistance to ecumenical cooperation. Pragmatic accommodation was one result in the broad center of the missionary movement, leading to greater willingness to engage with all sorts of organizational power, from imperial to ecclesiastical, even as imperial officials themselves generally continued to maintain the principle of religious neutrality and as religious purists questioned accommodation with worldly imperial entanglements.

The undeniable significance of the Evangelical revivalist subculture to the growth and success of the CMS in its "new era," as well as the success of Anglo-Catholic modernism in transforming the SPG, are both indicative of the importance of religious determinants and party identity to the relative success of foreign missionary societies in England. While such pietistic or holiness forces were potentially dangerous because of the anti-authoritarian, anti-intellectual, and anti-organizational biases of the most vigorous holiness practitioners (who argued for transcendence over worldly nations and empires), those societies that were able to harness the cycle of religious revivalism and the reinforcing dynamic of religious competition between high and low styles of belief often saw striking success because they were able to link other forces of relevance — gender dynamics, professionalization, imperialism — with a religious energy welcomed by their religious constituencies. These missionary dynamics were only part of the broader continuing power of religious pietism in an age when modernizing, secular ideals of efficiency grew in influence in university and governmental circles, but had far from claimed the English cultural stage. The growing resonance of Anglican foreign missions among certain highly motivated groups is demonstrated in part through one general statistic: between 1870 and 1913 the CMS saw income increase at a rate roughly 60 percent higher than the expansion of consumer expenditure, the SPG roughly 40 percent higher.[1] (See Appendix I, Figure 8.)

---

1. Figures calculated on the five-year averages of income for the CMS and the SPG 1870-74 and 1909-13 compared to consumer expenditure increases. In the same period, calculated by the same method, consumer expenditure increased by 80 percent, adjusted GDP by 83 percent. B. R. Mitchell, *British Historical Statistics* (Cambridge: Cambridge University Press, 1988), 831-85, Table 5.

While the importance of theology and religious party to the development of late-nineteenth-century English foreign missions is indisputable, concurrent social and cultural concerns also strongly influenced the cause of foreign missions. Most notably, feminized forms of expanding Victorian domestic charity and emerging patterns of popular entertainment provided both important models and an environment of acute competition that drove change and innovation in foreign missions. In the late Victorian period, foreign missionary societies redoubled use of the "worldly" methods of commercialized entertainments, despite the resistance to "sensationalism" expressed by older traditionalist supporters. For the CMS, the mixing of revivalist enthusiasm with techniques of popular recreation proved extremely effective, not least because of the way religious activists sanctified such profane activities. Engaging in this new strategy carried the CMS beyond the pattern of the clerically led organization that had been characteristic of the early Victorian period; the use of lay associations that were dominated by women and were more fully independent of the parish-based charity structure came to typify the movement. Missionary societies were leaders in the community of voluntary religious organizations that pioneered competitive religious activity in the Victorian era. Churches had to adopt these methods if they desired to grow in the nineteenth-century marketplace of activities and ideas. As such, churches operated to connect the world of religious belief and idealism to a society that was rapidly urbanizing, growing in wealth, and spawning a flourishing consumer culture that had knowledge and connections, not only in the empire but also beyond it, in growing transnational networks of trade, immigration, ethnic community, cultural affinity, and religious belief. It has been noted that the clerical conservatism of missionary societies tended to produce missionaries who lacked the training to interact effectively with foreign peoples and cultures.[2] However, if the societies failed in producing transculturally trained missionaries, they succeeded in producing English cultural commentators and entrepreneurs who understood and resonated strongly with English concerns and who, in domestic terms, successfully interpreted foreign cultures to a home audience in religious language that was explicable to English contributors. In this, missionary societies produced the largest number and the most popularly dispersed and effective translators of the world to domestic audiences, all rendered in English languages of faith.

The late Victorian strategy at the CMS that drew on the talents and organization of revivalism was very effective, but it had its greatest impact within certain identifiable social circles and geographical areas. Despite efforts to attract the "leisured" and the working classes alike, the movement became a growing

2. Williams, "Recruitment and Training," 116-17.

concern primarily in urban southeast England among the middle classes, as the artisanal and northern working-class networks that had contributed significantly to early Victorian missions declined.[3] This is not to say that missionary religion had little impact on working-class communities, and many Anglican clergy, engaged with the rising temper of popular imperialism, sought to use missions as a ramp to engage the industrial and urban poor, whom Church leaders perceived as their socially most crucial target.[4] The societies maintained high levels of commitment to full national coverage, including persistent and repeated efforts to connect with "the humbler classes," arguing that inducing them to liberality in the cause of the even more degraded heathen was to their spiritual benefit. In poor parishes the CMS maintained a strong commitment to door-to-door penny collections and to working parties designed to attract all classes.[5] At the SPG secretaries kept fees for association membership lower in poor areas to encourage the "humble classes," and they multiplied evening meetings, which appealed to "less educated" audiences.[6] Society directors were acutely aware of class differences in their constituencies, and they often referred to examples of the giving that came from working-class parishes, such as St. James's, Bermondsey, which in 1880 gave £71, almost all in copper pence, half-pence, and farthings, collected mainly through the parish's Bible class and Sunday school.[7] What such evidence suggests is that the formal contact of the working classes with institutionalized religion — whether with the institutions of the parish or the CMS — operated strongly through the Sunday schools, and that women's networks associated with juvenile education and welfare were the primary sites where the working classes encountered the missionary message. That this message revolved around the assertion that Christianity facilitated the growth of civilized values in savage, degenerate societies — the "gentleness, courtesy, and kindness" that operated as core values in working-class religiosity[8]

3. [C. R. Duppuy], "The Work of the Home Secretary," TS, [ca. 1918], p. 13, CMS Archives, G/AS 3/4.

4. On Anglican advances among the working classes in an atmosphere of rising anti-Catholicism, see McLeod, *Religion and the Working Class,* 38. Overall working-class religious loyalties remained relatively high for longer than has been traditionally accepted, particularly when a broader definition of religiosity is employed. Sarah C. Williams, *Religious Belief and Popular Culture in Southwark, c. 1880-1939* (Oxford: Oxford University Press, 1999), 2-8.

5. Letter to editor from *Gleaner* no. 697 and letter to editor from W. H. Griffiths, St. Paul's, Portman Square, *Home Gazette of the CMS* 2 (Feb. 1905): 16.

6. "Monthly Survey. February 1911" and "Monthly Review. April 1913," Committee for Women's Work Secretary, Monthly Summaries and Reviews, 1910-1918, USPG Archives, CWW 1.

7. "Three Hundred Pounds of weight in copper for the C.M.S.," *Church Missionary Gleaner* 8 (Feb. 1881): 24.

8. Williams, *Religious Belief,* 129-31, 154-56.

— meant that a natural resonance did exist between missionary religion and the outlook of many in the working classes. There were, in fact, significant numbers of parishes like St. James's, Bermondsey. Where activist clergy supported missions; where door-to-door collections were instituted; where missions were introduced as topics of interest in mothers' meetings, working parties, and parish sermons; and where, above all, Sunday schools were formed (special targeting of Sunday schools, which Anglicans implemented to a degree far surpassing other denominations, was particularly important) local organizational efforts elicited widespread interest across the social classes.[9] The degree of Anglican missionary support among the working classes was potentially large, as suggested by the nearly universal presence of missionary materials in prepared Sunday school curricula by century's end, but it remains largely unquantifiable. However, invigorated work of new cadres of largely middle-class female missionary volunteers ensured that the missionary message was constantly before English men and women across the social classes.

In theory the support of foreign missions was as wide as religious observance. The ideal was, as the SPG Women's Work committee put it, "to draw all closer in the work, rich, poor, trades people, women, men, children of all classes."[10] The practical strategy of missionary societies, however, was to concentrate on consolidating and expanding middle-class support because, in effect, the Anglican missionary movement was a middle-class affair, fully in leadership and ideology, substantially in support. Since the expansion of late Victorian Churches appears to have been based primarily on endogenous growth — that is, on recruitment from internal constituencies already affiliated in one way or another with a denominational tradition[11] — Anglican missionary societies naturally focused their greatest attention and found their greatest rewards among an internal, pious, middle-class constituency. As urban and suburban middle-class missionary supporters became progressively more important to the movement, the cultural constructions of Evangelicalism and Anglo-Catholicism operated as competing definitions of respectability. And the competition worked itself out in important ways on an imperial tableau: Evangelical concentration on spirited cultural criticism centering around morals and manners resulted in prescriptive denunciations of sinful behavior; Anglo-Catholic reliance on education and culturally sensitive discrimination in the diagnosis of social evils

9. On the widespread dominance of Anglican Sunday schools, see K. D. M. Snell and Paul S. Ell, *Rival Jerusalems: The Geography of Victorian Religion* (Cambridge: Cambridge University Press, 2000), 297-310.

10. Report of Mrs. Sunderland, 2 Nov. 1909, in Minutes of the Birmingham Women's Diocesan SPG Committee, USPG Archives, X 281.

11. Gilbert, *Religion and Society*, 198.

Domestic support for missionary activity was worked up in a variety of ways —
as at this children's missionary meeting — and on a variety of levels, appealing to
specific religious cultural and confessional identities and to national and imperial pride.
Overwhelmingly, local organization revolved around communities of children and
women, and increasingly employed methods drawn from popular entertainment.
Church Missionary Juvenile Instructor 12, no. 2 (1876): 124.

resulted in activist programs for social transformation. The division was not, of
course, always this clear cut, but the tendencies were recognized by contemporaries and reflected larger political dispositions. Within the movement, activism
was largely generated by visionaries. These were most often concerned with a
strongly gendered vision of international service, if women, and issues of party
conflict or theological innovation, if men. The agendas of women, students, aggressive imperialists, and interdenominational internationalists were primarily
developed and spread by these coteries of activists.

The transformation of the missionary movement in the late Victorian era
was strongly linked to religious changes that allowed women, for so long silent
and invisible supporters of missionary activity, to forge an open public role in

foreign missions and, in this role, to catalyze the late Victorian "new era" of missions. The clerical bias of society secretaries consistently masked the enormous contribution of women to the cause — not only at home, but also in the critical contribution of missionary wives as key field workers from the start, particularly in girls' education. However, from the 1870s, revivalistic religion publicized contributions that women had always made while legitimizing new departures in women's activity, at home and abroad, introducing large numbers of professionalized, unmarried female missionaries. On the one hand this was part of a broader trend to incorporate more of the laity into religious organization; on the other it was a reflection of the rapidly changing social role for women in England that was being pioneered by nurses, female educators, social purity activists, and missionary women. Linked to the growth of women's activity in missions was a growing fascination with the plight of foreign women — explicitly portrayed as victims of misappropriated male power that either suffocated them in domestic seclusion or terrorized them in the public market — that was catalyzed by the great imperial disaster of 1857, the rebellion in India. With the growth of women's missionary work, the importance of women — especially the unmarried — to field work increased, leading to clerical interest in women's missions, with the almost invariable result that these women's missions were absorbed into the authority structures of the societies. The narrativization of religious piety as feminine and irreligion as masculine that Callum Brown has outlined at the center of nineteenth-century British religious discourse was broadly extended by imperial experience into a narrative of worldwide dimensions by the end of the century.[12]

The process by which society secretaries and female organizers negotiated the place of women in the discourses and bureaucracies produced by the societies shows that, generally speaking, the men and women involved in foreign missions had identifiably different concerns. Anglican society secretaries and clerics were anxious to prevent women from undermining the authority of the clergy and church hierarchy, while women were concerned with creating structures that would cater to what they saw as the characteristically female needs of indigenous and colonial families and women. For some, these needs transcended traditional denominational boundaries, for others they seemed to require the particular denominational administration of sympathetic women, but the majority of English Anglicans pursued the ideal of women and men working cooperatively within the Church to advance both missions to women and missionary work more broadly. Among evangelical Anglicans the work

---

12. Brown, *Christian Britain,* chaps. 4 and 5. On the imperial dimensions structuring the nineteenth-century "woman question," see Midgley, *Feminism and Empire,* 13-40.

of women's missions thus fragmented along denominational and gender lines into three streams. Some women supported interdenominational cooperation in independent female-directed societies such as the Zenana Bible and Medical Mission; some supported independent activity by Anglican women, as in the Church of England Zenana Missionary Society; but most supported the work through the established channels of the clerically dominated CMS. These three streams taken together made a considerable current of missionary activity and led to the greater use of women in other societies, most notably the more socially conservative SPG, which increased the number of unmarried female agents and provided block grants that supported missionary sisterhoods, which were the primary female agency advocated in Anglo-Catholic missions such as the UMCA. While the influx of professionalized single women briefly highlighted the reality that missionary wives had been and continued to be critically important to foreign missions, the spread of professionalizing female agency ultimately served to re-subordinate missionary wives once again as underqualified agents.

English women's missionary activity, it should be noted, differed significantly from the pattern in North America, where women's work rapidly came to be directed by women's societies run by women and largely independent from the denominational societies. Greater clerical power and denominational cohesion set the context in which women's missions developed in Victorian England; enthusiasts who sought to expand the role of women in missionary work had to strive continually to counter the territorial concerns of the clergy. Nevertheless, despite the sense of crisis that grew in Victorian religion after 1890 as clerics, counting communicants and poring over other church-based statistics, grew anxious over apparent decline, the missionary movement continued to grow vigorously in England by linking its fortunes to the expansion of the subculture of holiness-based pietism — in both High Church and Evangelical circles — and to the growing opportunities for lay-based popular religiosity and the women's activism it encouraged. Despite the ideal of cooperation between male and female, however, women's missions particularly, and all Anglican missions overall, still relied heavily on the grassroots organization and activism provided by the largely independent "women's parallel church" of parochial feminine networking, which underpinned so much of Anglican life beyond ecclesiastical structures. Only after women's missions had flourished for two decades, from the 1880s, did the restrictions placed on women by the CMS begin to rankle enough to bring some Evangelical progressives to question the assumptions on which the movement had grown. But this only occurred after High Church women at the SPG negotiated considerable autonomy for themselves. The formula forged for evangelical women's missions in the aftermath of the 1860s began to weaken only after the turn of the century, as the women's parallel church was slowly infused with the greater expectations of new generations of educated young women, themselves facing the emergence of a wider set of problems raised by theological and cultural modernism and emergent colonial nationalisms. In this context many women were disposed to question presumed linkages between imperialism and evangelism. By the 1920s this had resulted in the development among Anglican mission women of an internationalist, pan-racial vision of cross-cultural "feminine redemption" that universally bound women together in a religious culture — most fully developed through the spread of the Mothers' Union — largely separate from the clerically controlled mission and ecclesiastical structures of the past.[13]

Despite a continuing evangelical emphasis on direct, unaffected preaching of Scripture, by century's end High Church missionary emphases on educational attainment, cultural sophistication, and social service — the model of the university-educated "gentlemanly" missionary — affected the entire missionary movement. Yet by the 1880s, radical holiness "higher life" evangelicalism, with its simple theology and emotional impulsiveness, had also created a powerful cultural and social response that was particularly encouraging to women and young university enthusiasts. University professionalism, working hand in glove with a type of religious institutional progressivism that suggested that buildings, schoolrooms, and educated elites could preserve and advance religious and national communities, whether at home or abroad, combined with holiness-driven evangelicalism to transform the late-century movement. Institutional emphases emerged out of the natural patterns of social engagement characteristic of clerical professionalism. They were also reinforced by the growing weight of women, formally barred from preaching, who tended to emphasize a social ministry. Also, professionalism and social service as missionary foci found substantiation in the ideas generated by a new "mission science" that served as the vehicle for a modern technocratic missionary urge. It was within this context that late Victorian programs for imperial engagement and changing missionary understandings of race and culture were worked out, as was the rhetoric of imperial trusteeship that came to dominate Anglican progressivism in the interwar period. This context, however, was largely the product of the new pietistic religious seriousness that grew after mid-century.

The critical problems of negotiating modernism at home and nationalism abroad confronted the British missionary movement after 1900, and the growth of student involvement in foreign missions only amplified their intensity. This was because student missionary involvement, while deeply rooted in the

13. Prevost, *Communion of Women*, 282-88.

evangelical holiness pietism of the Keswick Convention, progressively sought to broaden its theological basis in the 1890s and draw in High Churchmen. Through the enthusiastic style of American revivalism and the urban "missionary revivals" that holiness pietism spawned, missionary societies gained access to, and further cultivated, the evangelical undergraduate subculture of the universities, particularly in Cambridge. But the societies also found that competing pietisms brought continuing friction and controversy; they also brought radical forms of charismatic behavior that had to be controlled because they targeted for criticism respectable constituencies and established bureaucracies. Both the missionary societies and an emerging leadership in the student missionary movement, with its ambitions to extend its influence to a wider class of students, had an interest in expanding student activity beyond the restrictive bounds of radical pietistic subcultures, but in doing so they faced opposition both from the combative fringe of those subcultures and from traditionalists suspicious of "modern" ideas and methods.

Led by the SVMU, the student movement worked to transcend the bounds of evangelical holiness culture in order to embrace and unify a broader range of university Christians. To do so, it emphasized ecumenism and "mission science" — an attitude of open and critical study of missionary strategy — that succeeded in attracting the participation of previously exclusive High Churchmen, but at the expense of alienating "Bible Christians," who had founded and sustained the early movement but now moved rapidly toward a protofundamentalist position. The imaginative core of the Victorian missionary movement relied on a pair of evangelical attitudes: a fundamental spiritual chauvinism and an essential faith in the transforming power of the cross to achieve exotic conversions unassisted by worldly methods. Early in the century this imaginative core had been ever more frequently supplemented by institution building: schools, dispensaries, hospitals. And as women's influence reinforced social service strategies, the SVMU aimed to educate against the cultural ignorance that accompanied earlier forms of spiritual chauvinism. This had the effect, however, of weakening the intensity of feeling generated by the personal spirituality of pietistic evangelicalism. Resistance to this process expressed itself in a protofundamentalist reaction against both the progressive rationalization of missions and the emerging liberal evangelical position articulated by student leaders such as Frank Lenwood and Cyril Bardsley. The simple, faith-based enthusiasms of the 1880s had been discredited among many students both by their failure to achieve large-scale conversions among educated and socially privileged classes and by ongoing High Church criticisms of their cultural naiveté. After the turn of the century, then, the ingenuous belief that the Christian message leveled all cultures was more and more problematic in the context of missionary study emphasizing the complexity of the societies of Africa and the East.[14] Furthermore, the professionalism of student leaders diluted the ability of missionary propagandists to create compelling, simple, salable narratives of foreign exoticism. In the changing professionalized marketplace of ideas, the worth of a spiritual, emotional, anti-intellectual movement was decreasing. To a certain degree fashions had simply changed. The radicalism of Keswick was a powerful draw for the emotional evangelical youth of the 1880s, but by the turn of the century, "Keswickism" was no longer radical. As social reform movements caught the imagination of young High and Low Anglicans alike, the radical mystique of Keswick rapidly came to appear as a reactionary movement of an older generation.

Although the student movement created rifts in evangelicalism, it also appeared to offer a new opportunity for Anglican unity. The attraction of High Church students and younger clergy to the enthusiastic methods of the SVMU, often at the instigation of missionary-minded bishops, drew the SPG and Anglo-Catholic efforts into the mainstream of foreign missions in the 1890s. However, with the exception of small enclaves of fervent Anglo-Catholic support, mainly in the Home Counties, High Churchmen discovered that they lacked the spiritual temperament and conviction to generate fervent missionary support, and so they turned increasingly to the imperial idea to create zeal. Evangelicals at the CMS more weakly echoed the High Church emphasis on empire, but this new emphasis nevertheless served to draw the foreign missionary societies of the Anglican Church into the closest cooperation they had ever achieved. The CMS, which had been close in sympathy and temperament to Nonconformity in the 1870s, had more thoroughly embraced its Anglican identity by 1905 through energetic participation in Church conferences and congresses, closer cooperation with High Churchmen, and a new emphasis on the uniquely Anglican elements of CMS missions. Such "neo-Evangelicalism" appealed to many student leaders, who believed they were making the kind of adjustments and accommodations with the modern world that were necessary to prevent the missionary movement from falling into disrepute among the undergraduate population, upon which leadership in the movement had come to depend. At the same time, however, they became the carriers of ideas and attitudes that were to rend the evangelical world in the twentieth century, as con-

14. Mass conversions among single marginal castes in India were regarded with real ambivalence by many Anglicans due to doubts about the purity of spiritual motives in so-called "rice Christians." Stock, *History of the CMS*, 3:173-74. See also John C. B. Webster, "Dalits and Christianity in Colonial Punjab: Cultural Interactions," in *Christians, Cultural Interactions, and India's Religious Traditions*, ed. Judith M. Brown, Robert Eric Frykenberg, and Alaine M. Low (Grand Rapids: Eerdmans, 2004), 100, 104.

servative protofundamentalists and liberal evangelicals positioned themselves for the coming struggle. Anglican liberal evangelicals no longer perceived that the greatest threat to missions and to society was the "romanizing" tendency within the Church of England. Evangelical conservatives, however, still leaned toward conflating all the evils of "worldliness, unbelief, and romanism" into a single Satanic movement that had to be opposed at all costs.[15]

The student missionary movement among Anglicans generated an unprecedented drive for unity in the foreign missions of the Church of England. The new secretary of the SPG from 1902, Henry Montgomery, took up this drive and attempted to create an "imperial Christianity" that would unite and invigorate the entire communion. Early in the Edwardian period, both the CMS and the SPG seemed willing to adopt a new student-driven missionary imperialism, but very rapidly problems emerged with implementing a policy that would amount to a radical change from Victorian practice. The two foundational elements of the program — sympathy to students and younger clergy and an aggressive rhetoric of empire — both produced resistance from important traditional constituencies. Both elements alienated the societies from traditionalist Anglicans, whose first reflex was to deny the relevance of modernist challenges (so important to progressive students) and whose second reflex was to act as if missions were not implicated in the worldly concerns of imperial governance and control (which denied the relevance of "imperial Christianity"). The authoritarian impulse in an imperially oriented High Church progressivism found its greatest challenges in facing those who cherished the notion that human liberation lay in a free commerce in ideas, devotion to simple, revealed biblical truths, the opportunity for individual conversion, and the fellowship of shared faith.

The problem of Anglican modernism was so acute because it seemed to many to undermine not only older orthodox forms of piety, but also the holiness pietism from which the late-nineteenth-century movement derived its energy. The fringes of the Anglican spectrum — theologically and doctrinally exclusive forms of Evangelicalism and High Churchmanship — reasserted themselves in the context of Edwardian political upheaval over issues of colonial and social policy and the enfranchisement of women. Modernism rapidly became the issue around which criticisms of other aspects of the potentially unified Anglican missionary project grew, reinforced by older but still potent issues tied to the contest between "Protestant truth" and "papist heresy." This old division set the terms for Edwardian debates over mission strategy and formed the theological language for arguments over race, nationalism, imperial policy, and women's

---

15. Stock, *Recollections*, 181.

agency in missions, as they were subsumed within the larger set of disputes that took on the generic label of "modernism."

Theological language was hardly immune from racism, sexism, or cultural bias — quite to the contrary — but that language gave a particular color and emphasis to the consideration of such topics. Few missionary administrators used blatantly racist language. As the "race problem" became the subject of extensive discussion in missionary journals after 1905, the older traditionalists tended to emphasize the subordinate role of "daughter" churches and the authority of Church hierarchies defined in Western terms; younger progressives opposed this with an emphasis on sympathy, understanding, and the need for cultural synthesis. Both positions were obviously informed by race, but often in covert ways. LMS Secretary Frank Lenwood suggested the difference in attitudes of older, middle-aged, and younger missionaries to race when he commented, "[a]n observant Indian said that the old missionaries were fathers, the intermediate men were masters, and the men of the last ten years were brothers, and there was something in it."[16] Similarly, conservatives and liberals split over the role to be accorded women in the missionary movement, but they cast their arguments in biblical terms. Bishop Montgomery never expressed apprehension that his "progressive" editor Charles Robinson would cause a furor by raising issues related to race, gender, or imperialism in the SPG's "serious" periodical The East and the West; rather, issues of theology and denomination were the root of anxiety and identity, exemplified when Montgomery reined in a proposal to include articles in the SPG magazines that were written by Nonconformists and Roman Catholics.[17]

A general, centrist consensus over matters of race, gender, and empire existed within the mainstream missionary community. Thus, the editor of SPG publications was as unlikely to suggest that races had irredeemably fixed characteristics as he was that racial equality was an ethical necessity. An Anglo-Catholic bishop supporting the UMCA was as unlikely to assert that women were utterly unsuited for public life as that gender equality in the working and political world was a pure matter of justice. A CMS Foreign Group Secretary was as unlikely to argue that the British Empire was an unmitigated evil as that it was perfectly progressive and just. For the most part, missionaries persistently focused on issues of civilizational development and conditions of imperial rule,

16. Frank Lenwood, circular letter, 31 May 1914, CWM Archives (LMS), Home: Personal, Box 7, folder 10.

17. Nonconformists would cause enough problems, but Montgomery emphasized that it should particularly be remembered that "Rome hates us with a burning hatred; and they have no chivalry and their morals are not ours." Montgomery to Randall Davidson, 11 Mar. 1903, Davidson Papers, vol. 87, fols. 231-32.

inscribing in the institutional Church a more democratic and libertarian set of urges than found elsewhere in Anglicanism. On these matters — in their emphases on eradicating the Western liquor, opium, weapons, and forced labor trades — they often differed with imperial authorities, offering a critique of immoral empire while at the same time legitimizing imperial solutions as critical to the well-being of the nation and the churches. While the majority of missionaries rejected the scientific racism of many Victorian anthropologists, and thus theories of the genetic inferiority of non-Europeans, they still generally assumed indigenous cultures to be evil and inferior, and they often acted to eliminate indigenous "superstition" in order to allow the "child races" to attain civilization.[18] Among Evangelicals and High Churchmen, however, there was a surprising diversity of opinion regarding the importance of race, female capability, and the character of empire. In contrast, in the minds of conservatives, latitude of thought was unacceptable regarding the absolute evil of theological modernism (which of course informed the other subjects). Modernism was the conceptual and rhetorical center around which English Christians joined battle over other cultural and ideological issues.

Anglican unity and broader attempts at denominational cooperation failed in the Edwardian era largely because the project was tainted by a modernism that divided conservatives from liberals, and that divided those set upon defending established definitions of fundamental difference in matters of race, gender, and respectability from those endorsing greater openness and critical inquiry. While younger clergy, for example, emphasized the necessity of coming to terms with fraught issues of racial prejudice, many older and more traditionalist supporters balked. Thus when at the World Missionary Conference the young Indian priest V. S. Azariah, for fifteen years an organizer for the YMCA and influenced by its pan-racial aspirations, caused a minor sensation by appealing for true friendship in the missionary endeavor to the mostly British and American delegates, the response was largely one of avoidance. "Too often you offer us thrones in heaven," he acerbically observed, "but will not offer us chairs in your dining rooms."[19] Directly addressing the "problem of race relationships," he dryly commented on "a certain aloofness . . . a great lack of frank intercourse and friendliness" between European and Indian Christians, tracing much of the trouble to the fact that when "the missionary is the paymaster, the worker

---

18. On the absence — tied in part to the persistent influence of David Livingstone's writings — of hard social Darwinian ideas within missionary discourse, see John M. Mackenzie, "Missionaries, Science, and the Environment in Nineteenth-Century Africa," in *The Imperial Horizons of British Protestant Missions, 1880-1914,* ed. Andrew Porter (Grand Rapids: Eerdmans, 2003), 124-25.

19. Comment by H. F. Houlder, quoted in Stanley, *World Missionary Conference,* 124. On Azariah and the YMCA influence, see Harper, *Azariah,* 37-66.

his servant . . . we must admit that no sense of self-respect and individuality can grow in the Indian Church." The crowd he addressed was embarrassed, exhibiting some sporadic clapping, some grumbling dissent, and much shocked silence. The response of the missionary press, when the speech was noticed at all, ranged from condescending and self-justifying to bewildered and condemnatory.[20] Azariah was appointed the first Indian Anglican bishop two years later, precipitating conflict at the SPG, where the India Sub-Committee voted to oppose the plan, evidently supporting the objections of many older CMS missionaries that an inexperienced Indian was incapable of administering a diocese. Although objections were overruled by the bishops, including Montgomery as head of the SPG, centrifugal forces in the Anglican religious world seemed to be stronger than visionaries and progressives had counted on.[21] In fact, it was evident to many observers that Anglican missionary unity began crumbling as early as the aftermath of the 1908 Pan-Anglican Congress; this became clear in the months and years following the 1910 World Missionary Conference in Edinburgh.

Similarly, the imperial bid within the Edwardian Church proved to be more divisive than unifying. Recently, historians of empire have provided us with an enormous wealth of evidence on the wide diffusion and permeation of imperial ideas and symbolism in late Victorian and Edwardian society.[22] That many Churchmen hoped to forge stronger links between missionary enterprise and imperial activity is evident from the articles and books that flowed from the pens of Anglicans after the turn of the century.[23] Glowing ideas about the potential of empire to unite and glorify the nation flowed freely in this "imperial culture." But as the experience of the Anglican parties and missionary societies shows, the rhetoric was hollow unless it could be enacted in some positive program. The problem for missionary societies was to avoid giving offense to important constituencies, and what they discovered was that when imperial ideas were required to bear the weight of a concrete program — such as sending clerics abroad for colonial service — they often crumbled, not because of disputes over whether imperialism itself was a valid project, but over what precisely imperial engagement was supposed to be and do, and what its

---

20. Stanley, *World Missionary Conference*, 122-28.

21. Harper, *Azariah*, 130-32.

22. John Mackenzie's *Propaganda and Empire: The Manipulation of British Public Opinion, 1880-1960* (Manchester: Manchester University Press, 1984) set this research agenda, taken up in many following volumes in the *Manchester Studies in Imperialism* series.

23. See most prominently, for example, Wynne, *The Church in Greater Britain* (1901); Montgomery, *Foreign Missions* (1902); Ellison and Walpole, *Church and Empire* (1907), and the flurry of articles on empire as a subject at this time in the missionary magazines of the CMS and SPG.

relationship to the more expansive goal of Christian growth in the wider world was to be. The question of what it meant to be a Protestant Church and a nation with imperial and international responsibilities was amenable to no easy definition. Just as questions of imperial preference and Tariff Reform rent both the Liberal and Conservative parties in succession, the parallel divisions within the missionary movement had a widespread, but often local, impact on the larger national conversation about empire.

The pervasive imperialism in late Victorian culture surrounded and suffused the missionary societies, and quite clearly, despite the fervent desire of some visionaries, they could not escape being implicated in the imperial project. But imperialism had clear limitations as a primary means of motivating action and securing unity in the religious world.

Ultimately, the idea of empire itself proved dangerously amorphous, and, in a movement already racked by debates between liberals and conservatives, it seemed unwise to encourage yet another realm of dissension. Several influential Anglican leaders supported the missionary-imperial ambitions of Bishop Montgomery, intending to use his imperial program to reclaim political and social influence in England. His most important supporters, such as Archbishop Davidson, abandoned the initiative, however, when it became obvious that concrete imperial designs were dividing the Church without achieving any notable successes. Putting these ideas into practice in the Edwardian Church proved so difficult because the Victorian missionary movement in England as a whole had seldom closely or consistently allied itself programmatically with the imperial project as such, but rather had limited itself to educational and medical initiatives. These were designed primarily to advance evangelism as a distinct goal, certainly within and taking advantage of imperial systems, but also extending beyond them. This, at least, was how missionaries tended both to see and to depict these activities, and after the turn of the century they also understood that the heyday of imperial cooperation — perhaps most notably in the CMS's self-celebrated 1890s campaign for a Ugandan protectorate — had passed. Patriotic and imperialist enthusiasts, who were also often institutional moderates, remained vocal; however, diversity tended to rebel against a narrow imperial project. The debates and conflicts over imperial ideals that characterized Anglican discussions in the Edwardian period suggest that missionaries were more than simply purveyors of a homogeneous program of cultural imperialism.[24] Domestic religious culture was the primary and most important context for the

---

24. This position is strongly suggested in Greenlee and Johnston, *Good Citizens,* 6-68, although they divide missionaries according to attitudes toward imperial cooperation, with little attention to denominational or religious identities.

construction of missionary endeavors, and it determined the levels of support upon which their very existence depended.

Missionary ideologies were generated out of a complex interaction of influences — domestic religious culture, shifting gender relations, imperial anxieties, and encounter with foreign cultures — that intertwined reflexively in a feedback relationship of domestic and imperial factors and imperatives. When the World Missionary Conference convened in 1910 in Edinburgh, its temper was largely the result of student attempts to channel ideas about holiness and spirituality into an efficient and unified missionary program that could more effectively confront the challenges that increasingly independent indigenous churches and an internationalizing Christianity seemed to pose. As one delegate present put it, "The Conference was a modern Pentecost. Modern in its scientific preparation, and the business-like way in which it was carried through: Pentecostal in the manifest power of the divine spirit urging and quickening all who were present."[25] The theme of linking efficiency with spiritual power dominated Edinburgh. But the very premise on which the conference was organized — that scientific rationalism and spiritual emotionalism were mutually reinforcing — was antagonistic in England to the cohesion of the coteries of activists upon which the movement relied. Participants at Edinburgh understood that the activist support once enjoyed by the movement was waning, and they lamented that without it there was little hope that missionaries could take advantage of the overseas opportunities the twentieth century presented.

The Edinburgh conference has traditionally been understood as representing the high-water mark of Western missions and as crucially catalyzing the ecumenism that characterized world Christianity through the 1950s,[26] but the evident stagnation in England of missionary finances and recruits after 1906 meant that it also reflected a deep and persistent sense of anxiety over the future of the movement. Although the conference reports voluminously detailed the means of efficient home organization, ultimately most commentators urged a return to the power of the spirit: to Bible institutes, devotional conferences, retreats — in effect, a return to the forces that had made for advance in the 1890s. Ralph Wardlaw Thompson, who organized a holiness-style Forward Movement in the 1890s at the LMS, produced a characteristic post-Edinburgh lament in 1913: "[W]e have gone in for business methods but have dropped overboard

25. W. G. Allen, Scottish Agency Report, 31 Mar. 1910, CWM Archives (LMS), Home: Odds, Box 16, folder 1.

26. Andrew F. Walls, *The Cross-Cultural Process in Christian History: Studies in the Transmission and Appropriation of Faith* (Maryknoll, N.Y.: Orbis, 2002), 53.

silently and with some shame the great policy of faith in God."[27] Yet a policy of faith could not work without the faithful to support it. To many it seemed that "the spirit of commercialism and of the love of pleasure seeking" had hobbled missionary support, eaten away at the "sacrificial idea," and made church support of missions "formal and flabby."[28]

The science of missions had by 1910 developed a complex rational strategy for attacking the various world religions, but when missiology turned its eye to the anemic home base of missions, it could only urge regenerative spiritual revivals. This was hardly the vision of a confident Protestant nation and an imperial church that some had advocated a decade before. Churches and missionary societies were operating in a pluralizing society with greater philanthropic competition arising from the need to meet continuing challenges from domestic poverty and the distractions of increasing affluence, leisure, and education within the contributing classes. For a century missionaries had argued that healthy missions were the result of healthy churches and that healthy churches flourished in nations faithful to God's purposes. Yet when the delegates at Edinburgh looked around they saw materialism, consumerism, and skepticism. Despite an overseas world of rapidly growing opportunities and "open doors," the pessimism expressed by some at Edinburgh arose from the sense of spiritual paralysis in the home church.[29]

The failure of Evangelicals and High Churchmen alike to transform the missionary world led to demands for a return to party programs and the simple faith rationales and "spiritual revival" of the Victorian era, dealing a serious blow to the progressive ideals of student leaders.[30] The program of High Churchmen after 1900 to capture Anglican leadership and sidetrack party disputes had been as fruitless as Evangelical hopes that a unified missionary program would reverse their declining ecclesiastical influence within the Church. The plans introduced by student progressives were not popular in the traditional constituencies of support. Only by returning to the time-honored revivalist idiom and the old pattern of party confrontation — represented respectively by the CMS's 1913 holiness-influenced Swanwick Conference and

27. Thompson to G. Lyon Turner, 24 July 1913, TS extracts, CWM Archives (LMS), Home: Personal, Box 2, folder 9.

28. J. J. K. Hutchin to Thompson, 2 June 1911, CWM Archives (LMS), Home: Incoming Letters (Home Office), Box 14, folder 1.

29. "The State of the Home Church in Its Bearing upon the Work of Carrying the Gospel to all the Non-Christian World," in *World Missionary Conference, 1910: Commission I*, 348.

30. "Conclusions and Recommendations," in *Report of Commission VI: The Home Base of Missions*, vol. 6 of *[Report of the] World Missionary Conference, 1910* (Edinburgh: Oliphant, Anderson and Ferrier, n.d.), 271; Stock, *Recollections*, 400.

the 1913 Kikuyu Controversy over interdenominational communion embraced by Evangelicals in Africa — were the missionary societies able to reclaim the Victorian patterns of support on which their greatest age of expansion had been founded.[31]

If, as Callum Brown has noted, the full cultural dissolution of Christian Britain only actualized in the 1960s, to church leaders the decline of Victorian religion seemed to have begun in the 1890s and by the first decade of the twentieth century had resulted in a crisis of morale with the growing fear that regular church-going had become a minority affair.[32] By the 1920s, even members of the clergy pronounced the churches irrelevant to the needs of society, as the philanthropic structures of the Victorian era grew redundant with the rise of government provision for social welfare.[33] Suggestively, Anglican missionary societies — so long the focus of charity for the most stubbornly religious Anglicans — remained stable until 1928, when the Depression affected incomes disastrously.[34] Only in the 1930s did the social, ideological, and imperial context shift far enough to begin to call into question the sustainability of the Victorian pattern in which large, successful, centralized, bureaucratically organized, and culturally resonant English foreign missions were the primary avenue through which the churches engaged empire and world. Despite the strong persistence of religious belief particularly anchored in the religiosity of women, Anglican missions from 1903 onwards experienced one crisis after another. Once the structures of local charity, so extensively dependent on women's voluntarism, began to erode with the growth of opportunity for women, so too did missionary infrastructure that had supported itself on local networks of parish collections, lecture halls, charity bazaars, and fundraising entertainments. When in the 1920s agnosticism became socially respectable, the crisis of generations — presaged in the modernist debates and struggles over the boundaries of proper gender roles of the Edwardian period and amplified by the experience of war — ineluctably eroded networks of community-based missionary support. And in the interwar era the resonance that missions had previously enjoyed in the life of the church and the nation began to fade.

Justifications provided by successful missionary endeavors helped maintain religious identities in the Victorian era, but professionalism and liberal theology progressively discredited the idea at the core of naive evangelism: that the gospel was all that was necessary to effect change both at home and

31. On the importance of both Swanwick and Kikuyu to the (short-lived) CMS revival of fortunes, see "Memorandum submitted by Miss G. A. Gollock," 22 May 1914, CMS Archives, G/C 26 A.

32. Brown, *Christian Britain,* chap. 8.

33. Cox, *English Churches,* 272.

34. Stanley, *Bible and Flag,* 134-35.

abroad. Technocratic methods rose both in missions and in imperial governance, but the confident faith in the rightness of rule and English influence abroad — the eminent sureness of the great commission that church, nation, and empire had in the world — waned. The conditions that had allowed the growth and maintenance of a sophisticated, national, bureaucratized missionary movement in Victorian England, particularly within the Anglican church, had been produced by the dynamics of sectarianism and the unmuddied issues of denominational (and in the case of the Church of England, intradenominational) rivalry. The social authority of a professionalizing clergy and, most critically, the occupational ambition and availability of growing numbers of energetic women, produced a movement with strong competitive prescriptions for English imperial and international power and influence. These factors all began to shift after the turn of the century and to reverse after the First World War. Combined with the challenges posed in the mission field by indigenous nationalisms, challenges to the Victorian missionary synthesis multiplied. The balance of the 1890s between fiery sectarian evangelical and Anglo-Catholic drives, supplemented by the desire of many to extend a unitary Anglo-Saxon Anglican Church to transform the world, was increasingly challenged with the passing of the religious and cultural certainties of the Victorian age and the rise of liberal Anglican professionalism developed in the universities and driven by the spiritual ambition of young educated students, particularly women. But the imperial and international past of the Church of England, which carried on with substantial momentum into interwar Britain, can help bring into focus the legacy of the missionary enterprise, an enterprise wherein the chauvinism of spiritual expansion, seasoned by the social service imperatives that came to define the movement institutionally, ultimately developed into later ideals of international aid and development predicated upon the claim of Western peoples to moral duty, responsibility, and leadership. The tensions between humanitarian universalism and the very real manifestations of cultural, economic, and military power within a globalizing world system remain with us. But so too does the legacy of a now global Anglicanism, which, released from the shackles of European control, has more adherents in Africa than in the rest of the world combined, and which continues to be rent between theological conservatives and liberals. Like Rome and its empire, to which classically trained Victorian Anglicans were fond of referring, the most lasting and extensive global legacy of Britain and its empire may be — with all its historic divisions — its religion.

Statistical Charts and Tables

Figure 1. Global Protestant Missionary Incomes, 1899

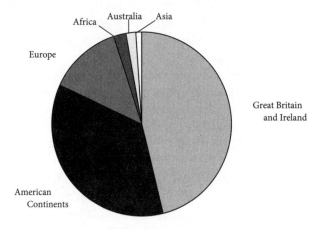

Great Britain and Ireland	£1,612,198	46.1%
American Continents (North, Central and South)	£1,250,616	35.8%
Continental Europe	£457,513	13.1%
Africa	£76,527	2.2%
Australia and Oceania	£60,845	1.7%
Asia (including India)	£36,044	1.0%
Total	£3,493,743	

Source: James S. Dennis, *Centennial Survey of Foreign Missions* (Edinburgh and London: Oliphant, Anderson & Ferrier, 1902).

Totals have been converted from US dollars to Pounds Sterling at a 5-to-1 ratio.

Figure 2. British Missionary Society Home Incomes, 1873

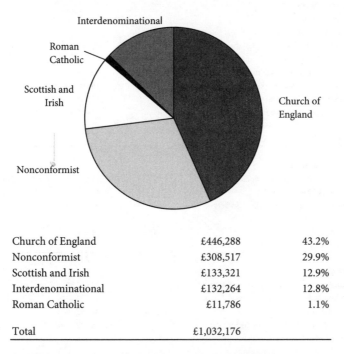

Church of England	£446,288	43.2%
Nonconformist	£308,517	29.9%
Scottish and Irish	£133,321	12.9%
Interdenominational	£132,264	12.8%
Roman Catholic	£11,786	1.1%
Total	£1,032,176	

Source: W. A. Scott Robertson, *British Contributions to Foreign Missions* (London: Church Printing Co., 1874).

Figure 2. British Missionary Society Incomes, 1873 *(continued)*

ENGLISH SOCIETIES

Church of England	British Income	Total Income
Church Missionary Society	251,610	262,670
Society for the Propagation of the Gospel	98,507	110,259
London Society for Promoting		
Christianity among the Jews	36,459	39,533
Society for the Promotion of Christian Knowledge	15,000	29,091
Colonial and Continental Church Society	17,043	35,239
South American Missionary Society	8,033	11,788
Universities' Mission to Central Africa	1,048	1,048
Plus 14 other smaller societies		
Total	£446,288	
Interdenominational		
British and Foreign Bible Society	80,000	121,615
Religious Tract Society	12,314	21,841
Indian Female Normal School Society	7,891	9,744
British Syrian Schools Society	5,380	6,322
Female Education Society	4,714	4,939
Plus 6 other smaller societies		
Total	£132,264	
Nonconformist		
Wesleyan Methodist Missionary Society	120,652	167,995
London Missionary Society	82,183	112,941
Baptist Missionary Society	34,792	50,710
General Baptist Missionary Society	8,622	13,947
Presbyterian Church in England	8,298	8,466
British Society for the Propagation		
of the Gospel among the Jews	7,563	7,657
Moravian Missionary Society	7,558	18,381
Methodist New Connection Foreign Missions	7,041	7,222
Primitive Methodist Foreign Missions	6,784	6,814
Plus 7 other smaller societies		
Total	£308,517	

SCOTTISH AND IRISH SOCIETIES

Free Church of Scotland		63,244
United Presbyterian Church Foreign Missions		39,470
Church of Scotland Mission Boards		31,524
National Bible Society of Scotland		14,214
Irish Presbyterian Missions		13,556
Edinburgh Medical Missionary Society		2,929
Plus 1 other small society		
Total		£133,321

CATHOLIC SOCIETIES

Society for the Propagation of the Faith	11,786	
Grand Total	£1,032,176	

Source: W. A. Scott Robertson, *British Contributions to Foreign Mission* (London: Church Printing Co., 1874).

Figure 3. Anglican Church Parties, 1853

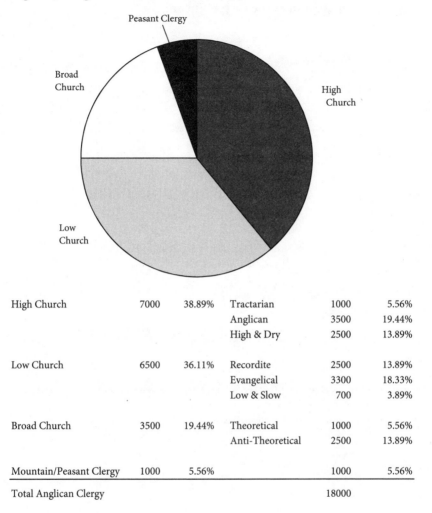

High Church	7000	38.89%	Tractarian	1000	5.56%
			Anglican	3500	19.44%
			High & Dry	2500	13.89%
Low Church	6500	36.11%	Recordite	2500	13.89%
			Evangelical	3300	18.33%
			Low & Slow	700	3.89%
Broad Church	3500	19.44%	Theoretical	1000	5.56%
			Anti-Theoretical	2500	13.89%
Mountain/Peasant Clergy	1000	5.56%		1000	5.56%
Total Anglican Clergy				18000	

Source: W. J. Conybeare: "Church Parties," *Edinburgh Review* 98 (Oct. 1853), 338.

Figure 4. Church Missionary Society and Society for the Propagation of the Gospel Income

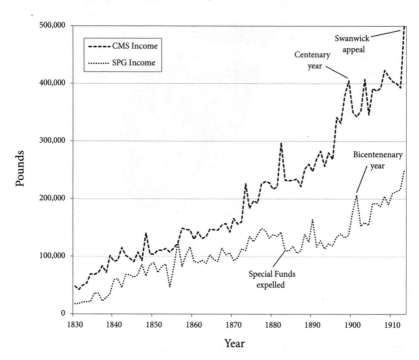

Source: *Proceedings of the CMS, 1913-14* (London: CMS, 1914), 36, and *Report of the Year 1913 of the SPG* (London: SPG, 1914), 273.

SPG totals are adjusted to remove income from Parliamentary Grants, Queen's Letters, and extraordinarily large bequests.

Figure 4. CMS and SPG Income, 1830-1914 *(continued)*

Year	SPG Total*	CMS Total	Year	SPG Total*	CMS Total
1830-31	£17,370	£47,959	1872-73	£113,124	£159,816
1831-32	17,801	42,081	1873-74	110,259	226,253
1832-33	20,687	49,557	1874-75	134,838	183,871
1833-34	20,773	53,051	1875-76	125,294	196,890
1834-35	21,474	69,581	1876-77	136,906	192,356
1835-36	36,347	68,606	1877-78	148,438	226,295
1836-37	35,773	71,727	1878-79	145,237	229,894
1837-38	22,325	83,446	1879-80	131,674	227,963
1838-39	28,265	72,050	1880-81	138,289	216,927
1839-40	34,759	101,197	1881-82	134,978	221,136
1840-41	58,992	91,471	1882-83	142,612	297,424
1841-42	60,923	93,202	·1883-84	109,572	232,448
1842-43	45,517	115,100	1884-85	110,039	231,541
1843-44	68,692	101,585	1885-86	117,971	232,219
1844-45	67,845	96,582	1886-87	105,712	234,639
1845-46	63,431	90,741	1887-88	109,765	221,330
1846-47	68,233	107,192	1888-89	138,367	252,016
1847-48	85,820	92,823	1889-90	125,039	260,282
1848-49	65,997	140,297	1890-91	164,383	247,737
1849-50	85,358	103,914	1891-92	116,520	269,337
1850-51	89,245	103,679	1892-93	127,149	282,805
1851-52	71,743	110,520	1893-94	113,079	256,662
1852-53	83,226	110,305	1894-95	122,327	279,685
1853-54	86,828	113,425	1895-96	118,258	268,526
1854-55	46,309	107,465	1896-97	133,516	341,395
1855-56	81,550	114,393	1897-98	139,532	331,598
1856-57	124,467	123,359	1898-99	132,356	379,827
1857-58	82,448	148,709	1899-00	136,846	404,905
1858-59	102,592	146,565	1900-01	178,396	350,492
1859-60	116,429	145,825	1901-02	206,799	342,619
1860-61	91,236	129,409	1902-03	152,535	353,164
1861-62	89,312	142,254	1903-04	158,642	407,502
1862-63	93,325	131,015	1904-05	154,154	346,058
1863-64	87,832	134,065	1905-06	191,957	391,911
1864-65	102,996	147,010	1906-07	192,436	387,298
1865-66	94,257	146,023	1907-08	186,613	392,296
1866-67	91,184	145,221	1908-09	204,666	423,325
1867-68	114,546	153,921	1909-10	189,923	412,551
1868-69	103,132	157,056	1910-11	209,481	403,610
1869-70	106,434	141,998	1911-12	212,918	400,674
1870-71	92,463	165,761	1912-13	216,519	392,938
1871-72	97,604	156,065	1913-14	250,585	508,214

Source: *Proceedings of the CMS, 1913-14* (London: CMS, 1914), 36, and
    Report of the Year 1913 of the SPG (London: SPG, 1914), 273.

*SPG totals are adjusted to remove income from Parliamentary Grants, Queen's Letters, and extraordinarily large bequests.

Figure 5. English Missionary Society Incomes, 1899

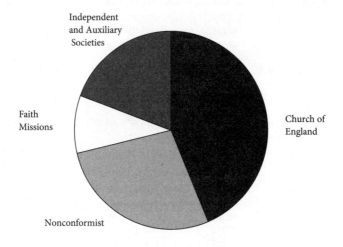

English Missionary Home Income

		Home Income	Foreign Income	Percentage of Total Home Income
CMS		404,906	49,507	32.0%
SPG		147,197		11.6%
WMMS		137,721	90,155	10.9%
LMS		122,858	26,072	9.7%
BMS		87,563	8,012	6.9%
	Sub-total	900,245	173,746	71.2%
Faith Missions*		119,109	18,114	9.4%
All Other Missions**		244,432	21,858	19.3%
	Sub-total	363,541	39,972	28.8%
	Total	£1,263,786	£213,718	
		Grand Total		£1,477,504

Source: James S. Dennis, *Centennial Survey of Foreign Missions* (Edinburgh and London: Oliphant, Anderson & Ferrier, 1902).

*Note: Faith missions include the CIM, Salvation Army, South Africa General Mission and Regions Beyond Missionary Union.

**Note: All Other Missions includes figures for 36 societies, many closely associated with the denominational societies.

Figure 6. English Protestant Female Missionaries, 1899

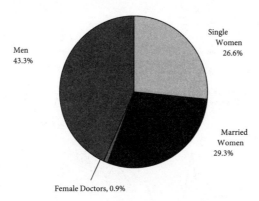

Women as a percentage of Anglican Foreign Missionaries

	CMS		CEZMS		ZBMM		CMS/CEZMS/ZBMM		CIM	
Single women	326	26.3%	224	95.7%	89	93.7%	639	40.8%	287	35.4%
Married women	349	28.2%					349	22.3%	196	24.2%
Female doctors	5	0.4%	10	4.3%	6	6.3%	21	1.3%	1	0.1%
All women	680	54.9%	234	100%	95	100%	1009	64.4%	484	59.7%
European missionary total	1238	100%					1567	100%	811	100%

	SPG		UMCA		WMMS		LMS		BMS	
Single women	75	6.4%	42	39.6%	51	12.7%	65	14.9%	72	22.2%
Married women	485	41.3%			126	31.3%	160	36.7%	109	33.5%
Female doctors	4	0.3%			3	0.7%	9	2.1%	3	0.9%
All women	564	48.0%	42	39.6%	193	48.0%	234	53.7%	184	56.6%
European missionary total	1174	100%	106	100%	402	100%	436	100%	325	100%

	Denominational Societies (BMS, CMS, LMS, SPG & WMMS)		Denominational Societies (including CEZMS & ZBMM)		Anglican Societies (including CEZMS & ZBMM)	
Single women	589	15.1%	902	23.1%	756	26.6%
Married women	1229	31.5%	1229	31.5%	834	29.3%
Female doctors	24	0.6%	40	1.0%	25	0.9%
All women	1842	47.2%	2171	55.9%	1615	56.7%
European missionary total	3904	100%	3904	100%	2847	100.0%

	All English Societies (excluding Salvation Army returns)		All British & Irish Societies (excluding Salvation Army returns)	
Single women	1426	26.1%	1627	25.9%
Married women	1548	28.3%	1757	28.0%
Female doctors	45	0.8%	66	1.0%
All women	3019	55.3%	3450	54.9%
European missionary total	5462	100%	6286	100%

Source: James S. Dennis, *Centennial Survey of Foreign Missions* (Edinburgh and London: Oliphant, Anderson & Ferrier, 1902).

For reasoning on the exclusion of Salvation Army data from English and British totals, see Appendix II.

Figure 7. CMS Income: Associations and Appropriated Funds

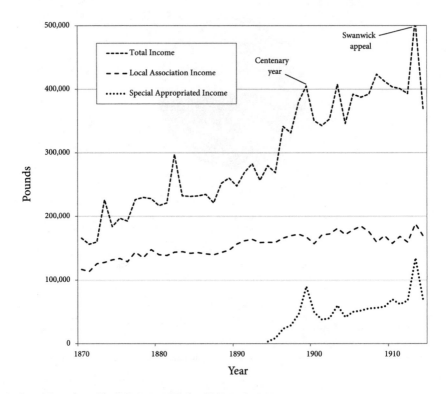

Source: *Proceedings of the CMS, 1915-16* (London: CMS, 1916), 32-34.

Figure 8. CMS and SPG Income as a Percentage of Consumer Spending, 1830-1921

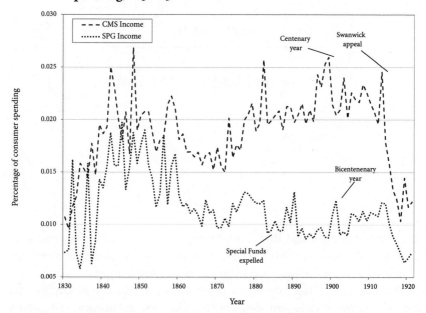

Source: *Proceedings of the CMS, 1923-24* (London: CMS, 1924), 31-32; *Report of the Year 1923 of the SPG* (London: SPG, 1924), 273; and B. R. Mitchell, *British Historical Statistics* (Cambridge: Cambridge University Press, 1988), 831-33.

SPG totals are adjusted to remove income from Parliamentary Grants, Queen's Letters, and extraordinarily large bequests.

APPENDIX II

A Note on Missionary Statistics

Missionary societies and their supporters compiled voluminous statistics. From the 1860s several made attempts at assembling comprehensive missionary data sets, and statistical compilation became something of a fetish through the 1880s and after. The interpretation of this data, which typically focused on converts, missionaries, mission workers, finances, and institution-building, was vigorously contested between missionary supporters and their detractors, as the battles over "missionary failure" in the late 1880s demonstrate. The task was a difficult one, as one of the first compilers, William Binnington Boyce, complained: "So defective are the Reports of some Societies, and so various are the modes of classifying labourers, adopted by different bodies, that it is not possible to gather . . . even the exact number of Missionary labourers . . . [and] ascertain who among the labourers are ordained Missionaries, who male and who female assistants from Christian lands, and who, in various capacities, native helpers."[1] These problems plagued subsequent attempts as well, and as the British missionary enterprise increasingly spun out its enormous variety of new missionary agencies and employed a large number of lay and short-time workers the figures become more complex and difficult to decipher. Missionary statistics are useful, but require careful interpretation.

While significant issues attend their use, they remain invaluable. The difficulties posed by compilation and interpretation proceed from several causes. First, and most seriously, missionary statistics suffer from the cultural biases of their compilers, nearly all clerical professionals, who either ignored or systematically undercounted both women and indigenous Christians and workers. Most

1. B[oyce]., *Statistics, 1861*, 3.

invisible in the statistics are indigenous female workers. Prior to 1890 most data sets ignore women, and prior tò 1900 most omit missionary wives (generally on the logic that clerical statistics for Britain did not include clerical wives). However, it is possible to extract precise data on women after about 1900 and on non-Western staff in most data sets from earlier: 84 percent of all mission staff, for example, were non-Western in 1910.[2] Second, missionary statistics were compiled from scattered, non-standardized society sources that muddle the origins of missionary incomes (between British and colonial sources, the latter also often under-reported), the different classes of contributors, the different kinds of missionary workers, and the different types of missionary agencies, not to mention the dependence of missionary societies on a vast amount of unquantifiable voluntary work. Thus, by one measure (data on "category I" societies engaged in direct proselytizing) British missionary societies collected over £1.6 million in 1899, yet by another (data on all societies, including those "indirectly coöperating" and "engaged in specialized effort" with "category I" agencies) the societies collected nearly £2 million.[3] The effect of complexity was compounded after the 1870s with the enormous proliferation of missionary societies (including in the colonies), many which were of a "faith" orientation and used large numbers of short-term lay missionaries and other "irregular agents." In addition the wide spread of independent churches, chapels, and dioceses meant that the assembling of overall statistics for Western missions often resulted in undercounting everything but the ordained European missionaries and the cash contributions that, in the eyes of the compilers, underpinned the movement.

For Anglican missions, manifestations of these problems were particularly acute. First, the SPG supported many overseas dioceses with block grants, various portions of which were put to missionary use, and often paid missionaries partial allowances to supplement poorly endowed dioceses. The commitment to episcopal control as an Anglican principle thereby meant constitutional ambiguity in SPG statistics and the definition of what, precisely, constituted a missionary. Second, many evangelical Anglicans supported both Church missions and interdenominational missions; the latter, while interdenominational in principle, were often, like the ZBMM, majority Anglican supported or, like the CIM, received substantial minority Anglican support. Third, donations targeted to overseas dioceses could flow through the SPG, the CMS, one of the smaller Anglo-Catholic missionary societies such as the UMCA, or be sent direct, without any central record, to overseas bishops or their commissaries.

2. Dennis, Beach, and Fahs, *Atlas of Missions, 1911.*
3. Dennis, *Centennial Survey,* 257-60.

Many High Church missionaries on furlough to England stumped for special funds directed to overseas dioceses of which no centralized records were made. And while money raised abroad was often reported in Nonconformist income totals, it seldom was in Anglican totals, being absorbed in many cases into diocesan finances.

In this book several sources of missionary statistics have been used. The most important have been Society reports, W. A. Scott Robertson's *Home Contributions to Foreign Missions* (1873), and James Dennis's *Centennial Survey of Foreign Missions* (1902). Each is subject to the problems indicated above, but each also has value. Most detailed in breakdown and categorization is Dennis's *Centennial Survey,* which to all appearances has accurate and detailed information on each of the individual societies listed. However, Dennis's aggregate totals are suspect, inflated as they are with 2,728 Salvation Army workers (which other statistical sets exclude and which, implausibly, omit mention of female workers for which the Salvation Army was particularly known). Furthermore, his totals liberally include missionary agencies and personnel that other compilers omit. When the Salvation Army data is removed, Dennis's aggregate numbers fit in reasonably with other data sets in indicating a total of British missionaries in 1899 of around 6,000, and his breakdowns for individual societies appear reliable.[4] For this reason I have removed the Salvation Army returns from many of the calculations I have made using Dennis's figures. Ironically, Salvation Army returns registering accurate gender distribution of workers would almost certainly confirm the general picture of a largely women's missionary movement.

All of these complexities mean that missionary statistics need to be assessed very carefully and that compilations of missionary statistics must be regarded with a variety of caveats in mind. Nevertheless, the voluminous, carefully collected and detailed data left by a movement obsessed with its vital statistics, compiled from the best sources of the day, were seen as essential to the success of the movement and treated with corresponding care. Despite their limitations, they provide generally reliable, useful data for comparison and analysis within the movement as a whole.

---

4. For other data sets, see Cox, *British Missionary Enterprise,* 270, Table 1.

Bibliography

I. Archives and Manuscript Collections

British Library
Asia, Pacific and Africa Collections, Robert Montgomery Family Papers

Lambeth Palace Library and Archives
Edward White Benson Papers
Bishops' Meetings
Archibald Campbell Tait Papers
Louise Creighton Papers
Randall Thomas Davidson Papers
Lambeth Conference, 1897
Henry Hutchison Montgomery Papers
Frederick Temple Papers

Bodleian Library of Commonwealth and African Studies, Rhodes House
Cambridge Mission to Delhi Archives
United Society for the Propagation of the Gospel Archives
Universities' Mission to Central Africa Archives

School of Oriental and African Studies
Council for World Mission (London Missionary Society) Archives
Interserve (Indian Female Normal School and Instruction Society/Zenana Bible Medical
    Mission) Archives
Melanesian Mission Archives

University of Birmingham
Church of England Zenana Missionary Society Archives
Church Missionary Society Archives

Emily Eugenia Barton Papers
Augustus William Bauman Papers
Graham Wilmot Brooke Papers
Arthur B. Fisher Papers
Gordon Hewitt Papers
Augustus Henry Lash Papers
Gaskoin Richard Morden Wright Papers
Society for Promoting Female Education in the East (Female Education Society)
    Archives

Windsor Castle
St. George's Chapel Archives
    John Henry Joshua Ellison Papers

II. Periodicals

Church Missionary Gleaner
Church Missionary Intelligencer
Church Missionary Juvenile Instructor
Church Missionary Record
Church Missionary Review
Edinburgh Review
Home Gazette of the Church Missionary Society
International Review of Missions
Occasional Paper of the Hawaiian Church Mission
Proceedings of the Church Missionary Society
India's Women: The Magazine of the Church of England Zenana Missionary Society
Report of . . . the Society for the Propagation of the Gospel in Foreign Parts
The East and the West
The Mission Field (SPG)
The Net Cast on Many Waters

III. Primary Printed Sources

Arden, A. H. *Objections to Foreign Missions.* London: CMS, 1902.
Arthur, William. *Woman's Work in India.* London: Woolmer, 1882.
Ashwell, Arthur R., and Reginald G. Wilberforce. *Life of the Right Reverend Samuel Wilberforce, D.D.: Lord Bishop of Oxford and Afterwards of Winchester.* 3 vols. London: Murray, 1880-82.
Barlow, Margaret, ed. *The Life of William Hagger Barlow, D.D., Late Dean of Peterborough.* London: Allen, 1910.
Barlow, W. H. *Diocesan Mission Boards: A Paper Read at the 14th Annual Conference, Cheltenham, June 6, 1871.* N.p., 1871.

Barnes, Irene H. *Behind the Pardah: The Story of C.E.Z.M.S. Work in India.* London: Marshall, 1897.

————. *In Salisbury Square.* London: CMS, 1906.

Barry, Alfred. *The Ecclesiastical Expansion of England in the Growth of the Anglican Communion.* London: Macmillan, 1895.

Barton, Cecil Edward. *John Barton: A Memoir.* London: Hodder and Stoughton, 1910.

Beach, Harlan P. *Dawn on the Hills of T'Ang; or, China as a Mission Field.* London: SVMU, 1898.

Bell, G. K. A. *Randall Davidson, Archbishop of Canterbury.* 2 vols. London: Oxford University Press, 1935.

Benson, A. C. *The Life of Edward White Benson: Sometime Archbishop of Canterbury.* 2 vols. London: Macmillan, 1899.

Benson, Edward White. "Missions." In *The Anglican Pulpit of Today: Forty Short Biographies and Forty Sermons of Distinguished Preachers of the Church of England.* London: Hodder and Stoughton, 1886.

Bickersteth, Samuel. *Life and Letters of Edward Bickersteth, Bishop of South Tokyo.* London: Sampson Low, Marston, 1899.

B[oyce]., W[illiam]. B[innington]. *Statistics of Protestant Missionary Societies, 1861.* London: Nichols, 1863.

Braithwaite, Robert, ed. *The Life and Letters of Rev. William Pennefather.* London: Shaw, 1878.

Bullock, F. W. B. *The History of Ridley Hall Cambridge.* 2 vols. Cambridge: Cambridge University Press, 1941.

Carey, William. *An Enquiry into the Obligations of Christians to Use Means for the Conversion of the Heathens.* 1792. London: Carey Kingsgate, 1961.

Cary, Otis. *Japan and Its Regeneration.* London: SVMU, 1900.

Charles, Elizabeth. *Three Martyrs of the Nineteenth Century: Studies from the Lives of Livingstone, Gordon, and Patteson.* London: SPCK, 1885.

Charlesworth, Maria Louisa. *India and the East; or, A Voice from the Zenana.* London: Seeley, Jackson and Halliday, 1860.

Chatterton, Eyre. *A History of the Church of England in India.* London: SPCK, 1924.

Church, R. W. *The Oxford Movement: Twelve Years, 1833-1845.* London: Macmillan, 1891.

The Church of England Zenana Missionary Society Jubilee Souvenir, 1880-1930. London, n.d.

Compton, Berdmore. *Edward Meyrick Goulburn, D.D., D.C.L., Dean of Norwich: A Memoir.* London: Murray, 1899.

Conference on Missions Held in 1860 at Liverpool. Edited by The Secretaries to the Conference. London: Nisbet, 1860.

Creighton, Louise. *Memoir of a Victorian Woman: Reflections of Louise Creighton, 1850-1936.* Edited by James Thayne Covert. Bloomington: Indiana University Press, 1994.

Cuddesdon College, 1854-1904; a Record and Memorial. London: Longmans, Green, 1904.

Cust, Robert Needham. *Essay on the Prevailing Methods of the Evangelization of the Non-Christian World.* London: Luzac, 1894.

————. *The Female Evangelist.* Hertford, UK, n.d., ca. 1891.

————. *Memoirs of Past Years of a Septuagenarian.* Private circulation, 1899.

Davidson, Randall Thomas, and William Benham. *Life of Archibald Campbell Tait, Archbishop of Canterbury.* 2nd ed. 2 vols. London: Macmillan, 1891.

Dawson, Edwin C. *James Hannington, First Bishop of Eastern Equitorial Africa.* London: Seeley, 1887.

———. *Lion-Hearted: The Story of Bishop Hannington's Life.* Seeley: London, 1890.

Day, A. Grove, ed. *Mark Twain's Letters from Hawaii.* New York: Appleton-Century, 1966.

Dennis, James S. *Centennial Survey of Foreign Missions.* Edinburgh: Oliphant, Anderson and Ferrier, 1902.

Dennis, James S., Harlan P. Beach, and Charles H. Fahs, eds. *World Atlas of Christian Missions.* New York: SVM, 1911.

[Dunn, A. H.]. *The British Empire and Its Spiritual Expansion: An Illustrated Address Delivered at Several Centres by the Bishop of Quebec in View of the Bicentenary of the Society for the Propagation of the Gospel.* N.p., n.d., ca. 1901.

Ecumenical Missionary Conference, New York, 1900: Report of the Ecumenical Conference on Foreign Missions. 2 vols. London: RTS, 1900.

Eden, George R., and F. C. Macdonald, eds. *Lightfoot of Durham.* Cambridge: Cambridge University Press, 1933.

Ellis, Harriet Warner. *Our Eastern Sisters and Their Missionary Helpers.* London: RTS, n.d., ca. 1883.

Ellison, John, and G. H. S. Walpole, eds. *Church and Empire: A Series of Essays on the Responsibilities of Empire.* London: Longmans, Green, 1907.

Ensor, George. *"Help These Women": A Plea for the Work of the Church of England Zenana Missionary Society.* London: Hunt, 1894.

French, Thomas Valpy. *The Proposed Cambridge University Mission in North India.* Private circulation, 1876.

Gairdner, W. H. T. *D. M. Thornton: A Study in Missionary Ideals and Methods.* London: Hodder and Stoughton, 1908.

———. *Echoes from Edinburgh, 1910: An Account and Interpretation of the World Missionary Conference.* London: Revell, 1910.

Giberne, Agnes. *A Lady of England: The Life and Letters of Charlotte Maria Tucker.* London: Hodder and Stoughton, 1895.

Gidney, W. T. *The Jews and Their Evangelization.* London: SVMU, 1899.

Gladstone, William Ewart. "Art. VI." Review of *Life of John Coleridge Patteson, Missionary Bishop of the Melanesian Islands.* By Charlotte Mary Yonge. *Quarterly Review* 137 (1874): 458-92.

Gollock, Georgina A. *The Contribution of Women to Home Work of the C.M.S.* London, n.d., ca. 1912.

Gollock, Minna C. "Women's Work." In *The Church and the Empire: Addresses at the Summer School at Eastborne, June 19 to June 26, 1915,* 197-214. London: SPG, 1915.

Gollock, Minna C., and Georgina A. Gollock. *Half Done: Some Thoughts for Women.* London: United Council for Missionary Education, 1916.

Goodwin, Harvey. *Memoir of Bishop Mackenzie.* Cambridge: Deighton, Bell, 1864.

Gregory, Robert. *Robert Gregory, 1819-1911: Being the Autobiography of Robert Gregory, D.D., Dean of St. Paul's.* London: Longmans, Green, 1912.

Grubb, Norman P. *C. T. Studd: Cricketer and Pioneer.* London: RTS, 1933.

Guinness, Henry Grattan. *The Approaching End of the Age Viewed in the Light of History, Prophecy and Science.* London: Frome, 1878.

H.A.S. [pseud.] *A Martyr-Bishop of Our Own Day.* London: Wells Gardner, 1881.

Harford, John Battersby, and Frederick Charles Macdonald. *Handley Carr Glyn Moule, Bishop of Durham: A Biography.* London: Hodder and Stoughton, n.d., ca. 1922.

Heanley, R. M. *A Memoir of Edward Steere, D.D., LL.D.: Third Missionary Bishop in Central Africa.* London: Bell, 1888.

————, ed. *Edward Steere: Notes of Sermons.* London: Bell, 1884.

Henson, H. Hensley. "The Church of England." In *Church Problems: A View of Modern Anglicanism,* edited by H. Hensley Henson, 1-31. London: Murray, 1900.

Hobson, J. A. *Imperialism: A Study.* London: Nisbet, 1902.

————. *The Psychology of Jingoism.* London: Richards, 1901.

Holland, Henry Scott. *A Bundle of Memories.* London: Wells Gardner, Darton, 1915.

————. *Personal Studies.* London: Wells Gardner, Darton, 1905.

How the Zenana Missions Began. N.p., n.d., ca. 1890.

Howe, W. F. *The Classified Directory to the Metropolitan Charities for 1880.* London: Longmans, Green, 1880.

Huff, Edmund. "Public Laws and the Colonial Church." In *The Church and the World: Essays on Questions of the Day in 1867.* 3rd ed., ed. Orby Shipley, 113-44. London: Longmans, Green, Reader, and Dyer, 1867.

The Indian Crisis: A Memorial to the Queen from the Church Missionary Society, on the Religious Policy of the Government of India. [London], 1857.

The Indian Crisis: A Special Meeting of the Church Missionary Society at Exeter Hall. [London], 1858.

Johnson, James. *A Century of Missions and Increase of the Heathen.* 2nd ed. London: Nisbet, 1886.

Kinnaird, Emily. *Reminiscences.* London: Murray, 1925.

The Land of Sinim: An Illustrated Report of the China Inland Mission. London: CIM, 1905.

[Lear, Henrietta Louisa]. Gray, Charles, ed. *Life of Robert Gray, Bishop of Cape Town and Metropolitan of Africa.* 2 vols. Edited by Charles Gray. London: Rivingtons, 1876.

Lewis, C. B. *A Plea for Zenanas.* N.p., n.d., ca. 1866.

Littledale, Richard Frederick. "The Missionary Aspect of Ritualism." In *The Church and the World: Essays on Questions of the Day,* ed. Orby Shipley, 25-50. London: Longmans, Green, Reader, and Dyer, 1866.

Livingstone, David. *Dr. Livingstone's Cambridge Lectures.* 2nd ed. Edited by William Monk. Cambridge: Deighton, Bell, 1860.

Lombe, E[dward]. *How is the Present Need of Missionaries to Be Met? A Paper Read Before the Cambridge Church Missionary Union, Oct 23, 1888.* London: CMS, 1889.

Longridge, George, and W. H. Hutton. *A History of the Oxford Mission to Calcutta.* 2nd ed. London: Mowbray, 1910.

Ludlow, J. M. *Woman's Work in the Church: Historical Notes on Deaconesses and Sisterhoods.* London: Strahan, 1866.

"Make Jesus King": The Report of the International Students' Missionary Conference; Liverpool, January 1-5, 1896. London: SVMU, n.d.

Mathews, Basil. *John R. Mott: World Citizen.* London: SCM, 1934.

Maurice, F. D. *The Religions of the World and Their Relations to Christianity.* 6th ed. London: Macmillan, 1886.

Melrose, Andrew, and T. C. Wilson. *Alexander Mackay, Missionary Hero of Uganda.* London: Sunday School Union, 1893.

M[ills]., C. M[ary]. *Edith Davidson of Lambeth.* London: Murray, 1938.

M'Kee, James. *Obstacles to the Progress of Christianity in India.* Belfast: News-Letter Office, 1858.

Montgomery, Henry H. *Foreign Missions.* London: Longmans, Green, 1902.

———. "Introduction." In *Mankind and the Church: Being an Attempt to Estimate the Contribution of Great Races to the Fulness of the Church of God,* edited by H. H. Montgomery. London: Longmans, Green, 1907.

———. *The Light of Melanesia.* London: SPCK, 1896.

———. *Service Abroad: Lectures Delivered in the Divinity School of the University of Cambridge.* London: Longmans, Green, 1910.

———. *The S.P.G.: Its Principles and Ideals.* London: SPG, 1915.

———. "With the Women," A Sermon Preached in Westminster Abbey on April 22nd, 1915, on the Occasion of the Commencement of the Jubilee Year of Women's Work of S.P.G. London: SPG, 1915.

M[ontgomery]., M[aud]. *Bishop Montgomery: A Memoir.* Westminster, UK: SPG, 1933.

Mott, J. R. *The Home Ministry and Modern Missions: A Plea for Leadership in World Evangelization.* London: Hodder and Stoughton, 1905.

Moule, H. C. G. *The Evangelical School in the Church of England: Its Men and Its Work in the Nineteenth Century.* London: Nisbet, 1901.

Murdoch, John. *The Women of India and What Can Be Done for Them.* 2nd ed. Madras: Christian Vernacular Education Society, 1891.

Official Year-Book of the Church of England. London: SPCK, 1886, 1887, and 1897.

Packman, Cyrus H. L. *The Establishment of a General Board of Missions: Being a Paper Read Before the Chapter of the Deanery of Liverpool North, September 26, 1871.* Liverpool, 1871.

Padwick, Constance E. *Temple Gairdner of Cairo.* Rev. ed. London: SPCK, 1930.

Page, Jesse. *Bishop Patteson: The Martyr of Melanesia.* London: Partridge, n.d., ca. 1888.

Palmer, Edwin. *Bishop Patteson, Missionary Bishop and Martyr.* London: Christian Knowledge Society, n.d., ca. 1872.

Parry, J. C. *What Is a Zenana?* London: Yates & Alexander, 1872.

Pascoe, C. F. *Classified Digest of the Records of the Society for the Propagation of the Gospel in Foreign Parts, 1701-1892.* 5th ed. London: SPG, 1895.

———. *Two Hundred Years of the S.P.G.* London: SPG, 1901.

Perry, Charles. *A Review of the Controversy Between the Bishop of Colombo and the Missionaries of the Church Missionary Society.* London: Hatchards, 1877.

Phillips, James Erasmus. *Woman's Work in Foreign Missions: A Paper Read at the Church Congress Held at Bristol, October 11th, 1864.* London: Rivingtons, n.d.

Pitman, Emma Raymond. *Central Africa, Japan and Fiji: A Story of Missionary Enterprise, Trials, and Triumphs.* London: Hodder and Stoughton, 1882.

———. *Lady Missionaries in Foreign Lands.* London: Partridge, n.d., ca. 1889.

Potter, Henry Codman. *Sisterhoods and Deaconesses: At Home and Abroad.* New York: Dutton, 1873.

Proceedings of the Conference on Foreign Missions Held at the Conference Hall, Mildmay Park. London: Shaw, 1879 and 1886.

Pusey, Edward Bouverie. *The Councils of the Church: From the Council of Jerusalem A.D. 51 to the Council of Constantinople A.D. 381.* Oxford: Parker, 1857.

Ranyard, Ellen Henrietta. *Life Work; or, The Link and the Rivet.* London: Nisbet, 1861.

Records of Missionary Secretaries: An Account of the Celebration of the Centenary of the London Secretaries' Association. London: United Council for Missionary Education, 1920.

Report of Proceedings and Papers Read at the Church Missionary Society's Conference Held at Lincoln. Lincoln, UK, 1878.

Report of the Centenary Conference on the Protestant Missions of the World. 2 vols. Edited by James Johnson. London: Nisbet, 1888.

[Report of the] Pan-Anglican Congress, 1908. 7 vols. London: SPCK, 1908.

[Report of the] World Missionary Conference, 1910: To Consider Missionary Problems in Relation to the Non-Christian World. 9 vols. Edinburgh: Oliphant, Anderson and Ferrier, n.d.

Restarick, Henry Boyd. *Hawaii, 1778-1920, from the Viewpoint of a Bishop.* Honolulu: Paradise of the Pacific Press, 1924.

Roberts, G. Bayfield. *The History of the English Church Union, 1859-1894.* London: Church Printing, 1895.

Robertson, W. A. Scott. *British Contributions to Foreign Missions. Analysis and Summary of the Receipts of Sixty-Five Societies for the Year 1872.* London: Church Printing, n.d., ca. 1873.

Rowley, Henry. *The Story of the Universities' Mission to Central Africa: From Its Commencement, Under Bishop Mackenzie, to Its Withdrawal from the Zambesi.* London: Saunders, Otley, 1866.

Ryle, J. C. *Holiness: Its Nature, Hindrances, Difficulties, and Roots.* 1877. Grand Rapids: Kregel, 1962.

———. *More Prayer and Work! Being Thoughts on Missions.* 7th ed. London: Hunt, 1886.

———. *What Do We Owe to the Reformation?* London: Shaw, 1877.

Sangar, James Mortimer. *Old Paths and New: Thoughts on the Centenary of the Church Missionary Society.* London: Wileman, 1899.

Smellie, Alexander. *Evan Henry Hopkins: A Memoir.* London: Marshall, 1920.

Smith, Herbert Maynard. *Frank, Bishop of Zanzibar: The Life of Frank Weston.* London: SPCK, 1926.

Smith, Stanley P., Charles T. Studd, and Reginald Radcliff. *The Evangelization of the World: A Three-Fold Appeal.* London: Hodder & Stoughton, 1885.

Sparham, Charles G. *Christianity and the Religions of China: A Brief Study in Comparative Religions.* London: Snow, 1896.

Spottiswoode, George A., ed. *The Official Report of the Missionary Conference of the Anglican Communion.* London: SPCK, 1894.

Staley, Mildred E. *A Tapestry of Memories: An Autobiography.* Hilo, HI: Hilo Tribune Herald, 1944.

Staley, Thomas Nettleship. *A Pastoral Address, by the Right Reverend the Bishop of Honolulu.* Honolulu: Hawaiian Gazette Office, 1865.

————. *Five Years' Church Work in the Kingdom of Hawaii.* London: Rivingtons, 1868.

Stanley, Henry Morton. *How I Found Livingstone: Travels, Adventures, and Discoveries in Central Africa.* London: Sampson, Low, Marston, Low, and Searle, 1872.

Stock, Eugene. *An Historical Survey of Women's Work in C.M.S. at Home and Abroad.* London, 1907.

————. *The History of the Church Missionary Society.* 4 vols. London: CMS, 1899-1916.

————. *My Recollections.* London: Nisbet, 1909.

————. *A Short Handbook of Missions.* 2nd ed. London: Longmans, Green, 1905.

The Student Volunteer Missionary Union: A Brief Statement of Its Origin and Growth, February, 1899. N.p., n.d.

Tait, Archibald Campbell. *Missions: Special Service St. Andrew's Day, 30th November, 1875.* N.p., 1875.

Tatlow, Tissington. *The Story of the Student Christian Movement of Great Britain and Ireland.* London: SCM Press, 1933.

Taylor, F. Howard. *These Forty Years: A Short History of the China Inland Mission.* Philadelphia: Pepper, 1903.

Taylor, Isaac. "The Great Missionary Failure." *Fortnightly Review* 50 (Oct. 1888): 488-500.

————. "Missionary Finance." *Fortnightly Review* 50 (Nov. 1888): 581-92.

Taylor, J. Hudson, ed. *China's Millions.* London: Morgan and Scott, 1885.

Thornton, Douglas M. *Africa Waiting; or, The Problem of Africa's Evangelization.* London: SVMU, 1897.

Tisdall, William St. Clair. *India: Its History, Darkness and Dawn.* London: SVMU, 1901.

Townsend, Meredith. "Cheap Missionaries." *Contemporary Review* 1-9.

Tristram, H. B. *The Daughters of Syria.* 2nd ed. London: Seeley, Jackson & Halliday, 1872.

Tucker, H. W. *The English Church in Other Lands; or, The Spiritual Expansion of England.* London: Longmans, Green, 1891.

————. *Memoir of the Life and Episcopate of George Augustus Selwyn.* New York: Pott, Young, 1879.

Vaux, James Edward. "Missions and Preaching Orders." In *The Church and the World: Essays on Questions of the Day in 1868,* ed. Orby Shipley, 152-88. London: Longmans, Green, Reader, and Dyer, 1868.

Venn, John. *The Revival in Wales.* London, 1860.

Ward, Gertrude, ed. *Letters of Bishop Tozer and His Sister Together with Some Other Records of the Universities' Mission from 1863-1873.* London: UMCA, 1902.

————. *The Life of Charles Alan Smythies, Bishop of the Universities' Mission to Central Africa.* 2nd ed. London: UMCA, 1899.

Webb, Allan Becher. *Sisterhood Life and Woman's Work, in Mission-Field of the Church.* London: Skeffington, 1883.

Weitbrecht, Mary. *The Women of India and Christian Work in the Zenana.* London: Nisbet, 1875.

Westcott, Brooke Foss. *The Obligations of Empire.* London: Macmillan, 1900.

————. *On Some Points in the Religious Office of the Universities.* London: Macmillan, 1873.

————. *Speech of the Rev. Professor Westcott at the Anniversary Meeting of the Cambridge Church Missionary Association, on May 11th 1885.* N.p., n.d.

Westcott, Brooke Foss, et al. *The Church and New Century Problems.* London: Wells Gardner, Darton, n.d., ca. 1900.

Wilberforce, Samuel. *A Sermon Preached at Westminster Abbey, on the Feast of the Purification, Feb. 2, 1863, At the Consecration of the Bishop of the Mission to Central Africa and the Bishop of the Orange River Free State.* Oxford: Henry and Parker, 1863.

Wilson, Roger C. *Frank Lenwood.* London: SCM, 1936.

Winter, Priscilla. *On Woman's Work in India.* London: Clay, n.d., ca. 1878.

Woods, Edward S., and Frederick B. Macnutt. *Theodore, Bishop of Winchester: Pastor, Prophet, Pilgrim.* London: SPCK, 1933.

Woodworth, Arthur V. *Christian Socialism in England.* London: Swan Sonnenschein, 1903.

Wynne, G. Robert. *The Church in Greater Britain: The Donnellan Lectures Delivered Before the University of Dublin, 1900-1901.* London: Kegan Paul, Trench, Trübner, 1901.

Yonge, Charlotte M. *In Memoriam: Bishop Patteson.* London: Skeffington, 1872.

————. *Life of John Coleridge Patteson, Missionary Bishop of the Melanesian Islands.* 2 vols. London: Macmillan, 1874.

IV. Secondary Sources

Ajayi, J. F. Ade. *Christian Missions in Nigeria, 1841-1891: The Making of a New Élite.* Evanston, IL: Northwestern University Press, 1965.

Allchin, A. M. *The Silent Rebellion: Anglican Religious Communities, 1845-1900.* London: SCM, 1958.

Allen, Hubert J. B. *Roland Allen: Pioneer, Priest and Prophet.* Grand Rapids: Eerdmans, 1995.

Anderson, Benedict. *Imagined Communities: Reflections on the Origin and Spread of Nationalism.* London: Verso, 1983.

Anderson, Olive. "The Growth of Christian Militarism in Mid-Victorian Britain." *English Historical Review* 86 (Jan. 1971): 46-72.

apRoberts, Ruth. *Arnold and God.* Berkeley: University of California Press, 1983.

Arnstein, Walter L. *Protestant Versus Catholic in Mid-Victorian England: Mr. Newdegate and the Nuns.* Columbia: University of Missouri Press, 1982.

Austin, Alvyn. *China's Millions: The China Inland Mission and Late Qing Society, 1832-1905.* Grand Rapids: Eerdmans, 2007.

Ayandele, E. A. *The Missionary Impact on Modern Nigeria, 1842-1914.* London: Longman, 1966.

Bayldon, Joan. *Cyril Bardsley, Evangelist.* London: SPCK, 1942.

Bayly, C. A. *Imperial Meridian: The British Empire and the World, 1780-1830.* London: Longman, 1989.

Bebbington, David W. "Atonement, Sin, and Empire, 1880-1914." In *The Imperial Horizons of British Protestant Missions, 1880-1914,* edited by Andrew Porter, 14-31. Grand Rapids: Eerdmans, 2003.

————. *Evangelicalism in Modern Britain: A History from the 1730s to the 1980s*. London: Unwin Hyman, 1989.

————. *Holiness in Nineteenth-Century England*. Carlisle, UK: Paternoster, 2000.

————. *The Nonconformist Conscience: Chapel and Politics, 1870-1914*. London: Allen & Unwin, 1982.

————. "Nonconformity and Electoral Sociology, 1867-1918." *Historical Journal* 27, no. 3 (Sept. 1984): 633-56.

Beeson, Trevor. *The Deans*. London: SCM Press, 2004.

Beidelman, T. O. "Altruism and Domesticity: Images of Missionizing Women Among the Church Missionary Society in Nineteenth-Century East Africa." In *Gendered Missions: Women and Men in Missionary Discourse and Practice*, edited by Mary Taylor Huber and Nancy C. Lutkehaus, 113-43. Ann Arbor: University of Michigan Press, 1999.

————. *Colonial Evangelism: A Socio-Historical Study of an East African Mission at the Grassroots*. Bloomington: Indiana University Press, 1982.

Bell, Duncan. *The Idea of Greater Britain: Empire and the Future of World Order, 1860-1900*. Princeton: Princeton University Press, 2007.

Bentley, James. *Ritualism and Politics in Victorian Britain: The Attempt to Legislate for Belief*. Oxford: Oxford University Press, 1978.

Binfield, Clyde. *So Down to Prayers: Studies in English Nonconformity, 1780-1920*. London: Dent, 1977.

Bowen, Desmond. *The Idea of the Victorian Church: A Study of the Church of England, 1833-1889*. Montreal: McGill University Press, 1968.

Bowie, Fiona, Deborah Kirkwood, and Shirley Ardener, eds. *Women and Mission: Past and Present; Anthropological and Historical Perceptions*. Providence, RI: Berg, 1993.

Boyd, Kelly. *Manliness and the Boys' Story Paper in Britain: A Cultural History, 1855-1940*. Basingstoke, UK: Palgrave Macmillan, 2003.

Brent, Richard. *Liberal Anglican Politics: Whiggery, Religion and Reform, 1830-1841*. Oxford: Oxford University Press, 1987.

Brock, Peggy. "New Christians as Evangelists." In *Missions and Empire*, edited by Norman Etherington. The Oxford History of the British Empire Companion Series, 132-52. Oxford: Oxford University Press, 2005.

Broomhall, A. J. *Hudson Taylor and China's Open Century*. 7 vols. Sevenoaks, UK: Hodder and Stoughton, 1985-89.

Brouwer, Ruth Compton. *New Women for God: Canadian Presbyterian Women and India Missions, 1876-1914*. Toronto: University of Toronto Press, 1990.

Brown, Callum. *The Death of Christian Britain: Understanding Secularisation, 1800-2000*. London: Routledge, 2001.

Brundage, Anthony, and Richard A. Cosgrove. *The Great Tradition: Constitutional History and National Identity in Britain and the United States, 1870-1960*. Stanford: Stanford University Press, 2007.

Burns, Arthur. *The Diocesan Revival in the Church of England, c. 1800-1870*. Oxford: Oxford University Press, 1999.

————, ed. "W. J. Conybeare: 'Church Parties.'" In *From Cranmer to Davidson: A Church of England Miscellany*, edited by Stephen Taylor, 213-385. Woodbridge, UK: Boydell, 1999.

Burstein, Miriam Elizabeth. "Reviving the Reformation: Victorian Women Writers and the Protestant Historical Novel." *Women's Writing* 12, no. 1 (2005): 73-84.

Burton, Antoinette M. *At the Heart of the Empire: Indians and the Colonial Encounter in Late-Victorian Britain.* Berkeley: University of California Press, 1998.

———. *Burdens of History: British Feminists, Indian Women, and Imperial Culture, 1865-1915.* Chapel Hill: University of North Carolina Press, 1994.

———. "Contesting the Zenana: The Mission to Make 'Lady Doctors for India,' 1874-1885." *Journal of British Studies* 3 (July 1996): 368-97.

———. "On the Inadequacy and the Indispensability of the Nation." In *After the Imperial Turn: Thinking with and Through the Nation,* edited by Antoinette Burton, 1-24. Durham, NC: Duke University Press, 2003.

———. "Rules of Thumb: British History and 'Imperial Culture' in Nineteenth- and Twentieth-Century Britain." *Women's History Review* 3, no. 4 (1994): 483-500.

Bush, Barbara. "Gender and Empire: The Twentieth Century." In *Gender and Empire,* edited by Philippa Levine. The Oxford History of the British Empire Companion Series, 46-761. Oxford: Oxford University Press, 2004.

Bush, Julia. *Women Against the Vote: Female Anti-Suffragism in Britain.* Oxford: Oxford University Press, 2007.

Cairns, H. Alan C. *Prelude to Imperialism: British Reactions to Central African Society, 1840-1890.* London: Routledge & K. Paul, 1965.

Campbell, T. W. "The Sisters of the Church and the Anglican Diocese of Sydney, 1892-1893: A Controversy." *Journal of Religious History* 25, no. 2 (June 2001): 188-206.

Cannadine, David. "The Context, Performance and Meaning of Ritual: The British Monarchy and the 'Invention of Tradition,' c. 1820-1977." In *The Invention of Tradition,* edited by Eric Hobsbawm and Terence Ranger, 101-64. Cambridge: Cambridge University Press, 1983.

———. *Ornamentalism: How the British Saw Their Empire.* Oxford: Oxford University Press, 2001.

Carpenter, Mary Wilson. *Imperial Bibles, Domestic Bodies: Women, Sexuality, and Religion in the Victorian Market.* Athens: Ohio University Press, 2003.

Carwardine, Richard. *Transatlantic Revivalism: Popular Evangelicalism in Britain and America, 1790-1865.* Westport, CT: Greenwood, 1978.

Chadwick, Owen. *Mackenzie's Grave.* London: Hodder & Stoughton, 1959.

———. *The Victorian Church, Part One: 1829-1859.* 3rd ed. London: SCM Press, 1971.

———. *The Victorian Church, Part Two: 1860-1901.* 2nd ed. London: SCM Press, 1972.

Chatterjee, Partha. "Colonialism, Nationalism and Colonialized Women: The Contest in India." *American Ethnologist* 16, no. 622-33.

———. *The Nation and Its Fragments: Colonial and Postcolonial Histories.* Princeton: Princeton University Press, 1993.

Christensen, Torben, and William R. Hutchison, eds. *Missionary Ideologies in the Imperialist Era, 1880-1920.* [Aarhus, Denmark]: Aros, 1982.

Clark, David. *Between Pulpit and Pew: Folk Religion in a North Yorkshire Fishing Village.* Cambridge: Cambridge University Press, 1982.

Clark, J. C. D. *English Society, 1688-1832: Ideology, Social Structure, and Political Practice During the Ancien Regime.* Cambridge: Cambridge University Press, 1985.

Claydon, Tony, and Ian McBride, eds. *Protestantism and National Identity: Britain and Ireland, c. 1650-c. 1850.* Cambridge: Cambridge University Press, 1998.

Clive, John. *Macaulay: The Shaping of the Historian.* New York: Knopf, 1973.

———. *Scotch Reviewers: The Edinburgh Review, 1802-1815.* Cambridge, MA: Harvard University Press, 1957.

Cnattingius, Hans Jacob. *Bishops and Societies: A Study of Anglican Colonial and Missionary Expansion, 1698-1850.* London: SPCK, 1952.

Coakley, J. F. *The Church of the East and the Church of England: A History of the Archbishop of Canterbury's Assyrian Mission.* Oxford: Clarendon Press, 1992.

Cohn, Bernard S. "Representing Authority in Victorian India." In *The Invention of Tradition,* edited by Eric Hobsbawm and Terence Ranger, 165-209. Cambridge: Cambridge University Press, 1983.

Colley, Linda. *Britons: Forging the Nation, 1707-1837.* New Haven: Yale University Press, 1992.

———. "The Difficulties of Empire: Present, Past and Future." *Historical Research* 79 (2006): 367-82.

Comaroff, Jean, and John L. Comaroff. *Of Revelation and Revolution: Christianity, Colonialism, and Consciousness in South Africa.* Vol. 1. Chicago: University of Chicago Press, 1991.

———. *Of Revelation and Revolution: The Dialectics of Modernity on a South African Frontier.* Vol. 2. Chicago: University of Chicago Press, 1997.

Constantine, Stephen. "Empire Migration and Social Reform, 1880-1950." In *Migrants, Emigrants, and Immigrants: A Social History of Migration,* edited by Colin G. Pooley and Ian D. Whyte, 62-83. London: Routledge, 1991.

Coombes, Annie E. *Reinventing Africa: Museums, Material Culture, and Popular Imagination in Late Victorian and Edwardian England.* New Haven: Yale University Press, 1994.

Cornford, J. P. "The Transformation of Conservatism in the Late Nineteenth Century." *Victorian Studies* 7 (Sept. 1963): 226-44. London: Epworth, 1993.

Corsi, Piero. *Science and Religion: Baden Powell and the Anglican Debate, 1800-1860.* Cambridge: Cambridge University Press, 1988.

Cox, Jeffrey. *The British Missionary Enterprise Since 1700.* New York: Routledge, 2008.

———. "C. F. Andrews and the Failure of the Modern Missionary Movement." In *Modern Religious Rebels: Presented to John Kent,* edited by Stuart Mews, 226-44. London: Epworth, 1993.

———. *The English Churches in a Secular Society: Lambeth, 1870-1930.* New York: Oxford University Press, 1982.

———. "George Alfred Lefroy, 1854-1919: A Bishop in Search of a Church." In *After the Victorians: Private Conscience and Public Duty in Modern Britain; Essays in Memory of John Clive,* edited by Susan Pedersen and Peter Mandler, 54-76. London: Routledge, 1994.

———. *Imperial Fault Lines: Christianity and Colonial Power in India, 1818-1940.* Stanford: Stanford University Press, 2002.

———. "Independent English Women in Delhi and Lahore, 1860-1947." In *Religion and Irreligion in Victorian Society: Essays in Honor of R. K. Webb,* edited by R. W. Davis and R. J. Helmstadter, 166-84. London: Routledge, 1992.

————. "The Missionary Movement." In *Nineteenth-Century English Religious Traditions: Retrospect and Prospect,* edited by D. G. Paz, 197-220. Westport, CT: Greenwood, 1995.

————. "Were Victorian Nonconformists the Worst Imperialists of All?" *Victorian Studies* 46, no. 2 (2004): 243-55.

Cracknell, Kenneth. *Justice, Courtesy and Love: Theologians and Missionaries Encountering World Religions, 1846-1914.* London: Epworth, 1995.

Currie, Robert, Alan D. Gilbert, and Lee Horsley. *Churches and Churchgoers: Patterns of Church Growth in the British Isles Since 1700.* Oxford: Clarendon Press, 1977.

Cutt, Margaret Nancy. *Ministering Angels: A Study of Nineteenth-Century Evangelical Writing for Children.* Wormley, UK: Five Owls, 1979.

Daggers, Jenny. "The Victorian Female Civilising Mission and Women's Aspirations Towards Priesthood in the Church of England." *Women's History Review* 10, no. 4 (2001): 651-70.

Davidoff, Leonore, and Catherine Hall. *Family Fortunes: Men and Women of the English Middle Class, 1780-1850.* London: Hutchinson, 1987.

Davin, Anna. "Imperialism and Motherhood." *History Workshop Journal* 5, no. 1 (1978): 9-66.

Deslandes, Paul. *Oxbridge Men: British Masculinity and the Undergraduate Experience, 1850-1920.* Bloomington: Indiana University Press, 2005.

Donaldson, Margaret. "'The Cultivation of the Heart and the Moulding of the Will . . .': The Missionary Contribution of the Society for Promoting Female Education in China, India, and the East." In *Women in the Church.* Vol. 27 of Studies in Church History, edited by W. J. Sheils and Diana Wood, 62 (1992): 16-39.

Donovan, Mary Sudman. "Women as Foreign Missionaries in the Episcopal Church, 1830-1920." *Anglican and Episcopal History* 62 (1992): 16-39.

Edgar, Robert. "New Religious Movements." In *Missions and Empire,* edited by Norman Etherington, 216-37. Oxford: Oxford University Press, 2005.

Elbourne, Elizabeth. *Blood Ground: Colonialism, Missions, and the Contest for Christianity in the Cape Colony and Britain, 1799-1853.* Montreal: McGill-Queen's University Press, 2002.

————. "The Foundation of the Church Missionary Society: The Anglican Missionary Impulse." In *The Church of England, c. 1689-c. 1833: From Toleration to Tractarianism,* edited by John Walsh, Colin Haydon, and Stephen Taylor, 247-64. Cambridge: Cambridge University Press, 1993.

————. "Word Made Flesh: Christianity, Modernity, and Cultural Colonialism in the Work of Jean and John Comaroff." *American Historical Review* 108, no. 2 (2003): 435-59.

Eldridge, C. C. *England's Mission: The Imperial Idea in the Age of Gladstone and Disraeli, 1868-1880.* Chapel Hill: University of North Carolina Press, 1974.

————. *Victorian Imperialism.* London: Hodder and Stoughton, 1978.

Elphick, Richard, and Rodney Davenport, eds. *Christianity in South Africa: A Political, Social, and Cultural History.* Berkeley: University of California Press, 1997.

Ensor, R. C. K. *England, 1870-1914.* Oxford: Clarendon Press, 1936.

Etherington, Norman, ed. "Introduction." In *Missions and Empire,* edited by Norman Etherington. The Oxford History of the British Empire Companion Series, 1-18. Oxford: Oxford University Press, 2005.

————. "Missions and Empire." In *Historiography.* Vol. 5 of *The Oxford History of the British Empire,* edited by Robin W. Winks, 303-14. Oxford: Oxford University Press, 1999.

————. *Missions and Empire.* The Oxford History of the British Empire Companion Series. Oxford: Oxford University Press, 2005.

Faught, C. Brad. *The Oxford Movement: A Thematic History of the Tractarians and Their Times.* University Park: Pennsylvania State University Press, 2003.

————. "Tractarianism on the Zambezi: Bishop Mackenzie and the Beginnings of the Universities Mission to Central Africa." *Anglican and Episcopal History* 66, no. 3 (Sept. 1997): 303-28.

Fischer, Benjamin. "The Evangelical Alliance in the 1840s: An Attempt to Institutionalise Christian Unity." In *The Church and Literature.* Vol. 48 of Studies in Church History. Oxford: Blackwell, forthcoming.

Fitzgerald, Rosemary. "A 'Peculiar and Exceptional Measure': The Call for Women Medical Missionaries for India in the Later Nineteenth Century." In *Missionary Encounters: Sources and Issues,* edited by Robert A. Bickers and Rosemary E. Seton, 174-96. Richmond, UK: Curzon, 1995.

Flemming, Leslie A., ed. *Women's Work for Women: Missionaries and Social Change in Asia.* Boulder, CO: Westview, 1989.

Forbes, Duncan. *The Liberal Anglican Idea of History.* Cambridge: Cambridge University Press, 1952.

France, W. F. *The Oversea Episcopate: Centenary History of the Colonial Bishoprics Fund, 1841-1941.* Westminster, UK: Colonial Bishoprics Fund, 1941.

Francis-Dehquani, Guli. "Medical Missions and the History of Feminism: Emmeline Stuart of the CMS Persia Mission." In *Women, Religion and Feminism in Britain, 1750-1900,* edited by Sue Morgan, 197-211. Basingstoke, UK: Palgrave Macmillan, 2002.

Frykenberg, Robert Eric. "Christian Missions and the Raj." In *Missions and Empire,* edited by Norman Etherington. The Oxford History of the British Empire Companion Series, 110-28. London: British Academic Press, 1994.

Gaitskell, Deborah. "At Home with Hegemony? Coercion and Consent in African Girls' Education for Domesticity in South Africa Before 1910." In *Contesting Colonial Hegemony: State and Society in Africa and India,* edited by Dagmar Engels and Shula Marks, 107-31. Oxford: Oxford University Press, 2005.

————. "Rethinking Gender Roles: The Field Experience of Women Missionaries in South Africa." In *The Imperial Horizons of British Protestant Missions, 1880-1914,* edited by Andrew Porter, 131-57. Grand Rapids: Eerdmans, 2003.

Garrett, John. *To Live Among the Stars: Christian Origins in Oceania.* Geneva: World Council of Churches, 1982.

Geertz, Clifford. *Interpretation of Cultures: Selected Essays.* New York: Basic Books, 1973.

Gibbs, M. E. *The Anglican Church in India, 1600-1970.* New Delhi: ISPCK, 1972.

Gilbert, Alan D. *Religion and Society in Industrial England: Church, Chapel and Social Change, 1740-1914.* London: Longman, 1976.

Gill, Sean. "The Power of Christian Ladyhood: Priscilla Lydia Sellon and the Creation of Anglican Sisterhoods." In *Modern Religious Rebels,* edited by Stuart Mews and John Kent, 80-102. Basingstoke, UK: Palgrave Macmillan, 2007.

————. *Women and the Church of England: From the Eighteenth Century to the Present.* London: SPCK, 1994.

Gilmour, David. *The Ruling Caste: Imperial Lives in the Victorian Raj.* New York: Farrar, 2006.

Grant, Kevin. *A Civilised Savagery: Britain and the New Slaveries in Africa, 1884-1926.* New York: Routledge, 2005.

————. "Human Rights and Sovereign Abolitions of Slavery, c. 1885-1956." In *Beyond Sovereignty: Britain, Empire and Transnationalism, c. 1880-1950,* edited by Kevin Grant, Frank Trentmann, and Philippa Levine, 144-65. London: Epworth Press, 1993.

Green, E. H. H. *The Crisis of Conservatism: The Politics, Economics and Ideology of the British Conservative Party, 1880-1914.* London: Routledge, 1995.

Greenlee, James G., and Charles Murray Johnston. *Good Citizens: British Missionaries and Imperial States, 1870-1918.* Montreal: McGill-Queen's University Press, 1999.

Grimshaw, Patricia. "Faith, Missionary Life and the Family." In *Gender and Empire,* edited by Philippa Levine. The Oxford History of the British Empire Companion Series, 46-761. Oxford: Oxford University Press, 2004.

————. "In Pursuit of True Anglican Womanhood in Victoria, 1880-1914." *Women's History Review* 2, no. 3 (1993).

Gundersen, Joan R. "Women and the Parallel Church: A View from Congregations." In *Episcopal Women: Gender, Spirituality, and Commitment in an American Mainline Denomination,* edited by Catherine M. Prelinger, 111-32. New York: Oxford University Press, 1992.

Gunson, Niel. *Messengers of Grace: Evangelical Missionaries in the South Seas, 1797-1860.* New York: Oxford University Press, 1978.

Haig, Alan. *The Victorian Clergy.* London: Croom Helm, 1984.

Hall, Catherine. *Civilising Subjects: Metropole and Colony in the English Imagination, 1830-1867.* Chicago: University of Chicago Press, 2002.

————. "Of Gender and Empire: Reflections on the Nineteenth Century." In *Gender and Empire,* edited by Philippa Levine. The Oxford History of the British Empire Companion Series, 1-31. Cambridge: Cambridge University Press, 2006.

————. *White, Male and Middle-Class: Explorations in Feminism and History.* New York: Routledge, 1992.

Hall, Catherine, and Sonya O. Rose. "Being at Home with the Empire." In *At Home with the Empire: Metropolitan Culture and the Imperial World,* edited by Catherine Hall and Sonya O. Rose, 46-71. Oxford: Oxford University Press, 2004.

Hall, Stuart. "The Multi-Cultural Question." In *Un/Settled Multiculturalisms: Diasporas, Entanglements, Transruptions,* edited by Barnor Hesse, 209-41. London: Zed Books, 2000.

Hamilton, Nigel. *Monty: The Making of a General, 1887-1942.* London: Hamish Hamilton, 1981.

Hansen, Holger Bernt. *Mission, Church, and State in a Colonial Setting: Uganda, 1890-1925.* New York: St. Martin's, 1984.

Harcourt, Freda. "Disraeli's Imperialism, 1866-1868: A Question of Timing." *The Historical Journal* 23, no. 1 (Mar. 1980): 87-109.

Harper, Susan Billington. *In the Shadow of the Mahatma: Bishop V. S. Azariah and the Travails of Christianity in British India.* Grand Rapids: Eerdmans, 2000.

Harrison, Brian. *Separate Spheres: The Opposition to Women's Suffrage in Britain.* London: Croom Helm, 1978.

Harrison, Peter. *"Religion" and the Religions in the English Enlightenment.* Cambridge: Cambridge University Press, 1990.

Hastings, Adrian. *A History of English Christianity, 1920-2000.* London: Collins, 1986.

Headrick, Daniel R. *The Tools of Empire: Technology and European Imperialism in the Nineteenth Century.* New York: Oxford University Press, 1981.

Heeney, Brian. *The Women's Movement in the Church of England, 1850-1930.* Oxford: Clarendon Press, 1988.

Helly, Dorothy O. *Livingstone's Legacy: Horace Waller and Victorian Mythmaking.* Athens: Ohio University Press, 1987.

Hempton, David. "Evangelicalism in English and Irish Society, 1780-1840." In *Evangelicalism: Comparative Studies of Popular Protestantism in North America, the British Isles, and Beyond, 1700-1990,* edited by Mark A. Noll, David W. Bebbington, and George A. Rawlyk, 156-76. New York: Oxford University Press, 1994.

———. *Religion and Political Culture in Britain and Ireland.* Cambridge: Cambridge University Press, 1996.

———. *The Religion of the People: Methodism and Popular Religion, c. 1750-1900.* London: Routledge, 1996.

Hempton, David, and Myrtle Hill. "Born to Serve: Women and Evangelical Religion." In *The Irish Women's History Reader,* edited by Alan Hayes and Diane Urquhart, 119-25. London: Routledge, 2001.

Hewitt, Gordon. *The Problems of Success: A History of the Church Missionary Society, 1910-1942.* 2 vols. London: SCM, 1971.

Hill, Michael. *The Religious Order: A Study of Virtuoso Religion and Its Legitimation in the Nineteenth-Century Church of England.* London: Heinemann, 1973.

Hill, Patricia. *The World Their Household: The American Woman's Foreign Mission Movement and Cultural Transformation, 1870-1920.* Ann Arbor: University of Michigan Press, 1985.

Hilliard, David. "Unenglish and Unmanly: Anglo-Catholicism and Homosexuality." *Victorian Studies* 25, no. 2 (Jan. 1982): 181-210.

Hilton, Boyd. *The Age of Atonement: The Influence of Evangelicalism on Social and Economic Thought, 1795–1865.* Oxford: Oxford University Press, 1988.

Hinchliff, Peter. *God and History: Aspects of British Theology, 1875–1914.* Oxford: Clarendon Press, 1992.

———. "Voluntary Absolutism: British Missionary Societies in the Nineteenth Century." In *Voluntary Religion,* edited by W. J. Sheils and Diana Wood, 370-76. Vol. 23 of Studies in Church History. Oxford: Blackwell, 1986.

Hobsbawm, Eric, and Terence Ranger. *The Invention of Tradition.* Cambridge: Cambridge University Press, 1983.

Howsam, Leslie. *Cheap Bibles: Nineteenth-Century Publishing and the British and Foreign Bible Society.* Cambridge: Cambridge University Press, 1991.

Huber, Mary Taylor, and Nancy C. Lutkehaus, eds. *Gendered Missions: Women and Men in Missionary Discourse and Practice.* Ann Arbor: University of Michigan Press, 1999.

Hunt, Nancy Rose, Tessie P. Liu, and Jean H. Quataert, eds. *Gendered Colonialisms in African History*. Oxford: Blackwell, 1997.

Hunter, Jane. *The Gospel of Gentility: American Women Missionaries in Turn-of-the-Century China*. New Haven: Yale University Press, 1984.

Hutchison, William R. *Errand to the World: American Protestant Thought and Foreign Missions*. Chicago: University of Chicago Press, 1987.

Hylson-Smith, Kenneth. *Evangelicals in the Church of England, 1734-1984*. Edinburgh: Clark, 1989.

————. *High Churchmanship in the Church of England: From the Sixteenth Century to the Late Twentieth Century*. Edinburgh: Clark, 1993.

Jacob, W. M. *The Making of the Anglican Church Worldwide*. London: SPCK, 1997.

Janes, Dominic. *Victorian Reformation: The Fight Over Idolatry in the Church of England, 1840-1860*. Oxford: Oxford University Press, 2009.

Jeal, Tim. *Livingstone*. London: Heinemann, 1973.

Jenkins, Paul. "The Church Missionary Society and the Basel Mission: An Early Experiment in Inter-European Cooperation." In *The Church Mission Society and World Christianity, 1799-1999*, edited by Kevin Ward and Brian Stanley, 43-65. Grand Rapids: Eerdmans, 1999.

Johnston, Anna. *Missionary Writing and Empire, 1800-1860*. Cambridge: Cambridge University Press, 2003.

Jones, Gareth Stedman. *Languages of Class: Studies in English Working Class History, 1832-1982*. Cambridge: Cambridge University Press, 1983.

Judd, Denis, and Keith Surridge. *The Boer War*. London: Murray, 2002.

Kanahele, George S. *Emma: Hawai'i's Remarkable Queen: A Biography*. Honolulu, HI: Queen Emma Foundation, 1999.

Kennedy, Dane. "Imperial History and Post-Colonial Theory." *Journal of Imperial and Commonwealth History* 24, no. 3 (1996): 345-63.

Kent, Eliza F. *Converting Women: Gender and Protestant Christianity in Colonial South India*. Oxford: Oxford University Press, 2004.

————. "Tamil Bible Women and the Zenana Missions of Colonial South India." *History of Religions* 39, no. 2 (Nov. 1999): 23-42. Providence, RI: Berg, 1993.

Kent, John. *Holding the Fort: Studies in Victorian Revivalism*. London: Epworth, 1978.

————. *The Unacceptable Face: The Modern Church in the Eyes of the Historian*. London: SCM, 1987.

Kidd, Colin. *The Forging of Races: Race and Scripture in the Protestant Atlantic*. Cambridge: Cambridge University Press, 2006.

Kirkwood, Deborah. "Protestant Missionary Women: Wives and Spinsters." In *Women and Mission: Past and Present; Anthropological and Historical Perceptions,* edited by Fiona Bowie, Deborah Kirkwood, and Shirley Ardener, 23-42. Providence, RI: Berg, 1993.

Kitson Clark, G. *Churchmen and the Condition of England, 1832-1885*. London: Methuen, 1973.

Knight, Frances. *The Nineteenth Century Church and English Society*. Cambridge: Cambridge University Press, 1995.

Knox, Edmund Arbuthnott. *Reminiscences of an Octogenarian*. London: Hutchinson, 1935.

Koss, Stephen E. *Nonconformity in Modern British Politics*. Hamden, CT: Archon, 1975.

————. "Wesleyanism and Empire." *The Historical Journal* 18, no. 1 (1975): 105-18.

Koven, Seth. "Borderlands: Women, Voluntary Action, and Child Welfare in Britain, 1840 to 1914." In *Mothers of a New World: Maternalist Politics and the Origins of Welfare States,* edited by Seth Koven and Sonya Michel, 94-135. New York: Routledge, 1993.

————. *Slumming: Sexual and Social Politics in Victorian London.* Princeton: Princeton University Press, 2004.

Koven, Seth, and Sonya Michel, eds. *Mothers of a New World: Maternalist Politics and the Origins of Welfare States.* New York: Routledge, 1993.

Kuklick, Henrika. *The Savage Within: The Social History of British Anthropology, 1885-1945.* Cambridge: Cambridge University Press, 1991.

Landau, Paul Stuart. *The Realm of the Word: Language, Gender, and Christianity in a Southern African Kingdom.* Portsmouth, NH: Heinemann, 1995.

Larsen, Timothy. *Crisis of Doubt: Honest Faith in Nineteenth-Century England.* Oxford: Oxford University Press, 2006.

Latourette, Kenneth Scott. *The Great Century, A.D. 1800–A.D. 1914: Europe and the United States of America.* Vol. 4 of *A History of the Expansion of Christianity.* New York: Harper, 1941.

Lester, Alan. "Humanitarians and White Settlers in the Nineteenth Century." In *Missions and Empire,* edited by Norman Etherington. The Oxford History of the British Empire Companion Series, 64-85. Oxford: Oxford University Press, 2005.

Levine, Philippa, ed. *Gender and Empire.* The Oxford History of the British Empire Companion Series. Oxford: Oxford University Press, 2004.

————. *Prostitution, Race, and Politics: Policing Venereal Disease in the British Empire.* New York: Routledge, 2003.

————. "Why Gender and Empire?" In *Gender and Empire,* edited by Philippa Levine. The Oxford History of the British Empire Companion Series, 1-13. Oxford: Oxford University Press, 2004.

Lewis, Donald M. *Lighten Their Darkness: The Evangelical Mission to Working-Class London, 1828-1860.* New York: Greenwood, 1986.

Lloyd, Roger. *The Church of England, 1900-1965.* London: SCM, 1966.

Lorimer, Douglas. "Theoretical Racism in Late-Victorian Anthropology, 1870-1900." *Victorian Studies* 31, no. 3 (Spring 1988): 405-30.

Lovegrove, Deryck W. *Established Church, Sectarian People: Itinerancy and the Transformation of English Dissent, 1780-1830.* Cambridge: Cambridge University Press, 1988.

MacCulloch, Diarmaid. "The Myth of the English Reformation." *Journal of British Studies* 30, no. 1 (January 1991): 1-19.

Machin, G. I. T. *Politics and the Churches in Great Britain, 1869 to 1921.* Oxford: Oxford University Press, 1987.

MacKenzie, John M., "Empire and Metropolitan Cultures." In *The Nineteenth Century.* Vol. 3 of *The Oxford History of the British Empire,* edited by Andrew Porter, 270-93. Oxford: Oxford University Press, 1999.

————, ed. *Imperialism and Popular Culture.* Manchester: Manchester University Press, 1986.

————. "Missionaries, Science, and the Environment in Nineteenth-Century Africa." In

The Imperial Horizons of British Protestant Missions, 1880-1914, edited by Andrew Porter, 106-30. Grand Rapids: Eerdmans, 2003.

———. *Propaganda and Empire: The Manipulation of British Public Opinion, 1880-1960.* Manchester: Manchester University Press, 1984.

Mackintosh, W. H. *Disestablishment and Liberation: The Movement for the Separation of the Anglican Church from State Control.* London: Epworth, 1972.

Mallampalli, Chandra. "British Missions and Indian Nationalism, 1880-1908: Imitation and Autonomy in Calcutta and Madras." In *The Imperial Horizons of British Protestant Missions, 1880-1914*, edited by Andrew Porter, 158-82. Grand Rapids: Eerdmans, 2003.

Mandler, Peter. *The English National Character: The History of an Idea from Edmund Burke to Tony Blair.* New Haven: Yale University Press, 2006.

———. "'Race' and 'Nation' in Mid-Victorian Thought." In *History, Religion, and Culture: British Intellectual History, 1750-1950*, edited by Stefan Collini, Richard Whatmore, and Brian Young. Cambridge: Cambridge University Press, 2000.

———. "Tories and Paupers: Christian Political Economy and the Making of the New Poor Law." *The Historical Journal* 33, no. 1 (Mar. 1990): 81-103.

Mangan, J. A. *Athleticism in the Victorian and Edwardian Public School: The Emergence and Consolidation of an Educational Ideology.* Cambridge: Cambridge University Press, 1981.

———. *The Games Ethic and Imperialism: Aspects of the Diffusion of an Ideal.* New York: Viking, 1986.

Mangion, Carmen M. "Women, Religious Ministry and Female Institution Building." In *Women, Gender and Religious Cultures in Britain, 1800-1940*, edited by Sue Morgan and Jacqueline deVries, 72-93. London: Routledge, 2010.

Marriott, John. *The Other Empire: Metropolis, India and Progress in the Colonial Imagination.* Manchester: Manchester University Press, 2003.

Marsden, George M. *Fundamentalism and American Culture: The Shaping of Twentieth Century Evangelicalism, 1870-1925.* New York: Oxford University Press, 1980.

———. "Fundamentalism as an American Phenomenon: A Comparison with English Evangelicalism." *Church History* 46, no. 2 (June 1977): 215-32.

Marsh, Peter T. *The Victorian Church in Decline: Archbishop Tait and the Church of England, 1868-1882.* London: Routledge & K. Paul, 1969.

Marshall, P. J. "Britain Without America — A Second Empire?" In *The Eighteenth Century.* Vol. 2 of *The Oxford History of the British Empire*, edited by P. J. Marshall, 576-95. Oxford: Oxford University Press, 1998.

———. "Imperial Britain." *Journal of Imperial and Commonwealth History* 23, no. 3 (1995): 379-94.

Martelli, George. *Livingstone's River: A History of the Zambezi Expedition, 1858-1864.* New York: Simon and Schuster, 1969.

Mason, J. C. S. *The Moravian Church and the Missionary Awakening in England, 1760-1800.* Woodbridge, UK: Boydell, 2001.

Mathers, Helen. "Evangelicalism and Feminism: Josephine Butler, 1828-1906." In *Women, Religion and Feminism in Britain, 1750-1900*, ed. Sue Morgan, 123-37. Basingstoke, UK: Palgrave Macmillan, 2002.

Maw, Martin. *Visions of India: Fulfilment Theology, the Aryan Race Theory and the Work of British Protestant Missionaries in Victorian India.* Frankfurt am Main: Lang, 1990.

Max Weber, Selections in Translation. Edited by W. G. Runciman. Translated by E. Matthews. Cambridge: Cambridge University Press, 1978.

McLeod, Hugh. *Class and Religion in the Late Victorian City.* London: Croom Helm, 1974.

———. *Religion and Society in England, 1850-1914.* New York: St. Martin's, 1996.

———. *Religion and the Working Class in Nineteenth-Century Britain.* London: Macmillan, 1984.

Meacham, Standish. *Lord Bishop: The Life of Samuel Wilberforce, 1805-1873.* Cambridge, MA: Harvard University Press, 1970.

Melman, Billie. *Women's Orients: English Women and the Middle East, 1718-1918: Sexuality, Religion and Work.* London: Macmillan, 1992.

Melnyk, Julie. "Women, Writing and the Creation of Theological Cultures." In *Women, Gender and Religious Cultures in Britain, 1800-1940,* edited by Sue Morgan and Jacqueline deVries, 32-53. London: Routledge, 2010.

Midgley, Clare. "Anti-Slavery and the Roots of 'Imperial Feminism.'" In *Gender and Imperialism,* edited by Clare Midgley, 161-79. Manchester: Manchester University Press, 1998.

———. "Can Women Be Missionaries? Envisioning Female Agency in the Early Nineteenth-Century British Empire." *Journal of British Studies* 45, no. 2 (Apr. 2006): 335-58.

———. "Ethnicity, 'Race' and Empire." In *Women's History: Britain, 1850-1945,* edited by June Purvis, 247-76. London: UCL Press, 1995.

———. *Feminism and Empire: Women Activists in Imperial Britain, 1790-1865.* London: Routledge, 2007.

———. *Women Against Slavery: The British Campaigns, 1780-1870.* London: Routledge, 1992.

Mitchell, B. R. *British Historical Statistics.* Cambridge: Cambridge University Press, 1988.

Montgomery, Bernard Law. *The Memoirs of Field-Marshal the Viscount Montgomery of Alamein, K.G.* Cleveland, OH: World Publishing, 1958.

Morgan, David. *Protestants and Pictures: Religion, Visual Culture and the Age of American Mass Production.* New York: Oxford University Press, 1999.

Morgan, Sue, ed. *Women, Religion and Feminism in Britain, 1750-1900.* Basingstoke, UK: Palgrave, 2002.

Mumm, Susan. "'A Peril to the Bench of Bishops': Sisterhoods and Episcopal Authority in the Church of England, 1845-1908." *Journal of Ecclesiastical History* 59, no. 1 (2008): 62-78.

———. *Stolen Daughters, Virgin Mothers: Anglican Sisterhoods in Victorian Britain.* London: Leicester University Press, 1999.

———. "Women and Philanthropic Cultures." In *Women, Gender and Religious Cultures in Britain, 1800-1940,* edited by Sue Morgan and Jacqueline deVries, 54-71. London: Routledge, 2010.

Murray, Jocelyn. "The Role of Women in the Church Missionary Society, 1799-1917." In *The Church Mission Society and World Christianity, 1799-1999,* edited by Kevin Ward and Brian Stanley, 66-90. Grand Rapids: Eerdmans, 1999.

Nair, Janaki. "Uncovering the Zenana: Visions of Indian Womanhood in Englishwomen's Writings, 1813-1940." *Journal of Women's History* 2, no. 1 (Spring 1990): 8-34.

Neill, Stephen. *The Interpretation of the New Testament, 1861-1961.* London: Oxford University Press, 1964.

Neill, Stephen, and Owen Chadwick. *A History of Christian Missions.* 2nd ed. Harmondsworth, UK: Penguin, 1986.

Newsome, David. *Godliness and Good Learning: Four Studies on a Victorian Ideal.* London: Murray, 1961.

―――. *The Parting of Friends: A Study of the Wilberforces and Henry Manning.* London: Murray, 1966.

―――. *The Victorian World Picture: Perceptions and Introspections in an Age of Change.* London: Fontana, 1997.

Nockles, Peter Benedict. *The Oxford Movement in Context: Anglican High Churchmanship, 1760-1857.* Cambridge: Cambridge University Press, 1994.

Noll, Mark A. "Revolution and the Rise of Evangelical Social Influence in North Atlantic Societies." In *Evangelicalism: Comparative Studies of Popular Protestantism in North America, the British Isles, and Beyond, 1700-1900,* edited by Mark A. Noll, David W. Bebbington, and George A. Rawlyk, vol. 5 of *Religion in Victorian Britain,* ed. John Wolffe, 135-75. Manchester: Manchester University Press, 1997.

Norman, Edward R. *Anti-Catholicism in Victorian England.* New York: Barnes & Noble, 1968.

―――. *Church and Society in England, 1770-1970: A Historical Study.* Oxford: Clarendon Press, 1976.

―――. *The Victorian Christian Socialists.* Cambridge: Cambridge University Press, 1987.

O'Connor, Daniel. *Gospel, Raj and Swaraj: The Missionary Years of C. F. Andrews, 1904-14.* Frankfurt am Main: Lang, 1990.

O'Connor, Daniel, and others. *Three Centuries of Mission: The United Society for the Propagation of the Gospel, 1701-2000.* London: Continuum, 2000.

Obelkevich, Jim, Lyndal Roper, and Raphael Samuel, eds. *Disciplines of Faith: Studies in Religion, Politics, and Patriarchy.* London: Routledge & K. Paul, 1987.

Oddie, Geoffrey A. *Hindu and Christian in South-East India.* London: Curzon, 1991.

Parsons, Gerald. "Rethinking the Missionary Position: Bishop Colenso of Natal." In *Culture and Empire.* Vol. 5 of *Religion in Victorian Britain,* edited by John Wolffe, 135-75. Manchester: Manchester University Press, 1997.

Paz, D. G. *Popular Anti-Catholicism in Mid-Victorian England.* Stanford: Stanford University Press, 1992.

Pedersen, Susan. "Hannah More Meets Simple Simon: Tracts, Chapbooks, and Popular Culture in Late-Eighteenth Century England." *Journal of British Studies* 25, no. 1 (Jan. 1986): 1-24. London: Routledge, 1994.

Pedersen, Susan, and Peter Mandler. "The British Intelligentsia After the Victorians." In *After the Victorians: Private Conscience and Public Duty in Modern Britain; Essays in Memory of John Clive,* edited by Susan Pedersen and Peter Mandler, 1-24. London: Routledge, 1994.

Peel, J. D. Y. *Religious Encounter and the Making of the Yoruba.* Bloomington: Indiana University Press, 2000.

Pennington, Brian K. *Was Hinduism Invented? Britons, Indians, and the Colonial Construction of Religion.* Oxford: Oxford University Press, 2005.

Perkin, Harold. *The Rise of Professional Society: England Since 1880.* London: Routledge, 1989.

Phillips, Clifton J. "Changing Attitudes in the Student Volunteer Movement of Great Britain and North America, 1886-1928." In *Missionary Ideologies in the Imperialist Era, 1880-1920,* edited by Torben Christensen and William R. Hutchison, 131-45. [Aarhus, Denmark]: Aros, 1982.

———. "The Student Volunteer Movement and Its Role in China Missions, 1886-1920." In *The Missionary Enterprise in China and America,* edited by John K. Fairbank, 91-109. Cambridge, MA: Harvard University Press, 1974.

Pickering, W. S. F. *Anglo-Catholicism: A Study in Religious Ambiguity.* London: Routledge, 1989.

Piggin, Stuart. *Making Evangelical Missionaries, 1789-1858: The Social Background, Motives and Training of British Protestant Missionaries to India.* [Abingdon, UK?]: Sutton Courtenay, 1984.

Pollock, J. C. *The Cambridge Seven: A Call to Christian Service.* Chicago: Inter-Varsity, 1955.

———. *The Keswick Story: The Authorized History of the Keswick Convention.* London: Hodder and Stoughton, 1964.

———. *Shadows Fall Apart: The Story of the Zenana Bible and Medical Mission.* London: Hodder and Stoughton, 1958.

Poovey, Mary. *Uneven Developments: The Ideological Work of Gender in Mid-Victorian England.* Chicago: University of Chicago Press, 1988.

Porter, Andrew, "Cambridge, Keswick, and Late-Nineteenth-Century Attitudes to Africa." *Journal of Imperial and Commonwealth History* 5, no. 1 (Oct. 1976): 71, no. 555-84.

———. "'Commerce and Christianity': The Rise and Fall of a Nineteenth-Century Missionary Slogan." *Historical Journal* 3 (1985): 597-621.

———. "'Cultural Imperialism' and Protestant Missionary Enterprise, 1780-1914." *Journal of Imperial and Commonwealth History* 25, no. 3 (Sept. 1997): 367-91.

———. "Evangelical Enthusiasm, Missionary Motivation and West Africa in the Late Nineteenth Century: The Career of G. W. Brooke." *Journal of Imperial and Commonwealth History* 6, no. 1 (1977): 23-46.

———. "Late Nineteenth Century Anglican Missionary Expansion: A Consideration of Some Non-Anglican Sources of Inspiration." In *Religious Motivation: Biographical and Sociological Problems for the Church Historian.* Vol. 15 of Studies in Church History, edited by Derek Baker, 349-65. London: Blackwell, 1978.

———. "An Overview, 1700-1914." In *Missions and Empire,* edited by Norman Etherington. The Oxford History of the British Empire Companion Series, 40-63. Oxford: Oxford University Press, 2005.

———. "Religion and Empire: British Expansion in the Long Nineteenth Century, 1780-1914." *Journal of Imperial and Commonwealth History* 20, no. 3 (1992): 370-90.

———. "Religion, Missionary Enthusiasm, and Empire." In *The Nineteenth Century.* Vol. 3 of *The Oxford History of the British Empire,* edited by Andrew Porter, 222-45. Oxford: Oxford University Press, 1999.

————. *Religion Versus Empire? British Protestant Missionaries and Overseas Expansion, 1700-1914.* Manchester: Manchester University Press, 2004.

————. "Scottish Missions and Education in Nineteenth Century India: The Changing Face of Trusteeship." *Journal of Imperial and Commonwealth History* 16, no. 3 (1988): 33-57.

————. "The Universities' Mission to Central Africa: Anglo-Catholicism and the Twentieth-Century Colonial Encounter." In *Missions, Nationalism, and the End of Empire,* edited by Brian Stanley, 79-107. Grand Rapids: Eerdmans, 2003.

Porter, Bernard. *The Absent-Minded Imperialists: Empire, Society, and Culture in Britain.* Oxford: Oxford University Press, 2004.

————. " 'Empire, What Empire?' Or, Why 80% of Early- and Mid-Victorians Were Deliberately Kept in Ignorance of It." *Victorian Studies* 46, no. 2 (2004): 256-63.

Prasch, Thomas. "Which God for Africa: The Islamic-Christian Missionary Debate in Late-Victorian England." *Victorian Studies* 33 (Autumn 1989): 51-73.

Prelinger, Catherine M. "The Female Diaconate in the Anglican Church: What Kind of Ministry for Women." In *Religion in the Lives of English Women, 1760-1930,* edited by Gail Malmgreen. London: Croom Helm, 1986.

Prevost, Elizabeth E. *The Communion of Women: Missions and Gender in Colonial Africa and the British Metropole.* Oxford: Oxford University Press, 2010.

Prochaska, F. K. "Little Vessels: Children in the Nineteenth-Century English Missionary Movement." *The Journal of Imperial and Commonwealth History* 6, no. 2 (Jan. 1978): 103-18.

————. *The Voluntary Impulse: Philanthropy in Modern Britain.* London: Faber and Faber, 1988.

————. *Women and Philanthropy in Nineteenth-Century England.* Oxford: Clarendon Press, 1980.

Putney, Clifford. "Man in Both Corners: Mark Twain the Shadow-Boxing Imperialist." *Hawaiian Journal of History* 40 (2006): 55-73.

————. "A Mother's Country: Mothers' Meetings and Family Welfare in Britain, 1850-1950." *History* 74 (Oct. 1989): 40 (2006): 55-73.

Ramusack, Barbara N. "Cultural Missionaries, Maternal Imperialists, Feminist Allies: British Women Activists in India, 1865-1945." In *Western Women and Imperialism: Complicity and Resistance,* edited by Nupur Chaudhuri and Margaret Strobel. Bloomington: Indiana University Press, 1992.

Reardon, Bernard M. G. *Religious Thought in the Victorian Age: A Survey from Coleridge to Gore.* 2nd ed. London: Longman, 1995.

Reed, John Shelton. " 'A Female Movement': The Feminization of Nineteenth-Century Anglo-Catholicism." *Anglican and Episcopal History* 57 (1988).

————. *Glorious Battle: The Cultural Politics of Victorian Anglo-Catholicism.* Nashville, TN: Vanderbilt University Press, 1996.

Reynolds, J. S. *Canon Christopher of St. Aldate's, Oxford, 1820-1913.* Abington, UK: Abbey Press, 1967.

Robbins, Keith. *History, Religion, and Identity in Modern Britain.* London: Hambledon, 1993.

Rose, Craig. "The Origins and Ideals of the SPCK, 1699-1716." In *The Church of England c. 1689–c. 1833: From Toleration to Tractarianism,* edited by John Walsh, Colin Haydon, and Stephen Taylor, 172-90. Cambridge: Cambridge University Press, 1993.

Rosman, Doreen M. *Evangelicals and Culture.* London: Croom Helm, 1984.

Ross, Andrew C. "Christian Missions and the Mid-Nineteenth Century Change in Attitude to Race: The African Experience." In *The Imperial Horizons of British Protestant Missions, 1880-1914,* edited by Andrew Porter, 85-105. Grand Rapids: Eerdmans, 2003.

—————. *David Livingstone: Mission and Empire.* London: Hambledon, 2002.

—————. "Scottish Missionary Concern 1874-1914: A Golden Era?" *Scottish History Review* 51 (1972): 51-72.

Rouse, Ruth, and Stephen C. Neill, eds. *A History of the Ecumenical Movement, 1517-1948.* 2nd ed. Philadelphia, PA: Westminster, 1967.

Rowbotham, Judith. "'Soldiers of Christ'? Images of Female Missionaries in Late Nineteenth-Century Britain: Issues of Heroism and Martyrdom." *Gender and History* 12, no. 1 (Apr. 2000): 82-106.

Rowell, Geoffrey. *The Vision Glorious: Themes and Personalities of the Catholic Revival in Anglicanism.* Oxford: Oxford University Press, 1983.

Rutherdale, Myra. *Women and the White Man's God: Gender and Race in the Canadian Mission Field.* Vancouver: University of British Columbia Press, 2002.

Sachs, William L. *The Transformation of Anglicanism: From State Church to Global Communion.* Cambridge: Cambridge University Press, 1993.

Said, Edward. *Culture and Imperialism.* New York: Knopf, 1993.

—————. *Orientalism.* New York: Pantheon, 1978.

Samson, Jane. "Ethnology and Theology: Nineteenth-Century Mission Dilemmas in the South Pacific." In *Christian Missions and the Enlightenment,* edited by Brian Stanley, 99-122. Grand Rapids: Eerdmans, 2001.

—————. *Imperial Benevolence: Making British Authority in the Pacific Islands.* Honolulu: University of Hawai'i Press, 1998.

Savage, David. "Evangelical Educational Policy in Britain and India, 1857-60." *Journal of Imperial and Commonwealth History* 22, no. 3 (1994): 432-61.

—————. "Missionaries and the Development of a Colonial Ideology of Female Education in India." *Gender and History* 2 (1997): 201-21.

Schlenther, Boyd Stanley. "Religious Faith and Commercial Empire." In *The Eighteenth Century.* Vol. 2 of *The Oxford History of the British Empire,* edited by P. J. Marshall, 128-50. Oxford: Oxford University Press, 1998.

Searle, G. R. *The Quest for National Efficiency: A Study in British Politics and Political Thought, 1899-1914.* Oxford: Blackwell, 1971.

Semes, Robert Louis. "Hawai'i's Holy War: English Bishop Staley, American Congregationalists, and the Hawaiian Monarchies, 1860-1870." *Hawaiian Journal of History* 34 (2000): 113-38.

Semmel, Bernard. *Imperialism and Social Reform: English Social-Imperial Thought 1895-1914.* Cambridge, MA: Harvard University Press, 1960.

—————. *The Methodist Revolution.* New York: Basic Books, 1973.

Semmel, Stuart. *Napoleon and the British.* New Haven: Yale University Press, 2004.

Semple, Rhonda Anne. *Missionary Women: Gender, Professionalism and the Victorian Idea of Christian Mission.* Woodbridge, UK: Boydell, 2003.

————. "Professionalizing Their Faith: Women, Religion and the Cultures of Mission and Empire." In *Women, Gender and Religious Cultures in Britain, 1800-1940,* edited by Sue Morgan and Jacqueline deVries, 117-37. London: Routledge, 2010.

Seton, Rosemary E. "'Open Doors for Female Labourers': Women Candidates of the London Missionary Society, 1875-1914." In *Missionary Encounters: Sources and Issues,* edited by Robert A. Bickers and Rosemary E. Seton. Richmond, UK: Curzon, 1995.

Sharpe, Eric R. *Not to Destroy but to Fulfil: The Contribution of J. N. Farquhar to Protestant Missionary Thought in India Before 1914.* Uppsala: Swedish Institute of Missionary Research, 1965.

Shenk, Wilbert. *Henry Venn — Missionary Statesman.* Maryknoll, NY: Orbis, 1983.

Shourie, Arun. *Missionaries in India: Continuities, Changes, Dilemmas.* New Delhi: ASA Publications, 1994.

Sinha, Mrinalini. *Colonial Masculinity: The "Manly Englishman" and the "Effeminate Bengali" in the Late Nineteenth Century.* Manchester: Manchester University Press, 1995.

Smith, Mark. *Religion in Industrial Society: Oldham and Saddleworth, 1740-1865.* Oxford: Clarendon Press, 1994.

Snell, K. D. M. *Church and Chapel in the North Midlands: Religious Observance in the Nineteenth Century.* Leicester, UK: Leicester University Press, 1991.

Snell, K. D. M., and Paul S. Ell. *Rival Jerusalems: The Geography of Victorian Religion.* Cambridge: Cambridge University Press, 2000.

Sohmer, Sara H. "Christianity Without Civilization: Anglican Sources for an Alternative Nineteenth-Century Mission Methodology." *Journal of Religious History* 18, no. 2 (1994): 174-97.

Soloway, R. A. *Prelates and People: Ecclesiastical Social Thought in England, 1783-1852.* London: Routledge & K. Paul, 1969.

Springhall, J. O. "Lord Meath, Youth, and Empire." *Journal of Contemporary History* 5, no. 4 (1970): 97-111.

Stanley, Brian, *The Bible and the Flag: Protestant Missions and British Imperialism in the Nineteenth and Twentieth Centuries.* Leicester, UK: Apollos, 1990.

————. "Christianity and Civilization in English Evangelical Mission Thought, 1792-1857." In *Christian Missions and the Enlightenment,* edited by Brian Stanley, 169-97. Grand Rapids: Eerdmans, 2001.

————. "Church, State, and the Hierarchy of 'Civilization': The Making of the 'Missions and Governments' Report at the World Missionary Conference, Edinburgh 1910." In *The Imperial Horizons of British Protestant Missions, 1880-1914,* edited by Andrew Porter, 58-84. Grand Rapids: Eerdmans, 2003.

————. "'Commerce and Christianity': Providence Theory, the Missionary Movement, and the Imperialism of Free Trade, 1842-1860." *Historical Journal* 26, no. 1 (1983): 71-94.

————. *The History of the Baptist Missionary Society, 1792-1992.* Edinburgh: Clark, 1992.

————. "Manliness and Mission: Frank Lenwood and the London Missionary Society." *Journal of the United Reformed Church History Society* 5, no. 8 (May 1996): 458-77.

————. *The World Missionary Conference, Edinburgh 1910.* Grand Rapids: Eerdmans, 2009.

Stephens, Geoffrey. *H. H. Montgomery — The Mutton Bird Bishop.* University of Tasmania Occasional Paper 39. Hobart: University of Tasmania, 1985.

Stephenson, Alan M. G. *Anglicanism and the Lambeth Conferences.* London: SPCK, 1978.

—————. *The First Lambeth Conference, 1867.* London: SPCK, 1967.

Stocking, George W. *After Tylor: British Social Anthropology, 1888-1951.* Madison: University of Wisconsin Press, 1995.

Stoler, Ann Laura, and Frederick Cooper. "Between Metropole and Colony: Rethinking a Research Agenda." In *Tensions of Empire: Colonial Cultures in a Bourgeois World,* 1-56. Berkeley: University of California Press, 1997.

Strobel, Margaret. *European Women and the Second British Empire.* Bloomington: Indiana University Press, 1991.

Strong, Rowan. *Anglicanism and the British Empire, c. 1700-1850.* Oxford: Oxford University Press, 2007.

Studdert-Kennedy, Gerald. *British Christians, Indian Nationalists, and the Raj.* Delhi: Oxford University Press, 1991.

Sugirtharajah, R. S. *The Bible and Empire: Postcolonial Explorations.* Cambridge: Cambridge University Press, 2005.

Symonds, Richard. *Oxford and Empire — the Last Lost Cause?* Oxford: Clarendon Press, 1986.

Temperley, Howard. *White Dreams, Black Africa: The Antislavery Expedition to the River Niger, 1841-1842.* New Haven: Yale University Press, 1991.

Thompson, Andrew. *The Empire Strikes Back? The Impact of Imperialism on Britain from the Mid-Nineteenth Century.* Harlow, UK: Pearson/Longman, 2005.

Thompson, David M. "The Christian Socialist Revival in Britain: A Reappraisal." In *Revival and Religion Since 1700: Essays for John Walsh,* edited by John Walsh, Jane Garnett, and H. C. G. Matthew, 273-95. London: Hambledon, 1993.

Thompson, H. P. *Into All Lands: The History of the Society for the Propagation of the Gospel in Foreign Parts, 1701-1950.* London: SPCK, 1951.

Thorne, Susan. *Congregational Missions and the Making of an Imperial Culture in Nineteenth-Century England.* Stanford: Stanford University Press, 1999.

—————. "Missionary-Imperial Feminism." In *Gendered Missions: Women and Men in Missionary Discourse and Practice,* edited by Mary Taylor Huber and Nancy C. Lutkehaus, 39-65. Ann Arbor: University of Michigan Press, 1999.

Thornton, A. P. *The Imperial Idea and Its Enemies: A Study in British Power.* 2nd ed. New York: Anchor, 1968.

Trentmann, Frank. "Introduction: Paradoxes of Civil Society." In *Paradoxes of Civil Society: New Perspectives on Modern German and British History,* edited by Frank Trentmann. New York: Berghahn Books, 2000.

—————. "The Strange Death of Free Trade: The Erosion of 'Liberal Consensus' in Great Britain, c. 1903-1932." In *Citizenship and Community: Liberals, Radicals and Collective Identities in the British Isles, 1865-1931,* edited by E. F. Biagini, 70-98. Cambridge: Cambridge University Press, 1996.

Turner, Mary. *Slaves and Missionaries: The Disintegration of Jamaican Slave Society, 1787-1834.* Urbana: University of Illinois Press, 1982.

Twells, Alison. *The Civilising Mission and the English Middle Class, 1792-1850: The "Heathen" at Home and Overseas.* Basingstoke, UK: Palgrave Macmillan, 2009.

—————. "'Happy English Children': Class, Ethnicity, and the Making of Missionary

Women in the Early Nineteenth Century." *Women's Studies International Forum* 21, no. 3 (May 1998): 235-45.

Urdank, Albion M. *Religion and Society in a Cotswold Vale: Nailsworth, Gloucestershire, 1780-1865.* Berkeley: University of California Press, 1990.

Valenze, Deborah M. *Prophetic Sons and Daughters: Female Preaching and Popular Religion in Industrial England.* Princeton: Princeton University Press, 1985.

Veer, Peter van der, ed. *Conversion to Modernities: The Globalization of Christianity.* New York: Routledge, 1996.

Vicinus, Martha. *Independent Women: Work and Community for Single Women, 1850-1920.* London: Virago, 1985.

Vickery, Amanda. "Golden Age to Separate Spheres? A Review of the Categories and Chronology of English Women's History." *Historical Journal* 36, no. 2 (1993): 383-414.

Viswanathan, Gauri. *Outside the Fold: Conversion, Modernity, and Belief.* Princeton: Princeton University Press, 1998.

Walker, Pamela J. *Pulling the Devil's Kingdom Down: The Salvation Army in Victorian Britain.* Berkeley: University of California Press, 2001.

Walkowitz, Judith. *City of Dreadful Delight: Narratives of Sexual Danger in Late Victorian London.* Chicago: University of Chicago Press, 1992.

———. *Prostitution and Victorian Society: Women, Class and the State.* Cambridge: Cambridge University Press, 1980.

Walls, Andrew F. "British Missions." In *Missionary Ideologies in the Imperialist Era: 1880-1920,* edited by Torben Christensen and William Hutchison. [Aarhus, Denmark]: Aros, 1982.

———. *The Cross-Cultural Process in Christian History: Studies in the Transmission and Appropriation of Faith.* Maryknoll, NY: Orbis, 2002.

Ward, Kevin. *A History of Global Anglicanism.* Cambridge: Cambridge University Press, 2006.

———. "'Taking Stock': The Church Missionary Society and Its Historians." In *The Church Mission Society and World Christianity, 1799-1999,* edited by Kevin Ward and Brian Stanley, 15-42. Grand Rapids: Eerdmans, 1999.

Ward, W. R. *The Protestant Evangelical Awakening.* Cambridge: Cambridge University Press, 1992.

Ware, Vron. *Beyond the Pale: White Women, Racism, and History.* London: Verso, 1992.

Warren, Max. "The Church Militant Abroad: Victorian Missionaries." In *The Victorian Crisis of Faith,* edited by Anthony Symondson, 57-68. London: SPCK, 1970.

Webster, John C. B. "Dalits and Christianity in Colonial Punjab: Cultural Interactions." In *Christians, Cultural Interactions, and India's Religious Traditions,* edited by Judith M. Brown, Robert Eric Frykenberg, and Alaine M. Low. Grand Rapids: Eerdmans, 2004.

Welch, Claude. *Protestant Thought in the Nineteenth Century,* Vol. 1: *1799-1870.* New Haven: Yale University Press, 1972.

Wellings, Martin. "Anglo-Catholicism, the 'Crisis in the Church' and the Cavalier Case of 1899." *Journal of Ecclesiastical History* 42, no. 2 (Apr. 1991): 239-58.

———. *Evangelicals Embattled: Responses of Evangelicals in the Church of England to Ritualism, Darwinism, and Theological Liberalism, 1890-1930.* Carlisle, UK: Paternoster, 2003.

————. "The First Protestant Martyr of the Twentieth Century: The Life and Significance of John Kensit (1853-1902)." In *Martyrs and Martyrologies*, edited by Diana Wood, 347-58. Oxford: Blackwell, 1993.

Wells, Julia C. "The Suppression of Mixed Marriages Among LMS Missionaries in South Africa Before 1820." *South African Historical Journal* 44 (May 2001): 1-20.

Wetherell, David. *Reluctant Mission: The Anglican Church in Papua New Guinea*. St. Lucia: University of Queensland Press, 1978.

Whiteman, Darrell. *Melanesians and Missionaries: An Ethnohistorical Study of Social and Religious Change in the Southwest Pacific*. Pasadena, CA: William Carey Library, 1983.

Wilkinson, Alan. *Christian Socialism: Scott Holland to Tony Blair*. London: SCM Press, 1998.

Williams, C. Peter. *The Ideal of the Self-Governing Church: A Study in Victorian Missionary Strategy*. Leiden: Brill, 1990.

————. "'Not Quite Gentlemen': An Examination of 'Middling Class' Protestant Missionaries from Britain, c. 1850-1900." *Journal of Ecclesiastical History* 31, no. 3 (July 1980): 301-15.

————. "'The Missing Link': The Recruitment of Women Missionaries in Some English Evangelical Missionary Societies in the Nineteenth Century." In *Women and Mission: Past and Present; Anthropological and Historical Perceptions*, edited by Fiona Bowie, Deborah Kirkwood, and Shirley Ardener, 43-69. Providence, RI: Berg, 1993.

Williams, Sarah C. "Is There a Bible in the House? Gender, Religion and Family Culture." In *Women, Gender and Religious Cultures in Britain, 1800-1940*, edited by Sue Morgan and Jacqueline deVries, 11-31. London: Routledge, 2010.

————. "The Language of Belief: An Alternative Agenda for the Study of Victorian Working-Class Religion." *Journal of Victorian Culture* 1, no. 2 (1996): 303-17.

————. *Religious Belief and Popular Culture in Southwark, c. 1880-1939*. Oxford: Oxford University Press, 1999.

Wilson, Kathleen. *The Island Race: Englishness, Empire, and Gender in the Eighteenth Century*. London: Routledge, 2003.

Wolffe, John. "Anglicanism." In *Nineteenth-Century English Religious Traditions: Retrospect and Prospect*, edited by D. G. Paz, 1-31. Westport, CT: Greenwood, 1995.

————. "The Evangelical Alliance in the 1840s: An Attempt to Institutionalise Christian Unity." In *Voluntary Religion*. Vol. 23 of Studies in Church History, edited by W. J. Sheils and Diana Wood. Oxford: Blackwell, 1986.

————. "Evangelicalism in Mid-Nineteenth-Century England." In *Patriotism: The Making and Unmaking of British National Identity*, edited by Raphael Samuel, 188-200. London: Routledge, 1989.

————. *God and Greater Britain: Religion and National Life in Britain and Ireland, 1843-1945*. London: Routledge, 1994.

————. *The Protestant Crusade in Great Britain, 1829-1860*. Oxford: Clarendon Press, 1991.

————. "A Transatlantic Perspective: Protestantism and National Identities in Mid-Nineteenth-Century Britain and the United States." In *Protestantism and National Identity: Britain and Ireland, c. 1650–c. 1850*, edited by Tony Claydon and Ian McBride, 291-309. Cambridge: Cambridge University Press, 1998.

Yates, Nigel. *Anglican Ritualism in Victorian Britain, 1830-1910.* Oxford: Oxford University Press, 1999.

———. *The Oxford Movement and Anglican Ritualism.* London: Historical Association, 1983.

Yates, Timothy E. *Christian Mission in the Twentieth Century.* Cambridge: Cambridge University Press, 1994.

———. *Venn and Victorian Bishops Abroad: The Missionary Policies of Henry Venn and Their Repercussions Upon the Anglican Episcopate of the Colonial Period, 1841-72.* Uppsala: Swedish Institute of Missionary Research, 1978.

V. Unpublished Dissertations and Theses

Frith, Eleanor Joy. "Pseudonuns: Anglican Sisterhoods and the Politics of Victorian Identity." Ph.D. diss., Queen's University, 2004.

Maughan, Steven S. "Regions Beyond and the National Church: Domestic Support for the Foreign Missions of the Church of England in the High Imperial Age, 1870-1914." Ph.D. diss., Harvard University, 1995.

Morawiecki, Jennifer A. "'The Peculiar Mission of Christian Womanhood': The Selection and Preparation of Women Missionaries of the Church of England Zenana Missionary Society, 1880-1920." Ph.D. diss., Sussex University, 1998.

Potter, Sarah Caroline. "The Social Origins and Recruitment of English Protestant Missionaries in the Nineteenth Century." Ph.D. diss., University of London, 1974.

Stanley, Brian. "Home Support for Overseas Missions in Early Victorian England, c. 1838-1873." Ph.D. diss., University of Cambridge, 1979.

Williams, C. Peter. "The Recruitment and Training of Overseas Missionaries in England Between 1850 and 1900, with Special Reference to the Records of the CMS, WMMS, LMS and the China Inland Mission." Master's thesis, University of Bristol, 1976.

Index